D1079775

Joan Littlewood was born in Stockwell in 1914 and won a scholarship to RADA when she was sixteen. Two years later she tramped north, planning to stow away in a boat at Liverpool. The Manchester BBC detained her, she broadcast her story and there met Jimmie Miller, singer, leader of the agitprop group Theatre of Action, which she joined, along with Gerry Raffles who was to be her lifelong companion. Reborn in 1945 as Theatre Workshop, the company toured the industrial areas of Britain, supplementing their meagre income with profits from tours of Germany, Czechoslovakia, Sweden and Norway. In 1953 they rented a derelict theatre in Stratford, east London, for twenty pounds a week. The attempt to stimulate a contemporary dramaturgy led to her creating legendary productions such as *Oh What A Lovely War!*, *The Quare Fellow* and *The Hostage* by Brendan Behan, *A Taste of Honey* by Shelagh Delaney; *Fings Ain't Wot They Used T'Be* by Frank Norman, music by Lionel Bart; *You Won't Always Be On Top* by Henry Chapman and the company, and *Sparrers Can't Sing* by Stephen Lewis. As Kenneth Tynan once remarked, 'Others write plays, direct them and act in them: she alone "makes theatre".' She died in September 2002.

'This is not a tidy elegant memoir, but it is a rather wonderful one. *Joan's Book* is funny, generous, warm-hearted, irreverent and bawdy ... a memoir that ought to become a classic of the kind she admires – vital, energetic, full of hope and riotous laughter.' Paul Bailey, *Daily Telegraph*

'This exhilarating autobiography: abrasive, impudent, grossly opinionated and, like her best theatre work, a fine piece of popular entertainment.' Jonathan Cecil, *Evening Standard*

'*Joan's Book* is big: nearly eight hundred pages. But then so is her life. For Joan Littlewood's unorthodox autobiography is a noisy, rumbustious, compulsively readable account of her attempt to create, through Theatre Workshop, something unseen in Britain

238   418

since Shakespeare's day: a high-quality popular theatre. What emerges is a graphic contradictory portrait of a brilliant, restless *animateur*: a romantic revolutionary with a strong streak of cockney common sense. You put down this turbulent, often moving book reflecting that the greatest paradox of all is that, although this particular Pope Joan has no children, she has left her indelible imprint on British theatre and has bequeathed us countless heirs.' Michael Billington, *Guardian*

'The tumult of *Joan's Book* is testimony to one of the great creative forces of our time. Like the Shakespearean character with whom she has most in common, she has, in her way, once again voiced her own unanswerable demands, betraying neither "faith, truth nor womanhood" in the process.' John Stokes, *TLS*

'This is a book that anyone who works in the theatre, loves the theatre or hates the theatre, is under an absolute obligation to buy. Joan Littlewood is the greatest theatre director of the present century, knocking possible rivals like Max Reinhardt and Jean-Louis Barrault into a cocked hat when it comes to intelligence, originality and the incalculable influence for good she has had on theatre all over the world.' John Wells, *Spectator*

'When the popular theatre movement reawakens and someone else sets off in pursuit of that entrancing mirage, Littlewood's example will come in handy as a treasure-island map. Until that time we can admire it as a story from the British theatre's heroic age.' Irving Wardle, *Independent on Sunday*

'You do not have to be even halfway interested in theatre to relish this welter of a book. It is compulsive, elusive and maddening. Read it.' Henry Livings, *Financial Times*

'There is about Joan Littlewood an admirable lack of self-pity and a feisty willingness to take on anything and anybody. Theatre people everywhere are in her debt.' Fergus Linehan, *Irish Times*

Joan's Book

NORWICH CITY COLLEGE

Stock No.	238 418		
Class	792.0233 LiT		
Cat.	SSA	Proc	3WL

The Autobiography of
Joan Littlewood

with a foreword by
Peter Rankin

Methuen

Published by Methuen 2003

Methuen Publishing Ltd
215 Vauxhall Bridge Road
London SW1V 1EJ

First published in Great Britain 1994
by Methuen London

Reissued as a Minerva edition in 1995
by Mandarin Paperbacks

Copyright © 1994 by Joan Littlewood
The author has asserted her moral rights

Copyright in the Foreword
© Peter Rankin, 2003

A CIP catalogue record for this title
is available from the British Library

ISBN 0–413–77318–3

Printed and bound in Great Britain
by Cox & Wyman Ltd, Reading, Berks

This book is sold subject to the condition that it shall not,
by way of trade or otherwise, be lent, resold, hired out, or otherwise circulated
without the publisher's prior consent in any form of binding or cover
other than that in which it is published and without a similar condition
including this condition being imposed on the subsequent purchaser.

Contents

Part One 1914–45

ONE : 3

Of my birth and parentage. Caroline Emily and Robert Francis, my grandparents, bring me up as their own. Of my Aunt Carrie, her brother Bob and sister Melinda, and Kate Daisy, my mother.

TWO : 11

We move to Stockwell. The house we lived in. Kate Daisy's suitors. Jim, her favourite, and his friends, the asphalters. Jim goes to War, so does Uncle Bob. They come through, without a scratch. I go to school.

THREE : 18

Christmas is merry at Number 8. Jim brings his comical friend, Harry Watson. Jim's rival, Alf Young, is home from Australia. A card game. Rivalry. A singsong. Tastes differ. Roll back the carpet. The evening ends on a randy note.

FOUR : 27

Caroline Emily tells her story with royal secrets. The usual bank holiday quarrel. Aunt Carrie is courting Harry Watson, but she takes me to the seaside for the first time. A mysterious lady visitor. Kate tells me she is going to marry.

TWENTY-TWO : 203

Time for voice classes at Nelson Illingworth's bungalow, once owned by Ellen Terry. Theatre Newsletter *befriends us. Our* Time *praises us. The debts are mounting. A young woman gives us a hundred pounds, says she can raise all the money we need. The Pennymans want us to run a residential summer school. Mike Thompson appeals to Art Council; is snubbed. Howard tries Lady Dugdale. His letter passed on to Sir Kenneth Clark, who recommends Arts Council. Ruth Brandes receives a letter from Ivor Brown of the* Observer. *He recommends Arts Council. The Summer School and bright students.*

TWENTY-THREE : 213

Gerry's lion cub. Au revoir, Ormesby. Pearl is going home to have her baby. Isla Gledhill will replace her. Margaret Greenwood, Edna Carson, Camel, John Blanshard and an exciting young writer, Benedict Ellis, join us. Freddie Piffard becomes our fourth director, with James Ford, Bill Maclellan and Hugh MacDiarmid. Bill Mac publishes Uranium 235. *Our first tour of Scotland. We gatecrash the Edinburgh Festival and attract all the poets of Scotland. Hospitality is great, but David and Ben spend a night in gaol. Jimmie receives plaudits from James Bridie. A surprise invitation.*

TWENTY-FOUR : 228

We play London for the first time. A group of MPs attend the show and a delegation from Arts Council. We are invited to lunch at the House of Commons. Arts Council finally turns us down. Tom Driberg likes us. At Ormesby, rehearsals for Jimmie's updated Lysistrata – Operation Olive Branch. *The police arrest him for desertion. Ben Ellis begs to take over his rôle, the deserter; succumbs to a violent attack of schizophrenia and has to be taken to the asylum. Let out for the first night and is cured playing the part. Freddie Piffard secures a tour of the British Forces in Germany. I stay behind to help Jimmie.*

TWENTY-NINE : 313

Jimmie's new play, The Other Animals. *Opinion divided. Tyrone Guthrie, Bill Davidson, Gerry (just returned) – against. An old admirer lets us have a house. We christen it the Parrot House, as the faithfuls reassemble, taking part-time jobs. Camel retrieves our equipment. Kerstin has a tour of Sweden in her pocket. With Gerry she obtains beautiful fabrics to clothe the play. Bill Davidson leaves. Difficulty with the setting. Carl Ebert from Glyndebourne and Nye Bevan attend the first night.*

THIRTY : 325

Gerry en route for Czechoslovakia. His adventures in Prague, trying for a tour. He is lent his fare to Stockholm, finds a hostel and all-night work, dishwashing. Swedish contacts unforthcoming, but the Czech tour is on. The company play Prague, a warm welcome, lively exchange with Czech actors. The Other Animals *received doubtfully.*

THIRTY-ONE : 340

Touring Czechoslovakia, following in Schwejk's footsteps. The feasting, the fraternisation, the speeches. A Moravian production of Twelfth Night. *Our hard-worked company looked down on by some Czech actors because we join in the manual work. Zoë Tauferova, the prettiest member of the Resistance. Bratislava, Director Bagar and the Slovak actors. A Bulgarian delegation joins us. Art for the People gives us a week's holiday among the pines before we leave their beloved country.*

THIRTY-TWO : 360

Through Poland – the Russian officer. A letter from Zoë. Gerry's note left on the ferryboat. Having visited Warsaw, he would like to live there. Kerstin meets us at Trelleborg. The Swedish Co-op have given us five thousand kronor, with which she had booked a tour. Gerry has already returned to England, to find a base. News of my friend Sonja Mortensen. We play the Stockholm Opera House. Royalty, and a packed house. Gerry finds premises at All Saints, Manchester. We need nine thousand pounds. Harold Lever is willing to help, but not Arts Council. I visit Sonja. The tour ends; not much cash, but new friends, Alf Sjöberg, Anders Ek, Birgit Cullberg.

THIRTY-THREE : 385

THIRTY-FOUR : 401

THIRTY-FIVE : 412

THIRTY-SIX : 420

Wanamaker watches a rehearsal, falls for the company. Next day, brings Michael Redgrave. We leave for Glasgow, Harry Greene driving. Gerry taken to hospital in Manchester. I return. He is ordered rest. We spend two weeks in Cassis. Recalled because Sam and Redgrave are presenting Uranium 235 *at the Embassy, Swiss Cottage. After a short season, we return to Glasgow, rent a house for the company. Jimmie leaves 'Theatre Workshop'. Jean Newlove, his wife, and Hamish, their son, stay with us. We commission* Le Malade Imaginaire, *but prefer our own version.*

Part Three 1953–63

THIRTY-SEVEN : 439

We move from Glasgow to London E15. The state of Theatre Royal. The generosity of May and Bert Scagnelli. Gerry asks West Ham to accept us as their Civic Theatre. They cannot. We live and produce plays on the barest minimum. The Safety Curtain falls during a performance of The Alchemist. *Harry Greene snatches George Cooper from danger. Harry Corbett and Avis Bunnage camping in France with Gerry and me during an enforced break. Farming, rehearsing in Tom Driberg's barn for* The Travellers *in Edinburgh. Harry Greene and Karl Woods given four pounds to take them there and construct the set* in situ.

THIRTY-EIGHT : 460

The Travellers *in Edinburgh. Obraztsov plays E15:* An Enemy of the People. *George Cooper's* Schwejk *transfers to the Duke of York's, our* Arden of Faversham *and* Volpone *to the International Festival of Theatre, Paris. George's* Volpone *proclaimed the finest piece of acting since Orson Welles performed there. Nina makes us bankrupt for a hundred pounds. Arts Council withdraw an offer of a hundred pounds. George Cooper and Harry Corbett leave us.* Mother Courage *in Barnstaple, Devon. The Italian Straw Hat with the original music. The Big Rock Candy Mountain for Christmas. Third tour of Scandinavia. Bankruptcy discharged. Edward II at E15. Visit from Jean Vilar.*

for 'unlawfully presenting parts of a new stage play not allowed by the
Lord Chamberlain', You Won't Always Be On Top. *Henry
Chapman is to receive a summons, also Gerry, Camel and Richard
Harris. We could be closed down. We need a lawyer. We circularise all
our friends, receive donations, support – only Michael Redgrave is loath to
associate himself with us, for fear we've been obscene. Wayland Young of
the* Tribune *takes over the appeal, but is against contacting the* Daily
Worker. *His QC is beyond our means. The notices may help – the only
adverse one, 'the workmen, peculiarly uninteresting',* Arts Council. *Harold
Lever, Chancellor of the Duchy of Lancaster, and Gerald Gardiner, Lord
High Chancellor in Wilson's government, defend us, without fee. The
result.*

FORTY-THREE : 513

G.B.S., J.P. Sartre and Paul Green, *American playwright, almost
unknown, certainly undervalued; an inimitable performance by John Bay
in* Unto Such Glory, *one of our best productions.* La Putain
Respectueuse, *with Yootha Joyce, incomparable. A quick trip to the
D.D.R., to receive my medal. Return to find another wild script awaiting
me. It could be worked on. I am alone in thinking so. I go ahead with my
reluctant team and kick the script into life – the lack of stagecraft covered
by Johnnie Wallbank's jazz links. Despite rejection by Arts Council and
flabbergasted reviews,* A Taste of Honey *brings 'em in.*

FORTY-FOUR : 521

Brendan in London for the launch of Borstal Boy. *The first hostage of our
time killed in Cyprus. There is a play in it. B.B. says he will write it, in
Ireland, and goes. The Royal Court try to take over Shelagh. Gerry tries
Arts Council for a bursary for her. She is given a hundred pounds. Graham
Greene praises us and gives Shelagh a typewriter. Brendan returns from
Ireland, drinking. Gerry chases him across Blackheath. He also attempts to
stop Shelagh spending all her money, which she resents. We try everything
to make Brendan write. He begins phoning bits of songs and jokes to the
theatre. We patch two acts together. Three days before opening night there
is no third act. We ad lib it. Shelagh's second play not good. I tell her to
study well-constructed plays. She says other people will work on it.*

FORTY-FIVE : 532

The Hostage notices. Brendan changes a line in one of his songs. And what about the Lord Chamberlain? We try for a war of the theatres with the Royal Court. They won't play.

FORTY-SIX : 539

Another packet on my desk. David Booth opens it. It's the genuine stuff. Frank Norman, Fings Ain't Wot They Used T'Be. Donald Albery takes Honey to Wyndham's. Arts Council asks what we're making out of it. Lionel Bart falls for Fings. Paris wants The Hostage. Frank, Brendan and Shelagh come with us to Paris. Acclaim. Brendan finishes up in gaol. In London we have three shows in the West End and nothing at E15. Success is draining us.

FORTY-SEVEN : 548

Two strangers at E15. A script from Wolf Mankowitz — a package production? Gerry needs one. Next day, conventional auditions for small parts. Victor Spinetti's name mentioned, he is working in a nightclub. I go to see him and very impressed. Wolf won't have a word of his play changed. Shall I quit? There's Victor, Roy Kinnear, Sheila Hancock in the cast and two of my own. They make it worth staying. To my amazement, this show follows the others into the West End. Arts Council lay claim to ten per cent of our profits. In fifteen years, they've given us £4,150. Richard Findlater quotes the grants awarded to theatres in Europe. William Saroyan comes to E15, improvising a play, Sam, the Highest Jumper of Them All. He likes it. The critics don't. He answers them. We prepare Every Man in His Humour for Paris.

FORTY-EIGHT : 558

Vic's nightclub won't release him for Paris. We close ranks and get by. Bob Grant wins an acting award. Wolf Mankowitz backs Shelagh's second play. We produce Sparrers Can't Sing by Steve Lewis. The play does well. Brendan is said to be writing Richard's Cork Leg. I go and see. He isn't. He records a passage — a disaster. He tries to buy champagne — violence in the grocer's — the police — a court case threatens.

FORTY-NINE : 569

The Hostage *is opening in New York. Gerry and I go ahead to contradict the bad press Brendan has been getting. A curious radio interview. The company and Brendan arrive, he is mobbed by press men. The backers worry about our accents. We play a joke on them. A brush with the Stage Manager. The first-night audience. Next day, Vic visits Lee Strasberg's studio. Dudley Sutton looks for Krushchev's boat. Studs Terkel corners me. We meet Libby Holman. Tom Driberg to the Labour Party Conference, Scarborough – Gerry and I to London, Brendan and Beatrice remain in New York.*

FIFTY : 579

Study Danton's Death *by Büchner, which we cannot afford. We take* Sparrers Can't Sing *to East Berlin. Harry Corbett directs an Alun Owen play while we are away. John Junkin falls for* They Might be Giants, *by Jim Goldman. Hal Prince finances it. The author attends rehearsals. To a man, the critics damn it. Disgusted, I quit theatre and Gerry. Sidney Bernstein arranges for Malcolm Muggeridge to interview me on TV. I go to Nigeria to work with Wole Soyinka, meet a young architect who sees me off. Goodbye, Europe.*

Part Four 1963–74

FIFTY-ONE : 591

Senegal. Exploring Dakar. The French colonials. The museum of the slave trade. On to Lagos. No Wole. No public transport. A lift through dangerous territory – a makeshift bed. The next day searching Ibadan for Wole and better quarters – witch-doctors – ju-ju – dances – a cultured concert – friendly people in a café. Mr and Mrs Hendrickse say I can rent their house.

FIFTY-TWO : 613

Ibadan – its hospital. Village carvings, the god of peace – a crocodile pet – a village festival. Removal to my new home – the snake-charmer. Work on film treatment of The Lion and the Jewel. *Wole turns up. A*

Lionel writes a song for Barbara Windsor. Gore Vidal and the fair
Elaine.

FIFTY-SIX : 657

Christmas in Casablanca. To Marrakech in an old, hired banger. The
Casbah and belly dancers with red noses. Beyond the walls, the Berber
entertainers. The remains of a harem. Among the sands, a forgotten Jewish
tribe. Our lives in danger – to the desert – across the mountains, making
for Agadir. Stopped by the floods – we must take the long road back. Gerry
exhausted.

FIFTY-SEVEN : 668

E15 needs a season of plays. Read a Vanbrugh and Genet, neither
suitable. Gerry plays me a tape, Songs of the First World War. *He*
wants them used in a play. Two writers have already tried and failed, a
third is working on it. Jacques Tati attends private showing of Sparrers,
offers me use of his studios at Charenton. A backer gives me the go-ahead
on needed pick-up shots. The third writer reads his play to us. There are
no songs in it. I could do better myself. Next day, I dictate a first draft to
Gerry. Say I can re-cut film and work on the play at the same time.

FIFTY-EIGHT : 677

BBC Singers dislike changes. Technical requirements are many.
Mornings removing schmaltz from songs, afternoons cutting film. BBC
Singers leave. John Gower (baritone), Colin Kemball (tenor) stay. Gerry
finds an army sergeant to drill actors. His language too blue to be repeated.
Ann Beach in tears over lack of script. With Camel on design, Dick
Bowdler on news panel, Ivor Dykes making slides and Gerry collecting
facts and figures, we shall have something.

FIFTY-NINE : 687

Sparrers film's East End première – I don't go – puzzling over
presenting the Irish in the 1914–18 War. Company have missed reaction
to film. Good idea for church scene and title, Oh, What a Lovely.
War!. Henri Barbusse books gives me an ending for it. First run, local

people as audience. Souvenirs of that War presented to us. The show works. We are indebted to the unnamed soldiers who wrote the lyrics we sing.

SIXTY-THREE : 736

Gerry visits Nigeria – proposes filming The Lion and the Jewel *in Tunisia. My 'commercial' production, a non-existent script. The composer's wild suggestions – a mixed cast – the choreographer and George Cooper. I quit. My successor fares badly. West Ham, now Newham, against the Fun Palace. The Greater London Council for their storm tanks, which were never built. We withdraw our appeal to the Minister for fear of endangering the whole Lea Valley Bill, which is to go before parliament. Deadlock. Gerry and Joan return to Tunisia, our only Fun Palace, for the second year's programme.*

SIXTY-FOUR : 748

Tunisia wants publicity for Le Centre. A well-known English critic comes to see our work, says that England shouldn't let us go. One more try in London. The Millwall Tenants' Association give us their blessing, but we have nowhere to go. The Evening Standard *publishes the story. One bit of land is free, the debris round the Theatre Royal, Stratford, left by the developers. We clear it, institute Learn-and-Play with local children and lost teenagers. We have festivals, a zoo, a riding school, in defiance of Local Authority. We call it 'Stratford Fair'.*

APPENDIX ONE : 763

Theatre Union Study Course, 1940. Each company member should prepare a paper or photomontage on their chosen subject.

APPENDIX TWO : 765

The Grosvenor Square Presbyterian Church and School at All Saints, Manchester.

APPENDIX THREE : 767

'Umeni Lidu – Art for the People' by Gerry Raffles, General Manager of Theatre Workshop, who have just completed a highly successful tour of Czechoslovakia.

Illustrations

8e   Glynn Edwards.
8f   John Blanshard.
9a   *A Christmas Carol.*
9b   *The Alchemist.*
10a   *Richard II.*
10b   *Richard II.*
11a   Sean O'Casey's *Red Roses for Me.*
11b   *An Enemy of the People.*
12a   Ewan MacColl's *The Other Animals.*
12b   Alan Lomax's *The Big Rock Candy Mountain.*
13a   *Edward II.*
13b   Brendan Behan's *The Quare Fellow.*
14a   Richard Harris.
14b   Dudley Sutton.
14c   Brendan Behan.
14d   Dudley Foster.
15a   Shelagh Delaney.
15b   Frank Norman.
15c   Frances Cuka and Jimmie Moore in *A Taste of Honey.*
15d   Lionel Bart.
16a   Murray Melvin.
16b   Roy Kinnear.
16c   David Booth.
16d   Victor Spinetti.
17a   Henry Chapman's *You Won't Always be on Top.*
17b   *Unternehmen Ölzweig* at the Maxim Gorki Theater.
18a   Valerie Walsh.
18b   Carole A. Christensen.
18c   Griffith Davies.
18d   Jane McKerron.
18e   Barbara Ferris.
19   Toni Palmer and Barbara Windsor.
20a   Ivor Dykes.
20b   Carol Murphy and Jo Benson.
20c   Dick Bowdler.
20d   Chick Fowler.
20e   John Bury.
21a   *Oh What A Lovely War.*
21b   Avis Bunnage in *Oh What A Lovely War.*

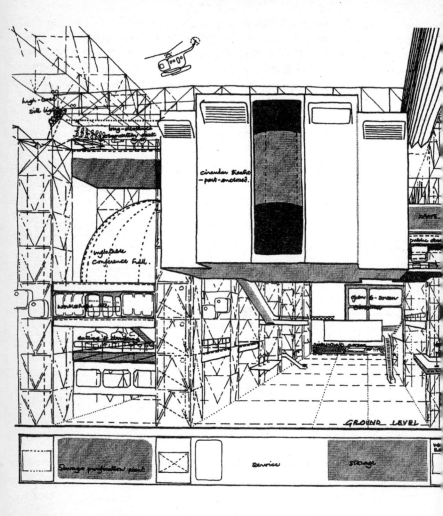

high-level
site lighting

long-distance
communication desk

circular theatre
- part-enclosed.

inflatable
conference hall.

workshops

open 6-screen
cinema

GROUND LEVEL

Sewage purification plant

service

storage

ARRIVE AND LEAVE by train, bus, monorail, hovercraft, car, tube or foot at any time YOU want to - or just have a look at it as you pass. The information screens will show you what's happening. No need to look for an entrance - just walk in anywhere. No doors, foyers, queues or commissionaires: it's up to you how you use it. Look around - take a lift, a ramp, an escalator to wherever or whatever looks interesting.

CHOOSE what you want to do - or watch someone else doing it. Learn how to handle tools, paint, babies, machinery, or just listen to your favourite tune. Dance, talk or be lifted up to where you can see how other people make things work. Sit out over space with a drink and tune in to what's happening elsewhere in the city. Try starting a riot or beginning a painting - or just sit back and stare at the sky.

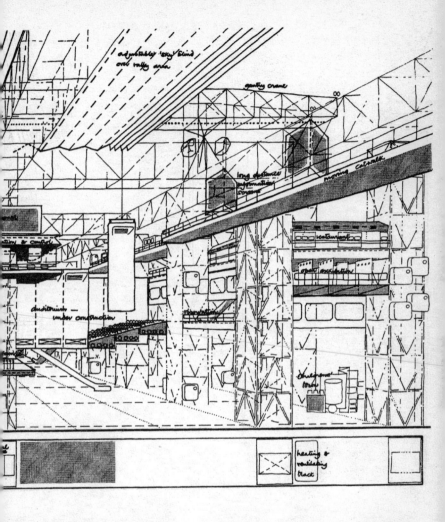

WHAT TIME IS IT? Any time of day or night, winter or summer - it really doesn't matter. If it's too wet that roof will stop the rain but not the light. The artificial cloud will keep you cool or make rainbows for you. Your feet will be warm as you watch the stars the atmosphere clear as you join in the chorus. Why not have your favourite meal high up where you can watch/the thunderstorm?

WHY ALL THIS LOT? "If any nation is to be lost or saved by the character of its great cities, our own is that nation".
— Robert Vaughan 1843

We are building a short-term plaything in which all of us can realise the possibilities and delights that a 20th Century city environment owes us. It must last no longer than we need it.

Foreword

When her beloved Gerry died in 1975, Joan made herself two promises. She would never set foot in the Theatre Royal again and she would never direct another play.

Promise number one she kept for twenty years. Then in January 1995, while rehearsing a new show, the writer-director, Ken Hill died. Joan felt she ought to be present at his first night. After all, Ken had started to learn about theatre with her. Any sentimental feelings ended abruptly as she crossed the threshold. She did not like the show. I had been working with Ken at the time but, like him, I was one of Joan's children. He, however, was dead. I was alive, so it was me that got it in the neck. How I wished she'd stuck to that first promise.

She stuck to her second promise good and proper. Joan never did direct another play. Some people were maddened by that. I just thought back to one evening in Paris towards the end of a troubled rehearsal period. 'It seems my only talent is for growing a show,' Joan said sadly, thinking about the Fun Palace and not having got it going. 'But whenever I've attempted anything away from Gerry,' – here she was talking about theatre – 'it hasn't worked. First *Twang!* And now this.' Perhaps you can see where I'm heading. After April 1975, she would always be away from Gerry.

Immediately after Gerry's death, Joan's mind ran back to the early days. A memo arrived on Ken Hill's desk. He was running the theatre at the time. 'Form a company and do the classics,' Joan wrote, but she'd never seen him direct a classic. It was stupefying. Nothing like that had happened at the theatre since 1955. Gerry's triumphs had always been new plays. You had to be older than I was then to realize that a company and the classics are a shield against the outside world and Joan no longer had a shield.

She didn't stick around. Instead, she went back to her pre-Gerry gypsy life, finding havens in other people's homes: Vienne, Pauillac, Paris, Brighton, Stockwell and my place in north London.

What mattered was the change of scene. Once installed, all she needed was dinner, a bit of company and a bed.

The words, 'she would never direct another play', are only there because they're easy to understand. According to Joan, she never directed a play at all, hence the expression, 'growing a show'. A journalist spent ten minutes arguing with her over what he would call her in his new book. Trying to be helpful, I proposed Concierge, a title she'd given herself many years earlier. 'All I do is watch things go by and when I don't like the look of something, I say, "No."' but she'd forgotten that one. 'Saboteur' was the title eventually settled on.

Young actors, on hearing Joan come out with this 'I never directed' line, would give me a sidelong glance. The funny thing is, it was true. It was also, as with a lot of things Joan said, misleading. No, she didn't tell actors what to do, nothing so boring. Nevertheless, she got what she wanted, ruthlessly on occasion. It was almost a relief when, in Paris, this time in Philippe de Rothschild's garden, she said, 'I was the only tough director England ever had.' Many of her actors, if they had been sitting there, would have nodded because that was the nearest to their experience.

What was Joan doing in Philippe de Rothschild's garden? Simple. Joan may have been ruthless at work but away from it, she was shy and vulnerable. Gov, as Joan called him, lived in France, away from people who knew her work, people who would have asked questions, wanted her to be *on*, to be the *Joan* they knew. He was a shield and he too had lost a partner. The archcapitalist and the one-time communist may have been an incongruous pair but sing the song, 'It's All Right With Me', and you might get the picture. When they were alone together, eating lunch and arguing by the waterside at Lacanau, a labrador eyeing them soulfully for scraps, they were OK.

Joan may not have directed again but she never stopped working. The plays, screenplays and adaptations, most of those didn't get done because she would build herself into them and have managers asking, 'But will Joan direct it?' Two books got published, though, *Milady Vine*, a thank you to Gov, and this one, *Joan's Book*, which took seven years. It would have taken less, were it not for Joan charging round the world breaking a bone here, knocking herself out there, but then, in her mind, she was always a teenager. When she did settle down to work, she would fight tooth and nail with her editors over one word. I liked to imagine these scenes affording amusement to the writers whose work she completely rewrote.

When you read the book, you'll find that the young Joan earned money in radio. The old Joan did too. She read her book and acted in plays. Here's a funny thing. Surrounded by actors, rather than watching them, she became a different person. In between takes, she chatted away, encouraging her fellow players, which they adored, and rubbishing directors, which they adored even more. It wasn't such an easy ride for the producer of the radio play. She had to get Joan to do some actual work.

When Joan got the news she would probably need an operation on her heart, she said, 'No hospital, no knife. Let me go in peace.' So when a few weeks later she did go, in a room she was familiar with, half asleep in an armchair, I had to stop myself from saying out loud, 'You've got your own way again, as usual.'

Peter Rankin
November 2002

Acknowledgements

My thanks are due to Josie Binns and Anne Murray for their patience and care in typing out my illegible script and to Peter Rankin for his critical nose and eagle eye.

My thanks are also due to the following for providing photographs of themselves and others:

Associated Newspapers for photographs numbers 16c and 19; Lionel Bart for 15d; Ken Blanshard for 8f; Dick Bowdler for 20c; Roy Brewer for 16d; John Bury for 5a and 20e; Romano Cagnoni for 21a, 21b and 23a; Carole Christensen for 18b; George Cooper for 7b; Harriet Crowder for 16a; Griffith Davies for 18c; Ivor Dykes for 20a; Howard Goorney for 3a and 3b; Harry Greene for 5d and 5f; Julia Jones for 6c and 6d; Ida Kar for 15b; Neil Libbert for 24a; George Luscombe for 5c; *Manchester Evening News* for 1a; Maxim Gorki Theatre for 17b; Tony May for 18a; Murray Melvin for 7c; Brian Murphy for 8c; Carol Murphy for 20b; Jean Newlove for 7d; The Press Association Ltd for 23b; Ken Ross-Mackenzie for 14a; ABPC Films for 16b; David Sim for 21c; John V. Spinner for 7a, 8a, 8b, 8d, 9a, 9b, 10a, 10b, 11a, 11b, 12a, 12b, 13a, 13b, 14b, 14c, 14d, 15c, 17a and 22a; Simon Trussler for 2b; Pearl Turner for 4a; Jeff Vickers for 18d and 18e; and Alan Vines for 8c. (Photograph numbers 1b, 1c, 1d, 2a, 4b, 4c, 4d, 5b, 5e, 6a, 6b, 15a and 20d are from J.L.'s own collection.)

Finally, I am grateful to Cedric Price for allowing me to reproduce his plan for the Fun Palace.

For Gerry

May his long fight encourage all those young artists oppressed
by our far-famed English philistines.

Part One
1914 – 45

One

*Of my birth and parentage. Caroline Emily and Robert Francis,
my grandparents, bring me up as their own. Of my Aunt Carrie,
her brother Bob and sister Melinda, and Kate Daisy, my mother.*

A cockney maid, in 1914, long before the Pill was a twinkle in your mother's eye, finding herself in the Pudding Club, if she was too young to know that Mrs Bunyan up Gateley Road could fix you with soap and water emetics for nine quid, might, all the same, have heard that strong purgatives taken in a scalding hot bath with a glass of gin could fix you up, but in any case hot baths were hard to come by, with or without gin. There were public baths at Kennington, but you'd never get past the dragon in the white overall with a noggin of gin under your coat.

Kate had a tell-tale face.

The dragon releases a gusher of boiling water with a large crank – glances at the clock – five minutes later it's 'Come on, Number 3! Out! Are you dead in there? Time's up!'

There was no one she could tell. Did Sister Carrie have her suspicions? She had given Kate an old-fashioned look when she caught her scrubbing away at those monthly pudding cloths, now white and bloodless, in no need of all that effort. She could never turn to her mother. What went on under your petticoat had to be kept secret. You mustn't even touch yourself there. How would she ever be able to look her mother in the face? She had put up with the sickness, the pain in the nipples, without a word to anyone. If it came to it, she would have it under a bush in the park. Who'd bother? They were too excited about the coming War.

She had never set eyes on him again. Well, only that once: when she told him. After that she kept a sharp lookout for him but he seemed to have vanished off the face of the earth.

'Kate! Turn round!' Here we go. Ma had caught her being sick in the sink.

'I thought so. Whose is it?'

'I don't feel well, Mum.'

'You'll feel worse before you feel better. You just wait till your father gets home.'

Kate rushed out into the street. It was the first time she'd stopped off work since she left school. The street looked unfamiliar. It was the time of day. Now that the cat was out of the bag she would have to talk to someone. She walked on, aimlessly. There was her best friend, Tilly. She was a shop-girl too, and nice. She could be in Queen Victoria Street when Tilly came out for the break at twelve.

They had a cup of tea and a Chelsea bun.

'Oh Lord, Kitty, you do go on. You're not the first and you won't be the last. Everybody's doin' it. I've got one in the oven myself, as it 'appens.'

'What?'

'A bun. It was all those knee tremblers down by the station. I told 'im not to go the 'ole 'og.'

Kate smiled and looked pretty again. Tilly admired Kate's black curly hair, blue-grey eyes, her trim figure and dainty feet, but what a firebrand she was. Well, she was tame enough now.

'I suppose it was that Jack?' Kate looked away.

'You'll never see him again.'

'I don't want to.' That was a lie, and Tilly knew it.

'Well, there's plenty more fish in the sea. What happened to that Alfie?'

'He went to Australia.'

'When is it?'

'I don't know.'

'You'll have to find out, won't you? Make plans, knit baby things and all that. Your ma'll adopt it, won't she?'

'I don't think so.'

' 'Course she will. After all, you've always been good to 'er, taken your wages 'ome on a Friday. You won't be able to go skylarking again for a while. Can't you see us pushin' our prams up the park of a Sunday, feedin' the ducks?'

There was no doubt about it, Kate felt so much better for seeing Tilly. The sun was shining on the river, she felt she could face the music. She let herself in at the basement. Her ma was at the copper in the scullery heaving a wet sheet on to a stick. Someone was talking to her.

'I'm not a bit surprised.' It was that old hag, Mrs Delaye, the local *Evening News*. 'You're not going to keep it in the family, are you?'

'What else?'

'Put it in an orphanage. The Bluecoats take 'em, I do know.'

Kate ran tiptoe towards the stairs.

'How has she taken it? I don't suppose she wants it.'

'I should hope not, the dirty little . . .'

'Well, then . . .'

'She's too far gone.'

'I always maintained that she'd come to no good, too wilful –'

Kate hadn't waited to hear that. She was sitting on the bed she shared with her Sister Carrie. 'Love locked out' leant his silly little bum against the door-frame in the picture. She threw off her shoes and punched the pillow. Old bitch! Carrie would make her life a misery from now on, too. After all, hadn't she made eyes at him when they all met that Sunday, round the bandstand in Hyde Park? But it was Kate he'd fancied. Worse luck. Still, Carrie was kind, really, though she was always making sarcastic remarks.

Kate whiled away the afternoon, examined her figure, counted her money, went through her drawers, and Carrie's, re-read her love letters – and Carrie's. It was so quiet. Tomorrow she would go to work. She didn't like being at home, it was as if the world had left you behind.

She heard her father come in. Ma would be telling him.

'Kate! Are you in?' The sudden cry sent a pain through her breasts.

'Yes, Ma.'

'What are you doing up there? Your father wants a word with you.'

Dad was pulling off his Post Office overalls in the passage. When he'd had a sluice he'd be ready for his grub. Ma was already dishing it out, a nice bit of silverside, carrots and mash.

'Kate's got something to tell you, Bob.'

'Have you, gel?'

She knew he wouldn't be cruel. He was hard with them but never unkind.

Ma was cutting a slice off the big crusty Coburg loaf, holding it against her breast.

Kate looked up at the family photograph on the wall, Robert Francis Littlewood sitting in his armchair surrounded by his family, Toby, his dog, between his knees.

'Are you waiting for me to tell him? Well, Kate?'

At that moment the basement door opened and Carrie came in, pushing her bike before her. She strode in, throwing her tam-o'-shanter on to the basket chair in the cupboard corner.

' 'Ullo, Katie, you home? Mum. Dad. The War's on. Kaiser Bill's told the Russians to take a running jump. Austria's in Serbia and the fleet's in Scapa Flow.'

'Never mind the War, sit down and have your tea.'

'Something wrong?'

'It's only a rumour.'

Ma sounded bitter. 'What's the matter with everybody?'

Kate passed the pepper-pot to her father and sat in the chair beside him.

'Oh, the news has broken, has it? I thought we all knew our Katie was going to be a mother.'

Kate leapt up. 'You shut up, you . . .'

'That's enough! Sit down the two of you,' said her father, mopping up his gravy. Then he turned to Kate. 'Is this true, gel?'

'Yes, Dad.'

There was another silence.

'Who've you bin with?'

'You don't know 'im, Dad.'

'Never mind about that. Who is 'e?' Kate turned her head away. 'You might just as well tell me, gel. I'll find out.'

'I'll not tell you with 'er 'ere.'

'I'm going. I know who it is anyway.' And Carrie flounced out.

Ma followed her into the scullery. Kate told Dad her secret. He was silent till he'd finished his mug of tea.

'Where does he work?'

'St Martin's le Grand. Don't go there, Dad, please don't.'

Then Mother's pride and joy arrived, dumped his plumbing tools and took his place at the table.

'Somebody dead?'

Kate was ready for him. 'Don't you start, Bob Littlewood, or I'll kill you.'

'What have I said?'

'That's enough. Try to keep your temper for once, Kate. Least said, soonest mended. Let's finish our tea in peace.'

Next day, Robert Francis took time off to find the man who'd done his daughter wrong. He'd finally got the name out of Kate and was even shown the face in her locket. He waited a long time by the gate but his patience was rewarded.

'You are Jack—.'

'You have the better of me.'

'I'm Kate Littlewood's father and I want to know your intentions as regards my daughter.'

'What should they be?'

'By rights, marriage.'

'Well, I'm certainly not going to do that.' The man spoke with a certain arrogance.

'I'll have to take you to court then, won't I?'

'You must please yourself, but I think you'd better understand that I have a position to uphold. I can't afford a scandal. As it happens I am to be married before very long.'

'I take it you don't dispute that the child is of your making?'

'I'm not prepared to admit anything, and I think it would be better for you and your daughter if this conversation went no further.'

Robert Francis ignored the advice and persisted to such effect that the case was settled out of court, the unwilling father having agreed to pay six shillings a week towards the child's maintenance until it reached the age of sixteen.

The summer before the War was the sunniest England had known for a long time. On Sundays, between Kingston and

Maidenhead, you couldn't see the river for rowboats and punts. Katie sat on the bank, resting her big belly. She was wearing her straw hat, trimmed with cherries. Somewhere a gramophone played 'If you were the only girl in the world'. She nearly cried.

While the boys over there were receiving their baptism of fire, in October she was delivered of a healthy girl. They called her Joan; it was the popular name that year. Maudie was added because everyone loved Maudie Edwardes.

Robert Francis dandled the new baby on his knee. 'Cor, what plates of meat,' he said. 'She'll make a good footballer.'

M y grandfather, Robert Francis, was an East Ender, proud of being a cockney, born within the sound of Bow Bells. He was a boy of thirteen at the time of the Paris Commune, but he knew nothing of that. His father was a Spitalfields weaver, and his mother spoke German like a native, or so he said, but nobody believed him.

'Yiddish,' they said. 'Anyone can see you're a Five-to-two, with your black curly hair and your ginger 'tache.' He was a good-looking man, though one eye was blue and the other one grey.

He'd always wanted to marry a country girl. Caroline Emily Burbridge came from Merton, which was country in those days when Peckham Rye was all green fields. He loved her at first sight. 'She 'ad a nose like a little shirt button,' he said. Whenever he told you about that first meeting, she would, as likely as not, be at her sewing, and she would bend her head and smile, then make a little mocking sound as she pricked another stitch. She wore her hair like a Degas girl, in a topknot, and he loved her till the end of her days, though he never used the word. She liked to tease him: she called him her John Willy, and always said she wanted to go first because she'd be lonely without him.

Her father had been a shoemaker, but a lazybones. When people came to collect the repairs, he was nowhere to be found, but she knew where he was – in the privy at the bottom of the garden, reading. He'd read anything he could lay hands on; he'd pick up a bit of newspaper in the street and read it. But neither his shoemaking nor his great reading brought him prosperity. Caroline Em was sent out to work before she was ten, skivvying, and though she was sharp and observant, she never learned to read and write. She could manage a few words, that's all.

Her John Willy was in a worse case, he too was out working by the time he was ten, ruling lines in a print shop. After a while he migrated to a soapworks and when, as a teenager, he took the Queen's shilling, 'They learned me to write me name,' he said. 'Then they sent me to India. My brother Dick did better. He disgraced himself and was sent to the boys' 'ome, but they eddicated 'im to read an' write.'

When Caroline Em went up to London, it was to work in a pub kitchen. Town life, she found, suited her better than the muddy lanes of Merton. She liked the bustle and hustle. One day, she heard there was a good job going in a high-class pub in Threadneedle Street. She went along wearing her pillbox hat and got it. Not long after, she was to be seen, of a Saturday evening, strolling in the park on the arm of her latest beau, a smart young fellow, tanned from his three years in India, with many a lively yarn to beguile her.

Soon they were married. They'd found a little house at the Elephant, Avonmouth Street, and there the family came along – Melinda, the saintliest; clever Carrie; Bob, the favourite; and Kate Daisy, the terror.

Robert Francis had a lineman's job, laying cable for the Post Office, nine hours a day; six hours Saturdays. Caroline Em still had to go to work, and take in a few lodgers. You couldn't bring up a family on thirty-two bob a week. 'The better-paid jobs allus went to the clerks, because they 'ad learning. Us linemen didn't stand a chance though we knew the practical side and we 'ad to tackle it.'

Life wasn't easy but the kids were well fed and shod. Round the Elephant, where a good many children still ran barefoot, that put you among the haristocracy. The Littlewoods were clever at school, but at twelve they had to go to work.

There were no holidays, but always outings on a Sunday in summer – a brake ride to Greenwich or Hackney Marshes, a singsong in the pub with the kids parked in the garden. Every year, Robert Francis took a few days off and walked to Dover and back, choosing the flowery lanes and dells, leaving the high roads to the cranky new motor cars. His sister Kit kept a boarding house there. Caroline Emily didn't go. She never had a holiday in her whole life.

At twenty-one, Melinda was preparing to marry a Canadian boy and go to live in Canada.

> *Melinda Littlewood is her name*
> *Single is her station*
> *Happy is the Little man*
> *Making the alteration –*

wrote Alf Little in her album, with a border of forget-me-nots round his signature. But, just as she was trying on her wedding dress, she collapsed. The doctor couldn't make out what was wrong with her. Her father's workmates clubbed together to pay for a specialist, but it was too late. She died on the eve of St Valentine's Day. The death certificate said 'enteric fever'.

Robert Francis was convinced he had carried the germ of her illness from India. Nothing could persuade him otherwise.

Two

*We move to Stockwell. The house we lived in. Kate Daisy's suitors.
Jim, her favourite, and his friends, the asphalters. Jim goes to War,
so does Uncle Bob. They come through, without a scratch. I go to
school.*

The Littlewoods moved. They found a nine-roomed house,
8 Stockwell Road, SW9. It would take the family and a few
lodgers. The area had seen better days, but the gentry, with
their horses and carriages, had moved on; only broken bell handles
and an empty mews testified to former glory. A coster with his
donkey and cart, and the Kennedys, car thieves, occupied the
mews. Number 10 was a dental clinic, and Mrs Nelson and her two
sons occupied Number 6. Her youngest, Eddie, used to torture his
cat, put it in harness and whip it to make it drag him along. When
it couldn't, he got up early and hanged it. Caroline Emily said
Mrs Nelson was a no-class person, and Robert Francis was at war
with the clinic because their cat chased his pigeons. He had built
a chicken run in the back yard, also rabbit hutches, a pigeon loft
and a bench, where he could sit for hours, pigeons feeding from
his hand, the chickens pecking round him. The chickens became
my friends. I would go and chat to them every day. When the
time came for one to have its neck wrung, I would run away and
stay away for hours. I never ate chicken.

In Caroline Emily's domain there was a meat safe, a mangle
and a woodpile under a tarpaulin roof. Her larder was the cellar
under the front steps of the house. Robert Francis also kept his
medicines there, home-made Black Strap, to keep your bowels
open, Paregoric, Boracic, Glauber's Salts and a sure cure for
baldness in a green bottle. 'Gunpowder and horse droppings,'
said Caroline Emily. 'Did you bring that back from India?'

By the time I came along, we passed most of our time in the

basement of that old house. My grandparents slept together in a dark room, front basement, with a good strong cabbage stick by the bed in case of intruders. Gran had ointments and bandages for her ulcerated legs, too. The passage was reduced to half its width by the old coats, macs and umbrellas hanging there.

In the kitchen a dresser ran the length of the room; the table was by the window, covered with patterned oilcloth. In the far corner, behind my grandfather's armchair, he had his pipe rack, and a small Japanese cabinet, inlaid with mother-of-pearl, where he kept the family's birth, marriage and death certificates. It smelt musty when it was opened.

As a baby Caroline Emily washed me in a zinc bath by the kitchen fire, and Grandad would sit in his corner watching till she handed me to him, wrapped in a warm towel. Then I was rocked and jigged to the bawdy songs he'd learnt in the army. The adults were not so privileged. Monday night was bath night, because Monday was wash day. All the dirty washing went into Gran's copper in the scullery; clouds of steam escaped every time she lifted the lid. The sodden clothes went through the mangle, then on to the lines in the back yard. In wet weather they had to be dried in the house, and that Robert Francis could not abide. He would wolf down his cold meat and bubble and squeak, and escape to the flea-pit on the corner. He wasn't keen on the pictures but where else?

When the wash was done, the hot grey water was baled out of the copper and lugged up two flights of stairs, bucket by bucket. The bathroom was splendid, with double doors, a wide window bordered with stained glass, a bath with claw feet – but no plumbing. My grandfather liked the bathroom; he reared his canaries there.

The house was impressive outside. Seven stone steps led up to the front door and its elephant-trunk knocker. A bay window, geranium window boxes, and lace curtains hid the best room, known as the sitting-room. Seven stone steps took you down to the basement, the dustbins, two coal cellars, and . . .

One two three, a lairy
My ball's gone down the airy –

Above the coal cellars was my grandfather's crowning glory, his front garden, a small square lawn bordered with Virginia stock or nasturtium; he alternated them. Hollyhocks stood by the railings, and delphinium, phlox and pansies grew in profusion. The centre-piece was the coal-hole cover, of figured ironwork. When the days lengthened into spring, he would spend his evenings gardening, straightening up occasionally to have a word with passers-by.

Caroline Emily brought me up as her own, though she was no longer young and there was still talk of a foundling hospital from time to time. Nobody saw much of the flighty one who had brought her trouble home. Aunt Carrie was good to me.

One of Kate Daisy's pre-war followers, Alf Young, turned up one day. He was in Anzac uniform and left Kate his photo. She put it on the piano and went upstairs to finish packing. She was off to Dover for Easter.

'It'll make a change,' she said.

'It's a house full of men,' said her mother.

It was: Jim, a young asphalter, and Harry, his mate, among them. They made a good pair. Harry was a comical bugger and Jim his appreciative audience. Kate said that Harry went too far, and Jim agreed as he strummed away at the old joanna.

K-K-K-Katie, my beautiful Katie
You're the only g-g-g-girl that I adore
When the m-moon shines on the cowshed
I'll be waiting at the k-k-k-kitchen door . . .

Kate bent her head and smiled.

Jim was doing quite well, till one Saturday night when he and Harry ran into the rest of the asphalters making for the music hall.

'Come and join us,' they shouted.

And they did. When they got in, the place was full of soldiers and sailors. Jim and his mates were the only ones in civvies, which caused a bit of a stir. It soon died down till, the acts proving a bit dull, the asphalters began to get restless, and during an over-long dog act began whistling and stamping. Even so the whole thing might have fizzled out if the management hadn't decided to ring the curtain down and give the signal for the national anthem.

Everybody jumped to attention – everybody except the asphalters. They, in their cockney way, started making for the exit. Jim tried to pass a burly customer who was singing the words out loud:

'Long live our noble King . . .'

'Can I get by.'

'God save our . . .'

'Oh, fuck the King,' said Jim.

And that did it. Wham! 'Take that!' Crash! Bedlam. The dogs began to bark. The manager called for order. Mind you, the asphalters had had a few, no doubt about that, and they weren't the only ones, with beer at tuppence a pint.

Tommie Jukes, Bert Storey, Jack Moss, Freddie Sapsford, Harry Watson and Jim Morritt laid about them like heroes. Harry found a bench loose in the back row. Suddenly Jim saw the funny side of it and started to laugh. That set them all off, the whole gang, and by the time they reached the fire exit, they were helpless. Luckily the police came in by the front door and began wading into the patriots.

When Kate heard the story, she was not amused. It was not that she was particularly patriotic, she just liked her suitors to be so, and Jim was by now well and truly smitten. What could he do? In the end . . . well, not quite in the end, but shortly after, Kate told him she thought he ought to do his bit. So, as his brother was already over there and had found a cushy job for the two of them, that's what he did.

He came to Stockwell, wearing his khaki, a round-faced, boyish-looking soldier. She wanted a photo of him to put on the piano, so they set off for the photographer's up Brixton, taking me with them. Jim had accepted me, with some surprise but no hard feelings. In any case there wasn't a chance of formalising his relationship with his girl. He was on embarkation leave.

As they walked along Brixton Road, a troop train slowed down on the railway bridge overhead. Soldiers were standing at the windows, the people in the street began waving. Jim held me up to have a better look. I see that train now, as I saw it then. The men were at the windows all along the corridor, looking down at us, but they weren't waving. The next stop was Victoria where they would take the train for Dover.

I remember, too, the great silver fish which appeared in the sky one day. Everybody was out watching, till the bomb dropped. It destroyed the school in Lingham Street and killed nine people.

One misty evening in 1918, Jim came home on leave which, by chance, coincided with Bob Littlewood's, Kate's brother. I was in the kitchen with Gran when the two men came lurching in, blue blind paralytic drunk, holding on to each other, singing:

> *I don't want to be a soldier*
> *I don't want to go to war*
> *I'd rather stay at home*
> *Around the streets to roam*
> *And live on the earnings of a . . . lady typist.*
> *I don't want a bayonet in me belly*
> *Don't want me bollocks shot away*
> *I'd rather stay in England*
> *In merry merry England*
> *And fornicate me bleedin' life away.*

It went to the tune of 'On Sunday I go out with a soldier', which had been greeted with wild cheers when the War was new.

Gran was struggling to push Jim up the stairs. Bob was being sick. They both stank. When Carrie and Kate came home they helped to undress them. Jim only woke up the next day. Kate took him out. All he wanted was to sit in Lyons and eat cream cakes, just cream cakes.

'Is the War over?'

'Not yet.'

The telegraph boy still came hurrying through the street, bearing the dreaded orange envelope.

'A comet with a fiery tail is approaching the earth,' said Gran.

I slept in the room which Carrie and Kate shared. One night when there was nobody in and the house and the streets outside were empty, I felt frightened. A tram went by, the gaslight flickered. I thought I saw the door opening. I looked at the pictures on the wall. Above my head was one I'd never really looked at. A lady was kneeling by a bed, her head down. There was a baby on the bed and a soldier's cap. Behind her stood an angel.

One day, Carrie came home with a roll of red, white and blue bunting and draped it from the upstairs windows. 'It's peace,' she said. Afterwards it was stored in the chiffonier and forgotten.

Uncle Bob came through without a scratch. Alf Young got a job on the boats, the Australian run, and Jim tried to go back to asphalting but there wasn't much work about. Bob was unemployed too. When Jim finally struck lucky, he tried to row Bob in. The two men didn't get on, but for Kate's sake . . . It was no use, Bob couldn't wield a nine-pound hammer. Jim showed you the corns on his hands with pride. Bob was a cissy, he said, and that was that.

Caroline Emily took me to school on my first day, and even walked into the classroom with me. She looked very proper in her black satin toque and her long grey coat. 'Was that your mother or your grandmother?' asked the teacher. I wanted to say, 'She's just Mumski,' the name Alf Young and I made up for her from Popski, the Bolshevik dog in the *Daily Sketch* cartoon, Kate's paper. Carrie read the *Daily Mirror*. Alf and I put a 'ski' on everyone's name in honour of Popski, but I thought I'd better say 'grandmother' to please the teacher, though I never thought of her as such.

School was a gorgeous place, with a bath full of wet plasticine, wooden lozenges, all different shapes and colours, red, bottle green, yellow and blue, so beautiful they made me catch my breath, and at Christmas I sang loud:

While shepherds washed their socks by night
All seated round a tub
A bar of Sunlight soap came down
They all went in the pub.

'Now each girl is to sing a song she learned at home,' said Mrs Frankish.

I started Jim's favourite:

I wish I had some bricks to build my chimney higher
To save those old Tom cats from pissing on my fie-er . . .

There was more of it, but I was interrupted.

'Some people come from nice homes,' said the lady.

Ours was a very nice home. Every head turned when our front garden was in bloom. 'They must be rich who live there,' said some girl. I heard her.

Three

Christmas is merry at Number 8. Jim brings his comical friend, Harry Watson. Jim's rival, Alf Young, is home from Australia. A card game. Rivalry. A singsong. Tastes differ. Roll back the carpet. The evening ends on a randy note.

We were rich all right at Christmas time when the puddings were mixed. Out came the deep earthenware vessel which usually held the bread, in went the dark fruity dough which gleamed and gurgled as Gran poured in the oatmeal stout and stirred it. Everyone had to stir, friends, neighbours, callers. When Mumski wasn't looking I scooped myself a fingerful. Scrumptious. And when nobody was looking Mumski stirred in all the silver threepenny bits she'd been saving; pudding bowls next, greased paper, pudding cloths, fastened with string and safety pins, and into the boiling copper and down with the wooden lid.

Then there was mincemeat, blancmanges, jellies, trifles and custards to attend to. One year Kate made chocolate mice. The meat caused a lot of controversy, but Mumski always had the last word . . . A good H-bone! And she'd go over to the City, to her favourite butcher and order a proper oven-basher. With plenty of veg, parsnips, carrots, sprouts and taters, good gravy and horseradish sauce, we wouldn't go hungry. Dinner would be quiet, just the family, friends could drop in later.

Harry Watson always brought a crate of stout.

'What we need is a barrel of ale,' said Jim.

'We're not made of money,' said Bob.

'Well, there's the Slate Club,' said Mumski, 'the Diddlum. We'll get a drop of gin and a Johnnie Walker out of that.'

'And some port and lemon,' said Carrie.

They had paid into the Diddlum all year. The local publican, Billy Borndrunk, held the bank. It was to be hoped there wouldn't be another to-do, like last year. The bloke round the Queen's Head had spent the lot and then hanged himself.

No use worrying. Life's too short.

The decorations? In the hall upstairs, mistletoe between the dark red drapes, holly and ivy over the pictures in the sitting-room, and a fluted paper bell under the hanging lamp was the centre of a maypole of paper chains. Faeryland!

I never wanted to catch sight of the mundane world outside. Here in our castle where Robert Francis and Caroline Em reigned, we waited, with beating hearts, for our Green Knight to come.

I wish you could have seen that sitting-room. It was always comfortable, plush curtains against draughts in winter, light pink with silver stripes in summer. Even the folding doors, which were never unfolded, were curtained, and the wallpaper was striped, saffron and silver. There were two armchairs in faded red and gold, with six single chairs and a sofa to match. They all had antimacassars crocheted by Carrie. There was a Turkey carpet, cleaned once a week with tea-leaves, a Persian rug by the fire and a light Axminster covering over the centre table. There was also an octagonal two-tiered marquetry table which at Christmas held bowls of tangerines, muscatels, almonds and boxes of sticky dates. The chiffonier stood by the folding doors with rows of glasses on it, some blue, some pink, all set on a runner of silky rosettes Alf Young had made on his most recent sea voyage. The overmantel with mirrored shelves sheltered china shepherdesses sitting in rustic chairs, or standing arm-in-arm with their lads. They all nodded their heads if you gave them a little shove. The mantelpiece itself was black marble, a large chiming clock in the centre of it, three blue vases, Dalton ware, on either side, not for flowers, just for their beauty.

'All pinched!' said Kate one day, when she was in one of her moods. 'They would be Aunt Kit's, if everybody had their own.'

Nobody took any notice. It was an old family feud.

Christmas day was peace on earth. In the front room the fire was blazing, the brass round the fender shone, the piano lid was open, the piano stool crammed with new sheet music. When the red candles were lit, the party would begin.

Oh, day of days. Selah. And I was five.

The morning's preparations had gone like clockwork. To crown it, Alf Young appeared with presents for everyone. He wanted to push the boat out.

'Everybody down the Swan.'

'Not me,' said Mumski. 'I'm just about to dish the dinner.'

Then we discovered that Carrie wasn't home.

'Come on,' said Jim. 'We haven't got long.'

I ran upstairs to see if the fire was all right. It was, and the tinsel was glistening in the unseasonable sunshine. I heard Mumski opening the oven and went down to lay the table. First it had to be extended, then we spread her best damask tablecloth.

'I'm chairman,' I said as I pulled the chairs up to the table.

Carrie came in, puffing and panting as she pushed her cycle into the passage.

'Where have you been, gel?'

'For my Christmas ride. I wouldn't miss it for the world. I got as far as Epsom Downs. Now I'm going to lie down for five minutes.'

'Dinner's nearly on the table.'

'I've got a stitch. Where are they all?'

'Down the Swan. Alf's home.' Carrie was halfway up the stairs. 'You towel yourself down before you lounge about in your clothes.'

'Yes, Ma.'

It wasn't too long before the pub contingent came rolling home. Jim and Harry Watson threw their capes at the hat-rack and went out to the bog. Kate looked flushed but pretty in her new satin blouse. It had a pattern of plums and black grapes. She went straight to the mirror and adjusted her hairpins.

'Delilah,' said Bob.

'You keep a civil tongue in your head,' said Kate, glancing at Alf, but he was giving my gran a hug.

'That's enough, you two.' It was Harry plonking a couple of bottles of beer on the table.

'Carrie in?' Grandad had been checking up on his pigeons.

'Getting 'erself pneumonia again, more'n likely. I'll get 'er,' said Bob and bounded up the stairs.

Jim came in from the back yard and began pouring the beer. When Grandad had taken his place, everybody sat down.

'You gels should 'elp your mother more,' he said as Carrie came in.

'Does she help me?'

'That's enough, Kate.'

I knew she wouldn't fight back in front of Alf. She helped Carrie serve the veg. There wasn't much conversation after that. I was next to my grandfather, my favourite place, because he would give me mouthfuls from his plate, and they were tastier than mine.

I could never understand why Kate flew into a rage so easily, but I knew it had something to do with me. Sometimes she couldn't stand the sight of me. Today, at least, she was leaving me alone. Too busy flirting with Alf, I thought. Bob was throwing his weight about. He'd got himself a packer's job at Raphael Tuck's before Christmas and they were keeping him on.

Jim kept clearing his throat, always a bad sign. Alf was telling us about a cannibal chief who'd been a prisoner on the voyage. He pinched Kate's arm and pretended to eat. 'Tasty,' he said.

'Alf, don't!' she said coyly.

'That's what this old feller did to me,' said Alf.

'Kate would need plenty of garnish,' said Carrie.

'Horseradish,' said Jim.

'Chestnuts,' said Harry. 'They don't eat the lot, do they, Alf? Only the tasty bits, the liver or the heart.'

'It's their ritual,' said Alf.

The entry of the Christmas pud was ours. Gran tipped brandy over it and set it alight with a long taper, while Carrie and Kate changed the plates. Harry told Carrie it was snowing, and while she looked out of the window he stuck a sixpence in her pudding; then Gran found a shilling, and Bob got a florin. Harry was a good conjurer. He finished up bringing a threepenny bit out of my ear. Afterwards he put on an apron and helped with the washing-up, all time complaining that with his big belly he couldn't bend.

Gran leant down to listen for his baby. Carrie couldn't dry the dishes for laughing.

Grandad was playing crib with Jim up in the front room. Alf sat on the sofa showing Kate the snaps he'd taken on the voyage, one of the knitting frame he'd made so that he could produce more table runners.

'It must be boring, all that sea,' said Kate.

Bob was picking out 'The Good Ship Yacky Yicky Doolah' on the joanna.

'Fifteen-two. Fifteen-four. Fifteen-six and a pair's eight . . .'

'After the Lord Mayor's Show comes a dung cart,' said Grandad, throwing down his cards . . .

'And one for 'is knob . . .'

'Shut up, Bob, will yer? We're trying to concentrate.'

The afternoon began to drag as even the brightest afternoons will when people are drowsy after so much food and drink.

About five, tea and Christmas cake arrived, and with it the first guests: the Masons, who'd been neighbours in Avonmouth Street. The families only saw each other once a year so there was always a good deal of news – births, deaths, and who'd run off with whom. I understood because I was in love with Tom Mason. He was twenty-three, but age didn't matter. Everybody knew, so it was quite impossible for me to utter a word when he was there. His mother was telling us how good he was on the piano.

'Give us a selection,' she told him.

So, after flicking his music case open, feeling his wrists and all that, he played some lively music. I loved dancing, so I hid behind the curtain on the door and when there was a suitable chord I leapt out to perform my running, jumping and twisting dance.

A sharp rat-a-tat-tat at the front door heralded the Simpsons. Mr Simpson was very serious and dignified. 'An artist,' said Bob, 'Sought after from the Horns, Kennington, to Austen Balls.' He even wore a droopy frock coat, green with age. Mrs Simpson had very frizzy hair and wore a black velvet band round her neck, with a diamond brooch in front. I thought the band was to hold her neck together; it looked rather scraggy.

Mr Simpson had a high regard for Bob's singing and had

brought along some appropriate music, but as they were getting together Caroline Em made her entrance. She had taken off her apron, changed her blouse and was wearing her silver brooch, the one with two love knots entwined. A cambric hanky, lavender scented, was tucked into the top of her skirt, and despite her bad legs, she moved gracefully.

'Here comes my queen,' said Grandad.

'Oh!' said Mrs Simpson. 'There you are! Well well well. Just another old 'ouse cat, like meself.'

Gran was barely seated when her sister Polly arrived with husband Fred and daughter Nellie. Polly was a merry old soul with a silvery laugh. She laughed at everything. Her Fred was very old; he had fought in the Zulu War till an arrow lost him his right eye. Daughter Nellie had a chalk-white face, thin lips and gold-rimmed spectacles. She looked rather sour on first viewing, but this was simply due to long service among the gentry. She could laugh as merrily as her mother if anything tickled her fancy.

What a soirée! The guests were gracefully dispersed and conversation hung in the air as everybody praised Gran's cake. Bob was looking slightly put out, but Mrs Simpson let out a shriek and silenced us all.

'Bobbie! What's holding you up? We're all waiting for you to start the ball rolling.'

'A song, a song!' cried Polly in her silvery voice.

Gran looked proud as Bob took up a pose by the piano, but Kate gave an audible sigh. Mr Simpson, already seated, looked up at the ceiling like a thirsty hen, and ran his fingers up the keyboard in a titillating glissando. Mrs Simpson bent over to whisper to my gran, but Bob gave a warning cough and Mr Simpson turned and subdued his wife with a cruel frown. Then he struck a chord. There was the beginning of a snigger from somewhere, followed by a slight hiss.

'Ssh.'

'Order, please,' said Mr Simpson. 'Our first number is from that delightful operettah, *Maid of the Mountains*.' And he launched into the intro.

Gran said quite audibly, 'Never starts till there's perfect silence.' Mr Simpson took it as a compliment, waved his head a bit, and continued elaborating his intro as Bob swelled and sounded off with 'A Bachelor Gay Am I', in a throaty tenor.

When it came to the chorus 'At seventeen he falls in love quite madly with eyes of tender blue', the whole room joined in, so Bob took a sip of water, but when he took flight on his own again, to the accompaniment of 'Lovely tone' from Mrs Simpson, and 'One voice, please' from Mr Simpson, it was too much for Jim, who started to laugh.

'Put a sock in it, mate,' said Harry, half laughing himself.

'Cor, crikey,' said Jim. 'I can't 'elp it. It's Caruso over there.'

' 'E must've 'ad a nasty accident,' said Harry.

That set Jim off; his guffaws could have been heard a mile away. Bob was trying to continue but Mr Simpson brought his hands down on the keyboard with a discordant crash and rose to his full height.

'Peppermint,' he said. 'Rum and peppermint. If you please.'

'Lovely touch,' said Gran.

'Ssh please, Mum,' said Bob.

'We are not amongst music lovers here, Birdie,' said Mr Simpson, sitting himself down by the chiffonier. He didn't speak another word all evening.

Jim went and sat at the piano. 'Alright, guv?' he said.

But the maestro merely lifted his head and looked at the ceiling again as Jim launched into a thumping medley. It was one of his specialities, and finished up with 'Knees Up Mother Brown'. At which, with a roar, the ladies stood up, formed two lines facing each other, and went into a cancan with a flashing of bloomers, lace-edged drawers and petticoats which would not have been out of place at the Old Bull and Bush. Harry rolled up his trousers, swathed himself in a tablecloth and joined in.

'Hold on,' said Gran. 'We'd better get rid of the carpet.'

Everybody joined in, the furniture was moved back, the carpet rolled away, while Jim brought out his mouth-organ and gave us his famous rendering of 'A little bit off the top will do for me'. Harry seized the fire-tongs and mimed extraordinary obstetric operations, chasing the giggling ladies up and down the passage, and finishing up in Aunt Polly's lap.

In the lull for drinks, Mrs Simpson struck a note on the piano and began to hum 'I dreamt I dwelt in marble 'alls' and, looking coyly at her husband, 'I also dreamt you lo-oved me still'.

'No, no, Birdie,' cried the ladies, with one voice. 'That song's unlucky. You'll bring misfortune on the 'ouse.'

All her husband said was, 'Do sit down, Mrs Simpson.'

She went back to her corner, trilling to herself, till someone blew a razzberry. Polly shrieked with laughter, which set Jim off again. He couldn't stop, so Harry took him out for a breath of air. The musical evening was drawing to a close, so Mrs Mason called for 'Just a Song at Twilight', and her son Tom obliged, adding twirls and arabesques, as the whole room hummed or sang along, and Kate and Alf pirouetted slowly round the recently cleared square of wooden flooring.

The two delinquents reappeared. Harry asked Carrie for a dance, and Jim tapped Alf on the shoulder.

'Excuse me, mate,' he said. And Kate languished into his arms.

'I think there's a bit of jealousy there,' said Mrs Simpson to Gran.

'Oh, definitely,' said Gran, as Alf gave Mrs Mason a hug. 'He's even proposed to her.'

'Why doesn't she have 'im? After all, the other one's only a common working man. Is it the child?'

'No, no, he says he's very fond of 'er.'

The dancing took over, foxtrots and bunny hugs, till Carrie came to announce a cold collation ready in the kitchen, cold ham and beef, pickles and beer. The merriment didn't flag. Poor plain Nellie found herself wedged in the corner with Harry next to her, and he started to give a commentary on taking her to bed, holding up a large teacloth to hide them. Everyone put their oar in, except Mr Simpson. Gran was the worst, asking how they were doing and how far he had got. Nellie took it in good part, shrieking with laughter at every bawdy suggestion. Then Gran pretended to make a note of the date and declared that she would be the midwife nine months hence.

It was pronounced a lovely party but I had an idea we'd only avoided trouble by the skin of our teeth and trembled when Kate went out to say good night to Alf, and after a minute Jim followed them.

Carrie said, 'Bedtime,' so I bade everybody good night and

went upstairs. As I lay listening to the last good nights, the storm which had been threatening broke. Kate was yelling at everybody. Then I heard the door slam. It was Jim going. Kate came running into the room, flung herself on to the bed and ground her teeth. I pretended to be asleep.

Four

I loved the winter, the dark cold nights, the warmth and firelight in Gran's kitchen. After tea she'd settle to her sewing and, with Grandad and I her attentive audience, move into a world of her own, impersonating all the characters who figured in her stories. Grandad would listen half-smiling, while I sat at the table marshalling all the buttons from her sewing box into groups and endowing them with life. She loved to relive her time at the pub in Threadneedle Street; she seemed to light on some image at random, then she'd be away.

'Every masher in the City came into the saloon at one time or another.' And she'd break the cotton with her teeth before continuing. 'We had the best bill of fare in the city. Take the dinner-time menu – boiled mutton and caper sauce, Monday; rosbeef, Tuesday; choice of boiled, with carrots, or tripe an' onions Wednesday; veal-and-ham pie Thursday . . . and of course there was wallies an' cheese an' onions on the counter every day. Help yourself. Friday was the best. Fresh fish alive, alive-oh, oysters, lobsters, salmon and skate, turbot, brill and finny haddock. The fishermen used to sail right round from Ramsgate, up the Thames to Billingsgate and a pint at the market pub. Old 'Alf-Past-Eight Feet always rolled in a barrel of live eels, of a Friday; 'e bought 'em off the Dutch brigs. When the guvnor's back was turned 'e'd try an' put one down your neck.'

By then we'd be back there with her in that steaming

underground kitchen, with the trays rattling up and down the hatchway to the accompaniment of a lively duet. And she would sing out both parts for us.

'Two o' pie, one ov 'ash an' make it snappy.'

'Two V & H, one wiv.'

'Four o' pie, wiv 'ash. One parsnip, one greens, one runners, one swede.'

'Two coming up.'

'And one plum duff, one treacle wiv, and any sign of my four down there? Gent's in an 'urry.'

'Ho yus, up there? Right. An' shove 'em where the monkey put 'is nuts.'

'You go and wash yer mouth out.'

'One day the rope broke and all the grub fell on 'im. We couldn't 'elp laughing.'

Young Caroline kept her eyes open at the sign of the Fox and Goose; that's where she learned to cook, just by watching, and her pies and puddings, cakes and pancakes were the best you ever tasted. She was such a sprightly lass, so good-humoured that her boss used to pack her off to his pub on the Isle of Wight for the summer season. That was where she blossomed, where she made her début.

'Of a Sunday evening, when work was done, the boss would drive us all round the island in a hired brake. Down to Cowes if the Royal Yacht was in. We went to Osborne once and saw all Prince Albert's personal things, just where 'e'd left 'em before 'e passed on. The old Queen wouldn't 'ave 'em moved. We visited Ventnor, saw the prison at Parkhurst.'

When she paused to replenish her cotton, Grandad might try to get in with his story of the man-eating tiger or the German sergeant who did it in his trousers one day, and when someone remarked on the smell, thought he hadn't heard it go 'plonck'.

'After that he was always known as Sergeant Ploncky,' said Grandad.

And Gran would turn up her little nose. India! She couldn't think what he was doing out there. Then she'd pick up the thread of her story.

'You know who 'e was, I've told you before.'

'Who are we speakin' of, gel?' Grandad would ask tentatively.

'I'm tracin' the German 'fluence for you. Nobody ever explained to me 'ow we came to be plagued with four of 'em. Same with the old Queen, 'ad to 'ave 'er German, she did. All interrelated, so some of 'em come out albinos or soft in the 'ead. There's one put away up north, somewhere, more a woman than a man, only 'e can't do nothin' for 'isself. Don't just sit there and let the fire go out, John Willy, give it a poke. Mind you, royalty's not been up to it since the old Queen. Might've been good for a few more years if that Teddy 'adn't driven 'is poor old father with sorrow to the grave, after the old girl 'ad a-begged an' pray'd 'im to curtail 'is wicked ways an' all, or at least shut up about 'em. 'E wasn't living on a bowl of tuppenny rice neither, talk about the life of Riley. Races, bad 'ouses, Gay Paree! An' that Jersey Lily. I saw 'er once, done up to the nines, like one of those sireens in Flappers 'All down the old Argyle, that class of place. She wasn't 'is only fancy bit, you know. The old Queen turned 'er 'ead whenever 'e turned up at an investyture for fear of seein' 'im with another one. This Prince o' Wales takes after 'im. Bob saw 'im over in Flanders. Swear? All because 'is 'orse got stuck in the mud. Bob said 'e'd never heard anything like it. Anyway, to cut a long story short . . .'

This always signalled a diversion, which sometimes strayed so far that Grandad would take a look at his watch and go and feed his hens. When he got back, Gran would continue quite happily.

''Er tears watered the bosom of the earth while 'e flew 'is kite in Freshwater, but 'is sins came 'ome to roost. 'Is first child was born with a stutter, so they tried again an' double-tried but nothin' doin'. After she'd been imported from Denmark for the purpose. You know why she 'ad to wear that 'igh collar to the end of 'er days, don't you? To 'ide the stains of 'is wickedness.'

And when the mood took her, she'd sing us this little song:

> *As I went down to Windsor, on a visit to the King*
> *The soldier there on sentry said he couldn't be seen*
> *But I looked through the window and recéi-ved* [she'd linger on the
>   second syllable] *a terrible shock*
> *For I saw Mrs Langtry sitting on his knee*
> *A-scratching his bantam –*
> *Cock-a-doodle-doo*
> *It's nothing to do with you*
> *Dickory Dock*
> *I know what*
> *Cock-a-doodle-doo.*

And as if that wasn't enough, she might fish out her one and only naughty story:

'Mrs L and Mrs K attended the funeral. "Don't cry, old dear," said Mrs L. "I won't," said Mrs K, putting away her black-bordered 'anky. "But don't you miss that dear bald 'ead between your legs?" '

Grandad would smile and sometimes, but rarely, he would remind her that he'd heard that one last week. Gradually her interest in royalty began to flag and when the Prince of Wales took up with Mrs Simpson she gave 'em up altogether. 'Not up to it, this lot,' and went back to her old favourites, with embellishments.

T he quiet evenings with Caroline Em and John Willy suited me well, but I dreaded the family reunions on bank holidays.

That was when the family feuds flared into open warfare.

'Where shall we go for Whit?'

'Golders Green.'

It sounded lovely, but we never saw the place. Though we were all up early, half the morning was gone before everybody was toffed up and ready. By that time the pubs would be open; relatives would turn up just as we were about to leave.

'Come and have one for the road, old dear. Nance can wait outside for a minute, can't she?'

Funny how often they'd changed my name. I'd been 'the kid', 'the child', now it was 'Nance'. Swallowing my disappointment,

I took my place outside the boozer. Two or three other kids were already there. We sized each other up. Grandad would bring me a glass of fizzy lemonade and an Arrowroot biscuit. Then I knew it was going to be a long wait. The sky clouded over. At last it was closing time. My lot came out pretty unsteady on their feet.

'Might as well 'ave a bite at 'ome first.'

Gran would unpack the ham sandwiches. Then the quarrelling started. I'd try to get them to stop, but they didn't even notice me.

'Leave them alone. They'll be alright when the pubs open,' said Gran.

I went and stood by the window in the sitting-room watching the buses pull up, gather up the queue and leave for Golders Green.

One bank holiday, Carrie took me to Dover and I saw the sea for the first time. When we passed a shop bristling with seaside paraphernalia, she asked me what I'd like. I'd noticed a small red bucket painted with yellow and mauve pansies. She bought it and held my hand as we walked on to the shingle. The wild waves came roaring at us and the spray touched my face. I looked at her, she was smiling. Tough with everyone else, she was always gentle with me. We sat down and I dropped small grey pebbles into the bucket, happy to be away from Stockwell.

Carrie was the voice of summer. 'Let's have a feast. Strawberries are here. I'll bring home a punnet.'

All over till next year. Well, not quite – Gran marked the changing seasons for us with raspberries and redcurrants cooked together and served with cream; cherry pies and gooseberry tarts; blackberry and apple – and then, Cox's orange pippin. Best of all, that mysterious wooden box which arrived every year on 6th October, my birthday. When prised open it revealed rows of William pears lying in whorls of tissue paper.

There was no message, but I associated the luscious taste with a strange woman who brought the box herself once. Gran called me into the kitchen. The woman was sitting in the wickerwork chair. She looked at me, then she left. I didn't hear her speak. Nobody ever spoke about the visit, and the woman never came back. No one said much about the pears either, just 'Not so good this year', or 'Better'. I doubt whether a thank-you was ever written because I don't think anyone knew where to write.

The house at Number 8 was changing. Bob was courting a new one, none of his previous flames having found favour with the family. I liked a pretty one, called Phyl, but Kate had snatched her photo from the top of the piano one day and told me to dance on it. Carrie was seeing a lot of Harry Watson, but still bicycling on Sunday mornings and coming home exhausted. Alf Young had only been back once, at Christmas time. He treated us all to the pantomime at the Lyceum. We queued for hours in drizzling rain, climbed a thousand steps to the back of the gallery and, among odours of damp clothes, oranges and dust, waited impatiently for the show to begin. When the orchestra began to play and the adverts flew away, the heavy curtain parted to show us, far, far below, a brightly lit patch of stage, but whatever was going on down there, it was lost in the racket the kids were making. Later there was a white form dancing in a limelight, and fairies flying with real wings. I would have given anything in this world for wings like that. Harry Watson said he'd get me some for my birthday.

That evening we said goodbye to Alf Young. Shortly after, Kate called me to her. She was in the bathroom, lying in the steaming water, half-submerged. I was hypnotised by those two globes floating above the water, and the black fuzz under her arms. I'd never seen anyone naked before. I was repelled, not so much by her nakedness as by the look in her eyes when she told me she was going to marry Jim. Either she was feeling lascivious thinking of her wedding night, or she wanted to see what effect her news would have on me, but I was learning not to show my feelings. In fact, Alf's going left a gap in my life. Everything had been good when he was around.

Five

*Preparations for Kate's wedding. Jim makes difficulties. Harry
Watson and Carrie get married. Number 8 fills up with lodgers,
casuals, a con-man, a child molester and a toff. The school takes us
to see The Merchant of Venice. I learn Shylock's part and act it
for my grandparents. My reading and how I read to them.*

Although Kate had often sent me out when friends from work
called, now that I was six she proposed to dress me in pale
pink and have me as her bridesmaid, her only bridesmaid.

'Not pale pink!'

'We'll have it made up in Peckham.'

So in a gloomy boxroom, yellow in the gaslight, this prickly
woman stuck pins in me.

'Prefixes and Suffixes,' and in went two pins. 'Can you name
a prefix? . . .' A very long pin.

I prayed for this séance to end.

'Three frills round the bottom,' said Kate.

'Can't I wear the brown velveteen that Grandad bought me
down East Lane?'

'Ssh!' said the dressmaker, her mouth full of pins.

'They teach them nothing nowadays,' said Kate.

'I'll still have enough left to make her a bonnet.'

'Dutch,' said Kate. 'With turned-up ears.'

The woman wrapped her tape measure round my head.

'Hm. Very big.'

'Swelled,' said Kate.

And we left.

The marriage was to be solemnised at St Michael's, Stockwell
Park Road, at twelve noon on the chosen Sunday. By eleven-
thirty, Kate was at the starting line, dressed to kill – white
silk dress, short, with tasselled kerchiefs hanging all round
the skirt, the bosom embroidered with seed pearls, and to

cap it all a veil, orange blossom, and of course a trailing bouquet . . .

'Anyone seen Jim?' she asked, suddenly.

'Sure! In the boozer with his best man,' said Carrie.

'What's he got on?'

'His best cap and white muffler.'

'No!' shrieked Kate. 'I won't have it. Tell 'im if 'e doesn't change that cap, the whole thing's off.'

Shortly after, against all the rules, Jim appeared in person. Kate looked at him, and burst into tears.

'What about that grey trilby we chose together?'

'I can't wear it,' said Jim.

'Why not?'

'It makes me look a pie.'

She ran out of the room. Jim lit a Woodbine. Gran said she knew something like this would happen and Grandad went out and talked to the pigeons. Then Carrie started smoking. She looked elegant in a light grey costume, bordered with a pattern of mauve glass beads.

'Where's Harry?' said Jim.

'Out,' said Carrie. 'You're surely not going to capsize the boat for the sake of a silly cap.'

Jim cleared his throat. It was an ominous sound.

At that moment, Harry appeared, the trilby on his head, whistling the Wedding March. He'd been to Jim's digs to retrieve the hat. Jim started to laugh, Harry started to fool about.

'Put it on, mate; it's only for two shakes of a dead lamb's tail. You can come down, Katie,' he called. ' 'E's wearin' it and 'e's ready for the noose.'

But she wouldn't come down till she saw Jim at the bottom of the stairs, wearing his brand new titfer.

At last we were off, in two taxis that had been waiting in the street since twelve noon. Considering how late we rolled up and that Mr Matheson, the clergyman, had never set eyes on any of us before, we did quite well. He prompted everybody right through the service, and Gran gave directions in a subdued whisper, which sometimes clashed with Mr Matheson. Jim was trying not to laugh but he managed the 'I will'. Back at the house, Gran had done her daughter proud, the cake Mr Debus made being the principal attraction. It was a two-tiered white plaster job with columns; but first we all had to make a wedding group for a photo. They put me on the floor cross-legged in front of Kate and Jim. I came out with the Dutch bonnet right down over my nose and me lace-edged knickers showing.

'Quite a pretty little wedding . . . ,' said Mrs Delaye as she sipped her glass of stout in Flappers Hall. 'No honeymoon, of course.'

'Always opening her mouth to fill other people's,' said Gran.

The newlyweds had strolled over to 33 Stockwell Road on the Sunday evening. They'd rented two rooms there from Mrs Preston. The bride left her bouquet, and me, for her mother. The marriage was the last celebration we had for a long time. It was the hungry twenties. No one ever saw that grey trilby again.

Carrie was married the next year, to Harry Watson, quietly, in a registry office, wearing that same grey costume. Bob walked the plank soon after; Lily was his bride and her people were well-to-do – well, compared with us. She reproached Gran for not giving Bob a better start in life. This upset Caroline Em who had given him all she had to give.

With the family gone, the house was quieter, but it wasn't ours any more. From the basement, you climbed thirteen dark stairs. Above those stairs was where Gran earned her living with Good Clean Beds for Single Men, twelve and six a week. The room behind the folding doors, formerly Bob's, housed the casuals. The small boxroom tucked away behind it was seldom occupied. Eleven more stairs and the bathroom; another seven to old Turner's. He was a permanent fixture, a toff – always wore a bowler hat and smoked a pipe with an amber mouthpiece. In Kate and Carrie's room at the front, Mr Ghisi. He was a waiter at the Savoy. The casuals were a bag of all sorts. There was Mr Frawley who came and went without a word, just came down for a jug of shaving water every morning, and that was the last we'd see of him for the day. Fusty old Chalmers kept Grandad entertained with stories of his adventures in Africa while he waited week in, week out for a postal order which never came. Finally Jim gave him his marching orders. I was sorry because he had kept Grandad amused, though

I knew he'd lifted those stories from the *National Geographic* up at the library. Mr Bensussan came next, and he told us all about the massacre of the Armenians and how the Turks had only spared him because he had red hair. When he went, Mr O'Donovan came. He never shed his overcoat but he sat in a corner of the kitchen, staring into the fire. He had no baggage. One evening he started talking and we thought he was never going to stop. He told us about the Black and Tans and the terrible things they'd done to his people. He left as suddenly as he came. Gran said he was a hunted man.

The white-haired old waiter, second floor front, was the one my grandparents liked best . . . Such nice manners. He had brought Gran a string of Ciro pearls in a maroon box lined with yellow satin. The hotel had been giving them to all their lady guests for Christmas and he had helped himself. Gran never wore them – pearls were tears, she said – but she appreciated the thought and put them in her bottom drawer.

Then, one Saturday night, when I was alone in the house, or thought I was, I noticed that the kitchen gas was lit.

'Who's there?'

No answer. I ran down the stairs. Mr Ghisi was standing with his back to the light, looking at me.

'Come here a minute,' he said.

I wanted to run, but my feet wouldn't move. Suddenly, he pounced and thrust his skinny fingers into the neck of my dress. Luckily Gran had made the dress with a small round neck, so he couldn't go far without tearing it. I pulled myself free. He grabbed hold of me again, shoving his bony knee between my legs.

'Christ, as big as a woman's,' he said, attacking my neck again.

'No,' was all I could manage. 'No.'

I knew I had no breasts. Now he was moving his leg between mine, pulling at my knickers. I didn't know what he meant to do but panic grabbed me as he pushed his distorted face near mine. I pulled away with all my force and ran right up to Mr Turner's room, where I hid under the bed and listened for any slight sound which might warn me of his coming. I heard him. The door creaked. There were people downstairs. It was my grandparents . . . laughing, talking to that old monster.

I crept downstairs to my room and scrambled into bed. Was

there a lock on the door? I was afraid to get up and look. I was afraid to be left alone in the house after that night. I couldn't tell anybody, but I kept well clear of Mr Ghisi.

My fear of this sweet old child molester was only banished by a special school outing. Miss Barnes, our new teacher, took us all to the Brixton Theatre one afternoon to see *The Merchant of Venice*. The kids started playing about till Miss Barnes told us off. I didn't care much for Antonio myself, nor Portia with her caskets, but when Shylock was on, I hung on his every word. When he made his final exit, he came down to the footlights, held his balanced scales high in the air, then let them fall with a crash.

I clapped like mad. Great.

Back in the classroom I took out the school issue of the play, and looked for my favourite speech: 'If you prick us, do we not bleed? If you tickle us, do we not laugh? If you poison us, do we not die? And if you wrong us, shall not revenge?'

My grandparents had never seen a play and all they knew of Shakespeare was Hamlet, 'I am thy father's ghost', Richard's 'A horse, a horse, my kingdom for a horse', and how Shylock would have his pound of flesh. Well, their education was about to begin. As soon as I got home from school I began my preparations, and at the witching hour, with the table cleared and the sewing box out, I leapt into the room crying, 'Let him look to his bond.' I had on a long coat which I'd found in the passage, and a moustache and beard of burnt cork. I made quite an effect.

'I am a Jew. Hath not a Jew eyes? Hath not a Jew hands, organs, dimensions, senses, affections, passions?'

'Bravo,' said Grandad. 'You make a proper Five-to-two.'

'And now go and wash your face, Jo,' said Gran.

As I left the room, Gran began telling him about the man who used to black up and sing 'Swanee River', down Thames Street. When I came back, Grandad was reminding her of the time he did a turn.

'When was that?'

'Weren't we laying cable under the City? And didn't we break into a charnel house with all the bones from the Old Plague there?'

'Yes, well?'

'Well, when we knew the overseer was coming, we lit candles in the skulls and I made me face white and started moanin'. He well nigh dropped dead. Hollerin' blue murder, he was.'

Gran bit into her cotton, and scraped her chair along. I wondered if they would like to hear the whole of Shylock. Of course, Gran was still a great entertainer; she couldn't take a penny ride to Brixton without coming back with a story. Perhaps they'd like a book better. I went through my private collection, lodgers' leftovers for the most part, three copies of *The Ring*, the boxing magazine; Marie Corelli's *The Sorrows of Satan*; Macaulay's *Lays of Ancient Rome*; *Opium Dens of the East End*, with grisly photos; *Under Two Flags* by Ouida; *She* by Rider Haggard; *The Iron Heel* by Jack London; *A Day in the Life of a Donkey*; and a Spanish–English dictionary. I struck gold the day Mr Chalmers went. In the fender, under a dirty sock and an old copy of *The Sporting Life*, I found a pile of *True Story* magazines. Here was riches. The juiciest one, 'Let not the sun go down upon your wrath', about feuding Arab sheikhs, sloe-eyed ladies lounging on cushions and a noble English officer. 'The Virtuous Maid' promised well, too. This maid was in service in London when the butler took advantage of her. Unfortunately, just when we were getting to the rude bit, Mr Chalmers had torn out the pages. I'd noticed that he used to wipe the lather from his cutthroat on them. Anyway, in the next instalment she'd had a baby, and by the end of it she had brain fever. I rather fancied an attack of that myself. It would make you really interesting.

'Don't ask her to go and fill the coal bucket, she's got brain fever.'

I didn't think any of these library efforts suitable for my grandparents. Grandad might laugh at a bawdy remark, but the next minute he would say to me, 'Cover yourself up. A girl mustn't show her knees.' He gave me a rap with his stick one day and I had to pull my white socks right up above my high black boots.

And there was the time he'd taken me to Hampton Court. We were walking round the galleries when he stopped to look at a painting of a nude woman; she didn't even have a veil blown across her mound of Venus. 'I don't think this is a suitable place for a young man like me,' he said, loud enough for everyone in the room to hear. I was rather embarrassed. So I took him by the hand

and led him to the next room, but as I turned at the door I was surprised to see everyone smiling, and Grandad was quite pleased with the effect he'd made.

Would they like to hear *Rory O'More*, the book left behind by the IRA man, Mr O'Donovan? I could easily soften the saucy bits and cut any rude words. I thought 'bloomin' ' was a swearword, that could go.

Thus began our nightly readings, a chapter a night.

Six

Now I'm wearing long stockings, and reading for my own pleasure – riding with Athos, Porthos and Aramis in a bid to save the queen's honour. I cannot believe my luck today. I am lying on the sofa in the sitting-room with my book. Nobody has called me for hours.

The afternoon was beginning to fade, the sun was setting over the red brick of the school opposite when I heard kids' voices down by the Swan.

'Throw out your mouldies.'

Of course, it's Derby Day.

I sat up and caught a glimpse of the race-goers riding home along the Clapham Road from Epsom. If they'd had a win they'd be throwing out showers of coppers. There were horses and carts, decorated with bright streamers, motor cars honking past them, crowds of kids diving into the road. Pearlies and Coster Kings poised like charioteers, charabancs with coloured wavers and paper trumpets and a donkey wearing ladies' long white drawers on his front legs.

He's coming our way. He's our donkey, from the mews. I went back to my book, but it was no use. They might return, any minute. I'd better go and look out for them; to be found reading would be worse than lying in bed all day.

The road was thronged with Epsom traffic, it was a long time before I spotted them, Gran, Grandad and Kate, strolling along the Clapham Road, all smiling, I'd never seen Kate look so happy. She was holding up the front of her dress; underneath you could see her dark sateen petticoat with the diagonal stripes, pink and green. She smiled and showed me what she held in her dress . . . a heap of silver and gold coins.

'Won on every bloomin' race,' said Grandad.

'Beginner's luck,' said Gran.

It may have been, but not for Kate. From that time on, picking a winner became a daily obsession.

> Land of our birth
> We pledge to thee
> Our love and toil
> In the years to be
> When we are grown
> And take our place
> As men and women
> Of our race.

Our Empire Day pledge, and as the piano joined in, we sang:

> Teach us to rule ourselves alway
> Controlled and cleanly, night and day
> That we may bring, when need arise
> No maimed or worthless sacrifice.

Young teachers from every corner of the Empire were standing beside Miss Birkin, our headmistress, looking grave. Then, for Miss Parker who had just arrived from Canada we sang:

> The thistle, shamrock, rose entwined
> The maple leaf forever.

And we all stood straight and felt important. The new war memorial had not long been unveiled, opposite the Swan. It would serve a double purpose, as clock tower and cenotaph. The patch of grass round it was to have benches, somewhere for the elderly to sit.

Mr Matheson had conducted the service and we'd observed a minute's silence. Then everybody sang 'Abide with me', accompanied by the Silver Band which usually played on a Sunday morning, outside the White Swan in the Brixton Road. Last of all, the flags fell away to reveal columns of names, inlaid in gilt. They occupied the four sides of the war memorial.

The crowd surged forward to check up on the names of their dead. There weren't many men about. Our Jim, for one, was up at the Labour Exchange in Brixton.

'Qualifications?'

'Skilled asphalter, tackle anything, domes, dormers, skirting, fillet, half-round channels, coves, piers . . .'

'Alright, alright.'

'Ceilings . . .'

'Get back in line. Wait till your number's called.'

'Another word out of 'im and I'll knock 'im into the middle of next week.'

'That's what you have to put up with for fifteen bob a week,' said the grey-haired bloke standing behind Jim. After an hour:

'Done anything about finding work lately?'

'You talking to me?'

'Yes, you!'

Jim was over the counter, chasing that senior clerk round his filing cabinets.

'You didn't hit 'im, Jim?' said Kate.

'No, no, no. It was enter the law, exit one asphalter.'

Kate took the rent book up to the cop shop and told them what she'd told Jim only that morning.

'I'm going to have a baby and that's why he went to the Labour in the first place, officer.'

Talk about the hungry forties, this was the starving twenties. The cops were uneasy. Everybody was. There'd been so many strikes, riots and mutinies lately. Even the police had been on strike. After that, their union had been suppressed. Now the unemployed were on the march, that's what they called the ex-servicemen these days – 'unemployed'.

'Fall in, lads, only another two hundred miles to go.'

'Look at them, bloody scarecrows.'

'So would you be if you'd traipsed four hundred miles, mate.'

'Want a crutch?'

'It's alright. I only left me toes at Wipers.'

Batallions of half-starved men were plodding along every road that led to London. I came home from school one day . . .

'No point in looking. There's nothing in the cupboard.'

The room at Number 33 was large and bare. My mother was standing by the window.

'What are we going to eat then?'

'Ask Jim's friends, the miners. It's about time they went back to work.'

'If the railwaymen and the transport workers had stood by them the strike would've been over by now.'

'What do you know about it?'

'I know that the miners have been left to fight their own battles.'

'I'll give you a battle if you don't shut up.' She looked very threatening.

'I'm going,' I said, and went.

I'd made up my mind to leave home long ago. I walked to Clapham, crossed two busy roads and made for the Common. It was deserted and looked unfamiliar. The sky was now a mountain of dark clouds. I saw a stretch of water gleaming in the dark and ran to it, took off my boots and socks, and walked in it, squeezing the soft mud between my toes. I came to a fallen tree and sat watching the last streamers of daylight fade away. The shops beyond the trees were all lit up. It must be late. I was shivering. If I was leaving home for good, I would have to make more preparations. . . .

Jim let me in. Kate hardly looked at me.

'It's long past your bedtime. Where've you been?'

I wasn't wearing my socks and my wet boots left a trail across the lino. I told them I'd been up the Common and I thought Jim was going to wallop me but he didn't.

'Don't come the acid with me, my girl,' said Kate. 'Stuck-up little bitch, too big for 'er boots, that's 'er trouble.'

I ran my fingers through my hair – thin brown stuff, not black and curly like hers.

'You'd think the school board would've taken her teeth out, got rid of that awful gap, wouldn't you?'

'Gran says it means I'll travel.'
'You'll travel if I put my hand across your face.'
'Alright, Kate,' said Jim.
'Takes after 'er bloody father.'

November 17th, 1923. As the squaddies from Kent marched through Deptford, the London Society of Asphalters, that is to say Jim and his mates, came out of the back room in the pub where they held their meetings and cheered.

'Long walks and short smokes,' Jim shouted.

MARCH AGAINST STARVATION read the banners carried by skilled men, trades unionists, ex-servicemen.

Jim's associates had not yet been granted trade union status. The leaders of the old established societies, some of them now boss's men, had written the asphalters off as a shower of Paddies and I-ties. The Italians had come to this country with the asphalt blocks and shown the natives how to use them.

The Kent contingent moved on towards Rotherhithe. Jim's mob felt sure they'd get a good hiding from the cops before they crossed the river.

'They won't let 'em get anywhere near the House of Commons,' said Tommie Jukes.

They didn't. The hunger marchers assembled in Hyde Park, and when the fiery speeches were over and the applause died down, they made their way to the workhouses which had been opened for them, hoping for a long kip and a few corn plasters. They stuck around London for ten days demonstrating and collecting a few more broken heads. When Parliament went home for Christmas the newspapers gave us the truth about the hunger march. It had all been a Communist plot, the organisers had been in daily touch with the Russians, who had supplied them with gold. No wonder the Prime Minister had kept out of the way.

Tommie Jukes landed a job in Cambridge and spoke for Jim. They hadn't the fare but Tommie's missus parted with a half sovereign she'd been keeping as a last resort, and they were off. Jim with two new wooden floats he'd made and a tool bag sewn together from bits of old carpet.

He wrote Kate that he'd found good digs and a friendly landlady, but Kate didn't like the thought of some Cambridge vixen making eyes at her Jim. She was pregnant again and lonely.

Unbelievably, Old Turner, the toff, had left Number 8 and moved in with the gold-digger who had hooked him in the Dog and Duck, Tooting Bec, lured him to her parlour and pleasured him. This revived the old boy's taste for it and we saw him no more. Aunt Fan was installed in his place. Now Mr Guy, top floor, was moving out and Kate asked if she could move in. She should have seen the dangerous reefs ahead. Grandad did, but he didn't stand a chance. The women had made up their minds. Not Carrie; we didn't see so much of her these days. Harry Watson had put his foot down: he didn't want her hanging around with Kate's brat.

It wasn't long before there was a row at Number 8. Aunt Fan objected to napkins drying on the landing, so Kate rolled saucepan lids down the stairs which banged into the old girl's door. One day she accused me of tossing my head at her, seized the carving knife and chased me round the house. Gran grabbed her arm or I might have been a colander. Poor Kate. Two rooms and a boxroom, no kitchen, a gas stove on the landing and Grandad had told her she would have to help her mother with the heavy work. She meant to, but each morning when she was bathing the babies (she'd had the second one, Milly, in '23) she'd get stuck into *The Sporting Life* and forget everything else.

She'd been clever at school, she told me. 'I was teaching the rest of the class when I was twelve,' she said. 'But I had to find a job. I might've got on, if she'd let me stay at school. We never had any luck, our side of the family, and always with a house full of lodgers.'

One day, exploring the old chiffonier, I came on a gilt-edged tome with *Picturesque England* embossed on the cover and tissue paper over its colour prints. Inside was a certificate:

Awarded to Kate Daisy Littlewood
of
Avonmouth Street School

by
Princess Alice of Athlone
at
The Crystal Palace
for her
Essay on Cruelty to Animals
(RSPCA)

'Carrie wrote the best part of it. She's always been the cleverest, but my handwriting was the best.' She didn't seem to care whether I was clever or not.

'Joan Littlewood, First Position in class.' Miss Barnes read it out at the prize-giving and handed me an adventure book. As a matter of fact I came first each term, and when I was ten they had put me among the ones selected to try for a scholarship. It would mean sitting an exam and exams made me sick. I tried to overcome it, but it was no use. Once I was sick in a drain on the way to school on exam day. They sent me back home and Gran wrapped me in her soft grey shawl, and sat me in Grandad's armchair and fed me on sponge cakes and soda water till I was better, always the moment I knew exams were over – but this scholarship business! As soon as the date of the first test was announced, I was sick.

When I judged it safe, I returned to school, but Miss Barnes had a surprise for me. I was to be allowed to take the exam all by myself, as she'd specially recommended me. I'll never forget that empty classroom, the dread of not coming up to expectation. My essay, 'A Day in the Life of a Penny', was a mess and so was I.

Seven

I win a scholarship. The uniform is a problem. The school is a convent. There is a General Strike. Playacting at school. Aunt Carrie has TB. Her daughter Marie comes to us. At the Old Vic, see Hamlet and Macbeth with John Gielgud and produce Macbeth at school. Carrie dies. We all go to Ramsgate on the insurance money. I'm drawn to the Pierrot show on the beach. At school the Roman Catholic ritual attracts me. Harry Watson marries again, takes Marie. I ask the Old Vic for a job. The nuns threaten to expel me. I skip matriculation and try for a scholarship at RADA, win it. Nick, my art teacher, takes me to Paris.

When the exam results were announced, I was amazed to hear my name called. I had won, I was a scholarship girl.

At the dinner break, I found Kate and Gran in the back yard, hanging out the washing. When I told them my news, Gran threw the shirt she was holding over the line, went indoors and came back clutching something. She put her wrinkled hand, with the two wedding rings, over mine. I was holding a gold sovereign.

Grandad was pleased too when he heard.

'She's the scholar of the family.'

Jim said he'd been through Oxford, on his bicycle.

Still, I knew they couldn't afford to let me take the scholarship. 'You have to wear a uniform,' I told them.

Gran said she'd make the blouses and wouldn't mind having a go at the gym slip.

'She'll have to have a cup and saucer 'at too,' said Grandad.

'There is a grant,' I told them.

Grandad's elder brother Dick made a contribution. He was in the workhouse but he could go out in the afternoons, and he came to see us.

'There you are, a proper school 'at for the girl,' and he produced a bright auburn velour from under his coat.

'Where did you get that, Dick?'

'It blew off the top of a bus.' And he gave the poor squashed thing a good punch to restore its shape.

'It would have to be black,' I said.

'What's the dyers and cleaners for?'

I wore the hat and I took the scholarship, and I attended La Retraite High School for Girls, which was five large houses and a red-brick annexe. A small, rosy-cheeked woman opened the side door on my first day. She was wearing a marine blue dress and a white coif. She spoke with a French accent.

'Take off your shoes.'

'I have no slippers.'

'You can't come in here with outdoor shoes.'

She produced some soft house shoes and when they were on she led me to the school hall. I could hear girls singing, and through the glass-panelled door saw a stage. There were pictures of holy-looking people everywhere and statuettes of JC and his mother.

'Sweet'art of Jesus! Found 'im love a mercy . . . ,' the girls were trilling away. It sounded too jolly to be a hymn. I liked the place. It was clean and airy – everything blue and white. The lessons were easy, the classrooms small. Outside the window you could see a playground, a large garden, and a football field.

'We play hockey,' said a girl with freckles.

She lived near me, so we walked home together. It was quite a walk, nearly three miles. Her name was Norah. She taught me the words of the song 'Sweet heart of Jesus, fount of love and mercy . . .'

The nuns were not nearly as strict as the London County Council teachers. One girl told Mother Austin a barefaced lie and got away with it. I was shocked. Still, I was taken up with my new school and almost forgot about home till it came to the school holidays, when I had to take the babies out every day.

'Alright if I call her Milly?' Kate had asked her mother.

'So long as it's not Melinda.'

'I thought Mildred.'

And Mildred was a fat, contented little being, so with Carrie's first-born, Marie, I had three of them in the pram.

Clapham Common Monday, Kennington Park Tuesday, Brock-
well Wednesday, and so on and on. I hated those parks. I would
hide my book in the pram, dump the kids on the grass and read.
One day I was deep in *The Iron Heel* and when the time came to go
home, Milly was missing. I packed the other two into the pram and
looked everywhere. Someone must have found her and taken her to
the police station. I'd have a look on the way home – yes, there was
Milly, gurgling happily on a policeman's knee. He seemed rather
good at the job, better than me. I didn't say anything at home; Jim
was moody these days.

One day in the spring of 1926 I heard shouting in Stockwell
Road, which for a week had been strangely silent – a bus was coming from Brixton with chalking all over it. Young men wearing plus
fours or Oxford bags were perched on the platform, others on the
steps, some were even hanging on to the driver's cabin. 'Support
us,' they were shouting. 'It's our last day.' A group of neighbours
stood on the pavement silently watching. My grandfather joined
us.

'Who are they?'

'University scholars,' the old man said.

I asked Jim about them later, and he said they were blacklegs.

'Blacklegs?'

'Scabs. The whole country is on strike, and they're trying
to break us. They won't. The strike's solid.'

But he was wrong. I read the paper to Grandad the next
day. 'Surrender of the Revolutionaries,' it said.

> The General Council of the TUC, led by Mr Pugh
> and Secretary Citrine, waited on Mr Stanley Baldwin,
> the Prime Minister, with J.H. Thomas, Ernie Bevin
> and Ramsay Macdonald in attendance.

'Shitting themselves,' said Grandad. 'They didn't think working-
class people had it in them.'

'But it only lasted ten days, Grandad.'

'What do you want, red revolution?'

'Why do they always leave the miners to fight on alone?'

By the end of that year, half a million men had given up their trade union membership.

A fter school each day, the girls prepared the Christmas decorations, making bunches of wistaria with mauve paper.

I got myself the only good job reading *Uncle Tom's Cabin* to them. Mother Mary Agnes told me I was useless.

'You'll be coming back to the reunions wrapped in an old sheet,' she said.

I knew I wouldn't because I'd no intention of attending any reunion.

Marguerite Renard was working on the set for the Nativity play and she worked me into the scene-painters' section so I gave up *Uncle Tom* and painted Jerusalem's gold roofs and minarets instead. Then I found I would sooner perform than paint, so I had a serious talk with Eileen Connor who was playing a king, and convinced her that the vista of Jerusalem badly needed her artistic talent. Then I approached the director, Mother St Vincent, our English teacher.

'You're rather young-looking for a visiting king,' she said, but she had a twinkle in her eye.

'I could make myself a fuzzy beard,' I told her.

I got the part and I enjoyed playing it; best of all I liked standing in the wings looking at bare boards, once the school stage, now a hill above Bethlehem where soon the star would appear to guide us.

One day, it was in 1928, Carrie came to talk to Kate. She sat by the door in her coat. Nobody spoke. I looked at her. She was crying. I'd never before seen tears fall like that.

'Who'll take care of Marie?' she said at last.

I went and hid in Gran's bedroom. Carrie had TB. They took her to a sanatorium, Pinewood, where she was kept in the open air, night and day. It didn't help. They transferred her to a hospital at Winchmore Hill.

When Kate and Grandad decided to let me go with them, I picked her some marguerites in the front garden. She lay on a single bed, alone in a bare room. The walls were green, dark green to her eye level, light green above that. There was one article of furniture, a plain locker beside the bed. Chairs had to be fetched for us. She was shockingly thin, her brown hair combed back, a black velvet band round her forehead. Her face and hands had no colour at all. Harry said that whenever he went she quarrelled with him but always wrote afterwards apologising.

Next day, at school, I went and sat among the damp-smelling plants in the conservatory by the chapel. Let her get well. Please let her get well. Presently I heard the soft click of rosary beads. The nuns wore them dangling from the waist. I stayed where I was and for the first time heard the mass from beginning to end. I thought it very beautiful.

'You can't go there. It's a blood tub.'

'What did you say, Aunt Fan?'

'Blood up to your knees in the first act. Your money back if you ain't satisfied by the end.'

'It's not like that nowadays. You are thinking of the old days. A lady runs it for God and Shakespeare now.'

Silly old bitch. She wasn't my aunt anyway. She was Robert Francis's sister, Frances. Her hair was badly dyed, she had a bulbous nose and a hairy wart and she looked down on our side of the family because her son-in-law had made it, with bananas. Did that give her the right to look down on the Old Vic?

We were going there from school. We were a bit late. When we got in, they were playing the overture – 'Fingal's Cave'. The play was *Hamlet*, with Gielgud, Wolfit, Martita Hunt and Robert Speaight. It had me on the edge of my seat all afternoon. Then I rushed home to read the play, and learned 'Oh what a rogue and peasant slave am I' by heart. From then on, I didn't miss a production down the Waterloo Road. Five pence late door and walk there and back. It wasn't that far.

I was considering a school production of *Hamlet*, when I saw *Macbeth*. Gielgud was too decorative, but I thought the play might be more suitable for school than *Hamlet* – more action, more murders. I tried out the best speeches on my grandparents. It would take time to lick the girls into shape. Of course, I'd have to persuade them to do it first; that wouldn't be difficult. I would play Macbeth and the Old Man at the end of Act Two. 'Threescore and ten I can remember well.' I could do character parts lovely. Marguerite Renard could be the woman. Her father was a saxophone player and he'd inspired her with a love of jazz. This maddened Miss McInnerny, our music teacher.

'A saxophone is an instrument of torture,' she declared.

I wondered if it would suit *Macbeth*.

Mother St Vincent could get the Assembly Hall for rehearsal after school and during the coming holiday, if she approved. I'd better present her with a cast list. She cocked her coif to one side when she saw it.

'Well,' she said, with a twinkle in her eye, 'if the others are as keen as you are . . .'

I started recruiting. Marguerite was okay. My best friends, Norah Cunningham and Phyllis Williams, fell in, and there was Ruby Baker, tall and rather gaunt, but with lovely dark blue eyes and a gorgeous smile. They were all a little bitten by the theatre bug at the time, having seen Reinhardt's *Miracle* at the Lyceum. I didn't fall for it, except for Tilly Losch dancing. Lady Diana was too bony and boring. The girls ganged up on me, said I was a cynic.

Cynic or not, I was the producer, and my word was law.

'We won't bother too much about the setting and lighting,' I told them.

It wasn't till four years later, when I saw the Compagnie des Quinze, that I realised what could be done with light.

'We'll have some sort of table for the banquet but stools are out. They'll limit the movement and I don't want to waste time getting furniture on and off.'

Props? Yes! Swords, blood, lightning flashes during the final fight. What about the head on a lance? Unfortunately we had to settle for the largest mangel-wurzel I could find in Brixton market.

The rehearsals were exacting and thorough, but one night when the opening was nearly upon us, I started clowning, stalking up and down hamming 'Is this a dagger?' I heard a chuckle from the shadows in the corner. It was Mother St Vincent; she'd been sitting there, watching.

If our audience, just the nuns and school fellows, expected to be bored, they were wrong. The play went like wildfire. Even the banqueting scene worked, everyone poised on thin air, pretending to be sitting. It worked so well that I've used the idea once or twice since. You've never seen much sitting around in my shows.

The morning after our performance, the headmistress, Mother St Teresa, sent for me. This usually meant trouble. On the contrary, she congratulated me on my verse speaking. What's more, she wanted the performance repeated. Mother Superior was coming from Angers-sur-Loire and it was felt that our *Macbeth* would be a credit to the school. I asked if our parents might attend. After a moment's thought she said, 'Yes, but only the cast's parents.'

I was tremendously bucked and started thinking of ways to improve the production. After all, the Mother Superior, Supreme Head of all the convents of our order, was not to be sneezed at. She duly arrived, and after being welcomed and refreshed, was installed on a dais in the middle of the Assembly Hall. The nuns sat around, looking grave and attentive. The parents, including Jim and Kate, were in rows at the back.

I'd vastly improved the music and sound effects. My first entrance, to kettle drum and trumpet, was made more touching by the 'Te Deum' sung by the school choir stationed in the corridor. My next great moment was Banquo's murder. This time it was to be performed in true Elizabethan style, and no messing. I'd added a sinister roll of drums to the scene, and as the third murderer (me, in a black cloak) produced an evil-looking knife and plunged it into a suitably hidden piece of meat, the blood gushed out on cue (cochineal). At that moment there was a terrible cry. The good lady, our Mother Superior, had fainted.

Despite the consternation, I couldn't help feeling gratified. This was it, theatre dynamic, but Mother Mary Agnes came running round and asked us to take it a bit more calmly. And they did, to my chagrin.

After that, I wasn't so keen on school plays; the audience was too timid. In any case I was going through my existentialist phase, walking by the river at night, contemplating suicide. Talk about the heartache and the thousand natural shocks – I'd endured them all.

There were many smells in the old house at 8 Stockwell Road which I disliked. Unlatch the ill-fitting panels under the stairs to the ground floor and you could distinctly smell mice as well as carbolic and Hudson's soap powder. In the kitchen corner, when the low cupboard behind Grandad's armchair was opened, it smelt like a graveyard, but none were as sickening as the reek of lilies which came with Carrie's body. It filled the room. For five days, the coffin lid was open. There were always those who wanted to see the face. Was it the smell of arum lilies, or death?

She died in that room at Winchmore Hill, alone. She couldn't reach the bell. They found the small vase of flowers spilt on the locker.

Kate and Gran went to the mortuary.

'When I came out, I hated the whole world,' said Kate.

Gran never spoke.

'If I'd known, I would have kept her here with us, I wouldn't have let her die in that place,' said Grandad.

She was thirty-nine. They laid her coffin on two trestles in the sitting-room along by the mantelpiece. Her presence took possession of the whole house. Harry Watson sat beside her for a long time one afternoon. When he came down, 'I've been arranging her hair,' he said, half-smiling. Had it been a pleasure?

So many people came to the funeral – relations of Jim's or Harry's? There were three or four fat women in black; one wore her hair in narrow plaits, which were looped under her black satin hat. She started to sob as she moved into the sitting-room, the rest followed, weeping loudly. I resented them. They didn't even know her. If they had, they would probably have disliked her, with that sharp tongue of hers. She certainly would have taken the mickey out of them. 'Blubbering' she would have called it. I cannot cry, I said to myself, and I loved her. Everybody moved out for the coffin to be screwed down. . . .

'Come and see your old man before he's screwed down.' I'd heard it so many times but I didn't know what it meant till I heard the screech of those screws turning.

We went to the funeral in two horse-drawn cabs, moving very slowly till we got as far as the Coach and Horses. Nobody spoke.

As I listened to the horses moving faster down Balham Hill, 'He went to the funeral, but just for a ride' kept going through my head. Men touched their caps as we passed. One or two crossed themselves. We were near my school. The girls would all be bent over their books. I felt sick.

That night I dreamt she stood by my bed. 'Oh, Carrie,' I said, 'I knew you weren't dead,' and woke up at once.

Her small daughter, Marie, stayed with us, and when summer came we went to Ramsgate on the insurance money. It was our first and last holiday. Jim was working there and we stayed in his lodgings behind the gasometer. I got up early every morning, walked the two miles to the beach and went swimming. I'd go far out, beyond the buoys.

Marie was a wistful little thing, with light fair hair. One day an old man bent down and patted her head.

'She's lost her mother,' said Kate.

'Oh, not for long,' said the silly old man. 'She'll soon find her again.'

My mother was in deep black from head to foot.

I didn't care for sitting around on the beach, so I explored the place and came upon:

> The Pierrots. Three shows a day.
> Seats threepence and sixpence.

I stood outside the palings watching them. They were in black and white; the girls wore frilly skirts, like powder puffs.

> *I wasn't born in Africa*
> *I wasn't born in France*
> *I wasn't born in sunny, sunny Spain*
> *I was simply born to dance.*

Each one had a song and dance to introduce them.

> *I am the baritone, I'll sing you songs galore*
> *And when I sing it's usual to give an encore.*

I was enchanted. From then on I stood in the same place at every performance. Soon I could tell what mood they were in as they took their places on their little stage. I tried to get in on the act. I entered a talent competition one evening and got one vote. I'd chosen 'My Mother's Arms'. I knew I'd made a mistake the moment I started; for one thing, I would have hated to be in my mother's arms.

The night before we left they had a special Carnival Night. I went early to watch them putting up coloured lights round their stand. The place was transformed. So were we.

'A retreat' at school meant a rule of silence, long hours outdoors, a hidden seat where you could read Thomas Aquinas or Francis Thompson in peace. Such books were at your disposal, laid out in the conservatory. Three times a day the bell summoned us to the chapel to hear Monsignor Gonne preach. This went on for a week, and though the grief for Carrie never left me, the calm of the convent was welcome.

One day I stole into the chapel as mass was being said. The place was full. All the girls wore black lace on their heads. I knew I didn't belong, but the place drew me and I thumped my chest on the 'Mea Culpa' with the best of them. When they all stood up and began moving towards the altar, I went too. A white hand was laid on my arm, very softly. I saw a white cuff, black veiling. I looked up. You had to look right into those narrow coifs before you knew who it was. Mother St Vincent looked at me seriously as she shook her head. I smelled arum lilies and fainted.

When I felt better, she explained Communion to me, and I understood that I was an outsider, but that I could be received into the Catholic Church. Meanwhile, I loved Benediction, the day's travail over, the candlelight, the dark sky outside, but especially:

> *Tantum ergo sacramentum*
> *Veneremur cernui*
> *Et antiquum documentum*
> *Novo cedet ritui:*

Praistet fides supplementum
Sensuum defectui.

Mother St Teresa called me to her study one day, sat me on a hassock and talked to me about a vocation. Some, she said, were called to serve God away from the world.

I told her I wasn't baptised, and instead of discussing vocations began asking her about the infallibility of the Pope, and trying to start an argument. She wouldn't bite, unlike Mother St Vincent, who sometimes got in such a paddy arguing with me that she'd clutch at her coif and a wisp of bright red hair would escape. If Mother St Vincent had been working on me, I might have proved more amenable. I told Mother St Teresa that in any case I couldn't desert my cousin Marie. She was quite irritated and told me that many refused the call but Jesus was used to excuses. At that I left.

As it happened, I was not to have Marie near me for much longer. By autumn Harry was courting again. It was the woman in the downstairs flat at 17 Pearman Street, off Westminster Bridge Road, where he'd lived with Carrie, a very gloomy place. The new love was small, dark-skinned, with a broken nose. She came from Uttoxeter, North Derbyshire, and spoke 'North Country'. Harry told Marie to run in and sing:

Ramona, I hear the mission bells above us.
Ramona, I'll meet you by the water fall . . .

Then say, 'Hallo Ramona.'

That did it. They hitched their wagon to the downstairs flat and took Marie away from us. Of course Kate hated the lady. If ever I started putting on a North Country accent, 'Shut up,' she'd say, 'You sound like that woman.' She didn't know the new Mrs Watson, but she enjoyed hating; that was perhaps why the family rows were more ferocious than ever and I was more determined than ever to get the hell out of it.

I wrote to the Old Vic, a beautifully written letter, offering my services. With my experience of Shakespeare, I could be pretty useful to them. I used what I believed to be my real father's name. They answered, but my mother intercepted the letter. She was in a cold fury.

'Don't you dare use that name.'

I never had, till then, nor have I since. I didn't care a damn about the name, or him, or her. I didn't give a damn about the whole stupid bastardy business. I'd begun to use the word to upset my cronies, especially Norah who was Catholic and worried because I wasn't christened. By that time I'd read Cervantes and enjoyed having a lost parent. It was good being an outsider, and it would make it easier for me to escape when my plans were laid.

Meanwhile I played the rebel, chalked 'The Masque of Anarchy' over three blackboards before class one morning, joined a march demanding 'Independence for India'. Gandhi came out to watch us from a balcony at the Dorchester Hotel.

'Put your trousers on,' shouted a comrade.

The next day I organised my own march. 'Form IVA! All out!'

I'd found a dead rat, so we made a procession round the playground with it, buried it with honours, crying 'Here lies the tyrant', and skipped school to enjoy the delights of Balham Market.

After that I was on the carpet.

'You are up for expulsion,' said Mother St Teresa. I didn't care, but Mother St Vincent stopped me in the corridor. 'You are losing your chance of going on to University.'

'University students are scabs,' I replied, and ran for it.

I thought they'd given me up. They hadn't. Perhaps they believed that rebels make good Catholics, or perhaps it was the news that I'd won another scholarship. On top of that, Nick – that is, Miss Nicholson, our art teacher – had been showing my drawings to Barnett Friedman at the Royal College of Art and he'd foretold a distinguished future for me as an artist. Nick thought she'd saved me from a fate worse than death.

'I saw that look in your eye.'

'No,' I told her. 'I outlived my Catholic phase long ago.'

I didn't tell her I'd written to the Royal Academy of Dramatic Art applying for a scholarship.

School was becoming a bit of a bore, even though I only

worked at the subjects I liked. I went to art galleries with Nick
on Saturdays and wrote long letters to her about 'art'. One day
she asked me if I'd like to go on holiday with her. I didn't fancy
it much. Nick all day. But I said yes. At least I'd be away from
home. Exams were going to be a headache but I'd get by, with a
bit of luck.

One day a long white envelope fell on to the mat. What's
this? Two set pieces to be learnt, *Tamburlaine*, *Hindle Wakes*,
sight-reading and an oral exam. It was for the scholarship to
RADA. Then I noticed the date, right in the middle of exams.
Ah, well! I started reading Marlowe.

I walked out of the house with my school satchel, took the tube
to Goodge Street, and found my way to this famous academy,
delighted to be skipping the chemistry exam. I was surprised to
find a roomful of young women chattering excitedly while they
waited for their names to be called. They were all fashionably
dressed. I was wearing school uniform.

When my turn came, I strode onto the stage, lifted my head
into the light and proclaimed:

> *If all the pens that ever poets held*
> *Had fed the feeling of their masters' thoughts,*
> *And every sweetness that inspir'd their hearts,*
> *Their minds, and muses on admired themes* . . .

and so on, a glorious speech.

Then came Fanny's refusal of marriage. I tried the new Mrs
Harry Watson's accent:

> *You're not a fool altogether. But you're not man enough for me. You're a*
> *nice lad and I'm fond of you but I couldn't ever marry you.* [Here I put
> a bit of laughter into the voice.] *We've had a right good time together,*
> *I'll never forget that. It has been a right good time and no mistake. We've*
> *enjoyed ourselves, proper. But all good times have to come to an end and*
> *ours is over now. Come along now, and bid me farewell.*

The sight-reading was easy. I'd had plenty of practice at that. After a while I was beckoned into an ante-room. A whole semi-circle of important-looking men and women asked me questions about the drama, then about school, and lastly, of all things, about that bloody gap in my teeth. Had I always had it? Still, some of the faces in the room were friendly and, as I went out, a Miss Burnett said, 'Good Luck.' I smiled back. I knew she would vote for me. There was one LCC scholarship, or rather one for a boy and one for a girl. I wanted to win more than anything on earth. I did.

Nick didn't seem very pleased, nor were the nuns. I heard Mother St Teresa telling the Schools Inspector of one more scholarship among the leavers, worth – she quoted a figure which she must have invented since nobody knew what the scholarship was worth. Nick reproached me because I hadn't matriculated with honours. I'd got through, but that missed exam had been a black mark. I thought she was going to cancel that proposed holiday but no.

What's more it wasn't to be sand in your pants and queueing for fish and chips. No, by God, it was PARIS.

Eight

*In Paris at the age of sixteen. Art and Nick's arty friends. She wants
me to be a painter, she wants to adopt me. Back in London, she takes
me to a Chelsea studio and helps me with my painting. I leave Kate
and Jim, go to live in Pimlico.*

I'm on the edge of my seat as the taxi races up the Champs
Elysées.

'Stop holding your breath,' said Nick.

The sky higher, buildings a gentler grey, street lamps shedding
softer light and the whores prettier. At the bus stop you pulled a
lever to release a numbered ticket, then when the bus came you
were called by rote.

At the teachers' hostel in Avenue Wagram, my room on the
third floor was long and narrow, with wash basin, mirror and
a mysterious kidney-shaped pan on legs. The polished wooden
flooring reflected a real French window. I lifted the catch – it
opened on to a small balcony – and let in the clamour of the
street, high-pitched motor horns, policemen's whistles. I could
just see the busy avenue where, a few minutes earlier, we had
driven past pavement cafés, waiters with long white aprons and
young ladies wearing tiny bowler hats tilted over one eye. There
was that perfume again – what could it be? It reminded me of lead
pencils. Was it the petrol? Even the petrol smells different over
here. No! It was the perfume of the hour – Soir de Paris.

Days of enchantment followed, and nights spent dreaming out
there on the balcony, making smoke rings with my Gitanes Jaune.
In Paris I had learned to smoke. Poussin, the posters on the Métro,
the Trocadéro and the ample folds of the stone goddess lounging on
the architrave of the Crédit Lyonnais opposite my window – they
all delighted me.

My favourite things? Rodin's Balzac wrapped in his stone cloak,

a mediaeval Madonna in Cluny and the spire of Sainte Chapelle. I
enjoyed Notre Dame when the colours cast by the Oriel windows
drifted across the paved floor. For a moment I was bewitched
again. 'Tread softly, this is holy ground.'

'Breakfast at five tomorrow.'

'Where are we going?'

'Les Halles, the market.'

Great, just the style. Jim's brothers and nephews had all
worked in Covent Garden market. Nick and I created quite a stir
– the English spinster in her brogues and tweeds and me. A huge
black porter with a mass of fuzzy hair stopped in front of me.

'Hé! Regardez le petit garçon! C'est une fillette, non?'

That was because I'd had my hair cropped like a boy's, Nick's
idea. She thought I had a well-shaped head.

Nick went everywhere armed with guide-books, maps and
timetables. She meant to show me all the sights. Fontainebleau
gloomy, the forest glorious, rocks to climb, bright orange slugs
laying about in the rain. Versailles, huge cobbled forecourt better
than inside, with all those acres of Louis' elephantine kitsch. Poor
Molière, having to work in a landscape tamed and tailored. He
would hardly get a look-in among all those water shows, fireworks,
masques and – Lully.

It was at Versailles that I first encountered this exquisite object.
It was on a yellow plate, on a white tablecloth, behind a neat box
hedge, in a modest restaurant.

'Un artichaut, mademoiselle,' said the *patron* as he placed a carafe
of red wine beside it. *'Vin à volonté,'* he added.

My first glass of wine.

Nick had given me a sketch-book, bound in linen, small
enough to use unseen and slip into your pocket. 'Take it with you
wherever you go and jot down everything that interests you.' So I
did. It made me use my eyes.

Two or three of Nick's friends turned up at the weekend.
They had been sketching in Spain and broke their journey home
to have a look at us. They were all artistic, but ladylike. One wore
a *gendarme*'s cloak, another a straight shift with tucks and peasant
stitching across the breast, and the third didn't stay long enough to
take off her coat. They all wore their hair in a page-boy bob or set

back in a ballet bun. Their voices were soft, they spoke in gently undulating sentences which never came to an end, leaving you in mid-air and in some suspense. 'As it were . . . So to speak . . . Don't you think . . .' They talked of Carrington, Lytton Strachey, Katherine Mansfield and that awful husband. . . . One of them was persona grata with Aldous Huxley. They only addressed each other by surnames, Bayley, Mason, Nick, and made rather consciously graceful gestures as they talked. Each pale hand bore an antique silver ring set with cornelian or jade. There were no wedding rings. Bayley was married to Tom, a sculptor, another awful man.

After a modest meal at the hostel, Bayley insisted on treating us to coffee on the boulevard and – another first for me – a liqueur. I chose Benedictine, curious to know if it would taste holy. Mary Cronin, from the sixth form, was hoping to be a Benedictine nun and she told me it was a very strict order.

I was going to sidle my sketch-book out when I noticed that the lady artists were already sketching, one under her cloak, another behind a menu card, Nick openly, holding up her pencil and closing one eye. Oh dear! Now the *garçon* is approaching, craning his neck to see what she's put on her pad.

'We got into terrible trouble in Spain,' said Bayley.

'How was that?' said Nick. She had a high voice and unlike the others a rather snappy way of speaking.

'We were drawing in a village and one by one the women came and stood looking at us. We carried on but they got rather cross and began to throw stones.'

'Did you throw them back?'

'We drew them. There they are.' And she giggled like a girl as she produced the sketch of the angry women. They looked very angry.

I took a sip of my strong sweet drink and sat on my sketch-book. The next day they went.

Half my Parisian days were gone and I began to dread the return to England. The security of school was gone for good, and the scholarship grant that went with it. The six shillings a week paid out by my putative father would cease on my birthday in October when I was sixteen.

'But you have a lot to go back for.'

There was a hint of mockery in her voice. I knew what she thought about contemporary theatre. 'The same routine, night after night, sometimes for months.'

'That's not the kind of theatre I want.'

Sitting on the balcony at night, I tried to explain my idea to her. Space, light and shelter, a place that would change with the seasons, where all knowledge would be available and new discovery made clear. It was a place to play and learn and do what you will. I could not define it philosophically, but its purpose was very clear to me.

I already knew that work was the only solution to life's problems, creative work with some manual labour thrown in. The inborn violence, murderous feelings, the hate and aggression which are part of us, even our petty feelings, can be transformed by creativity. . . . Was she listening? Her cigarette was glowing in the dark.

'Everybody an artist, or a scientist . . .' I stopped. She was laughing. 'Why are you laughing?'

'Because you pronounce the word artist the way a novice might say the word Jesus.'

I knew, by now, that above all she wanted me to be an artist. Funny old Nick, with her lovely slim figure, ugly face, and boyish stride. I knelt down, put my arms round her, rested my head on her lap and said I loved her. I don't know whether I did or not. I'd certainly never used the word before. We didn't talk like that round our way, and as for hugging and kissing – we might as well have been Bushmen.

'Ah, well,' said Nick. 'Better me than the first fellow-me-lad you meet.'

I didn't like that. Such fellers as I knew were eedjits. I told her so.

'Well,' she said, 'a nice young man might be a bit worried, you know, about your parentage.'

'Then to hell with him,' I said.

And to hell with her too, I thought. I didn't say it but I think that was the end of our beautiful friendship.

I found out later that Nick had written to my mother asking

if she might adopt me, and my mother had said no. Just as well, I said to myself – you won't be staying around with Nick all that long.

'Don't be so forlorn. We'll go back and paint. I have a friend who'll lend me his studio in Chelsea.'

Did she still think I might abandon RADA?

For our last night, Nick bought two tickets for the opera. I wasn't very enthusiastic. I'd seen an opera when Lilian Bayliss was trying her Sadlers Wells repertoire at the Old Vic. It was very nineteenth-century.

'Do we have to go?'

'It'll be an experience,' said Nick. 'And it's very cheap.'

'What's the piece?'

'*Rigoletto.*'

I dusted my shoes, changed my school blouse and off we went. As we mounted the steps from the Métro, there it was! A giant wedding cake! 'What style is it?' asked Napoleon III. 'Napoleon III,' replied Monsieur Garnier, the architect.

We entered solemnly, like gatecrashers at a funeral. But once inside, my art teacher was swept into a mad fandango. First the tickets – then the location – *La caisse – Le Contrôle – Eh bien!* Rubber stamp. At last we reach the Flunk-who-bars-the-way. Hm! Scrupulous examination of tickets. And everybody in a very bad temper, except the flunkey who has nothing but contempt for people who buy cheap seats.

The moment we are allowed through, all is calm, all strife is forgotten. Before us, pure theatre – and such staircases! Such curves, such splendour. And what a crowd. A smoothly coiffed head turns, to be admired; a platinum blonde raises a black gloved hand. Who is she looking for? Rastignac? Lucien de Rubempré? These stairs were designed for them.

I enjoyed the fashionable whirl. But I lost Nick. After a while she found me and we went in. I should have stayed outside. The crowd was more fun than the show. It was not my impression that the French company could sing, and what else is there to do in opera? Such a damn silly story could hardly be acted, except as a comedy. But if anyone on that stage had ever given the job a thought, they showed no sign of it. They just stood around looking useless, waiting for the cue to open their mouths and let out those frightful sounds. There was one good moment when Rigoletto's hump fell off, raising a cloud of dust, but nobody laughed, except me.

B ack in London, Nick took me to the Chelsea studio where we were to work. It was in a part of London almost as strange to me as Paris; the streets were tree-lined, the houses graceful. The studio itself was deep and square, with a narrow wooden balcony running round it. A Persian rug hung from one side, a touch of Delacroix in an otherwise austere setting. There were two easels, one large, one small, smears of paint on a large palette, an overall smell of turps and the blank canvas waiting for another Monet. Me, perhaps.

Early each morning I swam in the Serpentine, then walked to Chelsea, ready to start at nine. Nick set up a still life, fruit and pots and all that, but I wanted to work on my study of the coffee stall on the Embankment. I'd been there the last three nights, making notes. I'd walked home swiftly afterwards, only stopping to say good night to some lady who was clearly on the game. I was curious about such mysterious women, until I found that they weren't at all mysterious, more like the woman next door. Mind you, they wouldn't talk to me till I pretended I was a streetwalker. One of them actually believed me.

'Oh, well,' she said. 'You've got to do something.'

She was right, and I was going to do something. But first let's break the news to Mother.

S he didn't fly off the handle. She wasn't even surprised. All right, she would withdraw the cash which had been paid into an insurance premium. It would have been mine on my sixteenth birthday. The gold sovereigns Gran had given me, one each year on my birthday, she would keep. I didn't mind about the premium. I hated insurance anyway. As a child I used to close the door on their agent, Mr Vines, when he called at Gran's on

Thursdays to collect. I minded about Gran's sovereigns, but there was nothing I could do.

Jim listened, then he gave a dry cough. 'You go,' he said. 'And never darken my door again.'

Where had he picked up that expression?

W hen I was small, I always looked back when Aunt Carrie took me out. 'It's Paradise when you're away,' Kate used to say, and I expected to see the old house all shining. This time I didn't look back, I headed straight for Warwick Avenue, Pimlico, where Yvonne Rudellat lived. She was a dressmaker, French; her husband was an Italian waiter. I could stay with her, at a pinch, though all she could offer me was a camp-bed in the bathroom, five bob a week. It was a big bathroom. Her young daughter Connie slept there, she said, and I would only have to leave when somebody wanted a bath.

She was kindly. When she noticed I'd nothing but my school clothes to wear, she transformed the gym slip into a skirt and gave me a blouse which some customer had forgotten.

'There's a sale of shoes at Selfridges, a shilling a foot,' she told me.

'A shilling a pair of shoes?'

'No, one shoe. You have to look for the other one.'

It was hunt-the-slipper, as I rummaged through the mound of assorted shoes, till I had the pair, black and white, openwork.

Nine

I felt pretty smart when I crossed the threshold of RADA. The doorkeeper was doing the honest cockney with a snobbish girl student.

'Don't come it round 'ere,' he said. 'You ain't your father. Churchill's daughter,' he added as she stalked away.

I made for the cloakroom. It was crowded with girls wriggling their rubber girdles, comparing lipsticks and making bee-sting lips at the mirrors. They were all debs or rich Americans acquiring an English accent. I was the only outsider.

'Don't you have a *soutien-gorge*?'

It was the wardrobe mistress, trying to dress me for Rosalind. I'd only been given the one scene, the 'What though you have no beauty' bit; the part had to be parcelled out among a superfluity of girls – and what could you do with a fragment from that creaking old play?

At the end of the first term, the head of the Academy told me he was disappointed in me. I said I wasn't too happy either. In fact, I thought the place a waste of time. I only fancied Madame Gachet's French classes and Annie Fligg's Central European Movement, but the one cost a guinea a term and for the other you needed a pair of tights and I couldn't run to either on my scholarship grant, eleven shillings a week. I'd have to earn some money somehow. Meanwhile, Yvonne Rudellat came to the rescue again. She unearthed a bathing suit, salmon pink on top, black from the waist down, with a pair of school stockings cobbled on to the legs. I'd have my tights.

On the Saturday morning I walked into Annie Fligg's class, the legs of my outfit a bit stretched, but I was ready for action. And what action. Fräulein Fligg beat a drum and away we went . . . Up! Down! Leap! Stretch! Dyum da dee da. Dyum da dee. Forward and back. Dyum! It was great. I'd never felt so alive. My stretching out was putting a bit of a strain on those stockings, but what did it matter? Miss Bedell's ballet class had given me half-past-twelve feet, this was action, a first taste of Rudolf Laban's work which was to influence my whole life. I looked for any reference to him in the public library. There was none. I found an encyclopaedia of art in Zwemmer's bookshop. Yes here he is. But it's in German. I gathered that he'd revolutionised dance and opera while still in his twenties, that he was a crystallographer and a Dadaist. But taking it all in all, that Academy was a waste of time. I was quite shocked when George Bernard Shaw turned up to rehearse us in *Heartbreak House*. Why did he waste his time on such a place?

I was Ellie in the scene he chose.

'I don't want you to imitate me,' he said, but he gave a remarkably good reading of the part. Ellie, with a long white beard: 'When your heart is broken your boats are burned. It is the end of happiness and the beginning of peace.'

And my heart felt broken, but then he made us laugh playing the cockney burglar.

A titled girl approached me one day. 'It must be a frightful bore to be poor,' she said.

It was, but I found early-morning work cleaning – one and six an hour – and in the summer break I took a job in a knitting works. By autumn I managed a few luxuries, a steak-and-kidney pud at Lyons on Friday evenings, sevenpence, an occasional Promenade Concert, and an art card at Zwemmer's on a Saturday morning.

Yvonne Rudellat's husband owned the house in Warwick Avenue where I was living in the bathroom. They lived in the basement. Yvonne took my LCC cheques when they arrived and gave me back six shillings every Friday. Her other lodgers were a crazy cosmopolitan crew. The Hungarian chef and his wife lived in a big room on the first floor. It had carpets on the walls, enormous cushions, and a minute Turkish table always set with Imperial Tokay and Turkish delight. The husband, blond and fat, liked to lean on his balcony flirting with the girls in the flat opposite. His wife didn't seem to mind.

We had every kind of entertainment in that house, even French farce, when Yvonne hid her Parisian lover in the back room and her jealous husband nearly found him. I was given the trusted maid's role: I had to meet Monsieur Henri when he came off the boat-train at Victoria Station, wearing the coat in which she'd last said goodbye to him, smuggle him into the house, and take him his food. That part was tricky. Connie, her daughter, knew him and indeed it wasn't long before the whole house did.

M RUDELLAT: Yvonne! I can hear a man on the first floor.

The Hungarian chef bursts into song.

MME RUDELLAT: A man? You must be dreaming, *cheri*. There's no man here. (*In a whisper*) Joan, you must stand guard when I am with my friend . . .

CONNIE: Maman, do you know I could have sworn I heard Uncle Henri speaking.

MME RUDELLAT: *Tu plaisante, ma fille*. (*Nervously*) Who's that?

VOICE (*off*): I'm 'Enery the Eighth, I am –

CONNIE: That's the bookmaker from the top flat.

It was a wonder Monsieur Henri got back to France without a knife in his back. She always took him to the Strand Palace for a coffee if her husband slept late.

I was playing Cleopatra in *Scenes from Shakespeare*, BBC Overseas Service. Robert Speaight was my asp man. It was beamed to the far-flung Empire at 3 a.m. our time, but Yvonne insisted on coming to Broadcasting House to hear me. Archie Harding was the director; he had awarded me First Prize for verse-speaking at RADA. He was an upper-class Bolshie with a strong Oxford accent. Shortly after my début he was sentenced to internal exile in Manchester, and contrary to expectation loved the North, found it a breath of fresh air after London.

Meanwhile, I had to fall back on the knitting works at Tooting, but I attended art classes four nights a week and joined a literary circle which Nick's friend Bayley had organised in Chiswick. We read our compositions to each other on Saturday evenings, but often, just as you started it would be, 'Stop! That hand! The smoke ring! So sorry, do go on.'

The friend I'd made when I sneaked into the Slade School to draw, Sonja Mortensen, was now in Paris painting at the Académie Scandinave. 'Why not come here?' she wrote. 'What are you waiting for?'

Since the holiday with Nick I hadn't been able to pass Victoria Station without a pang. When did the next train leave? I would paint from the model all day, then sketch in the streets and write. What about eating? I'd nine pounds. I could get letters of introduction. Goodbye, London . . .

I found Sonja in an icy room in the Rue Daguerre. The rest of the clientèle lived by begging, selling bootlaces, or picking up odd jobs in the market. I watched them in the early morning downing a black coffee with Calvados before facing the cold streets. The lavatory was a hole in the floor of a cabinet. A dumb old man with his thick pebble glasses stirred it with a stick every morning, then swept the worn wooden stairs with the remains of an old broom.

The Académie Scandinave was still closed for Christmas, so Sonja painted by the window. I sat under the bed quilt in my coat making sketches. When my hands froze, I would leap up and warm both of us with exercises, adding a few fiery lines for Art's sake:

Roast me in sulphur, wash me in steep-down gulfs of liquid fire.

'To think of you here when you could be making a fortune reading poetry.'

Sonja hadn't much knowledge of the world. I liked her style, though. If some man annoyed her on the street – she was very good-looking – she would simply bonk him on the head with her umbrella.

My letters of introduction got me nowhere. A boyish-looking English girl? Useless. There was one exception, an eccentric old lady in radio. She saw me as a forgotten prince in a dark tower, playing with dolls, awaiting assassination. I was supposed to make up the script. We spent long afternoons in her stuffy salon discussing it. She collected dolls. One, life-size, with real eyelashes, lay in lace, smiling. I escaped early on a bitterly cold day and walked by the Seine. As I turned towards the Left Bank, the world blew up. Firework night, with gunshot – people running, a woman screaming – a line of coppers. . . . Back! Go back!

A young man dashed into the road and rolled marbles under the hooves of charging horses. One of those pretty cupolas which advertise the theatres of Paris had been uprooted and overturned. A barricade? Somewhere a crowd was roaring 'To the Elysées'. Then there were wild cries. . . . Gunshot again.

I flattened myself against a wall as a wave of human beings surged along the street. Is it revolution? It doesn't seem real, more like a film – Pudovkin against the elegant backcloth of Paris, but those cries were real enough, and the shots.

Crisis had threatened for a long time. Five presidents had come and gone in the space of a year, the word 'government' was a joke. France had a million and a half unemployed. Left, right and centre, every section of divided France was angry.

Two nights ago, Sonja and I had been in the market when *Paris Soir* arrived. Someone snatched it.

'*Stavisky s'est suicidé.*'

'*Non!*'

'*Regardez-moi ça!*'

On the front page there was a picture of a dead body, two coppers standing over it. Who was Stavisky? A dishonest but highly successful financier who had involved top-storey politicians and *haute-societé* speculators in his shady deals. Had he committed suicide? The people who knew their government decided he'd been silenced. He could have incriminated the whole corrupt clique running France, including the heads of the police force. The scandal brought the government down. That night's flare-up proved to be the popular answer to an attempted coup by the Right Wing.

As I ran down the stone steps which led to the Seine, I heard ambulance bells. An old hag was standing staring at me. She spat in my face. Along the cobbled quay lay mounds of rags, hiding the human beings who slept there.

Fifteen were killed on the street that night. Three hundred wounded were taken to hospital. Many others made their way home to nurse their wounds. My city of charming little restaurants, art, and René Clair *Sous les Toits*, was showing its other face. Sonja's parents wired her to come home. She didn't want to; she decided to move on to Italy. The violence in Paris continued. I wanted to move on too. But where to? London? Never. Was there another England? Better still, a New World. I would make for Liverpool and stow away on a boat.

Ten

Walking north, collapse at Burton-on-Trent. Taken in by poor people. Sleep. They find an envelope, 'Archie Harding, BBC Manchester', in my pocket. Despatch the letter. By return, my fare and an offer: In Town Tonight, *Saturday, Manchester. I am befriended there – a party, an offer of hospitality, entertained by D.G. Bridson, the local literary genius. Interviewed by the producer of the repertory theatre, I'm given a job.*

After a brief stop-over, visiting my grandparents – the old man mended my shoes for me – I was on my way. I intended to contact Harding in Manchester *en route*, in the hope that he would give me a job to help me along.

All that I possessed was tied up in the bundle I carried. It was my second-best skirt, stitched up at the bottom. I had two books with me, Thomas Aquinas and *The Diary of a Disappointed Man* by W.P. Barbellion; also notebooks and pencils. I walked all day and slept anywhere at night until, on the third or fourth night out, I was awakened by the roar of wild animals. In the morning I found I'd bedded down near Whipsnade Zoo. I changed my tactics, walked at night and snatched some sleep during the day. This was how it came about that a family of unemployed in Burton-on-Trent took me in. I'd found a patch of grass on some waste ground behind a row of working-class houses, plumped up my bundle for a pillow and gone to sleep. I must have slept a long time. Someone decided that I was dead. I woke to a row of faces looking down at me. A very thin, very poor woman was nudging my shoulder with her foot. I was still only half awake when she led me to her back door and thro' the yard to her small kitchen.

Over a mug of hot tea I fell asleep again, and the poor lady – they called her Beattie – went through my things to find out who I was. She came on a name and address in Manchester, Harding,

Programme Director, BBC, Piccadilly, and had actually posted a note to him while I slept.

The next day I went after a job in a brewery. I didn't get it. I found work as a charwoman instead. A week later, Beattie was very excited when I got back from work. There was a letter for me, from Manchester. It contained a contract for *In Town Tonight*. A two thousand-word talk to be prepared. Fee? Untold wealth – I can't remember how much – two guineas, I think, plus the expense of a night's lodging and my fare to Manchester on the Saturday. I wrote my talk, said goodbye, and took the train to my new world, and a new and wonderful life.

I loved the northern city at first sight. No Horse Guards, no South Kensington accents, no sir and madam stuff. The wind from the Pennines which swept through the Manchester streets had blown them away. In the Shambles, the timbered inn where Bonnie Prince Charlie had put up for the night still stood. Beneath the Free Trade Hall, and somewhere beyond, was the site of the Battle of Peterloo. This was the Classic Soil of Communism.

At Broadcasting House I had a friendly reception.

'How do?' said the lift man. 'Come and have a cup of tea. You'll be Joan.'

I was being escorted to the canteen by this friendly man who'd been at the door to meet me. As we crossed to the tea bar, a ringing baritone made me jump.

'Eighty-two thousand tons of cast iron segments from . . .'

The hiss of boiling water drowned the rest.

'Where?'

'Ilkeston,' boomed the voice.

'That voice! Where is it coming from?'

'Five hundred and ninety-four thousand, five hundred and eighty bitumen-grummeted boltings . . .'

'It's those damned speakers,' said my escort. 'They will leave them on.'

'One hundred and thirty tons of iron washers . . .'

'Do you take sugar?'

'. . . cast-iron segments . . .'

'Sorry?'

'Sugar?'

'No, thank you.'

'A scone?'

'Ferro-concrete built, brick or Portland stone finish . . .'

'Could you turn the sound down a bit over there?' The voice faded out.

'Archie's rehearsing Bridson's *Tunnel*. We've been at it all day.'

'His tunnel?'

'The King's opening the new Mersey Tunnel next Wednesday and Bridson is Archie Harding's latest discovery, the Voice was Jimmie Miller. You should try these scones.'

I did. They were home-made. A young man came to brief me. I was to start straight in with Cleopatra's 'Give me my robe, put on my crown' speech. After that I would be introduced and would give my talk.

It was all very friendly and exciting, but nothing to the scene after the transmission. *In Manchester Tonight* usually began with some old chap who'd grown a prize vegetable marrow or retired after fifty years' service on the Ship Canal. The glorious iambics delivered in vibrant tones must have come as a shock. Anyroad, as they say up there, a crowd of well-wishers showered praises on me. I was invited to spend the night at the home of a hospitable couple who happened to be in the building. Harding invited me to the rehearsals of *Tunnel* on the following day. People were falling over each other to be nice to me. What had I done?

'Your lucky tramp, love.'

Before bed I took a bath in Manchester's soft water and, for the first time in my life took a good look at my naked self in a long mirror in a real bedroom.

'You'll do,' I said.

Next morning I found a room in Grosvenor Street, Ardwick, and in the evening, after the *Tunnel* rehearsal, Bridson took me to visit a certain Jack Dillon. He and his wife Tanya kept open house on Sunday evenings; the BBC crowd, journalists and artists turned up with anyone interesting who happened to be around.

As we walked up a drive in Chorlton-cum-Hardy, I felt I was being surveyed by unseen eyes. Was I the lioness of the evening? I hoped they weren't expecting anything spectacular. On the other hand, I didn't look like a bum, either. My hair was short and clean. I had on my one spare shirt, my only skirt, sandals and a good-looking black silk coatee without collar which I'd saved for any unforeseen occasion. I looked quite smart, very smart for me.

I felt self-conscious when we walked in, but nobody took any notice of us. They were all wondering what had happened to Igor.

'Last seen lolling in the WC drinking eau-de-Cologne?' said Geoffrey.

'Thought you might have dropped him off at the infirmary for some treatment,' said a funny little man, as he darted about fetching drinks. This was Jack Dillon. He wore spectacles and talked incessantly in a high-pitched, hoarse voice, almost castrato.

'Tanya's gone to the Film Society with Manny,' he announced. 'It's the Eisenstein season. They're showing one of Grierson's tonight as well.'

'Pimm's Number One?'

I'd no idea what he was talking about but there was a bowl of punch swimming with fruit and veg on a side table beside plates of nuts and olives, and he was already ladling this exotic mixture into a tumbler for me. I tried to look as if I was used to Pimm's, though I'd seldom tasted anything stronger than a port and lemon in my life.

Two or three small groups were talking among themselves, flicking ash over their shoulders. Suddenly a voice soared above the rest. 'You're madly wrong. Lunacharski was a Blanquiste.'

Dillon sniggered. A pretty woman with faun's eyes and a gentle smile came in. Jack dashed up to her, knelt and kissed the hem of her skirt.

'She's mine, Rafe,' he said to a big soft bloke who had drifted alongside. 'Not that I'm getting anywhere. Look what I'm up against.'

'Norman Brown,' the newcomer announced himself. 'And my wife, Monica.'

Dillon handed him a beer.

Kenneth and Ruth Adam entered, took me in at a glance, and made for the drinks. 'Where is she? It's not a party without Tanya.'

'Don't worry, it'll get worse, especially if she brings any of her lovers back.'

Adam brought us up to date with the Igor situation. He had beaten up one of the *Guardian* night staff for waking him.

'Thinks he's still in Russia,' said Jack.

Adam started telling a story about Archie Harding. Everybody paid attention. Archie obviously went down well up here and his Oxford accent sounded even funnier imitated by someone with a North Country accent.

'So Archie was saddled with this big shot from London. He'd shown him round the building, given him a stirrup cup, and as a parting shot was pointing out the beauty of the Manchester skyline, when the entire contents of the office above came floating down past the window. "I say, what!" said the Big Shot. "Spring cleaning," said Archie. "Lancashire custom, very thorough. By the way, the BBC car is at the door – pity you've so little time left, but you should manage to catch a glimpse of Redbank before your train leaves." "What, what!" But Archie was chivvying him into the lift, to give himself time to phone for the car and be at the front door before the Big Shot, but he was beaten to the post. "Bit misty, what?" In actual fact it was pissing down. "Refreshing," said Archie, squinting at the sky. The car arrived, the BBC attendant opened the door. "Cheery-bye," said the Big Shot. "Frightful bore, pore thing," said Archie. "Yes sir," said the doorkeeper, picking up a couple of sodden files from the pavement. "See that Mr de Groot's things are returned to his office, will you, sergeant?" "Yes, sir, certainly sir. Mr de Groot feeling more like himself, sir?" "One hopes so. We don't want him ravishing any more of the secretaries." "No sir. As you say, sir –" '

'I thought that was what they were there for,' said Dillon.

'If so, they can sack ninety per cent of them right away,' said Rafe Parker.

Manny and Tanya came in. She was tall with a beautiful figure, and a plain face. Everyone kissed her except her husband. Manny made for the table where I stood, hiding my olive stone between finger and thumb, in the hope of secreting it in a potted palm. He asked my name, introduced himself – Manny Levy, a painter – and at once asked if I'd like to visit his studio.

'Enjoying the party?' said Jack Dillon, buzzing by. 'Manny's nice, isn't he? Your type.'

This is a party? I asked myself. This gathering was quite static and the talk so 'in'. I decided to go. Then one of the journalists started discussing Eisenstein, so I took another olive and stayed. It was no use, all they talked about was Eisenstein's private life and how homosexuals were being shot in the Soviet Union. Manny and Tanya said nothing.

'Tanya's silence is her strength,' said Kenneth Adam.

As I was trying to bow out, Adam's wife, Ruth, came up to Tanya and gave her a small bottle of *Je Reviens*. 'From Deauville,' she said.

'Don't forget to pack it for the hols,' shouted Jack. 'You may meet a nice man while we're away.'

It was time to go. I didn't want to arrive back late. I'd only booked the room this morning. 'And it's a God-fearing street,' I told Jack. 'The Salvation Army was playing "Whiter than the whitewash on the wall" when I left.'

'The poor fuckers had nothing better to do,' he said. That word came as a shock to me, but this crackpot used it all the time. As I said goodbye, he told me that he and Tanya were off to Robin Hood's Bay on the Tuesday, and I could stay in their flat for a couple of weeks if I so wished. I thought that was extraordinarily nice of them and said so.

'Not at all,' said Jack. 'Come round for a bowl of soup tomorrow night and bring your things.'

What could I say? It seemed too much to accept on such short acquaintance. Then I thought of the drum I had found, ten shillings a week, and the smell of stale bedclothes. As the landlady made for the stairs this morning, I'd heard a moan from the back room.

'Who's that?'

'He's blind,' she said.

The door next to mine was open. A thin old man was lying on the bed wanking, his red-rimmed eyes fixed on the ceiling as tears trickled across his cheeks.

'Disgusting, isn't it?' she said.

What could one do? Not much. I tidied his room next morning, tried to cheer him up, gave him a few bob. Jack and Tanya's place would be paradise after this. They and their friends were showy and bizarre, but they were kind too. I had an idea that all the talk about fucking and the frank paintings were part of the act. In fact I'd found Jack Dillon's free and easy talk refreshing, though he'd made me feel I came from a race of inhibited human beings. All the same, if I'd believed for a moment that he was a dangerous human being, I'd never have gone back.

What would my Stockwell Puritans have made of him? They fell about at the slightest allusion to the genitals, and a fart would bring the house down. Poor Prick had to go by the name of Little Willy – the bawdy hand of Time is now on Little Willy. I'd always had a frank tongue in my head. It had shocked the girls at school, but underneath I was a Puritan too.

'Only think, there's nowhere you can walk around naked except in the privacy of your own home.' Jack was right. How often I'd longed to run naked by the sea and plunge into the water, but I'd only done it in my dreams.

The morning papers did me proud. 'FAME COMES TO A GIRL TRAMP.' 'JOAN OF THE HEDGEROWS LIVED ON TURNIPS.' Amazing. So were the invitations – lunch with the *Daily Herald*, tea with the *News Chronicle*, drinks at six with the *Dispatch*. The *Manchester Guardian* had high praise for my talk, but didn't ask me out.

When I arrived at the Dillons' with my bundle, Jack sang 'Hallelujah I'm a bum'. I was awkward as they showed me the workings of the flat and the raspberry canes in their part of the garden. I knew I wouldn't touch the kitchen equipment, it was all too strange. I would eat raspberries, drink Manchester water, and try all those barm cakes, girdle cakes, potato cakes and bannocks I'd seen in the little bakeries.

I loved my room. When they'd gone, I closed the door, threw off my clothes and broke into a wild fandango. Suddenly the door opened and Jack walked in. I froze. So did he.

'I was doing my exercises,' I said, and I knew I was blushing.

He moved his hands towards me. I stepped back. 'I'd better go,' he said.

Next morning he found time to tell me he'd had to leave me, or he wouldn't have been able to prevent himself . . . I felt false. I was not a virgin, but the deflowering had been so unsatisfactory that I'd tried to forget it.

My fortnight in the Dillon flat was 'Time out of life'. Their friends came to call and I invited my new friends. When Hazel and Carter of the *Daily Herald* arrived – you rarely got to know a person's Christian name in those days – they seemed as amazed to light on this Abbaye de Thélème in Manchester as I had been. They looked at the books, picked up *The Apes of God* and *Ulysses*, peered at the paintings and tried to make out how my host and hostess earned their living. I couldn't tell them Manchester was a bigger place than I'd imagined. I thought everybody here knew everybody else, but poor old Hazel and Carter lived in bachelor flats in Barlow Moor Road, Didsbury, and never seemed to meet anybody but their boozing companions on the paper.

Manchester was then about the size of Balzac's Paris. When I told Dillon that I'd spent an evening with Carter and Hazel, 'We drink our beer with the *Herald*,' he said. 'But we wine and dine with the *Guardian*.'

Manchester was very proud of the *Guardian* and Scott, its famous editor, the pillar of Liberalism. 'A bulwark against the south.' 'What Manchester thinks today, London thinks tomorrow.'

On a sunny day, I washed all my clothes, put on the kimono which was hanging on the back of the door, and went out to gather raspberries. A dusty figure appeared at the gate pushing a bicycle. Who was it? As soon as he spoke I knew. It was Beattie's husband from Burton-on-Trent. I had written telling them about the broadcast and my new friends, but had hardly given them another thought. When he saw the flat, his jaw dropped. He glanced at the blue kimono, and I could see that he was ill at ease. I had a job to make him sit down and take a bite to eat. 'No. Now I know you're alright, I'll make tracks.'

He had cycled all that way just to be sure I'd come to no harm. I was touched. I tried to explain the situation but he'd decided that I'd gone wrong. My story didn't make sense to him. Even in Burton they'd taken me for a bit of a mystery. I asked him to rest for a while but he got up abruptly and left. I never saw or heard from Burton again, but I'll never forget them.

Bridson cropped up again, though, and Monica, the lady faun

who lived in the flat downstairs with Norman, her newly-wed husband. Bridson's home would be austere, I knew. Monica's was voguey, red and black. Everything was red and black, even the papers round the sweets. She told me that Norman was a pillar of Toc H. I wondered how he could put up with Jack Dillon's flamboyant passes at his young wife. 'He knows that I love him,' she said, giving me her gentle faun smile.

Bridson lived with his mother in Prestwich and insisted on knowing which train I was taking. 'Otherwise I tire myself out with fruitless journeys to and from the station.'

I thoroughly enjoyed the train ride between the cliffs of sandstone where heather sprouted. Everything I did in Manchester was enjoyable; I'd never been so happy in my life. It seemed that till then I'd never been happy at all. At Prestwich station I received a slight shock. It was himself, standing by a hedge, wearing a kilt. And when his mother opened the door with the stained-glass panels, she was kilted too.

'Our name is pronounced "Bride-son", not "Brid" as it is writ. We're Manx.'

Bridson was Harding's reigning genius, that's all I knew. Widow Bridson's house was desperately neat, but she didn't smile much. The furniture was mainly bookcases, all under glass, some under lock and key – the first editions. I was shown around; there were rows of Fron Frolico and Kelmscott and all the Nonesuch series. They looked as if they'd never been opened.

'My life's reading,' he told. 'I've planned it all.'

'You mean you know what you'll be reading till the end of your days?'

'I do.'

And he pulled one side of his long gingery moustache. Widow Bridson brought us two cups of pale tea and four shortbread biscuits, then, discreetly, she left us alone. Over tea her son spoke of his idols, Pound, Eliot, Wyndham Lewis and their leader, and his, the old bannerman of lost causes, A.R. Orage.

'Social Credit?'

'Yis!'

'Aren't you just trying to avoid the beaten track? Major Douglas hardly faces up to reality.'

He pulled that gingery whisker again. We didn't agree about poetry either. I told him that I preferred the Yanks.

'I'm deep in *The Waste Land* myself,' he said.

'Then tell me one thing. Why should a Bradford millionaire look any sillier than anyone else in a silk hat?'

After tea he extracted some typewritten poems from a neat portfolio and asked me to read one or two out loud. My performance excited him. 'Everyone will think I'm great if you read my poems. . . .'

Was he propositioning me? I fancied his books, but not him. In any case, he'd just mentioned that his fiancée, Vera, was his inspiration. I was curious to know how he earned his living.

'In an office,' he said. 'Like T.S. But in the evenings Vera and I analyse poetry.'

All Dillon's gang wrote the young lady off as a bad influence on him. I couldn't wait to meet her. I invited them both to tea. What a disappointment! She was thin and pale, a droopy girl with a voice so weak and an accent so refined, you couldn't make out a word of what she said. Her young man had no great regard for the Northern vowel sounds either.

'Ai'd laik a bit less charter in the par-sage,' came over the speaker during the *Tunnel* rehearsals. We'd been in the passage waiting for our cue to enter the studios and I guess our chatter had got a little noisy.

When Bridson and Vera arrived at the Dillons', the garden was bright and summery, but Vera walked straight into the sitting-room, took off all her clothes and lay on the floor draping a thin grey scarf across her scanty breasts. She made gooseberry eyes at her man, her breast gently heaving. So that's why they came, I thought. They can't do that at Widow B's. They had brought a colleague from Geoffrey's office with them. He was lurking by the door, like a dog eyeing the cat's meat. Geoffrey gave Vera a dry kiss.

'Hold on a second.'

'Ai'm doing mai best,' he said.

'Don't go,' said the colleague. I was already halfway out of the door.

'I need some cigarettes.'

Outside, the sunny streets were deserted. It was August Bank Holiday. I walked the endless road past Southern Cemetery, through Stretford, Urmston, as far as the swing bridge at Barton. Then all the way back. I had no money to waste on buses and trams, but in any case I'd sooner have slept out again than get mixed up in the love life of the Prestwich poet.

A note, signed Bayley, was left at Broadcasting House inviting me to lunch at the Squirrel. I turned up to be greeted at the entrance by a young woman with piano legs and a quizzical expression on her rather plain face. Over our Welsh rarebits she explained that we had been contemporaries at RADA. She'd heard my broadcast and wanted to assure me that my hard times were over. RADA had put me off theatre completely, but I was intrigued when Miss Bayley told me she was about to join the local repertory theatre as an actress.

'However did you manage it?'

'Daddy is a director.'

I changed the subject.

Shortly after, I met a local theatre critic in the *Guardian* pub on Cross Street. He'd read my story in the papers, so I asked him for a job.

'Come and see me at my office,' he said.

Whether he had a job in mind, I'll never know. Hardly had I been ushered into his gloomy back room in Deansgate, when he started touching me up with long, pale hands covered with sticking plasters. I pulled back. He grabbed me and plunged his long, thin tongue into my mouth.

'Didn't the nuns teach you how to kiss?' he said.

'And didn't anybody teach you to keep your sick hands to yourself?'

'I got these sores working on radium,' he shouted after me.

I learned afterwards that it was true, he was a scientist as well as a director of the local rep; the only one who knew anything about twentieth-century theatre, actually; the rest were businessmen.

Anyway, if I didn't get a job soon I'd make for Liverpool and my trip to the New World. By chance I met Manny Levy on Oxford Road. 'There's some genius at the Midland looking for you,' he said.

'Who is he?'

'You don't look like their idea of an actress.'

'I should hope not.'

Everybody knew everything about everybody in Manchester. I went along to the Midland Hotel, a big Germanic pile, made some enquiries and got the name of Mr Carol Sax, an American producer. He was in a small sultry room on the fourth floor. With the single bed and two standing trunks there was hardly room for tubby Mr Sax.

'Ah, the gal who knows how to get publicity for herself,' he said. That had never been my intention, but I let it pass. 'Well, what are you going to do for me?'

'It's more like what are you going to do for me,' I replied.

'I don't know what I'm doing here,' he said vaguely. 'There's no money in it. This room alone is costing me five pounds a night.'

I decided to give this old zany a taste of theatre if it was only for the hell of it, so I launched into Lady Macbeth's invocation before he had time to stop me:

> *The raven himself is hoarse*
> *That croaks the fatal entrance of Duncan*
> *Under my battlements.*

He looked quite startled. I let rip, doing my best to put the wind up the old flanneller. When I died down, he smiled.

'You'll play that one day.'

'I doubt it,' said I.

'Have you heard of the great American dancer, Maud Allen?'

'No.'

'She will be performing her artistic Dance of the Seven Veils in the second show of our coming season. We aim to shake things up a bit around here.'

'Great! And what about me?'

'Maybe. Why not? How would a salary of two pounds ten a week suit you?'

'Fine,' I said.

'You're on.'

I couldn't believe it and left double quick in case he changed his mind.

'Rehearsals start next Monday, half past nine,' he shouted.

A ctually Mr Sax's reign lasted for one show only. He began simply enough with *The Swan* by Molnar. I was Assistant Stage Manager and small parts but only had one line, as the maid.

'At least we could hear you,' said Bayley's father.

When Miss Maud Allen turned up for the second show, a middle-aged dancer with dusky eyes, there was a slight snag. The building was surrounded by policemen and she was escorted away. So was Mr Sax. We heard that her Dance of the Seven Veils had been banned as immoral in the US, and in England her name had appeared in some black book of sex scandals. Mr Sax was an escaped lunatic.

The stories were blown up, then suppressed. Miss Bayley said he hadn't actually been in a loony bin, it was only that his relatives had paid him to stay away from the USA. You couldn't blame them for that. As for his theatre technique, it derived from Belasco, according to Audrey Cameron, our Stage Manager who'd worked on Broadway. All I saw was Mr Sax sitting at rehearsals in a swivel chair with his back to the actors, only swinging round to shout at them when he had an idea, which was rarely.

His replacement was a tall, raw-boned barnstormer, Dominic Roche. He'd learned his technique in Irish fit-ups and belonged to the rogue and vagabond school. He carted a large old wife around with him, but managed to service most of the female members of the company.

Before starting work I left the Dillon flat, leaving wild daisies in a blue china vase to welcome them. When I was paid my first week's wages, one pound, five shillings, half pay for rehearsals, I bought a box of Terry's, half a crown, and went to return the keys.

'We're visiting Manchester's answer to the Old Vic,' said Jack. 'Want to come?'

'I'd love to. Who's the director?'

'Don't think they have one. A friend of ours, Noel Barker, keeps their books for them and . . . all the pretty women. He was caught on the job, recently. "I'm a nudist," he declared. "Come and join us." '

The door to 111A Grosvenor Street was anything but inviting. It hung open to reveal a pitch-black nothingness. We lit matches to find our way up a worn wooden staircase. Jack shoved open a door on the first floor. The scene was from Daumier – a semicircle of dark-clad figures, their backs to us, and, beyond them, in a circle of light, two men dishing out mugs of tea. Sitting beside a dying fire was a slightly saturnine figure.

'Noel Barker,' said Jack.

In his brown tweed jacket he looked rather better dressed than the rest. He was trying to collect subscriptions, but nobody had any money. In front of the fire, naked legs slightly apart, stood a brown-haired, pale young man with freckles. As we entered a cloud seemed to pass over his face. I felt sure it was because of us.

'Who's that with no trousers on?'

'A crank.'

'What is this place?'

'Their rehearsal room.'

Tonight being Sunday, they were not rehearsing. It was a social evening, and everyone was drifting around. I discovered that the crank, as Jack Dillon called him, was Jimmie Miller. I'd heard that name, somewhere.

'He's off to Moscow soon,' I was told.

'Interested?' said Jack. 'He's got nice legs.'

Eleven

Walking into that gloomy studio, on that cold Sunday evening, sealed my fate. I still thought of leaving Manchester.

The only thing was, Manchester had taken me to its heart and after the life I'd led it was a very nice feeling.

Jimmie Miller was wearing sandals, very short shorts and a large hand-knitted jersey. 'Why are you dressed like that?' I asked him when we came face to face.

'I've been camping in the dales with Stooge,' he said, self-consciously.

Stooge, real name Gerard Davies, was in identical kit, but his head was shaved and he didn't bother to speak, he just clowned. His nickname came from *The Three Stooges*, a knockabout act at the time of the Marx Brothers, but he was much better looking.

After a while I identified Jimmie Miller's voice. Had he been declaiming all the facts and figures for Bridson's *Tunnel*?

'That's right, and I know who you are. You're Littlewood. Archie Harding wanted me to come to Burton-on-Trent and collect you.'

'Why didn't you?'

'I didn't fancy it.'

'What's this gathering all about?'

'Theatre of Action.'

'Not a bad name.'

'You're not bad yourself, despite your Southern accent. Don't think much of the company you keep, though.'

'What's wrong with them?'

'Well that bloke Dillon was in the Army of Intervention, if you know what that was.'

'I do. They went to crush the Russian Revolution.'

'In fact there were three armies of intervention. Friend Dillon was with Denikin. Now he's just a clerk in Inland Revenue trying to brown-nose his way into the BBC.' This Jimmie Miller had a way of talking to you as if he would like to knock you down; I wanted to know more about his Theatre of Action, and Jimmie could talk – aggressive perhaps, but well-informed about politics, and about a theatre movement of which most people in England had never heard: worldwide agitprop. He'd met Bert Brecht and picked up enough German to sing, or rather singspiel, Brecht's songs. He had the only typed copies of Brecht's early plays, in German. It was to be another twenty years before Ken Tynan discovered Brecht for the readers of the *Observer*.

Jimmie knew a lot about the German agitprop troupes, and had formed his own Red Megaphones – in Salford – 'A propertyless theatre for a propertyless class'. They took their name from a parent band which had sprung up in Red Wedding, a working-class district of Berlin. Jimmie's Megaphones had appeared on the streets, in parks, at open-air meetings all over Lancashire. He seemed to have sources of information not available to the rest of us, news of Maxim Vallentin, for instance, the leader of the Berlin Megaphones. He was still alive and free and what's more functioning, despite the Nazis.

'Functioning? How?'

'They turn up at street corners, or in the courtyards of tenements – any place where they can raise a crowd and make a quick getaway. Then out come the megaphones: "*Fenster auf! Fenster auf! Wir sind die Rote Sprachrohr!*" And the show begins. They have great songs but no written text. Their job is to disseminate news of resistance to Hitler. All such items are cut in the heavily censored German press. The show over, sometimes only half over, interrupted by a warning from their scouts, they vanish.'

'It sounds very brave. People forget how much opposition there is to Hitler in Germany.'

'Of course; more than here.' Hadn't I heard of the great protest march through Red Wedding? Hadn't I heard the song that Hanns Eisler had written specially only the night before?

And without further ado, he began half singing, half chanting, at the top of his voice. Nobody seemed surprised, some even joined in, or hummed along:

> *Links, links, links, links! Die Trommeln werden gerührt!*
> *Links, links, links, links! Der 'Rote Wedding' marschiert!*
> *Hier wird nicht gemeckert, hier gibt es Dampf,*
> *Denn was wir spielen ist Klassenkampf*
> *Nach blutiger Melodie!*
> *Wir geben dem Feind einen kräftigen Tritt,*
> *Und was wir spielen, ist Dynamit*
> *Unterm Hintern der Bourgeoisie.*
>> *'Roter Wedding' grüsst euch, Genossen,*
>> *Haltet die Fäuste bereit!*
>> *Haltet die roten Reihen geschlossen,*
>> *Denn unser Tag ist nicht weit!*
>> *Drohend stehen die Faschisten*
>> *Drüben am Horizont!*
>> *Proletarier, ihr müsst rüsten!*
>> *Rot Front! Rot Front!* *

---

*Here is my very rough translation of these words:

> *Left! Left! Left! Left! Hear the drums beat!*
> *Left! Left! Left! Left! Red Vedding's on the street!*
> *Here there's no mewling, herein lies power,*
> *What we bring you is the class war*
> *In a bloodstained melody!*
> *Against the foe we will charge and strike,*
> *What we carry is dynamite*
> *At the end of the bourgeoisie.*
>> *Red Vedding greets you, comrades,*
>> *Raise yours fists on high!*
>> *Close your ranks, our day is nigh*
>> *The Fascists stand 'gainst a threatening sky!*
>> *Working people, arm yourselves!*
>> *Red Front! Red Front!*

Sounds great, but what are we doing, in England? Nothing theatrically anyway.

'I don't know what you expect. There are still half a dozen agitprop groups in Lancashire. "The Dark Lamp" works the Wigan coalfield, "The Red Cops", the Rossendale valley. There were far more up till 1932. ("Cops" means the cones on spinning frames, by the way, not Old Bill.) They all went to the World Olympiad of Workers' Theatres in Berlin and came back with an inferiority complex. The German and Czech groups were so brilliant technically, they felt they couldn't compete. When power was handed over to the Nazis, the Party pundits in London decided that agitprop was too sectarian. Traditional theatre might be more useful if we were to form a United Front against Fascism. Curtain theatre, they called it.'

'Agitprop sounds more exciting.'

'Have you ever tried bawling through a megaphone from the back of a lorry – or competing with a fairground?'

'Still, it's more in line with the nineteenth-century fairground theatre of runaway clerks and chimney sweeps or the Miracles and Moralities. I'd rather have them than *Box and Cox* – Greeks before Galsworthy.'

'Only the best is good enough for the workers,' said Jimmie Miller. 'Agitprop is crude in the age of Appia. Don't discount beauty. We wear a uniform, blue overalls, our basic costume, blokes and polones. If you want to change your character, you change your hat – a top hat for a capitalist, a cloth cap for a prole, miners' helmets for pitmen. All our props are as simple as we can make them – a row of poles to represent prison, if we are playing the Meerut sketch. You've heard of the prisoners of Meerut, I suppose?'

I hadn't, so there was a detour while I was told the story of the fight for Indian Independence, the Cerni Camghar strike of the railway men in Meerut in particular. Their leaders had been imprisoned, Lester Hutchinson, a Manchester progressive, among them. Jimmie's sketch was a demand for their freedom.

'I like the sound of agitprop. Couldn't it be tuned up?'

'Possibly, but it may be played out.'

'So this Theatre of Action is your Curtain theatre?'

'Well, we still perform sketches, songs and poems at meetings, indoors and out. We were at the Ramblers' Rights demo at the Winyates Pass this year.'

The idea of agitprop suited me. A bare platform, everything created by the actor – tempest, sun and rain, swimming rivers, drowning in storm-tossed seas.

Curtain theatre? The very words depressed me.

J immie had loved the excitement of agitprop. I could tell when he told the story of the Red Megaphones. During the strike against the eight looms, a year ago, he had prepared an up-to-the-minute sketch to be performed in Wigan marketplace. In 1932, Burnley and all the weavers of Lancashire had struck against the introduction of eight looms; they weren't winning and they weren't eating too well. The miners of South Wales collected food up and down the valleys, and despatched a convoy of well-stocked lorries to Lancashire. Jimmie's troupe knew they were due to arrive in Wigan, during a mass meeting aimed at raising morale among the cotton workers.

The square was thronged, a sea of cloth caps and shawls as far as the eye could see. The union men spoke first and were heard in silence. Then, at a given signal, the red flag was hoisted in the middle of the square; stewards cleared a way through the dense crowd and the Welsh lorries drove in, their banners flying. . . .

> Food from the South Wales miners to the Burnley strikers. Solidarity for ever and the Union makes us strong.

A great cheer swelled into 'Cwm Rhondda', led by Jimmie.

The company in that cold studio had thinned out and a shilling was needed for the gas meter. A mate of Jimmie's found one, Alf Armitt, a serious, good-looking chap, obviously second in command.

'It's no use saying one thing and thinking another,' said Alf. ' 'Is Nibs there *is* the agitprop movement. Can you count the number of times we've had to do the trick on our own because the rest got cold feet? It's not all dramas and brotherhood, sister. Nine times out of ten the police break us up, smash the props and arrest one of us. Remember the night I came and bailed you out with your old lady's rent book and you were still clutching the rim of our only bowler hat?' And Alf burst into a loud laugh.

Work at the Rep theatre seemed irrelevant after that meeting with the 'Theatre of Action'. I looked forward to seeing their work and dropped into 111 Grosvenor Street.

'Another refugee from Hitler found us, last night.'

'The Popular Front against Fascism and war is gaining strength. Stafford Cripps is addressing a meeting in Manchester, Friday evening.'

'Can't go. I'm working.'

'Come to our meeting at Hyde Socialist Church on Sunday, then.'

I went and found them in a bare hall, the platform hung with a white screen. Everybody was busy, arranging chairs, laying out props. A small group on the platform was going through a Thälmann spiel with Jimmie. Alf Armitt was up a ladder rigging a small, unusual-looking lamp.

'What sort of spot is that?' I asked him.

'I don't know. I only made it.'

'Alf was a lens grinder, by trade.'

'I've been checking up on Adolph Appia's ideas,' he said as he focussed the light on Jimmie's group.

'Hey there, big fella. John Bull wants you for the next war,' was the response.

'I should have coloured shadows tonight,' said Alf.

Jimmie's rehearsal over, he came and asked me to hear him through 'The Fire Sermon', a Symbolist poem by the American, Funarov.

'John Bull was sent to us by the New York agitprop,' he said. 'There it was "Uncle Sam wants you".'

'You need two voices for this,' I told him, handing back the poem.

'Yes, but who?'

'Me. I practically know it already.'

'Great!' And with two or three trials, we were ready.

Free Ernst Thälmann needed lighting adjustment. The shadow of a manacled man must appear on the screen, while the chorus declaimed downstage. Then us! And did we let rip? It was exhilarating and we finished up in a red glow, courtesy of Alf. The evening was rounded off with a group of Eisler songs, sung by Jimmie. He sang well and when the applause died down most of the audience stayed, asking questions or arguing while cups of tea and sandwiches were handed round. Jimmie threw a worn-looking typescript at me. 'From the WTM, in London,' he said.

'What's the WTM?'

'Worker's Theatre Movement, the usual stuff, preaching to the converted. We need new ideas. Got any?'

'Sure.'

I didn't tell him I was writing a Nativity play for the Rep. Roche needed a fill-in and we needed the money. There wasn't much satisfaction in my work there.

'Drawing-room comedy next week.'

'She can play the cockney maid.'

'Then it's *The Sport of Kings*.'

'Can't see her fitting into that.'

But I'd play the maid with a consumptive cough and delicate hands and as Lady Muck I'd turn up in jodhpurs and bowler hat with a riding crop – which could wreck anybody's laughs. The directors had, at one point, decided to sack me, till they found I'd become the company's resident comic. The audience was greeting my every appearance with gales of laughter and when it got about that Stan Laurel's talent scout had recommended me for a place in his team, I was reprieved.

Mind you, I could act if I got the chance. For the old dancing mistress in *Mädchen in Uniform*, I streaked my hair with red dye, dug out some whalebone corsets and high-heeled satin shoes, too tight for me, and minced on to the stage in a halo of the long-ago.

My Nativity play went on and at the end of the week I was handed my two pounds, ten shillings, with an extra guinea in the envelope.

'Thanks,' I said. 'And I'll have my cards at the same time.'

Roche appeared. 'You can't go now,' he said. 'We're putting on Toller's *Draw the Fires*. It'll be our biggest production yet. He's coming for it himself.'

Well, Toller was one of my heroes. His first play was written when he was in prison for his part in the Bavarian uprising of 1918. *Masses and Men* was the great play of the German Expressionist movement. I couldn't miss working with Toller. And he turned up sooner than expected. I found him strolling through the auditorium early one Monday morning – a small, rosy-cheeked man of about forty; his black wavy hair streaked with grey. A girl walked behind him, a slim young blonde with an Eton crop. She didn't speak a word of English. It turned out that she had been a Nazi, but changed her ideas when she met him.

He hardly waited for introductions but called for the actors; opened the piano and picked out the notes as he sang:

> *Vee don't fight for our countree,*
> *Vee don't fight for our Gott,*
> *Veer fighting for ze Ruditoffs,*
> *Who keek us in ze mud.*

'Does he mean Romanoffs?' I asked Keith Pyott, a serious actor who had been imported specially for this show.

'Ruddy toffs,' said Keith, seizing the prop shovel that Teddie, the gentle ASM, was holding. 'You'd have to have a better grip on it than that as a stoker,' said Keith.

'A stoker! Am I?'

'We all are. We're mutineers in the German Navy. 1917.'

'Was there one? How revolting!' And he giggled. Nobody else laughed. They were being asked to shovel coal as they sang.

After a while I could stand it no longer. I went up to Toller. 'You need men who know how to work,' I told him.

'Where are zey?'

'Not far away. They can sing Eisler too.'

'Bring zem.'

But it took a lot of argy-bargy before Alec Armstrong, Alf Armitt, Gerard Davies, Bob Goodman and Jimmie Miller agreed to come. Everybody was very impressed with them at first . . . but it wasn't long before the fat was in the fire, and when Jimmie demanded a subscription towards the work of Theatre of Action, it burst into flames.

'Zat young man!' said Toller. 'He sinks he is everybody and he is nobody!'

Somehow that show went on, but neither Roche nor Toller had proved capable of making a team of their bag of allsorts. Toller had secured a Sunday night showing at the Cambridge Theatre, London, but on the Saturday night as we started packing for the journey, Alec Armstrong held up the proceedings.

'No donation. No Theatre of Action,' he said.

No donation was forthcoming, so Theatre of Action departed. Then I couldn't find the prompt script. I'd searched everywhere but the train left at midnight. There was no time to unpack and repack.

'We'll find it on the train,' said Teddie.

The company was asleep before we'd pulled out of the station. Roche on his wife's ample bosom, Mr Johnstone, the Stage Manager, on the two dressing baskets in the guard's van. Teddie and I found him there when we went in search of the script. We couldn't wake him.

'Drunk again,' said Teddie.

There was no sign of the script when we unpacked at the theatre in the morning. Johnstone declared that one of those bogmen had gone off with it and departed for the boozer.

'I'll make another,' I told Teddie. 'I know every sound and light cue. After all, I've been working the corner for a week.' And I began sticking pages in a ledger, while Roche conducted the rig and walk-through, replacing the lost stokers as best he could. At lunch-time the barman in the pub next door asked me if we were all Bolshies.

'Why?'

'That big Ulster fella who was in here said you were.'

Johnstone! And he'd disappeared into the wilds of WC1 taking our script with him. I'd have staked my life on it. Anyway, we did our best without him and there wasn't one technical hitch. On top of that I played my part, as the barmaid, better than ever, singing:

Who wants a sailor's girl?
Who wants a shilling a day?
There's nothing so fair, as can compare
With a girl on sailor's pay

in full voice – but at the end of the evening I asked for my cards. I'd done my best for Toller and the company, but I'd had enough.

Twelve

I was out of a job, had to give up my digs. I thought I might manage if I could camp out at 111 Grosvenor Street, but that wasn't acceptable. So Jimmie persuaded his mother to let me stay at their two-up, two-down at 37 Coburg Street, Salford 7. Bill Miller, his father, hadn't much to say, he'd hardly breath to speak; lost his health after long years as an iron moulder, followed by victimisation for union activity.

Betsy, his wife, was thin and bent, old before her time. Though her body was covered with psoriasis she was out cleaning from dawn to dusk each day, managing her own home somehow on the Saturdays. She had lost three children in infancy, Jimmie was her only surviving child, and her darling. No matter how hard the going, the best was for him, the best food, the best clothing. 'She'd take the skin off her back for him,' said Bill Miller.

Jimmie was registered at the Labour Exchange as a motor mechanic, but he did better busking, singing Hebridean songs to the cinema queues. Someone drew Archie Harding's attention to him and from that time on he appeared in North Region's features whenever a 'proletarian' voice was needed.

I worked my way into radio too – reading poetry, acting and eventually, and for the first time in radio, interviewing real people. In the library Jimmie and I started our long collaboration – first *The Voyage of the Chelyuskin*. We sent it to Moscow, where it was translated into Russian and broadcast on Moscow Radio.

Poor old Betsy didn't take to me, nor anyone else for that matter. She would always speak of 'the class enemy' with studied venom, and that meant just about everybody but Jimmie and her husband. Then one Sunday afternoon after I'd heard Jean, the cocker spaniel, barking and discovered Bill Miller with a length of rubber tubing in his mouth connected to the gas tap, she actually turned on me. She'd been asleep but had heard me go to Jimmie for help.

After that the house was not easy to live in. Bill turned to Christian Science, the old lady seemed to be wasting away. I began to feel sick. Why had I ever come to live there? I remembered how long it had taken me to get away from my mother and Stockwell.

'You know what they'd call Joan, don't ye?' said Betsy one day, in her musical Scottish voice. She'd spotted what was wrong with me before I did. With every penny I could lay hands on I fled to London. I had an idea where I might find a backstreet Celestina. And I did. It was a brutalised, sordid business but not as bad as being trapped in Coburg Street.

I went back there. Where else could I go? Bill received me kindly. 'You look weak and wasted,' he said. Betsy took Jimmie aside and talked of marriage. He told her I wouldn't have it. Her husband had been saying how much he'd've enjoyed nursing the baby.

'Coming out for a coffee?' I asked Jimmie. When we were sat down in Lyons I began telling him what was on my mind.

'It needs totally different staging. Make a satirical ballet of it.'

'What are you talking about?'

'That script you threw at me. I took it to London. Of course it needs words, but we should use mainly music, song and speech intercut. Alf would have to make a switchboard for a brilliant lighting plot. The set? Constructivist.'

Jimmie looked a bit nonplussed. 'How do you present the characters?'

'Stylised. Put the three capitalists on three high stools, the master banker on the highest, dressed in rubber rings, like the Michelin tyre advert. The coupon clipper on the lowest with a long cigarette holder and a trailing dressing-gown.'

'And the press lord?'

'He's the middle one, swathed in ticker tape. Upstage, a platform serves for chorus movement, bathing belles wearing gas masks, unemployed, singing in the street, wounded soldiers. And do you think we could invent a moving news panel? It could relay news, grave and trivial, counterpointed against the action. "War in Manchuria. Film star divorces his loved one because he says she bites her nails." '

'We've two or three bright engineers from Metro-Vicks interested in us these days. They might be able to put something together for you.'

I was excited by my idea and presented it to the gathering at Grosvenor Street that very night. The repertoire hadn't varied very much lately, apart from the addition of *Newsboy*, an exciting sketch from USA. Nothing of our own. I thought they'd be excited.

'Sounds like a lot of twaddle to me,' said Jack, our most ardent Party member. 'Why not give 'em the message, straightforward and no messing.'

'Yes, it does sound rather arty,' said Nellie. 'I mean ballet . . . all that jigging about. . . .'

It's true that I had thought it would give me the chance to introduce a bit of movement training, which they badly needed.

'Curtain theatre, that's the line.'

'Well, they've put forward their ideas,' said Harold Olsberg. 'Shall we give it a go? All those in favour?'

'Do leave off,' I said. 'You can't decide on a creative experiment by vote. Let's try it, at least. Is anyone prepared to work with us?'

A few hands went up.

'Strikes me we've been barking up the wrong tree ever since we wasted all that time at Manchester Rep,' said Jack as he turned aside.

'Address your remarks to the meeting,' said Jimmie. 'Crummy, as it is . . . why not pack it in, the lot of you? There's nobody here who's managed to turn up on time to every rehearsal for the last three months, do you know that?' And he whipped out a small pocketbook and began to read out names, dates and the number of minutes each one had lost. . . .

'Put a sock in it, Jim, for Chrissake,' said Harold. 'Don't let's waste any more time. Let's do something.'

'Right,' I said. 'Any of you wanting to join in, get on your feet. Give me Mossolow's "Music of the Machines". Good, now let's try stepping forward, one. And two steps backward. Go.'

With a week's evening work, two weekends and a day at the Round House, Every Street, Ancoats, our show was on. We called it *John Bullion*. We were at our favourite venue, the best theatre space in the whole of Manchester. It had been built by the followers of Swedenborg at the beginning of the nineteenth century.

> Theoretically brilliant. The finest piece of expressionistic craft ever seen in England.
>
> *City News*

> The nearest thing to Meyerhold the British theatre has got.
>
> *Manchester Guardian*

Not so our critics. They even suggested expelling us.

'Don't worry,' said Jimmie. 'We're going anyway.'

'Where to?'

'Moscow.' A shock wave ran through the room.

'Why did you say that?' I asked him as soon as we were alone.

'Because it's true. A letter came this morning, offering us two places at the Moscow Academy of Cinema and Theatre.'

The word soon got about and I was greeted with my photo in the papers again, with 'She's off to Moscow, now.' One paper declared that I'd given the best performances ever seen at the Repertory Theatre.

'All very fine,' I said. 'But what about the fare?'

'We'll have to borrow it.'

'You mean write begging letters?'

'Why not?'

'I've never done that.'

Jimmie was a great commander, but I wasn't used to being commanded. I took him up on his bossiness, told him I was the one getting replies.

'We'll have to go to London soon to apply for our visas.'

'Have we the fare to Moscow, then?'

'Nearly. We still need money for the licence.'

'Which licence?'

'Our marriage lines.'

'To hell with that. I've told you I don't believe in it. The French Communists don't either.'

'They get married.'

'Well if they do, the women keep their single name.'

'It would bring the Party into disrepute, if we were arrested and the police discovered that we weren't married.'

'Oh to hell with the Party. Stuffy lot from what I can see of them . . . and the police.'

All the same, we went to London. I went first, of course, to try and find somewhere for us to stay. I fancied Cheyne Walk, with its literary connections and the 'Sweet Thames' running softly and all that. I made my way along, knocking at every door. No luck, until one, a sweet old dear, smiled at me.

'What do you do?'

'Well, I write, and . . .'

'God sent you. Come in.' It turned out that God had sent me to translate a book she'd written. . . .

'Into which language?'

'Into a film treatment.'

'Oh good. My co-worker knows all there is to know about films.'

'Your – ?'

'Jimmie Miller. We write together.'

And so we did and while we worked on the film, we lived rent-free in her basement. Her name was Mrs Algernon Newton. She seemed a little off-key; so did her children Bobbie and Joy. Her other son, Nigel, had fled to some desert island to paint in peace. We were glad when that treatment was done, what with Bobbie stuffing his dress suit into the copper fire, introducing

whores to his mother when she was lying in bed and robbing the
gas meter. . . .

'God never made a woman without a shilling,' was all she said.

After a grand reading with Anthony Asquith, the film director, Algernon Newton R.A. and his second wife, we made our
escape. We'd found a room in Battersea, across the water. We
could hole up there till our visas came through. We gave classes in movement and drama and attended political meetings. I
refreshed myself at the art galleries, but we weren't going all
out. We were really just waiting. It was worse when Mr and
Mrs Miller decided to join us. Betsy felt we couldn't take care of
ourselves.

Would our visas never come through? When the Peace Pledge
Union wrote asking us to put on a Peace play in Manchester, with
their support, we jumped at the chance.

'What about Moscow?'

'I think we should carry on the fight here. We'll learn more
about theatre that way than studying in an academy.'

Jimmie agreed. He was only too anxious to pack up and
leave for the North. So was I – I'd hoped to put London behind
me for good. Apart from anything else I loved the Derbyshire
moors and longed to climb again among the peat hags and the
heather.

The play we chose was Schlumberg's *Miracle at Verdun*. It
needed a large cast and for the final scene, set in the League
of Nations, we would have to find men and women of many
nationalities.

We wrote to every drama society in Lancashire, advertised
for technicians, musicians, actors and actresses. We contacted the
Manchester University Students Union hoping to interest foreign
students. We chose a new name, Theatre Union, and the Quakers
lent us the Friends' Meeting House for our rehearsals. We started
work, Jimmie and I rehearsing alternate scenes. It was good to be
back in the North.

In the play, the dead of the First World War rise from their
common grave and return home to see what their sacrifice has
achieved. Schlumberg had already been murdered by the Nazis
who feared the truth in his play.

During rehearsals I celebrated my birthday.

'Look, you're twenty-one now, you don't have to wait for your mother's consent.'

'My mother's consent? For what?'

'Marriage.'

At that we had such a flaming row that it came to blows. We were on the main road to town, at Rusholme, and the tram driver who saw us stopped his tram and came over to separate us.

'He only wants me to marry him.'

'Well it looks like a good beginning,' he said, and went back to his tram. And for better or for worse, I gave in. 'Fine birthday present,' I said as we signed on at Pendleton Town Hall, one Saturday morning. Enid and Ronnie Finnemore were our seconds. Ronnie was theatre critic on the *Daily Dispatch*, the only journalist who'd come out in the General Strike. It all went according to plan, until the bloke officiating asked for the ring.

'I don't wear rings,' I said.

Enid hastily slid hers off and handed it to Jimmie. Afterwards the four of us went and had lunch at the Squirrel.

On the Sunday, back to work. A bright, enthusiastic crowd had come together for the production, and the actors performed with such ardour that they carried the audience along with them. We played to packed houses at the Lesser Free Trade Hall and the word 'peace' was on everybody's lips.

'So now, what are you going to do about Spain?' asked Ben Ainley. Ben was a schoolteacher and a Communist Party functionary. He was a great bloke. The kids loved him. So did we. He would always reason with you, never tried to put anything over on you.

'Seen anything of Alec Armstrong or Bob Goodman lately?' Jimmie asked.

'They're in Spain.'

'You mean they've joined the International Brigade? How did they do it?'

'Well, all volunteers have to be passed by London first. Then they leave for France with a forged passport. In Paris they receive a ticket to the Spanish border. Walter Lever tried but he was turned down on medical grounds. Les Preger's gone, so has Sam Wild. The rest of us are trying to raise money to send a foodship to Barcelona. Can your "Theatre Union" do anything for us?'

'We can put on a play,' I said.

'Might be better to go round the pubs, collecting. Jimmie's a dab hand at a topical lyric.'

Spain for me was Cervantes, Tirso de Molina and Lope de Vega, the glories of Velasquez, El Greco and Goya. Spain and its people merited the highest tribute we could bring them and that, I believed, was Lope de Vega's *Fuente Ovejuna*. The republicans still used the lines that Lope wrote. . . .

'Death to the tyrant band. All for Fuente Ovejuna.'

'The village of Fuente is still holding out, Ben, the place where the people stood up against tyranny three hundred and fifty years ago.'

Ben thought I was arty, he always had, ever since he sent me out selling the paper and I'd been so busy chalking *Daily Worker* in beautiful letters on the roadway that I hadn't noticed the big, shiny boots standing right beside me.

'Lope was in the Armada,' I called out after Ben. 'He was probably drifting round Dublin Bay writing our play.'

'Ancient history,' Ben shouted back.

Could we do justice to the poetry, and music of that great play? Despite the objections raised by Ben and other orthodox allies we tried. It seemed to be working. Bill Sharples, sculptor and engineer, designed a magnificent set and carved a great ram standing on its hind legs beside the well. Ern Brooks painted a backcloth, using the colours one associated with Spain. Barbara Niven designed the costumes. Jimmie arranged the music and Harold Lever became our business manager. People were deeply moved by the tragedy of Republican Spain, left to fight alone by the forces of democracy, so-called, in France and England. Manchester sent a food ship, many of her sons gave their lives, including our comrades, Alec Armstrong and Bob Goodman.

Honour forever, to the International Brigade
They are a song in the hearts of all true men.

HUGH MACDIARMID

We heard, much later, that Alec had been found dead in a trench at Jarama, with his throat cut. He went to Spain in the boots he had worn rambling in Derbyshire. The tragedy of non-intervention weighed heavily on us. It was clear that Hitler and Mussolini were using Spain as a rehearsal for the war they were preparing.

We lived by our work for the BBC. Jimmie wrote the story of Chartism, and worked on a novel. I brought men and women from the farms, mills and mines of the North to the microphone. It was a staunch group of young men and women who kept Theatre Union alive. Jimmie received a copy of Erwin Piscator's adaptation of *The Good Soldier Schwejk*, by Jaroslav Hašek. 'It's too Germanic,' he said, 'like the English trying to write a play set in Ireland, but I guess we can get nearer to the Czechs in production. They say that in 1918 the Czech soldiers laughed so much when they read the book that they threw down their rifles and went home.'

Again we advertised the forthcoming production and again an army of artists and technicians arrived, joined by refugees from Central Europe and Howard Goorney, a boy of seventeen from Higher Crumpsall. The play involved many changes of scenery, so for the first time we used a revolve; each turn revealing another Ern Brooks cartoon to set the scene. Cartoons and costumes were all black and white, with occasional flashes of colour for delight. No khaki. It became the most popular play we ever produced.

In the world of 1938, sanity was balanced on a knife-edge. Chamberlain was banking on Hitler turning against the arch enemy, Soviet Russia, and Halifax was supporting him. Austria had already been sacrificed and Czechoslovakia threatened; 'a far-away country of which we know nothing', we were told, but Czechoslovakia had a pact with France and Soviet Russia. So, in September 1938:

MUNICH

Betrayal – A cover-up.

Sudetenland and Czechoslovakia left to face naked aggression. It was time to confront people with the facts. They had been kept in ignorance, like the people of Germany. The government at Westminster must be condemned out of their own mouths. Jimmie and I made a list of sources. Hansard, Labour Research, relevant White papers, Claud Cockburn's *The Week*, International Press Correspondents (Inprecor). The Tory press was available in bound volumes at the Central Library. Friends in politics and journalists would supply us with titbits. We established hotlines to some surprising places. In those days there were more Reds on the *Daily Express* than on the *Daily Worker*.

Each member of the company researched a different theme. Jimmie and I correlated the results and thrashed out problems of presentation with the technical group who frequently grounded our flights of fancy with 'We can't afford it. You'll have to use your imagination.'

MARCH 1939. HITLER INVADES CZECHOSLOVAKIA. CHAMBERLAIN FORCED TO GUARANTEE POLAND.

Every evening you would find rows of us in the Reference Library hidden behind barricades of books. 'The Left-wing Buttresses,' Rafe Parker called us. He was a dodgy journalist on the *News Chronicle*. And, when we finally staggered away with our notes, 'Did you find what you were looking for?' asked friendly Firkin, the doorman who had known us of old and even lent us the price of a coffee when we were broke.

SEPTEMBER 3RD. POLAND INVADED. CHAMBERLAIN DECLARES WAR ON GERMANY.

Hurry! But we need film. Too dear! The electronic news panel? They don't exist. We must have it. Hurry! The electrical engineers from Trafford Park invented one.

AT LAST. MARCH 1940. WE'RE READY.

LAST EDITION
at
THE ROUND HOUSE

We built two narrow platforms on either side of the auditorium. They ran the length of the hall. The stage area was unusually wide, divided into three by pillars. The side stages were curtained off, but we needed the space. The curtains came down. Intercutting between five acting areas or opening up on them all at once should make for lively theatre. Our audiences had never seen anything but variety shows or pantomime; to hold them we would have to use every trick in the trade and some never seen, before or since.

Ada Tootill, as a miner's wife, covered the length of the right-hand platform bringing news of the disaster in the Gresford pit. Leon Blum and Attlee discussed the merits of non-intervention on the central stage, while refugees from Guernica struggled along both platforms. Revue, dance, newsreels followed. Daladier, Mussolini and Hitler appeared as gangsters, Chamberlain went fishing for a four-power pact.

The seats cost sixpence and one and six. We evaded the censorship by calling ourselves a club. It was an old dodge, the seat money was receipted as a subscription. It would have been a waste of two guineas sending the script to the Lord Chamberlain. For one thing, we altered items every night according to the news, and for another, representation of living people was forbidden by law and we were impersonating them all.

Jimmie and I functioned as narrators, standing on either side of the central stage. Passages from MacDiarmid's *Flaming Poetaster* linked the Spanish Civil War scenes. General Mola had boasted that he would soon be riding into Madrid in triumph.

> *But while he was waiting, the Internationals came in*
> *And the Anarchists from Barcelona*
> *And the Communists from Asturias*
> *And Mola's white horse turned out to be a bloody white elephant*
> *Have a ride on it Campbell.*

As few people in our audience would have heard of the South African poet Roy Campbell, I changed the name to Chamberlain.

The show was red-hot, frank, funny, and very popular. One night the bluebottles came in. One of them asked the ticket office why we weren't displaying a letter licensing the performance. Nobody knew. Owing to popular demand, we transferred the show to the centre of Manchester. The bluebottles came as well. One or two timid spirits drifted away. We closed ranks and took on the parts they abandoned.

This had to be the moment when I was laid low with an attack of quinsy. Jimmie gave me a detailed report on the night's show when he came home. 'Two new blokes came in tonight. Just when we needed them. One's a giant, looks good too. I've already put him in a couple of scenes. The other one's helping on publicity.'

'You warned them about the cops?'

'Sure.'

I managed to get to the Round House the next night, apprehensive as always. It wasn't too bad – the audience was as keen as ever; even one of the undercover policemen was laughing. There was no sign of Jimmie's giant in the early scenes, but when it came to the Prague street scene, there he was, a big, broad-shouldered young man with dark curly hair, listening to Vivian Daniels, as a Czech worker, explaining the partition which was to be imposed on their country. Text by courtesy of Chamberlain's hatchet man, Runciman.

Thirteen

University students join us: Gerry Raffles, Rosalie Williams, Graham Banks. A girl from Manchester Rep denounces me to the police. Last Edition *is a wild success. The police close it down. Jimmie and I taken to court. Harold Lever helps us. We are fined and bound over. The BBC blacklists us. Lancashire backs our theatre.*

The young man with the dark curly hair was Gerry Raffles, aged sixteen, and he was walking right into the lion's den.

He had known Graham Banks, who was already with us, at Manchester Grammar School. Graham told him about the show. Gerry only wanted to see what all the fuss was about, but when he saw us, he joined us. I went backstage to meet him.

'Fine thing,' I said. 'I turn my back for five minutes and someone steps right into the middle of my carefully careless choreography.' All I got from this incredibly beautiful young man was a smile.

Rosalie Williams, an attractive, saucy-looking girl, was listening. I told her how I'd enjoyed her new bit with Neville Chamberlain which Jimmie had written specially for her. She was a Good Fairy, and danced up to Chamberlain to whisper, 'The Link are having a party tonight and Lord Halifax is the chief guest.' And her eyes popped with pleasure. Gerry knew Rosalie; they were both at Manchester University. She was studying English. Gerry, Political Economy.

'I've had visitors,' she told me. 'Two policemen knocked at our door last night. They gave my poor father quite a turn.' Her father was headmaster of Urmston Grammar School. They invited themselves in to tell him that his daughter was mixing with the wrong people. He didn't know what they meant. They asked to see Rosalie and waited for her to come home. 'I was shattered when I walked in, especially when they started questioning me about the Communist Party and Jimmie.'

'Our Jimmie?'

'Jimmie Miller.'

Graham Banks overheard. 'Don't let it worry you. They've been round to my place too. The old man was a bit fussed but then he's like that.'

I asked if anybody else had been visited. They hadn't. It looked as if working-class parents hadn't merited police attention.

Next day Alison Bayley met me on the street. She was the director's daughter who'd been at RADA at the same time as me.

'Have you time for a coffee?'

'Old times chat?' I asked. I hadn't seen her since joining Theatre of Action.

'I've denounced you to the police,' she said, and took a sip of Kardomah's wartime best.

'What did you tell them?'

'About your being a Communist.'

'Oh, that's all right. They already knew.'

She put her head on one side, pulling a wry face, as she stubbed out her half-smoked cigarette. 'I felt I had to tell them, Littlewood.'

I was more intrigued than upset. Why was she telling me this? Was I supposed to grant absolution? She was top-drawer Manchester and miserable. I was an outsider and happy. I began to feel sorry for her, but she was enjoying playing Mrs Judas. I left her lighting another cigarette and went to have a look at our new stage in Deansgate. The notices had been blown up and Gerry and Graham were mounting them on a board outside the building. They looked very pleased with themselves.

Graham followed me. 'Gerry's old man has had a friendly warning from Police Superintendent Valentine. He had police photos of Gerry at the head of the May Day march, carrying a huge red flag.'

'And winking at the pretty girls,' I added. 'Is Gerry upset?'

'Not in the least, but then he doesn't need a political party, he's a revolution in himself.'

'His father will try to get him away from us.'

'He won't succeed. Have you seen these?' He had copies of the notices. I didn't want to see them. I was afraid that attacks from the bourgeois press would dishearten the company, already disturbed by the police visits.

> *Last Edition* is an experience not to be missed. The script is well written with fewer false notes than strokes of genius. Its transformation into loosely merging dramatic episodes is brilliantly conceived. The acting and production are of such quality that weak spots go unnoticed in a pervading sense of urgency, relieved at times by an interlude of delightful fantasy and witty satire, rising on occasions to a climax of startling emotional force.
>
> *Manchester Guardian*

> Theatre Union demonstrates that it is possible to be political and still retain a sense of humour. It has bitter passages, but it is a lively fancy that has inspired the episodes leading to the present war. Their actors are well trained, and not afraid to tackle new forms and give extraordinarily good performances.
>
> *Daily Dispatch*

> Months of research . . . Realistic staging, combined with mime, ballet and satirical verse . . .
>
> *News Chronicle*

> Ingeniously, expertly, the story of National and International events was dramatised.
>
> *Daily Express*

Our audiences were giving us a standing ovation each night. The police closed the show. Gerry kept those crits. Jimmie and I were summoned to appear in court. None of the political parties wanted to know. We were in No Man's Land. On the night they closed us down, Hitler invaded France. 'Anyone spreading alarm and despondency is liable for prosecution.' Bellringers were on standby for fear of invasion. Foreigners were arrested and shipped to the Isle of Man. Pro-Nazi, anti-Nazi – all lumped together.

The day of the court case was drawing near. Even summer days are gloomy at such a time. We still had no legal representation. Then, one morning, our old friend, Harold Lever, blew in to tell us he'd found the right barrister. All we had to do was give him the ammunition.

When the dreaded day arrived I put on my best . . . well, my only suit; I lived in bib and brace overalls. Then I gave my hair an extra brushing, and breathed deeply. Walk tall, I said to myself, and sailed into that courtroom with Jimmie Miller like a star at a photo call. Gerry was already there with Graham. Several members of the company slipped in at the last moment. The reporters nodded and smiled.

We listened to the case preceding ours. Two rather raffish characters stood in the box looking very sorry for themselves. What had they been up to? Their solicitor was explaining. They were variety artists, a double act, they'd been impersonating Hitler and Mussolini, embracing, declaring eternal friendship, then turning away to make rude signs and blow razzberries at each other. I thought it sounded rather funny, but the magistrate was not amused. Had they been brought to court for mocking Hitler and Musso? No, impersonating living people was against the law.

'Let's hope they get off. He can't make fish of one and fowl of the other,' said our man.

He had assured us that we were only being prosecuted on technical grounds, but the beak looked a proper Tory and there were all those notes in the policemen's pockets. I would have liked to give the sad comics an encouraging smile but they didn't once turn their heads, just stood there staring into space. One had a prominent Adam's apple, which kept moving up and down though his face was expressionless. Still, they got off. It was our turn. We moved towards the box.

Whatever one's opinion of courts, criminal or royal, they are well designed to put you in your place. The sinking feeling came when they called my name, but I saw Gerry smiling at me and took heart. The theatre was our cause, the court case a joke. I stepped up to take a bow. The police prosecutor began his harangue. Oh dear. He wasn't in the least concerned with technicalities. He opened up straight away on the political content of the show. It was dangerous, inflammatory, scandalous, and he quoted police notes taken during performances. The beak looked very severe. The gates of the female prison opened before me. Those notes weren't very accurate, rather muddled, in fact.

Ah good, our man is on his feet, he looks a real barrister, the right shaped head, smooth dark hair, a slight suntan . . . Good casting. He's objecting to the introduction of politics. We are not here on a political charge. This is a very highbrow, artistic company, they do all sorts of strange and wonderful plays with unpronounceable names – and here he waved our beautifully designed programmes for *Fuente Ovejuna* and *Schwejk* at the magistrate, and had some fun pretending he could hardly pronounce the names.

'This one is so artistic that no one has ever heard of it.'

He gave the magistrate an 'in' smile as if they both knew we were merely a collection of cranks. Then he pursued his argument. These young artists had merely failed to cope with the technicalities of presentation, engrossed as they were in their art, and not understanding that for a club performance time must be allowed to elapse between the payment of the subscription and admittance to the club area.

I was still playing the carefree gal, though in truth I'd given up. And it had all seemed such a fuss about nothing at first. I tried to keep up the act but my mouth was as dry as a bone. Our man was still talking . . . very convincing. I was beginning to believe him myself and swore that if we got off I would direct nothing but pure art, *Pelleas and Melisande* or *The Tidings Brought to Mary*, and win plaudits for my sensitivity and respectability.

The magistrate was summing up. What was he saying? Were we free? We were bound over for twelve months. Fine? Five guineas apiece. It was not a negligible sum when you could buy five Woodbines for tuppence and Liebfraumilch cost two shillings a bottle at the wine shop in Albert Square. Outside in the fresh air we forgot the fine as Howard Goorney started mimicking the beak. Howard was already one of our faithfuls.

Not long afterwards, Jimmie and I, sailing into the BBC to take part in a Children's Hour play, were stopped by the burly Lancashire doorman. He put his arm across the door.

'I have instructions not to admit you two.' He knew us very well.

'Not to admit us? But we have a rehearsal. We'll be late.'

'Sorry, but you are not allowed in Broadcasting House.'

We had no alternative but to go and phone the friendly director, Olive Shapley, and tell her we were barred. She seemed amazed and none too pleased, having to replace us at such short notice. She obviously hadn't been warned. What could we do? Our relations with the Communist Party were not good but we asked them who else had been blacklisted. It couldn't be just us.

'Well!' said Mick Jenkins, a local Party functionary. 'You have access to microphones.'

'Do they think we're going to read the Communist Manifesto over the air, with the director and the engineers bound and gagged in the control room?'

L.C. Knights of the National Council for Civil Liberties was at Manchester University. We wrote to him and he saw us, noted all the facts and promised to do what he could. We admired his work on Ben Jonson, but he was better at that than at fighting for freedom. We never heard from him again. We offered our story to the newspapers. They didn't publish it, not even the *Daily Worker*. So there we were, no means of support, no redress . . . The BBC didn't even send us our two-guinea fee and it was they who had broken the contract, not us.

A letter arrived from John Coatman, top man at the BBC, Manchester. It was an invitation to lunch, not in Broadcasting House but at a small businessmen's dive near the Stock Exchange. He was a big man, and wore loose clothes which looked very ordinary but weren't. He was pale, even his eyes were pale, but they didn't miss much. He had a ready smile and a friendly manner, which went with his comfortable Lancashire accent. Surprising to learn that he'd served with the Indian police, fought on the Afghan frontier and lectured on political science at Delhi University.

During a documentary on the Manchester BBC, a snatch of Coatman talking to the lift-man was included, and an old lady phoned in. 'Why was the head of the station calling the lift-man sir?' she wanted to know.

The lift-men were all ex-army sergeants with authentic British Army accents. One of them asked Tina Bonifacio, a harpist in the Hallé, to kindly refrain from talking foreign to her son in the lift. She was talking French to her half-French son, Jean-Christophe Déjèy.

John Coatman was a Manchester Liberal of the old school, none too keen on taking orders from London. He didn't see the justice of depriving Jimmie and me of our livelihood. He didn't regard us as a threat to the country. 'This is a lot of nonsense,' he told us. 'I know Sammy Hoare. I'll have a word with him when I'm in London.' Then he told us about his army days, and the comradeship of the First World War. 'If they want me back,' he said, 'I know what I'll ask for. The Poor Bloody Infantry – no responsibility.'

Hugh MacDiarmid took a similar line. 'If they call me up, I'll ask for my old job back.'

'You had a good job?'

'Quartermaster sergeant.'

Coatman had shaken hands with us warmly when he said goodbye. We went our way feeling quite hopeful, but weeks went by and no contracts dropped through the letter-box. Despite Sammy Hoare, we were out. We heard that Beatrix Lehmann, Michael Redgrave, André van Gyseghem and Walter Hudd had been barred at the same time. One of them denied that he had ever had any sympathy with the Left. He was afraid of losing a film contract. He kept his film.

Coatman saw us again but only to report failure. No access to mikes, no contracts with the BBC, no entry into defence areas for the duration. I was already barred from working in Sheffield because I'd broadcast a criticism of the housing there.

'And the Nazi sympathisers?' I asked. 'The extreme right?'

'The same ban applies to both sides.'

We knew there was a deeply reactionary core in the BBC. They kept their jobs.

After the high peak of *Last Edition* the company settled for a period of study. Jimmie put up a reading list, each title accompanied by the book's number in the catalogue of the Central Reference Library. Gerry suggested forming a library of our own and offered to organise it. He was immediately appointed librarian. His first act was the donation of all his personal books, each one neatly labelled and numbered. The only other contribution was the books Jimmie pinched from the bookstalls of Hanging Ditch. For a good book he'd have Gibbs' bookshop quote a price before he acquired it. At other times, if he had the ha'pence, he'd buy a book and sell it at a profit to be squandered on coffees all round in Lyons. He believed he had a God-given right to any book he needed, and had no scruples about plundering them. One day he invaded a friend's flat and took every book he fancied. Years later he returned them, to the amazement of his victim, who strangely enough remains his friend to this day.

Recently I came across the theatre's Study Course among Gerry's papers. You can find it at the end of this book.

Despite the ban on our work, Theatre Union clubs sprang up all over Lancashire after *Last Edition*. Rossendale Valley wanted a living newspaper on cotton. There was a demand for classes and weekend courses on theatre technique on every side. Bacup became our rural stronghold. We would arrive in a borrowed truck on the Friday evening and work all night preparing the hall. The bakers would bring us fresh rolls and mugs of tea as we worked and in the morning, early, the public baths would be opened for us. Saturday and Sunday would be given up to classes and shows for club members only. One Sunday night the town band saw us off after a march up the main street. An old weaver pressed sixpence into my hand. 'For the theatre of the people,' he said.

Gerry kept his list of research for *Cotton*:

1. Locate all leaflets issued by the Burnley Weavers Winders and Beamers Assn, 1931–1932.
2. Check up on the Northern Counties Textile Trade Federation, 1932.
3. Locate the early strike committees' call for action, 1932.

The *Cotton Workers' Leader*, organ of the Solidarity
Movement, 1933.
The *Cotton Spread* No 1, 1935.
The Nelson and District Weavers' Assn, 1936.

By this time Gerry had left the shelter of home and university
and was finding out how the other half lived. How he managed
his researches while driving a large carthorse round Salford all day
I shall never know, but he did. Then again, Gerry had an endless
capacity for hard work, and a zest for life.

Fourteen

We need premises, and move from pillar to post, finishing up in a crypt. Call-up diminishes the company. Love affairs break out. London being badly bombed, my family are in danger. ENSA? Not for me, the ban operates. Given freelance journalist work in Manchester. Bill Sharples, a pacifist, called up. We rehearse Lysistrata. *The crypt is bombed. Howard's prowess. Jimmie is called up. I hear from Marjorie Banks.*

As Laban movement and vocal exercises, often carolling to each other across non-existent valleys, now formed an essential part of our training, the old studio in Grosvenor Street was too confined. We needed space. We fire-watched a disused warehouse and in return they let us have the use of it, but the first time we danced a jig the floor gave way. We would have to find somewhere safer. We tried pubs, clubs, even the Band of Hope, but if you didn't drink, gamble or pray you were suspect.

Barbara Niven had now joined us. She was tall and slim, wore her dark hair in a bun, and was not only attractive . . . she could twist men round her little finger. There was an enormous room above Hardy's furniture emporium at 42 Deansgate. Hardy himself had already succumbed to Barbara's charms. When she organised 'Art from the Spanish Republic', he let her hang the paintings there. Customers in search of a tasteful three-piece had been rather startled when they came upon Picasso's 'Guernica'.

'A *rehearsal* room? Oh, I'm afraid not. Evenings only? And weekends? Well, there'd be nobody about at weekends.' Barbara gave him her wry smile and a small study of a pebble painted while staying with Hugh MacDiarmid and Valda in the Shetlands. Mr Hardy prided himself on his appreciation of modern art. He gave her the keys.

We revelled in the place. Jimmie wrote a song about it. Our

classes were well-attended and the address became well-known –
all sorts of visitors dropped in. The actress Luise Rainer arrived
one day. She was married to Clifford Odets at the time and in
contact with 'The Group' in New York. We had always exchanged
scripts with them and she knew that we had been the first English
company to produce *Waiting for Lefty*. She found us swimming in
an imaginary sea. Jimmie invited her to join us. She laughed but
said she'd sooner see some of our work. We ran two or three scenes
from *Cotton* and *Fuente*. Then she began to ply us with questions.
She was shocked by our poverty. In those days America snapped
up talent regardless of class or opinion. In any case, anybody who
was anybody in Hollywood was red.

On top of that, the stream of refugees from Hitler tended to
flow to America, though many stayed with us. Each new arrival
was questioned for news of Friedrich Wolf, Maxim Vallentin,
Gustav Wangenheim, Anna Seghers, Ernst Busch – Had they
escaped? What had happened to Rudolf Laban?

We began to feel the draught in the autumn of 1940. The first
to receive call-up papers was Harold Bowen, one of our mainstays.
He had brought the house down as Chamberlain in *Last Edition*. Of
course he was getting on, well into his twenties. His farewell binge
was our last party before the War overwhelmed us.

'It'll soon be over,' said H.B.

We carried him to the train, drunk as a lord, and Clare Ffoulkes
sang 'Will ye no' come back again' as the train moved out. Harold
was shouting something but I couldn't catch it.

'It was Long Live the Illustrious Theatre,' said Jimmie.

Back at 42 Deansgate, we held one of our company meetings.
The electricity bill had just arrived and it was heavy. Our spacious
room had been a luxury. Our only income now was from one-night
stands up and down the valleys. We would have to find more modest quarters. I dreaded a return to the slums. Was there no place for
an indigent theatre to work out its destiny? One afternoon I called
on our friends, the Finnemores, and found Enid drinking tea in the
front room with a burly, sunburnt man. Ronnie was finishing his
theatre column but came flittering in to introduce me: 'Joan, the
rebel – Etienne Watts of All Saints.'

'You walked to London with the Hunger Marchers, didn't

you?' I said.

'And was beaten up with them,' said Enid.

Etienne Watts was one of the vicars in the Anglican Church who believed that Communists were the only true Christians. He was not alone, quite a brotherhood believed as he did. He opened his church for the homeless at all times, endeavouring to put Christ's teaching into practice. As a result he was looked upon as a dangerous eccentric.

Enid asked what was wrong. I was not often seen abroad at tea-time.

'I'm looking for a secluded workplace where there'd be no risk of complaints from neighbours.'

'I've just the thing,' said the Reverend Etienne. 'It's very private and there's absolutely no risk of interference from the other occupants.'

'It's already occupied?'

'By the quietest of people. The dead.'

We all knew his church at All Saints, the nineteenth-century building at the crossroads which divides Ardwick from Chorlton on Medlock. It had been surrounded with gravestones but Etienne had removed them to make a children's playground.

'You'd better come and have a look, before I put you in the crypt.'

The inside of the church was pleasantly bare. Behind the altar he had placed two banners: one red, bearing a gold hammer and sickle; the other, the cross of Christianity. Descending a circular stone stairway from the vestry, we came to the crypt. There were quite a lot of occupants, a coffin in each alcove, sometimes two. They looked rather mouldy. In one corner there was a very small one covered in leather which had once been green. It was fastened with brass nails. They looked insecure. When I described the place to the company, nobody was enthusiastic but no one actually opposed the idea. There was no alternative and it was rent-free. Bill Sharples wanted to know about the flooring.

'Beaten earth.'

'We'll have to put down some planks.'

Within a week a section of wooden flooring was laid, and our precious gear was safely stowed.

'Our personal bunker,' said Bill Sharples. 'Now they can do their worst.'

'Down among the dead men,' said Jimmie. 'What are we rehearsing, Euripides?'

'*The Birds*,' said I.

We had a crack at it and soon forgot our surroundings. Two ghouls in the company actually enjoyed the place. One night as we left, I heard 'Fell open . . . long golden hair'. Necrophiles!

W hether it was the influence of Aristophanes or the boredom of war, love affairs were sprouting all over the place – dark-eyed Ada Tootill with Robert Dyson, one of Barbara's young artists; sprauncy Ruth Wilson who danced so well, with Vivian Daniels; actor Les Goldman, the Commander in *Fuente*, with anyone he could get; and Jimmie Miller, more than ever combining his courtships with recruitment to the Communist Party, was now surrounded by a most unsuitable collection of young ladies, all carrying the Party card. The happiest lovers do not seem to need such a large turnover, but Jimmie, no longer hampered by the rivals and critics he'd suffered in Theatre of Action days, thoroughly enjoyed being cock-of-the-walk.

One fine Sunday evening I saw Gerry and Clare Ffoulkes strolling along on the other side of the road. Clare was talking, Gerry listening, his right arm round her shoulder. They were a pretty sight. Clare, her gold hair hanging loose, Gerry wearing white shorts under a long, dark-blue dressing gown, a left-over from his prosperous days – and both oblivious to the world. It all looked perfect but in fact she was telling him that they were through, she was leaving him for another member of the company. Soon everyone knew, because Gerry looked so desolate, except when Clare was present – then he couldn't take his eyes off her.

'He's touched,' said Jimmie, quite forgetting his own lovelorn performances.

As it turned out, they were both upstaged by Graham Banks. He proposed to our nymph from *Last Edition*, Rosalie Williams, call-up papers in his hand.

'It's the RAF,' said Graham. 'So you might not have to put

up with me for long.'

No one said so but we all knew that Graham's chances of survival were slim; mortality among bomber crews was very high. Jimmie told Rosalie that if she married Graham he would commit suicide. She wasn't impressed, so he said it again and added, 'By this hand . . .' He wanted to thrust his hand into flames, but unfortunately there was only an electric fire so it all fell a bit flat. Everybody enjoyed the story and almost everybody was surprised to hear about Rosalie and Jimmie. I wasn't.

Since August 1940, the Luftwaffe had been invading southern England nightly. The planes flew over Croydon, then across SW London where my family lived. We all knew the casualty lists were tailored, but sometimes you heard the truth. . . .

'Direct hit on a shelter in Kennington Park last night.'

'I thought it was a near one.'

'What about Balham tube station?'

'They all got drowned in the sewers. Never go down those places myself.'

Officially tube stations were regarded as the safest refuge during a raid, but many wouldn't use them. Too dirty, and you could be trapped down there.

I wrote to my grandparents and Kate, my mother. I wrote telling them they'd have to leave Stockwell. Was I crazy? Leave? It hadn't even occurred to them.

It was cold but I was snug enough, perched in the driver's cabin of a giant lorry, somewhere in the middle of blacked-out England. Suddenly, a gigantic chandelier of fire lit the sky. The driver pulled up. We watched in silence. 'That was Coventry, that was,' he said, and drove on into the night. We had seen the opening of Reichsmarschall Göring's provincial bombing tour.

London stank of charred timber, chloride of lime and foul drains. The tenements had been sliced from roof to basement, and patches of faded wallpaper marked the areas where people had passed their lives. I was looking for Kate and family. The street was roped off. An air-raid warden told me they'd been moved to a house round the corner. They hadn't expected me, but Jim brewed a pot of tea and we sat down and talked.

'We ran out in the street and cheered,' said Kate, 'when we first heard our guns.'

'You mean there's been no defence at all?'

'That's right.'

'You must go down the tube.'

'No fear.'

'If they come too close we all get under the table.' They had a steel table supplied by the government.

'When it's over Dad makes a cup of tea and we all go to bed.'

'Sometimes it's not worth going to bed.'

'The boys love it,' said Milly. 'Young Jeremy spends his time looking for unexploded bombs.'

As I was telling them they ought at least to send the kids away, the sirens went. It was a chilling sound. We sat listening. I heard a few anti-aircraft guns. Jim got up, went out into the back yard and shouted to a neighbour. Milly went for a bucket of water and a stirrup pump. When the All Clear sounded, I ran round to my grandparents'.

It was hell being so far away when they were in danger. I tried to persuade them to come to Manchester. Gran began to cry. I had never seen her cry before, but instead of putting my arms round her I went on till Grandad told me to shut up. 'We don't want to leave our home.'

I went away upset by their attitude. I thought I knew best! I passed deserted streets smelling of damp rubble and charred wood on my way to Drury Lane, the HQ of ENSA. I had written them about engaging Theatre Union, but received no reply. Maybe face to face I could talk them into it. That would be something. It might even mean exemption for the rest of the boys. The stage door was hidden behind a wall of sandbags.

'Identity card.'

A phone call to Drama Section, a long wait. At last . . . In . . . Some raddled comics, a scented woman, her face covered with white powder, a corridor of plywood cubicles . . . dressing baskets piled up against the wall. They were to be sent to far-away places. Would they ever get there?

I found the door marked 'Drama. Mr Oscar', and as soon as I

set eyes on him I knew I'd seen him hanging around a churchyard in some old B picture. He told me to sit down, and while I was removing a pile of playscripts from the only seat, asked what I'd done.

'Hm, rather "family",' he said and turned his attention to a blonde head which popped round the door.

'I'm back, sweetie,' it said. 'Death warmed up.'

'You look ravishing, duckie.'

'Double bookings again. We ran into *Soldiers in Skirts* three times. The boys need a little more SA, those pansies are too camp.' As she revealed herself full length, I took a close look at Mr Oscar's desk. More dog-eared plays, a tumbler with smudges, two used teacups, and an overflowing ashtray.

She was now shuffling her new photos at him. 'Take a peek at those plays, while I go thro' these,' he told me.

There followed a long discussion on tours, heat, flies and camera angles. I got up to go. The blonde undulated to let me pass. Her bosoms were lapping over her low-cut scarlet bodice.

'Don't forget the plays, dear,' he called after me. 'I want your verdict on them, you know.' I collected two or three and fled.

As I passed the stage door, I asked the lady's name.

'Sounds like one of the MMs,' said the doorman.

'MMs?'

'Maria Martens. *Murder in the Red Barn*. Melodrama. Nothing like the old blood an' thunders.'

I sat in the park and read Mr Oscar's plays, fast. They were very depressing. I wrote a report on each one and took them back to Drury Lane. This time the doorman barred my way, just like the BBC sergeant in Manchester. It was the same ban. I dumped the plays and went back to Stockwell.

Mr Oscar didn't find time to acknowledge my reports or ask if I had the fare back to Manchester. I had, and intended to return there as soon as I could persuade my grandparents to leave London. I had some success. It was not so much the bombs, but because the old house was now too much for them. I set to work and scrubbed and polished it from top to bottom. It got Mr Oscar out of my hair but made me think of all the times the old people had coped on their own.

Jimmie's mother would be prepared to come and help with the removal. I told them they'd enjoy the North.

'There's no place like London, Jo,' was Gran's parting shot.

B ack in Manchester, Bill Sharples had started making masks for *The Birds*. Rosalie had taken a job with some weekly rep.

I daren't ask her what she was playing, in case it was Maria Marten. It was.

I decided to find myself a job. So I went back to my old haunts, finished up in the *Manchester Guardian* pub on Cross Street which was packed with faces I used to know. I even got a cheer as I walked in.

'Where have you been?'

'On the Murmansk run.'

'All that Moscow gold still getting through?'

'Sure.'

I'd been away too long.

'Come on, J.L., tell us what you've been up to.'

'Reading *Essays on a Dying Culture* with Basil Dean.'

Bob, an old mate from BBC days, brought me a glass of wine.

'Want to try your hand at journalism?'

'Why not?'

He wrote an address on a scrap torn from the *Evening News*.

'They'll want it in before six, but you'd better let me have a look at it first. Peel Park, Salford family entombed – that's your story.'

I found the place, got the picture and wrote my two hundred words in a local café.

Bob read fast, wriggling his nose occasionally. 'Not enough suspense there, needs a few tears in the last paragraph, and more punch in the opening.' Drama everywhere, I said to myself.

That story changed my luck. Bob handed me several more. Arrival of German wounded at Manchester Infirmary; Hull fishermen's wives wait for news; first crèche in a cotton mill. Then a windfall – a film script, *The Making of a Great Newspaper*. Guess which? The *Daily Express*, Manchester edition. The newspapers didn't seem as scared of Reds as the BBC. The journalists I knew were a cynical lot, rebels themselves, most of them.

The next bit of news that came my way was harder to swallow.
Bill Sharples had been called up. 'But he's a pacifist,' said Howard.

'That's right, so they're only giving him non-combatant duties
– on an oil tanker.'

'The most dangerous job in the War,' said Jimmie. 'Did he
go before a tribunal?'

'Yes, Bill's a confirmed pacifist, like his father before him.
It made no difference.'

We would have to postpone *The Birds*. Bill was a great
designer, unique. We put away the masks he had made, carefully
wrapped.

'We'll do *Lysistrata* instead. At least there are plenty of women
in it.'

The American translation was the best and Jimmie started
work on the music. For the chorus of warmongers we'd plenty of
specimens in the government. We decided to model our old men
on them. Evening rehearsals kept our mind off the bombing, but
we dreaded the mornings – the post, call-up papers. The blackout
was very strict. If your curtains let out a chink of light, the police
would have you in court.

> *Dancers, come forth, the Graces with you. Bring Artemis, Lord of
> Pleasure, our Apollo. Bring Dionysus and his maenad maids . . . See
> how his eye darts flames.*
>
> *We sing Athens, Queen of cities, fair citadel of the golden height,
> the dream of men, the child of fair women . . .*

Aristophanes knew how to bring light to his people even in
the darkness of their never-ending war.

Ada Tootill was Lysistrata:

> *O Zeus, with your Queen bring lightning. Come! Come all the inhabitants
> of the earth and sky. Come ye gods, witness this honourable peace, now
> concluded.*

Oh God! How I wish it were.

It's late, time to stop – to go out into the reality of blackout and the boredom of war. I called good night but the company were tidying up and arguing. It was best to get home early these days. I left. Toots (Lysistrata) and Ruth (Lampito) followed me. We went scurrying along Oxford Road and had reached the first turning when there was a thunderous explosion and we were flung against the wall. I was scared to look back in case the church had suffered a direct hit. It had. By the time we got there, the fire engines were arriving. Etienne Watts was scrambling over the fallen masonry. Why don't they start digging? The company's in that crypt. Of course, it wouldn't occur to them that there'd be anybody in the church, let alone under it.

They knew. Etienne Watts had already told them. The firemen were moving towards the only remnant of the structure left standing. Two home guards approached from the Moss Side end. Then came the miracle. From the vestry area a dusty figure stepped out. It was Gerry. He turned to help the others, as they tottered out into the night. They were dusty and shaken but unhurt.

'How did you escape?'

'By the stone steps which lead up to the vestry. They're intact. Mind you, when that bomb dropped we thought our last hour had come.'

The arch of the roof had opened and a long crack appeared. Then, thank God, it had closed again. The two halves came together. I think we all gave silent thanks for the strength of the stone and the skill of the builders.

Howard, faithful ever since *Schwejk*, was unusually absent, the night the bomb dropped. It was the girls' doing.

They'd decided that he always looked sad because he was starved of love and it was the company's duty to help him.

'Especially now,' said Toots, 'because he's just fallen in love and if he isn't satisfied he will be inhibited and perhaps remain – till the end of his days – a virgin.'

A vote was taken. It was decided unanimously that he should be provided with:

1. A love nest, with gas fire.
2. Food and drink, ham sandwiches, Guinness and Babycham.
3. A gramophone, with Bix Beiderbecke records.
4. Two French letters.

It was all set up and the key of Nat Kellner's flat was handed to him without a word.

'Alright, Howard?'

Next day we were all anxious to hear the result. He shook his head. 'The sirens went just as I was getting down to it. I had to make straight for the hospital. Well, I was on fire-guard duty.' He didn't tell us that the nurses' home had been hit, and he was there all night, bringing them out, the living and the dead.

As for the rest of us, with the destruction of the church we were completely stumped. We met in each others' homes, read plays, made plans, tried in vain to keep up our spirits. I had bad news from London.

My friend Sonja Mortensen had lost both parents when Richmond was hit during a heavy air raid, and Margie Debus, all her family when a land-mine fell behind the Swan, Stockwell. I would have to get my grandparents away. They could hardly run for their lives. Then Jimmie's call-up papers arrived.

> *I'd never been out of Salford town,*
>> *the place where I was born*
> *Until one day I joined the ranks and wore a uniform*
> *But I'd rather never travel if the only way to see*
> *The world is through the rife sights of a Mark 4 303.*

Jimmie's exit took the cake. The company mourned its leader even before he was lost. Gerry offered to go in his place, but Clare put her foot down.

'No, you won't,' she said. And Gerry was delighted.

'Jimmie's genius stifled before it has had time to develop,' said Rosalie.

'You're all ridiculous,' said Clare and flounced out to the pubs with Gerard Kelly.

F or the actual departure, Jimmie made a heroic speech, bidding us hold fast and carry on! But he'd hardly been in the army twenty-four hours before the mood changed. His letters were so utterly dejected that we all had to hitch-hike up to Richmond, Yorkshire, on the Sunday to cheer him up. After that he cheered himself up, to the tune of Clementine:

> *Down in Wathgill, Richmond, Yorkshire, by the*
>   *winding River Swale*
> *There's a camp where browned-off soldiers tell a*
>   *very sorry tale . . .*

But we still had to make that trip to Wathgill every week, laden with delicacies, mostly supplied by his adoring mother.

Jimmie's updated version of 'Browned Off' went the rounds of the British Army:

> *The medical inspection boys is just a bleedin' farce*
> *He gropes around your penis and he noses up your arse,*
> *For even a Private's privates boys enjoy no privacy,*
> *You sacrifice all that to save democracy.*
>
>   *Oh, I was browned off, browned off, browned off as could be*
>   *Browned off, browned off, an easy mark that's me*
>   *But when this war is over and again I'm free*
>   *There'll be no more bloody soldiering for me.*
>
> *The Colonel kicks the Major, then the Major has a go*
> *He kicks the poor old Captain who then kicks the NCO*
> *And as the kicks get harder the poor Private you can see*
> *Gets kicked to bloody hell to save democracy.*
>
>   *Oh, I was browned off, etc.*

Soon he was turning out a song a day and it was obvious that the CO had no intention of letting him be transferred to a regiment which would offer some activity more fascinating than square-bashing. Only the Medical Officer resented the entertainment. 'Write another song about me, Miller, and I'll give you an injection in a place you will never forget.'

Jimmie wrote me every day, mostly jokes and nostalgia. So were mine to him. It must have been disappointing for the police who were opening them all.

Howard's call-up came next. Then Gerard Kelly's. How long before Gerry's? Graham came home on leave, proposed to Rosalie again and was turned down again. After he'd left we heard that this had been his last leave before being sent on night raids.

A letter arrived asking me to visit M. Banks, Features and Drama, London. At first I was delighted, then I thought about it. Why go all the way to London to be shown the door again? I wrote M. Banks saying that I'd had enough of BBC manners. A secretary replied arranging a meeting at the Stag, a Features and Drama boozer, and enclosing my fare. Good. I would be able to see my grandparents at the same time. I found the pub empty but for one or two BBC soaks. I'd hardly got to the bar when the door swung open and an elegant, very beautiful young woman stepped in.

'I'm Marjorie Banks. You're Joan.'

Now why had I expected a Plain Jane and no nonsense? Well, the BBC had favoured frumps at one time. Marjorie was the first intellectual lovely I'd ever seen. She interviewed some Yanks who'd just landed; they threw away their Rita Hayworth pin-ups and adopted Marjorie instead.

I wasn't sure she knew about the ban. She did. What's more, she'd decided that if my name wasn't flashed about I could at least earn a living, and should we go and have a decent lunch? We downed our dry Martinis and made to go just as the rush began. As we left I heard a high falsetto. 'Littlewood and Banks? Where's Willie Gallagher?'

I knew that voice, though I hadn't heard it for a long time.

Jimmie's words came back to me. Dillon – army of intervention. So Marjorie was a known Red? We were living in strange times. Had I been too long in my crypt? I asked Marjorie about Dillon. Jack, now Francis, Dillon was safe in the arms of the BBC for the duration, writing fairy stories for adults, after Oscar Wilde – a long way after. Quite a jump, Manchester Inland Revenue to Frog Princes and Sugar Plum fairies in a well-furnished office at Rothwell House.

Over lunch, I tried to tell Marjorie about Theatre Union. She wasn't very interested. She was a journalist; so was her husband – both courageous people, good to have on your side.

Fifteen

Marjorie finds a way to let me work. We write a series together.
D.G. Bridson remembers me, gets me a job writing and directing
an Overseas series. My grandparents leave London. My grandmother
dies. Gerry and I become lovers. He is called up. Graham's plane shot
down over Germany. My grandfather dies. Gerry is kicked out of the
RAF.

Marjorie managed to get me a temporary pass. We wrote a series between us, 'Front Line Family', precursor of today's soaps. We became friends although, apart from work, we had little in common. She thought my theatre ambitions daft. Why make things difficult? Why not work inside the existing racket?

Marjorie and other good friends could work inside the established order – I couldn't – but she never gave up trying to get that ban lifted. She didn't succeed, but she talked and put work in my way, so that even my old friend Bridson recovered his memory. A green contract arrived offering a programme a week for six months – to be written and directed by J.L. Geoffrey was now in charge of Overseas broadcasts and America wanted stories of everyday people, and as I was the only one who'd had contact with such glamorous creatures, I was offered ten pounds a week, a secretary and a desk of my own.

Bridson only knew the way he'd worked in Manchester, pre-War. 'Assemble your characters, invite their workmates and relatives, find two or three good songs and you have your show. You'll need a good MC.'

I chose a quiet Canadian, Kent Stevenson. The general run of BBC presenters sounded like Bulldog Drummond. I had no problem finding a lively bunch of people in Warwickshire. Bridson had booked a BBC studio in Birmingham. The first busload arrived and the back-slapping and wise-cracking commenced.

'I'm not performing in front of all those people?' said Kent.

'That's the idea.'

He walked to that microphone like a lamb to the slaughter. At the end I showed him my stopwatch. 'Dead on time,' I said.

'So am I,' said Kent. 'An hour's broadcast in one take! Jesus! Can't we record them one by one in the privacy of their own home or in a pub, anywhere they feel at ease? That way you keep taping till you get what you want.'

'How do we put the programme together?'

'In the cutting room.'

I'd never come across the taping technique before, neither had anyone else at Broadcasting House, but Kent was so keen it was worth a try. For the next transmission we took a small recording unit and captured our prey in the most unlikely places – by hedgerows, up to our waists in the River Don, over the garden wall. When we arrived back in London, the van was stacked with cans of tape.

As we were unloading, the phone rang. 'The engineers tell me you've enough tapes to start a factory.'

'That's right, Geoffrey.'

'What are we going to put out tomorrow?'

'You'll be surprised.'

The phone gave an angry grunt. And I prayed, because I'd never spliced a tape in my life. We recruited the best team in the building and worked all night. You only appreciated Kent's microphone technique when you heard those recordings. The show sounded different to anything I'd ever heard.

I found myself at home with Kent and his Canadian colleagues. They were stationed in the basement at 200 Oxford Street, but they longed for excitement and danger. My work was too gentle for Kent. In a wood, recording birdsong, you'd find him staring up at the sky as a bomber flew overhead.

'Where are you, Kent?'

'Flying. I want to tape a raid over Germany.'

It took him a long time, but he managed it. Unfortunately we never heard the recording. His aircraft was reported missing.

S outh-west London was suffering badly and Jimmie's mother was keen to go there, sort out my grandparents' affairs and bring the old people back to the cottage where the Millers now lived, at Werneth Low above Hyde, Cheshire. I had to agree. I couldn't go myself; I was the breadwinner, fully occupied with BBC work. In any case, Mrs Miller seemed better equipped to deal with the situation.

I got back to Hyde in time to welcome them, put a vase of tall marguerites in their room and made a meal, brisket of beef and carrots. Then to my horror, they arrived with little more than the clothes they stood up in. All their furniture, bedding and crockery, all Caroline Emily's treasures had been sold or given away. I was so shaken that all I could say was, 'What about Spot . . . the cat?'

'It was only when I had them take him away that your granny broke down and cried,' said Mrs Miller sorrowfully. 'But I couldn't have him here.'

What had I done? They might have survived the bombing, even enjoyed it, sharing the experience with neighbours, but this heartless charity . . . I tried to tell them how dangerous London had become, that they were well out of it, but in fact their old house was not hit and they pined for London.

On the first sunny day of 1941, Gran had a bad turn. She'd been sitting outside sewing all afternoon, then suddenly she keeled over. We gave her a drop of brandy and put her to bed. The next morning, grey skies came down again. She leant towards the window surveying the bleak industrial landscape in the valley below.

'Not very gay,' she said. Then she made her way to the WC and collapsed. It was a brain haemorrhage.

She was unconscious for twenty-four hours. Mrs Miller and I took turns to sit by her. I took the night shift. Grandad slept alone in the small spare room upstairs. I listened to the croaking, snoring sound all night. I thought it must be the end, though it was the first time I had watched the approach of death. I went to the kitchen to drink a cup of tea at eight in the morning as Mrs Miller took over. While I was away the end came.

I went to tell the old man. He looked at me and his still handsome face dropped stupidly. His bowels gave way, for the first and last time in his life. 'I should have been with her.'

'She didn't know anybody, Grandad.'

Mrs Miller was used to coping with death, unlike the doctor who arrived too late from his surgery a mile away, and didn't even go in to look at Caroline Em. Mrs Miller said he was scared of death.

Later, when the sun came out, Robert Francis and I sat together in the garden. I played some Bach for him but Mrs Miller was very disapproving: a mourning house must be silent. 'I think Jo was only trying to help,' he said and we sat there in silence for a while.

'Do you think we go on?' he asked quietly, glancing up at the blue sky.

I couldn't say yes, I just looked at him and put my hand on his.

'It was because her poor legs healed,' he said. 'It went to her head.' They had healed because she hadn't had to be on her feet all day as in London. She'd been able to rest. After a long while he spoke again, 'It's better the way it is. She would have been lonely without me. She told me so.'

The funeral was hard for him to bear, an old man of eighty-four. She was buried in the churchyard halfway down the hill. The very house-proud widows of Werneth can be seen every Saturday morning scrubbing and polishing their husbands' tombstones, even those with RIP boldly displayed. The poor old fellers had no peace, even in the grave. Kate came to the funeral with her brother Bob.

'Now she's gone, I feel old,' she said. But not too old to start bickering with her brother. It was a relief when they went.

I t must have been in the doldrums between Christmas and New Year 1942, that I found myself trying to suppress a dose of flu while inspecting a prefab hospital somewhere on Salisbury Plain, donated by America. I had a fever, my teeth were chattering and my face was flushed, but the very superior young doctor I was interviewing didn't even ask how I was going to get back to Salisbury.

I hitchhiked in the rain. Then, wrapped in a blanket, crouched over a mini-gas fire, I tried to write the story of my day, gave up, took a hot toddy and went to bed. In the sweaty dark I woke with a thump and grabbed the phone. 'What day is it?'

The dozy night porter worked it out.

'I should be in London . . . What am I doing here?'

'I'd forgotten the Round-the-World-on-New-Year's-Eve broadcast for which I'd found the participants. The speeches they'd written out would already be in the censor's hands to be passed for tomorrow's recording. Nothing could be broadcast unless it had been censored and stamped.

On the train, I had a high fever. At BH I was raving. Karel, my Czech find, had not sent in his contribution.

'See that it's here by nine in the morning or there'll be a nasty hole where Prague should be,' said the editor.

At midnight, after fruitless phone calls, I abandoned Karel. It would be easier to write the schmaltz myself and find someone to mug up a Czech accent. The Prague of my delirium was pure Hašek, with Wenceslas Square and the Charles Bridge thrown in for good measure, and at a quarter to nine the following morning it lay on the editor's desk. What a relief.

'Hold on. Haven't you forgotten something?' said I to myself.

'No.'

'You don't need a Czech to read it?'

There was only one place where you could pick up anything. I took a taxi to Soho. It was deserted but for two angry Poles fighting over a brass, but no Czech. In Goodge Street I gave up and had a coffee. One more call and then – bugger it. One of Karel's flatmates answered. 'He was here, dear, but he's gone.'

'Where?'

'To the BBC to do his thing.'

Outside the studio, the red light was on, the recording was in progress. Karel was in the corridor waving a sheaf of closely written pages and demanding to be let in to read them. The studio manager was trying to quieten him. 'But we already have your piece, it's been censored. You can't change it now.'

'You're too bloody late, Karel,' I said. 'Take it or leave it.'

I knew that all the poor bastard wanted was to let his parents know he had reached England safely. What did it matter if at the same time he had to read a lot of English piffle? He read it.

Three letters arrived while I was sleeping the New Year in. One looked official, two were love letters. I count all letters love letters if they're not in official envelopes. The first was from Philo, a young Austrian refugee who'd attached himself to Theatre Union. He'd been interned as an enemy alien but was about to be released to marry a passport. The other was from – of all people, Gerry. I didn't open the official envelope.

Work was going well in Manchester. They were reading *The Devil is an Ass*. 'P.S. When will you be back? I'm thinking about you far too much.'

Whenever possible I visited Werneth Low to be with my grandfather. I would take any little extras I could lay hands on, a tablet of soap, my sweet coupons, a little sugar. Whatever you gave Mrs Miller, her first thought was to put it aside for Jimmie. All the same, she did her best for Robert Francis, but I knew he was lonely without his Caroline Em. He liked it best when I sat and listened as he retold the old tales about India, but all too soon I would have to go – I had to earn.

Gerry always came as far as the bus stop when I left for the Millers. We would just sit on the bench and wait. He never said very much, but I liked teasing him because he took me so seriously. If he gave a rueful grin I'd stop and try to be nice. One Friday night I was sitting quietly when he bent over and kissed me. I got up and ran, boarded the wrong bus, jumped off and ran for the right one. I saw him laughing at me and shook my fist at him, then clambered up to the top deck and sat by the window. I didn't read, just sat there dreaming. Once I touched my cheek where he'd kissed me.

Gerry was nineteen, sexy, a very desirable young man. I was just twenty-eight, plain, hardly what you'd call attractive, moody often, amusing sometimes, but Gerry didn't see me as I was. He called me beautiful. Perhaps, when he looked at me, I was.

One day I told him I had to go to Chester for the next script. He asked if he might come with me. It would mean an outing rather than routine, but I knew that he knew that I would most probably have to stay overnight. Had I been flirting with Gerry? Yes. You should be ashamed – the director and the youngest member of the company. Well, there wasn't much of a company left and we were happy together. In any case it wouldn't last.

My routine on these visits was programmed:

- Quick survey of ancient monuments and historical remains.
  Any radiogenic characters picked up on the way – bagged.
- Try paper shops, auction rooms, pubs for local wits and wiseacres.
- Avoid mayors, clergymen, headmasters, police chiefs and managers of football teams.

I relied on chance.

'Where did you find those marvellous people?'

'I just went out on to the street and there they were.'

In Chester I meant to spend as much time as possible with Gerry, but for once I kept drawing blanks. The plumber who told very good stories wanted nothing to do with broadcasting. An amusing old girl only wanted to have her budgerigar recorded because he could recite the ten commandments. It was lunch-time. Gerry had been browsing round the bookshops and found a Victorian guide to Chester with prints of Roman ruins. When I said I hadn't had much luck, he offered to come with me in the afternoon. I'd never gone hunting with anyone before but there wasn't much else for him to do. It worked rather well; people fell for him, and by evening we'd collected a regular Crazy Gang. In a candlelit Roman basement we were served a powdered-egg omelette and no coupons asked. Over the ersatz coffee I wrote up my notes.

'I've still got to find a hotel,' I said.

'I've found one,' said Gerry. 'Remember you once said you could share a bed with a pair of nice legs?'

'I said that?'

'In front of the whole company.'

'I'd say anything at a rehearsal.'

'You didn't mean it?'

'I might have.'

'It's only that I happen to have nice legs, lots of nice things as a matter of fact.'

'I know.'

And you've guessed the answer to that. Well, despite the difference in age, or any qualms I might have had, Gerry was the most wonderful thing that ever happened to me – and still is. In the morning, he was down first. When I joined him in the breakfast room I felt like an awkward girl. He took my hand.

'You're too young to stay out all night with strange men.'

We went rowing on the River Dee, sang the old song and felt like staying away from the rest of the world for ever. He told me that his strength was all for me. And it was.

S oon after our one-day honeymoon, Gerry was called up. . . . It was the RAF, to be trained as a pilot. . . . Report to London.

He was given a weekend's leave almost immediately so on the Friday I took the train to Euston. He was waiting by the barrier. If he hadn't approached me I wouldn't have recognised him: the uniform, the biggest pair of boots I'd ever seen, and his beautiful dark hair cropped. His head was almost shaved. It made him look younger than ever. I had on my light tweed suit and I'd bought a green Chenille cap specially for the occasion. I thought it rather smart. Gerry gave it a dirty look.

He was stationed in St John's Wood, and had booked a room nearby so as not to waste time getting back to barracks on the Sunday evening. He never talked much but he was more silent than ever, holding my hand as we walked along. Then we just made love, and on the Saturday I took him to the Blue Lantern in Old Compton Street. Almost everyone there was in uniform, but when the door was shut and the curtain pulled, war became a joke. You weren't counting the minutes till goodbye, you were in love, now and for ever.

On Sunday evening we were back at the hotel early. One more time before . . .

A clock was chiming somewhere. He leapt out of bed. 'I'll have to rush,' he said.

I threw my clothes on and picked up my green Chenille.

'Oh, do leave that silly hat and hurry, Joan!' he said.

I laughed. 'Say it again, Gerry. That's the first time you've ever been cross with me.' He kissed me and we ran. Outside he flagged down a speeding taxi. Gerry was taking the RAF seriously.

There was bad news from Manchester. Graham's plane had been shot down over Germany. He had not long celebrated his twenty-first birthday. And my grandfather was poorly. I had been feeling so bad about him. I knew, too late, that I should never have brought my old people away from London. He would listen but he was quite lost when Mrs Miller started ranting against the class enemy and she could barely understand his old cockney chat. What could I do? I couldn't take him back. He was well into his eighties, though still strong as a horse. He wore no glasses and his eyes were as clear as day. I was quite shattered when he came for a stroll with me, bringing a walking stick.

'Ah, well, I've had a good innards,' he told me.

Before long the nights began to trouble him. You would hear him shoving his bed about and cursing someone. There was nobody there. As I said goodnight and closed the door, I'd hear him say, 'That was Joan Littlewood!' Who did he see there, in the lonely room? He had only his phantom for company.

I wasn't there when the end came. I rushed back but I wasn't in time. At the graveside, the parson said, 'He had a good long life.' It wasn't long enough for me. I rushed away from Werneth Low. The only person I wanted to see was Gerry, who'd been transferred to Ludlow.

'Have you been in trouble?'

'No. Well, yes but only over the morning papers.'

'You can't get them?'

'They're delivered, all except the *Daily Worker*.'

'I must say it's a treat to see it back, and the ban lifted, but you'll never get it, not in the RAF.'

'It took a bit of an argument but I got it. I complained about the lack of organisation too. We were supposed to be building this large hut, but no one knew how to run the job.'

'I bet you took over.'

'More or less. And they'll have to do something about the grub: it's diabolical.'

'Are you with a good mob?'

'Great. It's only one or two of the officers who are ridiculous.'

Perhaps because he went on complaining, he was suddenly transferred to Stratford-on-Avon. 'Easier for you to get to,' he wrote. 'Come this weekend, we'll have two whole days together.'

As the train clattered on through the open countryside I moved into the corridor and opened a window. The world was wonderful. Soon I would be with Gerry. It was a quiet room, Stratford Tudor, with chintz. The hotel was friendly. We made love straight away, then strolled down to the river. An old boatman offered us a swan's egg. 'It'll make you a good custard.'

The swans glided by looking disdainful. We declined the egg.

There was no avoiding that Festival Theatre, which looked anything but festive. 'I'd like to see the stage machinery,' said Gerry.

'It seems very shut.'

But he'd spotted a workman opening the side door, went and spun him a yarn and got us in. The curtain was up. We moved to the centre of the stage. Extraordinary! It was the only place where you could be seen by the whole house. A mediaeval cart must have been a more functional performance area, and even Palladio allowed for airborne chariots and sliding transformation scenes. Not this place, which was the prizewinning design in a competition backed by Flowers' Brewery. Nobody had noticed that the doorways giving on to the stage were too narrow to allow the passage of an Elizabethan farthingale.

I didn't fancy the evening performance but Gerry wanted to see the lighting. He was soon satisfied, so we went out on to the riverside balcony for a drink. It was the best part of the building. Gerry began talking about flying. It fascinated him. I asked him the difference between air speed and ground speed and he explained it to me carefully, but I couldn't grasp it.

'Are you getting on any better with the officers?'

'Sure.'

But I knew he wasn't.

'Don't worry, sweetheart. Just be sure we have the longest night of the year, together . . . always.'

In the morning we had breakfast early because he had to look in at the camp.

'Is something wrong?'

'No, no. I'll be back in no time.' And off he went.

Gerry was never one for unnecessary explanations, but when ten o'clock chimed and there was still no Gerry, I began to worry. I tried to read, took a walk in the garden. Eleven o'clock . . . no Gerry. Something had gone wrong. It was just on twelve when a pleasant young man in RAF uniform walked into the lobby and began looking for someone. It was me.

'I'm Roy, a friend of Gerry's.'

'What's happened?'

'He's all right, but he can't get out.'

'Why?'

'He's in the guardroom. All leave was cancelled yesterday but he'd arranged to see you, so he skipped. We tried to cover for him but Gerry's absence leaves quite a gap.' I must have looked crestfallen.

'It's all right, they won't shoot him.'

'But it could be serious.'

'Two of the whippersnappers have their knife in him.'

'Let's have a drink.'

'I'm afraid I have to get back. I don't know how I got away.'

'Thank you for coming. Give him my love.'

'Of course.'

'It's no use staying on the off-chance?'

'I'd say not. He won't be out again this week.'

This Roy seemed to have enjoyed playing his rôle, though I didn't look right for my part in Gerry's *All for Love*.

Back in Manchester, weeks went by without a letter. Had they locked him up and thrown away the key? Then one day there was a knock at the door and it was Gerry, smiling and in civvies. 'They kicked me out.'

'What for?'

' "Averse to discipline." '

Sixteen

*The call for a second front. A day in Blackpool with Gerry before he
starts work as a miner. His experiences in the pit. An accident – the
amputation of his left leg threatened. He goes to stay with his mother
and sister. The Normandy Landings. Gerry's leg is saved. Russia's
gains. Gerry's study course for actors.*

E ver since 1943 when the Russians took back Stalingrad, and a
quarter of a million Germans surrendered, we'd believed the
War was over.

'What have they got that we haven't got?'

'Generals,' said Nye Bevan.

Each night the Russian guns thundered as new victories were
announced. We marched and demonstrated and petitioned. 'Open
a second front, now.' One day Gerry headed a column moving
along Market Street, then found himself under arrest. It wasn't
his politics, it was his overcoat, cinnamon with green lapels. They
decided he was a French deserter.

'Why aren't you in the forces?'

He produced his discharge papers, and when they'd checked
them, reluctantly they freed him.

'Nobody wants me,' said Gerry, and rented himself a large barn
of a room looking out on to Central Station. One bed, a table and
chair, home-made bookcases, and it was furnished. The plumbing
was his own and one gas ring was enough for his cuisine. While he
was still looking for work, a BBC job took me to Blackpool and I
asked him if he'd like to come with me. At the end of the morning's
prospecting, we passed the town pool. Gerry bought tickets and in
we went. My God, I'd never seen anything like it. Gerry dived and
swam like a dolphin.

'Where did you learn to swim like that?'

'At school.'

Later I found out that they wanted him to train for the Olympics but he'd lost interest. I was poodling around, watching him. He dived under me and came up smiling. 'What do you think you're doing? Bring your legs together. You must trust the water.'

We lunched on pale-blue rabbit masquerading as chicken, then struggled against the wind till we came to the Tower Ballroom. An enormous crowd was shuffling around to the tune of 'White Cliffs of Dover'.

'Shall we dance?'

'I do have a job to do, Gerry.'

I didn't like to admit that I'd never been in a ballroom before. He put his arm round me and sidled me in among the dancers, making for the uniformed commissionaire who was directing the crowd, like a traffic cop.

'Keep movin'.'

'How many do you reckon you've got on this floor?' asked Gerry amiably.

'Keep movin'.'

'How many . . .'

'You're causing a jam, mate.'

The music changed to 'Roll out the Barrel' and everybody started jitterbugging.

'Keep circling now, clockwise.'

'Must be three thousand at least,' said Gerry.

'Lookin' for trouble, are you? Keep movin'.'

And the crowd took up the cry.

Suddenly there was a piercing shriek. 'Keep your 'ands to yourself, sailor.'

'Looks as if there's going to be a spot of bother,' I said.

We'd had enough anyway and made for the nearest exit. We didn't take our re-entry tickets. On the train back: 'That was my last fling. I've taken a job.'

'What in?'

'Coal.'

'You don't mean you're going mining?'

'Pendleton pit.'

'That's the hottest pit in Lancashire,' I said.

But I couldn't stop him, nor could anyone else. They took

Gerry on as a ripper, glad to have him. So many young pitmen had joined up before mining was made a 'reserved occupation'. A ripper, sometimes called a stoneman, had the toughest job in the pit. He made the tunnels, breaking through stone and rubble till a new coal seam was laid bare. Pendleton was so hot that the men worked naked but for a loincloth. Gerry drank a gallon of water a shift. One night he grabbed the oil can by mistake and swigged it.

He was in Harry Ogden's gang. Harry was a lean, rangy man, all muscle and bone. He would hear the first drip of water where no water should be.

'She warns you,' he told Gerry. 'Every sound she makes means summat.' The earth was always a she.

'There she goes.' That was Elijah Asprey at three in the morning. When the earth turned over in her sleep, he said.

Corny jokes were repeated endlessly. 'Late again, Stan? Missus lying' on your shirt-tail, was she?'

If sound carries in the pit, so do smells. You can smell a freshly-cut apple a mile away so if anyone farted, it was: 'Cor, Christ, Ben, why don't you tell your missus to shop at the Co-op?'

' 'E could bottle it and sell it to the Russians.'

Before long, Gerry constituted a one-man Communist party, launching his campaign from his one-man party cell.

Man or Mouse?
Does two tons of coal = two ounces of cheese?
CPGB
Pendleton Pit

Two ounces of cheese was the miner's weekly ration.

Each day there would be a new version of the leaflet slipped into every locker. God knows how he found time for the printing and distribution, but Gerry revelled in his strength and his ability to work round the clock. The miners made him a shop steward. Sometimes I would be presented with a great lump of shining coal, smuggled out in the now famous overcoat. I asked how he was getting on.

'Fine,' he said. 'Except for rolling out of bed at four in the morning. I think I'll transfer to the night shift.'

I didn't think night work was such a good idea. Gerry would never sleep in the day with the rest of the world up and about.

I was in a Kendal hotel room writing about Lake Windermere when the landlord came to tell me I had a call from a phone box in Manchester. It was Gerry, sounding very faint. He wasn't well, he said. This was unusual; Gerry was never ill. The phone call itself was unusual. We didn't phone each other: I had no privacy, he had no phone. I went back as soon as I could to find him resting his right leg. The knee looked terrible.

'What happened?'

'In the pit . . . a tub.'

'When?'

'About ten days ago.'

'And you've been here on your own ever since?'

He wouldn't hear of a doctor or a hospital and he was in pain. What was I to do? I tried the herbalist on the street corner. He advised a hot poultice of comfrey leaves. Poor Gerry, I am a terrible nurse. Next day he was feverish and I was frightened. He needed care and attention. That bare room was impossible. I had no place of my own – there was Rosalie's, the old Millers'. He said no. Well, then he'd have to go to his mother and sister. They were living at St Anne's. He would recover there by the sea, if he would go. He had to agree, and I took him to the train. When he'd gone, I stood on the platform feeling terrible. I'd let him go, alone. I made excuses for myself. I had to earn money, I had people to keep, but Gerry had to face that painful journey on his own and he hadn't uttered a word of complaint.

When I phoned at the weekend his knee had been operated on and the doctor warned his mother that it might be necessary to amputate. I wanted to be with him, night and day, but the family knew nothing about our relationship. When I phoned, I changed my name, but Manny, his father, always recognised me straight away.

Was this deception? I didn't like it, but then again why upset everybody for what could only be Gerry's passing fancy? His knee recovered. When he came out of hospital, he asked me to visit him in St Anne's. He'd squared it with his mother. As I approached the little seaside villa, my heart beat fast. It was a charming place, the front lawn bordered with pansies. It was all so clean after Manchester.

The door opened . . . There he was, Gerry, sunburnt and handsome, on crutches. He wore a blue sports jacket and grey trousers, his shirt was dazzling white. How well-cared-for he looked. Mother and sister eyed me over his shoulder. They must have suspected. We took lunch at a polished table with lace doilies and cornflowers in a cut-glass vase. French windows opened on to a garden with white walls and neat flower beds. Conversation was stilted, till Sister Doris described how they'd found his poor knee covered with dirty leaves. I felt I was being accused. All right, but soon I'd be in the sunshine with him. I was to be allowed to take him out in his wheelchair.

He managed those crutches very skilfully, and after a lot of warnings and hand-waving we were off. He'd planned the path we should take and soon we were quite lost among the sand dunes.

'You needn't look so sad,' he said. 'I'm not altogether incapacitated.'

Indeed he wasn't. His loving was as wonderful as ever. As we lay there, the sky pale blue, the sea softly murmuring, I felt at peace with the world.

'I'm always happy when I'm with you, Joan.'

Tea was laid when we got back. I lingered in the hall, to be sure the last grain of sand was brushed from my coat. There wasn't much time left. I was still working in Kendal, it was a complicated journey. Parting was a farce, keeping up the sensible older woman act. When the taxi they'd ordered arrived, I made a dive for it.

'Goodbye! Goodbye, Gerry. I'll write tonight.'

I found I had just time to phone at the station – one more word with him, after thanking the ladies. The train missed the connection at Carnforth, so I arrived in Kendal long after midnight. Nothing stirred on the main street. My bed-and-breakfast was shuttered for the night, so I threw stones at the landlady's window. When she finally put her head out, she threw down the keys and shut the window with such a bang it set her dog barking, and all the other dogs in Kendal followed suit.

I sat on my lonely bed and wrote the promised letter.
A few days later, the balloon went up. It was June 1944 . . .

> *It's here chum, it's here chum*
> *It's the Second Front for you*
> *In spite of their old Atlantic Wall*
> *We're the boys to see it through.*
> *It won't take long to finish it*
> *When we have got their range*
> *And then we can all go home*
> *And live like humans for a change.*

JIMMIE MILLER

I rode back to Manchester in the engineer's van. They sang all the way. Everybody was rejoicing. It was happening at last. We were back in Europe. They put me down near Central Station. I glanced up at Gerry's place, and was surprised to see the light on. He couldn't be there yet, but he was, still on crutches – but whatever about dainty rooms and cut flowers, he wanted to be back in Manchester.

For days we could hardly find time for everyday business. We stopped for every news bulletin but got very little news. Still, we knew we were there to stay. It was not another Dieppe Landing. Gerry was afraid to go out. With his blue sports jacket and his crutches people thought he'd been with the Second Front. They didn't stop to think that he could not possibly have got back from the Normandy beaches so quickly.

'If I get on a bus, some frail old lady insists on giving me her seat,' he said.

Indeed, he must have been on his feet too soon. The knee flared up again. He was back in hospital, facing another operation. I was terrified. He looked so ill.

But there was more bad news to add to our misery. Bill Sharples' oil tanker had been blown up at the mouth of the Clyde. All hands were lost. Bill, wonderful artist, gentle pacifist. Our beloved Bill was gone for ever.

They saved Gerry's leg and he convalesced slowly, at Rosalie's house. There he began his fight for compensation from the coal owners. The money, he said, will finance our theatre. In the evenings we played chess and listened to the news.

The Russians were striking back. Each night we waited for the Chaliapin voice of the Russian announcer. Vitebsk . . . Zlobin . . . Orska. Three orders of the day. On June 25th, Mogilev, Lepel . . . places we had never heard of, yet the heart leapt. Soon it would be over. The War that need never have been. Soon we would pick up the broken threads . . . our life's work . . . Theatre Workshop.

Part Two

1945 – 52

Seventeen

I find a pearl and a lily. The War is over, the old hands reassemble.
Pearl Turner and Lilian Booth join us. Then David Scase and Ruth
Brandes from the BBC. Henceforth, we shall be known as 'Theatre
Workshop'. We celebrate with a ramble in Derbyshire. Jimmie with
us. Rosalie and David marry secretly. John Trevelyan finds us ideal
premises in Kendal. We pack. The ideal premises fall through. Still,
we go!

I let myself in quietly and tiptoed up the stairs
The thought of being home again had banished all my cares
In the bedroom there I murmured, 'Nell, your soldier boy has come'
When a voice replied, in sharp surprise,
'Say, Nell, who is this bum?'

JIMMIE MILLER

After four years of war, I was on my own, in Chichester.
It was Sunday evening. On no account must I miss Pearl,
I was told. She's on at the local dancehall. The place was
packed when I got there. I stood at the back, out of the way of
the jiving couples. Presently the lights dimmed and an angel in
Land Army uniform appeared in a spotlight and sang Schubert's
'Ave Maria'. There was silence when she finished. Then came a
roar of applause which shook the roof.

I went looking for her. Would she sing for a programme
on Chichester? No! Ask our cowman, he's broad Sussex:

Oi be fresh as a daisy as grows in the fee-elds
An' they calls I Buttercup Joe.

And she played the cowman with a straw in her mouth. She was great and I managed to persuade her to sing 'Sussex by the Sea' the following morning.

I sent the recording of her singing to the musical director at the BBC Manchester, and straight away he offered her a role in *The Bartered Bride* and sent her the score. She learned her part by heart and turned up for the first rehearsal dressed in her best. Everything went well till . . .

Rat-a-tat-tat, the conductor's baton on the music stand.

'You are hanging on to that A, Miss . . . Turner, is it?'

'Pearl.'

'Take a look at the score, please.'

She looked. He tried again.

Rat-a-tat-tat! He came and pointed to that A.

'Oh, I don't read music,' she said, giving him her sweet smile. 'Let someone play it over to me and I'll have it in no time.'

'What are we doing here? Coffee break, gentlemen.'

As the musicians made for the door, Percussion left a note on her music stand: 'I'll beat it out for you, pet.'

Pearl had the loveliest voice. She sang her part beautifully. She was young and quick. Wouldn't you have thought it worth their while to teach her to sight-read? But no, she was never offered work at the BBC again.

'Soon I'll be starting my own company,' I told her. 'It'll be different from the others. Come with us.'

A few weeks later, in Oldham, Lancashire, I found Lilian Booth. I'd written a radio play, *My first day in a cotton mill*. The producer wanted a Children's Hour auntie to play it. 'Can imitate a boy, has dialect, age thirty-five, plays younger.' I'd heard some of that BBC dialect. It was so thick that you couldn't understand them, they couldn't even understand each other.

'I'll find you the right girl,' I told the producer and ran for the bus.

I turned left by the Greaves Arms, and soon found a girls' school near a mill. The headmistress was friendly, quite willing to let me have a quarter of an hour with the school leavers. She didn't even try to be helpful, just left me alone with them.

First I let them have their head impersonating their teachers; then they acted a scene from the recent past, leaving for school in the morning, with a volunteer playing the mother. Next came the difficult one, the future, schooldays over – a job in the mill? Lilian, with a face like Buster Keaton's, told us it would be very noisy and pretended to take her place at a loom. I asked her how she'd like to play such a game in a BBC studio. She said she wouldn't mind, and I booked her then and there. The day she came to Manchester I took her to the canteen and asked her if she'd mind collecting our cups of tea. Two actresses were standing by the counter. One, a famous beauty, was waving her arms about.

'Excuse me, luv,' said Lilian.

She was perfect as the mill girl. I asked her if she'd like to join us when she left school. She wouldn't mind, she said.

In Kendal, Westmoreland, I'd talked to John Trevelyan, Director of Education, about my ideas.

'Why not settle here?' he said.

Kendal, the gateway to the Lakes, a sleepy old market town? Still, Trevelyan would be a powerful ally. He was already talking about getting help from CEMA, the Council for the Encouragement of Music and the Arts, forerunner of Arts Council.

Well, wherever we started, it had better be soon. We were all rearing to go. Gerry had been to Oak Cottage to inspect our pre-War lighting equipment stored there. Howard was writing frantic letters from Belgium: 'What's happening? I'm wasting my life. Soon I will be twenty-four.'

I sent him a card: 'I aim to start this summer, come what may. So get out of the army, end of July latest.' Gerry sent him a copy of his plan for a new lighting system, and a bar of soap.

John Trevelyan wrote that he'd been scouring Kendal and thought he might have something for me. I left by the next train and we visited a building which had been requisitioned at the outbreak of War, but with Victory in sight, he thought a little pressure would release it. The name of it caught my fancy – Howie's Rooms. I went straight to the Post Office and expressed a letter to Manchester, enclosing some rough sketches and a plan:

Dear Rosalie,

I have such news, I must tell it you right away. We have a
theatre. It is down by the river and there is a car park nearby. The
main room is 70' long, 30' wide. There are three side rooms, one
40' long but only 10' wide. Altogether enough space for exercise,
training, dancing and a flexible programme area. There are two
exits, windows, lavatories, suspended heaters.

J.T. is very keen for us to tie up with Education. He's asked
me to sit on the County Drama Committee. It might help to get
us a grant. He says he is confident of CEMA backing.

He sees us as educators, functioning as a teaching unit,
influencing the village drama societies and schools, giving classes
in play-writing and the use of sound and light. Paul Rotha, who
runs a village film unit, is a friend of his and he would work with
us. He has already written John Coatman at the BBC to have me
appointed BBC rep here.

Best of all, he promises to build up a theatre library. He thinks
we should not always be putting on shows but spend a good
deal of time on research. Would we make enough to live? I'll tell
you how it strikes me. Why not come as we are? Just the few of us.
Why pay people we have to train in our ways? It would be fairer
if they paid us. We say there is talent everywhere. Let's find it here.

My letter set the cat among the pigeons. When I got back we met
at Rosalie's to discuss it. We'd hardly got started when there was a
knock at the door. It was Howard Goorney, in civvies. There was
a roar of delight.

'They let you out!'

'I was going mad.'

'Going?' said Gerry.

'How's your wooden leg?' Howard came back.

'Two hundred and twenty-five pounds' compensation and he
gave it all to the theatre.' That was Rosalie.

'You can have my bonus too,' said Howard. 'But I'd better
be treasurer. When are we starting?'

'Any time now.'

'Which play?'

Miss JOAN LITTLEWOOD, a London girl, who, after walking from the south in the hope of joining a repertory company, is to appear at the Manchester Repertory Theatre

1a Joan, the tramp.

1b Jimmie, the young fanatic.

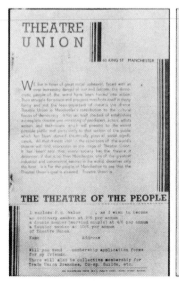

1c 'Come and join us.'

1d 'For the Spanish Republic.'

2a The pioneers in Kendal: (*left to right, standing*) Bill Davidson, Howard Goorney, David Scase and Nick Whitfield; (*sitting*) Kerstin Lind, Pearl Turner, J.L., (*behind J.L.*) Harold Bowen, Gerry Raffles, a friend and Jimmie Miller.

2b (*left to right*) John Blanshard, Rosalie Williams, J.L., Mrs Pennyman, Howard Goorney and Colonel Pennyman.

3a Howard Goorney, who joined us
aged seventeen.

3d David Scase's last job
at the BBC.

3b Bill Davidson quits aircraft design
for Theatre Workshop.

3c Rosalie Williams with us
before the War.

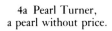

4a Pearl Turner,
a pearl without price.

4b Benedict Ellis,
a rare poet.

4c Tom Driberg,
lifelong friend.

4d Kerstin Lind,
our Swedish nightingale.

5a John Bury,
fresh from the Navy.

5b Ruth Brandes, our first
costume designer and sound operator.

5c George Luscombe, dancer,
choreographer, actor from Canada.

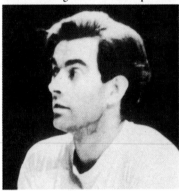

5d Harry Greene, 'Wait!
I'm coming with you.'

5e Josie Wilkinson, costume designer.

5f Marjie Lawrence, actress and
singer.

6a (*left to right*) Margaret Greenwood, Denis Ford and Edna Carson.

6b Barbara Young and David Scase jitterbug.

6c Julia Jones, writer and actress from Liverpool.

6d Edmond Bennett, actor who became Julia's husband.

7a Gerard Dynevor, Aumerle,
Dunlavin, versatile actor,
brilliant always.

7b George Cooper,
the best of actors.

7c Harry Corbett and Avis Bunnage, twin stars.
7d Jimmie Miller's wife, Jean Newlove, with their son, Hamish.

8a Barbara Brown.

8b Yootha Joyce.

8c Brian Murphy.

8d Maxwell Shaw.

8e Glynn Edwards.

8f John Blanshard.

'Depends how many we can rustle up. I haven't written everybody yet.'

Howard brought out his fountain pen and cleared a space on the table. By lunch-time he'd written Hugh MacDiarmid, Bernard Shaw, Rudolf Laban, Kurt Jooss and Nelson Illingworth informing them that our resurrection was imminent, and I added Pearl Turner and Lilian Booth to the list asking them if they still wanted to join us.

'I think our discussion should continue in Derbyshire,' said Howard. 'I can't wait to taste pure water again.'

O n the following day we met at Central Station. It already felt like a celebration, and to make it complete – 'The dead arose and appeared to many' – Jimmie Miller was standing by the ticket office, waiting for us, shorts, Bergen pack and a new ginger beard.

'Call me Ewan,' he said before we'd got over the shock.

'What for?'

'It's my pen name, Ewan MacColl.'

We knew that the Scots liked pen names – Hugh MacDiarmid, James Bridie, Lewis Grassic Gibbon . . .

'He was the one who gave me Ewan. It's from his trilogy.'

'And MacColl?'

'Plucked it from the air.'

I knew it was a precaution. Jimmie had gone on the trot some time ago with Toots' husband and you could face severe jankers if they caught up with you. Well, it was his problem, no longer mine, and it was a fine day. Forget it.

The French silk mill at the end of Lathkill Dale looked elegant as shafts of pale sunlight played across it. In Monsaldale we took off our clothes and swam. Howard wasn't very good and Jimmie couldn't swim at all.

'Whenever I try,' he said, 'I go straight to the bottom.'

Gerry, the Manchester Grammar School champion, offered a lesson, but as he was about to give them a brief demonstration Jimmie launched into a long lecture on the science of natation. We couldn't help laughing. The old Jimmie was back.

Strolling through these dales, enchanting at any time, but particularly pleasant on this day of reunion, we fell silent as we passed the calm water of Wathkilldale. I think each one of us took a silent vow to be true to our theatre. I was with Howard; the others were sauntering along behind us. I heard Gerry's laugh as we walked under the great rock which bellies out above the path. Ahead of us were high tors of limestone. Jimmie's voice rang out loud and clear, singing his own song:

> *There's pleasure in dragging thro' peat bogs,*
> *And bragging of all the fine walks that you know*
> *There's even a measure*
> *Of some kind of pleasure*
> *In wading thro' ten feet of snow.*
>
> *My rucksack has oft been my pillow*
> *The heather has oft been my bed*
> *And rather than part from the mountains*
> *I think I would rather be dead.*

Once this dale had been a giant cave. The rocks which strew the river bed landed there when the roof caved in.

On the train back to Manchester Jimmie wanted to know why we weren't restarting in Glasgow. Didn't we know there was a Scottish Renaissance? Then he brought out his version of *The Flying Doctor*, which he'd been carrying in his pack, and read it to us. Molière with a touch of *Il Medico Volante* and some of his own jokes thrown in, Marx Brothers' style. With some musical-box tunes and a ballet it would pass a merry hour.

'What are we calling our theatre?' asked Howard. 'When it's christened it's born.'

'Well, we've had Action and Union.'

Someone hit the right note. I wrote it across my diary: 'The Workshop'. A theatre, a workshop? Everybody made fun of it, but years after, 'Workshops' sprang up all over the place. Everything was a Workshop, from two councillors meeting in the pub to a baby show.

Next problem. What were we to put on with *The Flying Doctor*?

I had some good material collected in Hull during the War, including the story of a merchant ship which survived an attack by Nazi war-planes. Add a simple human story, set it against the traditional music of the North-East with some new songs of Jimmie's, and we'd have a winner. After a week he came up with a ballad opera, *Johnnie Noble*.

'I could sing the male narrator, this Pearl of yours the female, if she's coming. Rosalie's right for the girl, she dances so well, but who for Johnnie?'

'And all those music and sound cues?'

'One hundred and fifty up till now.'

'We'll need a wizard sound operator.'

The best I knew was David Scase. I'd worked with him on BBC programmes. No one could select, cut and shape sound like David. What's more, he could lay hands on the best effects in the BBC library. But could I nobble him? I'd talked about our theatre, of course, but he was a breezy, happy-go-lucky chap, with a girl in every port. I didn't think he'd want to be hooked.

I asked around Broadcasting House, Manchester, for news of him. There was a honey-haired girl in the engineering department, Ruth Brandes. When I mentioned the theatre, 'I can cut costumes as well as tapes,' she told me. And she had news of David. He would be visiting Manchester in the near future.

When the day came, I had Rosalie standing by. I introduced her, we had drinks together and they got along famously. But rather too soon Rosalie had to go. She was taking a dancing class at the University. 'If you've nothing to do, David . . .' she said.

'Is Bright Eyes in your company?' he asked me.

'She certainly is.'

'Then I'm in.'

He was, and before long he and Rosalie were married. They still are. Rosalie was one of our best actresses. David became Master of Theatre Workshop's Musick and Ruth our first costume designer. David decided to build the sound equipment we needed himself, and he did. It was superb. He also concocted the most spectacular scene in *Johnnie Noble* with Jimmie: men at sea, manning a Bofors gun under fierce aerial bombardment. Clever falls, the sound of dive-bombing and explosive light effects made the stage appear to heave and roll. The sound effects were the best that could be found in the BBC archives.

David knew his subject. He'd been in the Merchant Navy, torpedoed and badly wounded. They stitched his head together but the wrinkles on his forehead didn't match. More and more we began to see Johnnie Noble in him. If David was Johnnie, why shouldn't Johnnie be David?

'Funny idea of casting.'

'Why? David's good-looking, the right age, he can sing and move. A real sailor plays a sailor? Better than *In Which We Serve* with that mournful trio Noël, Dickie and John doing their bit for J. Arthur Rank in a tank at Pinewood.

David was rehearsing as Johnnie when a telegram arrived from Pearl: 'See you Friday. Arriving 16.40. London Road, Manchester.'

I was afraid that the first sight of that station might put her off and asked Gerry to go and meet her.

'We managed to avoid the posters with "100,000 men in Manchester wear a truss" by diving down the steps,' said Gerry, 'but we walked straight into Seven Belly Stott.'

'Who?'

'You know Seven Belly, the geezer who won the pie-eating contest at Dirty Dick's.'

'He had such a nice, friendly smile,' said Pearl.

T he costumes for *Johnnie Noble* were simple. Fittings for the men at the ship's chandlers down by the docks, with Ruth seated among the sea boots, presiding. For the women, sea colours: blue-grey, green and oyster pink. Material that will light well, I told Ruth.

'What about their feet?'

'We can't afford footwear, they'll have to go barefoot. We'll say it's a stylised production.'

'You can't do that with *The Flying Doctor*.'

'That's the least of my problems. What about the set? An interior and an exterior, with door and window.'

That evening, I had an idea. Can anybody draw a cloud? Everybody tried, including me.

'What's it for?'

'We fly in a cut-out cloud for the outside, and a chandelier for the house.'

The chandelier was easier, and Gerry managed to scrounge some grey and blue velveteen for costumes. Howard found a bundle of ballet shoes, a job lot; only none of them were big enough for Gerry.

'I'll wear my old man's slippers,' he said.

'With rosettes on them,' said Ruth. 'But you still haven't got a set. You can't put the play on with only a chandelier and a cloud. Sganarelle has to leap in and out of a window and handle a practical door.'

'I'm thinking about it.' I knew we'd no wood. I also knew that our total wealth was three hundred pounds. Gerry had spent a lot on lamps and resistors. The sooner we got going, the better. We began packing.

I had a surprise phone call. It was John Coatman, head of the BBC, Manchester, inviting me to lunch at the restaurant where Jimmie and I met him when we were barred. He was there before me and he didn't beat about the bush.

'How would you like to be head of Features and Drama in the North Region?'

'It would be marvellous, but didn't John Trevelyan write to you . . . ?'

'Put the unfair treatment you received behind you.'

'I have done so, but the rest of my life is for my theatre.'

He seemed disappointed. I was quite touched. Next day, I was properly touched. A letter arrived postmarked Kendal. I tore it open . . . 'Howie's Rooms are not available nor will they be in the foreseeable future.' The bottom had fallen out of our world and we didn't even know why.

'What do we do now? Stay here? Go where?'

'We do have contacts in Kendal and the surrounding villages,' I said

'We could find a hall and open as planned,' said Howard.

The top and bottom of it was – we went. On 21st July 1945,

we climbed on to the back of a hired lorry and set out on the long road to heartbreak, near despair. We never lost faith in our ability, but if we'd known what lay in store for us we might have stayed home.

Eighteen

The pleasures of Kendal. Rehearsals in Tory party rooms. Mrs Fawcett's good digs. Bill Davidson, aircraft designer on holiday, designs and makes our first set. The wood given to us by Mr Barchard of Hull. Kerstin Lind, from Sweden, joins us. The Labour Party sweeps to power. Our first night. The bomb on Hiroshima. Trevelyan asks us to entertain orphaned children freed from Nazi camps.

Arrived in Kendal, I kept well away from the riverside and Howie's Rooms. For the moment we were working on a top floor in the High Street. If you leant out of the window far enough you could see the mountains and there was a patch of wild land next to the building which could be used when the weather was fine. Frederic Wilson, a local printer, had found the premises for us.

'Ideal,' I said, as we walked in. 'Who's underneath?'

'The Conservative Party. This is their building,' he said.

Mr Wilson was a keen amateur actor. I'd first encountered him at the BBC. I soon discovered that for the citizens of standing in the town, culture meant a yearly production of *Lilac Time* by the amateurs, or Wilfred Pickles telling smutty stories at the Rotary Club, and the BBC was an establishment where only Tories got past the door.

Kendal itself was paradise. We'd found good digs and ate regularly. Gerry and I were at Mrs Fawcett's. She took in lodgers at her house on the hill. It was very pleasant strolling home to her midday meal after the morning's work. We had to pass under an old stone arch and we always snatched a hug and a kiss there for, of course, despite all I had said about having to part when the company restarted, we were still lovers, secret lovers. Even Mrs Fawcett didn't know that we slept together. She knew we shared a room but she thought Gerry slept on a put-u-up in a curtained recess, having given up his bed for me. One morning she came in at the wrong moment, with two cups of tea. I quickly pulled the bedclothes over him.

'Where's Gerry at?'

'I don't know.'

'He must have gone out,' she said.

Gerry was tickling me to make me give the game away. I didn't, but only just. She was short-sighted but, in any case, she had taken such a shine to Gerry that I don't think she would have minded whatever he did.

Flushed with the heat of the stove, smiling at us all, she would dish out steaming broth, her wooden spoon in one hand, an iron saucepan in the other, to Seamus and Sean, the building workers; Martin the quarryman; Noble, her brother; Gerry and me; all waiting, hungry as hunters.

Seamus never stopped trying to talk us into making poteen. ' 'Tis great gargle. Noble's shed in the back yard would serve the purpose, and I'd find you the worm for the distilling.'

Martin seldom spoke, he would just sit dreaming, a far-away look in his eye. Noble was amused by us all. Why did he never take his cap off? After a while Mrs Fawcett told us he'd lost all his hair when he worked in the pyrites mine. He'd been no more than a boy, she said.

We'd given ourselves a fortnight to put the two shows together – with dance routines for *The Doc* to the music of Kodály's *Háry János* to be mastered, sessions on style and long rehearsals for *Johnnie*. It was a tight schedule. When the costumes were made, Ruth operated the sound, music and effects. David said nobody else could cope. He was doing well as Johnnie, with Rosalie as his beloved. There was only one snag. If, at any time, even during the tenderest love scene, a cue was infinitesimally late, he would leap off, give Ruth a rapid bollocking as he inspected the equipment, then leap back to pick up where he left off.

One day, when the men were being divebombed on their imaginary *Johnnie Noble* trawler, a stranger wearing a battered pork-pie hat and a dark mac strolled in.

'MI5?' I asked.

'Six,' he said and sat down to watch us.

When we broke for a cup of tea, 'Got any jobs that want doing?' he asked.

'Could you build a set?'

'Depends . . .' He had a cool accent, rather posh. I'd worked out a minimal *Flying Doctor* set.

'Two pieces, light, portable and stable. They must revolve at a touch.' We showed him the action which involved the door and window.

'No problem, if you have the right wood.'

'Tell us what you want and you'll have it.'

While we got on with the rehearsal, he made sketches and scribbled calculations. At the first break I wrote Hilary Barchard, a junior production engineer at the BBC, Manchester. Her father was a timber merchant in Hull. I told her the type of wood we needed and asked if she thought her father would let us have it, at cost price. She wired back, 'I'm sure he will.' In two days, that wood was delivered to our doorstep, that set . . . a gift from our first patron, Mr Barchard, and Bill Davidson, the laconic stranger.

Next? Of all people, Lilian Booth arrived. It was a gloomy afternoon and we were vainly trying to capture the mood of a dockside street on a warm summer evening. She watched, listened to David's tape of sirens, kicked off her shoes and walked right into the imagined street and, with imaginary chalk, marked a hopscotch oblong on the floor. One after another, the others began watching as she hopped around and wobbled on one leg as she bent to pick up her imaginary chalk. You couldn't take your eyes off her.

'Does your mother know you're here?'

'Oh yes. Is there still a part for me in the play?'

'You just made one for yourself.'

I would fit her into *The Flying Doctor* too, if Ruth could raise a costume. It would have to be a small part, but it would mean that she would learn to dance.

Sleepy Kendal woke up with a start when the next recruit

appeared. She strolled along the High Street, her long legs dividing her silk skirt, her deep breasts sunburnt, almost naked. Heads appeared at shop doorways, curtains quivered upstairs. Bill Davidson put down his hammer. It was Kerstin Lind, our Swedish girl, promised by Vivian Daniels in the days of *Last Edition*. She was tall and dark, her voice low and seductive, quite unlike anybody's idea of a Swede.

On the following Sunday we took a break to show the latest arrivals the beauties of Kendal. It was fine and bright as we set out to climb the nearest peak, our packed lunches in our pockets. Kerstin went on ahead after looking at the route on Jimmie's ordnance survey map. He had arrived a few days earlier, under his own steam. The rest of us lingered along the way, chatting, gulping in the pure air as we began the climb and the chain of blue mountains to the north came into view.

When we breasted the first ridge there was no sign of our new beauty, but we could hear her voice echoing back from the rocks on the other side of the valley. Then Pearl recognised Kerstin's multi-coloured skirt where it hung on a bush. She collected it and we moved on. Another ridge, and not a sign of the songbird. Then Bill spotted a bra on a bush.

'Kerstin! Where are you?'

No reply. On and up we went. Nobody spoke, though we had our second wind by now. At last, near the peak, between two rocks, we found her little white briefs.

'Kerstin!!'

'Marvellous view from here.'

'There she is!'

And there she was, naked as the day she was born, stretched out on a grassy knoll.

She was a child of the sun. No matter where she was, in the frozen north or the deep south, if a ray of sun appeared, her clothes would be off. In the heart of Manchester she sunbathed on the roof of the Central Library. God knows how she got there. But then Kerstin could get anywhere. Few could resist her; yet her life had not been easy. Many lovers and little love, so many conquests but no friendship.

O n 26th July 1945 we were, as usual, in our top room working when David flew in with a radio.

'The whole country's falling to Labour,' he said. 'It's a landslide.'

We'd been so absorbed in our great theatre that we'd forgotten all about the Election. And it was an unbelievable victory. Somebody flung open the window and began shouting the news to the street, but there was nobody there. We were still jumping for joy when the door opened and Miss Hilary Overy, OBE, the Tory agent and a former Wren, marched in, carrying a large Union Jack. For a moment we stared at each other. We tried not to look triumphant, but she couldn't help noticing our joy.

'Lieutenant Colonel Vane holds his seat,' she said.

Pearl smothered a giggle. Well, the honourable and gallant may have held Kendal but we, at that moment, lost it. Miss O. moved towards a wall ladder and clambered up to a trap door. The radio went on intoning, 'Blackburn – Labour returned; Bolton – Labour returned; Bury . . .' We broke early and rushed down into the street to celebrate, but there wasn't a soul in sight. David pointed up. Miss O. had hoisted her banner the wrong way up.

The Tories imagined that the Labour Party was made up of red revolutionaries and Labour's overwhelming majority threw them into a panic. 'From now on, we shall be living in Woolworths,' said Harold Nicolson. Some fled to Canada, others to the Channel Islands or the Isle of Man. They needn't have bothered, five years' collaboration with the Tories, in the national interest, had blunted the keen-edged blade of socialism. There were men of integrity and talent in the new government, notably Nye Bevan, chief architect of the National Health Service. The nation's health had been improved by rationing – brown bread, limited sugar, school meals and milk. Nye Bevan meant to go further – a healthy nation, free medical advice for all. Stubborn resistance was put up by many of the doctors, but they were defeated, and William Temple, Archbishop of Canterbury, dubbed England 'The Welfare State'.

Gerry took a day-trip to London to see if any of our new bosses were interested in us. He said you could see new Labour members sitting around the lobby scribbling notes on bits of paper. Some of them had never had a typewriter, let alone a secretary.

For us it was a time to forget everything but our first night which was fast approaching. Apart from rehearsing we'd addressed the Young Farmers, the Professional Women and the Clarion Club, but we hadn't managed to penetrate K Shoes or the Buffaloes. Bill Davidson's set, complete and gaily painted, turned merrily to the Kodály. I gasped.

'It looks as if it could fly.'

'Well, I was an aircraft designer,' said Bill. His fortnight's holiday was up, but he showed no sign of going.

'Too many new characters arriving,' he said, went back to London, turned in his job, came back and joined us.

One of the new characters was Lilian's mother. We all tried to make her feel welcome.

'I know,' she said, 'but it's lonely for our Lily without her folks.' Then she packed the girl's bags and took her home.

That left a hole in the two shows. How could we replace her? What would be the use? It would mean constructing a replica. You can't replace someone who has been a creative element in the production. I had cold feet. Everything depended on our première. After all those years of waiting I dreaded an anti-climax. The opening night was upon us. With another week we might pull it off. I put it to Howard and Gerry. They held the purse-strings.

'Another week? All those mouths to feed and nothing coming in?' It wasn't possible.

The day dawned. The technical team had worked till 3.15 a.m., then they went home to bed. The rest met at 4.30 p.m. to tune up. We couldn't have been more serious if the hall at Kendal Girls' High School had been for the Pope's lying in state.

By seven the audience was trickling in, the *beau monde* of Kendal and a sprinkling of friends and supporters who'd come all the way from Manchester to support us. We played the Molière first. Then, our *pièce de résistance* – 'Here is a stage, a microcosm of the world.' Pearl and Jimmie were in great voice – but there was an intake of breath as we played a hunger march, and when Jimmie sang:

> *So Johnnie shipped aboard a craft*
> *Well known in the coasting trade*
> *She sailed to Barcelona*
> *Through the fascist sea blockade.*

You could feel the reaction of the locals. In the short time we'd been there we'd noticed how cut-off they'd been from the War. We'd even heard stories of black market locally.

Even so, at the end we were surrounded by smiling faces. Fred Fairclough from Wigan Little Theatre invited us to play there. John Trevelyan particularly admired *Johnnie Noble*. Our Manchester friends walked us home, but they were tired so we arranged to meet at the Woolpack for coffee the following morning.

A s we strolled along the High Street to keep our date, the newspaper placards blazed at us with WAVE OF HORROR, RETURN TO THE DARK AGES. Surely we couldn't have been as bad as that. Gerry bought a paper; the crit would be inside. On the front page the news: THE BOMB! Hiroshima had been wiped out. Despite all the agitation, Truman had pressed the button. Why? Japan had been suing for peace.

'It was to stop the Russians moving in,' said Gerry.

There was no mention of our show in the paper. I was relieved. In face of the terrible news I felt irrelevant. A local scandal merited a headline though: DEN OF VICE FOR YOUNG BULLS, referring to a modern farm up the road which was using artificial insemination.

At the Tudor lounge in the Woolpack we were greeted with applause and congratulations. All the parents were there, Rosalie's, Gerry's and Jimmie's, and there were several friends from the days of *Last Edition*. Were we as good as we had been? Opinions differed, but there was nothing but friendship and good wishes for the future. Someone suggested lunch, but we said we had a company meeting at two o'clock. In fact we felt a bit awkward;

we hadn't been in a hotel or restaurant for many a long day. The happy meeting broke up with fond farewells.

The company was in good spirits but anxious to hear the best about themselves. Everyone repeated everything they'd heard and it was all good. Only Howard gave it as his opinion that Kendal, having seen us, had written us off. Ruth changed the subject and started a wake for the poor Japanese.

David came in late, having been waylaid by John Trevelyan down by the Town Hall. 'He wants us to entertain some children from concentration camps. . . .'

'Children?'

'Orphans. They were flown here from Germany, every nationality. . . .'

'Do they speak English?'

'No, every nationality except English, but they all understand German.'

'Where are they?'

'In a disused ordnance factory about eight miles from here.'

'Robin Bagot speaks German; he was a prisoner of war,' said Kerstin.

'Then call forth Bagot,' said Howard.

'Yes, but he lives a few miles away at Levens Hall. He gave me a lift one day. When I was stranded at Carnforth.'

'But will he help us?'

Kerstin phoned him and he turned up straight away. We piled his green Lagonda high with our props and costumes and he set off, taking Kerstin with him. The rest of us took the bus. The conductor knew the place, a hangar off the main road. The concrete of the forecourt was cracked. Inside, it was quite dark but we could make out children's faces looking at us. Some couldn't have been more than three, others perhaps sixteen or seventeen. They were wearing any old clothes, but nearly all the boys sported army caps, American, British or Russian.

Robin Bagot held out his hand to one of them. '*Wie geht's?*' The boy put his hand behind his back. I noticed the tattoo mark on his wrist. He raised his sleeve to show me a number. Then others began to uncover their tattoo marks. A big boy, wearing a Balaclava, pointed to his sunken left eye; it had been kicked out.

We were their first visitors. They wanted to know what we wanted. David connected the sound. *La Vie Parisienne* echoed through the room. There was no reaction. We set about making the place more attractive; we'd brought Chinese lanterns and paper chains. They watched gravely, incurious, still suspicious.

We had plotted a clowning version of *The Flying Doctor*, adding bits of custard-pie comedy for laughs. The opening ballet met with no response whatever. Robin Bagot then began to tell the story of the play in German, but he'd hardly finished a sentence when the children started to boo, a dull menacing sound. The Englishman in charge walked on to the stage and explained, in Yiddish, that Robin wasn't German. Like them, he'd been a prisoner of the Germans. Later we learned that the children had booed every time anyone had been taken away to the gas chambers.

We cut Robin's story and tried to make our meaning clear with mime and funny gibberish. All the characters wore bright colours save Bill Davidson, as the lawyer. He wore black with a comical black hat and had made himself a long thin nose, but the kids decided that he was a villain and booed every time he came on. At the slightest suggestion of aggression, with a clown's slapstick, or even a feather duster, they booed. It was the only sound we heard from them till after the show. Then they began to talk, in German, or broken German. I thought they'd never stop. A boy of eight started the ball rolling

'Mutti and my papa went into the ovens . . .'

His neighbour chimed in with: 'That's nothing. Mutti and Papa and Grossmutti were taken away.'

And the next one capped that. Bill asked one of the boys where he'd found the red star on his cap. 'The Red Army freed our camp. They gave us guns and told us to shoot the guards.'

'And did you?'

'No.'

Children had been found working on V2 launch sites. The rockets were still at the experimental stage and could kick back and kill them. Cigarettes had been used as bribes by the camp guards. One girl, daughter of a Reichstag deputy, had been a child prodigy on the piano when she was taken away with her family. On her release, she could still play. On the whole, the boys had survived the camps better than the girls. As we left, I asked what we should play for them next time we came.

'The camp,' said one.

And the others repeated it: 'Yes, play the camp.'

Though I'd known the healing power of theatre all my life, those children taught me a great lesson. Playing the camp can banish the camp; playing fear can drive out fear; and aggression ritualised sometimes becomes art.

Back in Kendal it was: 'Do you mean those Jew boys? What use are they to anybody? Have you seen the way they smoke?'

The children were adopted in the UK or the USA soon after, in twos and threes, or separately. We kept in touch. Some sent photos of themselves in their new homes. They were unrecognisable: smiling, well-dressed. Perhaps, having known what they had known, they would help to make this world a better place. Maybe not.

Nineteen

The Lake District not viable financially. Gerry becomes manager.
Will Arts Council assist us? Success at Wigan Little Theatre. Gerry
makes heavy demands on the town's electricity. We prepare Lorca's
Don Perlimplín. Dr Luis Meana, who was in Lorca's company,
helps us. The play shocks Kendal. Jimmie proposes an anti-atom-bomb
play. Lancashire dates. I visit Bill Sharples' parents. Laban and Lisa
Ullmann see our work. Howard and I visit Arts Council.

A t the end of the week, when Gerry and Howard went
through the receipts, they found we had taken less than
a hundred pounds in Kendal and we were committed to
even smaller halls at Grange-over-Sands, Windermere, Staveley,
Kirkby Stephen and Penrith. Our lectures and classes, secured
through the Education Department, were unpaid.

'This isn't going to work,' said Gerry. 'We need better bookings.'

'Someone'll have to drop out and find them,' said Howard.

O n the Monday, hitchhiking to Grange, Ruth Brandes and
I were discussing the problem.

'Well, Gerry's the best-looking,' said Ruth.

Gerry, who was walking behind us, heard and chased her
up the hill. Someone sounded a horn and a battered old banger
wheezed by. Gerry waved. It was Mrs Fawcett's lodger, Martin,
at the wheel.

'Got room for us?' shouted Ruth.

'Don't be daft, he's got all our gear in there,' I told her. Gerry
persuaded him to borrow his guvnor's van for the morning.

Another ten miles and Robin Bagot's Lagonda flashed by us
for the third time. Kerstin had wheedled him into ferrying the
entire company to Grange. We were the last and by the time we

got there, Gerry was actually volunteering to go on the quest for bigger and better bookings.

That night we had a good house, wild applause, and when we got back there was a letter confirming Fred Fairclough's invitation to play a week in Wigan. Great! We were saved.

We rehearsed wherever we found ourselves, after we'd cleaned the hall, rigged the stage, balanced the sound, set out the props and pressed the costumes. Rigging might mean shifting a grand piano, which meant getting permission from the 'committee', which meant finding them, and often persuading them that it was a bit inhibiting to play a show round a grand piano.

'You the party for the drama again? What is it now?'

Each day we worked on Lorca's *Don Perlimplín* and warmed up for the evening show, with games and parallels, often finishing flat on our backs listening to flamenco. The villages we played were austere and grey but then so were Lorca's, I guess, for all their glamorous Spanish names. What is 'Westmoreland' in Spanish?

Howard presented me with the figures for the week as I sat reading an article by Maynard Keynes, chairman of CEMA: 'The day is not far off when the economic problem will take the back seat where it belongs and the arena of the heart and head will be occupied, or reoccupied, by our real problems – the problems of life and of human relations, of creation and behaviour and religion' – sixty-seven pounds, five shillings and ninepence – and a batch of essays written by the local children after they'd seen *Johnnie Noble*. Most of them described the docks, the streets, the seas and storms or the raids they'd imagined as they watched the show, played on a bare stage.

I pulled out of the loading and wrote to the Drama Director of CEMA, a Mr Michael Macowan. I knew that John Trevelyan had already approached him so I simply asked whether CEMA ever gave direct assistance to companies such as ours.

After the Saturday night de-rig we usually met to divide the spoils. This week there were none. When the digs were paid, there was nothing left at all. How would we get to Wigan where there would be good digs, friends and, please God, an audience? Railways and buses were now beyond our reach.

'The first few quid we make,' said Gerry, 'I'll buy a lorry and drive you all about in it.'

He knew exactly where the best second-hand lorries were to be had – at the Post Office auctions.

But as yet we hadn't the few quid. We hitched and on the Sunday night straggled into Wigan Little Theatre by twos and threes, lugging the necessary props and records in packs. We were met by Fred Fairclough and two members of his committee, kindly people with a great love of theatre. Their programme of plays was outstanding; only first-rate works were produced and it was by no means a conservative selection. International authors unknown to the commercial producers found a place in the Little Theatre. The acting and direction were of a much higher standard than the repertory or touring companies.

Fred's colleagues wondered when the actors and actresses would be appearing. We were always dressed for work in the open air; overalls, duffel coats, woolly scarves. After the unloading each one would get on with their allotted task. Gerry was in charge of lamps, cables and switchboards, and when everything was rigged and plugged in, he'd run through the light and sound cues with David operating.

With black velvets up, the outlines of the stage were blotted out, the floor space lost its shape in pools of light. Searchlights tore across the hall as guns roared and flares were dropped, in Wigan with unusual brilliance. Gerry must have been enjoying himself with the Little Theatre's spanking new equipment. It was a stimulating atmosphere. The audience rose to us. The bombing raid in *Johnnie Noble* had them lifted out of their seats. The persistent ringing of a phone somewhere backstage added to the tension. Even if we'd wanted to, we couldn't locate it – all the doors were locked.

The applause at the end stopped suddenly as the caretaker went on stage to announce that the street lamps had gone out. Gerry was still at the switchboard.

'Nothing to do with us, is it?' I asked.

'Wouldn't be surprised if Gerry had used up the whole town's supply,' said David, smiling happily.

Worse was to come. The local trams were at a standstill and the ringing telephone had stopped. Fred and his committee members walked in. They looked slightly shell-shocked.

'How did you think it went?' I asked nicely.

Gerry was busy unplugging some of his cables. 'Smashing,' he said, grinning and slapping Fred Fairclough on the back.

'The whole district is in darkness,' said one of the committee men, the chairman. 'We've just had the Electricity Board on the phone.'

'They'll be alright now,' said David, as Gerry replaced a little metal plate in the floor.

'You must have broken the seals,' said the chairman.

'I had to,' said Gerry, 'or we wouldn't have had enough power for the special effects.' Gerry loved bright lights. If he could have had his way the streets of Manchester would have had Blackpool illuminations.

Wigan never forgave us for plundering their city's electricity, though our week there was a great success with their public, and we came away with our pockets so full of money that we were able to hire the St George's Hall for the next show. The posters were already up:

> The Love of Don Perlimplín for Belisa in his Garden.
> An erotic Allelujah in 5 scenes . . .

magenta Gil Sans on a banner across the High Street, and our new Workshop symbol (we really should have patented that name of ours).

CEMA, now Arts Council, wrote that Mr Macowan and his deputy, Charles Landstone, would be too busy to come to Kendal, but as they had heard from John Trevelyan that we were doing very good work, they would be sending Walter Hudd in their place. Walter Hudd? Forget it, a mediocre actor. We'd written him off before the War.

Rosalie had persuaded Dr Luis Meana, lecturer in Spanish at Manchester University, to come to some of the rehearsals of *Perlimplín*. He had been a member of Lorca's travelling company, La Barraca, so we should learn a lot. At our first run-through he sat spellbound as wild flamenco gave way to grave pavane and black paper birds flew across the white brick wall at the end of the room. When black lace fans were folded across Perlimplín's nuptial couch by two naughty sprites, he asked, 'How long has the old boy got with his new bride?'

'As long as you like.'

He went for a coffee and we set up the props for the next scene. Morning – and on each of the bedroom's five balconies, a different hat – tricorn, sombrero, top hat, Harlequin hat and a sailor's tammy. We'd added to the enigmatic atmosphere of the scenes which followed with strains of Manuel de Falla. Jimmie's was the voice of the unknown serenader. As Belisa listened, a letter was thrown in at the window, a love letter.

Luis came back, bringing me coffee. Belisa was singing, imagining herself in bed with her unknown lover. Another letter arrived inviting her to a rendezvous in the garden at night. Garden scene. Belisa waits. A figure muffled in a red cloak appears, and falls at her feet. She lifts the cloth from his face. Her lover is none other than her old husband Perlimplín, with a dagger in his heart.

Luis said, 'Enchanting. Kerstin as Belisa adorable. Howard great as Perlimplín, but which play is it?'

'You mean you don't recognise it?'

'That's right.'

'But the story comes from Tirso de Molina.'

'Lorca would certainly enjoy what you've made of it, but in Spain it can only be played as a puppet show.'

'Why?'

'Well, Perlimplín is an old cuckold, a figure of fun there.'

Dr Meana stayed to see how Kendal would take its first taste of Theatre Workshop eroticism. He finished up in the wings, playing the maracas. There wasn't a sound out front when Kerstin finished her first aria. Was the hall empty? No, there was plenty of coughing. It was the same all the way through, and at the end? Silence. Silence, followed by a few hisses and cluckings, till one or two began to clap wildly. Luis looked at me. 'Why are you so surprised? Lorca had just such a reception.'

While he was telling me how shy Lorca had been, the Hudd appeared so I listened to Luis intently and let Howard cope with the visitor. Luis was saying that he'd often had to pretend to be Lorca when the company arrived in a strange village. The poet simply couldn't take recognition. Neither could Gerry and we escaped. Howard told us next morning that Hudd had been delighted with the show.

Then we were told that the supper party arranged in Luis Meana's honour had, at the last moment, been cancelled. As he was about to leave, a message came to his hotel. Supper postponed indefinitely. The hostess had been taken ill.

J immie rounded on us all at the next company meeting, when somebody suggested *L'Étourdi* for the next production. Hadn't we had enough frou-frou? A live theatre should be dealing with live issues.

'Like living and the cost of it,' said Howard.

'No, the bomb!' said Jimmie.

'The A-bomb's already out of date. Does anyone know anything about cobalt?' That was Bill Davidson.

Rosalie didn't believe they'd ever drop another bomb.

'Don't be daft,' said David. 'They can't wait to have their atomic war.'

'Frying Tonight,' said Bill.

'We've got to put on an anti-bomb show,' said Jimmie.

Gerry took the despatch case and hitched to Newcastle in search of a big theatre. Rosalie went to Lancashire to publicise the dates already booked there. She was glad of the break; Jimmie had taken to prowling round her lodgings at night, wading in the river and threatening to commit suicide. David was not a light sleeper but the ructions if he did wake up would be nobody's business.

Bill Davidson took Jimmie through the history of the atom from Democritus to Einstein. The rest of us tagged along, trying to visualise the space–time continuum, time bending back on itself, MC squared = E, and Mendeleev's table of the elements. Our world became a mass of electrons, protons and neutrons, and the millions of stars at night mere molecules in a Milky Way. Jimmie was banished to the library and left to thrash out a first draft of *Uranium 235*.

Gerry returned from Newcastle to tell us that the North East held far more promise than the Lake District. He had secured several dates with the help of Alf Simpson whose People's Theatre would sponsor *Bomb Show*. Gerry didn't hang about, he was off to Liverpool, Blackpool and Wallasey trying for dates.

Rosalie brought good news. At Bolton Little Theatre the tickets were going well, largely because the leading lights there, Jack Wardle and Norma Wilson, were old friends. That was how it went. If a live theatre had built an audience, we were in clover; if not, we might as well have stayed home. In Bury the word went round that we weren't theatricals at all because we slept with the windows open and didn't want Guinness for breakfast.

As soon as we reached Bury Technical College I escaped, leaving the company to tackle the rig. I climbed the long, lonely road to the house where Bill Sharples' parents used to live. It was, as I remembered, laid back from the main road, the only approach a grassy cul-de-sac. I had no difficulty in locating the place. There was no other house within sight, just the one Victorian mansion, slightly menacing, even in broad daylight. Hitchcock would have jumped at it. The gate had to be lifted from its hinges, the driveway was overgrown with weeds, the garden a tangled mass of briar, with here and there a dead rose, withered in the bud. The house looked deserted, the windows black and grimy.

I pulled at the china stopper hanging from the front door. A bell clanged. I waited. There was obviously nobody there. As I turned to go I heard slippered footsteps. The door opened. It was Mrs Sharples – or was it? Her hair had turned white, but there was still something of the air of a young girl about her: with her little side curls, bright blue eyes and rosy cheeks.

'It's Billy's friend, i'n't it? Come in,' she said.

The voice was young too.

The house was, as I'd remembered it, a rambling antique shop. I edged round a parrot cage, a stack of *Pearson's Weekly* and a Napoleonic cannon; every available space was hung with musty curtains or tapestries, all faded to a nondescript grey-brown which, when the sunlight entered, looked like a tawny old cat's coat.

'Somebody there, Mamma?' It was Bill's voice.

'It's one of Billy's, Dada.'

Mr Sharples approached. He was tall and grave, like Bill. Behind the opened door was a vast kitchen, tall glass containers were ranged along dark green shelves, which had been placed rather high up. It looked as if portions of animal anatomy were floating inside them.

'You'll have seen this before,' said Mr Sharples as he flung aside a woollen curtain, maroon-coloured, to reveal a billiard room dominated by the rampant sheep Bill had made for *Fuente Ovejuna*.

'Did he ever show you his underground railway system?' A labyrinth of model stations and tube tunnels was spread over the green baize. 'It worked on a vacuum system.' He gently tapped the model, which was clean and shining, free from the overall dust.

'You saw the car he built?'

'Yes.' There was a model of Bill's 'Flying Cigar' on a side table.

Mr Sharples took me to his lumber room. Mrs Sharples disappeared into the kitchen. He showed me a cluster of rubber tubes, needles and washers, his version of a milking machine, a loom which could have replaced the Jacquard. A strange collection of objects which puzzled me . . .

'A failure,' he said. 'Birth control, but it involved an Artesian system. Still, as Mamma put it, it was worth a try . . .'

There was a large portfolio leaning against the wall. It was Bill's – photos of completed sculptures, drawings of projects, architectural studies. He was twenty when he was blown up in the Clyde.

'Tea's infused.' It was Mrs Sharples calling us. On the stairs going down I noticed engravings of Leonardo's works lining the walls. I stopped to have a look.

'Dada inherited these. He gave everything else to the movement,' said Mrs Sharples. 'But Billy loved the Leonardos.' And she moved to a round table covered with sage-green velvet and poured me a cup of very strong tea. 'Dada doesn't believe in private property,' she said, as I sipped my tea from a mug issued to commemorate Charles Bradlaugh.

I didn't like to ask which movement. I only knew that Bill had been brought up a pacifist. She wanted to show me a picture of him. I said I remembered him vividly. 'He should have stayed with us. They never would have found him. You know that a lot of Billy's friends came here, after he was taken. I never turned them away.'

That night we had quite a good audience, all Mr and Mrs Sharples' friends, and Bill's, the Jehovah's Witnesses.

In Blackburn, the hall was grim and the stage looked like a letter-box. I went to meet Rudolf Laban and Lisa Ullmann at the station. I had visited their studio in Manchester when I was looking for a dancer to take classes at Ormesby and there I saw this fair girl moving like a solitary leaf, caught in the wind . . . Jean Newlove.

Finding Laban in Manchester had been a miracle in the first place.

'Why on earth did he come here?' Howard wanted to know.

'Well, there's Barton Swingbridge and the Ship Canal, Trafford Park and the docks,' said Rosalie.

'Engineering,' said David. He was right, the head of a large engineering firm, F. C. Lawrence, had studied Laban's analysis of moving forces, his kinaesthesis, and wanted his engineers to understand the theory.

The industrial North appealed to Laban. As a refugee from Hitler's Germany he had, for a time, enjoyed the peace of Dartington Hall in Devonshire, where an American couple, the Elmhursts, had sheltered distinguished refugees; but Manchester lured him.

'I'd hardly left London Road Station,' he told us as we crossed a windy street, 'When I saw this gang of loaders heaving crates on to a truck and stopped to watch.

'"Looking for a job, guvnor?" said one of the men. He looked like the foreman.

'"Not the way you're tackling it."

'"Think you could do better?"

'"I'm sure of it."

'And without more ado, I lifted a crate and swung it to the gentleman.

'"Quick! Now, we bend, throw! Yes, find your own space!

Have you got the rhythm? Lift and swing. . . .'

He was still swinging when we got to the hall. It was raining and the hall was empty except for a little lady in a corner making notes. Another one entered like the headmistress prepared for prize-giving. I gave the company a quick pep talk, put a bucket under the leak in the lavatory, and went and sat beside Laban and Lisa, mainly to shelter them from the draught. A few senior citizens straggled in. It was raining heavily outside now.

Laban was delighted with the show and gave us a lot of encouragement. The note-taking lady was from the *News Chronicle* and disliked us. The headmistress was Arts Council's representative from Manchester. She loathed us. I asked the company if it mattered what the *News Chronicle* and Arts Council thought so long as Laban was on our side? They weren't altogether sure.

The next morning we were due to have a crisis meeting, but on the way there I tripped and fell in the street, banged my head and lost my memory. When I came to, I'd no idea who or where I was. No wonder. I was in a nunnery. The females in the company had been given a bed there for the night. Presently I heard Ruth say, 'Poor Gerry.' He'd found his way in.

'Where have you been?'

'Liverpool.'

'Are we doing well here?'

He shook his head. 'But we have the David Lewis Theatre for Christmas.'

'If we last that long,' said Howard, and reminded me that we had a meeting with Arts Council in London the following morning and I'd better pull myself together. Everything depended on the outcome. Debts were mounting. Wages were no more. It was 'to each according to his barest needs'.

We climbed into a dingy old railway carriage at midnight and slept.

Twenty

An unsatisfactory meeting. A Blackpool date cancelled. We do well, thanks to James Ford, at Wallasey. Liverpool at Christmas. Jimmie's play, Uranium 235, *progressing. Professor Rotblat helping. Three shows a day at the David Lewis Settlement. The kids, morning and afternoon;* Perlimplín *evenings. Hodgkinson of Arts Council at an evening performance; congratulates everybody. Mrs Summerfield of Kendal sends us fifty pounds. We remember the party she gave us. Report from Arts Council. They will have nothing to do with us unless our actors are replaced or retrained.*

We waited in an impressive hallway; there were Matisse prints on the stairway. A very important person checked our identity on the first floor, and a very businesslike woman ushered us in to the presence of the Drama Director, Mr Macowan, an unsmiling little man. How very sorry he had been to have missed Kendal and John Trevelyan, but he had heard all about us. Howard threw in a safe question for a start. How could we get off entertainment tax? We couldn't pay it in any case.

'Well,' said Mr Mac, 'you would have to be taken over by a disinterested committee or a board of directors who could constitute the disinterested committee required by law before you could even apply for exemption, but I'm afraid it would be difficult to find a board of directors who would be sympathetic to the experimental nature of your work.'

Should I rush out into the street and collect a disinterested committee then and there? 'It would appear that the best method would be for Arts Council to take you over completely. . . . Why didn't you consult us before deciding to start your company?' He took out his little Eversharp. 'Business manager, twelve pounds a week . . . Transport thirty-five pounds a week, which could be reduced if Arts Council purchased a lorry. Wages, speaking off the top of my head . . . eight pounds a week per person. By relieving

the company of all financial and organisational worry they would
be free for creative work . . .' He scribbled some more. '. . . at a
cost of, say, two hundred pounds a week.'

The thought of so much money made me dizzy, but Howard
looked composed as he handed over a list of our returns and
running costs, two pages.

'Your business organisation appears to be weak. A group
earning an average of eighty pounds a week is hardly a financial
proposition. Might this be due to the type of play you present?
Or the locale?'

Howard agreed that we needed help on the organisational side
and the district was proving more difficult than we had foreseen.

'I'm thinking of Lincolnshire,' said Macowan. 'The folk there
would serve as an antidote to those ultra-arty tendencies which
develop in groups like yours. It would be preferable to finishing
up an adjunct to the Left Book Club in Edinburgh, for example.'

I could think of nothing better than a link with Victor Gollancz
and his highly successful publishing house, but I held my peace.

'Have you thought of O'Neill or Bridie?' said Macowan. Howard
asked if they would go down well in Lincolnshire. 'Perhaps not,'
said the Drama Director.

'Well, you produced documentary plays in the army,' I said.

'Yes, but how long does it take you to mount a new play
on the road?'

'Six weeks.'

'Impracticable. I must stress that Arts Council will not consider
a company which is continuously losing money.'

Howard brought out a press cuttings book with raves from
the small towns where we'd played and articles about our work.

'Our capacity for hard work has not gone unnoticed,' he said.

The Drama Director did not appear to hear him. He was
changing the lead in his little Eversharp. 'Limited appeal,' he
said. 'There is a Major Northcut and a woman called Heller in
Lincolnshire; they've already ploughed the land. Now they are
asking for a group . . .' The secretary hurried in with a sheaf
of letters for signature. Macowan cast a lacklustre eye over us.
Howard picked up his press book. We left. Howard thought we
were being considered for the Lincolnshire project and from that

time on kept in touch with Mr Macowan, always enclosing a list of forthcoming dates, but pointing out that they were provisional and could be cancelled when the Lincolnshire project materialised.

From 3rd to 6th December, we were booked in at the Jubilee Theatre, Coronation Street, Blackpool, but by the first of the month not one seat had been sold. We had to cancel. We were broke, grounded. It turned out to be the very place where Mr Jo Hodgkinson, Mr Mac's new Manchester rep, decided to visit us. When he found the place there was no one there. Howard wrote at once, apologising for the inconvenience but pointing out that we had not been notified of the visit, and couldn't have anticipated it.

'More ammunition for them,' said I.

If Blackpool sank us, Wallasey salvaged us. The spacious hall at Oldershaw School had one of the best-equipped stages in the country. James Ford, the headmaster, produced the classics there, ancient and modern. He was familiar with every theatrical technique and loved the art so much that his enthusiasm spread beyond the school to the whole community. He was our white moth. He sensed us from afar, helped us on our way, and at the end of a week of good shows, lectures and ideas exchanged, James Ford became a firm friend and staunch supporter.

'I'm nipping over to Liverpool to see Rotblat,' said Jimmie one day. 'Bill's coming along to interpret.' Professor Rotblat had agreed to help with *Uranium 235*. Jimmie was proud of the Germanic title. A few scenes were already on paper. He'd emerge from a dressing room with: 'David! Give us the opening of the Thomas Tallis. I've got as far as Giordano Bruno.' And we'd stop whatever we were doing – at the ironing board, swabbing the decks or up a ladder – and listen. By the time we broke for a cup of tea, everybody wanted to know more about the church and Bruno.

Uranium 235 was likely to become a sermon or an illustrated lecture. Well, both forms had provided great entertainment in their day. What wouldn't I have given to hear John Donne preach or Rutherford lecture on electrons? Apart from anything else, the lecture hall at the Royal Institution in Albemarle Street is just about the most attractive theatre in London.

Gerry and I had rough digs in Liverpool. Our sink hung from the wall like a dead tulip, the mattress was lumpy, and the theatre, in a street where the sun never shines, on a beat where the cops never walk, was dumped under a hill crowned with some half-built cathedral. Below was all thuggery, buggery, hunger and war, with white-slave trafficking in the pub on the corner. I didn't believe it either till one night Bill was offered a hundred pounds for Pearl in the urinal. Howard asked him why he hadn't taken it and Pearl chased him all round the canteen of the David Lewis to the amazement of three old wankers eternally seated at a well-scrubbed table, occasionally refreshing themselves with a cup of tea and a biscuit for tuppence halfpenny. Through a broken glass panel we could see the pit and the stage where we were to perform. The billiard room would have to be our communal dressing-room. The air was perfumed with Lysol. 'All the same this place could be something,' I said.

'Yes? What?'

'A morgue?'

'An abattoir?'

'No, a centre for enjoyment, work and play. Those old geezers look as if they've never had any fun in their lives.'

My friends looked at me and shook their heads.

Whatever we thought about the place, under-used and neglected as it was, David Lewis, who owned a large store in the centre of the town, was a major public benefactor; this building was one of his many charities. Gerry had impressed several of his trustees or we would not have been booked for the festive season, three shows a day, morning 10 a.m., afternoon 2 p.m. for children, evenings for strays.

On the first morning the theatre began filling up with children of every colour, but mostly Chinese. Were they speaking Liverpool with a Chinese accent or Chinese with a Liverpool accent? And what on earth could we play for them? Instant pantomime? Jimmie would have to abandon his atoms and do his monkey act. Ruth fixed him a costume. Music, lights, drums. Jimmie leapt on to the stage. Bill chased him with a butterfly net. Jimmie produced a banana, pretended to eat the skin and threw the fruit at Bill. Then he took a ladder up to the dress circle and started balancing dangerously along the edge while the kids shrieked with laughter and tried to pull him down. I signalled to Howard to lead the company on in a dance. The manager was waving at me from the orchestra pit. A minute or two later he appeared at the pass door.

'It's going too far,' he said. 'I'm responsible for these children.'

The dance was still going on, but its appeal was limited. They wanted more monkey tricks. Howard tried clowning. The company smiled and blew kisses. Bill shook his fist, and that did it. There was a roar like the crowd on the Giant Racer at Belle Vue. Bill suppressed Howard, and Jimmie, now thoroughly in the mood for *Hellzapoppin*, raced on with a trombone and gave it to Bill. He had found a set of band instruments under the stage and was bringing them on, one by one, awarding them to everyone. Howard finished up with the euphonium. Then Pearl came on got up as the Fairy Queen and suggested a band practice. It was cacophony but the kids loved it.

When I finally brought the curtain down, Howard was in a state of revolt and flatly refused to have anything more to do with such nonsense. 'It's chaos,' he said. 'At least let's try organised chaos.'

We planned a more structured entertainment for the afternoon, leaving gaps here and there for improvisation. Years later, we would have known how to encourage them to make their own improvisations. For the moment, we set competitions when we ran dry. They entertained themselves well enough at least part of the time.

By the end of the afternoon, the company was whacked and there was still the evening performance of *Don Perlimplín* to come. As a crowd of kids jostled out of the building, a middle-aged gent in a dark suit came fighting his way towards us.

'Who's that?'

Ruth Brandes had rescued him.

'Arts Council's Manchester Representative,' she said, and aside, 'The one who'd made the fruitless trip to Blackpool, Mr Joseph Hodgkinson.'

So, in the evening, we played our beautiful *Perlimplín* to him as he sat amongst a group of old beggars, behind a crew of dusky

Lascars who spoke very little English. Curtain down, Mr
Hodgkinson congratulated everyone in sight, including the fireman. I made myself scarce. As far as I was concerned, it was
antipathy at first sight. He was everything I disliked in the
professional theatre, charm as removable as pancake make-up, a
fashionable accent, a liquid smile. The company listened to his
compliments and thanked him very much, aware that financial
assistance in the New Year depended on him. I was impervious.
In my pocket was a cheque for fifty pounds donated by Mrs
Summerfield of Kendal.

She had given a farewell party for us on the eve of our
departure for Liverpool – sherry, little sandwiches and gramophone music. David had looked through the records and played
'John Peel'. When it came to the 'View-Halloo-oo', several voices
started baying like hounds. It was two or three locals who had
strayed in. Bill Davidson was standing by the piano. He asked
Pearl to give him a note. Jimmie looked worried.

'He's not going to sing!' he said. 'He only knows one song.'

'A little ditty in honour of the occasion,' said Bill.

  Oh, they were large *****

– Pearl smothered the offending word with chords –

  ***** as heavy as lead
  With a single twist of his dex-ter-ous wrist
  He could toss them right over his head.

One of the hounds roared with laughter. Bill ploughed on. This
time Jimmie had a fit of coughing and David whispered 'boots' on
the offending word. Mrs Summerfield smiled and Bill sang, 'Boots
as heavy as lead.' But Pearl had had enough; she led the company
in wild applause. Bill looked crestfallen.

'Spoiled my laughs,' he said.

'No, dear,' said Mrs Summerfield. 'It should have been balls,
not boots!'

Arts Council were not so accommodating. Mr Hodgkinson could not recommend us to his superior officer in London. If Arts Council were ever to be associated with us, some of our actors would have to be replaced while the rest underwent a lengthy period of retraining. Learn to time bitchy lines while drinking tea? Drop your trousers while running in from one door and out through the other? We might even aspire to the high camp which passed for Shakespearean acting.

'A lorry driver's son playing a king!' said Sir John Gielgud one day, when we were discussing a young actor's performance of *Richard II*.

'Could the king play the lorry driver . . .?' – J.L.

A rts Council sent me their latest drama bulletin. They noted that their production of a new Bridie play was 'pregnant with the romance and mystery of Gaeldom'. That should be good.

I did not want the company to see the Hodgkinson letter. Well, not at that moment. I showed it to Howard. He was furious, not so much with the criticism, but because the critic had been so full of praise when he met the company face to face. Howard wrote back straight away, asking if one could change one's mind so radically, so quickly? He said he would raise the matter with the Drama Director in London, and he did.

It was after Liverpool that I committed my first murder. No, it wasn't Jo Hodgkinson, it was a gentle soul with brown eyes and long dark hair, an actor of the old school. There had been no one to play Gorgibus in the original *Flying Doctor* and the rôle had suited his style. Unfortunately, he was very much out of place in *Johnnie Noble* and he would be in *Uranium*, but I couldn't face hurting him. He hadn't complained even during the worst weeks. I did the cowardly thing. I announced that we were disbanding. I said goodbye and disappeared. He believed me and went. Someone must have told him the truth. I don't know, but I swore I'd never cast to type again and I never did. Some time later, though, we exchanged friendly letters. He was a gentle soul.

Twenty-one

In January 1946, a short version of Jimmie's *Uranium 235* was launched at the People's Theatre, Newcastle, to cries of 'Author!' and general acclaim. It was deserved. The preparation had been mind-bending but in the end we had managed to produce a historical pageant for the Advancement of Science, with an ambiguous figure at the centre of it – the Scientist. Bill Davidson had to undertake the part, he had the right presence and knew the subject, a necessary qualification since in one section we provoked interruptions and questions from the audience and he would have to answer them.

The first half, 'Democritus to Dalton', had been inspired; the dance sequences, the mime had been a joy to work on. There was a dodgy moment on the first night – Gerry emerged from the night as Theophrastus Bombastus Paracelsus, wearing a Queen Mary toque which was too small for him and wobbled. Luckily the Chorus of Alchemists upstaged him. My *Pietà* was a cinch – a half-naked man carried along by three bowed figures. The second half of the show was more difficult. There was no time to spare. It needed sharp cross-cutting from scene to scene. John Dalton lectured at a table which was merely a roll of velvet, held flat by two top-hatted colleagues who squatted on empty air, a throwback to my school production of *Macbeth*.

We wanted to show the 'Release of Energy' and explain it.

Our atomic ballet certainly looked marvellous but I doubt whether anyone was any the wiser at the end of it. Jimmie, half-dominie, half-preacher, then launched into a morality play. Energy appeared on a leash held by Greed, Lust and Death – an attractive *ménage à trois*, with Gerry as Energy very winning with a few strings for a shirt and tights. One after another the scientists, whose discoveries led to the making of the Bomb, were confronted by the Unholy Trinity. To add light and shade, enhance and contrast these vignettes had been the challenge. The Curie scene, the most impossible, became my favourite. I presented Marie and Pierre's life as a waltz, interrupted by flights of verse. When Death took Pierre off in a slow dance and Marie stood alone in a silver cone of light, she described the actual discovery of radium. Rosalie as Marie glowed. It was one of Jimmie's best bits of writing but Rosalie's discovery of a cache of original Victorian costumes at Minnie Bleazard's shop in Hulme had something to do with it. The Curie dress was our greatest treasure. It was of striped grey satin, the stripes made by using the reverse side of the material.

Jimmie's epilogue was a powerful impeachment of the forces of evil. One had to be careful that it didn't appear to be aimed at the audience, who by their presence and forbearance had earned remission. At the end of the show the stage was packed with young people arguing, questioning, examining our sound and lighting equipment, wanting to know how to start a 'Workshop'. A young man, Mike Thompson, offered to come and help us on the business side. Jimmie and I were to give talks and classes on the Saturday and Sunday. It promised to be a lively weekend.

It was, and in the evening our new friends showed us round the town, and introduced us to genuine calypso, which was all the rage in Newcastle at that time. So much so that we fitted a short calypso show into the repertoire as we went off to try our luck in the mining towns of the North-East, perked up by our reception at the People's. That was how it used to go, weeks of dreadful dates, empty halls, icy digs, then some wonderful character would open the door to a welcoming world where theatre and the arts flourished. It was individuals who kept good theatre alive, Alf Simpson, James Ford, Fred Fairclough, the Wardles in Bolton. Never, I noticed, the appointed representatives of Arts Council.

Mr Macowan had written Howard a rebuke in which he said that from now on he would only accept his own judgement, all the reports he received were so contradictory. It was either opprobrium or adulation – nothing in between. One day he would see for himself.

Meanwhile Gerry was chasing up and down the country, often sleeping rough, trying to storm the castles where the theatre barons were entrenched. He believed he would find an impresario who would put us on the map. Gerry's belief in us was boundless. One night after rigging the worst hall we'd ever played in, we found a notice on the front row, middle chair: 'Reserved for Jack Hylton.' From then on it became a running gag; we even reserved a seat for the Pope in Glasgow. Gerry had just arrived back from London where he had seen Wilson Barrett, Jack Hylton, James Brennan and two powerful sirens, Daphne Rye and Kitty Black, who guarded the labyrinth where the minotaur Binkie Beaumont lurked.

'So what?' said Jimmie.

'So I've got the Empire, Dewsbury, for a week,' said Gerry.

I t was the merry month of May and Gerry smiled as he opened the loading bay doors at the Dewsbury Empire to admit a line of girls, carrying white cubes, hatboxes and sewing baskets.

'What's that smell?' said Pearl.

'Wild animals,' said Rosalie.

'There it is again, piss!'

'It's only the lions,' said Gerry. 'They've just moved out.'

'Are you sure?' said Pearl.

Beyond the semi-darkness, we saw an enormous stage. High up in the gloomy flies a white dove fluttered. Ruth was rather moved. 'I'll go and buy it some maize.'

Gerry was climbing a wall ladder to inspect the switchboard which was on a platform above the prompt corner.

'Our velvets are going to be much too small.' I was talking to myself, the others had disappeared into the deep recesses of the wings.

Two or three big lumbering blokes emerged from some dive where they'd been playing cards.

'Flats? Scrims?' said one. 'Any trucks?'

David tried to convey some idea of our rig. The chief stage-hand winked at his mates. David was irritated. He could work with anyone but after one glance at the Dewsbury crew he called us together and in no time our props and costumes were unpacked and small quick-change tents rigged. Nobody had time to change in the dressing rooms when we played *Uranium 235*.

Gerry was cursing up in the gantry, he'd just stumbled into a cache of empty beer bottles. Howard had set up an office in the nearest dressing-room. I was prowling round the back of the stalls checking the sight lines when three seedy old gentlemen wandered in. The first two were carrying violin cases. Number Three climbed over the orchestra rail and opened the piano lid.

'How do?' said David.

'How many numbers?' said Number Three.

'That's OK, mate. Our music's canned.'

'You'll want an overture, won't you? And you can't have an interval without a medley, let alone a walk-down.'

'I leave it to you,' said David and went back to the rig.

A few scratchy sounds followed, then some strains of *Desert Song*. When David tried the speakers, the three old men went out to the boozer. The stage-hands followed them.

Gerry had left the building to visit the local Labour party and check up on block bookings. He'd been promised real support in our first real theatre. Howard had written to youth groups in all the neighbouring towns and we looked forward to good houses. David had barely run through the sound and light cues when the chief stage-hand walked to the middle of the stage.

'Reight then, that's it, lads.'

'What's it?' said David.

'Twelve o'clock, lock-up.'

'We've rehearsals after this.'

'Re'earse? What's that? No, no, you'll 'ave to find somewhere else to bugger about. All theatres shut from midday till 6.30 p.m. You know that.' And he locked the doors and pocketed the keys.

Gerry had left me the name of the pub where we were staying.

'You go up by the ginnel and continue on till you come to a snicket,' said the old dear in the box office. 'You can't miss it.'

You could, but it didn't matter, the locals were very friendly. So was the pub, with a coal fire blazing in the bar, the only bar. We had a small room on the first floor, with a high old-fashioned brass bedstead, a patchwork counterpane, a comfortable armchair and a round table. What a place! A slap-up supper when we got back each night, boiled mutton and caper sauce, or shepherd's pie, or toad-in-the-hole, all served with Yorkshire pud doused in gravy and two veg on the side. And of course the pleasure we took in each other's company, when we climbed those stairs after a long day.

Gerry was so pleased with his big theatre and his audience organisation that he invited his father to come over from Manchester and see how well we were doing. Manny was still very dubious about the harum-scarum career Gerry was pursuing.

'Dewsbury? A one-off,' he said. 'You'll still be faced with draughty halls and no public.'

He arrived to find a contented company, but the theatre looked vastly empty even with Gerry's hard-won audience carefully disposed to look more. The Empire Dewsbury couldn't pull them in. Neither could we. All we had to show at the end of the week was a well-fed company. Even Howard put on a little weight and David could be heard singing as he hung out his washing in the back yard, sailor fashion. All the blokes seemed to be getting their ettle driven and their grateful landladies fed them like fighting cocks. As actors, they had the edge over the local beaux, in that they were here today, gone tomorrow.

Our next date, Leeds, was a let-down. And the City Palace of Varieties . . . ? Zero. Gerry and I shared our digs with a donkey. He was part of a variety turn, a cut above us socially, though in Chapeltown we were all equal, a pound a week, do your own cooking. After the show, all the lodgers would arrive in the kitchen – a basement room with a copper in the corner – and start preparing supper. The donkey would enter by the front door, take his nosebag in the back yard and retire to the ground floor back with his mistress, a bareback artiste.

At our weekly meetings there were no more inspiring speeches. We knew that this touring, without a base, was a dead loss. I had always believed that we should function where the need was greatest. What about acquiring the David Lewis? Jimmie didn't fancy Liverpool. For him Scotland was our only hope. Mike Thompson, who had joined us after Newcastle, said he thought we'd come nearest to realising our aims in the North-East, and as he'd had some encouragement from the British Council and Tyneside Radio, pending Gerry securing Drury Lane or Jimmie resurrecting the Scottish National Theatre, he proposed to book us a North-East tour, with guarantees. He'd already sounded Newcastle Arts Council and they were not unfriendly.

'They'll be excommunicated,' said Howard.

Gerry said nothing but he went on assembling a list of theatre moguls.

Jimmie and Bill Davidson skipped to Glasgow one weekend and came back born-again Scots. They'd undergone conversion in a river of whisky at 240 Hope Street.

'What goes on there?'

'It's William Maclellan's place.'

'A pub?'

'A publishing house.'

'Not only is there a poet on every street corner,' said Bill, 'but they're all sleeping at Maclellan's, among the presses, wrapped in their own galley proofs.'

'Nationalism's really on the up and up,' said Jimmie.

'It's even managed to produce its martyrs,' said Bill. 'Douglas Young for one. He's been in prison for the cause.'

'He has a long black beard,' said Jimmie, as he began acting all the parts. 'He's a giant. Robert Blair Wilkie, who's a wee feller, used to run to the gaol every day carrying everything Douglas asked for. They're still inseparable.'

'Characters!' said Bill.

'We couldn't see one bloke because he retires to his bed for nine months of the year, only gets up to hoist his supplies by pulley.'

'But you saw Chris Grieve?'

'Of course. All he talks about is The Scottish Renaissance.

Scotland attracting the brains of the world, the place for everyone, not just the Scots. All the young poets flock round him. "He's the comet, we all issued from his tail," Hamish told us.'

'Hamish Henderson? What's he doing?'

'Bringing out his collection of war songs,' said Bill.

'Does Chris still write in the Lallans?'

'Not only Chris. Robert Garioch is translating the Greeks into Lallans.'

'Won't that limit the number of readers?'

'Not as much as writing in dead English. Sorley Maclean writes only the Gaelic these days and Sidney Goodsir Smith has invented a language of his own. His Edinburgh epic is still unpublished. Nobody will touch it.'

'Like the Flaming Poetaster? Has Chris won that battle yet?'

'Not a chance, too hot to handle.'

'I'm glad we used it in *Last Edition*. So you think we should settle in Scotland?'

'We shouldn't miss what's happening up there. Even Glasgow Unity is wide awake these days. They're preparing a play about the Gorbals, the first bit of proletarian writing to come from anywhere outside the USA.'

'Mike's doing well in the North-East,' I told him. 'We're already booked to give classes and lectures at every date, hospitality all along the line and several guarantees. People want to know what makes us tick.'

'We'll be talking all night,' said Bill. 'When will we get some sleep?'

'We never do,' said Howard, who liked his eight hours.

The North-East was stimulating. We stayed in the homes of scientists from the ICI labs, coalminers, chemists, steelworkers, dockers. We ran into charming eccentrics like the Deputy Town Clerk at Stockton-on-Tees, who took us to the local sweet factory and swore it had once been a theatre. He was right. The area which had been the stage could still be discerned, and on the wall treadmarks showed where there had once been a staircase. The tiring room would have been a loft. I could easily imagine Hogarth's strolling players preparing for their show there, the actresses nursing their babies.

At Aycliffe we played to children who'd been abandoned, ill-treated or written off as delinquent. They seemed so gentle. One young boy was holding a length of dark-green satin to his cheek. He wouldn't part with it, held it to him night and day.

In Blythe, Bill and Jimmie's new friend, William Maclellan, appeared at the end of a long grey street, kilt flying, fair hair lifting in the breeze. He had come south to see *Uranium 235*, but having alighted at the wrong station he'd had some difficulty locating us. Nevertheless he seemed quite unperturbed and greeted us with grave courtesy. Without waiting for an introduction or small talk, he began telling us about the great new work on ecology he was publishing, 'before we make a midden of the planet,' he said. He was very knowledgeable on the subject and still talking when we arrived at the Miners' Hall to prepare for the show.

He was lecturing a member of the audience on the subject when the curtain fell. When Jimmie appeared, he declared his readiness to publish *Uranium 235* as soon as the ecology book was launched.

'We stand at the threshold of a new era,' he declared and began quoting Krishnamurti in a soft lilting accent. Then he asked what else Jimmie had written. How many times had I heard that someone was going to publish Jimmie's work? I'll believe it when I see it, I said to myself.

I n Whitley Bay there was no hospitality, and we were all in the same awful bed-and-breakfast. The show kept us warm but out in the street the north wind had a cutting edge. There wasn't a chip shop to be found, so we had to face the prospect of going to bed hungry. Thank God the landlady took pity on us and made a pot of tea. After that we all scrambled into our beds. We'd hardly snuggled down when Jimmie came rushing round to announce that Bill Davidson was turning his toes up and we might want to be there for a last farewell. Bill was lying on a truckle bed, his old green trilby pulled down over his nose, and his pyjamas pulled on over his working clothes.

Someone started to sing, 'His eyes do show his days are almost done.'

'Piss off,' said Bill, opening one eye and quickly closing it again. 'I'm concentrating on being in the most pleasant place on earth, the warmest.' This was one of my pet exercises when we were frozen. Mind you, Bill was a shivery mortal at the best of times. Every year he wore his long johns till May was out and even then he only changed to woolly combinations with slightly shorter sleeves. Roll on Saturday and Middlesbrough. We'd a half-day school there and hospitality.

The hall was ramshackle, a bit draughty, but not unsympathetic. That is to say, you could move the chairs around and even take the piano off the stage without attending a committee meeting. A tall, elegant person, who looked sixty one minute and no more than thirty when she smiled, was quietly making sure that we had everything we needed. There had been hot coffee waiting for us as soon as we'd finished unloading.

'You are all staying at my house tonight,' she said, as if we were old friends.

She must have a pretty big house, I thought. She told Howard that she had seen *Perlimplín* in Newcastle and loved it and that, I think, was how we came to be staying at Ormesby Hall, the home of Colonel Pennyman and his wife, Ruth, the lady we met in the hall. One night starving, the next warm and welcome in a beautiful stately home. Whatever else, our life was not monotonous.

The company came into the palatial dining-room by ones and twos, without formality and wearing no finery, but they looked good, refreshed and polished. I was proud of them. No one was making small talk or being clever. I think we were all a little dazed by the brightness of the log fire, the haze of turquoise and white everywhere, and the smell of good food. Our host and hostess took their places at either end of the long table. There were no placements, we just sat by our usual partners. I was near Ruth Pennyman but I heard her husband telling Pearl and the others, 'Bin here since 1500; had to move out – Cromwell and that crowd. Politics?

Worse than religion. Pennyman? Always been top man round here. . . .'

His wife was talking about Lorca and the Civil War. She had been in Barcelona at the bitter end. Bill managed to find out why. She was collecting orphaned children and bringing them back to England, as many as she could manage.

The conversation became fragmented as the food went round, good soup and fresh fish. The Pennymans began to draw us out about our travels and soon our favourite stories were being told, half-myth by now – drily related by Bill, with sardonic comments from Howard and gales of laughter from the rest. While everyone was laughing, Gerry slowly got up, walked over to the fireplace and scraped the fishbones from his plate into the fire. Then he turned with one of his smiles and took his place at the table again.

'It's all right . . .' Mrs Pennyman began, but she didn't finish.

The next day being Sunday, we were invited to take our ease and enjoy the house and grounds. 'We're very lucky,' said Ruth Pennyman, and invited us to stay on while we played the surrounding towns. Gerry and I strolled past the Tudor wing and on through a cobbled courtyard just as a clock in the Vanbrugh-style archway chimed the hour. I could see my companions here and there, in the park, figures in a sunny landscape. When we passed each other we smiled, rather foolishly, as if in a dream.

At lunch, Ruth Pennyman started asking me about the training session she had seen at St John's Hall. I had noticed her there, watching, too shy to join in. What about acting, she said, can it be taught? 'Everybody can act,' I said. 'Aren't we all acting most of the time? Performing is something different. Our politicians, popes, barristers and rabble rousers are all actors, but con-men, spies, crooks and plain-clothes policemen are even better.'

'What is a good actor?'

'Part priest, part poet, part clown.'

'And what were those exercises for yesterday?'

'To develop initiative, excite curiosity, exercise the imagination.'

'Too much sensitivity may only cause more pain.'

'I think that has to be risked.' I began to talk about reversing rôles in an argument when we were joined by her husband.

'Put on *Henry V* here once,' he said. 'Did you see that ancient oak down there by the village?' And he pointed to a far corner of the park, almost out of sight.

'That was my starters post. I was the messenger. At a given signal, rode split-arse across the fields and arrived dead on cue.' He loved rolling his tongue round his well-chosen phrases.

'Rather large lady is my sistah,' he said as he strode off to meet her.

For Ruth Pennyman, theatre was almost an obsession. She wrote plays for a local drama group, entered competitions with them and travelled to any out-of-the-way village where she might find some old custom surviving. She was fascinated by our exercises and the training. Before we left, she asked if we would come back and conduct a weekend school for local youth clubs. I said yes, wondering if it would be possible.

Soon after Ormesby we faced the most bizarre of all our North-East bookings – a week at Billy Butlin's Holiday Camp at Filey. Who would have thought of that but Gerry? He had kept it a close secret, partly because he liked secrets, but mainly because he had seen how disappointing it was when things fell through.

'This will show whether we're popular or not,' he said. 'All we need is a chance.'

Some chance. We were well paid, fed and housed and the all-in wrestlers showed us some of the tricks of their trade. There was only one performance area for all the different entertainments. We came on after the wrestlers, so they told us to watch from the back and learn, which we did. The shows were continuous, and free – one never-ending variety show. The large audience gave us the same treatment as they gave everyone else, whistling, shouting comments and clapping each scene in *Uranium 235* as if it had been a music-hall turn. The title had not been announced, which was probably just as well.

Billy Butlin's stewards, his Redcoats who ran the place, were amiable tough guys who'd been with him since he started. Even so he'd turn up unannounced and snoop around to be sure everything was being run exactly as he'd ordained. They respected him for it and worked their balls off for him. They wakened you in the morning with 'Good morning, campers', called you at meal-times, 'Grub-up, campers', announced the day's programme, ran the sports events, games and competitions, told you where to park your kids if you wanted a few hours without them and where to find them when you lost them.

It may sound like hell to you but it was happy hell for the campers, and cheap. Holidays were rare for most people unless some elderly relative fell off the perch and you got a share of the insurance money. Even then it would only mean a few days of squalling kids, sand in the ham sandwiches, peeling shins and a knotted hankie over your head against sunstroke, or worse still, rain, rain and nowhere to go.

The waiters dropped us second helpings at every meal as they swayed around balancing a great pile of dishes on a tray. The dining-hall was enormous and every time a piece of crockery was dropped there'd be a roar of applause from a thousand throats.

'We did have fun, luv.'

At night the last dance was always a rumba and the entire population would form a line, each one holding on to the backside in front of him as they snaked about all round the camp, but never beyond it.

'We enjoyed ourselves so much we didn't want to go anywhere else.'

'Good night campers. Lights out.'

One day Gerry and I climbed the fence next to our chalet and made for the beach. It was only a hundred yards away but nobody ever went there. As we stood on the shimmering sand there wasn't a soul in sight.

We'd been installed in camp only a day and a half when notes in code began to appear under our breakfast plates and muttered messages were passed as we queued for a second cup of tea. 'Mass break out during Housey Housey.' Plan rejected. Bill Davidson had started an escape game and passed round a plan for a tunnel with 'Digging starts after the show in Stalag 111'. Daft sod. It was a good game though.

It was a good-tempered week, but what with all-in wrestling tricks and learning Old-Time dancing, we didn't manage any

rehearsals. On the Friday a crowd of journalists turned up. Some of
them, for want of anything better to do, wandered in to our show.
Afterwards Gerry and I had a drink in the bar with Ian Mackay, a
jovial journalist from the *News Chronicle*. He looked up at the lurid
fresco behind the bar.

'Well,' he said, 'the place isn't as bad as it's painted.'

Nelson Illingworth, our friend the Australian opera singer,
came all the way to Butlins to see us and to inspect the camp.
Afterwards he invited us to spend a week at his home on the
Thames near Staines. There he would give our voices some much
needed attention. We were all keen to go – good voice training is
rare. You may develop a wonderful operatic noise but ten to one
nobody will understand a word you're singing. That's all right for
Covent Garden; actors have to be understood. The visit to Staines
depended on our having a week out and a little cash in hand. The
Butlins date provided the cash, so when a firm date at Pilkington's
Glassworks fell through, we packed our rucksacks and took the
road south.

Twenty-two

Time for voice classes at Nelson Illingworth's bungalow, once owned by Ellen Terry. Theatre Newsletter *befriends us.* Our Time *praises us. The debts are mounting. A young woman gives us a hundred pounds, says she can raise all the money we need. The Pennymans want us to run a residential summer school. Mike Thompson appeals to Arts Council; is snubbed. Howard tries Lady Dugdale. His letter passed on to Sir Kenneth Clark, who recommends Arts Council. Ruth Brandes receives a letter from Ivor Brown of the* Observer. *He recommends Arts Council. The Summer School and bright students.*

Nelson's place had been one of Ellen Terry's homes, a rambling riverside bungalow where the Thames was green, the trees were green and the main rooms were covered with faded frescoes of male swimmers in knee-length bathing suits and ladies in straw boaters waving at them from houseboats. Even the rooms seemed bathed in a pale green mist. Here and there wood carvings, perched on pedestals, discouraged arm-waving and wild gestures. They were the work of Leon Underwood, a friend of Nelson's who had taken his Prix de Rome in Iceland rather than Italy. We seemed to have stepped back into a past which seemed remote but yet was part of our lifetime. A record of Chaliapin was playing as we arrived, and Nelson's rowboat was slapping up and down at the water's edge. His garden was inviting. How pleasant it would be to sit by the weeping willow and read and talk.

'We're the Moscow Art Theatre taking a day off at Stanislavsky's dacha,' said Howard as Chaliapin got deeper and deeper and slowly came to a halt.

'Sorry,' said Nelson, bending his head as he came out from the door which led to his den. 'I didn't wind him up enough.'

He wound us up, straight away. No respite till we could count to fifty with the merest intake of breath at twenty-five. There we were every morning, singing, chanting, producing pure vowels and throwing consonants into them like straws into a stream. Half an hour of Nelson and I felt quite drunk.

I thought Kerstin sang like a bird of morning but Nelson didn't agree: 'You've thrown away pure gold for a silly head voice,' he told her. She got mad and denounced him. 'That's it. That's your true voice,' he told her.

I was rather glad that Pearl had gone home to Chichester for the week. She was pregnant and though we said we'd all help with the baby and bring it up among us, she was not converted. She loved her husband and he had told her that he wanted her home.

Jimmie turned up late, very broody. Either he was in love again, or it was still Rosalie. In any case he didn't think there was anything to be learnt from *bel canto*. To make matters worse, Nelson thought Gerry marvellous, virile, handsome, born to act. Next morning Jimmie disappeared. I explained to Nelson that he was suffering from an obsession.

'Tell him to go to the pictures,' said Nelson.

Then David Scase arrived. He'd been to visit his old pals in the BBC. He was amazed to hear Bill Davidson singing away with the rest of us. We were all used to Bill's croaky voice and Nelson didn't seem to mind it, but he kept detecting those flattened Cambridge vowels of Bill's and picking on him. Colonel Pennyman had put it in a nutshell: 'Bill? Clever chap but not an enunciator by naytchah.'

'Vowel is voice,' said Nelson sonorously. 'Let it come from the solar plexus. No, Bill, that's a diphthong. Like this . . . ,' and he gave out a siren sound which shook the window-panes.

David was smiling at the thought of Bill singing like Nelson or Chaliapin.

'Try "Pluck thy strings, proud gipsy, palpitant with passion . . ." '

Nothing would have induced Bill to recite anything of the sort.

'You don't hear any accent when I speak,' Nelson went on . . .

'Oh yes I do,' said Bill, his cool drawl more pronounced than ever, 'a distinct Australian twang,' and he turned his eagle eye on his tormentor. There was a moment's silence, then Nelson tugged at the woolly bonnet which he always wore and launched into the death of Boris, in Russian.

'You don't hear it when he sings,' said Bill magnanimously.

I sometimes thought he modelled himself on Dr Quelch, the

headmaster at Greyfriars. Bill knew whole passages of *The Magnet* by heart.

Early each morning, Kerstin and Gerry set off for Staines by rowboat. They did the provisioning. The rest of us went swimming or cleaned up. We slept all over the house or out in the garden, in sleeping bags. After the voice sessions, we read plays. Tirso de Molina's *Don Juan*, Lorca's *Blood Wedding* and Jimmie's adaptation of *The Agamemnon*.

Why was Kerstin sad?

'Midsummer night,' she said. 'At home, we celebrate the longest day with bonfires and midnight parties.'

As a rule, Kerstin wouldn't be seen dead at a party . . . but at midnight, she stood quite naked by the river, singing, then dived in and swam towards the opposite bank. Gerry stepped out of the darkness and went in after her. He beat her to it, diving under her. Then the two of them went gliding with the tide – a couple of water babies. I knew Gerry loved her. Was he falling in love with her? I suppressed a feeling of jealousy. Kerstin had so many lovers, so many wanted her. In any case, jealousy destroys reason and has nothing to do with love. I loved Kerstin and still do.

*O*ur Time published a glowing article about us. *Theatre Newsletter* called us the most exciting theatre company on the road.

On top of that, Ossia Trilling and Andrew Campbell, who edited *Newsletter*, offered us a desk at their office in Dean Street, Soho. Arts Council still ignored us and we were as broke as ever. Our creditors were threatening. Even so, we would have to mount a new show. Meanwhile. . . . Rig – de-rig. Load – unload. Stockton. Aycliffe. Darlington. Brancepeth. . . . Marvellous house at Brancepeth, my beloved Basher Marshall and family in the audience. No one at all at Crook, but just as Howard and Mike Thompson were totting up the debts a wild young woman burst in on them. 'I'm Nina,' she said, 'and I'm mad about you. I've read all your notices and I want to join you.' When she heard about our financial situation, she was heartbroken.

'Here, take this. Please,' she said, handing a wad of notes to Mike. 'I'm going straight back to London to raise all the money you need.'

Our first weekend school at Ormesby had been well organised and the weekend went so well that the Pennymans asked us to spend the whole summer running a residential school with regular weekend sessions for local people. They would organise it. We said yes, wonderful, and hoped we wouldn't be in the Debtors' Prison by then.

Nelson Illingworth wrote from the Blasket Isles where he was on holiday, to say how keen he was to work full-time with us and that with a real effort we could revitalise the dying English theatre. That's what we thought once, but the dying English theatre had proved a good deal stronger than us. It showed no sign of giving up the ghost.

'You should all go and be stockbrokers – the English don't want art,' George Bernard Shaw once told me. Why didn't we give up? Why go on playing those sad little halls? Was that where we thought the theatre should be?

Mike Thompson had not set much store by the flamboyant Nina. He wrote to the head office of Arts Council in London, asking for the forms which had to be filled in when you applied for a grant. He followed it up with a letter to a Mrs Fox in Edinburgh and a Mr Mather in Newcastle, regional reps of Arts Council. He asked them for help in organising tours in their areas. From London came the reply, 'There are no such forms.' From Edinburgh, after a second letter asking for a reply to the first, 'Do not presume to mention Arts Council in connection with your company when organising a tour of this area.' From Newcastle, a friendly note, offering a guarantee of fifty pounds for a school booking.

Inspired by the Pennymans, Howard wrote to Nancy, Lady Dugdale, their neighbour, asking for help with Arts Council. She passed the letter on, with cuttings and photos, to Sir Kenneth Clark, who was on the Central Committee of Arts Council. He replied, 'A well-reasoned application should do the trick. Your Theatre Workshop is obviously a very serious affair.'

Gerry went off to London and tried the cultural attaché at many embassies. He knew that somewhere in the world a door would open to us. We all took to letter-writing. Anyone and everyone who might be interested in our survival received a letter. Ruth Brandes added a postscript, 'Even a donation would help.'

Bonamy Dobrée, who had liked us in Manchester, forwarded my letter to Ivor Brown of the *Observer*. Brown replied, saying that I should apply to Arts Council.

The weather could not have been fairer as we hitched to Ormesby to prepare for our much-heralded summer school.

The place was transformed. The Tudor wing had been redecorated throughout. The refectory with its late sixteenth-century fireplace was now furnished with two long tables. The kitchen and scullery had been modernised. Upstairs there were single and double bedrooms, and two dormitories. From the passage which ran along three sides of the building, you looked down on a central courtyard. It gave the place a cloistered atmosphere. The rooms had been given plain beige floor-covering, and light blue curtains and coverlets. A bed, table and bookshelves completed the picture. For rehearsals there was a long room over the stables. The stables themselves would house our equipment. There was a kitchen garden, ours to cultivate.

Ruth Pennyman's locals had done the work. They were all coming to our first weekend school, which would be followed by a fortnight's residential course. Students were coming from every town where we had played. There had been no need to advertise. We could not accommodate all the young people who applied. The company would function as guides, entertainers, cooks and bottle washers. They would also assist with the classes and keep everybody happy. And the reward? Bed and board at beautiful Ormesby.

I was pinning up the weekend's programme as the first students arrived. I felt as nervous as they looked.

'Oh, hullo! Do come in. Make yourselves at home and . . . welcome.'

And from then on it was TOTAL THEATRE. I don't think anyone stopped playing or play-acting night and day. It was beautiful summer weather, so the morning started with deep breathing and dancing on the lawn. This was not obligatory; nothing was. If you wanted to tune up on your own there was a park and woods to wander in, your solitude made more pleasant by the knowledge that, at any moment, you could join the rest of us. The long room was available if we needed it but nearly all the work took place outdoors. Any time of the day you would hear young people singing or calling to you as they revelled in the wide, sloping parkland. Our classroom was boundless, limited only by the distant fringe of trees which hid the village.

Explaining our sources was Jimmie's territory. The agitprop movement, the American Left Theatre and the Revolutionary Theatre of twentieth-century Germany and Russia were unknown in England, so Jimmie had an open-mouthed audience, and when several refugees from Hitler dropped by they were bombarded with questions about that extraordinary flowering which had been so savagely crushed in Germany.

Jimmie had not lost his power to hold an audience. He would launch himself with a short peroration, and then his rhetoric would flow in a turbulent stream with quotes flung on the air like paper darts. His conclusions were often allusive, and sometimes made your hair stand on end. It was heady stuff. He would analyse a society by its dramaturgy and vice versa, jump from the apple in the Garden of Eden to the tree in Marvell's garden without a pause for breath. He would enlarge on Shakespeare's fear of civil war, drawing on the old queen's bastardy and the usurpers waiting in the wings – Essex and Jamie, her Macbeth. It was not long since Jimmie had started reading Shakespeare, and he was enjoying him all the more for not having read him at school.

One day he took a crack at *Lear* – the same theme, usurpation. Only in this case Lear was usurping himself, said Jimmie, and that was just as bad as usurping the other fellow. To crown it he sang the ballad of King Lear and his Daughters. Where had he found that tune? Was it his own or dredged up from some forgotten book of airs? You never knew with Jimmie.

I've seldom been known to give a good talk. I'll start on the wrong foot and get into a tangle of tongue-twisters, all the profound thoughts I'd sorted out beforehand having flown out of my head. As well I didn't accept all those invitations from American universities much later on. I would have had to give them their money back.

Rosalie, a graceful dancer, ran the movement classes and had everybody jumping, whirling, gliding and twisting to the tinkling beat of the tambourine. By this time we had absorbed the rudiments of Laban, but still used some of the Dalcroze exercises and methods of relaxation we'd developed ourselves. The Colonel was always nearby watching, Mrs Pennyman sometimes. When she came they would both join in. On the first Saturday a group of young people from the village was pirouetting across the lawn, led by Rosalie.

'Little brunette, rather nubile – the one with the pink knickers, can't help noticing.' It was our host standing beside me. He had a definite penchant for the pretty gals. On the Sunday he came upon Pearl sitting on a fallen tree.

'Have you ever been kissed?' he asked her. This was funny because she was by now heavily pregnant. 'Because you're going to be kissed now.' And he gave her a peck on the cheek and strode away.

He was an innocent creature, with his Edwardian English – slightly army, which improved his jokes. He loved to pass judgement with a good round phrase. Watching Kerstin . . . 'Magnificently straight in the leg, rather deep in front, for a Swede.'

He had us all taped. I heard him telling someone that I was the CO keeping them all in order.

'Howard? Pure Persian.'

Among the students there was a tall young man who had arrived in the uniform of the Fleet Air Arm. He didn't seem awfully good at dance movement but waved his arms around dutifully when Rosalie told him to float. In fact he couldn't take his eyes off Rosalie and it wasn't her pert little face. I followed his gaze – Rosalie was wearing a well-cut leotard, a very short one without arms or legs, so that only a bar of silk separated her pretty and rather plentiful little bush from the outside world. This young man was early for all the classes and decided that he wanted to stay with us. I always thought John Bury was won by Rosalie's pretty mound of Venus. He had been trained as a chemist and was also attracted by Gerry's amazing collection of gelatines. He would have liked to take over the switchboard but he knew nothing about lighting. 'Call me Camel,' he said, but we never knew whether it was because he could drink enough to last him a week or because he had a camel's aloof expression above his deeply cleft chin.

My contribution to the school was pure chicanery. I didn't talk, I just made everybody work. They would all be sitting there, waiting to be entertained, or at least edified, and I'd say, 'Right? All out. Come into the room exactly as you did the first time. Follow the same people, say the same things, walk the same way, recapture the same mood.' It was always chaos, then correcting, checking up on each other, talking to a stranger, maybe for the first time, the ice would be broken. It would be quite a time before such a simple scene could be reproduced in the mood and atmosphere of the first entrance. It might be simple but it had to be carefully manufactured, the beginning of the art of acting.

'Every performance a first time . . .'? A world of problems opens up. Many give up trying to find a solution. They play in a curious past tense, nearly all the 'marvellous performances' are played in this way. If a performance is truly marvellous, you do not notice it as such, you watch the play.

For these first encounters I might propose an identity game, asking each one to step through an imaginary doorway and tell us who they were. We all have to face this at some time in our lives. Few can stand feeling tall enough, broad enough, important enough to just be themselves. This one is inaudible, that one needs opposition, a third needs a title, or forgiveness. If it does nothing else, this game moves the party along. Soon we know everybody's name. If we don't, try a memory test, eyes shut. Then if you don't remember the name, think of a nickname which summarises the person. If we are to contribute to a work of the imagination we must first free ourselves, and find each other. It's Blind Man's Buff. In fact this is another good game to start the ball rolling. As work progresses you will find useful stimulus in parallels. And if a problem vexes you, don't keep picking at it. Move away. Try the opposite. Who can draw the right line, first time?

A company of actors doing their best one day. Each one playing his part for all it's worth, but it's dull. What's wrong? This one is standing with his back to that one, and not even noticing him. They are all unaware of each other, and they are supposed to be part of a small community governed perhaps by fear. Stop! Let's pretend we are a shoal of fish swimming through dangerous waters. It worked, and partly because the game was amusing and everyone had stopped working on the precise problem.

With the company's help it didn't take long to break the ice at Ormesby. Shyness vanished and there was no pretentiousness or snobbery. When a feeling of quiet confidence was achieved, the imagination games began.

On the Sunday morning we were all outdoors, quietly trying one of Laban's movement scales, when the Colonel, dressed in his Sunday best, came striding across the park. 'I say, where's Kerstin?' It was a question almost everybody asked at some time or other.

'Doing her voice exercises somewhere, Colonel.'

'She's doing very well. Nobody's listening to the vicar. Rather afraid he'll throw in the sponge if we don't put her on soft pedal.'

We dispersed, looking for the lady. Ruth found her – sitting up a tree, almost naked, singing a Swedish love song. I could see that the Colonel was amused, though he tried not to show it. Anyway, he didn't go back to church, and when the service was over some of the villagers went bustling about, trying to find the owner of that disturbing voice.

The evenings passed very pleasantly. Supper over and the chores done, music came into its own. Some would gather round the piano in the rehearsal room and sing part songs, others would sit listening to Jimmie singing with Bill or young Denis Ford accompanying him on the guitar. Denis was Mr Ford's son, he'd come from Wallasey for the school.

One night Bill came strolling into the refectory wearing his old titfer and a pair of dark glasses. He'd been one of the *plongeurs*, as he called them, and when he'd finished his stint at the sink he'd picked up the slate, rubbed out tomorrow's menu and written 'Take one'.

'OK everybody, settle down. We're taking it from the shoot-up. Props! Guns please. Lights. Cameras.'

In no time everybody was in on the act . . . Bill directing, improvising the plot as he went along. Everybody played their favourite part and made up their own dialogue. Denis loved leaping in the air and falling flat when he was shot. Jimmie was a gangster, Pearl a gangster's moll. Bill chivvied his team of difficult technicians from set-up to set-up. Jimmie changed rôles, became a cameraman, using a biscuit tin for a camera. The shooting was transferred from room to room over the whole house, then out into the courtyard and up on to the roof. Everybody was included, even two sweet ladies who suddenly appeared. Denis threatened them with a death ray and they fled to the Pennymans' house in terror. It was well past midnight when Denis Ford finally expired in an acid bath.

The amazing feats performed that night, acrobatic and histrionic, made you realise how lively invention is when everybody is in on the act and enjoying himself, instead of standing around waiting to give a performance. The only snag was those two sweet ladies. They were from Arts Council. Well, they should have realised that the death ray was only a pocket torch.

The film game went on night after night, till everybody had invented somebody or something they'd had in mind, perhaps all their lives. We had Westerns, horrors, historicals, gangsters, and the pace was fast and furious. I think we felt the need for fantasy, the War wasn't far behind us. Bill had not fully recovered from Peenemünde despite his cool manner, and a young man who called himself Benedict Ellis turned up and he was an even worse case. At first he enjoyed the exercises, then he'd go off and spend hours listening to Mozart. One night he confided in Gerry. He'd been an officer in the army. At Caen, badly wounded, he lay buried under his own men. Some dead, others in great pain. He could not forget it. Ben was striking-looking with black hair and brilliant dark eyes. He wrote, designed, and loved working on the lighting.

I hoped that all I had learned would be of some use to these enthusiasts who looked at me so expectantly. Theatre is therapy for the sufferer, created by sufferers such as the man who had both Iago and Othello in his head, and knew such fear of the dark.

At Ormesby there was a lot of laughter as we worked and played, slept little, and enjoyed ourselves.

Twenty-three

Gerry's lion cub. Au revoir, Ormesby. Pearl is going home to have her baby. Isla Gledhill will replace her. Margaret Greenwood, Edna Carson, Camel, John Blanshard and an exciting young writer, Benedict Ellis, join us. Freddie Piffard becomes our fourth director, with James Ford, Bill Maclellan and Hugh MacDiarmid. Bill Mac publishes Uranium 235. *Our first tour of Scotland. We gatecrash the Edinburgh Festival and attract all the poets of Scotland. Hospitality is great, but David and Ben spend a night in gaol. Jimmie receives plaudits from James Bridie. A surprise invitation.*

Gerry and I shared a room. I was still reluctant to let anyone know about us. It wasn't shame or love of privacy. I just wanted to stave off Jimmie's attacks on Gerry. The sight of our happiness seemed to infuriate him; he didn't like anyone to go their own way. He was still trying to keep his hold on Rosalie. Perhaps all these attractive new arrivals would take his mind off us. They did. First a local girl, Margaret, who arrived early each morning on her bicycle to smile up at him as he stood by the window of his room, waiting for her. That didn't last. Jimmie was in his Don Juan period.

Gerry was a very private person, but he would look in on any class I was taking, watch for a while, then be off, always with some job to attend to. I noticed that Camel was always disappearing with him. They would make for the room in the stables where all our gear was stored. Tidying the cables, Gerry explained. I couldn't see what interest Camel would have in cables. He and Gerry seemed to be developing some secret bond and would mumble to each other, completely unintelligibly. Then they would give a secretive grin. What was going on?

I could get nothing out of Gerry. Nobody could. I tried Camel. It was no use. All I got was an inarticulate murmur, turning his

head and plucking at the beard he was cultivating. I pressed on
. . . 'Sorry. What did you say?'

More mumbling, but I definitely recognised the word 'lion'.

'You didn't say "lion"?'

'Cub,' said Camel.

'A lion cub!'

'Only a young one,' he said, indicating the size and glancing
round to see if Gerry was about.

'We've been preparing a stall for her, a trough and playthings,
all that.'

'Is Gerry starting a zoo?' Gerry heard his name and came
towards us, grinning.

'She'll be here tomorrow, sweetheart.' And he gave me a hug.

'Does anybody else know?'

'The Pennymans, and they've no objection. I'm only afraid
she may be lonely.'

How had he found her? Well, as usual, Gerry, always looking
for alternatives to our village halls, had bought *World's Fair*, the circus paper, but instead of finding a circus ring to work in he found
'A lion cub on offer, female. Due to meat rationing the circus is no
longer able to feed this splendid young animal. Anyone willing to
offer a good home and feed should apply.'

'But how can we feed her?'

'Camel and I are both prepared to give up our meat ration.'

We three kept the next day's arrival secret but someone else
who was in on the plot could hardly contain himself. Gerry had
disappeared after breakfast but all morning a lithe figure, wearing
grey plus fours and a Tyrolean hat, kept hovering round the stables. Finally he buttonholed Camel.

'Gerry not back yet?'

'No, Colonel, though he should be,' said Camel. 'They told
him to be at the station at 12.10 to meet her coming off the train.'

The dinner bell had gone when Gerry arrived, completely
crestfallen, and he had on his blue shorts and his bright blue
windjammer. He unwrapped a large meaty bone and dumped
it in the scullery.

'Not on?' said the Colonel.

'The police,' said Gerry. 'They won't have her.'

There was a long silence. The master of Ormesby got on the phone but the constabulary were adamant. Gerry was very sad. So was the Colonel.

Our summer school ended on a seashore at Redcar. At our last-night party someone said sentimentally, 'Let's see the dawn break over the sea before we say goodbye.' And so we did and parted with declarations of eternal friendship, drunken tears and from each and every one an offer to stay and work on, even if it meant living off the dole.

'One way of getting a government subsidy,' said Howard.

Kerstin called down to us from a high rock's edge. 'I'm going back to Sweden, to book us a triumphal tour.'

'You can't go yet, Zany,' I shouted. 'You are needed for the next show. Besides we haven't got the fare.'

Parting with Pearl was very sad. She was going home to have her baby and I didn't think she would ever come back. Isla Gledhill, a songbird from Newcastle, would have to replace her, and Camel, Ben, John Blanshard, Margaret Greenwood and gentle Edna Carson joined us after the summer school.

Despite Arts Council's opposition, Mike Thompson had managed to book a healthy-looking Scottish tour. I would have to return each weekend to run the weekend schools, and as Rosalie couldn't be spared from the shows, Laban's dancing star, Jean Newlove, had been invited to take over. Jimmie suggested gatecrashing the Edinburgh Festival. Theatre nobs would be there from all over the world. The Festival was still a draw, though this year's visiting companies sounded prestigiously dull. We could outshine them all, but where?

Our first directors' meeting was scheduled for the following weekend. Mike would have to attend, so Gerry offered to go to Edinburgh and find a venue. The Workshop had four directors: Hugh MacDiarmid, James Ford, William Maclellan, and Freddie Piffard who was head of BBC Variety, London, at the time. David had worked on his programmes for a while and, when they found they were chasing the same pretty secretary, they became friends. While we were playing Middlesbrough, David heard that the Variety team were combing the North-East looking for talent, and advised them to come and see our show. Afterwards they invited Gerry, David and me for drinks at Middlesbrough's best hotel. This was itself an event. We hadn't been in a pub since that first hopeful day at the Woolpack in Kendal.

Freddie Piffard had fallen for the show, hook, line and sinker. The style, the company's versatility, pace and *joie de vivre* won him. We could talk to him about the daily training without receiving that supercilious smile which usually greets the mention of such unprofessional behaviour. It turned out that he had once worked in a circus. We parted with warm good wishes on either side and that was that. When David suggested that Freddie might join our board of directors, I didn't think he would accept, but he did and he was coming to Ormesby with the rest.

The meeting was prepared with great care. While Howard and Mike typed out the agenda and the reports, four rooms were made ready, wild flowers gathered for the breakfast trays and succulent dishes planned and executed with a skill that might have made our fortune in the catering business.

William Maclellan arrived first, wearing his kilt, of course, and carrying a bulging briefcase full of books, among them, amazingly, the proofs of Jimmie's *Uranium 235*. James Ford next, quiet and charming; then Chris Grieve – looking wilder than ever, his hair turning grey but standing on end in perpetual amazement at the world's stupidity. 'I've no time for anything between genius and the common man.'

Freddie took us all in his stride and suggested we have a look at the agenda before lunch. William Mac had just launched into a long description of his latest publication, *Sorabje*, though none of us had a clue who Sorabje was.

Financial report after lunch, then artistic progress and plans. Our four champions shook their heads over the figures and their fists over the Arts Council story. Chris was particularly vehement in his condemnation of 'that rag-bag of mediocrities'. He had already come up against the Scottish Arts Council, so at least we could expect a column of glorious vituperation in his periodical *The*

Voice of Scotland, where, like Dostoevsky before him, he contributed many articles under different names.

Rosalind Goodger, who was giving us much needed secretarial help at the time, wrote to Mr Michael Macowan on her own initiative and asked why Arts Council existed if it was not to assist companies such as ours. She actually had a reply and was told that it was our outlook which was hindering our progress – a pretty frank admission at last, as if it hadn't been clear all along, of the strong political prejudice against us. To hell with them.

Freddie, like Gerry, was not particularly interested in Arts Council. He'd had a good idea, which would yield us a reasonable income for a couple of months at least. He was on the committee which selected entertainment for the British Forces in Germany, and would persuade his colleagues to send us there. We didn't believe him, but we were wrong. In January and February 1947 we played to the British Forces in Germany.

The day after the directors left, thanking us for our Oriental hospitality, we were on our way to the land of mists and braes. Gerry had hired a lorry for our journey and on a fine autumn morning we set forth. I think we all had a romantic idea of Scotland, the tragic history of the Highlands, the heroes of our fathers' time – Maclean, Keir Hardie, Willie Gallagher.

'Can we go by Hadrian's Wall?'

'That's miles off course.'

It had always seemed to me the natural frontier between England and Scotland, but of course I was wrong and soon, careering across the wide hills of Northumberland, one forgot old Roman stones, breathing the clear air of that exhilarating land. Gerry was taking the panoramic route.

Jimmie sang 'The king has ga'en frae Bamborough Castle'. It lasted till we passed the Holy Isle of Lindisfarne. Denis Ford had asked Gerry to stop at the village before the border. I was half-expecting to see customs men in tartan kilts and bonnets when we got there but in fact we zoomed on till we came to a small village. It looked as if it had just been scrubbed, very austere but with gardens crowded with yellow, pink and crimson roses. Every shop belonged to Mac somebody or other, the name announced in gilded Victorian letters. The buildings and paving stones were the colour of red lead. When the lorry stopped at the lights, Denis started shouting to Gerry. Camel came round to the back.

'Anything wrong?'

'I asked Gerry to stop before we got into Scotland.'

'Why?'

'I wanted to be sure of some . . .'

'If you've time for that,' said Camel, 'you're not pulling your weight.' And he strode off.

'What makes you think you can't get them in Scotland?' asked Bill.

'They're Puritans, aren't they?'

The lorry lurched forward, fourteen miles to our first date.

> *The king sits in Dunfermline town*
> *Drinking the bluid-red wine –*

Jimmie was shouted down this time. We've no blood-red wine. My backside's gone to sleep. And it's raining! Who booked this date?

'Come on,' shouted Camel. 'All out! Unload! Rig before tea.'

'Is this where we're playing? What's it in aid of?'

'Andrew Carnegie.'

'What a dump!'

'No wonder he got the hell out of it.'

'What've you got in these crates?'

'They're just wet.'

'How are we going to dig up an audience in this hole?'

'Sound a trumpet and run up a flag.'

> *Parade the streets with drum and fife*
> *And give them the show of their life.*

We did, but Gloomtown liked talk more than shows. We talked all week to the Women's Guild, the Men's Guild, the Bird-watchers and the Dog Fanciers. By Friday I was glad to get away to the silence of Ormesby where our new dancing mistress, Jean Newlove, would be waiting, with her pumps on, ready for the weekend's rally.

We'd no money to waste on rail fares. If you didn't travel in style with the lorry, you hitchhiked. That may sound jolly. In practice it was boring as hell. Hours on some rainswept tarmac, with occasional lorries splashing past you. What a bloody waste of time. And if a kindly-looking character did stop for you, as likely as not he turned out to be a groper.

I passed a station and the thought of all those trains speeding south was too much for me. I turned back, bought a platform ticket, found the right platform and a train waiting just for me! I found a seat beside the corridor, and relaxed. What luxury! The feeling didn't last, every door opening, every footstep, could be the ticket inspector. I'd better get off at the first stop. It didn't stop. I was on the express. What's more, it wasn't going anywhere near Middlesbrough. Out in the corridor, I leaned on the rail and willed that train to stop or at least to slow down. I trailed along to the WC and opened the door. The roar of the wheels grew louder. You could see the rails thro' the dirty hole. No use shutting myself in there when the ticket inspector arrived. He would simply bang on the door till I came out. Then what would I say? I couldn't give Ormesby Hall as my address. He was coming. No, he wasn't. I thought I heard 'Tickets, please'. I stood by the door. I pulled the window down. The train was slowing down. I grasped the door handle, shoved and – jumped.

That train was going a lot faster than I'd thought. I almost got caught in the door and fell awkwardly, rolling down a gravelly bank of weeds and prickles. I let myself roll and kept my head down, scared to look up lest the train had stopped and an army of angry ticket collectors was searching for me. I heard a mournful toot, the train gathered speed and was gone. I was alone in the world, crouching on a bed of cinders, God knows where, and I'd twisted my left ankle, and ricked my back. The long hours of hitchhiking which followed are best forgotten.

It was after midnight when I saw the roof of Ormesby Hall

in the distance. Jean Newlove would let me in if she'd arrived to take the weekend's dance sessions. She had. She put a cold compress on my ankle, a hot water bottle at my back, and promised to buy me a railway guide for Christmas. That weekend I took my classes leaning on a stick, and told everyone I had lumbago. Colonel Pennyman said I was lucky to be able to stand. He'd once had an attack of lumbago and been forced to take the salute bent in three. He gave me a demonstration.

G erry phoned from Edinburgh, from a hall right in the heart of the Festival area. 'It's great.'

'Come on, what's wrong with it?'

'Nothing. All the local shows are held here – pigeons, canaries, poodles.'

'At the same time as us?'

'No, no. We move in each day as the livestock move out. Our banners are already strung up across the road: "Theatre Workshop is here".'

Nowadays gatecrashers outnumber official festivities. We were the first. The Fringe, they called us, and the name stuck. The local shopkeepers were not very friendly, apart from the Italians who ran the café next door. They knew what we were up against. It didn't matter much. Soon the world hikers, stopping off in Scotland for a bit of culture, came by to find out what this Workshop was all about. It was a year after Hiroshima. So, 'Let's see the world before they blow it up' and many young people only worked till they had enough money to be off. Newspaper reporters from far-away countries came buzzing around as well.

We felt at the hub of things and it was a good feeling. People waved at us from the tops of buses as they passed under our banner. In the hall two blokes in kilts were helping Ben rig the lights. We'd no idea who they were, they'd just walked in offering to help.

The rig progressed, despite the flow of visitors. Nobody had given a thought as to where they would lay their head. Camel came in and pinned a list of addresses to the notice-board, but who had time to go looking at digs?

At tea-time a brawny chap in Highland dress drifted in, followed by the caretaker who had six poodles yapping at his heels. The Scotsman read out one of his poems and the caretaker asked what time we would be leaving. We knew, did we not, that the dog show had been postponed, perforce, in our favour.

'Hamish Henderson's the name,' said the Scotsman, handing the caretaker a copy of the poem. He was given a severe look and left standing.

Several poets wandered in with beer tankards in their hands looking for Hamish and as the sun set over Edinburgh's romantic skyline, which we had yet to see, more pints were sent in from the pub and a young middle-aged man accosted Bill Davidson. Were we the theatricals who interested themselves in the properties of *Uranium 235*? Was that a hint of a Highland accent?

'Yes,' said Bill, 'but we're a bit pushed at the moment.'

'Come round to my place later for a beer and we'll talk it over. Simon's the name.' He wrote his address on a card.

'You come as well,' he said to me. 'And you – and you.'

He went round the hall. I thought he was going to invite the caretaker who returned at that moment carrying a macaw.

'A scientist, I guess,' said Bill when Simon left. In fact he was in charge of the rivers and waterways of Scotland and a voracious reader, interested in any esoteric manifestations of nature, which included us. It was 3.30 in the morning when the conversation petered out, and the beer.

'You can't go anywhere at this hour,' he said, as his beautiful wife came in with an armful of bedding.

It was a capacious apartment. Just as well, because we slept there, all fifteen of us. I was up early, showered to wake myself up, and tiptoed round the flat checking on the sleeping forms draped over settees, camp-beds and carpets. Yes, they were all there.

I enjoyed my walk over the heights of Edinburgh and found the caretaker brushing the pavement outside the hall. 'Looking for two of your brood?' he said.

'No. We've all been together.'

'Then what are they doing here?' He nodded towards David and Ben who were drinking coffee outside the Italian cayf. Ben was sketching.

'Where were you?' I asked.

'Where were you?' said David. 'You forgot all about us.'

'When we left Ben was still sorting gelatines and you were painting the sound box. I hope you didn't finish up in the hall.'

'We finished up in the cooler, with a board and a wooden headrest.'

'It gave me an idea for my play,' said Ben. 'Grey, greyer and black.'

'One blanket and the door locked,' said David.

'But how was it you had nowhere to go?'

'It was late. You were all gone. We tried to find you but they ran us in.'

No recriminations! And we did do our best to compensate for their night in the nick. They had two dinners, a helping of Italian ice-cream, and the best sleeping bags at Simon's that night.

He liked our company, so did his beautiful young wife. They insisted on us staying at their flat for the whole three weeks. Pity we weren't playing *Uranium*. It might have interested them but they weren't that keen on any sort of theatre. They just liked us.

All Scotland's wits, poets and gossips appeared in the local pub during the Festival. They didn't attend any of the concerts, operas or theatrical performances, yet they seemed to know exactly what was wrong with everything, and they had a fund of scandalous gossip about each other. Each one held court in his own particular corner at his own particular time and if frontiers were violated fighting could easily break out. Although none of them would admit it, they enjoyed meeting these foreigners washed up by the high tide of culture. They needed a new audience for their diatribes and dithyrambs and if the payment was only a pint of the best, it was welcome.

We enjoyed the sound of the bagpipes echoing from every art and part but, as Hamish assured us, outside the Festival, Auld Reekie was as dull as ditchwater. Give me Glasgow every time, said he.

Our many-purpose hall was lively enough. There was something going on morning, noon and night. To supplement the dogs and canaries, we organised lunch-time debates, a damned good argument being the only form of theatre flourishing in Scotland at that time. We were pulling in the audiences for the show too. Not surprisingly, since all the newspapers had written about the gatecrashing group, and a strong attack had been made on us in the *Scotsman*, which proved useful. We were alive, they said, and vital, but too wedded to unorthodox opinions.

After that, the poets clustered round us more than ever, declaring that we were the only live thing in Edinburgh. Dr Mavor, James Bridie the playwright, announced his intention of visiting us, and Bill Maclellan brought him along. Gerry went over to the Lyceum, captured Wilson Barrett, the theatre owner, and insisted he came to the Saturday show.

An enormously fat man appeared one lunch-time. We'd just curtailed our rehearsal because the dogs were appearing and barking madly. 'Where can I buy a ticket for the play?'

'I'd buy three if I were you,' said Jimmie. The chairs weren't very wide.

'All right, all right,' said the fat man.

'Name?' said Rosalie.

'Henry Sherek.' His name in the West End theatre was bigger than he was.

One way and another we were getting our full share of the limelight and thoroughly enjoying it. We were eating well too. Luncheon at the British Restaurant down the road cost one shilling and sixpence, and it was good. Each night after the show, Hamish would carry some of us off to the pub. We were hungry and we weren't great drinkers, but we enjoyed the stories, the rivalry for the hand of the countess who lived on Princes Street, Sorley's child bride, and Sidney Goodsir Smith's latest bender.

'Sidney's work will never see the light of day,' said Norman McCaig. 'And Chris Grieve'll always be in the dog-house.'

It sounded a bit more robust than the works of those delicate buggers down in London.

One night, Gerry and Joan were to be smuggled into the Festival Club, with no thought of paying the large subscription fee, naturally.

'Members only,' said the doorman as we sailed in.

'Honorary members,' said Hamish and took Gerry's arm.

They were both tall, robust and looked quite striking together, but not, as you might say, orthodox. What's more, beyond the paid-up toffs in evening dress seated at tables, a whole row of poets could be seen lounging at the bar. One or two of the wild ones would be let in, they were good value and lent the place a little local colour. But we were six – no, seven. Eight as I arrived with Bill Maclellan, who'd just tagged on.

The *maître d'* advanced on us.

'I'm sorry, but . . .'

'That's all right,' I said. 'The doorman couldn't have known who we were.'

I was wearing my tartan skirt and a white cardigan. Respectable but definitely not chic. The poets picked themselves up from the bar and came towards us.

'We shall need a table for nine,' said Hamish. 'We're expecting our Poet Laureate.'

Gerry let out such a roar of laughter that all heads turned in our direction. The *maître d'* gave a signal and two tables were joined together. We sat at ease as Hamish ordered ale and chasers.

'Who's our Poet Laureate?' I asked.

'Chris, of course,' said Hamish, and he downed a good half-pint in one.

Everyone else was concentrated on a square of parquet in the middle of the room where eight middle-aged ladies were forming up. They wore white cotton shifts, black plimsolls and had plaid scarves draped across their bosoms, but no bras underneath.

'Highland dancing,' whispered Duncan, the painter.

They looked nothing like the girls you see on shortbread tins or the illustrations to the Waverley novels, and the dance was more like something invented by a parson's wife in 1910 than an eight-some reel. How can you dance a Highland dance without men? All they had was a piano and a fiddle. Before long Hamish made for the bar, where he seemed to have a place reserved, and we weren't long after him. Soon we were all happily installed with yet another tankard of ale, while Hamish gave us 'Brave John Maclean's coming back to the Clyde'.

As we were being escorted out, we noticed a group of young men in black, with shaved heads, coming in. Bill Mac said they were from Gustav Gründgens' company.

'Gründgens'? You must be mistaken.'

'I'm not mistaken. They're opening in *Faust* on Monday.'

'Wasn't their visit cancelled?'

'That's what we thought, but here they are.'

There had been a great deal of protest over this invitation. Gründgens was not just an eminent Nazi. He had personally been responsible for the murder of Hans Otto, Germany's most popular actor and head of German Actors' Equity until the Nazis took over. It was unbelievable that Gründgens should have been allowed to come to this country. Was it only anti-Nazis who were turned away? Rudolf Bing, the Festival organiser, was himself an Austrian Jew. He had been at Nuremberg when the Nazi war criminals were on trial. He'd heard the first batch sentenced to death. After the encounter at the Festival Club, we ran into the men in black everywhere. You'd see them strutting in and out of the big hotels or window shopping in Princes Street. We were told that there was to be an organised protest when the Gründgens show opened.

Jimmie had received a flattering letter from James Bridie, the Scottish playwright, and was feeling pleased with himself. Gerry had one from Wilson Barrett, the London theatre owner, and was folding it away. All the same, I managed to catch a glimpse of it: '. . . excellent performance. If at any time you want a job, I should very much like to have you in my company.'

'Gerry!' said Jimmie. 'All he's fit for is shifting pianos.'

'What keeps you together?' asked Bill.

Gerry laughed.

Howard had a letter too, an angry one, from Michael Macowan. A young architect had taken as his 'diploma project' the designing of 'a school for Theatre Workshop' and the drawings had been sent to Michael Macowan for his opinion. 'Apart from Theatre Workshop,' the young man wrote, 'there has been nothing of artistic significance in the English theatre for the last fifty years.' This put Mr Mac beside himself. 'Nothing of artistic significance?' he wrote, as if we were responsible for the young architect's opinions. 'What about the last three seasons at the Old Vic?'

We didn't know the architect, but he obviously felt as we did about the Old Vic. Whoever he was, we were pleased to have him on our side and couldn't help enjoying the rage into which he'd plunged poor Mr Mac. 'Your work is boring,' the artistic director went on. 'I was bored and I had the impression the audience was bored too.' Apparently he had been to see us after all, though he hadn't made himself known. We never met the young architect or saw his plans.

We had decided to update Jimmie's *Operation Olive Branch*, his version of the *Lysistrata*, for the next production. He had added a chorus of front-line soldiers and a deserter written in Lallans. Lallans had been invented by Chris Grieve. It was a brilliant synthetic language and Jimmie had been longing to have a crack at it. The deserter became an expression of his own isolation, and he wanted to play the part himself. 'The Lallans must be spoken correctly,' he said. This was only an excuse. His character was to be murdered by Gerry, a Pirandello situation which appealed to Jimmie's peculiar sense of theatre. The chorus of old men bore a distinct resemblance to Churchill, Pétain, Patton and their crew. Howard, as their leader, was playing his old man so deaf that he had no idea which war he was in.

After the *divertissements* of Edinburgh, we were doing well on a tour of the Scottish mining towns. Then, one day, Mike Thompson threw us a surprise packet. Could we play *Uranium 235* in London, or rather, at Hanwell, just beyond Ealing in London? Our friends at *Theatre Newsletter* and two of the North-East MPs thought it would be good to challenge Arts Council on its own doorstep. I wasn't happy at the thought of curtailing the *Olive Branch* rehearsals, but Howard and most of the company were in favour of putting political pressure on Arts Council. 'Hanwell is near enough to attract all the MPs in the new Labour government who are interested in Art for the People,' said Howard.

'By the People,' said Karl Woods, a miner's son who'd joined us after Newcastle. He was named after Karl Liebknecht.

Personally, I had not noticed that Labour MPs were any more interested in art for the people than the Tories, but the Hanwell faction won, the booking was accepted and everybody was delighted when Arthur Blenkinsop, Nye Bevan, Tom Driberg, Benn Levy, Ian Mikardo and Alf Robens accepted our invitation to attend the performance. Then we asked Arts Council to send a delegate. As their funds depended on the goodwill of the government of the day, they immediately arranged to send someone along when they heard how many Labour MPs were coming.

Twenty-four

*We play London for the first time. A group of MPs attend
the show and a delegation from Arts Council. We are invited
to lunch at the House of Commons. Arts Council finally turn us
down. Tom Driberg likes us. At Ormesby, rehearsals for Jimmie's
updated* Lysistrata – Operation Olive Branch. *The police arrest
him for desertion. Ben Ellis begs to take over his rôle, the deserter;
succumbs to a violent attack of schizophrenia and has to be taken to
the asylum. Let out for the first night and is cured playing the part.
Freddie Piffard secures a tour of the British Forces in Germany. I stay
behind to help Jimmie.*

The theatre at Hanwell may not be a very inspiring showcase, but at least it was packed. Many Londoners who'd heard of this controversial company braved the journey. It was our first appearance in the South and they gave us an enthusiastic reception. The Arts Council delegation did not reveal itself. The Labour MPs did. The curtain was hardly down before they were up on the stage, poking around like kids at the end of the school play. I caught one of them fooling around in our one and only top hat, but at least they invited us to lunch at the House of Commons next day and we accepted with alacrity, always happy at the thought of a good meal.

Kate Daisy and Jim, her husband, had turned up, amazed to discover what I'd been up to all these years.

Howard was on the phone to Mr Macowan the following morning. 'Well, you've been turned down by the powers that be,' he was told, 'and they are right. From now on, if Miss Littlewood wishes to continue, she must finance the work herself.'

On the other hand, the MPs' lunch was tiptop, though I found it rather warm. My tartan skirt was at the cleaners' and my long pants too old, so I had simply rolled up my pyjamas under my coat. By the time we'd drunk the wine and warmed to the compliments I was definitely overheated, but I couldn't take my coat off. Alf Robens made a moving speech and there were so many promises of support and interest that we left feeling that we would at least be offered the National Theatre, if they ever built it.

Gerry and Howard were nobbled by Tom Driberg who wanted to know more about us. They tried to persuade him to come to Ormesby for the first night of *Olive Branch* and see for himself. We knew that he was the world-famous columnist who had won Maldon from the Tories in 1944, standing as an Independent. We also knew that he had a name for discovering new artists. He was a tall, handsome man who made no secret of his carefully cultivated taste. He was attracted to Gerry at once, but tended to regard women as enemies.

Anyone less likely to succumb to Tom's advances than Gerry it would be difficult to find, but Tom preferred confirmed heterosexuals. He agreed to come to Ormesby, and Gerry and Howard were well pleased with themselves.

'He said that I reminded him of Lady Oxford and Asquith.'

'You, Howard?'

'Yes, me.'

Inspired by our visit to the House of Commons, as soon as we got back to Ormesby we started redoing all the old men's scenes, one in the Athenian parliament, with Speaker, Mace Bearer and all the ritual of Westminster. We were enjoying the joke one afternoon when I heard Colonel Pennyman's voice, then a silence broken by his footsteps on the stairs. He came in, without ceremony, apologised for the intrusion, and asked where our resident playwright was to be found.

'He'll be working in his room.' No, the Colonel had looked there. 'He may have taken Jean for a walk,' said Rosalie. Unlikely.

I followed the Colonel to the door. In the courtyard below two men were waiting and even though it was growing dark they were identifiable.

I felt like running to the village to warn Jimmie but I hesitated and it was too late. He appeared in the drive strolling towards the house with Jean . . . then suddenly stopped in his tracks. One of the plain-clothes policemen looked at Colonel Pennyman and

together they approached my ex-husband. I couldn't hear but I
knew what was being said and I knew that Jimmie wouldn't
deny his name. They moved towards the house, the two cops
with Jimmie, the Colonel following. Jean stood still for a second,
then she ran up the stairs to us.

'I think we'd better carry on with the . . .'

Jean sat by the window. My mouth went dry. If they were
going through the lines, I couldn't hear them. Presently Ruth
Pennyman came in and suggested going back to the house. We
all walked quietly to the refectory. David was laying the fire.

'Where is . . . ?'

I followed David's glance. At the end of the long table, the
two cops sat waiting.

It seemed a very long time before Jimmie walked in, and when
he did he was unrecognisable, his beard was gone, his face was
ashen, his chin seemed to have disappeared. He gave a wild look
round and before anyone had time to do or say anything, he was
gone – the two plain-clothes men hid him from sight as he moved
towards the door. If he did turn to us, we couldn't see him.

I heard the police car drive away. Jean said they had seen it
as they came up the drive and Jimmie had told her that they had
come for him. Perhaps he'd kept the dread of arrest to himself for
so long, that the actual event came as a relief. I would have to face
the Colonel at once. He would probably show us the door. He was,
after all, an army man. I found him. I faltered, trying to give him
some sort of explanation.

'Yes,' he said. 'I see, but then some of these artistic chaps
simply can't stand army life.' He showed then, and was to continue
to show, far more compassion than many of the artists and writers
to whom we appealed for help.

The company had the right to an explanation. In any case, I
did not want them to think that Jimmie was merely a shirker. It
was always difficult to understand other people's motives, I told
them, though we may think we do. Jimmie's gift for song-writing
had made him popular in the army from the outset, he could easily
have had a cushy War. Why had he 'riz to his feet and shauc'led
awa' ' like the deserter he had written into his play? Why had he
chosen solitude rather than the comradeship of army life?

'Was it a political desertion?' asked Bill. I didn't think so.

'It took a bit of courage,' said Ruth.

'A lot of people must have helped him,' said Camel.

I didn't answer though I knew they had. Whatever Jimmie's motivation had been, the company was sympathetic, especially to Jean who was shattered by the turn of events. She came from a very conventional family and she had already had to swallow the news that her lover was still legally married to me. Now this. I told her to buck up, that nothing serious would happen to him. We would have him back in no time. All this was rather more optimistic than I felt, but Jean trusted me; she thought I was tough. 'You'd better be,' I said to myself.

Legal help? Would he be court-martialled? I didn't know. Did the army allow you a civvy lawyer? I doubted it. I would have to find out, at once, but first . . . to locate him, get some pocket money to him, and a food parcel. It was winter, nearing Christmas. What a time to land in an army detention barracks! All the gruesome stories told about those places began to surface.

'Who's to play his part in *Olive Branch*?' asked Howard.

Ben could not stop talking about Jimmie. He said he knew exactly why he had left the army. Ben had lived through the hell of Caen, where so many British soldiers had been destroyed by British guns. He might have resented Jimmie. He didn't, not for a moment. Like Jimmie, Ben had changed his name when the War was over. He had come to us to start a new life. He too wanted to be a playwright. He asked quietly if he could take over Jimmie's part in the play.

On the second day a letter arrived from him. The first night of captivity had been spent in Middlesbrough police station, the next day he was taken to army detention barracks at Northallerton. Ruth was already collecting food for a parcel. Everybody contributed. We put together a long letter with reports on work in progress, old jokes, slanderous comments on each other and one pound note which Howard extracted from the cashbox.

Gerry, Howard and I made a list of all the people who had admired his work and wrote asking them to appeal on his behalf. But who to? What was the correct procedure? We would have to hurry. We couldn't leave him shut up in that place. Lights burned in every room till the small hours. They were all writing letters for Jimmie.

Ben had his own idea. Using his best Lieutenant Ellis accent, he phoned the War Office every day, enquiring after the playwright James H. Miller, wanting to know when he would be released. He was an important playwright but in delicate health and so on. It was an impressive performance. It seemed that we would be well-advised to plead incompatibility. A character unsuited to army life, but that called for an established psychologist. How much would that cost? Bill Mac wrote that a fund was being started in Scotland.

'That will have to take care of it,' said Howard. 'We can't.'

My refugee friends in Manchester recommended a Jungian practitioner. I wrote to him at once, and he replied asking to see all Jimmie's writings, including his earliest efforts.

Our première was only three days away. The letters and phone calls would have to die down.

'The best service we can render Jimmie now,' I said, 'is to make a success of his play.'

Ben was reluctant to rehearse the deserter until he received a letter from Jimmie wishing him luck and saying that his arrest had been a question of mistaken identity. The James Miller on their list was a much older man. Someone had told the police that there was a deserter named Miller in our company, calling himself MacColl. Who could have done such a thing? Someone who knew us. I didn't want to think about it.

The dress rehearsals were flat. At the postman's approach everybody's concentration went. We were up all night making props, finishing costumes. On the Friday evening, I passed the lamp room. Ben was examining a cable. The night was calm, the house unusually still. Camel passed me, carrying a large light-bulb. Then . . . had he turned back? I heard footsteps coming my way. Was it Camel?

'You've stopped, Ben,' I heard him say.

There was no reply. Ben appeared. He didn't see me, his eyes fixed on something ahead. What was he looking at? There was nothing there, nothing but darkness.

'I think he's . . .'

There was a sudden crash of breaking glass. Camel ran. Some lights went on. Who was in Jimmie's room? I'd forgotten. Ben had moved there after the arrest.

Gerry was standing by the door now, looking at the glass and frame of Ben's engraving of Mozart which lay smashed on the floor. The bookshelf was empty, the books had been swept on to the bed, except one, his treasured *Metaphysical Poets*. He was tearing it in two with a giant's strength.

I picked up what was left of Mozart. Gentle Ben turned on me a face distorted with rage and hate. Gerry pulled me away. Ben's eyes slewed round in his head, till they almost disappeared, and that's how they stayed, as if he were listening for something he couldn't quite hear.

'He's very ill,' said Gerry. 'We mustn't leave him.'

Ben was a quiet man and sensitive, slight of build with delicate hands and feet. The giant's strength he had suddenly displayed was unbelievable. But as suddenly as he had fallen into this terrifying state, as suddenly he emerged, his usual gentle self.

'Don't let them put me away,' he said. 'You are my family. If I stay with you, I will be all right.'

But he wasn't. With the approach of darkness he heard voices. They were telling him what to do. He would hurl a mirror to the floor, seize a knife and rip the bed open. Four of us tried to hold him down, that slender man, but he would rear up with the strength of a lion, his back arched, his eyes turning in his head. It was terrible to see.

'And dangerous,' said Ruth, when Gerry carried the exhausted man to the WC. She had been helping nearly all night.

'He seems to want to destroy the things he loves best, maybe the people too. I think we should hide all the knives.'

I went to join Gerry, scared that Ben might become uncontrollable. Gerry was whistling, turning on the tap, trying to get Ben to pee.

In the morning we were all whacked. It was Saturday; the first night was on Monday. At the moment it was taking half a dozen of us to watch over Ben, see that he did not harm himself. Howard and David wanted him to be taken away, for his own sake, but as if he had heard them he grabbed Gerry's arm. 'You won't put me away? I have to play Jimmie's part on Monday.'

'I'll never put you away, Ben,' said Gerry, 'unless you want me to.'

An hour later he made a terrifying attack on Isla, who was bringing him a lunch tray. When Gerry and I got there the room was a shambles, the bedding half out of the window, but Ben quiet again, his head in his hands.

'I think you'd better take me,' he said. 'I might hurt you.'

We knew we'd have to do as he said. Ruth did the phoning while Gerry washed and dressed Ben with great care. The house was utterly silent as we walked with him to the Colonel's car.

The 1880 building had no name in the book, its red brick had blackened with age. The doors were barred. We were admitted by a wicket gate. Inside, two tough men in uniform waited for us.

'Is he certified?'

'No,' I said. 'He is not.'

'Does he need a jacket?'

Gerry shook his head. We were told to follow these men. We made a grim procession through bare corridors, the walls dark green and chocolate brown. I glanced at Gerry. He was scowling, tight-lipped. He put his arm round Ben, who let himself be led along, in a daze. We passed heavy oak doors, inset in the thick walls. On each door there was a card in a small brass frame. We came to a door where the brass frame was empty, and stopped.

'We can't leave him here.' It was the office of the physician, or psychiatrist in charge. All I wanted was to get the interview over and take Ben back with us. One of the guards opened the door, the room looked like the corridor except for a heavy roll-top desk and the sandy-haired young man standing by it.

'The party from Ormesby Hall,' said a guard.

The young man dismissed the guards with a glance. He wasn't actually young; when you saw him close to, his face looked careworn. His suit, ill-fitting, might have been a demob suit. Gerry began to give Ben's particulars and a brief account of his army experience. Ben looked at the window.

'I have only just been demobbed myself,' said the doctor.

What a relief! This place might be a leftover from the days of straitjackets and whips but here was someone who'd been through the same experience as Ben. I began talking, found myself explaining that Ben was due to play a rôle, very important to him, on the following Monday, that he had identified himself with the character.

'If he does not play it,' I said, 'he will be in worse case. If we let him stay, please let him come out and play the part on Monday, even if he has to return afterwards.' The doctor gave me a funny look. I thought he was going to put me in a straitjacket.

'All right,' he said, 'but he must be brought back here at once when he leaves the stage.'

Ben was still staring at the window. Gerry repeated what the doctor had said and asked him if he was willing to stay where he was for the weekend.

'Yes,' said Ben firmly.

Gerry gave him a hug.

'May I come back and see him tomorrow?' he asked.

'Of course,' said the doctor.

As we left the two guards moved in.

Sunday was our last rehearsal day. On top of that Tom Driberg was arriving. I wouldn't be able to visit Ben. Ruth wanted very much to see him, so she went along with Gerry.

Driberg arrived in time to take lunch with the Pennymans. Afterwards he asked if he might sit in at the rehearsal. Usually I would have said, no, not unless you join in the work.

'I could prompt,' said Tom.

'We don't,' I said sternly. 'The way we work we don't have to learn by heart.'

He seemed surprised. What did we do instead?

'We work round the words till they come right.'

Over lunch he'd heard about the real-life dramas which were besetting us. He was a journalist. I didn't want the questions to start. I gave him a copy of the script and asked him to time the pages. David lent him the company stopwatch, rather reluctantly. We ran the last scene. Peace, garlands of flowers, lovers united. Kerstin finished the paean to life which ends the play. Tom clicked the stop watch, but Jimmie had written in two more lines.

LYSISTRATA: Won't you join us, soldier?

There was no reply. Rosalie, who had been reading the deserter's lines, told Driberg that you never spoke the last line of a play till the first night.

'The actor who should speak it is not with us,' said Howard.

Something made me turn my head. Gerry and Ruth were waiting quietly at the back of the rehearsal room.

'How is he?'

'Joan and I had only just left yesterday when he made a violent attack on a guard.'

Silence.

'Are they still going to let him out tomorrow?' I asked.

'Yes, but all knives and mirrors must be kept out of sight and he will be accompanied by two guards.'

'What about the scene with the armed struggle?'

'What are we to do with two large guards?'

'I don't mind having them in the prompt corner,' said Driberg.

It was almost the hour call when an ambulance drove up. Gerry got out, then the two guards – then Ben. David had unscrewed all the mirrors in the men's dressing-room. We had cut all the weaponry in the fight scene, and hidden the swords and daggers. In the event of any outbreak of violence Ben would be overwhelmed. But the actors were tense, uneasy.

'We don't want those guards coming on stage.'

I was accused of enjoying the situation, but my heart was in my mouth. I could only pray that the performance would purge the madness. Ben looked white, haggard, and thinner. He put on his ragged costume himself. Gerry fixed his hair. Ben hadn't uttered a word. The two guards looked on.

Curtain up. The women's scene went well, if a little overexcited. The old men got their laughs. The soldiers' scenes were too quiet. Here it comes. Gerry moved into the wings with Ben, who looked like a man going to the scaffold. I shouldn't have done this. I could see Tom Driberg half-hidden in the shadows, vainly trying to look as if he wasn't there. The two guards had moved to the pass door. The drama of Ben would overshadow anything we could produce. I hid by flattening myself against the wall. I couldn't have gone out front to watch.

A moonlit night at the front. A sentry on guard on the brow of the hill. The rest passing the night as best they could, dozing, grumbling, talking about anything but home. Gerry's soldier comes on with a prisoner – Ben.

'What have you got there?'

'A deserter.'

Questioned roughly by the soldiers, the deserter begins his great apologia. Ben spoke quietly, simply, but with passionate conviction – pale as he was, half-naked, the effect was profoundly moving. In the audience, absolute silence. It was as if they all held their breath. I caught Tom Driberg's eye. We knew that the danger point was passed. If great acting is akin to madness, we were witnessing it.

Rosalie's brother Rory was in the audience. The curtain was hardly down before he was with us, on the stage.

'What a fantastic performance. Who is that?'

Ben was being hurried out to the ambulance. The guards wouldn't let him wait for a cup of tea. Gerry threw on a long jersey and went with them.

Ben came back each night to play his part and each night the storm that had overwhelmed him grew calmer and the performance more ordinary. At the end of the week, Ben was his old self but weak.

Tom stayed on to watch us at work, questioned us about our lives, our aims, our politics, and went away to write a review of our work. He could not then tell Ben's story, or Jimmie's, but felt he had to add a comment on the company.

Any of these people could be earning ten times their

present income in the commercial theatre. Several have refused good offers. They just believe in what they are doing. They have certainty in their mission – plus humour and a notable lack of conceit.

As they sit round their log fire at Ormesby at the end of the day's work, they break easily into singing – folk songs, American work songs, bawdy army songs.

I have never come across any community, religious or political, or any group of stage people, so free as they are from personal pettiness. They are completely and unselfishly single-minded. In fact, they illustrated for me the meaning of the Gospel text, 'If thine eye be single, thy whole body shall be full of light.'

TOM DRIBERG'S COLUMN
Reynolds News, Sunday January 12th 1947

Christmas came and went with Ben and Jimmie still away. Gerry and Edna baked a cake. The Colonel gave us six bottles of wine. Ruth proposed a toast, 'To absent friends.' And we sang 'Comfort and joy' with a will. Then the good news came. Freddie Piffard's tour of Germany was on, and we'd barely a fortnight to prepare for it.

M ichael Macowan was leaving Arts Council. Ben was recovering, he would be discharged from hospital at the end of the run of *Olive Branch*. Jimmie was still on hard tack. Ben was so weak and thin that I didn't think he would be able to stand the strain of Germany. Yes, he dreaded the 'Sturm und Drang', he said, but wanted very much to go. I thought a few quiet days in the Lake District might help before any decision was made. Ben said OK, but he couldn't go alone and as he spoke his eyes strayed towards gentle Edna, a new girl. After that, everyone regarded her as the virgin chosen to be chained to the rock. She let herself be persuaded, and went.

I had planned to go to Germany with the company but Jean and everyone else looked to me to rescue Jimmie. Everyone, that is, except Gerry. 'You're not going to spend the next three months springing Scrooge,' said Gerry. 'What about me?'

I told him how lonely I would be without him. He didn't believe me. Howard said he would send me weekly reports. He was taking over as company manager. Rosalie would have to be responsible for training; Jean wouldn't leave England with Jimmie locked up.

As a company we had taken a decision not to touch the black market. There were too many stories about the Army of Occupation trafficking and trading.

Gerry said he would organise visits to theatres and concerts.

The weather turned bitterly cold after Christmas. A hard winter was forecast. We bought duffel coats and friends knitted woolly scarves for us. Our boat was to sail from Hull on the morning of 28th January. We would have to be up and away by 6.00 a.m. No need to worry, John Blanshard was always up before dawn; that was why he had been appointed porridge-maker. But as there is always a first time for everything, John B. overslept.

No time for porridge, no time for showers, no time for good-byes. Everyone was scurrying up and down the passages. It took my mind off the coming parting. We made it by the skin of our teeth, Lord knows how. I found myself standing on the quayside alone as they went aboard.

'Don't forget to write.'

'I'll write every day.' And he was gone.

The ship was grey, the sky was grey, the horizon the colour of iron; wild white waves broke surface beyond the harbour walls. I would wait till she sailed. An Admiral of the Humber came and stood beside me. He gazed out to sea.

'She's in for a bit of weather,' he said.

Anchors aweigh. I couldn't see anybody on deck. I waved. Where's Gerry? I turned and retraced my steps along the deserted quay. I felt utterly desolate.

Twenty-five

The letters which passed between Gerry, Howard and me while they were away on a 'Combined Services Entertainment' tour of Germany in 1947.

GERRY to JOAN   Wednesday Morning
                                           29th January 1947

My dear love,

I watched you grow smaller and smaller, as we sailed up the Humber. A dozen times I felt I wanted to jump overboard and swim back to you. How can I live away from you for so long?

                                           Thursday, 30th January

Almost everybody felt sick and went to bed early. David was completely unaffected. Ruth and Kerstin haven't been seen at all today. There are lots of German POWs on board. David and I had a word with some of them. They said they would try to see our show if we came anywhere near their home town.

This is a very fast ship. It carries more passengers than the Queen Mary, but these days you hear speakers blaring everywhere you go. 'Holders of Number 3 tickets and troop deck sergeants, your dinner will be ready in fifteen minutes. Don't forget your lifebelts. No lifebelt, no dinner.'

Send a formal application for the Library Theatre this week and a copy of the press verdict leaflet.

We are surrounded by an ice-pack. At first I thought it was the surf breaking against the ship, but it's ice, two feet thick. The sea sweeping over the bows freezes before it touches the deck. Sometimes one sees a signal lamp flashing a message or a klaxon horn gives a raucous blast.

Joan, I love you more than I could ever tell you. Neither the excitement of a sea voyage, nor the prospect of a new country can put you out of my mind. It is not just physical desire, as you well know, but the need to share my experiences with you and yours with me. Without you, life is drab. And to have left you alone in dreary England . . . it's unbearable. Come soon, my love, as soon as you can, and dress warmly. I have on two pairs of socks and my feet are still cold. Thank heavens for your Balaclava. If I believed you were coming I could live in hope. If not . . . I may not last out.

We've passed the Elbe lightship and pilot. We're breaking the ice in the Elbe estuary. At 4 p.m. we will be in Cuxhaven.

I send you all my love.

Gerry

P.S.   Morale is high. Everyone is excited and interested. Kerstin was bemoaning her fate and ours, without you.

GERRY to JOAN

The Darlington Hotel,
Cuxhaven,
which used to be a
small seaside resort.
Thursday, 10.15 a.m.
30th January

My Joan,

It took us an hour to dock last night. Then the POWs went ashore with a couple of British Warrant Officers in charge of them.

'Anyone want their baggage taken ashore?' All the hundred or so women on board rushed to load the Germans with baggage. Only one of ours exercised her rights as a conqueror.

Ashore, passport identification and money changing. It took them fully five minutes to let me through the passport barrier. Then to this huge, ultra-posh hotel, where we were given perforated red slips, which read:

     1 whisky
     1 gin
     1 breakfast
     1 lunch
     1 tea
     1 dinner
     10 cigarettes
     1 haversack rations
     2 cognac
Our rations for one night.

For the ten cigarettes you get twenty-four Kensitas, a bar
of Cadbury's dairy milk chocolate, a box of matches, a bar of
good soap, and a razor blade – cost one shilling and sixpence.
Everyone's first instinct was to try the cognac. It was very good,
a shilling a glass.

The food is excellent, served by efficient German waitresses
who manage to look graceful while juggling armloads of soup. Bill
Davidson was so busy waggling his eyebrows at one of them, he
couldn't find his mouth with the soup spoon.

                                                          Gerry

GERRY to JOAN   Hamburg
                                       'Boccaccio Casino'
                                       [Ein Fürst Bismarck Hotel]
                                       About midnight
                                       Thursday, 30th January

Darling,

We were wakened at 4.15, to be ready to leave at 5.50 for
Hamburg. The others went for the train but someone had to wait
for the gear which was to go by road. I said I'd stay. It would give
me a chance to see Cuxhaven and write to you. I prefer travelling
by lorry anyway. The driver will be German and I am going to
speak German whenever possible.

If this letter breaks off suddenly it means that the truck has
arrived . . .

Good job we didn't bring our lighting equipment; the cases and

trunks have been badly knocked about. In the sling which brought
our stuff up from the hold, there were one or two other crates; one
of them came crashing down and smashed to smithereens on the
dockside.

No sign of the lorry. The sun was shining in a clear sky so
I went for a walk but it was unbelievably cold, eighteen degrees
Fahrenheit, below freezing. The Germans all wear black patches
over their eyes.

They are as friendly as people anywhere. A 'Guten Morgen' is
returned with a smile, perhaps because I'm not in uniform. Some
of the girls appear to be rather more than friendly.

The truck didn't come until 1.30. By that time there was no
one to help load the gear. Some POWs were roped in but I
couldn't make them understand that our equipment was precious.
In the end I tackled most of it myself, watched by about twenty
German POWs and two British sergeants who gave me a word or
two of advice now and then. In the end the curtain rails projected
about six feet from the tail of the truck. One old chap told me to
tie a red flag with a hammer and sickle from them. It is about a
hundred miles from Cuxhaven to Hamburg, the landscape more
like Holland than my idea of Germany . . . flat, with windmills
and canals. Ninety-nine per cent of the houses have steeply
sloping thatched roofs. All waterways frozen solid – predominant
footwear, clogs and sabots.

At the outskirts of Hamburg the devastation was complete,
gaunt ruins standing alone in an ocean of rubble. For the first
time, I saw the black peaked caps of the German workers and
the chimney sweeps with their top hats, their boys trotting
along beside them. Every time the truck pulls up a crowd of
children appear, clamouring for food. The crippled and maimed
are everywhere, often so badly maimed that at home they would
not be seen at all. I saw one hobbling by, still in his field grey.
Only the old men hold themselves erect.

Arrived about 5.45. The others had been in the hotel since 9
a.m. They had been warned not to go out unescorted for fear of

returning with 'shreds of clothing clinging to their pulped flesh'.
A fate which befell some other Army Entertainment unit – or so
they were told.

   David, Camel and Ben had looked at the theatre. They say
it's huge. There is plenty of lighting gear but the switchboard is
under the stage, operated by periscope. They were told that some
of the theatres on the tour are badly fitted and we shall have to take
a complete lighting unit with us, switchboard, cabling, lamps. Back
to our days on the road with a vengeance. A couple of technicians
will accompany us, which should make rigging a bit lighter.

   We only needed to bring one evening's entertainment. They
don't mind what we do for a second show. Berlin the second
month of the tour. Do try to be there, sweetheart. Everything
I want in life becomes possible when I'm with you, dear one.

                                                 Gerry

P.S.   Everyone tips with cigarettes. The company is setting an
example by giving theirs away with no thought of return. Good
on them!

GERRY to JOAN   Hamburg
                                 Late the same night

There is a German opera season at the theatre this week. Tonight *A
Masked Ball*. Most of the company went. They were tremendously
impressed by the lighting and décor and the marvellous orchestra,
but Howard found the production too conventional. I didn't go.
I ran into a mild middle-aged chap in the bar. He works in
censorship and kept me intrigued over innumerable, well, at least
a dozen, glasses of cognac. He said there were some good German
theatres in Hamburg, so I went to look for them, found my way
to the working-class district, and the very smart Flora Theatre,
smart outside – inside more like the Riley Smith Hall, Leeds.
Out of bounds to allied troops. They were playing some German
musical comedy, could have been English, but for the language. I
soon left.

   I tried German cinema, also out of bounds. The film resembled
one of those unfunny Ealing comedies. Afterwards I queued for a

tram. It was dark, icy cold. I was inconspicuous, so I stood with the Germans, to avoid being identified with the conqueror. Do they know I am English? Superficially, one is accepted in a friendly way by these pinched, grey-faced people, but sometimes your eyes meet theirs and they cannot hide their feelings. I saw a famous German opera singer at the Town Hall today. He was pleading for an issue of clapboard or even cardboard. He'd found no glass for his windows since they were shattered by the bombing.

Howard has called us for 10 a.m. so I'd better get some sleep. This is a hotel de luxe. I have a room to myself, solid German comfort, a big washbasin with hot and cold water, bedside lamp, bedside telephone, writing desk . . . but I can't forget the smell of garbage and cabbage soup which hangs over the back streets, nor the faces of the crowd waiting for the tram. I didn't have to pay my fare. I was simply asked for my military permit. All the passengers on board, packed in like sardines, took a look at me. Were those actors, exploring on their own, really cut to ribbons?

Joan, it is only three days since I saw you but it feels like a lifetime. Are you looking after yourself? Are you keeping warm? Did you buy yourself a woolly hat? Do try to stay on your own, darling, you like it better than being with other people. Come over soon. I kiss your mouth, and pray that I may dream about you.

Gerry

GERRY to JOAN   Friday 31st January
                                 Hamburg Opera House

Howard rehearsed the script changes all day. One of the technicians here worked with Kurt Jooss and knew Laban's work. This was the biggest theatre in Hamburg, but it was badly bombed. What was the stage is now the auditorium, the present stage was formerly the wings, prompt side. It still seats six hundred. After an evening at the opera, *The Pearl Fishers*, discovered that my tin trunk is definitely lost, stolen. Now I've no change of clothes.

Gerry

JOAN to the COMPANY   77 Dean Street
                                       Soho W1
                                       Friday 31st January

First I must tell you how much I miss you all. I am a tree
in winter, very lonely without you.

   I must congratulate you on even the worst of your performances
of *Johnnie Noble*. This is not softening of the brain, I've just listened
to the BBC's interpretation of our show. What a travesty – I'm glad
you missed it. I hope you are all surpassing yourselves. You owe it
to your future.

   Since you left I have heard reports of conditions in Germany
and of British behaviour there. I know you all realise what power
you have; a group of people behaving well towards fellow man can
have a tremendous effect. I wish I were with you. I cannot wait
to hear every detail of your achievements – as individuals and as a
company. I trust the rigging and travelling is not too exhausting. If
anyone needs warm clothing, let me know. You could learn a great
deal in Germany, so visit the theatres whenever you can.

   I'm working on a plan which should provide new opportunities
for each of us. Difficult to write to everybody. But believe me you
are all in my thoughts, every day. Let me hear from you. Offers
are coming in for the summer.

                                           Joan

P.S.   JOAN to HOWARD

Made a flying visit to the psychiatrist who is studying Jimmie's
writings. I stressed the urgency of the situation. He is a very
serious character but so obscure with his pronounced German
accent that I could hardly understand a word he said. In any
case he hasn't got halfway through Jimmie's first work yet, the
Salford novel. I was noting the titles of the books he's written.
They are many. He offered to lend me one on dreams. I tried
to read it on the train back to Ormesby. It was strong stuff.
Our dreams, unedited, seem to be quite disgusting. Compared to
this, Hirschfield's *Encyclopaedia of Sexual Aberrations* reads like Jane
Austen.

   Bill Maclellan wrote to all our Scottish supporters. James Bridie replied, 'A gifted writer, but this does not excuse his desertion. I have no sympathy with his behaviour. His friends must have known and helped. If there is to be a fund, I will contribute – Mavor.'

J.L.

GERRY to JOAN   Celle
                                                 Sunday 2nd February

Beloved,

Have been looking forward to Celle, to seeing the oldest court theatre in Germany. The town is untouched, and there are many fine half-timbered houses. The Schloss? Imposing. The theatre is small but very lovely, all white and gold, the ante-rooms lined with silk and velvet. There is a Chinese room, nothing but softest green, blue and grey. It defies description. This theatre is Renaissance Germany, 1695. It holds three hundred and twenty but it is beautifully equipped and still functioning. The Germans seem to take more care of their treasures than we do.

I went on to the stage to get the feel of it. I could have stayed for hours, but the guide came to show us the chapel and the picture gallery. One portrait there I can't forget, the head of a young girl, in profile. Her hair – dazzling red gold, flowers in her hand. A Renoir of surpassing beauty.

I shall have to go back to Celle. It is so beautiful and it cherishes its precious possessions, yet only a few miles away a name remains which is not to be found on the map . . . Belsen. An exhibition there included letters sent to the manufacturers of the gas ovens: 'We thank you for the efficiency of your machines . . .' etc. I saw Germans weeping as they walked by.

I have just read your letters through again, Joan. I am so lucky to have known you. Life itself is not more precious to me nor more stimulating. God, how slowly the time passes. When will I be with you again?

Gerry

JOAN to HOWARD   77 Dean St
                                    Soho W1
                                    Tuesday 4th February

Hope the responsibility isn't proving too much, with your
performances to think about as well.

Kerstin may have told you that she wants to try and book
Sweden after Germany. If she's really going I can't give her a
part in the next play.

Jimmie was in London this weekend seeing the psychiatrist.
Apparently he suffers from a form of epilepsy, which accounts
for the hysteria and blackouts. He looks frightful at the moment.
He was told he needed immediate treatment. God knows whether
the army will comply.

I have sent *Blitz Song* to George Bernard Shaw, and asked
Harold Lever and our new friend Driberg if they could intervene.
Try to locate John Trevelyan at the Control Commission. I'm sure
he would give Jimmie a testimonial.

Look out for Gustav Wangenheim in Berlin. Will you be allowed
into the Soviet zone? Laban is looking out old contacts. This tour
should clarify the company's ideas. I hope so.

                                    Joan

GERRY'S DIARY   Minden,
                                    Tuesday 11th Feb

Today I have given up writing to Joan. I haven't heard a word
from her.

JOAN to HOWARD   77 Dean St
                                    Soho W1
                                    14th Feb

My dear Howard,

I'm afraid I'm not feeling very cheerful and London's grim, there's
no heating anywhere. The cafés aren't open for long so Mike and
I missed lunch today; we were copying all Jimmie's evidence for

Arthur Blenkinsop MP, who is helping.

Jimmie arrived after an all-night journey, no food. For the last two days he's been in despair. The battalion commander told him he would be sent overseas when he'd done his stint in the glasshouse. I can't see any light at the end of the tunnel. If we give up you must carry on. We've always worked closely together. They have the power to break Jimmie, and that would finish me. I took on the fight with him because it needed both of us. Please don't mention how I'm feeling to Gerry. The court-martial is next Monday, the 17th. His number is 3779986, if anyone wants to write. The address is the same till the sentence is promulgated; that means at least a week.

I am glad you are meeting artists. It is fantastic that defeated Germany can produce good theatre while London goes on turning out tripe. We cannot imagine it can be colder than London, anywhere. I can't believe I'll ever see you all again.

I've been toying with the idea of *The Ghost Sonata* for the repertoire, I think Strindberg's great. I want so much to know about all the successes and failures, but don't worry if you haven't time to write and don't worry about us. The next letter may bring good news.

Yours,

Joan

JOAN to the COMPANY   17th February
                                             77 Dean St
                                             6.30 p.m.

Jimmie's court-martial is cancelled on medical grounds. So some success after all our efforts. The case will be dealt with summarily by Jimmie's CO. The barrister says that will mean 28 days' detention at the most, perhaps none at all. Meanwhile he will be taken to a military hospital. Hopefully from there to be discharged altogether. Drink to that. Mike and I drink to the hope that we will all be together again soon, with Jimmie free and the company in good heart. Don't think I can come to Germany while Jimmie's situation is unresolved. It was the psychiatrist whose report quashed the court-martial, but to be left alone in a military hospital . . .

There is only one cure for all ills – work. At least I have
the weekend schools. Are you all giving superb performances?
Is Howard addressed as Herr Regisseur and are you the best
company to tour Germany since Wangenheim?

Keep warm. I've never been so cold. But we had dehydrated
potato for supper last night with dried egg and London town in
candlelight. I shall be so happy to see you all again, but how long
will that feeling last?

Your ever-loving producer,

J.L.

Tuesday 18th Feb
Wuppertal

A STATEMENT BY MEMBERS OF THE THEATRE WORKSHOP COMPANY

After our performance on the evening of 17th February 1947,
we were told that supper would be served at the Golden Eagle
Officers' Club, Wuppertal. The meal ordered, several members
of the company refused wine, asking for water.

A Major who was standing at the bar sent eight drinks across to
our table. One of the actresses went to thank him but met with an
embarrassing response. The Major and his companions were the
worse for drink.

The meal over, some of the company started dancing and
couldn't help hearing this same Major making obscene comments
as they passed. The men were referred to as 'bearded bastards'.
Howard Goorney, the company's Producer, suggested that we
leave. While collecting our coats in the foyer the drunken Major
(Brown of 14th/20th Hussars) stuck his head round the door and
shouted, 'You had better get out of here quickly, you have got
long noses,' while one of his companions started objecting to our
presence in the club.

'Why do you want us to leave?' asked one of the actresses.

'You've got long noses', was the reply. David Scase, our Stage
Director, asked him what he meant by this remark.

'Another Yid,' said Major Brown to his friends, and a stream of anti-Semitic abuse followed.

Howard Goorney persuaded David Scase to move away.

'That's right. We don't want you Irgun Zvei Leuni in here.'

'I completely associate myself with my friend's remark,' said the second Major.

The company decided to leave rather than rise to the gross provocation which followed.

It seems to us that such behaviour calls for a public apology.

> Howard Goorney,
> Producer
> David Scase, Stage
> Director
> Benedict Ellis,
> Lighting Director
> Rosalie Williams,
> Gerald Raffles
> Düsseldorf, 18th Feb 1947

Next day

P.S.   Called on Power, the Welfare Officer, to get reaction to our protest – a shifty response. Officers' Club very sympathetic. They made forty thousand pounds this year.

GERRY'S DIARY   Friday 21st February

Some German actors came to see the show but at first were refused admittance. After a lot of persuasion we got them in. They were impressed by our work. Joan writes from Ormesby complaining of lack of letters.

HOWARD tO JOAN   Saturday 22nd
                                     Düsseldorf

Told Power our publicity was bad, suggested improvements. He seemed friendly, told me Major Brown had been reprimanded and barred from the club.

Düsseldorf
                                        Saturday 22nd

Four letters from Joan. Wired back. I have a hundred and
twenty-six pounds, thirteen shillings. Went to a party. Some big
shots in MI5 among the guests. Isla told one of them, 'You should
talk to Gerry, he's a Communist.'

GERRY to JOAN   Hagenfurst
                                        26th February 1947
                                        Wednesday
                                        Late at night

My Joan,

Today I organised a trip to the Schloss at Ketwig. Seven of
us went. It took two hours. No joke in our coach. We were
petrified with the cold, but it was worth it for the riches of
Van Gogh, Gauguin, Renoir, Corot, Fragonard, Manet, Franz
Hals, Brueghel the Younger, and Daumier's 'Spurning of Christ'.
All human life was there. I cannot forget Daumier's magnificent
monochrome, but we landed back only forty-five minutes before
'Curtain up'. I wish I could go back again, but that would
mean a day off, and Howard insists on training and exercises,
daily.
     Yours,

                                        Gerry

P.S.   Beloved, I am so miserable. No news of you. It doesn't
mean that you haven't written, the postal service is chaotic. We
all went for a fortnight without a single letter at the beginning.
Maybe something terrible has happened . . .
                                        G.C.R.

GERRY to JOAN

Hagenfurst
Thursday Night, 27th
Friday morning before the
post, 28th

My Joan,

I was almost sick with excitement when I opened your telegram.
I couldn't believe I was going to speak to you. I had over half an
hour's wait before the call came through, and almost gave up. The
curtain is at 8.00. I changed at 6.00 to be ready, phone calls have
to be between 7.15 and 8 p.m.

When I heard your voice, I could have cried. We are so far
apart. The three minutes passed in a flash, but time enough for me
to hear that you are ill. Why? Why can't you look after yourself?
It doesn't matter when I'm there, I can look after you. But whilst
I'm away, who else will? And if anyone does, they take their toll.
I wish I had never come on this trip.

Friday 28th February

Howard reports that the company are tired of his repeated
criticisms! And Rosalie is off sick. Her roles have been recast.

GERRY to JOAN

Friday 28th February
Late

Dearest love,

I tried to phone you tonight. From 7 p.m. until three minutes
before eight. I waited in the small office which contains the magic
kiosk, all ready to go on. At five minutes to eight they said the calls
were coming through, but I had to go. Tomorrow I'll try again – if
only the calls would come through on time.

Rosalie saw a specialist today. He said she would be a fool
to go on playing! She has a very sore throat, a fever and feels
bloody awful. Edna can take over the *Proposal* but *Johnnie Noble*
without Rosalie is insuperable. You will have to come and play
it. The army have promised to lay on a plane to bring you.

Are you over the flu? What happened? Did you go out too

soon? That is the way to lay the seeds of another illness. Why
aren't you here? I could have enjoyed this tour with you, despite
all the frustrations. There is so much to see and hear and we could
have walked in the forest, visited the galleries, tasted fine wines and
liqueurs. Together we would have enjoyed it all. Alone I have no
desire for these things.

Tomorrow is mail day. Will there be a letter from you? If I
don't succeed in getting thro' on the phone tomorrow night, God
knows when I shall hear your voice again. Do try to come. The
company needs you terribly, though not as much as I do. And in
a fortnight's time we are due to play Berlin.

Your, and only your

Gerry

JOAN to HOWARD   Friday 28th February
                                 Ormesby

Ormesby is now an Arctic outpost. We are quite cut off. The
courtyard is impassable, there are snowdrifts in the passage and
over the walls and ceilings the snow casts an unearthly white light.
I have hardly ventured out of my room. I had to keep to my bed
for a day or two with a dose of flu. Getting to the Post Office is a
major expedition, which all goes to explain this delayed reply.

Jimmie has been ill. On Wednesday he was moved to Northfield
Military Hospital, Birmingham, an army nuthouse. He is in the
'violent' ward, guards, locked doors, straitjackets and isolation cells
(padded cells, I suppose) but there is some hope of his getting his
discharge.

About the anti-Semitic outburst, I think it is not to be wondered
at with the situation as it is in Palestine and the demoralisation of
the British Forces in Germany. It must be very unpleasant to have
to rub shoulders with these types but I don't think you should
make any more protests. And don't be depressed when you get
small houses. The troops have been conditioned by the rubbish
they've had dished up to them.

You seem to be organising the training excellently. You are
right, we must raise our standards. I don't want production to

have to cover up weaknesses. It is important that results are
assessed and criticisms made by the whole team, at your weekly
production meetings.

I am not too proud of *The Proposal*, and you cannot do
much with your character without a completely new concept.
If you have an idea, take time, work on it, but don't put it into
practice too soon. For the moment do what you can about the
others but concentrate on your own rôle. It was very interesting
when I last saw it. Make good use of those large theatres, go
through chunks of dialogue purely for voice but voice with
nuance.

I would like Ben to feel free to write his play after the
tour and the company to have a chance to improve technically
using Ormesby as base. We can earn our living playing and
teaching locally. It would be self-defeating just to go on mounting
shows. Our work must shine. Those who don't like the idea, will
go.

I'm discussing this with Mike today. He'll probably shoot
me.

Keep your heart up,

J.L.

GERRY to JOAN   Iserholm, 1st March
                                       Saturday night

Dearest beloved Joan,

Just a line to tell you how much I love you and miss you.
Tonight we gave an excellent performance to a large, responsive
audience. Rosalie was well enough to sit and watch out front. She
said it was the best she had ever seen it.

A letter from you today, written on Monday in Middlesbrough
Post Office. You must have been there while I was phoning
Ormesby. I hope you are really fit now, and getting plenty to eat.

The company has earned itself an exemplary character with
the various CSE units as the only group not solely occupied in
exploiting the black market. It's terrible the way people tip with
cigarettes.

I will write fully tomorrow.
Your

                              Gerry

P.S.   Martial law was declared in Palestine today.

HOWARD to JOAN   Sunday March 2nd
                                  Hanover

Last night Ben left his bedroom and wandered about. He needs
help. Rosalie has suggested certain changes. Dinner party at the
Officers' Club in honour of Isla's birthday. Wine and a huge cake
laid on back at the hostel. The party went on till nearly morning.

GERRY to JOAN   Sunday March 2nd
                                  Hanover, 4.15 p.m.

Dearest,

The mails due yesterday were delayed by the snow. You say
that you haven't had a letter from me for a long while. For your
information I wrote to you every day, at least once, and posted the
letters every day, until Tuesday Feb 11th at Minden when I hadn't
heard from you and was feeling suicidal. I didn't write any more till
Feb 18th when I heard from you and realised that at least you still
remembered me. I have written every day since, occasionally two
days spilling over into one envelope. So now you know.

   Don't be misled into thinking that we are doing a triumphal tour
mobbed by crowds clamouring to see us. We most definitely are
not!! The audiences seem to be getting smaller and more restive,
but their cracks are marvellous. Unfortunately they destroy David
and poor old John B., especially when the already sparse audience
is made even sparser by the defection of a large crowd of clod-
hoppers. Rosalie was pretty scathing after watching the performance. She liked Howard, David and John Blanshard – and she
thought I was good. She thinks the weak spots are inherent in
the writing.

   Howard feels low, he says he feels like cancelling the rest of the tour and returning us to England. You really should come and help us over this bad patch. Indifferent audiences night after night destroy the company's morale.

We have had a lot more snow; many of the roads are impassable. On the way here we saw several abandoned lorries. Most other companies have refused to move from their billets. We have a very good German driver so we made the journey from Iserholm in six hours. But the lorry with the equipment still (10.30 p.m.) hasn't turned up and he's been on the road since 8.30 this morning.

Dear Joan, another day nearer to the time when I shall see you. By then I shall be a jaded, drink-sodden wreck. Apart from the company needing you, I need you so badly that I've been trying to work out a scheme for flying back to England and kidnapping you – or just flying back!!

Gerry

P.S.   A gang had to be sent to dig the truck out of a snowdrift. It didn't arrive till 5.15 p.m. the following day.

G.

P.P.S.   We can't go wrong at this hostel. They say we're the nicest company they've ever had, can't do enough for us. The CSE theatre manager, young, pro-T.W. and very much against the black market, knows some great calypsos.

GERRY to JOAN   Hanover
                                               Tuesday night, March 4th

My darling,

Things are looking up. Howard (at the company meeting): 'It was so dark on the stage last night I had to carry a torch to find my way about.'

Edna and Ben have split and with the minimum of fuss, at least in public. It can't have been very pleasant for Edna, but she took it with her usual pride and self-control. I don't think she minds being away from that whirligig. He celebrated his release from marital bliss by making notes on 'Masters of the Drama' in preparation for his play. And he has gone back to Jung. We all have to differentiate between empirical and cognitive thinking.

The German interpreter saw the show tonight. She says the Germans understand it better than the English.

Your

Gerry

GERRY to JOAN   Hanover
                                                 Wednesday, very late
                                                 March 5th

My dearest love,

At eleven-fifteen tonight I received three wonderful letters from you, the latest dated March 2nd, only three days away from me. I have been so occupied with reading and re-reading them, finding out what you wrote to the others and looking at your handwriting, that I felt reluctant to start writing myself. It has been a long empty week since I last heard from you, but these letters make up for it. I don't want to make this a love letter even though my being is filled with love for you and I long for your presence. There seems to be a lot to tell you but I am tired. If I let my feelings run riot there will be no time for anything else.

John Blanshard and Margaret undertake Herculean labours together. Starting early morning, John holds Margaret's diaphragm or rehearses her parts (i.e. rôles!) Rosalie thinks their vocal work shows some improvement. I am not sure it's worth it. They are so prim and self-righteous about it all. I know voice production is all-important but when they refuse to go to a concert or see paintings because they must do their exercises, it is surely time to think again. John B. always gives an efficient performance, which is more than can be said for some of us. On the other hand, it is impossible to look at Margaret on stage. She is always so self-conscious. I'm sure she isn't helped by the way they work together.

We have cut the recordings of Jimmie singing. Denis sings 'Love Love Alone' and makes an excellent job of it. You may find this difficult to believe but Jimmie couldn't sing it better. Bill accompanies Isla in 'Man Of Our Time' on the guitar and it's now interesting and audible.

Morning

Joan,

Do you intend to go on for ever with this cast? The size of the company dissipates your energy and makes this a very expensive outfit to run. Apart from anything else, Jimmie's work is no longer sublimated here. There is a lot of criticism of the way he insults the audience. If all the bits were cut that people want cut, there would hardly be anything left. I've never thought much of *U235* as a play, though I've not let my work in it grow stale.

Now the audiences here are dwindling with each performance, but they do get more appreciative. I must close, the post is going. Goodbye for now. I love you with every fibre of my being.

Gerry

GERRY to JOAN

BERLIN NEXT WEEK
(24 DAYS TO GO)
Lüneburg
Sunday evening
9th March 1947

Well, difficult one,

How are you? I have a touch of flu so I am not really at the top of my form. We wait for the bus each morning in the market square, which gives us plenty of time to admire the sixteenth-century houses.

Ben is happy. He's having a beautiful *affaire de coeur* (*et de ****). Don't mention this to anyone, because Ben feels it all very deeply and, except for Camel and I, nobody knows anything about it. There was a dark-eyed waitress at the hostel called Joanna who for a time caught the eye both of Ben and Howard. It remained on that plane until Saturday when she went out for a walk with Ben. 'She is only twenty but she's seen everything – such terrible things that there is nothing left for her to see' – and on Saturday night he took along a bottle of whisky and slept in her arms.

There were half a dozen young women in Hanover who were of the right shape and size for dalliance, but not for me, though I got an offer as I was sitting in the lounge writing to you. It was about 2 a.m. Friday. A buxom peasant girl with black hair and black eyes came out of the kitchen and stood right next to my chair. She laughed at me, ran her hands through my hair and said, 'I'm twenty-one and have never had a man.' I told her that I had a beautiful wife at home but she said, 'England is a long way away. It's not good for a man to be always alone.' Fortunately John B. came in and saved the situation.

Dear heart, I must leave you and rest up for the rig. I have to get rid of this flu. If I were John Donne I could write you such a poem but as I'm only me I will have to wait till I'm with you and try to show you by direct action. Clasp each warm breast for me. Tell them how much I wish I were there to do so myself.

Your

Gerry

GERRY to JOAN   Tuesday 11th March
                                 Lüneburg

Good morning, beloved,

Last night we had a large but very rough house.

DAVID: You can't kill all of us.
VOICE (*from the audience*): I could.
DAVID: Can you give me something?
VOICE: Yes. Potassium cyanide.
JOHN B.: In a few minutes the audience will leave this theatre.
VOICES: We're going now.

I didn't get all of them. We often get homosexual cracks when Energy draws his circle on the floor. Last night they really went to town during the whole Energy speech. I don't find it annoying, rather the opposite. But I must say the audience made a shambles of the last scene, though they were very appreciative at the curtain call.

Ben really is in love. Having to leave after only one night
with his Joanna, he is even more in love. He has sent her his
cigarettes, his rations, and spent his wages on silk stockings and
soap for her. He is intensely serious, very sweet and up half the
night trying to translate his letters into German, with the help of
Camel's pocket dictionary. You mustn't mention this to ANYONE.
Love makes him so beautiful. I wouldn't hurt him for the world.

About us, if you want the truth, the only element which
will militate against us becoming a popular theatre is Jimmie. I
come more and more to the conclusion that his overall influence
is directly opposed to the sort of theatre that you and most of
us want. Soon you will have to realise it or another ten years of
your life will be wasted. Dearest Joan, don't do me the injustice
of thinking I am just grinding my own axe. I am old enough to
have critical faculties and they are not dependent on my emotional
responses.

I make no comment on your writing a Derbyshire script
for the BBC – I can't think of anything polite enough to say.
Whatever you do, look after yourself and live on your own.
You've enough money to stay at that little pub in Rusholme.
Don't drag all the way up to Werneth Low. You allow yourself
to be put-upon in personal matters which means you never get
enough privacy. So far as I can see, you might as well have been
working in a factory for all the time you've usefully had to yourself
lately.

Dear love, I wish I were with you. I feel as if I never will
be again. I can't tell you how much I love you because at this
moment I am only conscious of your absence.

Gerry

P.S. Edna plays Rosalie's Neutron in *U235*, now. She has
made it completely her own. It's an excellent performance, but
she seems terribly unhappy. Howard says she wants to leave.
So does he. 'Nobody wants training or rehearsal any more,' he
says.

GERRY to JOAN   Lüneburg
                                 Wednesday night
                                 March 12th 1947

Beloved Joan,

The German stage-hands at the theatres always watch the show
and their comments are very instructive. Tonight one of them
told me, 'These English soldiers don't understand. The ones who
fought in the war, they understand.' And these chaps can't even
speak our language!!! There is really very little demoralisation in
Germany. We saw more of it in peace-time Glasgow than here.
Almost every German we've spoken to has been looking for a way
forward, deeply conscious of the state their country is in. 'There
will be no spring for us this year,' said a hospital cleaner to Bill.

   If only the Occupation Forces had given a clear, progressive
lead, there would have been some hope, but with the British
troops behaving like Nazis, there's nothing but frustration and
despair.

   Life will be emptier with Ben away writing. For me, he is
the only real oasis in this desert. Howard is a rock and you can
depend on Camel, though he's passive and undeveloped, but of
the rest, only John B. gives water from his own well. Ben will be
a serious loss. He is worried about earning enough money to live.
He talks about BBC scripts. Can't the theatre grubstake him? He
is probably going to Mrs Stewart's in Kendal, two pounds a week
board and lodging. Surely to God we can afford to pay him three
or four pounds a week whilst he is writing a play for us. If you
agree, do write and tell him so. It's causing him a good deal of
anxiety.

   I have been meaning to tell you what an excellent job Howard
has been doing. He is influenced by neither fear nor favour and
nothing is too much trouble. We have had more regular training
than we had in England and weak spots in the shows are always
refreshed. He has been tired just lately, that's why he thinks the
company has had enough. In fact, they all want his warm-ups to
continue.

   Sweetheart, soon I shall see you, but not soon enough. If I
were going to see you an hour from now, it would still be three

thousand, six hundred seconds too long. And it is exactly three weeks. Twenty more dawns after this, now breaking, till you are the sun and I the surrounding sea.

Gerry

HOWARD to JOAN   Lüneburg
                                        Thursday March 13th

HOWARD'S REPORT

When this tour finishes, from what I can make out:

David intends to earn money. Rosalie intends to lose her appendix and acquire a baby. Edna and Margaret, to fulfil themselves as schoolteachers. Ruth to fulfil herself. Kerstin is going to Sweden and will probably never come back. Denis is leaving too. Seven left out of fifteen. Looks as if you're going to need a new company and start all over again. If you insist on a company of the same size, you will recreate all the problems. If you don't, you can't play the same repertoire. I have tackled the dissidents, each in turn. David will postpone his departure. (How far this is due to your letter, which he received today, I don't know. Largely, I think.) Rosalie will go when he goes (connubial bliss). Unless, of course, we're successful in the meanwhile. Edna is determined to go and I had a helluva job with Margaret and Ruth. Margaret now thinks she may stay and write. Ruth wants to talk to you. All these dramas! Can't Mike just give her a fortnight's notice? I know I'm just evading an unpleasant task. And now Bill wants to know what's going on. He wants to stay and be an actor! But will he ever be?

Howard

Stop Press Margaret has quit John B. and taken up with Camel. Now she has no intention of leaving us. Alas. Last night I went to pieces in *The Proposal*. Tonight the shows picked up.

Lüneburg
                                         Thursday March 13th
                                         3.30 p.m.

My Joan,

It is your absence which has brought this situation to a head.
If you had been here, they would have sustained themselves on
your talent. What a lot of energy we waste. For God's sake, from
now on choose plays which have only a few characters. Let's be
small and beautiful instead of, as now, smothered in shifting sand.
If you concentrated your efforts on a few people, had David doing
nothing but sound, Camel nothing but lights, got rid of everybody
who showed no promise, we'd crash the big time much sooner.

I have no doubt you will do what you think best. I only hope
Scrooge stays in gaol long enough for you to decide without
him. Otherwise, we will have a new influx of *demi-vierges* stirred
to attempt creativity after a few nights' clumsy love with a red-
bearded playwright.

You ask me to tell you whether anyone ever thinks of Jimmie.
Well, the only person who ever mentions his name not in a
derogatory way is Rosalie, who often asks about him and says,
'Oh, Joan won't come, she won't leave him.'

Otherwise, I think people here have a far more objective view of
him than you've ever had. Several believe that he is a real menace
to the Workshop's future and have said so.

I must go now, sweetheart.

I still don't believe in our holiday in Paris.

Auf wiedersehen. Mit alle meine Liebe,

                                                      Gerry

Berlin
                                         Monday 17th March
                                         3.30 p.m.

Dearest,

By half-past twelve last night, the gear was loaded and we climbed
on to the night train to Berlin. Ben was away till the last moment

saying goodbye to his Johanna. (Note the 'h'.)

Owing to the transport people's muddle, there were only six sleepers. Despite strong opposition from me, these, by popular gallant consent, went to the young ladies of the troupe; the male members of the cast spent the night in discomfort, struggling for sleep.

The engine on German trains is much bigger than ours and a larger part of the works is outside, so it looks like a towering dragon in the low night light. The train doesn't speak English either. Instead of the stolid 'di-di da di-di da', it talks faster, in a more excited fashion, 'tsse, cling cling cling cling; tsse, cling cling cling cling.'

Unfortunately it was a troop train, and it's when you are among our troops that you are conscious of the German reaction. Many of our people say they feel it all the time. I pass for a German at first sight, so I am usually accepted – not when mixed up with soldiers, though. The hatred inspired by these seventeen-year-old 'conquerors' wells up at times like this. The train staff carry loaded guns very conspicuously. One wanted to throw me off because he thought I was a German civilian.

Even so, this was an exciting journey. I pulled down the sprung window in the corridor, watching for the lights which shone occasionally from the high mounds of rubble. All the time the train talked to itself in its high-pitched voice. What was it saying? 'The night train to Paris, the boat train to Paris, the night train, the night train.'

We arrived about 7 a.m. and after breakfast proceeded to the rig, fortunately not difficult. It seemed very small after the places we've been playing. Actually it's bigger than the Queen's, Glasgow; a twenty-four-foot opening, twenty-one-foot depth.

We tried to phone you yesterday, but after waiting three hours we were told that the lines were out of order. Tomorrow we will try Dean St. As you are holding auditions there, we may get you.

There are new and quite respectable posters advertising the show. The fuss Howard made weeks ago has borne some fruit, now that the tour is almost over. Goodbye for now, sweetheart. I am going to try for an hour's rest before the show. I wonder if we really

will get to Paris. If we do . . . you'll see. I wish I were there now.
  Your

                                             Gerry

HOWARD to JOAN   Berlin
                                        Monday 17th March

Dr Wilhelm Pieck came backstage after the show. Very friendly,
talked of us playing to a German audience. A British officer would
have to be consulted.

GERRY to JOAN   Berlin
                                        Tuesday night
                                        18th March 1947

Dear love,

Tried to phone you again but the lines were out of order, due to the
gales. From now on I don't even know where you will be. Bill and
Kerstin went to the offices of *Our Time*, the paper which published
an article on us. They were introduced to Friedrich Wolf. He
is about fifty now, went to Moscow when Hitler seized power,
fought in Spain in the Thälmann Battalion, interned in France,
on his release went back to Moscow. During the War he made
his way to France and fought with the Maquis. In Germany at
the end of the War he worked with the underground in Stuttgart.
  Still twelve more days here, but the nights are the worst. How
could you leave me to face sixty-three days and nights alone? If I
could have left the company without hurting the show . . . I can't
write any more.

                                             Gerry

HOWARD to JOAN   Wednesday 19th March
                                        Berlin

With Gerry to see Pieck and a man called Lynch. They had
watched our show again and arranged for the company to see

The Adding Machine. Lynch is very anti-Soviet but dead keen on our work.

Gerry and I tried to get to a theatre in the Russian zone, without success. Saw the Kurfürstendamm. So many signs of luxury, shops full of wonderful antiques. To the Volksbühne. Splendid acting, excellent staging, but had to leave at 7.00.

HOWARD to JOAN   Friday 21st March
                                                 Berlin

With Kerstin and Rosalie to the Soviet zone to attend a rehearsal of Friedrich Wolf's *Cyankali*, performed by students. They were young, but old enough to have seen the horrors of war. They live in unheated houses, they are badly paid and underfed, but there was an enthusiasm and a love of their work which gave tremendous life to the performance.

It was heartening to see life springing up in the shambles that was once Berlin. After lunch we saw Ernst Busch in *Sailors of Cattaro* at the same theatre. Again the audience was mainly students. Their reaction as the red flag was hoisted to the strains of 'The Internationale' coming, as it were, from across the water, left no doubt as to where their sympathies lay.

The theatre will play a tremendous part in the re-education of German youth, if it is allowed to do so. Most of the theatres seem to be in the Russian sector, though Bartog, who was said to be the most progressive producer, works in the American zone. The British officer responsible for German theatre in our zone told us the Russians spoiled German actors in order to keep their hold on them.

Friedrich Wolf dined with us at our hostel; an inspiring man. Thank you for your letter and your training plan. I am disappointed because I'm impatient to act. I'm not satisfied with my work. I want to move on to the next stage. I know there's no short cut to being an actor. I only hope the auditions have brought us some new talent.

The week in Berlin has been full and fruitful. Friedrich Wolf is Bill and Kerstin's 'baby', a wonderful chap and a useful contact.

He can put us in touch with young writers all over Europe.

There's a lot I want to say, Joan, but I'll have to cut this letter short as I've made a morning call and this afternoon we are visiting a Schloss near here to see some Rembrandts.

Yours,

Howard

P.S.   What about Isla? She's lazy, gets on my nerves and doesn't know what day it is but she has talent. Thank Christ it's your job to decide who's worth keeping.

I'm preparing a report on the tour covering the shows, audience reactions, company behaviour and development, or otherwise. You may find it useful and it will serve to clarify the position in my own mind. I'll let you have it before the next company meeting.

Jimmie out yet?

Twenty-six

Gerry and I. To Paris. The shadow of the War. Jimmie is free. Revisit my favourite places, see Jouvet's École des Femmes, Jean-Louis Barrault's Hamlet. Back in UK, Mike, Gerry, Kerstin try for dates. Felixstowe – the Isle of Man – and a very eccentric hostess. In Manchester, at last, we play the Liberty Theatre. An unforeseen outbreak on the streets.

I was in London when the boat docked at 6 a.m. on Monday 31st March 1947. Gerry went straight to Manchester, spent the evening with his folks and the following day combed the town, looking for a theatre.

See you Wednesday April 2nd, 4.00 p.m., London Victoria, No. 8 platform, Continental Express.

Joan

Gerry had never seen France, and as he stood at the barrier, the tickets in his pocket, he began to think he wasn't going to see it now. Suppose Jimmie Miller was still under lock and key? Five to four. A harum-scarum figure came dashing across the station.

'Where were you? We almost missed the train.'

No hugs and kisses till we were aboard, then, with those grey-blue eyes on you and your hand in his, the world could get lost.

'Scrooge free?' he asked at last.

'Any day now.'

'It took you long enough.'

'I wouldn't have managed it at all without good friends, and the psychiatrist helped. He said Jimmie was a paranoid personality with strong Oedipal tendencies.'

'That's an understatement.'

'What does it matter? It's all a lot of tosh . . .'

With the sun gilding a steel-grey sea, I wanted to forget Jimmie and the company, everything but our being together. We stayed on deck till it was almost dark and the French coast a shadow on the horizon.

'Let's spend the night in Dieppe.'

It was pleasant to linger while everybody hurried towards the waiting train, speaking French. All we had to do was find a bed. The houses in the dockside streets were already shuttered, but the restaurant offering *Sole Dieppoise* was still open. Madame gave Gerry the name of a small hotel and he went off to investigate. I'd scarcely had time to order when he was back.

'All fixed.'

'What a relief.'

I hadn't wanted to produce my passport. It bore the name Miller.

T he sun shone on us through flimsy curtains. We lay abed till the whole room was flooded with light. Bowls of coffee and lengths of buttered bread arrived. We went and breakfasted out on the balcony. There was a statue in the square below; market stalls were being set up all around it. Could it be the square that Sickert painted? It was. I have never located that hotel since, though I have often looked for it. On that first morning together, after a hard winter's separation, we were just happy to be alive. The *rapide* for Paris went clanking by.

'Never mind. We'll take the stopping train, see more of France.'

'Anything you say.'

A *gendarme* was on traffic duty. Gerry asked him the way to the town station. He touched his cap and smiled. I was relieved. After all, the Allied invasion had not been exactly popular on this coast. 'The English gave their machines, the French their *poitrines*.' I wanted to ask him if he'd been in the Resistance, but just then two young men in kilts wandered across the road, without waiting for the green light. He blew his whistle and administered a short, sharp reprimand. On our way to the station, the hoardings were plastered with fly posters of De Gaulle's long face. 'He's back.'

The stopping train lived up to its name and at every station Gerry hoisted some old lady up into the carriage and placed her bundle on the rack.

'*Anglais?*' said the little man opposite. '*Plus gentils que nous.*'

> *Bien que leur chapeaux sont bien laids*
> *Goddam, moi, j'aime les Anglais.*

He went on, explaining in rapid French that we were of course a nation of eccentrics, eating jam with our meat and living in perpetual fog. Then he translated the notice about not leaning out of the window for us. Gerry, to stem the flow, asked him what all the De Gaulle publicity was about.

'*Rassemblement du Peuple Français.* 'E will launch 'is campaign Monday next, in Strasbourg. All France awaits 'im. 'E will unite us. Too many strikes, too many Socialists. We French are not disciplined as you English. Everybody distrusts everybody – but De Gaulle has powerful friends. Monsieur André Malraux 'as joined 'im.' And he went on till the train swung into Rouen, whereupon, waving his dispatch case, he disappeared.

By the time the tall grey tenements of Paris appeared we'd had enough of our stopping train.

'*Ça marche à Paris,*' said the old lady with mittens, as Gerry helped her to the platform.

We were hungry. The only part of Paris I remembered was the rue Daguerre. We took the Métro. It still smelt of garlic, lead pencils and 'Soir de Paris'. Gerry noted the famous names given to the stations, Louise Michel, Jaurès, Robespierre, Dumas, Ledru-Rollin, Etienne Marcel, and we renamed some of our London stops: Sylvia Pankhurst for Trafalgar Square, Gerard Winstanley for Charing Cross, Wat Tyler for the Tower. Change at George Lansbury for Geoffrey Chaucer.

We took a room with balcony, bidet, double bed with sausage pillow, eleven francs a night, rue Vavin. There were yellow flowered curtains and a yellow quilt. The bathroom was at the end of the passage; you obtained the key from Madame.

We dined at Le Bon Acceuil, rue Daguerre, which I'd known in

my youth. It looked very different, smaller. We walked past twice
before entering. A bell clanged loudly; the *propriétaire* stopped
swishing her dishcloth across the counter. Was it the wrong place?

'Can we eat?'

Madame shuffled to a table, screwed up the stained paper
cover. 'Beans, salad, paté and vermicelli,' she said.

'We'll take them all,' said Gerry.

'*Comme boisson?*'

'*Rouge.*'

Four card players had been watching us. They resumed their
game.

'Shall we find somewhere else?'

But Gerry was already seated and hungry as a hunter.

As we paid I asked what rue Daguerre had been like during the
Occupation. I thought they hadn't understood, till one of the card
players turned down his cards and came to the bar. He swallowed
a Calvados, then moved to the door.

'You see the corner of rue Général Leclerc, the *supermarché*? It
was there the women made their protest. The Boche were taking
all our food. They dispersed the women, *très vite.*'

S hrill klaxons woke us in the morning.
'It's only the Paris traffic.'

We snuggled together again and made love. Our time was
our own.

'Let's take *petit déjeuner* on the grand boulevard and watch
the world go by.'

I brought out my new cap and put it on at a Parisian angle.
Gerry tried to snatch it and chased me along the passage. I took
refuge in the lift. He was waiting when I landed and my beautiful
cap was whisked off my head. I never saw it again. At a small table
on the Boul. Mich. I made my first *faux pas*.

'*Bonjour, m'sieur, 'dame.*'

'*Café et croissants, s'il vous plaît.*'

The waiter, a tall faded man, gave me such a look as he
plonked a small basket of dry bread in front of me.

'Did you 'ear about the War?'

After that the War haunted us. We imagined jackboots in the Louvre, *Interdit aux Juifs* on the phone boxes . . .

'I wouldn't have lasted long, they'd have got me for something more serious than a phone call,' said Gerry and bought himself a sausage that hummed with garlic. With two Uniprix glasses and a litre of *rouge* we went and sat by the Seine.

'*Bon appétit*,' said an old lady who was leaning on the parapet.

And as I scattered crumbs for the sparrows, she asked if I believed in God.

'No.'

'You think this is the end of it all?' She looked up at the mountains of white clouds. 'Yes, it is difficult to believe in God after all we have lived through.'

We'd 'done' the Louvre. I'd renewed acquaintance with old favourites and Gerry had found it all a bit overwhelming.

'But you must see Rodin's Balzac,' I told him. 'I haven't, since I was a schoolgirl.'

It was still on view at the Rodin museum, my favourite – the one with the leonine head and the body wrapped in a cloak of stone. Gerry loved the figures half-plunged in marble, the ones which had once so shocked the critics. Afterwards we inspected the stone queens in the Luxembourg Gardens, so respectable and Victorian after Rodin. The children were launching model yachts on the round pond as they have always done, War or no War. Then we wandered through the streets. The shops were rather bare but we admired the glass paintings of laundresses, style – Belle Epoque; the plaster lobsters above the fishmongers in rue Mouffetard; and the old suitcases full of books so tattered that no one would dare unfold them.

Next day we went to Montmartre to look for the place where Louise Michel and her fellow Communards had held out to the last, but we couldn't find it. We talked of bringing our theatre to Paris – in triumph, of course – as we sat in Le Chat qui Fume. We'd decided it was the place where the decadents had talked the night away in the nineties and drank a *fine* in their honour. On the other side of the road the old red windmill was still turning and a gaping dragon lit you to a select cabaret which was just about to begin. We went, paid our five francs, groped past a heavy

curtain and found ourselves in a room where a small audience sat
in mournful anticipation. A peroxide blonde in red bra and shorts
told us that drinks were obligatory. The droopy red curtain slung
across the room was bulging and a tinny gramophone gave out 'Ta
ra ra Boum dee ay'. Two tepid white wines arrived on a tray. The
curtain rose and three peroxide blondes stood there, red stars on
their nipples and spangles on their suspender belts. They marked
time to the music, then suddenly made a beeline for Gerry and
pulled him out of his seat. He struggled manfully . . . No use.
They hauled him up on to the stage and the curtain fell. The
youngest girl pulled it aside to announce, 'M'sieu Géri is off on
a voyage to the Moon.' Fanfare on the gramophone and M'sieu
Géri is revealed lying on a tilted disc between two of the girls. He
waved as the disc began to spin and stars and moons went jerking
by on clotheslines. Applause, the space travellers waved. Curtain.
Gerry staggered out, smiling ruefully.

On 8th March, the day of Jimmie's release, Gerry wrote
'Scrooge out' in his diary. To me it didn't sound an appropriate
nickname, but it was funny when Gerry said it and reminded me
that we hadn't given theatre a thought since we'd left London.
Louis Jouvet was playing at the Athénée. We'd better see that,
said Gerry and went to the French actors' Equity and acquired
two comps.

As he wended his way through the usual ticket ritual in the
foyer, I studied the large map which showed all the countries
where Jouvet's company had played during the Occupation. They
escaped to America in good time and he wanted everybody to know
it. Women known to have slept with a German were dragged to the
public square to have their head shaved brutally but the famous
Arletty, who'd lived with a Nazi officer, was merely given a quiet
trim, in private. Apparently this was doubly offensive to the Don
Juans of Paris, since until the Occupation she'd been a lesbian. I
was brooding about this when Gerry took my arm and guided me
to the stalls entry. He looked so handsome in his best white shirt
that I was proud to be with him, and for once we weren't climbing
to the back of the gods. . . . I noticed a picture of Dominique
Blanchar who was playing Agnes. Was she Pierre's daughter? I
saw him as Raskolnikov in Gaston Baty's production of *Crime and*

Punishment years ago. If she was as talented as Pierre . . .

A middle-aged woman in a black dress steered us to the far end of the back row, let down a small folding seat. Gerry would only be able to get one buttock on to it. A man, already seated, turned and let down a second bucket seat for me. I sat on it quickly. The lights were dimming, the orchestra tuning up and the woman stood holding out her hand.

'She expects a tip,' I whispered.

Gerry found her some small coins.

'*Vous n'êtes pas généreux, Monsieur,*' she said.

We found out, after, that her only remuneration was tips.

Everyday thoughts vanished as Christian Bérard's enchanting set was revealed. For Molière's *École des Femmes* he'd designed two white-walled theatre streets which converged downstage. Arnolphe and Chrysalde approached *Côté Jardin*, gossiping, but Jouvet was overstating Arnolphe, representing instead of being. Too much shaking and fumbling. Had he been distracted in the wings? Perhaps he'd arrived too late to think himself into the rôle? After all it was his company; he had to shoulder the responsibilities as well as act. As the scene wore on he found the right pitch, the superficialities disappeared, the language had more nuance. In the second scene he was Arnolphe, playing with all the art which conceals art. Well, we'd had to watch him doing his warm-up; it was edifying.

The stage mechanism at the Athenée was ingenious. The two white walls rode smoothly away to reveal a garden with flowerbeds, well-trimmed trees and climbing roses. This was where Arnolphe's young ward, Agnes, took the air in a garden overlooked by a tall white tower. The douce Dominique gave her such an air of sweet simplicity that, against better judgement, you were convinced of her innocence. Hidden from the world she might be, but she was never bored, apparently quite content to sit stitching her guardian's nightshirts. What's more, the alexandrines tripped from her tongue so spontaneously that Monsieur Molière himself might have been her mentor.

The cleverest set change was to come. We would have missed it had we not been in the worst seats in the house. Jouvet left the garden, entered the tower and a moment later appeared on a balcony,

high up. It would have been an impossible climb even for a young
and agile performer. We saw the trick. He was whisked up in a lift.
After the show we walked home relishing Molière as never before.

'Now we ought to see Barrault's *Hamlet*.'

'Shakespeare in French? It's worse than Molière in English.'

But Gerry didn't want to miss it and we had to stand. I'd
seen Barrault's *Enfants du Paradis* and disliked it . . . Deburau
in silk pyjamas. It saved a lot of French actors from deportation,
Gerry told me. 'That's why there was such an enormous cast.'

His Hamlet was just as I'd expected, good taste – no vulgarity!
'Lady, may I lie in your lap?' It sounded as if he wanted to take his
ease on her sofa. Well, Jean-Louis certainly managed to rid the play
of Shakespeare's *'ordures'* to which the famous French librarian had
objected.

Too soon the time came to face life again. Life? The survival
of our Workshop. There was to be a company meeting at Laban's
studio in Manchester the following Monday. I dreaded it – half the
company leaving, the rest jaded. *Adieu la liberté.*

W e were in danger of becoming court jesters at Ormesby,
said Ben, opening the discussion on premises.

'There's nothing wrong with patronage,' said Rosalie.

'It isn't that the Colonel wants us out,' said Howard. 'It's
just Joan.'

'I didn't like that pack of hounds in the courtyard,' I said.

'I wrote Littlewood from the army nuthouse and told her to
get Lever to buy the Arcadia cinema.' Jimmie had returned from a
holiday in the Lake District with Jean, and was looking more like
his old self.

'She didn't,' said Gerry. 'It's no cop. The empty synagogue
on Cheetham Hill would do better, or even the old boxing ring
at Ardwick.'

'What do we use for money? Our summer tour has fallen
through because we asked for guarantees. There's only Felixstowe
left – and us.'

'We could play Ewan's, I mean Jimmie's, *Blitz Song*,' said Jean
– she'd only known him as Ewan – 'It only has a cast of four.'

My heart sank. What had Bernard Shaw said about it when Jimmie was in the nuthouse? 'Powerful, but depressing.' Worse than that, it was a replay of his flutter with Rosalie when he was supposed to be married to me. At the time he'd only wanted me to play the wife!

Soon I would be taking another weekend school in Ormesby. I'd probably be able to replenish the company there. I hadn't mentioned the offer of a BBC programme on Swaledale to the meeting, Jimmie having accused Rosalie and David of selling out to the fleshpots because they'd landed a few *Children's Hour* jobs at two guineas a time. It was a relief to take the train to Middlesbrough, put my feet up and admire the splendour of the Industrial North. Anyway, Gerry had agreed to work on the Swaledale programme for me. We needed the cash too.

The railway journey from Manchester to Leeds was pretty grim, nothing but rusting machines slumped in pools of oil, empty sheds with blackened windows, the sheen of verdigris here and there among banks of rosebay and bindweed. So much for the workshop of the world.

Ormesby was deserted. The Colonel and his lady were away. The old house looked lonely. My spirits revived when I started work and I managed to collect enough young enthusiasts to play Felixstowe with us, if we could raise the fare, but what could we play? Well, we'd more girls than fellers. Ben had gone to write his play, so Jimmie would have to take back his original role, the deserter. That should please him. Gerry was making a good job of Swaledale. He'd added quite a few country lyrics to his repertoire. Now he wanted to take up the quest for premises again. Kerstin too wanted to be off. 'I could help fix a tour,' she told me. 'And who would play Lysistrata?' I asked.

Shaw always said, 'Theatre Workshop will get by – they always do.' And we did. Everybody took any work they could find, helped lick the newcomers into shape, pooled resources, and on a glorious June day in 1947 we arrived in Felixstowe. I got up early each morning to swim in the blessed sea. The day's work began on the grassy lawn beside the Pavilion. We sang and danced and rehearsed Margaret as Lysistrata, watched by a crowd of holidaymakers. We'd sell a few of them tickets before they drifted away.

Kerstin and Gerry were off on the quest.

On the Friday night, a handful of gravel was thrown at my window. It was Gerry standing there, arms outstretched. He came in and handed me a carrier bag.

'Present from the smoke,' he said.

I shook out a summer dress, dark green with bronze patterns. I loved that dress, the only dress I've ever worn.

'Where's Kerstin?'

'I've no idea. She came to see Chico Marx with me at the Palladium, then vanished.'

'Is he coming to see us?'

'How can he leave his show? He said he'd like to see our act and we told him how much we admired the *commedia dell'arte*. He said he'd never heard of them. Anyway, Tom Driberg's coming tomorrow and Michel St Denis. I tried for Stephen Mitchell, he runs the Coliseum, and the new head of Arts Council, Landstone – he doesn't seem much livelier than Macowan. By the way, we've got another date, on the Isle of Wight.'

On the Saturday evening, I went to hear Tom addressing the local Labour Party. They were mesmerised by his impeccable Oxford accent. Towards the end, 'I see comrades looking at their watches,' he said. 'Thank you. I thought for a moment you were shaking them.'

'No indeed, Mr Driberg,' said the chairman. 'You 'ave charmed us.'

Gerry stayed long enough to come to the Isle of Wight and swim with me in a shallow cove near Ryde, where the water was warm and rose-red tendrils swayed around you. Kerstin wrote us a card from the Isle of Man. She was doing well. All we had to do was get there . . . I can't say that we were exactly popular on the island. Neither was J.B. Priestley. 'He's a Bolshevik,' we were told. 'We don't want his sort living here.'

By dribs and drabs we arrived at Liverpool, Gerry and Camel driving with the gear stacked on the back of an old truck. There we embarked on a pleasure boat bound for the Isle of Tail-less Cats. Kerstin met us on the pier at Douglas. 'You're going to eat,' she said. 'You'll see.'

'How did you ever get here, Kerstin?'

'Hitched.'

'What, over the sea?'

'In a plane.'

We didn't doubt her. She was mistress of the Impossible.

'You are all staying in a magnificent house, for free. It was owned by Captain Bligh of *The Bounty*. No, not Charles Laughton, the real Captain Bligh. Wait till you see it!' And we all piled on to a bus, alighted by a crumbling stone wall, and trekked along a dusty road between bushes of flaming gorse till the sound of rifle fire stopped us in our tracks . . . Two bursts. Should we take cover? A figure appeared, running towards a clump of bushes, followed by another. A raucous female voice pursued them: 'I'll teach you, you fucking idle bastards. . . .' We couldn't see the owner of the voice.

Kerstin was quite unperturbed. 'She is a little eccentric,' she said, and shepherded us to the house. As we entered: 'Come in and have a drink, fellers.' It was the Voice.

We were in a large ancestral hall, antlers, guns, leopard-skins, all the trimmings, but in a small ante-room to the right of the entrance there was a smart bar – the drinks shelves lined with pink mirror. Just above the bar, from a bodyless head, two eyes surveyed us, two eyes and a strand of dark hair, part of an Eton crop.

'Lynne,' said Kerstin. 'The company.'

Lynne was so short she couldn't appear above the counter without climbing on to a box. 'I'm so goddamned fat,' she told us as we knocked back our unaccustomed Martinis. It soon became clear that she had fallen madly for Kerstin, who didn't seem to mind. She simply ignored Lynne's whole performance.

'One night with me,' declared our hostess, and as her head turned we could see the imprint of a lipstick kiss on her neck, 'one night with Lynne and you won't want any goddamn men.' She had lipstick on the other side of her neck too.

A Tudor panel in the hall swung open and one of the flying figures from the park appeared. A cosy woman with a Manx accent. 'Like to see your rooms, ladies and gentlemen?' As she guided us upstairs she lowered her voice.

'Two divorces on 'er 'ands. The husbands have threatened to kill 'er – alienation of affections . . . It has to be that, because a man can't cite a woman as co-respondent.' She was obviously very proud of her mistress.

'What was all the shooting about?'

'She was a bit peeved with our Terry because the cat had got into the buttery. She's hasty when she's ruffled, but she's very nice.'

Camel and Gerry went off to inspect the next day's rig. It was another seaside pavilion. Kerstin and I were invited to take pink champagne in the hostess's private snug. She wanted to warn us: 'You won't get much change out of the islanders. They're all half-mad – interbred. I rely on folks flying in from London for a bite to eat – I'm a great cook.' That was an understatement, as we discovered when the company sat down to a delicious supper. We weren't long out of bed afterwards. Everybody was tired from the journey.

In the wee small hours, when we were all fast asleep, the deep silence was shattered by the opening chords of *Scheherezade*.

'Wake up, wake up.' The Voice sounded above the music. 'Come out and listen to God's glorious music!'

I got as far as the passage. Two wizened old ladies in long nightdresses were peering over the bannisters. One wore curl papers under a nightcap. Lynne was standing in the hall, fully dressed.

'Come on down. Life's too short for sleeping.' Heads, startled, furious or sleepy, were looking out all along the corridor. 'Come on, then. Bring a blanket with you. Shift yourselves.' And she turned the music up full blast as we all went tottering down the stairs.

Might as well, not much sleep to be had this night. In the hall we lay around, lapped in music, till dawn, and as its rosy fingers prodded the dark clouds, there was an issue of drinks all round and Lynne went off to bed. The old lady in curlers shouted after her, 'Lovely, lovely, lovely Lynne. You always do something to surprise us.' She and her sister were rich Salmon and Gluckstein heiresses who spent most of their life becalmed in St John's Wood.

Our hostess was the only woman ever to have escaped from Ellis Island by swimming ashore, or so she told us. I believed her.

'Why were you there in the first place?'

'I was a gun-runner.'

I believed that too. She was certainly a *femme–homme fatale*. Whenever you saw her there'd be at least two women hanging round her neck, good-looking ones, kissing and stroking her, but she'd always shake them off if Kerstin came by.

She never came near our show, her own performance kept her fully occupied. In fact you could not imagine her outside her own setting. All the same she could put the finger on any character on that island who had the slightest spark of fun in them and they were all duly rustled up and ordered to come and see us, entertain us and talk about us. She liked us.

We were sorry when we had to move to the other side of the island for a second week's booking. It started with a performance for local grammar schoolboys. Never, anywhere, not even among bored BBC actors at long rehearsals, have I heard so many ordinary phrases given a dirty double meaning. After the show Gerry and I fled, mounted on hired bikes and pedalled up the lonely coast road, taking in deep gulps of salty air, then free-wheeled down through mist and moonlight.

One morning the hall where we rehearsed was full of mist. It moved in eddies across the floor. In the distance we could hear a low boom. It was the foghorn, but suddenly, amazingly, it broke into a scale . . .

'That's no foghorn. It's Gerry doing his voice exercises.'

It was.

Our next date was in our home town, Manchester. It should have been our home. Its marvellous library had been our Alma Mater; the theatre which was in that library had always been closed to us. Every application we made was turned down by Charles Nowell, chairman of the Libraries Committee.

When we were about to leave for Germany I asked him, 'Aren't you happy to see us go?'

'Yes, so long as you don't come back,' he said.

Well, we came back and still we were barred until –

Monday August 4th
Theatre Workshop
presents
Operation Olive Branch
at
The Library Theatre, Manchester

What had changed his mind? Not all the pleas, requests and letters in the press from all sorts of influential people in the town. It was a line in the *Radio Times*.

> BBC North Region. From Kendal to Berlin. Tuesday August 5th, 7.30–8.00 p.m. The Theatre Workshop players tell the story of their troubles and tribulations over the past two years.

Our friends in broadcasting were still with us.

'You're the mouse and we're the elephant,' said Hugh Middlemass. 'But you make more impression than we do.'

We didn't make much of an impression on the cloakroom attendants as we trundled our gear down the stairs at the library to the basement where the theatre was housed.

'They supposed to be actors?'

We looked much more picturesque – sunburnt, wind-blown, in bright shorts and tops of every period, left over from discarded plays – Camel, our minor prophet, with his long beard and sandals, grunted when he noticed the mucky marks on the cyclorama.

'That'll have to be cleaned.'

We went to it with a will and by the time we finished the stage was as clean as a new pin, and we were as black as Newgate's knocker. Not on the first night, though, that was all garlands and shining limbs and warm embraces. We stayed for the triumphal curtain, then made for the friendly little restaurant near All Saints. It was still light on this sunny evening of the August Bank Holiday.

A few sunburnt ramblers, returning from the High Peak, went swinging by, married folk who'd spent the day in Whitworth Park, were carrying their children home to bed. We found places upstairs, ate our fish and chips, asked for more bread and butter, and were just about to sup our second cup of strong tea when we heard the crash of breaking glass, followed by a burst of laughter. Our ordinary was on the edge of Chorlton-on-Medlock, a rough old place; anything might happen there, especially on a bank holiday. Another crash, this time followed by a burst of cheering and shouting.

Maggie and Camel were at the window.

'They're smashing the window of the shop next door.' Two or three of the company started for the stairs. The rest of us trailed after. Downstairs the proprietor was already at the door.

'What's wrong?'

'It's the chemist's next door. He's a Jew boy.'

Twenty-seven

*The troubles in Palestine. We witness two outbreaks of anti-Semitism
in Manchester. We wish to show people what we have seen and find
a vehicle. The play* Professor Mamlock *will serve. We can parallel
what we have seen with events in Germany. The Lord Chamberlain
warns us not to mention what we have seen in Manchester; despite
protests from journalists, the ban holds. We mount a castrated version.
While playing* Operation Olive Branch *in Manchester, I invite some
lonely-looking German prisoners to the play. The company disapprove.
I am invited to the prison camp to see the Germans acting. Gerry and
I try to shelter at the Rudolf Steiner Hall, see Ken Tynan rehearsing
Hamlet.*

The troubles in Palestine! We'd forgotten them – the reprisals,
counter-reprisals, beatings, summary executions, massacres.

A young Jew tied up and whipped. (A Terrorist? A
Freedom Fighter?) The next day a British officer captured
and horse-whipped. Arab raids on Jewish settlements, the Jews
fight back. Schlomo ben Yossef was working on the kibbutz at
Rosh Pinna. It was raided many times. When yet another busload
of Arabs arrived, he fired on them. No one was hurt, but Schlomo
ben Yossef was hanged.

What was this strip of desert, the size of Wales, for which men
fought and died? 'This bloody country,' General Allenby called it
when he captured it from the Turks, in 1917. A legion of 'little
tailors from Whitechapel' formed part of his army – because

A man without a homeland is a man without a shadow.

and

His Majesty's government views with favour the
establishment of a National Home for the Jewish

people and will do its best to further this project.

ARTHUR BALFOUR, 1917

During the Second World War, Anthony Eden (Conservative) refused to let Jews take refuge in Palestine, and when Jews were freed from the concentration camps and columns of them set out for the Mediterranean, Clement Attlee and Ernest Bevin (Socialists) had them turned back. Any who escaped the net and managed to board the vessels which had been provided by their compatriots, were fired upon. Many finished up in camps on the island of Cyprus; those who reached Palestine were attacked. By 1947, a new generation had learned to fight.

> We will not be exploited, humiliated, pillaged and dishonoured ever again. Nor will we wait for someone else to emancipate us, we shall see to it ourselves.

The proprietor of the café fished out a copy of the *Daily Express*. Across the front page there was a photograph of:

HANGED BRITONS: THE PICTURE

THAT WILL SHOCK THE WORLD

> Radioed from Jerusalem last night, this *Daily Express* picture was taken in a eucalyptus grove south of Nathanya, Palestine. The bodies of murdered Clifford Martin and Mervyn Price – British security sergeants – hang from saplings.

Daily Express, August 1st, 1947.

Circulation 3,842,410.

On the previous day two members of the Jewish Resistance had been hanged by the British not a mile from where the bodies of the British soldiers had been found. I don't think the screaming crowd in the street outside had much knowledge of Palestine or Bevin, or even Hitler for that matter; they just fancied a good racist lynching.

The proprietor told us that the chemist's shop was owned by

a local man, Manchester born and bred, 'but the feller who works for him has a foreign name – Resdikian, or some such.'

'An Armenian name,' said Howard.

'Not much difference, is there?' said the proprietor. 'They're all Wogs. Anyroad, I'm closing now, so if you don't want to be washing the pots . . .'

Outside, the crowd had grown. For the moment they were well pleased with themselves, shoving and shouting, a typical Bank Holiday mob. We left them to it and turned into Grosvenor Street, the heart of that blighted area from which most of these happy hooligans had sprung. At Ardwick Green I was reminded of a May Day long ago when we passed this way in procession carrying the red and gold banners of the Manchester TUC. Some old biddies standing on the pavement shouted, 'Go back to bloody Russia.'

'Give us the fare and we'll be glad to,' Bill Riste yelled back.

On this beautiful evening Ardwick Green was deserted. We said goodnight and went our way. Howard had to cross Cheetham Hill Road on his way home. Next morning he reported seeing an old man mobbed by a crowd of youths. They were throwing lumps of hard filth at him. Until then I would never have believed that crossing the poor Jewish quarter of Manchester could be dangerous. I suppose we all believe that it starts on someone else's plot until, one day, it happens to us.

No account of these two unusual events appeared in the local papers.

If nothing else, we believed in democratic communication. So much news never appears in the newspapers. It is suppressed and bias accepted. My country, right or wrong. One of the arguments against those who were fighting for a Jewish National Home was that they were all Communists, and as far as the general reader was concerned that settled that. Not far from our chemist's shop Matthew Hopkins, Witchfinder General to James the First, located a witch, who confessed under torture that she was in association with a yellow devil with blue spots. She was burnt to death. We are the witches now.

'What can we do about it?'

'What we do best, put on a play.'

'Write it ourselves?'

'Put down what we have seen.'

Gerry suggested *Professor Mamlock* by Friedrich Wolf, the story of a famous doctor, a German patriot, wounded and decorated in the First World War, who argues against his son's militancy when Hitler's followers begin to show their colours. In the doctor's own clinic racial prejudice appears and we learn that Mamlock is himself a Jew. The struggle between father and son, the mother's feelings – she is not a Jew – are the fabric of the play. Finally, Mamlock is attacked on the street, wounded and humiliated. He dies.

I wasn't thrilled with this play. I had seen the Russian film version . . . a cast merely efficient, too many white coats. Bill Davidson suggested Brecht's *Round Heads and Pointed Heads* but Brecht, like Sartre, never seemed to know exactly what he was saying. *Round Heads and Pointed Heads*, as the argument collapses, becomes almost anti-Semitic. In *Mutter Courage* his admired heroine is nothing but a cheap Jack, profiting from the country's war. Better to use Swift's *Gulliver's Travels*, the war over the way you crack your egg, for instance. Make a play from that.

Friedrich Wolf had sent Kerstin the *Mamlock* script in German. She read it to us, making a rough translation as she went along. The conflict between father and son rang true, the setting moved from Mamlock's clinic to his home. Plays set between four walls are almost sure to be all talk. If we could add street scenes, using Wolf's dialogue, we could suggest parallels with the Manchester events but we would have to add the fact that we had witnessed such scenes ourselves, if we were to make our point.

Next morning, in the Library basement, we began throwing ideas around. Howard recapped what he had seen and Gerry went to the reference section and turned up 1933 newspapers. By the end of the day we had two or three street scenes sketched in. I added the Reichstag fire. It would only need a few onlookers standing watching the fire reflected on the night sky . . . three floodlights and six silk handkerchiefs.

By the dawn's early light the script was ready for typing. Then to the Lord Chamberlain with a postal order for its return clipped to the flyleaf and his fee for the reading, one guinea. Set, props and costumes would have to cost nothing.

That script came fleeing back – the long white envelope with the Lord Chamberlain's stamp on it fell on the mat with an ominous plop. All scenes representing the street events of the 4th August 1947 TO BE CUT.

'The whole point in putting on the play will be lost.'

'Let's try an appeal.'

We had included the words, 'We saw these events ourselves on the streets of Manchester.' If we cut that? No. We got friendly journalists to protest. It made no difference.

'All the scenes . . . etc. No further appeal can be considered.'

Should we drop it? We had worked night and day to have the show ready while the story was still hot.

'Couldn't we just tell the audience about the parallels?' said David.

'*Last Edition* is already chalked up against us.'

Could we afford another court case? No. Could we rely on support from the Left? We could not. They preferred mourning the fallen to winning the battle. And the answer to the chastising hand of English censorship? Compromise. We put on our castrated show, pointing up the parallels, with music and mime.

British première – *Professor Mamlock*
by Friedrich Wolf
adapted by Joan Littlewood

This, the third production of Joan Littlewood's that I have seen, confirms my earlier estimate of her great talent, a talent that is for staging a play in three dimensions in such a way as to make the most of the author's text.

In this production she chose to avoid the realistic convention in which the original was written. . . . Playing the scenes alternately on two sloping platforms, with brilliant overhead spotlighting, a documentary technique was created for which our audiences seem unprepared.

Although the play deals with the usurpation of power by the Nazis in 1933 and the hounding of the

Jews, Liberals and Radicals, it has remarkable topi
cality when viewed in conjunction with current newspaper headlines. In fact, Miss Littlewood wrote a
prologue based on an incident which the company witnessed in a northern town in August and which, I was
informed, was almost identical with an incident in the
play. The Lord Chamberlain refused to grant a licence
unless the prologue was omitted and even directed that
no mention of the English town in question be made
in the programme. I am yet to be persuaded that the
documentary presentation of anti-Semitic excesses on
the stage is against the public interest.

OSSIA TRILLING

Ossia Trilling was the only journalist to publish the story of the
Lord Chamberlain and the Manchester outbreak. Kerstin and Bill
Davidson had written to Wolf about the difficulties over *Mamlock*.
He wanted to know why Kerstin was not playing young Inge
instead of the mother. He didn't know how prejudiced middle-aged
English actresses were against plays of social significance. We had
to rely on young people. Wolf went on, 'What Bill writes about
English theatre sounds right. Tradition can become a burden and
the stronger the white collars, the weaker the theatre. Today we
definitely stand at a social and theatrical turning point. We were
merely the storm birds. G.B. Shaw writes in his foreword to *Plays
Pleasant*, "The theatre as a social organ grows in importance. Bad
theatres are just as pernicious as bad schools and bad churches!"
Could you not (like our Volksbuehne) get support from the trade
unions? Do they not have an interest in theatrical culture?'

Forty years on, coming upon Gerry's carefully annotated text, I
realise how strongly the father and son relationship in the play
appealed to him. Rolf Mamlock's arguments with his father
echoed Gerry's fights with Manny over politics, lifestyle and
theatre. The liaison with me was never called in question, though
Manny was well aware of it. It seems so obvious, reading Gerry's

notes, that he thoroughly understood the father he quarrelled with so fiercely, and loved him, as Manny loved his prodigal son. If Gerry had played Rolf and a mature actor, say Frederick Valk, Professor Mamlock, the play would have gained great strength. The youth of our company was, on this occasion, a drawback, though in the dancing caricatures we often used, an advantage.

Going through Gerry's notes, I also discover how many trade union leaders, theatre owners, eccentric millionaires and theatre speculators showed him the door. I put Gerry's *Mamlock* script away safely. It reminds me of things I would rather forget – his lone fight to keep a record of our history and my indifference.

W hile playing *Olive Branch* in Manchester I put my foot in it with the company. Crossing St Peter's Square on my way to a Saturday matinée I passed a bunch of miserable-looking squaddies. They were wearing some dull uniform, and standing around by the war memorial. They looked so desolate I asked if I could help. A smiling young English officer emerged from the crowd and told me he was in charge. 'They're German prisoners, you know.'

'You've been showing them the sights of Manchester?'

'Yes indeed, but we seem to have run out.'

On the spur of the moment I asked if they'd like to come and see our show; it only meant crossing the road.

'I'm sure they'd be delighted,' said the young officer. 'But they are prisoners of war, you know – Nazis, what's more.'

The word came as a shock. He was muttering something about formalities but I didn't really hear what he was saying. I was looking at this pathetic mob in their worn-out uniforms. He was asking if the following Saturday might be convenient.

'Yes, of course,' I said, without thinking.

During the week I received a formal note informing me that twenty German POWs would like to avail themselves of my kind invitation. I replied saying that I would reserve twenty seats at the matinée. I hadn't said a word to the company. It was not until I was told that a crowd of uniformed men were at the box office waiting for me that I broke the news. And then . . . Revolt.

'Nazis!'

'We'll be part of their re-education.'

Someone was calling Beginners and I was still getting nowhere. I wondered if they would refuse to take the curtain up. David was the most upset.

'But you must have played to ex-Nazis in Germany,' I said.

'We may have, but these are declared bastards.' Everybody agreed.

They were right, of course. I tried pleading. If they'd come across a set of miserable-looking characters hanging around . . . I thought of adding the rain. I didn't but I went on a bit, and one by one they walked away. I couldn't throw the Germans out now. I'd be lucky not to be thrown out myself. The curtain rose. The company gave a good performance. At the end the Germans shook hands with me and thanked me with exemplary courtesy as I stood in the foyer asking them if they'd enjoyed the play. Had they understood it?

'Oh, yes.'

And they identified themselves to a man with the character Ben had created, the man left behind when the rejoicing died away.

LYSISTRATA: Aren't you joining us, soldier?

SOLDIER: I have joined you.

LYSISTRATA: Then why are you so melancholy?

SOLDIER: I am tired.

LYSISTRATA: Stay with us and rest a while.

SOLDIER: I have a long way to go yet.

LYSISTRATA: Where is your country?

SOLDIER: I have no country. I am a slave.

LYSISTRATA: But the war is won.

SOLDIER: Not for me. While there is a slave anywhere, peace is only a dream.

LYSISTRATA: Will you fight for a dream?

SOLDIER: There is a girl in Thrace . . .

LYSISTRATA: The road to Thrace is a long one.

SOLDIER: The road to freedom is longer.

The English officer said that the men would like to invite our company to see their show. They had written and mounted it themselves. I accepted but only one member of the company offered to come with me, Yvonne, young, blonde, very good-looking, a recent discovery. She asked if she might bring her mother. The three of us met at Central Station. The camp was somewhere in the wilds of Cheshire. It was Sunday evening. The train was empty. Mamma began talking about their holiday in Switzerland.

'You couldn't help noticing how clean the German Swiss were compared with the French, could you, dear?'

'No, Mutti.' I hadn't noticed that her mother had a slight German accent.

We nearly went past the small station and the camp was hard to find. We arrived late. The young officer was waiting for us outside a large Nissen hut. He hurried us in, led us past rank on rank of prisoners who seemed to be sitting at attention. As we were ushered to our privileged seats down in front, the stony silence was broken by a low, but unmistakable, hissing. An elderly man on the other side of the aisle was sitting up, straight as a ramrod. His hair was flecked with white, he had a huge Kitchener moustache. He wasn't hissing, just staring ahead, not even glancing at us, though both the ladies with me were handsome and well-dressed. I asked the officer to apologise for the hold-up but he thought better of it; the curtain was being flapped by someone on the stage side.

The play told the everyday story of a German family in war-time – the women's parts taken by men, of course, but there was no suggestion of men in drag. In that sex-starved gathering the 'women' were accepted for real. All the paraphernalia of the show, even the spotlights, had been made by the prisoners, constructed from any bits of flotsam they could lay hands on – a lady's fur coat from wool waste dyed brown with coffee, tankards from coffee tins covered with silver paper. Although we applauded with all our might and Mutti made a little speech of thanks in high German, the only prisoners who talked to us were the ones who had seen our show. Two of them managed to draw me to one side. I put my finger to my lips. Then I whispered that they could always find me at the Library, if they ever got there again. On the train back, I told Yvonne's mother that the ingenuity displayed by the soldiers was not just a German trait, as she thought. Robin Bagot had told me how English soldiers in German camps performed the same miracles of improvisation.

I was reading in the Reference Library one day when two men in grey uniform slid into the seats beside me. I looked up. 'The comrades wish you to know that they understood the message of your play, perfectly well.' I thanked them and they left.

The camp was split up soon after and the prisoners were sent back to Germany, some to an Allied zone, some to the Russians, but every now and then I would hear from one or other of them. Peace is war's twin sister, one of them wrote.

Our days in Manchester passed all too quickly. Soon we would be on the road again, taking our mutilated production of *Mamlock* to any place that would have us. If they didn't want *Mamlock*, what would they like? Shakespeare? Music hall? A one-day school? Somebody in London liked the sound of *Operation Olive Branch*, our *Lizzie*, as we called it now. They actually offered us a date. That's how it came about that Gerry and I stood surveying the Rudolf Steiner Hall. We had come to measure up and confirm the booking.

'Do you think we might con them into letting us stay the night?' We had about five shillings and fourpence between us and nowhere to go.

We entered the holy-looking building, all curves and harmony, presented ourselves to the caretaker and asked if we might look round.

'Well, the stage is occupied by another production at the moment.'

What did it matter? We were in. Gerry went and investigated the wiring. I sat on a dressing basket, making sketches. The caretaker was obviously anxious to lock up and leave. If we didn't bring things to a head soon, the shops would be shut and we wouldn't even have a roll and butter for our supper. I explained that there were one or two things we just had to check. Couldn't we lock up for him? Otherwise we'd have to come back very early in the morning. It worked. The keys dropped into my hand.

I crossed the hall, looking busy. Gerry nipped out for a bottle of milk, a loaf and a pat of butter. The caretaker left. In the quiet of the evening we ate our simple meal, found a dressing-room with a couch and an armchair and slept fitfully. In the morning we had only to tidy up and look over the switchboard before we left. We were almost ready when there was a loud banging at the front door.

'I'll go,' I said. Gerry was brooding on stage.

The caretaker already? No. The door wasn't fully open before a pack of alien beings came surging in. At their head a tall, kingly figure who strode over the parquet and threw his cloak over the dressing basket. I melted into the shadows, Gerry grunted. They didn't notice us. They were absorbed in some shared fantasy and waited. The kingly one uttered a word of command; they flew about in every direction. We made for our hideaway. It would be best to make ourselves scarce, and when possible escape.

The troupe stopped in their tracks as certain individuals took up prearranged positions on the stage. Then one produced a bell and another a large prompt book.

'I'd love to watch for a moment.'

'Well, don't let them see you.'

The kingly one inspired enormous respect as he ordered his cast here and there with crushing authority. I couldn't imagine what they were working on because I couldn't hear. Everything was conducted in a low mumble.

A broom lay near at hand and inspiration seized me. I lowered my woolly cap over my nose and began sweeping the parquet, at the same time drawing nearer to the stage. . . . No, it can't be – but it was – spoken in a strange dialect, almost unrecognisable . . . Shakespeare. *Hamlet*, what's more.

The leader called a halt and had words with a young woman who frowned intelligently, then gave a great bound and landed back on the stage. She gave a piercing shriek which flowed into a torrent of words, all on the same high note. The few words I caught told me we were in Ophelia's mad scene, and terrible, schizophrenic though it was, it was not terrible enough for the director. She should stalk up and down as she spoke. She tried – still shrieking . . . No good. She tried again, silently. He gave a satisfied grunt. I remembered from a remote past the story of a mermaid who was given legs, in order to satisfy her mortal lover – but when she tried to walk they pierced her like swords. This poor girl's walk was perfect mermaid.

I went on sweeping but stopped at the sound of glass smashing. Ophelia had dashed a mirror to the ground. Was she going over the top? No. Her tormentor was satisfied, just what he wanted. . . . What was he doing to the poor Ophelia? The woman-hater. A halt was called as two men trundled in a large dressing basket, and the characters began trying on various eighteenth-century outfits. I felt sorry for them, thinking it had been a mistake at the costumiers. It wasn't.

'Let's go.'

As I went to return the broom, a sixpence was pressed into my hand.

'That young man,' I said to Gerry – 'is destined to be a London genius in no time at all.'

And I was right. He was twenty years of age and theatre-struck, but soon someone noticed that he could neither act nor direct. He became a critic, clever, too, when it came to dealing with the old guard. He ousted Beverley Baxter from the *Evening Standard* and took his place. Sad that, with all his brilliant reforming prose, he should finish up in the clutches of the most stupid ham that ever conned people into taking him for an actor. 'I'd sooner have him on my side than shooting at me,' said Sir Laurence and offered Ken Tynan a job. 'Dramaturg!' said Ken and was accepted, though I doubt whether Laurence Olivier had any idea what a dramaturg was.

Our short season at the Rudolf Steiner was disappointing. So was Tynan's. What else could you expect in such a glory hole? With no money for publicity, and not a critic to be seen. One bouquet came our way; it was from Robert Muller in his Stage Door column:

> Theatre Workshop's visit has not been a commercial success. This is the public's loss. This company offers the most original, skilful and progressive productions that England has seen since the end of the War.
>
> It would be invidious to blame the ordinary theatre-goer for his lack of discrimination. The fault lies in the apathy of the critics on whose taste the public – for better or worse – seems to rely. I am not attacking the

critics who went to the Rudolf Steiner Hall and came
back to condemn the play. That is their prerogative.
What is a scandal is that several important papers
(including four dailies and several Sunday and weekly
papers) completely ignored the production. None of
the millions of readers of these journals could have had
an inkling of the fact that Theatre Workshop was in
town. The fact that the show's first night occurred in
a week that was crowded with such frightfully important events as the last night of *Perchance to Dream* may
justify the absence of the busier critics.

Theatre Workshop had to win success in Germany, France,
Norway, Sweden, Russia and Scotland before the English critics
deigned to notice them. When we moved to Stratford, E15, in
1953, no critic came. It took eighteen months, during which time
the best of our classics were mounted – before any London critic
took the tube to Stratford station.

Twenty-eight

Christmas. Michel St Denis offers us a room at the Old Vic.
The company splits up. Gerry and Joan head north. A room with
Mrs Staunton at Ardwick Green. Howard and Kerstin follow. The
company will wither without a base. Gerry campaigns for the David
Lewis Settlement, Liverpool. We enjoy a pleasant day in Sherwood
Forest. Gerry's project is put to T.W. Jimmie is opposed. The rest
are more interested in Jimmie's new play. The David Lewis turns us
down. Gerry goes away.

The very thought of this time in our life, and I go wandering round the room, rearranging books, sharpening pencils, sorting papers, anything rather than face it all again. We were a flop, a disaster. Blame the critics, blame Arts Council, blame everyone but ourselves. And then face facts. It was all right saying our standards were not their standards, our concept of theatre completely foreign to them. So what? There was an audience for us, somewhere, we never doubted it, but where? If there wasn't, we might as well give up. But never, for one moment, did any of us think of giving up.

All we needed was a place of our own, said Gerry, and set out each morning to look for it. From Gatti's cinema in the Westminster Bridge Road to an old music hall in Wapping; from a pub with a stage in Hoxton to a disused factory East of Shoreditch. He was working from *Theatre Newsletter*, 77 Dean Street, where our friends still let us use a corner of their office with desk, phone and filing cabinet.

Christmas was approaching, everything else was fading away, a second German tour, a visit to Hungary, a week in Worcester . . . No one in the UK was interested in even taking a look at us, let alone promoting us. Nevertheless, Gerry noted every movement of this threatened species – the impresarios and their agents.

One day, Michel St Denis, who was running a theatre school at the Old Vic, asked if we'd like to work there during the

Christmas holidays. We accepted, though some of us had already found Christmas jobs and others were looking. Even so, we could meet there in our spare time. I couldn't have resisted the Old Vic, anyway. That stage was my holy ground. An elderly man under a Cavalier hat showed us in. I asked him if he was a painter.

'Scene painter,' he replied. 'Acting Stage Doorkeeper.' He had a cockney accent with an arty flourish to it. 'There's no scene-painting nowadays. They don't even have scenery. There was always a painting dock in a theatre in my time, a bridge and pulleys, as in the days of the old masters . . . paint you anything from Tutankhamun's tomb to the Last Judgement. I accomplished an entire and complete Channel crossing once, with shipwrecks, sharks, giant waves, sunshine, rainbows – and it all moved smoothly across the stage, upstage of course, where we now stand being the deck.'

'How did it move?'

'Giant rollers. Simplest, always the best. I'll light the auditorium for you.'

I didn't recognise it. The restoration after the bomb damage in 1941 had completely altered it. My recollection was of an intimate theatre. We were given the use of a large airy room on the top floor, and people came when they could. At the first lunch break I took Isla for a walk along the Cut, the Lower Marsh, that is. And there it was. 'A little bit orf the top, darlin'?' 'Umpy-back bananers. Lovely ripe bananers.' 'Squeeze me an' I'm yours.' It was the world I came from and you could still buy pease pudding, bread pudding and saveloys for coppers. On our way back to the rehearsal room, we saw girl students in ankle-length black skirts, queueing in a passage. There was a smell of coffee in the air. 'A canteen!'

Next day Isla and I followed the coffee trail and tagged on to the queue. We were quizzed, discreetly. Isla asked one of the girls why she was wearing a long skirt.

'We wear them all the time. It's Surea Magito's idea, to give us grace and carriage.'

I liked the look of the girls at the costers' barrows down the Cut. They wore bright colours, short skirts and tall, curly hairdos; the blokes, zazzy neckerchiefs and earrings. We had an arty girl once who sewed toy bells inside the hem of her long skirt. At least she was original.

We took advantage of the subsidised grub in that canteen. Someone must have noticed. We were asked if we'd like to have our Christmas dinner there. We accepted joyfully, and it was good nosh. Bill Davidson crowned it with, 'It was Christmas Day in the workhouse. The snow was falling fast.' We had taken the drastic decision to split and swore we would not come together again till we had a permanent home. Gerry and I were staying with Ben. He was renting two unfurnished rooms on a top floor in Edith Grove and made us very welcome. One night we were talking about the German tour when Ben turned on me.

'It was too long for Gerry to be away from you,' he said.

'I know, and he told me about the German girl.'

'He didn't feel guilty?'

'No, why should he?'

Ben had accepted a course in radio production at the BBC. I hardly dared ask how his play was going.

'The great playwright has resigned,' he said.

'But you can't do that. We're all waiting for Benedict Ellis, his first play.'

'That's not even my name,' he said. 'I invented it.'

This surprised me, but of course I didn't ask him what his real name was. Benedict suited him so well.

'You can be the genius now,' he told me. 'At least you seem to enjoy whatever it is you do. Play-writing should come easy, mine has been drudgery. . . .'

'Then don't bother.'

'Look! Six months' slavery.'

He threw a thick black folder at me. 'You don't have to read it. I don't want to spoil your fun.'

'What fun?'

'I heard all that laughter and voluptuous slapping when you went to bed last night.'

It was true that I had been trying to do Laban's exercises in a long skirt, one of Ben's sheets. Gerry was laughing so much I thought he'd break the bed.

'You shouldn't live alone, Ben.' All the same, our rough-and-

tumble life was too much for him. We could never quite forget
that Ormesby attack.

'I must abandon the world of make-believe,' he said.

'And we must leave this unreal city.'

I was happy to say goodbye to London. I'm much more at
home in the North. On the bus I told Gerry I'd written to
Hugh MacDiarmid. I wanted him to write 'The true story of the
Great King Macbeth and Gruach his queen, their resistance to the
Saxons and the long march they led to save the Scottish army from
annihilation. . . .'

'Where did you get all that?'

'From Ruari Erskine of Mar. He has all the documents, and
if MacDiarmid isn't interested there must be a poet north of the
border who will write us a true Scottish *Macbeth*. Shakespeare was
too insular.'

Gerry didn't think we'd get a play out of Scotland. 'They
haven't had a playwright since David Lindsay wrote *The Three
Estates*.'

'Lorca would come alive in Scots or Irish,' I said.

But Gerry was thinking of more practical problems.

'I'm going to get a base for us this year, if it's the last thing I do.
If I don't, we'll wither away. Tomorrow I shall be in Liverpool.'

'Why?'

'To have another look at the David Lewis Settlement, a vast
building like that, under-used.'

'Misused.'

'I've a plan which would revitalise the whole area.'

'You are an oyster, Gerry.'

'I'm going to discuss it with James Ford.'

After our night ride, he went straight to Victoria Station and
took the train to Lime Street. I looked for a room. It was good
to walk round Ardwick again. We might be dispersed and in debt,
but we would hold on to our lifeline, each other.

John Bury and Margaret Greenwood had married at some
point. (Such arrangements were usually kept secret. None of
us could afford presents and in any case marriage was reckoned
rather bourgeois.) Margaret had long since become Maggie, but
John always remained Camel. This was the first chance he'd had

to introduce his new wife to his parents in Eaglescliffe. They would hitch back immediately if anything came up. Meanwhile Maggie could always earn, teaching ballroom dancing; she had been a gold medallist before joining us.

Bill Davidson needed a break. At the end of '47 he had an attack of alopecia. It left him without a hair on his body. It could have been a delayed reaction to Peenemünde. He had met Karl Fuchs there, who believed, as Bill did, that all scientific discovery should be shared regardless of national boundaries. Fuchs was later imprisoned for alleged spying. On his release he went back to Germany – East Germany.

Bill's work for Theatre Workshop, the sets he designed and made, his music, his translations, were simply the reverse side of his scientific work. Such a brilliant man, cool, cautious and witty, but while we were at the Old Vic he took to wandering the streets of London as if he'd never been there before. He would join us in the evening, his old green hat pulled right down over his bald head.

'I've got to go,' he said one night.

'Where?'

'I found myself crying as I watched the Lord Mayor's Show.'

Whatever the cause, atomic power, us, or the wild *affaire* he'd had with the most beautiful girl in the company, he needed peace. I prayed that he would soon recover and come back. His quiet arguments were a tonic among our wild enthusiasms. He went to his parents' home in Dulwich and made a living correcting exam papers for his old university.

Gerry and I moved into a furnished room at Ardwick Green, within walking distance of the railway station. Howard took the room above us and Kerstin moved in with him. Rosalie and David were back at her father's house in Urmston. She was pregnant, and David had a job directing *Carmen* for the Altrincham Garrick. Mike Thompson and Isla were in Dundee where an old friend, Marie Hopps, was now directing; and the rest found work in Manchester. Whatever happened, most of us were in the same city, and still afloat.

Gerry was now our General Manager, and our only hope.

Jimmie retired to Oak Cottage to write, and I took the train to

Worksop for yet another 'visit' programme, this time to Sherwood
Forest.

Gerry's Liverpool project reawakened in him all the hope and
enthusiasm which had taken us to Kendal in '45 – a school, a base
– continuity. We already had friends in the district and James
Ford, one of our directors, was as keen as Gerry. Night after
night Gerry sat on our bed writing and rewriting his 'Proposals
for the Conversion of the David Lewis Centre at George Place,
Liverpool 1':

> . . . The composition of the district has complete-
> ly changed since the David Lewis settlement was
> founded. Most of the former inhabitants, the poorer
> working-class for whom the building was intended,
> have moved out to the north side of the city. These
> days the area houses newcomers, immigrants mainly,
> of many nationalities. There seems to be little sense of
> community and a good deal of demoralisation. . . .

The pennies in our landlady's rickety gas meter under the stairs
would give out and for once I would be the one to propose bed. . . .

'You have looked over the whole place again, Gerry?'

'Of course, and it's better than I remembered, the theatre holds
five hundred and forty. There is an outside workshop, a canteen,
lots of large rooms for lectures and classes.'

'And the old dodos who run the place, have you seen any
of them?'

'Edwards, their Chairman, showed me round. He seemed
favourably disposed, but I'll have to win over half Liverpool
before I budge the Trustees.' And he folded away the formidable
list of contacts he'd made.

On Mondays our ways parted, Gerry to pound the pavements
of Liverpool, I to wander in the Sylvan groves of Sherwood. But
after a week stalking any forestry workers, farm hands or eccentrics
who might have something to say for themselves, I was happy to
get back to our little drum in Ardwick. Gerry wasn't home this
Friday but the landlady, Mrs Staunton, was somewhere about.
She rented us her front room for twelve shillings and sixpence

a week, and let us do our cooking in her kitchen. You had to be careful not to tread on her cats; there were a lot of them. She fed them on cats' meat, bought on a skewer, and rabbit, which could only be found at Lewis's.

Gerry's 'Proposals' were on the table:

> It is unrealistic to perpetuate the *Love on the Dole* mentality, alleviating the effects of city life without touching on the cause of so much discontent. Rather, we should show them the good things in life. If we give them high standards, we may awake in them an appreciation of quality and they will no longer be satisfied with the second-rate.
>
> At the David Lewis, works of art could be presented, studied and analysed. In time, individuals would seek their own liberation in creativity and find a fuller, richer life. Such facilities do not at the moment exist in Liverpool. We are in contact with distinguished artists who would be happy to participate in the experiment; companies of players would visit a centre unique in this day and age.
>
> Theatre Workshop has already made an impression on artists and critics from many countries. The latest issue of *Theater der Zeit* calls on the theatres of Berlin to weigh their achievements in the light of the standards set by the English Theatre Workshop. . . .

The door flew open. It was Mrs Staunton.

'Jesus, Mary and Joseph,' she cried, and collapsed on to the one chair, hiding her face in her apron.

'What's wrong?'

'Baby Bunty.' She let the apron fall. 'I ran into the road to stop her but the tram came. I looked down – Baby Bunty's guts is out.'

My God, her favourite cat. There was nothing I could say. I went to her corner cupboard to look for the drop of Irish she kept there. Luckily Gerry arrived and we all sat at the kitchen table and drank to the memory of the unfortunate little cat.

Gerry was bursting to tell me his news, so we left Mrs S. to finish the whisky. He'd seen every influential soul in Liverpool: Archbishop Downey, Dean Dueley, the Vice-Chancellor of the University, the Curator of the Walker Art Gallery, Professor Rotblat. The only two who'd shown no interest at all were Malcolm Sargent and Lord Leverhulme. Ruth Lever had been more than helpful. And had I read his Proposals?

'I was just reading them when the news of Baby Bunty broke.'

'I have fifty copies. One of my girlfriends rolled it off for me. It's pretty good. I took some to London.'

'Gerry, you do tear about.'

'I had to see this David Webster. He may be the *éminence grise* at the David Lewis, but he's mostly in London. He administers Covent Garden Opera House.'

'Was he sympathetic?'

'He listened. I hadn't long, I had to catch the four o'clock back, but I managed to see John B. and Bill. They say all the young companies are in trouble. Diana Britten has just been evicted from the Gateway because she couldn't pay her rent.'

'Have you any money left?'

'I had to borrow off brother Eric. Well, he has a regular wage.'

'Must be nice. Don't you think you should let the company in on Liverpool?'

'Don't want to raise their hopes. In any case I'll have to report to Scrooge first, I suppose.'

'I'd like to go to the pictures. *It Always Rains on Sunday* is on at the fleapit.'

'Let's go.'

But at that moment Kerstin came in to see if we had any tea. 'Our future will begin in Stockholm,' she said. 'I don't suppose there's any sign of my fare yet?'

'What about my socks?' said Howard, entering dramatically. 'And this Nina!'

'Who's Nina?'

'That young woman who gave us a hundred quid. She's going around seeing anybody who's anybody, using our name and asking them for money, and my socks are full of holes.'

'It's no use worrying about things we can do nothing about,' said Kerstin. 'Why don't we all go to the cinema?'

We went.

On the Saturday morning, Gerry went to see Jimmie. When he came back he didn't say a word, but sat writing. I looked over his shoulder.

> *Oh, with what virtue lust should be withstood*
> *Since 'tis a fire quenched seldom, without blood . . .*

He put his hand over the page.

'You shouldn't look. Have you finished your piece about the D.L. scheme yet?'

'Here it is.'

He read it quietly and liked it.

'There's to be a Workshop meeting on Monday. Tomorrow is my last day in Sherwood,' I said. 'I only have to check the text with the characters. I'd like you to meet them. Afterwards, we could explore the forest.'

'Did you visit the model pit at Cresswell?'

'I have a miner from there in the programme. He's a castrato.'

'What!'

'It was an accident at the coalface, but he's a very cheerful man, and a great raconteur.' I told him about the others, the bird-watcher, the herbalist, the geologist, the erudite cowman and the woodman who had presented me with a model of shire horses harnessed to a wagon loaded with felled trees. He'd carved it himself and it was perfect in every detail. But it was the miner who interested Gerry.

We couldn't visit the model pit, unfortunately, but we had a drink in the local with the miner, then made our way home to prepare for the next day's meeting.

Camel and Maggie had hitchhiked from Eaglescliffe. Benny, a new lad, came from Haydock. There was Howard and Kerstin, Gerry and me. We all sat on the bed with the patchwork quilt or made the most of the available floor space. Jimmie and Jean came in while Gerry was reading the letters he'd received.

From BILL:

We need a Theatre Workshop firmly installed at the David Lewis, with a school functioning every day, shows every night and tours to places within easy reach. Leave all talk of experiment till we get the place. Don't talk about it, just do it. These people know nothing about theatre and you mustn't frighten them. Offer to call it the D.L. Theatre. This might flatter them and appeal to Arts Council. When somebody asked Laban what he called his theories, he said, 'What does it matter? It's just dancing.'

From WILLIAM MACLELLAN:

Dear Gerry,

Delighted to get your memo ref. the Liverpool project. This is exactly what you have been searching for and it is brilliantly presented. I don't see how the Trustees can ignore it. Education Authorities have been hunting for curricula such as you can provide.

Gerry continued with his report on the David Lewis building:

> At the moment, admission to the club costs two-pence, to the theatre fivepence, OAPs threepence. There is no Adult Education, only whist drives, a billiards school, table tennis and darts matches, three dances a year for the blind, performances by local dramatic, operatic and musical societies. A military band rehearses on Sunday mornings, orchestras on Sunday evenings. OAPs meet on Wednesday afternoons, and Liverpool dancing schools use the theatre. Nevertheless, the problems of cohabitation can be overcome. Ten thousand pounds will be needed to underwrite the first year. I propose to launch a public appeal in Liverpool to raise this sum. The equipment which

Theatre Workshop will provide is valued at two thousand pounds.

Most theatre schools are situated in London. A regional school for young people interested in theatre and prepared to devote themselves to it, should form part of the scheme. Paying pupils would help to finance the enterprise. Part of the training would consist of work with local people, particularly the unemployed, immigrants, OAPs and Youth Groups. Lectures on Social History, Art, Architecture, Linguistics, Appreciation of Music and Stage Technique would be open to the public. Joan would head the project, assisted by Laban, Jimmie, Jean and Nelson Illingworth, Bert Lloyd and Hugh MacDiarmid. Myself as General Manager. David Markfeldt has already been approached for assistance with drama.

I have prepared a list of plays which could be presented in the first year: *Angelica*, *Bartholomew Fair*, *The Playboy of the Western World*, *The Three Estates*, *Blood Wedding*, *The Tower*, *The Gardener's Dog*, *L'Étourdi*. Plays promised include a documentary on coal by Syd Chaplin, *A Scottish Macbeth* by Hugh MacDiarmid and *The Other Animals* by Jimmie Miller. Films include *Shoe Shine*, *The Stone Flower*, *To Live In Peace*, *Open City*.

He paused for breath and there was a long silence.

'Don't all speak at once.'

Howard was about to open up when Jean jumped in.

'How long would we have to rehearse these difficult plays?'

'I should say a fortnight – at first,' said Gerry.

'Have we all forgotten the difficulties we had there at Christmas?' said Howard. 'Those unruly kids.'

'And the dirt and demoralisation!' said Jean.

Gerry passed her a copy of his Proposals.

'You'll notice that one of our aims is to improve the quality of life there.'

'We are only a crowd of hungry bastards looking for somewhere to sell our peculiar talents,' said Benny. 'If they'll have us, let's go.

It would be somewhere to park the gear, if nothing else.'

'And that's very important,' said Camel. 'At the moment it's dumped all over the place. If we lose it, we won't be able to start again anywhere.'

'I've written to all our well-known supporters asking if they can help me win over the rest of the trustees. . . .'

'And the old boys who run the building,' said Howard.

'I know . . . all five of them . . . the Committee!' said Gerry.

'Our new General Manager seems to take it for granted that the scheme has merely to be implemented.' It was Jimmie, who looked as if he were about to explode. He was. 'If you want my opinion, the whole idea is completely impractical. Certain factors are being ignored altogether. It is very sad that Mike Thompson felt he had to resign and seek a safe job because the financial situation got him down. Now, it seems, Nina Somebody-or-Other wants her hundred pounds back and if she doesn't get it, threatens us with bankruptcy. Gerry talks glibly of raising ten thousand pounds – in Liverpool. As I remember, the only offer of money we received there was a hundred pounds for Pearl Turner. Perhaps Gerry would find the offer still open. . . . As for Bill's arguments, they are simply unacceptable. So we are to drop the name Workshop and abandon the experimental side of our work, just to please the custodians of this nineteenth-century charity. Frankly, it's not on. We will never accept dictatorship. We rejected it from the Communist Party; we left Ormesby because we were in danger of being patronised. No, we want complete autonomy. And as for Joan being put in the position of a hack director, a show a fortnight – out of the question.'

Jean burst in: 'I should like to ask why only one of Jimmie's plays is listed. . . .'

'Thank you, Jean. It's true, I and my co-workers have given our lives to the theatre. For months now, I've given up the comradeship of the group to write a play to Mahler's music, passages from the *Second Symphony*, and it's either the best thing I've ever written or it's rubbish.'

The mention of a new play excited the company, so instead of finishing on a low note, the meeting broke up to a buzz of questions and interest.

'It's not finished yet,' said Jimmie.

Gerry was silent, but in his diary he wrote:

'Meeting no cop. Letter from Nancy, Lady Dugdale, no help.
Kerstin has gone, trying to make it to Sweden, on her own.
'I'm afraid I don't know any of the trustees you mention,' wrote
Lady Dugdale, 'but I do think this is the opening you seek to
fill in England, that which the Compagnie des Quinze filled in
France. The only drawback is the sameness of Ewan MacColl's
[Jimmie Miller's] plays, always the biased political theme, the
eternal underdog.'

I thought she was being biased. I'd collected the authentic
material for *Johnnie Noble* myself – and Jimmie's version of
Molière was hardly political.

One morning I was awakened by the unaccustomed sound
of shoes being brushed.

'Trustees day?'

'Yes. Keep your fingers crossed.' That night he was home early.

'Well?'

'We won.'

'You mean we've got the D.L.?'

'Practically. The trustees are converted. They can't make any
financial contribution and we will have to pay the rates and maintenance, about one thousand, three hundred and thirty-one pounds
a year. Also they reserve the right to veto any Theatre Workshop
production.'

'That's not going to please Jimmie.'

'He'll see the light, but I've still got to contend with the
Committee. They're decent enough blokes, all good Labour
Party members, I'm sure, but they seem to have a prejudice
against what they call the Bohemian element. Anyway, I'm seeing
them all before the end of the week.' And at that he sat down to
report progress to Bill and everybody who'd been at the company
meeting.

Bill replied by return:

Your news is very good indeed. It's difficult not to get worked up.

The physical amenities of the D.L. are magnificent. I remember a
wooden shed at the back stuffed with scenery and useful wood. I
gather that a certain element in the company was for throwing the
D.L. back in their face if we weren't given absolute autonomy.
This attitude has nothing to do with twentieth-century England.
You never get anything for nothing. Once you have the place it
should be easy to convince them of the value of this or that play.
In any case we are against crude propaganda. If the company turn
down the D.L., for whatever bloody silly reason, I shall reserve the
right to play no part in any future activities.

Gerry underlined 'activities' and scribbled 'We're broke' under it.
   'I've had a good idea,' he said to me.
   'Not another one!'
   'Yes. And David Lever, the solicitor, Harold's brother, is
helping me with it.'
   'What is it?'
   'If Nina and all our other creditors can't touch our gear, we're
safe.'
   'We have to pay our debts.'
   'Yes, but we can't at the moment.'
   'So?'
   'Our Board of Directors will have to say that all our equipment
belongs to them.'
   While Gerry continued his fight for the D.L., I visited the
Millers' cottage. Jimmie had finished his new play and wanted
to read it to me. Mahler's *Resurrection Symphony* had inspired him
and he played sections of it as he read. A summary can hardly do
justice to the work, but I will try.

> A prisoner is being dragged back to his cell, delirious
> after torture. He is a political prisoner. His gaoler
> enters and tries to reason with him. Left alone, the
> phantoms of three comrades appear and accuse him
> of betraying the cause for which they died. As their
> image fades, a fourth being taunts him. 'Who are you?'
> 'Yourself.' This other self resents the shackles which
> the prisoner has laid on him, and a recapitulation of the

prisoner's life begins – first a girl as a moon breaking through clouds; then an elusive virgin, followed by a fertile wife; and lastly a woman all lust and carnal appetite.

Next comes a scene in an asylum where the victims of too much thought are cured with Pentathol. The chief psychiatrist is the gaoler, in a white coat. The despairing prisoner is then visited by a Chartist, a Communard and a Spanish Republican. They were all defeated but they still believe in the cause for which they died. They are replaced by three small-minded people who mouth the usual clichés about life. The play ends on a note of defiance. The prisoner pours scorn on his gaoler, who shoots him dead. The gaoler finds that he is now the prisoner and calls to the victim who has escaped him.

These bare bones give no indication of the poetry of the work. The writing was often dazzling, so dazzling that it tended to obscure the meaning.

Jean had been listening, quietly.

'There is scope for marvellous choreography,' she said.

'It will need marvellous technique all round.'

'You are the only one who can tackle it,' said Jimmie.

'What with?' I asked, and left.

I saw little of Gerry that week, but he seemed quite cheerful. The T.W. directors had agreed to accept ownership of our theatrical effects, and Kerstin had received favourable letters from Sweden. Several theatres would be interested to discuss a visit – but when?

On 9th March, the David Lewis trustees' decision was overturned by the Committee, and their Chairman, J.T. Edwards, wrote to Gerry:

Your project would seriously interfere with the activities being carried on at present and for which the D.L. organisation was designed. In the circumstances, therefore, we can make no recommendation to the trustees and so far as we are concerned, we cannot assist you.

Gerry took the blow quietly. In fact he could not accept such an end to the story. He went to Liverpool again to talk to Edwards, but all he got was:

I can only say how deeply I regret the decision. I was looking forward to seeing your plan working.

'I'm going,' Gerry told me. And I could see that the wind had gone out of his sails.

'Where are you going?'

'To the Texan oilfields to drive a truck. It's well-paid.'

'And dangerous.'

'That's OK.'

And he walked out. On the table he left a pile of letters to be posted. They were to all the people who'd helped him on the David Lewis scheme.

Twenty-nine

Jimmie's new play, The Other Animals. *Opinion divided. Tyrone Guthrie, Bill Davidson, Gerry (just returned) – against. An old admirer lets us have a house. We christen it the Parrot House, as the faithfuls reassemble, taking part-time jobs. Camel retrieves our equipment. Kerstin has a tour of Sweden in her pocket. With Gerry she obtains beautiful fabrics to clothe the play. Bill Davidson leaves. Difficulty with the setting. Carl Ebert from Glyndebourne and Nye Bevan attend the first night.*

I knew that there'd been a meeting called at the Millers' to read the new play. Some had not attended. What was the use – we were defunct. Before the reading, the rest had decided to look for work but be ready to come together when things looked up. Afterwards there was such enthusiasm for the play that harebrained schemes were suggested which had little basis in reality. Many had joined us attracted by the ideals for which Jimmie stood, held by his flow of words, at once mystifying and exciting. Before he left, Gerry had expressed little interest in the play, now called *The Other Animals*, but I had been sending copies to people who might help us.

Tyrone Guthrie replied:

Sorry you are having a discouraging period just now, but hope you will see a clear way, suddenly and unexpectedly. As regards the play, though I think it is the work of a poet, I have no desire to see it on the stage. Much of the verse is unintelligible. This is no condemnation of it, as verse. I'm sure it will be perfectly intelligible in another thirty or forty years, but at present I don't feel attracted to works of art which express confusion and an almost psychopathic preoccupation with violence and destruction.

Bill Davidson seemed divided:

There are passages where one says, 'All very clever, but what does
it all add up to?' On the other hand, it has a breadth and nobility
which is refreshing after so much decadent writing; a completely
intellectual approach to the emotional problems of existence, which
confirms what I've always suspected, that an emotional problem
can be reduced to an intellectual one.

The company may have been enthusiastic about Jimmie's play
but all they did when they met was moan.

'If only we had a place to play,' said Doreen. 'I'd sooner
be in *While Parents Sleep* than washing up in Woolworths.'

'Go and get a job in weekly rep, then,' said Howard.

'I've got to be available for my rôle as the elusive virgin.'

'Typecasting,' said David.

'We must hang together,' said Benny.

'We probably will,' Howard replied.

Rosalie and David, now Jimmie's ardent advocates, had whole
passages of *The Other Animals* by heart. One night they went for
a curry in Sadar Bahadur's new restaurant in the centre of town.
He sat under a palm tree, folding table napkins and reminiscing.

'He remembered us all from *Fuente Ovejuna* days and sends
his love to you, specially,' Rosalie told me.

'I know. If he sees me in the street, he gives me a round
of applause.'

'Well, now he's got a house in Fallowfield, empty.'

'There's room for everyone and we could rehearse Jimmie's
play.'

Where was Gerry? He was our property expert. Had he really
gone to Texas? I was too lonely without him. He disappeared for
two or three days, and when he did walk in he went straight to the
cupboard, without a word.

'Empty!' he said. 'I knew you wouldn't take care of yourself
while I was away.'

'I've been perfectly well fed, thank you.'

It was no use asking him where he'd been. He'd tell you
nothing till he was ready. 'Do you think you could draw a

thank-you for my old man and send him a flower?'

'Of course. Shall I say thank-you for anything special?'

'For paying all our trading debts.' I had to sit down. 'Not Nina. He thinks she had her money's worth out of us.'

'I'll go to the flower market early tomorrow.' I went. He still hadn't told me where he'd been and I was dying to know. I phoned his father. He chuckled.

'He's been here with me,' he said. 'We've been making a film of the waterproofing process, with me at the centre of it.'

I took him his posy and a drawing I'd made of Gerry, then hurried home. Gerry was out. Rosalie had told him about Sadar's house and he'd been to take a look at it.

'I've signed the tenancy agreement,' he said when he returned. 'Twenty-six pounds, one and eightpence a month. Everybody'll have to pay their whack.'

'There's room for all of us?'

'Unfortunately, yes.'

Camel and Maggie moved in straight away. They'd been sleeping in a single bed in a lodging house in Hulme. Even the Means Test inspector had felt sorry for them. Gerry and I left Mrs Staunton's and joined them. Howard went home, and Kerstin hitched to Tilbury, determined to get to Göteborg. We christened our new residence 'The Parrot House' in honour of the green parrots on the wallpaper in the front room. We were all sleeping on the floor. To Camel fell the task of hitching to Ormesby, recovering the lighting equipment and getting it back to us by train, or bus, whichever he could manage. Bill Davidson and John B. were to recover our London property.

By now we were all used to tackling any impossible job which came our way. Maggie, Gerry and I scrubbed and polished. Benny turned up and lent a hand. John B. arrived driving a decrepit-looking van which looked as if it had been rescued from a car-crusher. The *Proposal* sofa, chair and jardinière, still gaily painted, furnished the Parrot Room. Benny claimed the oval sloping bed from *Perlimplín*. The rest of us made do with rostra from *Operation Olive Branch*, except for Doreen: she got the hammock, and John B. awarded her the purple cellophane aspidistra as a consolation prize. He moved into the basement where he could continue his jam-making and pickle-bottling undisturbed. As soon as Camel got back from Ormesby, he and John B. started digging up the back garden to grow vegetables.

One evening David and Rosalie dropped by to see how we were faring. Everybody was busy painting the woodwork or cutting up vegetables while they discussed the advantages of packing books in Hanging Ditch over hawking fly-papers in Market Street.

'I'm glad to see you're all nicely settled,' said Rosalie as we drifted into the front room to see how they were.

But suddenly she burst into verse:

> *Shags opened the breast of the wheeling gull*
> *As he rode the shifting currents of the air*
> *His perfect flight*
> *Was a reminder constantly before their eyes*
> *Of the gulf which lies between*
> *Their world, half-fish, half-bird*
> *And his, all bird – perfect*
> *Man, the other animal*
> *Men, the other animals.*

'We are neglecting Jimmie's genius for a mess of pottage,' she said.

'I didn't think my stew smelt that bad,' said Gerry.

David froze him with a look.

'It is our duty to show his work to the world. No one else will.'

'The Elusive Virgin' put her oar in: 'It's very beautiful.'

'Great stuff,' said David. 'And I know Jean can't wait to get her hands on the choreography.'

'Bill Davidson's opposed to it,' said John B.

Gerry, who was standing by the door, said nothing.

'Why did we cancel *Blood Wedding*?' asked Benny. 'It was simpler than this play.'

'We couldn't odds it,' I said. 'I wanted to use A.L. Lloyd's translation but Lorca's sister had given the English rights to Roy Campbell, the South African poet.'

'Fascist poet,' said David. 'He joined forces with Franco.'

'That's not the point. He has the rights, that's the incontrovertible fact. A.L. Lloyd says he doesn't even know the Spanish language.'

'Why don't we do *Hindle Wakes*?' said Gerry. 'An honest Lancashire play, with no complications.'

'It's not Workshop,' said Rosalie.

The aroma of Gerry's stew brought the impromptu meeting to a close.

'Adjourned till the next time.'

'It's a fantastic play,' said Rosalie to Gerry as she left with her husband.

The news must have been carried on the wind. Bill Davidson wrote:

I hear there's a move afoot to put on Jimmie's play at all costs. At Christmas we decided not to come together till we had a permanent home. To put this show on, if we had the D.L., would be one thing, but to reassemble just to mount Jimmie's play would be even madder than is usual with Theatre Workshop. It needs a lot of preparation, not only of the cast, above all of the audience. For God's sake bring the company down to earth. Where's the money coming from?

On a fine Monday morning I wished Gerry a happy week.

'So long as I don't hear that you're putting on this new play of Scrooge's.'

'I'm not convinced that it would be the right choice myself. I admire Jimmie's talent but he has no sense of structure.'

'You've always supplied that.'

'In this case, the Mahler supplies a certain amount of conflict, but the rest is schizophrenic; the conflicts are self-made. It's strange the way some of the company are wild about *The Animals*.'

'Rosalie and David have always been sold on his writing.'

'Rosalie thinks David should play Jimmie's other self. I'll have to read it again.'

'You know Kerstin's on her way back from Sweden?'

'She made it?'

'God knows how.'

And she arrived back breathless with enthusiasm.

'Our clear way lies through Stockholm,' she declared. 'They love the idea of a play set to Mahler. Emwall is mad about it and he's our leading impresario.'

It had some brilliant writing in it and the possibility of exciting acting and dancing.

'But Kerstin,' I said, 'we've no money, no rehearsal room. . . . All we've got is a lot of old tat.'

'You've never let little difficulties like that stand in your way.'

'And what do we do about costumes?'

She went into a huddle with Gerry and the next day they disappeared altogether. I went into the kitchen to prepare a special evening meal. I was chopping the onions when Howard found me. He was worried about Nina's threat of bankruptcy.

'But there's no need to cry over it,' he said.

'It's not Nina, it's the onions. And you stop worrying and write out a menu. It's a proper Swedish meal tonight, in honour of Kerstin's return. Put the blue-and-yellow flag at the top. Right? Meatballs with tomato sauce. Green salad with seaweed. Afters – redcurrants.'

'Is it real seaweed?'

'Of course.'

'I'm still worried about Nina and her hundred quid.'

'Tell her we'll pay her when we come back from Sweden.' It was Kerstin, followed by Gerry, both laden with huge bundles.

'Lengths of silk, brocades, seamless nylon and a new voile that's not even on the market yet.' Kerstin was flushed with excitement. 'For the Mahler play. We've been to the biggest warehouse in Manchester.' All for free, thanks to Kerstin.

'No, in exchange for an advert in the programme on our Swedish tour.'

'Have we got a Swedish tour?'

'Sure, all we have to do is write a few letters.'

'They're glorious fabrics,' Gerry said. 'But they don't have to be used for Jimmie's play.'

'They have to tour Sweden,' said Kerstin.

'The Library Theatre's free for two weeks in July,' said Howard, 'but I didn't think we'd have anything ready. Do you think we might use the Yackypack Club for rehearsals, Gerry?'

'How do you spell it?' Kerstin had her notebook out.

'Who knows?' said Gerry. 'That's what the Yiddisher people call the Sephardi.'

'Oh, the aristocrats!' she said. 'The ones from Spain and Portugal.'

'Gerry knows all the Yackypack birds,' said Howard.

'Then you must get this club, Gerry.'

And sure enough, Gerry found himself walking along Palatine Road next morning, looking for the place. He had known one or two Yackypack families when he was at Manchester Grammar School, but he hadn't set eyes on them since.

Once found, the next problem was the doorman. No, he didn't think the secretary was about. He'd take a look. Silence descended till the click of counters was heard and the soft shuffling of cards.

'Gamble their lives away, they would. One of 'em 'ere staked his wife on the turn of a card, and lost.'

It was the doorman. After a minute, a slithery-looking man joined him and looked Gerry up and down.

'Manny Raffles's boy?' Gerry winced and then explained the problem.

'Do anything for 'im. The place is yours. Mind you, there's only the music room. It's not used very often. See that you clean up after you. My best to the family.'

Gerry's success was announced to general rejoicing.

'I suppose it's to be the Scrooge masterpiece, then?' said Gerry.

'Everybody's very keen on it, but they've all got part-time jobs.'

'You'll manage,' he said.

Bill Davidson pulled out. He joined Mike Thompson and Marie Hopps at the Dundee Repertory Theatre. I made a night and day work schedule, wrote articles till the small hours myself and slept during Jean Newlove's dance rehearsals. Margaret made hotpot that lasted a week, and Doreen, the Elusive Virgin, made so much Swiss porridge that the company held a protest meeting.

Jean was on form. She limbered everybody up to such effect that after the first workout, nobody could walk upstairs and after the second they couldn't walk down. Jimmie conducted the analysis of his lines. . . .

Golgotha was built of skulls, Paris and Byzantium
Colchis was built on a fever swamp
And Nineveh was plagued with flies that swarmed
from Tigris River . . .

That was Benny, who was playing a deranged architect. . . .
'*Bone and blood built Troy town, but the blood was . . .* green?' asked
Benny.

'Green, boy,' said Jimmie. '*And men were poisoned by the sewers
of Babylon.* Continue.'

And Benny roared out:

Give me a plot of ground, a river and two hills,
A tenth part of the energy dissipated in a day of war,
And I will build a city like a song, where nothing will
offend the eye and nothing will be hidden.

'There should be a crescendo there,' said Jimmie.

Peter Varley, a Tyrone Guthrie discovery, suddenly turned
up to offer us his talent, and proved excellent as the sadistic
gaoler. Rosalie, heavily pregnant, came in from time to time to
encourage us. Jimmie was playing the hero, David his alter ego, at
the same time working miracles with the Mahler. He would allow
no one else to touch it. Jean was the Moon, a non-speaking part.
The Elusive Virgin was quite happy, despite snide remarks from
the male members. Maggie was the fertile wife, and Kerstin the
Duessa of the piece.

Gerry was busy writing letters – but he liked to prepare lunch
for the two of us in our room. One day, after a good morning,
I noticed the laburnum and lilac for the first time as I walked
home. Gerry laid some crisp Cos lettuce on my plate with a slice
of Wensleydale beside it, and we sat happily munching, till a loud
rat-a-tat on our door made us jump. It was Camel, with John B.
standing behind him. The food cupboard on the landing had been
flung open. Camel pointed at a white plate.

'My prize lettuce.'

'The only one in the garden,' said John B.

'There's a bit left,' I said.

'That is not the point.' John B. sounded like the headmaster.

Gerry looked crestfallen. 'It was very good. . . .'

When the silence became a bit silly, Camel turned on his heel and strode away, muttering.

I had wanted to show him some sketches I'd made for the set. I'd have to wait till he simmered down. Sets were never finalised till we'd analysed the play and decided on the essential visual elements. Mostly we had to re-work materials already used, but the shows always looked good and felt good. However beautiful, sets conceived before the play is rehearsed, superimpose on the production. The director deciding on the interpretation alone cannot compare with the work of a composite mind.

Our costumes evolved with the characterisations. They had to allow for dancing, possibly acrobatics. The pockets must be practical and the cloth and trimmings suited to the characters' station in life. When we were playing *Henry IV* for schools, and too poor to make our costumes, the Old Vic kindly lent us some of theirs. Ralph Richardson's Falstaff padding was the funniest; it stood up on its own. It was quite impossible to move in it. The costumes and trimmings all made of the same material, whether for rich or poor, may have been effective at a distance, but gave no stimulus to the wearer.

For effect, though, you've got to hand it to Noguchi. Did you see John Gielgud's *Lear* directed by Mr George Devine? I was at the first dress rehearsal, and watched one of the actors unwinding these long black swaddling bands. Noguchi came by to help him. 'Anything wrong?'

'Yes! I'm dying for a pee.' The designer burst out laughing.

The Other Animals was not easy to design. The play took place in the hero's mind. A bare stage wouldn't do though; the changes of mood could be helped by the lighting. At first the hero is physically confined, but a realistic setting would be inappropriate. I imagined a disc, suspended in space at an angle, surrounded by silver rods which converged towards the vertex. It should look like a pendulum, arrested in space. It would have to appear to move and the imprisoning rods to disappear.

To convey the prisoner's claustrophobia, then his sense of boundless space, we settled for a distant arch, at times so small that it would be necessary to crawl through it, then so high that the stage was suffused with light; sometimes it appeared to be merely a normal door.

Camel didn't draw but he kept my sketches and made life-size mock-ups, simple but adjustable: doll's-house models give such a false impression. With Ben and Bill Davidson gone, Camel was responsible for lighting and sets. He would have to pull the stops out for this one.

The design of the dresses decided on, the girls made their own, scared at first to touch the shimmering fabrics so splendidly acquired. Gerry came out of his shell and invited all the newspapers to the first dress parade. It was a sight to be seen: the girls wafting round the stage in their luscious frocks with very little underneath, lights flashing, cameras clicking.

Jean's Moon dress was proving difficult.

'She's young, riding the clouds,' I said. 'She should be as naked as possible.'

'That's all right, but I've my b.t.m. to think about,' she said.

'Try this.' I threw a silver drape at her as she stepped out of her kimono. The cameras redoubled their clicking. The *News Chronicle* tapped my arm and made me look through his camera: a cheek of Jean's lovely Renoir rump had freed itself from the silver. I leant forward and drew the veil. Kerstin looked gorgeous in the new unmarketed cloth. David had a white silk ballet shirt and tight trews.

We'd hardly dispersed when a call came through from the *Daily Dispatch*: 'The big Swedish girl – the frock she was wearing doesn't photograph. She comes out half-naked.'

'Suppress it.'

'We'll have to.'

The *News Chronicle* next: 'I'm afraid it's a naughty shot of Miss Moon's *derrière*.'

'Oh, dear.'

'We daren't publish it.'

But the cotton firm were intrigued by the story of the disappearing nylon. I wonder if they ever marketed it.

Gerry went to London after the photo call. On the day of our first night he sent us a telegram saying that Aneurin Bevan wanted a seat. He had just launched his National Health scheme and would be in Lancashire visiting hospitals. At the hour call, the company was excited, but very nervous. The stage looked enchanting when Camel switched the lights on. He had been up all night rigging and trying out his special effects. Old rostra were heavily disguised and the silver rods had been conned out of a scaffolding firm.

David looked the complete romantic hero when he entered. Jimmie, his darkling other half, was in grey. Visually surprising, at times erotic, at times terrifying, the play was now a ballet with words, and the words, proclaimed in full voice, with passionate conviction, generated almost enough excitement to stop you wondering what the hell Jimmie was getting at, apart from 'exposing his self-mutilated ego', as one of his old flames put it. Fred Isaacs, of the *Manchester Evening News*, was so taken with it all that he sat through every dress rehearsal, became a Mahler addict and a confirmed Theatre Workshop fan.

Our opening night coincided with Rosalie's. Annabel, her first-born, arrived just before the interval. David was on top of his form in the second half. Rosalie's parents were at the show and very taken with the acting. 'Jimmie reminded me of one of the stars of former days,' said Mrs Williams.

'Johnston Forbes Robertson,' added Mr Williams. Luckily Jimmie had never heard of the gentleman.

There was a lot of fun on stage, after the show. We hadn't the money for a party but we drank the health of Annabel, youngest member of the company. At the last minute I'd been recruited to come on stage just before the final curtain, an avenging angel, come to gather up the remains. A sharp camera man caught me with Nye Bevan and the next morning we appeared on the front page: MINISTER OF HEALTH MEETS DEATH.

Nye told us we should play Ebbw Vale. 'The company there asked me how they could lose money. "Give them a Greek tragedy," I told them. Well, they did and made more money.'

Then Carl Ebert from Glyndebourne told me I should be producing opera. There'd be no competition.

'There's only one man who can do it and he's in Germany.'
'What's his name?'
'Felsenstein.'

Thirty

Gerry en route *for Czechoslovakia. His adventures in Prague,
trying for a tour. He is lent his fare to Stockholm, finds a hostel there
and all-night work, dishwashing. Swedish contacts unforthcoming, but
the Czech tour is on. The company play Prague, a warm welcome,
lively exchange with Czech actors.* The Other Animals *received
doubtfully.*

I'd had no word from Gerry since the telegram announcing
Nye's coming. What was he up to? I knew he hadn't much
money and he was too proud and shy to stay with friends.
Where was he sleeping? He'd spent the night on Euston station
more than once. It was Thursday evening. The phone rang. Long
distance.

'Where are you?'

'Paris.'

'What are you doing there?'

'Trying for dates abroad. Tell Kerstin to make sure of Sweden.
I'll tackle Czechoslovakia, Hungary, Poland and Romania.'

'How? You can't go to all those places. What with?'

'I took thirty pounds out of the kitty. I bought my ticket
to Prague out of it.'

'You're mad.'

'For you. I know.'

'Have you a visa?'

'Yes. The Cultural Attaché in London said it would take four
days. I got it in seven and a half minutes, largely by main force.
Tom was terribly dubious about the whole trip. I slipped into the
House to say goodbye to him and nearly missed the night train –
I made it with thirty seconds to spare.'

'Where are you now?'

'At David Rothman's flat. He offered me a farewell call.'

'You really are going?'

'I didn't think so till midday. The American Embassy here said a military permit to cross Germany would take three weeks at least. I tried drama, I tried charm and won. I must go, beloved. That train won't wait. It's supposed to stop at Bucharest and Budapest. If it does, I can drop off and try them. Take care of yourself. I love you.'

'It's you who'll have to take care. Please do. Good luck, Gerry. Good luck.' The line went dead.

I tried to concentrate on *The Animals* but the thought of Gerry on that uncomfortable train haunted me. Manchester to Prague on small change. The play was pulling them in. Perhaps the mixed notices intrigued them. We'd had a lot of publicity, and Kerstin was optimistic about Sweden. I'd have to keep the company together. I asked Howard to try and extend our stay at the Library Theatre and dug up a comedy of Jimmie's that might do well. It had a dog in it.

Gerry was writing to me as his train crossed France, but the letter didn't arrive for a week:

> Thursday 22nd July 1948,
> 10.15 p.m.
> Bar-le-Duc

My Joan,

It's almost dark, there's only the faintest streak of light across the horizon. I hope you will be able to read this scribble. I am very tired and the train jogs like hell. If you can't, don't worry. It's hardly literature.

At 6.30 this morning Paris was displaying her usual elegance. I treated myself to a *café fine* and a copy of *Humanité*; then phoned Rothman. He offered me a bath and breakfast. I accepted gladly, only worried lest after that night on the ferry, I might fall asleep. In the cafeteria there were five hundred pilgrims on their way to Lourdes. I asked the waiter for a *ficelle*, cheese and a carafe of *rouge*. It was a French boat, so I spoke French. An old priest had been watching me. 'You notice the Continental style,' he told his pilgrims. 'Wine with everything.'

It was sunny when I left David's – the same brilliant weather as we had, but no time for meandering. . . . Darling, I'm falling asleep. I'd better say good night and get forty winks while I have the compartment to myself. Sleep well, my love. How I long for you.

A beautifully polite *poilu* has just wakened me. Blast it! We seem to be at the frontier. This train does not go through Bucharest and Budapest; the schedule was a mistake. Now for my passport, visa and hard-won military permit. I may as well eat my supper while we wait. Before leaving Paris I took the precaution of buying a litre of *blanc*, a bottle of Chateauneuf du Pape, two fresh baguettes, some Brie and a garlic sausage. I hoped to pass this dull journey in a state of semi-inebriation, but in fact it has been fascinating, though some of it a little queer.

In the lost hours I was roused from my slumbers by two happy *poilus*, lumbering into the compartment singing, '*On dit en Italie* . . .' One fell on top of me. '*Pardon! Pardonnez-moi, mon vieux.*' He stank of beer. 'Ssh!' said his mate. '*Britannique?*' He made sucking noises. '*Oo, là, là, les Britanniques sont tous pédés.*' As he lurched towards me, I jumped up and thrust the two of them out into the corridor. 'Get lost! *Va t'en!*' And I shoved the door shut. I heard them invading the next compartment as I tried to go back to sleep. It is now 2.45 a.m. and we are entering Germany. It will be evening when we reach Czechoslovakia. The frontier town is called Cheb.

Friday 23rd July, 5 p.m.

Good evening, sweetheart.

The countryside is beautiful. Soon I will be leaving Germany. Everywhere people stare up at the train as if they would like to be aboard. Next stop, Czechoslovakia.

7.30 p.m., Cheb

This is it!

A Czech customs official went through my papers. He kept looking at our photos. '*Divadlo?*'

My first Czech word – 'Theatre?' I nodded. He smiled and called to his colleague. They found the photos fascinating and patted me on the back. We're away and I'm in a world of giant sunflowers and trailing hops. We passed Mariánské Lázně, the station decorated with clusters of bright flowers. I saw a church spire, green. Can't read the names of the stations, but they all have flowers.

Now we are in a dense forest of fir and pine.

I hope I have enough cash to stay in Prague till Monday, Praha in Czech. I must not slip into German. Andras, the Cultural Attaché, gave me the address of a cheap hotel.

I am worried about you because I know you won't be eating or looking after yourself whilst I am away. Please do. Howard has your money. Oh, Joan, I need you desperately. If only there would be a letter from you at the hotel – but I know it's not possible. I must wait till I get back to Manchester for your news.

8.40 p.m., Křinice

A fellow traveller has entered the compartment. Luxury is at an end. My belongings were spread over six seats. I have gathered them up. We must be getting near to Prague. I'd better close this letter. I want to post it as soon as possible. The hardest part of my journey is now to come – selling us to the Czechs. Then on to Stockholm, God knows how. I only hope Kerstin has paved the way for me there. Courage, dear one.

Gerry was mistaken, they weren't so near to Prague. He arrived much later.

Saturday 24th July 1948
Hotel Beranek

My love,

I couldn't finish the letter on the train because I'd packed the writing materials and was too uncertain of the time of arrival to risk unpacking them.

I was going to tell you about the man who gave me such a *frisson* when he entered the compartment with '*Revisor*' on his badge. I jumped up, waved what was left of my bottle of wine at him, dived into my pack to locate the phrase book – and all the time he just smiled indulgently. I suppose he took me for a loony. He'd only come to clip my ticket.

Arrived in Prague, the language problem became acute. No one spoke French or English and they closed like a trap if you tried German. The Czech language looks and sounds like nothing I ever saw or heard. Life is not going to be easy. It was by pure chance that I found this hotel and it took to well after midnight. Nevertheless I secured a room, on the top floor. It has a comfortable bed, with a single eiderdown for covering, as in Germany; a bedside lamp, wardrobe, chairs, a table, a divan, even a single ante-room with washbasin and boiling hot water. Sixty-two crowns a night, about six and threepence, not cheap but very nice. Came the morning, I awoke bright and early, had a thorough wash-down and set off to find the Ministry of Information.

Saturday evening
24th July

Prague is more beautiful than they say. It makes you feel young and energetic. Nobody looks rich and there are no spivs about. Along the shores of the Vltava, people lie about in boats, pretending to fish. It's an aristocratic, pleasure-loving river, but occasionally it turns a high, narrow water-wheel.

At the Ministry of Information I found Madame Hortova. She had little English but managed to let me know that all the theatres were closed and all the important people away. I would have to come back in the autumn. All the same, as I was here I

should call on the Minister – on Monday. She couldn't make any
decisions.

I hope you've managed to book two more weeks at the
Library.

In the afternoon, feeling a bit lost, I started skimming through
the telephone directory and noticed an English name. On the spur
of the moment I called the number. It was a girl's voice, and
friendly. She invited me round for tea. It was a posh hotel, the
Flora, and she even offered me a bed in her room to save expense.
I declined; I felt at home at the Beranek.

At six o'clock I tried the PEN club. The secretary, Jirina
Lümovà, was there; a slight woman with a sad face, aged about
fifty. She spoke very good English and seemed to have a working
knowledge of many languages. During the Occupation she was a
link in the chain which helped people to escape. She was caught
and sent to a concentration camp. She would have died there but
for the swift advance of the Red Army and the Prague Uprising.
Her husband, a doctor, was murdered by the Nazis a fortnight
before the Liberation. She took me to the Narodni, the Artists'
Club, for a meal. She knew all the theatre people. Afterwards
I asked her if it was far to the synagogue. I knew it was the
oldest in Europe. 'Twelfth century,' she said. 'It's a wonder it
survived.'

We went. Of course, it couldn't compare with the great
cathedrals, it's a simple building – but for me, as old as civilisation.
We couldn't go in, there was a service on. Prague has always been
proud of its Jews, she told me. And now they've given a splendid
château to the Israeli ambassador, though the Belgians and the
Americans and British had applied for it. Lümovà is a Catholic
who loves Communism, a charming European who is proud of
her native country.

She asked me to prepare an article on Theatre Workshop
which she would translate on the Sunday. 'We will meet at
nine,' she said. 'Morning or evening?' 'Morning! So that I can
show you picturesque places.' It was gone eleven when we said
good night.

Late Sunday 25th July
Hotel Beranek

From 9 a.m. till 10 p.m. Madame Lümovà walked me from Slav Baroque to Gothic, to Roman and blisters. I gave her my article. She invited me to supper at her apartment. In the evening Madame Lümovà checked her translation with me, made copies and had them delivered to the Czech papers. Over a cold collation we dissected latter-day French writers and Czech theatres. She had been an actress in her younger days.

And how are you, beloved? I miss you so much. I long to be near you, even to hear you, but it would cost about four pounds to phone you from here, and as things stand I can't afford it. I will have to leave for Sweden tomorrow, or Tuesday at the very latest. Has Kerstin written the friends whose names she gave me? I shan't have enough money to stay at a hotel. As yet I haven't even got my fare. I trust no urgent problems have arisen, nothing that cannot wait till I'm back at the end of the week.

Late Monday 26th July
Hotel Beranek

Dearest Love,

Today I came near to complete defeat. The Minister of Information, Loewenbach, stated categorically that a tour this autumn is out of the question. He is a discourteous man – with everybody, I noticed, not just me. Still, he offered me lunch and we sat there for nearly an hour before he introduced me to a leading theatre critic who was at the next table. We had only my Anglo-French and the critic's Czech-French, but it was obvious that he was very keen on us coming. 'To contrast with the official English theatre which came last year,' he said. Apparently the Arts Theatre brought *Hamlet*, with Alec Clunes. Every aspect of our work interested him, our technique, philosophy, you – especially you. He said that three or four important directors were returning to Prague the following day and I should not leave without meeting them.

With two powerful allies, Jirina and this critic, hope returned, but I shall have to stay another day. I must be sure of this tour. The journey through Poland takes longer than I thought and you have to pay with foreign currency. As I have no currency, I am in something of a dilemma. Everybody has been very kind, inviting me out for almost every meal. The only drawback has been having to pretend that I like beer. Luxuries are dear here, necessities cheap. Cigarettes, twenty for four shillings and indifferent quality. The CP looks prosperous. They have an impressive corner block on a main street. And the girls are beautiful.

It was so hot this evening that I took off my clothes and lay on the bed to cool off. When I woke up, my watch had stopped. I decided it was about five in the morning. It was 11.30 at night and a girl in the room across the street was undressing. As I turned over on my empty bed, a wave of self-pity came over me. It's not Theatre Workshop I'm homesick for, it's you. Good night, my queen. Or are you mine? Have you taken up with some homosexual hanger-on and completely forgotten

> Gerry?

> Midnight
> Tuesday 27th July
> Prague

My darling,

I am afraid to write. It may all be wishful thinking. Well, here goes. In all probability we shall open in Prague on 13th September, on very good terms: three hundred and fifty pounds for ten days guaranteed, and seventy per cent of the gross takings. If we are a success, we stand to make a great deal of money. We can't take it out of Czechoslovakia so it won't be much use, but we will feel good.

This evening I met Ota Ornest, producer and director of the Realistische Divadlo and chairman of the Theatre Council, the government body which controls theatre policy. He said he would be 'enchanted' to offer us his theatre from September 13th. What delightful English, and what a miracle that he should offer us the very date I wanted.

Publicity will start immediately. Maggie must collect and collate the crits which will translate well, and the best photos, Ursula Hartlebens's. Her address is in the bottom drawer of my desk, the file marked 'Publicity', and I need photos of you. There is a plate negative in the top drawer, right-hand side. Chick can run off half a dozen copies, three glossy. Nothing to be sent till I get back.

It could still fall apart. Tomorrow, at 9 a.m., the whole issue will be reviewed by the organisations who will have to finance the project. You will know the result before this letter reaches you. If you haven't had a telegram – Amen. Life starts early here. My first appointment tomorrow is at 8 a.m. with the National Bank, where I will try to borrow my fare to Stockholm. I've had a helluva time getting a Polish visa. I trust I shall be able to leave tomorrow afternoon. We're having a heatwave. Prague is in holiday mood, with short-sleeved shirts or no shirts at all, while I'm dolled up in my best and only suit. Today I even had a touch of sunstroke.

These dispatches from the front don't leave much space for love, which is the mainspring, but I long for you as the parched earth longs for the rain, and when I get back I will find you, as always, hellishly busy. Where do we go from here?

Your

Gerry

P.S. Ota Ornest sold us to Umeni Lidu (Art for the People). The tour only needs official sanction, a mere formality.

P.P.S. A complete stranger has lent me 2,500 crowns. I'm off.

Late Wednesday 28th July
Somewhere in Poland

My darling,

Here I am, reclining on bare boards, forty hours' travel ahead of
me – and no food. What a life! My first experience of Poland, an
encounter with the frontier guards, was extremely pleasant. My
second – being charged four shillings for two buttered buns and
ten shillings for a bottle of wine – very unpleasant. I've tried my
best to be sure I'm on the right portion of this train, to no avail.
Maybe I'll finish up in Moscow. Who cares?

G erry left Prague at 4.00 that summer afternoon, praying that
the small supply of sterling he had left would get him from
Stockholm to England. To relieve the tedium of the journey,
he noted all the stations:

4.45 Zachady, 5.05 Nymburk, 5.17 Podelbradyhazne. 8.15, an
hour and a quarter's wait at the Czech frontier, Lichkov. 9.30,
an hour's wait at the Polish frontier, Myedzylezie. 1.35 Wroclaw,
5.15 a.m. Poznan. All the engine drivers in Poland sport Lenin
beards. The firemen are clean-shaven. I have just passed the most
uncomfortable night of my life. 9 a.m., approaching Stettin.

Thursday 29th July,
2 p.m.
Odra port

Swedish boat, *Kung Gustavus V*. The Baltic as calm as a duckpond. I
fell asleep in the sun and woke quite brown. 9.30 p.m., Trelleborg,
Sweden. 10.30–10.50, Malmö. 11.10, train leaves for Stockholm.
   Darling, here I am on an electric train, very comfortable.
For the last thirty hours I have been given food by people I
had only just met. A Viennese shared his slice of bacon with me,
a Danish diplomat presented me with a huge lump of Gruyère and
a tin of liver pâté. He added a Swedish crown when he saw that
I couldn't change any money at Malmö. A Polish bloke wanted

me to break my journey and rest at his house. I had offers of hospitality from three strangers. I only hope we are as kind to people we meet. Not once did I ask for anything, you may be sure.

Poland looked so poor, the detritus of war everywhere. In six hundred and seven kilometres I saw not one single building which had not been torn apart by shell-fire, shells more devastating than bombs. There were empty buildings, ruins everywhere, and every twenty miles or so a graveyard of tanks, guns, armoured cars and burnt-out buses. The Red Army fought its way to Berlin over this territory. Now the weaponry is covered with rust and it's impossible to tell which side it belonged to. What does it matter now?

Friday early, 30th July

I was sleeping peacefully at midnight when a horde of young Swedes invaded me, packing the compartment to suffocation. I've been trying to sleep ever since, without success. Now a new day has dawned. I have had a wash – the first since Prague. Most of the brown washed off, too. Now I'm ready for battle. I'm worried about two things. Doing any good here. Getting back to England in the foreseeable future. If you and I don't get together soon, we'll be too old.

Still Friday 30th
7.50 a.m. Stockholm

The buildings *en route* looked Germanic, many built of wood. Here the towers are knights' helmets. And the knights? Rich and fat.

Mid-morning

I am sitting in a bank because it's cool and there's a table. The clerks eye me with suspicion, but they did change me a little money, extracting a large discount for risks. The other banks refused to take English, French or Polish money. Emwall is away till Monday. Ingemar Lundgren also. All Kerstin's friends seem to be away. Greta Almgren may be back tomorrow, and I cannot have a place on the boat before Wednesday.

The shops are crammed with eggs, bacon, cheese and every sort of fruit and vegetable. I've only been here three hours but already I've taken a dislike to the place. There is no native courtesy as in Czechoslovakia. I hope it's not as hot as this in Manchester; you will be having a thin time if it is. It's a long time till Monday. I'd better book that boat, else God knows when I'll see you.

Don't mention my reaction to Stockholm to anyone. I know you understand my feelings. It is a very handsome city.

Goodbye for now.

G.

Saturday 31st July,
Stockholm

Beloved,

I found a hotel about 9.30 last night. Once in my room, I sat on the bed and began to change my shirt. Hours later I woke, half-dressed, undressed and slept till morning. I asked for a bath, desperately needed. This is the cheapest hotel I could find, but it costs twelve shillings a night, without breakfast, and is not nearly as nice as the Beranek. Perhaps one of Kerstin's friends will offer me a bed tonight.

I have a place on that boat; should be in Tilbury 10.30 a.m. Friday. If only Emwall had been here yesterday, I could have arranged anything there is to arrange by now. I wrote him from Prague, telling him when I was arriving, but there was no message at his office. It is frustrating having to hang about, an unwilling tourist, and being treated like one.

About midday

Greta Almgren has just invited me to a meal Monday evening, but not a word about staying there. I shall have to choose between eating and sleeping; both cost so much that I doubt whether I'll be able to do either. Another scorching hot day. I'll be with you later. I must find somewhere to stay tonight.

Later

Words are unsatisfactory, a faint echo of my feeling for you. I
long for you with my whole being, and perhaps it's all in vain.
Will we ever again enjoy the peace we have known together, the
understanding which overcomes love's battles? Will we ever have
time for any kind of love? Not some weary routine, like bourgeois
marriage, but that which *makes hungry, where most it satisfies*.

   We have known it, so we must have it.

   I do miss you so.

                                              Gerry

                                              Saturday night, 31st July

Darling,

After a long search, here I am at the KFUM, Swedish for
YMCA. Three shillings a night, fifty in a room, which would
only be pleasant if there were two in it, you and me. The bed is
a two-tiered affair, with no sheets, so sleeping will be a bit hairy.
We are high up, overlooking the water and a busy tram
terminus.

   That hotel charged me two and six extra for the bath. Was I
pleased to leave it? I hired a canoe and paddled around a lake for
a couple of hours. There are very pleasant waterways and lakes in
Stockholm. I found a quiet wooded stretch, but all of a sudden a
hundred motorboats came roaring by, almost upsetting my
canoe.

   Tomorrow, another day to waste before I can do anything
useful. To enjoy this place you need a high-powered car and
a bag of money, but the simple life would do, if you were by.

   If Bill Ward [a railway worker, an old friend of Theatre
Workshop, J.L.] hasn't been to the show yet, get Howard to invite
him and his missus, and be sure that he gets comps. They can find
him at the marshalling yard.

Sunday morning,
1st August

There are young people from all over the world in this hostel.
The Finns are particularly friendly. They kept me up till after
2 a.m. talking a hybrid German. I couldn't have slept anyway,
it was too hot. A Viennese girl started teaching me how to say
'please' and 'thank you' in Swedish when a young Liberian seaman
walked in. He'd been sleeping on the floor of his consulate for a
week. Nobody would take him in because he's coloured. The kids
on the street shouted 'nigger' after him. A crowd of Czech students
were listening and they all began criticising Sweden's attitude to
the Nazis, all that. We had to bring it to a close at 9.30 – that's
when you're turned out. I went and slept on the river bank. It will
be a relief to get on with the job tomorrow.

Monday morning,
2nd August

This morning I felt like jumping from the window into the
cool water below. I looked round the dormitory – bearded faces,
fevered faces, sweating bodies in dark-brown bunks. It's a Belsen
of a place. I have that *malaise d'esprit* which completely left me in
Prague.

*   *   *

Months later, I found out why. With a couple of Czech students
who knew the ropes, he'd spent Sunday evening and all that night
dishwashing.

'I can't imagine you dishwashing, Gerry.'

'I didn't, much. I talked to them about theatre and at least
I had enough to eat.'

At 2 p.m. he saw the impresario, Emwall. At 6 p.m. he
had a meal with Kerstin's friends. At 9.25 he was on the train
to Göteborg, and on Wednesday he was on his way to England.
The boat docked at 7 a.m. on the Friday. He took the first train
to Manchester and found me in a dressing-room, padded and

bewigged to play a silly old woman.

'And Prague?'

'No news.'

It was another two weeks before the Czech tour was confirmed. Gerry's marathon had cost him nineteen days, many sleepless nights, and thirty pounds. Nobody seemed very impressed. By that time we were all expected to work miracles, especially Gerry; yet his was the hardest stint. The subsequent tour was, by comparison, a pleasure trip. Gerry was twenty-five, handsome and could charm a bird out of a bush. Without him, we would never have seen Prague, or anywhere else for that matter. We would never have been heard of.

Thirty-one

Touring Czechoslovakia, following in Schwejk's footsteps. The feasting, the fraternisation, the speeches. A Moravian production of Twelfth Night. *Our hard-worked company looked down on by some Czech actors because we join in the manual work. Zoë Tauferova, the prettiest member of the Resistance. Bratislava, Director Bagar and the Slovak actors. A Bulgarian delegation joins us. Art for the People give us a week's holiday among the pines before we leave their beloved country.*

He stood on the railway station at Cheb
He shook us by the hand and said,
'You're welcome to Czechoslovakia.'

FROM JIMMIE'S SONG

Jan Stedry, Beatrice Broumlicova and Zoë Tauferova were representatives of Art for the People. They had come all the way from Prague to meet us.

Zoë was the youngest – petite, with shining red-gold hair swept into a bun, her green eyes framed in delicately blackened eyelashes. Beatrice was older, a sumptuous blonde, dressed in a well-cut, brown velvet suit. Jan had a tired, cynical look. He'd been with the Free Czechs in England during the War.

A bus was waiting for us. We were greeting the driver when Jan said; 'You don't say "Hi" or "*Ciao*" in CSR, just "*Čest práci*" – "Honour Labour".'

The sun shone and one by one the company nodded off as we sped through our new-found land. Julia Jones was sitting with Chick Fowler. They had joined us for the tour, Julia to replace

Kerstin who would have to be released as soon as possible to go
to Sweden, and Chick to augment the technical team. We had also
kidnapped Peter Smallwood, a charming light comedian who'd be
right for the short plays we'd brought. Our skips were packed
with *Johnnie Noble*, *The Flying Doctor*, *Perlimplín*, *The Proposal* and
The Other Animals. Gerry was brooding. Was he still mad with me
for bringing *The Animals*? The bus pulled up.

'Coffee,' said Jan.

We entered a small farmhouse, more like somebody's home than
a wayside café. Bowls of milky coffee and hunks of home-made
brown bread, thinly buttered, were placed on the long wooden
table. As we sipped our coffee, which tasted of nuts, the farmer's
wife made a speech of welcome. Not one word was comprehen-
sible, but it sounded so warm and kindly that we clapped and said,
'*Čest práci*.'

When we were all back on the bus, we were told, 'Lunch will
be at Carlovy Vary. Anywhere else would be a disaster.' It was
Jan, of course, in his impeccable English.

'Carlovy Vary?'

'Formerly Carlsbad,' said Camel. 'The playground of crowned
heads.'

'And Goethe and Schiller,' said Gerry.

'Healing waters are just what we need,' said Howard. Jimmie
didn't hear; he was adding a verse to his song about the journey.
It went to the tune of 'I met her in Venezuela'.

Ahead of us was a steep hillside dotted with palaces, gilded
by the sun.

'Lunch,' said Jan.

'Are they hotels?'

'Rest homes for working people, these days.'

We wanted to stretch our legs first. It was a place for dawdling
and dreaming. 'Make it a quarter of an hour,' said Jan.

Benny was talking French to Beatrice, and Zoë was trying her
English on Peter Smallwood. I joined them as they strolled towards
the river. We all leant on the warm stone parapet and watched the
fishes, basking all in a row.

'Look at them!' said Peter. 'Toeing the party line.'

I'd noticed the small Union Jack flying with the Czech flag on the bonnet of the bus. 'Do we have to display the British flag?' I asked, for I felt uncomfortable at the thought of 1938.

'It is good for people here to know that there is another England,' said Jan. I felt we were hardly representative of any England. Still, it takes all sorts.

Despite an excellent lunch, we were all wide awake for the rest of the journey. I don't think we missed a thing. It was seven when we arrived at the outskirts of Prague, and the shops were dark.

'They close early,' said Julia.

'An electricity cut,' said Camel.

There were candles burning in every window, and when we were stopped by the traffic we saw that they were lighting portraits of President Beneš draped in purple or black.

'He died today,' said Zoë. 'The whole country is in mourning.' For us, too, his name was synonymous with Czech freedom.

A reception had been laid on in our honour at the House of the Trade Unions. Out of respect for Beneš it was quiet and brief. Dr Freilinger, the Minister of Culture, was there, and many leading trade unionists. Vladimir translated their speeches for us. Freilinger stressed his country's ardent desire for understanding with the British people. I felt so inadequate. All I could do was raise my glass: 'To Friendship! To the Czech unions and the TUC.' The glass of white wine was taken from my hand. I looked round – it was a union official.

'You are being photographed.'

What was wrong? I asked Jan.

'They don't want you to be seen drinking.'

'I wasn't drunk.'

'But we were, a generation of drunks when the Germans went.'

I slept like a top and woke thinking I was in Edinburgh, but looking down on the roof-tops and the Baroque towers emerging from the mist, I remembered that we were in the land of Dvořák, Janáček, Smetana, Kafka, Čapek, Hašek, and Jan Hus.

After breakfast of tough bread, spread with cheese, a small dollop of plum jam and coffee, still ersatz but very welcome, we went to work. Our rehearsal room was high, wide and very handsome. The parquet floor shone, the windows opened on a garden. What wouldn't we give for such a room back home? We changed into our rehearsal kit. Luxury wasn't going to spoil the Workshop.

'This is the Baletni Sal,' said Zoë as we checked the day's schedule and took our places, ready for action.

We'd hardly lifted a foot when a polite young man walked in to announce an imminent press conference. We tried again. This time it was an invitation to meet all the staff of Umeni Lidu – 'Art for the People' – at a luncheon. And so it went on, all day – invitations, greetings, flowers. We had to exert all the discipline at our disposal to get any work done at all. In the evening, a four-course meal before we left to attend the Burian theatre. The following night it was to be Ornest's show at the Realistische. We were rather disappointed not to be playing there, after all Gerry had told us about it, but Ota Ornest felt we should be in a bigger theatre and Burian had changed his programme to accommodate us. We were being treated like stars before they'd even seen us.

We all longed to see Prague, but we only caught glimpses of it as we hurried from reception to Baletni Sal and back again. On the way to the Burian theatre for the first time, we sensed the great wave of Czech Baroque which meets old classical Europe in Prague. The theatre itself was a large, slightly ramshackle place, and E.P. Burian looked like a William Saroyan character. He told us, with a twinkle in his eye, that he was now an MP and a newspaper editor, as well as number one Czech director. He had become famous, after the Liberation, for his *Romeo and Juliet*, set in a concentration camp. Tonight's play was rather static. Perhaps it was the unknown language, or the dumplings and sauerkraut we'd just eaten, but most of us had a job to keep our eyes open.

Afterwards, the actors greeted us like long-lost comrades and toasted the English theatre in slivovitz.

'That one speaks English very much,' said the doyen among them, pointing to a humorous little chap who'd had the funniest part in the play. 'Give the English friends your Shakespeare, Josef,' he said.

Josef needed no coaxing. 'Amlett,' he announced and launched into a long spiel of pure gobbledegook. It sounded remarkably like dull English: no change of pace, no inflection, and very peculiar vowel sounds. It would have been monotonous if it hadn't been so very funny, particularly as the actor never changed his expression but looked all the time like a perplexed Labrador.

'Alec Clunes to the life,' said Peter Varley.

The Czech actors were in stitches, and I gave them my impersonation of John Gielgud.

Next day was remarkably similar to the first: receptions, meals, interviews, but we managed to find time to explore the Burian stage. Our things had already been unpacked and the set was being rigged by Czech stage-hands, helped by Camel and Chick, with David of course superintending the sound.

The Press had already written about the way we tackled the off-stage jobs. They thought we were unique and seemed to imply criticism of Czech actors. We had noticed how many wore the Czech Communist badge. Surely they wouldn't be shirkers.

As we walked to the Realistische, sunburnt crowds were making for home, boats were being tied up on the Vltava, and as we stopped to admire the façade of an eighteenth-century palace, the carved wooden doors swung open.

'*Entrez, entrez!*' It was the concierge, wiping the last of the shaving soap off his chin. We walked into the courtyard where a fountain played and a flock of doves swooped up to the roof-top. We stood there, smiling. The old man, proud and delighted, tried to explain the palace to us, with a little English. We waved goodbye when we went and the last we saw of him was that smiling face.

I looked forward to visiting the Realistische, where Gerry first heard that our tour was on, and Ota Ornest was waiting there like a guardian angel, ushering us into his charming, intimate theatre. There was no alien territory between the stage and the auditorium, which was so comfortable. The play was by Ilya Ehrenburg; the production glowed. Ornest had put a shine on it, quite impossible to define. Altogether it was an unforgettable evening. In my mind's eye, I always see that theatre as Aladdin must have seen his cave, a wish come true.

No soothing music or tranquil relaxation could suppress the excitement of our first night. Jan, with intuitive wisdom, had invited us all to tea in his booklined study with its pale-green walls. We tried to talk about things far removed from theatre, but nothing is removed from theatre, as you have no doubt discovered.

Howard asked Jan about the relationship between the artist and the state in CSR. He shrugged his shoulders.

'It means working to rule,' he said. 'What else?' And he went to the bookshelf and handed Howard a copy of *Candide*.

I kept glancing at the clock. Would we come up to their expectations? I looked at Gerry; he was feeling the same way. I was glad when the time came to leave for the theatre. And it was a packed house. Beginners please . . . the familiar strains of Mahler as a wandering spot moved across the bare stage. Silence, the audience utterly still. The concentration was tangible; a pity the poetry would be lost on them.

In the wings, every entrance was jammed with stage-hands, curious to see what all the fuss was about. You couldn't get on or off the bloody stage. I tried waving them away. They didn't even see me. I couldn't see what was happening on stage but I could sense it. The actors were tense; at times their feelings bordered on hysterics. Was something wrong? I decided to go round to the front and see for myself.

Such a gulf separates you from your company when you go out front. The lighting looked terrific, the dances were going well. Jimmie wasn't overdoing it. There was a burst of applause after one of his speeches. They were getting the gist of the argument, I felt sure, but there was no audible reaction.

At the interval I saw Benny looking completely disheartened.

'We're not getting through,' he said.

'Some of them are getting it,' said Maggie.

I tried to buck them up. 'It looks divine and the movement of the play is getting them.'

Jimmie didn't say a word, and Gerry hadn't come round.

'We might do better if we could clear some of those stage-hands out of the wings.' That was David.

'I'll get a translator,' I said, glad to get away. The bar bells were ringing. Another hour of it. I would go and sit in the audience.

At the end, the stage was packed. Translators were called for as questions, congratulations and criticisms were voiced on all sides. Didn't the author know anything about recent history? Did he know how many lives were lost in Prague when the city rose against the Nazis? Was England still insulated? 'Your author is an Existentialist.' 'No, he is a pre-War Expressionist.'

The top and bottom of it was that a book by their national hero, Fučik, had just been published, *Report from the Gallows*. The work had survived but the author hadn't. He had been taken to a hill above Prague by his gaoler and asked, 'What do the people in that city care whether you live or die?' The temptation was similar to the situation in *The Animals*, but Jimmie's play was all beauty and great music. Fučik died in a sordid gaol. He had spurned the tempter and his offer of freedom and forfeited his life. On top of that, like so many Czechs, Fučik was blessed with a sense of humour; and in Jimmie's play there was none. Fučik had distributed his anti-Nazi tracts on the streets of Prague, disguised as a Koh-i-noor pencil.

The crowd on stage showed no sign of diminishing. Every member of the company was being quizzed. Some made a splendid defence, others made for the bar. The arrival of a stage-hand staggering under a pile of huge tomes created a diversion as each one of us received *The Union of Art and the People*. Gerry accepted his with a smile, then, catching my eye, he gave me a rueful look.

Next night we played *Johnnie Noble*, our story of a Hull fisherman, his life in unemployment, and war. The audience lapped it up, they loved the songs. We had a wildly enthusiastic reception. We were asked to record the play, and arriving at the radio station next day, I walked straight into an old friend from England, Vladimir Tošek. We'd met in war-time Manchester when he was a refugee. It was so good to see him. He was now head of the overseas department at Radio Prague.

Soon we would be leaving Prague to tour the major towns of CSR and Gerry was not coming with us – there was still a lot of paperwork to be tackled.

One of our first ports of call in Bohemia was Pilsen, home of the Skoda works as well as the famous lager. We were escorted to the man-made caverns where the beer is stored, treated to its history and given a sample. Then the Mayor arrived wishing to address us. He called on Jan to translate.

'Throughout the War,' he began, 'Pilsen was untouched, but when the Americans knew that the Red Army was advancing on Prague, they bombed us – Skoda works, railway sidings – then they occupied us. I took them bread and salt. General Robinson was the man I met. Nevertheless, we do not wish to be dominated. We thank the Soviets, but we are a democracy. Personally I should like to know more about the Marshall Plan.'

He finished by welcoming us and sending his greetings to the Mayor of Manchester.

It looked as if our tour would be following the wanderings of the Good Soldier Schwejk. We knew the book well, since staging Piscator's version, or thought we did, but as we met real people and learned their songs, it seemed that our production had been hopelessly wrong. Even so, when we reached Upper Vltava, Howard, Benny and Chick started quoting from the book as they tried to decipher the names of the towns on the signposts.

'We'll never get to this bloody Budějovice,' said Benny. Everyone laughed. It was Schwejk's line as he trudged away from the front when he was supposed to be making for it.

'We'd better,' said Jan, 'or we'll get nothing to eat.'

It turned out to be a delightful place. The town square looked like a *commedia dell'arte* setting. The Mayor was waiting for us and made a long speech, not about peace and friendship, it was a list of invitations – from the Town Council, the Koh-i-noor pencil factory, the Education Committee, three Trade Union branches, and two youth clubs, and they were all invitations to eat.

'No wonder he's so fat,' said Julia.

David whispered, 'Shall we refuse them?'

'It would be rude,' I said. 'They'll probably be giving us their rations.'

There was no getting out of it, the dumplings stuffed with spinach, cream and yolk of egg, the pork chops, goulash, diced beef with paprika and garlic, the sweet dumplings with plum jam and the black bread, ham and slivovitz with everything. Halfway through each meal we were served with little pots of stewed fruit, cherries or prunes.

'Half time,' said Jan. 'It refreshes you for the second half.'

At the third meal, I noticed that the dumplings were disappearing rather rapidly. I was listening to the secretary of the Education Committee when I saw Doreen secreting one in her handkerchief.

'The last line of *The Good Soldier Schwejk* is quite incorrect in German and English translation,' said the secretary.

'What should it be?' I asked.

'There is no Kaiser at the Pearly Gates, with wounded soldiers in Hašek's book. No, no, the good soldier turns to his comrades. "Don't shoot!" he says, pointing to the enemy lines. "There's human beings over there." '

At the end of the eighth meal, Jimmie called to me: 'Joan!' in a strangled voice.

'What's wrong?'

'Lamp the confectionery!' An enormous cake had arrived, oozing booze and wearing a crown of bright pink icing. I'm afraid the show was a little slow that night, and Jan was discovered sound asleep in the back row at the end.

Next morning an emergency meeting was called.

'We cannot eat eight meals a day and give a good performance at night,' said Howard.

'I propose we stagger the meals,' said Chick.

'Refuse them altogether,' said Julia. 'We're here to work.'

'But these meals are the best part of the visit for our Czech friends,' said Camel. 'Have you seen their ration cards? Fifty grammes of bread, fifty grammes of meat, ten grammes of butter, fifty grammes of confectionery and fifty grammes of sugar.'

'They went a bit over the top yesterday,' said Howard.

'You mean they're sacrificing their rations for us?' That was Julia.

'Invitations staggered?' said Howard. 'All in favour? The ayes have it.'

As we were taking our places on the bus, the 'Youth for Peace' turned up with a huge bouquet of red carnations and made a speech. We thanked them; Jan made a short reply and we left. It was a shame to let the flowers fade on the bus. Luckily we passed the hospital on the way, so we left them with the janitor.

That last line of *Schwejk*, missed in the German translation, haunted me. I decided to re-work our adaptation and asked David to collect records of Czech songs and dances.

One Sunday we went through a small town so beautiful . . . but then all the towns in Czechoslovakia are beautiful, not just Prague. Two pretty girls, arm in arm, a soldier carrying his baby, a young couple with a bassinette, a policeman sporting his upturned moustachio . . . they were all promenading to the music of the band . . . Smetana. I would put that into my new *Schwejk* too.

Gerry was rejoining us at Brno, Beatrice and Zoë with him. I'd been hearing the hurdy-gurdy of a fairground somewhere down the street and as soon as Gerry had settled in, I took him exploring.

First thing we saw was a roundabout with a panorama of wolves chasing troikas through deep snow. We went for a ride.

'How have you been, Gerry?'

'All right. Had a difficult time with Beatrice, though. She'd taken a shine to me, wouldn't leave me alone.' Gerry never realised how attractive he was.

'Never mind, love,' I said. 'I'll protect you.'

We were staying at the Grand Hotel. What splendour! As dinner was about to be served, the imposing white and gold doors swung open and two columns of waiters came flying along on either side of the long table, holding their loaded trays on high.

'Very Ernst Lubitsch,' said Gerry, stroking an imaginary moustache.

After dinner, Jan rose to announce the next day's programme. 'A visit to the Moravian National Theatre in the evening, after an excursion to and, we hope, a glimpse of, the Abbess's bottom . . .'

Maggie (who'd been squinting at her guide-book): 'You mean the bottom of the abyss?'

'Oh, your English accents,' said Jan.

The Moravian National Theatre was honoured to have us, and gave Gerry and me a box on our own. The production was 'Elizabethan', but utterly incomprehensible till suddenly an actor called out, 'Good evening – how are you? – very well, thank you – good night.' Every head turned to smile at the English guests.

'Gerry!' I exclaimed. 'That was Sir Andrew Aguecheek! And this is the tattiest, dreariest production of *Twelfth Night* I have ever seen.' The following night it would be our turn, but at least the dreaded *Animals* looked good.

In fact, the company played well and a packed house dutifully applauded. In the interval, the Mayor thrust his way on to the stage and made a very long speech. By now we could recognise the words 'peace' and 'friendship', but he went on and on. Jan whispered the English for one or two phrases but then got bored and gave up. After fully twenty-five minutes, the Mayor piped down, and Jan rose. 'The Mayor says you are very welcome,' he said, and sat down.

His Worship looked thunderstruck. He said nothing, but later at the reception I saw him buttonholing Beatrice. I hoped he wasn't putting the knife in Jan. Beatrice already disapproved of him. She was all for the new Czechoslovakia, and Jan was, unquestioningly, a sybarite. We were also aware of a growing rift between us and some of the successful Czech actors. In every town, newspapers commented on our ability to cope with any problem that arose.

'But we concentrate on our art. Menial tasks are not our concern.'

I only hoped we weren't getting soft with all this flattery and good living. All the same we did go around looking like a band of brigands. 'Must you look so scruffy?' I asked Camel when we assembled for a visit to a hat factory.

'And must you interfere with Camel's personal liberty?' said David. All the same, Camel did go back and change his shirt.

When we got to that damned hat factory, I was still ruffled. The machinery looked old hat, even dangerous, and I decided to stop being tactful. 'That thing should have a guard on it,' I said, pointing to a Heath Robinson contraption with a moving belt schlepping around it.

On the bus to Bratislava, crossing the broad plain of Slovakia, I perked up, listening to a good-looking middle-aged doctor who had cottoned on to us. 'The trouble with Brno,' he said, 'is its lack of Jews. That fool killed them all off. Did you see what we're left with?'

Then Zoë passed me a snapshot of herself, slim and trim, carrying a large revolver. 'In the Resistance,' she said.

'Watch her,' said the doctor. 'She put paid to a hundred Nazis with that thing.'

I couldn't believe it – pretty, green-eyed Zoë! But it was true, and Jimmie wove her into his Czech ballad as we rolled along. We were all looking forward to playing the famous town on the Danube, in fiercely patriotic Slovakia, where the people rose against the Nazis in the name of Catholic Slovakia, just like the followers of Hus in the fifteenth century.

> *Czech people! After the tempest of God's wrath shall have passed, the rule of thy country will again return unto thee.*
>
> COMENIUS

We were to meet Director Bagar and say goodbye to Beatrice in Bratislava, but everybody wanted to see the Danube before anything else when we got there. 'Unaccompanied females should not be out after dark,' said the doorman in German. We came across old buildings, half-demolished, propped up with scaffolding, as we approached the muddy-grey river.

'It isn't blue at all,' said Howard.

'Forty miles to Vienna,' read the signpost.

When we got back we found the hotel lobby busy with waiters attending to shifty-looking characters carrying dispatch cases and in the lift there was a small man wearing a grey overcoat and a soft grey velour. He carried a black portfolio and neither smiled nor returned our 'Good Evening'. The climate had changed.

At the goodbye soirée for Beatrice, there were the usual speeches, but Jan didn't bother to translate at all. 'You must know it by heart by now,' he said.

Next morning, an attempt to refresh *Johnnie Noble* was interrupted by the entrance of the mighty Bagar. He swept in, embracing all and sundry and, thumping his chest, cried, '*Ich bin primitiv*. Come!'

'Where?'

'To my new theatre.'

We went. Progress was slow because once in the street he was greeted by all and sundry. There were hugs and smiles, handshakes and greetings all along the way.

First, he showed us the actors' apartments. 'Good,' he said, 'and cheap. Not free. For the artist, every comfort. Not that they deserve it, cutting rehearsals to make a few crowns at the radio.'

Then his new theatre, half-built, big and conventional, like him. In a town which looked poor, it seemed out of proportion. 'That is mine too,' he said as we passed a seedy-looking cinema. 'We favour the cinematic art here. Have you seen *Bila Tun*, our film of the 1944 Slovak rising?' There was fierce pride in his voice, the pride of a Slovak who has known oppression. Actually, Gerry had seen the film in Prague. Afterwards I asked him if it was good.

'Exciting. But the Bratislava actors have nothing much to do but stand around looking unshaven – which they do very well. It's a Russian actor who steals the show; he plays the leader of the partisans' revolt.'

The evening produced a boisterous public and a lively show. More stage-hands than ever crowded the wings, but we were getting used to them and they joined in the applause at the end, enthusiastically. Our capers in the wings, changing and preparing to go on, had been the best part of the show for them. We were glad to sit down to supper, but behind a curtain we could hear toasts roared out and gales of laughter.

'It's the Bulgarians,' we were told. 'They were at your show.'

They must have known we were there, for before long the curtain parted and the Bulgarians invaded us. They were broad and handsome, the men and the women. Only Gerry among us was a match for them.

'We are the Bulgarian artists' delegation. Greetings!'

Most of them wore large red stars, and they all carried bottles of Bulgarian wine. Each one claimed a partner. I asked the lady who landed next to me what her star was for. She replied in Bulgarian, which was translated as 'shooting so many Nazis'. The wine went round, the crowd swelled. A party of Slovak actors joined us; the room became one big scrum, with greetings in half a dozen languages. One or two of the Bulgars produced bagpipes, the tables were thrust back, dancing was about to begin. The waiters, huddled together by the kitchen door, lunged in and rescued china, decanters and bowls of half-eaten food. A sharp young Slovak was calling for hush. One of the Bulgarians was pouring wine into his pipes and the Slovaks were beating on the tables. The sharp young man leapt into the centre of the room and fought heroically against an imaginary enemy.

'First round Slovakia!'

Wild hurrahs.

Our hero tore off his shirt, leaving only the collar and a stringy tie dangling from his neck. He wanted Gerry to wrestle with him. So Gerry tore off his own shirt and presented it to the challenger.

'On the table!' cried the Slovak.

One of the waiters was praying as Gerry charged into the fray like a mad bull. The table collapsed. The fight went on while the room roared and the chandeliers shook. Someone declared the contest a draw.

Uproar as the dancing recommenced, with renewed vigour. But while the bodies hurtled by and the music rocked the rafters, an ardent Slovak bent over me demanding, in broken English, how many Slovak plays were shown in London and whether I was taking the film of the '44 rising back with me. . . . He didn't stop but I couldn't hear for the noise. My deliverance only came with a general sortie.

'Where are we going?'

'To the tziganes!'

I caught a glimpse of Maggie being chased up the stairs by a very athletic Bulgar.

'We'd better keep together. We have to leave at the crack.'

'We'll get you back. Come on.'

I tried to collect the mob, but one or two shirkers had sloped off to bed. There was no sign of Maggie but Camel didn't seem worried. Outside, the air was cool and the town square was sleeping as we climbed into two or three old bangers and careered off through the deserted streets. Here and there we stopped, but the doors were locked and the houses asleep. Beyond the town we came to an isolated hut.

'This is it.'

Someone hammered on the door. . . . Silence. More hammering. To our amazement the door opened. In the light of a single oil lamp, we saw two or three real gipsies. But they had drunk their last bottle of slivovitz and were half-asleep. So we sang our own songs to them.

Dawn was breaking as we drove back. We'd left ourselves only enough time to collect our bags and wave goodbye. Maggie looked bright enough. I asked her how she'd fared with the Bulgar.

'Alright,' she said with her flat Yorkshire accent. 'But do all Bulgars have sech long tengues?'

Our tour was to finish up in the industrial towns of CSR, Olomouc and Ostrava. As we went through Zlim, Howard wanted to be dropped off at the Bata factory in the hope of acquiring a pair of shoes without coupons. We couldn't stop. At Olomouc we were invited to a chocolate factory, and Howard cheered up. But there was bad news. Our truck had been hitched on to the wrong train. Someone would have to locate it and get it to Olomouc, or there'd be no show. We drew lots. Howard got the black spot.

At the chocolate factory, the former owner met us at the gate. 'I am now the Workers' Representative,' he told us. 'You see, if you have started from nothing you can't give up. It doesn't matter what I am called so long as we still make beautiful chocolates.' And they did, but only for export. 'To Switzerland and the US. I'm afraid not Czechoslovakia, not yet. . . .'

Everybody saved some nice ones for Howard, so he didn't do so badly, and willing helpers had recovered our gear so the day ended well, as did the show.

Ostrava was smoky and grimy, surrounded by coalmines. It reminded us of home, that is to say, Manchester. Here we were to say goodbye to Jan and Kerstin, who was leaving for Sweden, and Gerry, off on his own, as usual. From now on Zoë would be in charge of us. Everybody wanted to know how Kerstin would get to Stockholm. Nobody had any idea that absolutely nothing was fixed.

Then Umeni Lidu offered us a week's holiday before we left their country, or alternatively we could spend the week playing the small towns in the former Sudetenland. We took a vote. The company decided, unanimously, for work after a couple of days' rest. Jan would take the message to Prague. We were all sad to see him go. Jimmie sang his ballad, with Jan in it, and our friend looked acutely embarrassed. Kerstin held out her arms as if to embrace the world, and Howard walked away, almost in tears. Gerry jumped on the train and waved to us.

We were glad to have the show to distract us. Zoë was the only one who looked perfectly happy. She had been flirting with each male member of the company in turn. She had an infallible technique: making a yashmak of her pretty diaphanous scarf, she would invite her prey to fix her blind, or look at her window cord. All the same, I think Peter Smallwood was her favourite.

'I 'ave been on ze river wiz Peta Small, and now I know ze all,' she told me. Poor Peter didn't know where to put himself. He was a very shy young man. He joined the priesthood when he finally left us.

After the show, our friend the doctor came to give us a phone message. We were to spend our two-day break at Hude pod Smrikem (the hut among the pines). He stayed to tell us how much he admired our efforts. 'As for us,' he said, 'if the good fellowship which exists now is to endure, we will have to make an all-out effort. Fine words are not enough, there must be selfless giving.' His name was Doctor Fuch. He had come to CSR from Hungary to take care of the people newly released from the camps. 'Many of them died on the road home,' he told us. He was now a miners' doctor.

When we left for Hude pod Smrikem, it was with a reduced load. We'd cut down the rig for the smaller places, and Karel, a happy-go-lucky giant, was our driver. The hut among the pines turned out to be a holiday station high up in the mountains. When the bus can climb no further, you alight and inhale the heady perfume of pine and woodsmoke. Nearby there is a log cabin where forest guards and lumbermen are downing pints of lager. They shouted a greeting and insisted on buying us all a drink. Then someone produced a concertina and played us such a merry tune that I started to dance.

'Joan's hornpipe,' said Benny.

'We mustn't linger, there's quite a climb before we're home,' said Zoë.

There was. We were puffed when we arrived. After lunch we found a game of skittles in the garden. Nobody knew the rules, so we invented them. Howard and I wandered off and started climbing steadily among the pines. The sun was warm, the path carpeted with needles. Paradise after weeks of theatres, visits and receptions. We didn't even have to talk. On the skyline a glossy black horse appeared; the rider wore a black jacket and cap. It was growing dark as we retraced our steps and the path was a mini-galaxy of stars.

'Glow-worms,' said Howard. *'Vers luisants.'*

After supper we all strolled down to the woodmen's cabin. This time there were two or three concertinas playing, and as soon as I crossed the threshold I was asked for my hornpipe. I couldn't oblige. I tried to explain that I'd made up my dance on the spur of the moment. So we all danced and sang all the Czech songs we knew, and learned some more.

Our mini-tour through the border country was easy-going, the hospitality modest but warm and friendly. When the trade union-ists brought their wives along with them, they were such shy women, not at all used to strange company. We were told that the good things we were eating came from over the border. In Poland, food and drink were more readily available.

There was a different atmosphere in the Sudetenland. Doubtful characters sported red stars. The Sokols wore a semi-uniform. And the black market . . . ?

At Hradiste there was a large meeting in the town square. It was the anniversary of Munich. The crowd was quiet and attentive until the mention of the word Chamberlain, when there was an angry murmur. We had to hold the curtain till the meeting dis-persed. Many of the participants came to the show. They were not hostile, in fact they were a good audience. Afterwards there were questions. Why had the English people turned against them? Why hadn't Munich been prevented? We couldn't fail to notice the tattoos and brand marks from the camps. How could we explain the English Tory to them? One brawny chap announced that Hitler and Stalin amounted to the same thing. 'All leaders turn into monsters,' he said.

At Vsetin a peculiar person introduced himself as a leading Communist, but as we sat at lunch he began making lewd sugges-tions to Doreen. She was our youngest and had to be protected. Zoë arranged for our meals to be served away from the public rooms.

The next time we walked through the dining-room we were treated to a parody of 'The Internationale'.

On the other hand, the meetings with artists and actors were better than in the big towns. Karel who drove our bus attended them all and revelled in the discussions. I was amazed at how much of our work he'd understood. It turned out that he'd been an active member of the drama group when he worked at Bata and now had a better grasp of the meaning of theatre than many of the Czech critics. He loved the art; so did many of the audiences. At one small town they'd just finished building their own theatre.

Our bus journeys were idyllic. Karel would lead the singing as we rode through the sunny autumn landscape. On my birthday there was sunshine, flowers, contentment. This time it was the company who had given me flowers, which made it all the nicer and completely blotted out the fact that in the little town of Sumperk there was no welcoming party, merely some black-market types hanging around. At the theatre, waiting for me, was the best present of all:

Beloved,

A happy birthday to you in Czechoslovakia. May you have lots more in every country in the world and may we be together always. Au revoir, darling heart.

Your

Gerry

And the next day, in his farewell letter:

I enclose a hundred crowns which Zoë lent the company. The situation with Beatrice is resolved and we now have a good camaraderie. She is a pleasure to be with.

I met the head of Umeni Lidu who 'is extremely satisfied' with us. There will be no difficulties next time.

You won't be leaving Czechoslovakia until 13th October. Beatrice wants you all to have time to relax before packing.

Do not change any Czech money into Polish zlotys. They are useless outside Poland and not much use there. Unless you have

Czech money, you will not be able to buy anything to eat on the boat crossing the Baltic.

My darling Joan, it is getting very cold and I am extremely worried as to whether you are warm enough. If we play Poland, I will bring out some warm clothing for you but I'm afraid you will be cold till then. Do please look after yourself.

Now I must go to bed. It's not that I want to sever this tenuous link between us but merely that I can no longer feel my feet.

P.S. None of the Czechs I have met will ever forget Munich, but they still blame the French more than the English: perhaps because they had always liked and trusted them more. At a meeting I attended, every speaker was disillusioned with the French and poured scorn on their war record. 'Individualists! They will never revolt.'

I did not agree.

Goodbye for now.

Good night.

The last few days were glorious, the sun shone, the bus rolled merrily along, decorated with flowers, flowers from our friends in Knov where we'd had a hilarious night. The safety curtain stuck, not for the first time, but the Mayor profited by the occasion and made a speech, all the time in imminent danger of being crushed to death by the threatening iron. We fell back on the usual get-out and sang. Camel was heard, unmistakably, singing 'I wish that I were home in bed' to the tune of 'Sadila'.

At our last port of call, Val Mezeritsi, we were playing at the Sokol HQ, and there was no mistaking the hostility from a section of the audience. Sad, because we were about to leave a country we were all in love with and we sang all our Czech songs on the long moonlit drive to Ostrava.

Without a word to me, Gerry had left Prague for Poland at 4 p.m. on my birthday. He couldn't have arrived at Warsaw till the following morning. What was happening to him? I knew he wanted to secure a tour of Poland above all things. If only he would send me a word.

Goodbye Czechoslovakia. Ostrava, 11th October 1948.

The big event of the day was the farewell meeting at the Miners' Hall at midday, which left us two hours to pack and chase round looking for mementoes on which to spend our spare crowns.

The Miners' Hall was packed. I looked down at faces I already knew, in Derbyshire, South Wales, Scotland, Pas de Calais — miners' faces. The speeches were simple and heartfelt, as delegates stood up, one by one, to convey respects to their opposite numbers in Great Britain, and inevitably the old questions arose. Had Great Britain forgotten them? Was the Right Wing still powerful? Were the people in our country more politically conscious than the Czechs?

We had no comforting answers. We could only offer our friendship. Each member of the company promised to do all in their power to further the cause of peace and friendship. One old miner wanted to know about conditions in the pits at home and I was able to describe them.

Jimmie sang a miners' song from the North-East:

> As me an' me marrer was ganging to wark . . .
> I met with the de'il, it was in the dark. . . .

And the men clapped in time. Then we all sang. I was presented with a miner's lamp and a gorgeous bouquet with a ribbon inscribed in gold, 'Miners of Ostrava to the Workshop'.

We left the hall singing. We were leaving with such warm feelings, such a strong desire for international understanding and a better world to come. We waved goodbye.

Beatrice, Jan and Zoë were on the platform to see us off. Zoë was near tears. So was I. Jan said, 'See you in London, maybe.'

Beatrice called out, 'Come back next year' when we leant out of the windows. The train was already moving when Zoë remembered that she had a letter for me. She raced along the platform and David grabbed the envelope.

There was to be no next year for us, nor for many of our friends in Czechoslovakia. The wave of optimism which had borne us along, broke. Jan, for one, disappeared. We never saw or heard from him again.

Thirty-two

Through Poland – the Russian officer. A letter from Zoë. Gerry's note
left on the ferryboat. Having visited Warsaw, he would like to live
there. Kerstin meets us at Trelleborg. The Swedish Co-op have given
us five thousand kronor, with which she has booked a tour. Gerry has
already returned to England, to find a base. News of my friend Sonja
Mortensen. We play the Stockholm Opera House. Royalty, and a
packed house. Gerry finds premises at All Saints, Manchester. We
need nine thousand pounds. Harold Lever is willing to help, but not
Arts Council. I visit Sonja. The tour ends; not much cash, but new
friends, Alf Sjöberg, Anders Ek, Birgit Cullberg.

On the Polish train we were wedged among Poles, Czechs
and Hungarians, taking turns to rest half a buttock on a
corner of the wooden bench. A smiling Polish woman was
determined to get through to us. She pointed to her man. We
understood that she had met him in the *konzentrationslager* and
. . . Here she uncovered a huge breast to reveal her baby happily
sucking away. Then she fumbled in her straw holdall, produced a
green apple and offered it to me. I took a mouthful; the flesh was
white and frothy, a beautiful apple. As I passed it round, her man
told us, in halting German, how much they'd weighed when they
were freed and how much they weighed now.

I was standing beside a smart young Russian officer. He was
reading and declined his turn at the seat. 'Do you read English?'
I asked.

He shook his head.

'I have read Pushkin,' I added rather foolishly.

'I, Dickens,' he replied, smiling.

'I, Turgenev.'

'Robert Burns.'

And we went on trumping each other, till he left us at Łódz.
The two bundles laid along the luggage racks were snoring.

The rest tried to sleep, except for a man with a dirty bandage round his head, who stood propped up in the corridor and smiled at you every time he caught your eye.

When daylight came, we saw the devastated land which Gerry had crossed twice. Where was he now?

I remembered the letter from Zoë which David had grabbed just as the train was leaving the station.

Praha, 11th October 1948

My dear Joan,

You don't know how much I would be on the train. There are so many questions about which I would speak with you. I am sorry I am not a fakir to conjure magically one flying carpet which will bring me to Sweden. In place of it I'm writing some words.

I was very happy with you, Joan, and with all the members of your troupe. Indeed they were days full of friendship, of collective work, successes and international bringing together, despite the language troubles. They were days full of merry events, as the singing in the bus, dancing in Hude pod Smrikem, Jimmie dressing up as a girl, battle of chestnuts and so on. Days with failings too, no stage-hands, no bathrooms – 'Oh the silly buggers', 'Bloody dumplings again' – but no one has shown dislike in such times. I will always remember smiling Chick when there were troubles with the riggings. This was why I liked you all so much.

I'm thinking of you, very anxious to know how you are faring. I did not like my food when I thought of you in the cold train without enough to eat, or money. It was terrible for me to be unable to help you.

I wish for you a very successful tour in Sweden. Write, darling. I have a great interest in the all about it, your work, your experiences about the country and the people. And where is Gerry? I hope it is all right for him too.

For you, darling Joan, the greatest successes. Be sure to write very soon.

My best love,

Zoë

On board the ferryboat carrying us to Sweden, I wandered
into the bar hoping to buy myself a coffee, and there on the
shelf among the adverts I saw a letter addressed to me, in Gerry's
handwriting. How lucky that I came in, but I suppose one of the
company would have spotted it.

                                    8th October 1948

Dearest love,

If you came this way you will have found this. If not, it will
lie here till, covered in beer stains, it drifts into nothing.

I bet you spend more time thinking of Jan than of me. I thought
of you as I traipsed through Warsaw. If we play Poland, I would
very much like to play in *Johnnie Noble* again. I've watched it from
the front and the play suffers a great deal from my absence.

On second thoughts, if we play Poland, let's stay there. I
am sick at the thought of going back to England. Churchill
has made what amounts to a call for war on the USSR. The
English papers are full of aggression. In Poland they know how to
live and they have a live theatre. In England, breaking our hearts
trying to achieve the impossible, that's the way of the martyr. The
task we've set ourselves is incredibly arduous, frustrating, draining
– and may never be achieved in our lifetime. If you are willing, let
us go now, before necessity drives the rulers of Britain and America
to submerge us all in another war. Think it over.

Must I be the one to forge the chains which will bind us
for life? What a prospect! You have only to say 'Come' and I
will wipe Manchester from my memory. To forget England may
take a little longer, but there will be no regrets. I love you, Joan.
You will never find anyone who will love you more. The thought
of travelling further away from you is unbearable.
                                    Gerry

He sounded very low. Obviously he hadn't done so well in
Warsaw. His was a thankless job. No wonder he wanted to
act again.

When we arrived at Trelleborg, Kerstin was there waiting for us.

'You all look wonderful,' she said. 'Welcome. Tomorrow night you are playing Norrköping and everybody is living in excitement at your coming.'

'And the tour?'

'Östersund to Malmö, Göteborg to Stockholm, and for everybody a bed and a meal everywhere.' On the train we all crowded into the same compartment to hear how she had brought it off. 'I don't know,' she said. 'It was a miracle. Ten years since I left Sweden, I knew nobody, and there I was trying to sell an unknown company with unknown play by an unknown author.'

'Where did you start?'

'I landed at Göteborg and went straight to the Municipal Theatre. The Director could not have been friendlier. "I will be the first to present the Workshop in Sweden," he said. He phoned Falk in Norrköping, who was just as sympathetic – and that started the ball rolling, town after town, all for us.'

'What about the money?'

'Fifty per cent of the takings; travel and publicity paid by Riksteatern. They're a sort of Arts Council of Sweden. We will play the Municipal Theatre for free; they will pay staff and publicity.'

'We've still got to get back to England.'

'I know, and someone told me to try the Co-op. So I made a date with the president, Albin Johansson. He listened to me without saying a word. At the end he said, "I understand your aims. I am in favour of your fight against commercialism. I will be glad to help you and your comrades. Would you please take this note to the office on the first floor." I did so and an envelope containing five thousand Swedish kronor was put into my hands. I'd never seen so much money in my life.'

'Where is it?'

'In the bank, though I don't suppose it will be there for long.'

It was unbelievable. Sweden was unbelievable – these tall, pale people with their lilting voices, all speaking English, and such correct English. We composed a letter to Mr Johansson, saying thank you.

In Norrköping the autumn leaves fell softly on to the clean

pavements and were soon brushed away. We were received by a group of young actors who led us to a table set with white china, a glass of milk, a plate of Swedish crispbread and a pat of butter at each place. After a nourishing meal, we were taken to meet our hosts. I was to stay with Baron and Baroness Mannerheim. In the evening they were entertaining the whole company to dinner. I didn't think we'd be dancing on the tables there. All the same, it was all very pleasant, if a trifle formal. Wine was gently poured, but we were told we couldn't touch it until the Baron had toasted his wife. We played the game rather well, I thought.

Next night, the audience reaction was overwhelming. They took us to their hearts. I thought they understood us better than an English public. The *Svenska Dagbladet* certainly did:

> A striking experience. The audience stamped with joy. There is something of Vachtangov and Meyerhold adopted by this company, but most of it is new. The means of expression, rhythm, movement, design of light and shade, the spoken word, all were worked together to create a liberating, expressive whole. The packed audience applauded with southern spontaneity.

And the *Östergötlands Dagbladet*:

> The company went to work with passion, subtle precision and teamwork rarely seen. *Johnnie Noble* gripped the audience. Chekhov's *Proposal*, a splendid example of theatrical parody, with extravagant mimicry and gesture, was irresistible, the work of a lively imagination. At the fall of the curtain, the applause was almost endless.

On our last night in Norrköping, the Stadsteater gave a party for us and brought out their most prized possession in our honour, the décor for the first production of *As You Like It* in their theatre – gauzes, cut cloths scattered with red-gold leaves; branches high up on the scrims, mossy rocks on the stage itself. It was magical, and supper was served there in a softly-lit Forest of Arden. There were toasts and flowers. Mine had a card which read, 'Many thanks for your magnificent, unforgettable performances in Norrköping. Signed, the Mayor.'

GERRY to JOAN   11th October 1948,
                                          Wednesday, 3.15
                                          Aboard *M/S Saga*

My darling love,

On the quay at Göteborg I thought up a dozen excuses for staying in Sweden long enough to see you. What changed my mind? It's quite simple. Kerstin told me the ticket would cost a hundred and twenty kronor third class. So I took a hundred and seventy which should have seen me to Manchester. She forgot the fare from Stockholm to Göteborg, another fifty. So I'm broke.

Whenever I move from one country to another I'm doomed to penury. Added to that, I haven't had a laugh since I left you in Ostrava. In eighteen hours I shall be in London. Alas! Last time I made this trip you were in Manchester and every stage in the journey brought me nearer to you. Then my heart pounded as the boat moved forward. Now my desires are in the ship's wake. All I want is to reach some mythical destination, where you are.

Parliament is in recess. Tom Driberg is in Haiti. In a way I'm relieved. It's pleasant to talk to him but I dread having to fight him off all the time. Between Beatrice and Tom I feel like a doe or a young hart upon the mountain. Escape was easier with the lady; with Tom I have the disadvantage of speaking the same language.

A happy Polish chap has just buttonholed me. 'Swedish men are cold,' he told me. 'But their women . . . They take you home, feed you – and afterwards they introduce you to their girlfriends.'

By the way, did Jan come back to Ostrava to see you off? I suppose you told me you'd written to him to cover yourself. It must have come as a shock to learn that I'd stayed on in Prague for a couple of days. You never know, I might have returned unexpectedly. How cruel you are. If you have fallen for Jan, or anyone else, the whole basis of my existence collapses. I knew it would come, sooner or later. I'd hoped it wouldn't be quite so soon.

Now I understand why you urged me to return to England – to leave you free for Jan. What a bitch you are to make me so mad with jealousy when I'm so far away.

It's only 6.10 p.m., but already night is falling. In the morning, England – six hundred miles away from you.

8 a.m., waiting for disembarkation. We are tied up but not allowed off yet. All my feelings are merely a dull ache.

9.30, in the train at Tilbury. Everything grey, the morning, the train, the grass beside the track. Trying to carve out a future for the theatre, I may find a brighter England, if one still exists. This stretch between Tilbury and London is like a Victorian lithograph by an artist with no imagination.

We have just passed a dirty old shack labelled 'The Evangelical Mission to the British Isles'. Goodbye for now. London approaches, half-hidden under a grimy pall, and I must leave you.

> *Day and night*
> *My fancy's flight*
> *Is ever with my Joan*

> > > > Gerry

JOAN to GERRY   Linköping

Dearest Gerry,

A clip for your notebook.

Ostgöte Correspondenten:

> The English group Theatre Workshop fascinated the audience from the start. The whole performance was a great success. The actors are like acrobats. *Johnnie Noble* concluded with an ovation, the producer was cheered.

I have been staying with a headmistress deeply interested

in eighteenth-century English literature. We spent half the night arguing about Sterne and Smollett. I happened to mention the Mortensens over breakfast, Sonja's parents. Her father was a professor at Uppsala University before he settled in England, at Richmond. 'You're not the Joan that Sonja always used to talk about?' 'Yes. Where is she now?' 'On a farm, near Ljusdal, in the very far north, the topmost tip of Sweden.' 'I would love to see her.' 'You would find her much changed. She has never recovered from the loss of her parents.'

As soon as I can take a day off I shall visit her, Gerry. She always thought of others. Poor Sonja. She arrived home one day to find the house a pile of rubble, her father and mother under it. She now lives a hermit's life, completely cut off from the world. Her relatives are rich but they give a farmer very little to keep her. She was an obsessive artist when I knew her. Now she has no money to buy paints. I must go, but it looks as if I shall have to travel to her from Stockholm. What an unbelievable coincidence, my staying with someone who knows Sonja.

Is anything happening at home? Did your visit to Poland come to anything? You tell me nothing, Gerry.

Do put our crits together and write an article for the *Guardian*. It would help in our quest for a theatre. And don't be so moody. Moods and feelings are all very well, but we are a revolutionary theatre and subjective feelings have to be sacrificed. If I let my feelings run away with me, I'd spend my time with sybarites like Robin Farquarson and Tom Driberg.

And there'd better be a letter from you soon. I have to adapt the shows to a different stage every day. It's easier for you to write; you don't have to tear yourself away from a wildly different activity.

Na sdar.

Joan

P.S. I've written a new ending for *The Flying Doctor*.

GERRY to JOAN   Manchester, 16th October

Dear Joan,

I came here on the midnight; there was no point in staying
in London, especially as I'd nowhere to sleep.

We have had quite good publicity in Manchester. Fred Isaac
wrote an article for the *Standard* based on my letter to him
from Prague. The *Evening News* and the *Guardian* have printed several news items about us. Yesterday I gave all three
papers some new stuff. The *Guardian* has printed a very good
piece.

This morning, at long last, I received a letter from you, but
judging by the tone of it I don't know whether we're still lovers
or merely fellow campaigners.

Farewell. I hope my next letter is not signed by the same
belle dame sans merci, should she remember to write to me
again.

G.

Gerry was having a great time playing the cuckold. True, I
found Jan attractive, but that didn't mean I wanted to go to bed
with him.

JOAN to GERRY   On the train,
                                 Västerås to Stockholm
                                 Friday 22nd October

Gerry!

Kerstin arrived from Stockholm with letters for everybody but
me. In the dressing-room I was still hoping that she had mislaid
your letter and would be bringing it to me. But no.

Västerås was great, an industrial town. Eight Communists,
eight Conservatives and thirty-two Social Democrats on the Town
Council.

Our audience was terrific. In fact, our performances have made quite a stir everywhere. Today we are giving a special matinée in Stockholm. Kerstin has secured the Opera House, quite a scoop. The train gets in 11.20, quick lunch, play 4 p.m. It has to be *The Animals*; the sets and costumes for the other shows are dirty. I dread the panic.

How is the successful young manager fresh from his triumphs in Europe? I can just see you.

Na sdar.

J.

P.S. I shall not be able to write to you tomorrow or Sunday, which will doubtless throw you into a jealous rage.

Later the same day

The Opera House holds twelve hundred. The orchestra pit could house the Hallé. Backstage is a labyrinth of corridors, *ascenseurs* and numbered doors. The stage-hands are very well-dressed and only have to press buttons which send ramps and rostra swinging and swirling about. I left Camel and Chick to deal with them and went looking for the wardrobe with Jean. When I came back, Chick was on his knees extracting tacks from the stage floor, and Camel was left with ten minutes for his lighting rehearsal. Nevertheless the curtain rose at four, punctual to the minute.

To set your mind at rest, the thousand kronor which the place cost were in the till by two o'clock. Then the *beau monde* turned up, including three members of the Swedish Royal Family. The Czech Ambassador was there and blew me a kiss. Actors, students and artists filled the upper rungs. As Jean's first entrance was coming up, she was nowhere to be seen. Chick and I went in search of her. My fault, I'm never satisfied with that damn Moon costume and I'd changed it yet again. She was in wardrobe being sewn into it when she heard her music coming up on the tannoy. She gathered her flimsy drapes and fled, but she didn't know which floor she was on, nor which lift button to press. Chick caught her as she was descending for the second time to the basement. The Moon was rather breathless, but only two bars late.

Although the show had been flung on, it went very well, and afterwards a young man called Torsten declared his love for me.

I swore at a diplomatic gentleman from the British Embassy and stepped back into a floral arch which was intended for Kirsten Flagstadt who was singing there that evening.

And here are some snippets for you.

Svenska Dagbladet:

> British theatre makes a revolt at the Opera House. The storm of applause for Theatre Workshop was fully justified. It was an excellent experience. . . . [Amusing, too, the critic said to me, to see a beautifully dressed audience applauding Red propaganda.] It is not very often we see such high standards in Sweden. Joan Littlewood is a great producer. Her use of light is especially important.

Stockholm Tidningen:

> English theatre is often tame and sleek, although highly developed professionally. The movement in opposition has brought out what is finest in English theatre, and one of the most interesting examples of that opposition is Theatre Workshop, a fine example of group theatre. Their use of sound is wonderful, full of nuance. The performance has a richness and film-like quality.

GERRY to JOAN   Manchester,
                                      Friday 22nd October

My darling,

Wonderful day, two letters from you. The first sign for nearly a week that you actually remember me. A day that brings no letter is never-ending; seven – a lifetime. I had to consult my diary to be sure that only a week had passed. When we drift apart I lose all desire to do anything. You see what power you have over me.

I have found the ideal place for us, the old Presbyterian church at All Saints. It has tremendous possibilities. It is clearly visible from two hundred yards away in every direction. If we painted it white, no one could miss it. Lever would be prepared to raise £4,500, about half the money we would need at the outset, and he could secure a mortgage for the rest. We would repay in rent. It might be thirty or forty years before we were straight, but what's the alternative?

I might be able to raise the money in small contributions. A Mr Nightingale has offered to put up five hundred pounds if there was a chance of the venture getting off the ground. Another bloke said he'd buy the place and let it out to us, but that would be no use. We must have control, it must be ours. I tried Arts Council a week ago. No reply.

If only we had somewhere to work, we could start a Building Fund. An agent tells me he has a building that would suit us, another church, already converted. He hasn't said where it is. If it's at all possible, I shall snap it up, and I've found a domicile for the company. God knows I cannot face another period *en famille*, but storage space, nine bedrooms, two bathrooms and three lavatories for five pounds a week, plus two pounds' rates, is not to be sneezed at. If the company want it, let me know and I'll have the gas and electricity turned on.

I will have to leave my father's house soon. I'd hardly said hullo before an argument started about politics. It soon reached boiling point. Now I'm scarcely tolerated and Brother Ralph doesn't speak to me at all. This sullen hate depresses me, it reminds me of Jimmie Miller.

It's about 2 a.m. and I'm so tired that the words take longer and longer to extract themselves from the pen. I wish you were here. The memory of you is like autumn remembering summer. Thank you for the letters, my love. They brought me back to life.

Your

                                        Gerry

JOAN to GERRY   Stockholm,
                                                Saturday 23rd October
                                                Riverside café

My dear Gerry,

This ordinary is the only human retreat I've found in this city.
'Respectable' places won't serve women unaccompanied. I'm the
only woman in this place. No wonder the blokes, mostly dockers,
look morose. This beer doesn't help either, but if I drink any more
milk, I'll hallucinate.

How are our creditors? And Nina?

I'm afraid we won't be bringing much loot back with us. I
could write a book, that might help, but how can you write about
this work? Can you describe the process of thought?

Have you seen our copy of *Eastward Ho*? I'd like to include
it in the repertoire, if we ever have a theatre.

I never tell you about all the good things here – like meeting
Alf Sjöberg, the only director who makes Strindberg live again.
Great! And the actor, Anders Ek, marvellous and mad. He sleeps
in a four-poster with a large portrait of Stalin for a bedhead, arrives
at the theatre hours before the performance, and tries all the seats.
I saw him in Kafka's *Trial*, very expressionistic, his two whores,
black knickers and pink suspenders. Birgit Cullberg is the Laban
choreographer and dancer in Sweden, and pretty good. She wanted
to meet Jean, but afterwards said she was surprised to find her 'a
charming young *petite-bourgeoise*'. I wonder what she expected?

Na sdar.

                                                Joan

P.S. Tomorrow morning, at 5.30, I am setting out on my long
journey to the North.

GERRY to JOAN   Manchester,
                                                Saturday, 23rd October

Dear Joan,

As usual, England is busy with anti-Communist propaganda.
There is real danger of another war, with the Americans looking for

world domination. They won't make it, for all their atom bombs, but they could press that damn button by mistake and we'd all fry together, as the man said.

Already a revolutionary situation is developing in France. The miners are defending the pits against the police. Each day brings news of other unions striking in sympathy. The dockers of Brest and Calais have refused to unload ships carrying coal. Will they be strong enough to beat de Gaulle? A branch of the NUM has sent a thousand pounds to the French miners. Solidarity, the brotherhood of man, is not forgotten and the French strikes will go on spreading. Even the French Socialist papers are supporting them. All the English papers, save *Reynolds* and the *Worker*, go on repeating the same old story – a Communist manoeuvre.

Have you heard from Madame Bick, the Polish Cultural Attaché in Stockholm? If not, ask Kerstin to phone her and find out if Poland is still interested in having us. I had just enough time to see two companies in Warsaw. They were impressive, the performances and the audiences a hundred per cent alive. If it's the theatre artists' job to be part of a living interaction between all the elements in a production, they fulfilled this function admirably.

You are right to tell us never to lose humanity. Smartness, superficial cleverness, they're for the blasé, but they alienate a popular audience and prevent them from participating. Audiences respond to a love of life. If there is none, I, for one, want no part of it. Our work has such a short life. A painting lasts till the canvas rots; ours fades the moment it is accomplished. Joan, you must exercise as critical an appreciation of the text as you apply to every other aspect of the production, or I fear your own great gifts will go awry.

I hope the company brings some money back from Sweden. As you say, there are bills and no obvious means of paying them. Nina has not reared her ugly head yet because she expects to be paid the moment you get back. There are so many difficulties to be faced. I know of no other enterprise which creates so many complications. Our search for support has been too circumscribed. We've tried HM Government, the town councils, the unions. . . . Where do we go from here? The rich? I know very few rich people. On top of that, I'm not cut out to be a money-raiser. You may represent a poverty-stricken theatre but you daren't be poor yourself. I'll have to enter society, hang around the Midland; that's where the monied types lay about.

However it turns out, I intend to have a full private life, with you. There are so many experiences to be shared, none without you. I never want to finish a letter to you, it's a tenuous contact. Sometimes I only half-believe that you are real. I dream about you and love the dream.

Your

Gerry

P.S. I have a ten-shilling note and can't make up my mind whether to send it with this letter.

Monday, 25th October
1948, midnight
Manchester

Joan. No letter from you.

Today I've been trying to organise a civic reception for your return. How do you find the proper title for a Lord Mayor when he's a she, I mean a woman? I will meet you at Tilbury, if you ever come back. I still have the return half of my ticket to Manchester.

I am all yours, but where are you?

Gerry

JOAN to GERRY   Tuesday 26th,
                                       on train to Göteborg

My very dear Gerry,

I have been to the land where everyone wears a fur hat and moves along icy roads on skis or snowshoes. Still, apart from my knees and fingers, I managed to keep from freezing.

I had been told to take a bus from Ljusdal station, then hire a car at the terminus. I was making for a remote farming community.

There were no buses so I had to take a car all the way. The few
people I met stared at me as if I'd been a head-hunter. Boys and
girls were skating on ice, they looked like Brueghel's children, but
the landscape was dull, apart from the sky. And the doors and
window-frames of the farm buildings were painted with red lead,
that coagulated blood colour.

I walked up a steep track where the car could not go and
came to a poverty-stricken farmhouse with tiny windows. No
one answered when I knocked, so I plodded round the house,
finding no sign of man or beast. I was about to give up – sixteen
hours' travelling, the problem of making oneself understood, for
nothing. . . . Then I saw what I took to be a poor peasant woman
coming out of the stable, carrying a bucket. It was Sonja. Sonja
who had always looked so elegant, beautiful Sonja.

They told me she'd never smiled since she'd been there but
she smiled at me, though it was as if she took me for a dream. I
felt like one. I thought of Dostoevsky's *House of the Dead*. Her room
was pitiful; so were her clothes. The people at the farm think she is
mad, but when we talked about Paris and painting she was as bright
as ever. She is no more mad now than she was then. She cannot
bear evil and ugliness, she never could – a strange, lonely person,
too sensitive for the world she found herself in. Her millionaire
relatives pay the farmer barely enough for her food. The word has
got about that she is schizophrenic. I don't think she is.

She has to go to bed at eight each night because they will
not keep the stove on after that and the place is very cold even
on summer evenings. She cannot even go to Ljusdal because she
has no money, no bicycle and, as far as I could see, no suitable
clothing. Even Ljusdal, a small place – a few shacks – would be
an event for her, though the people there would hardly offer lively
companionship.

She doesn't grumble or moan about her situation. She seems
quite unable to indulge in self-pity or pettiness. She has three
old copies of an art magazine, some drawings of peasants cut
from a calendar, a few strands of coloured wool and an old box
of water-colours. Her relatives do not believe in 'Art', as her
father and mother did. She says she no longer has any desire to paint
but I'm sure the desire could be reawakened in her. She gets up

at six, walks for hours in the woods and sometimes helps in the
fields.

We sat in her room. It is bare apart from two chairs and an
old narrow settee on which she sleeps. She has no wireless. I don't
want to bore you with my story, it's just that my mind is full of
her. On the journey there I thought I should try to bring her back
to England, but it would be impossible. You couldn't just take her
away. She has built a wall between herself and the world for her
protection. She is a person with rare depths of feeling, devastated
by the blows fate has dealt her. They slaughter cows at the farm
quite often, and when it is going to happen she runs away into the
woods and hides. She thinks they are coming for her. That isn't
mad. I have known the feeling myself.

If only she could express it all in writing or painting but in
that place her spirit is broken. I love her. I am the only person
she has ever had as a friend. What can I do? How does one help a
bird that is dying in a cage? Out in the world she would die, too.
When she smiles she looks young, a girl again, but she is so thin.
How can she live without human companionship? It's terrible the
way she is treated, the way they look at her. Such cruelty, cruelty
and grossness.

I must stop writing about Sonja. After all you don't even
know her. I wish I could help her find happiness – what a
presumptuous wish. Happiness? Another myth. Nevertheless we
must try. We must do what we can. I hope there will be a letter
from you in Göteborg. How much longer before I come home to
you?

I've not seen the company since Friday night. It's been refreshing
to be on my own. A bath would be even more refreshing.

David has been very sympathetic and considerate. You know he
takes charge of the money now. He lent me fifty kronor from the
funds in case I got stuck. Thank God I haven't touched it because
it looks as if we may run short. Our Saturday matinée has been
cancelled. The publicity had been completely forgotten. I hope,
if any love letters have arrived there for me, that you haven't been
reading them, but I bet you have, you b******. What's more, you
won't even mention them to me.

If I descend into drivel it's because I must keep writing. If

I lift my head, three pairs of watery eyes fasten on me like
jellyfish. When I joined this train during the night, most of
the compartments were unbearably hot and the corridors were
crowded. I made for a darkened section. When the ticket collector
came round, he told me I was in second class. Anyway, I pleaded
non-comprehension and he gave up.

It was comfortable in the seat I'd found, but so hot, burning
hot. I began little by little to shed my clothes. On the bench
opposite there were three huge female backsides, no heads or
shoulders, just backsides swathed in wool and fur, all grey,
brown and black. As I turned over, trying for comfort and
sleep, the backside nearest to me seemed to quiver, in the
half-light it loomed as large as the highest hill in Sweden and it
definitely quivered. Why? It was about to emit a long-drawn-out,
wet, fluttering fart – which smelt like all the milky breaths of
Sweden. I thought the lady might be about to say something,
but almost at once the horrid emission occurred again, and this
time with an unmistakably Swedish inflection. The large grey
woollen bottom stirred as I closed my eyes. The ladies went
on dreaming their milky dreams. In the dawn light, when they
arose, they were all three comfortable, well-dressed Swedish
bourgeoises.

I saw a strange landscape this morning – fog obscuring a
city . . . lovely.

Gerry, why a reception for us on our return? Alderman
Kings-Ball or one of his ilk would be bound to come out with
some dirt about Czechoslovakia.

I wonder if you have had any luck with All Saints. I'm saying
au revoir now, darling. This has been a murderous trip. I haven't
had my clothes off for two nights, but it was worth it. I cannot
believe in your hugs and kisses. I cannot believe you exist, but I
love you.

Cheerio, me old two an' eight.

                                        Joan

GERRY to JOAN   Friday 29th October 1948
                                                 Strand Corner House,
                                                 London, 3 a.m.

Dearest love,

Received your letter, written Tuesday, only two and a half days
away from me. I'm so glad you saw Sonja. I can't wait to hear more
about her. As things stand, we couldn't offer her much comfort in
England, could we? Here I am lucky to have a table for an office
in this all-night dump. The waiter has just told me that service is
closed.

   Tomorrow, or rather later today, I am seeing the head of the
Co-op's Cultural Section. Tonight I shall go back to M/C on the
night bus – and tonight the clocks go back. Will I ever get that
extra hour in bed, with you. . . .

                                                 Same day,
                                                 Leicester Square, 4 p.m.

I had to break off. A young seaman had cottoned on to me and was
telling me all about his latest voyage on a tramp steamer. In the end
they'd had to chop up every bit of timber aboard, the coal had been
used up. That was the end of the story. The waiter showed us the
door.

   This trip has been a dead loss so far. The Co-op bloke wasn't
in his office this morning. They said he'd be in this evening, but
too busy with *Reynolds News* to see anyone. I'll give it another try.
He would surely have written me if it was no use coming, though
I can't say I was impressed by the efficiency in his office – the place
looked half-asleep. . . .

                                                 Two and a half hours
                                                 later
                                                 Charing X Road Post
                                                 Office, 6.30 p.m.

Sorry, darling, I had to go for a walk to wake myself up. London
is crowded with people just walking about. It feels foreign to me.
I don't even understand what they're saying.

I've just phoned the Co-op. Hoskins, my target, isn't in yet. I'll try again at seven and the bus company say there are no seats left for tonight. What a life! I couldn't stand another night in London, nowhere to sit even.

7.15 p.m.

Hoskins still isn't in. Of course he is. He just won't spare the time to see me. We should introduce him to our Swedish co-operator, Mr Johansson. I must make a dash for Victoria and try for that bus.

À bientôt, sweetheart. Come back, I can't stand much more of this.

Gerry

P.S. Eric is at the Dorchester. Do you know how much they're charging him? Two pounds fifteen a night, plus six and six for breakfast. Isn't it disgraceful? I'd sooner do what I do than be rooked like that.

JOAN tO GERRY   29th October
                                                        Johnnie Noble

My Gerry,

I shouldn't be writing during the show, but I must, I am miserable without you, and there's nothing much left of me.

My cue's coming up. I'll be back.

Later

It's the interval. I gave an abominable performance. At the cue, as I braced myself, I heard Chick switch the sound on. It hissed right through my speech. Then the fireman clumped through the wings. Excuses! Say rather I've lost my marbles. It's all these receptions. Who cares about the show? It's the least important item on the programme. Tonight we will have the Anglo-Swedish Society, *smörgås* and *eau de vie*, and after that, hospitality, which means explaining us, with a dictionary, half the night.

Don't worry, tomorrow I'll probably be twice as miserable!
I'm on again, they're just going into the Taffy scene.

J.

P.S. Don't take the nine-room house if there's no chance of
a theatre. What's the use?

GERRY to JOAN   2nd November, M/C

Dearest Joan,

If you were to have half as much patience with me as I must
have with this job, I should be a very good actor. So little gets
done. Today I've been rushing around trying to prepare England
for the return of the company, and achieved nothing. I wrote
Llewellyn Rees at Arts Council a fortnight ago. He hasn't even
acknowledged my letter. If this goes on much longer I'll be fit for
nothing; suppressing one's emotions, denying personal prejudices,
kills the imagination and I shall never be an actor.

I meant to work through the night, but I'm too tired to think.
Even so, I can't face that empty bed.

Goodnight, sweetheart. Your

Gerry

JOAN to GERRY

Hi, Gerry,

Last Thursday . . . was it Thursday? I've lost all sense of time.
Anyway, whenever it was, I was posting your letter at the railway
station when I heard a dull thud. It was a young workman who'd
fallen to the floor and was lying there, unconscious. Women were
running towards him, jostling each other to be first; one was trailing her expensive fur coat on the floor as she ran. But they weren't
coming to help, only to look. . . . The behaviour of people who'd
never known war, or bombs.

I'd made an afternoon call that day to refresh the show
and improve the lighting. The Czech Cultural Attaché was

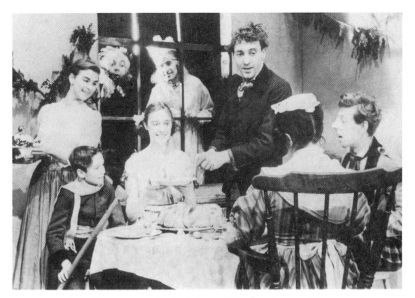

9a Our *Christmas Carol* with (*left to right inside*) Margaret Greenwood, Alan Nunn, Shirley Dynevor, Harry Corbett, Avis Bunnage and Bill Ormond; (*outside*) George Cooper and Howard Goorney.

9b *The Alchemist* with (*left to right*) Howard Goorney as Subtle, Harry Corbett as Face and George Cooper as Sir Epicure Mammon.

10a *Richard II*, the company. Set by Harry Greene.

10b *Richard II* with (*left to right*) Howard Goorney,
Harry Corbett and George Luscombe.

11a Sean O'Casey's *Red Roses for Me* with (*left to right*)
Gerard Dynevor, Julia Jones and Isla Gledhill.

11b *An Enemy of the People* with (*left to right*) Julia Jones, John Blanshard,
Jim Pounder, Tom Pounder, George Cooper, John Bury and Howard
Goorney.

12a Ewan MacColl's *The Other Animals* with (*left to right*)
George Luscombe and Jimmie Miller (Ewan MacColl). Set by John Bury.

12b Alan Lomax's *The Big Rock Candy Mountain:* our male chorus.
Set by John Bury.

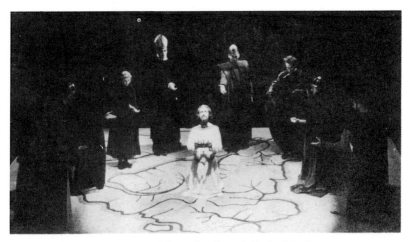

13a *Edward II* with Peter Smallwood. Set by John Bury.

13b Brendan Behan's *The Quare Fellow:* the prisoners' exercise.
Set by John Bury.

14a Richard Harris.

14b Dudley Sutton.

14c Brendan Behan.

14d Dudley Foster.

15a Shelagh Delaney and
A Taste of Honey.

15b Frank Norman and
Fings Ain't Wot They Used T'Be.

15c Frances Cuka and Jimmie Moore
in *A Taste of Honey.*

15d Lionel Bart
the music man.

16a Murray Melvin,
a hostage.

16b Roy Kinnear,
his wonderful walk.

16c David Booth,
the one and only.

16d Victor Spinetti
of Wales and Italy.

bringing a representative from the East German Volksbühne in the evening. The company knew and the show bucked up considerably. Afterwards we enjoyed reminiscing with our Czech friend and the possibility of a tour of East Germany was discussed.

David has had a straight talk with Riksteatern, and last night gave us all an extra ten kronor. He thinks we were not given good terms at the outset, but it was all fixed in a hurry and they couldn't have foreseen that we would make such a hit. Next time we should do better. So many small halls, at a great distance from each other, has meant too much spent on transport.

Did I tell you that we visited Drottningholm when we were in Stockholm? That theatre is the loveliest thing I have seen here, and Callot's *commedia dell'arte* drawings! One of the French Ambassadors brought them here, from Nancy. They are so small; from the detail in the reproductions I'd imagined them much bigger. The King's chair was still set in solitary state, the stage sloped gently, the sets changed sliding on and off on tracks, and all was exquisite. You would have loved the sound effects, especially the thunder, made by rolling a cannon ball across the loft above the stage. You can see the current King playing tennis in the grounds of the neighbouring palace. His brother works in the tax office in Stockholm.

Denis and I should have travelled with the lorry today, but we were so wet when we'd finished helping with the load that we decided not to risk it, and David gave us some kronor for breakfast. We celebrated – a boiled egg, coffee and a cigarette – and missed the train.

Julia has lent me a mac and I have your pullover and gloves, so I don't need anything, Gerry. Must go now.

All my love, dear Gerry.

J.

The failure to get any joy from the Co-op was discouraging and, as anyone could have told Gerry, a wedding reception was not the place to try a hold-up for money. Still, a doctor who'd seen *Last Edition* offered fifty pounds towards the purchase of All Saints, but immediately after, Freddie Piffard phoned wanting to know how soon Nina would receive her hundred pounds. To crown it all, the Polish tour fell through, partly because relations between East and West were at freezing point.

I wrote scolding him for going without food and sleep:

David has enough money to get us all back to Manchester and pay your wages. Rather than sit up all night, you could have asked for a sub, as you're too proud to stay with any of our friends. Are you training to be a Trappist monk?

And I don't want any more about 'carnal relations with anyone else being out of the question'. You are as full of lust as an egg's full of meat. Thank goodness.

J.

His next letter was more cheerful:

Tom Driberg is back from Haiti and the new *Daily Worker* is out. It really is an achievement. Here is the first copy. I only hope the contents will now improve. I've sent my article on Umeni Lidu to the Co-op. It will let them know what they should be about.

Last night I was treated to a Segovia concert – disappointing. I prefer my recordings.

The tour was drawing to its close. We were homesick for each other. All I dreamed about was a quiet room, with books to read, and Gerry, but before I left Sweden I wanted very much to visit a steel mill. So one morning, before dawn, I set out. Day broke over a countryside fast disappearing under snow. I knew Sweden specialised in luxury steel, but I wasn't prepared for the sheer elegance of the place I came to. No foul air, no oily rags. The floor was like a ballroom, nobody smoking, nobody drinking beer. In one corner, enclosed from the working area, was a room you could only describe as a withdrawing-room, with tall, well-kept indoor plants, light oak seats and tables, and the legend,

'No smoking, but if you must, please do so in this area.' I was told there had never been a strike in this mill. I could believe it. I got chatting to a friendly steelworker before I left and he invited me home. It was almost my last night in Sweden and his was the first working-class home I'd visited. It was a simple apartment, not much furniture, but good, lino on the floor. His wife apologised for the meal: *Hors d'oeuvres*, sausage and egg, cakes and coffee. It tasted good to me. They talked about the War, how Nazi officers travelled first class across Sweden to Norway, while Swedish soldiers were transported in cattle trucks. The university was reactionary too, he said. An English Liberal booked to give a series of lectures on post-War Europe gave one lecture only, then he was dropped. Still, we have forty thousand Party members in our country now, he added.

'Which party?'

'The Communist Party.'

At our last company meeting, Peter Smallwood announced that he'd been accepted for the priesthood and Kerstin said she wanted to stay on in Sweden; Howard asked if he might stay and enjoy a short farewell holiday with her. Peter Varley simply told us that he was going back to Prague.

And you and I, Gerry? We'll walk in the sun and lie together, my beautiful one. We are free, you and I.

J.

GERRY to JOAN   Saturday

Beloved,

This is my last letter to you. On Monday night we'll be together so what does it matter that the Lady Mayor is unable to receive us, and the Trades Council never received the greetings from their Czech counterparts, and the Co-op has returned my article?

In two and a half days you will be boarding the *M/S Saga*, bound for Tilbury.

A) Money change is open from 2 to 3 p.m. Work out how

much you should get and check your change.

B) If you want to avoid the rush, take your bags to the
FIRST CLASS HALL outside the dining-room and leave them there,
against the wall, or the porters will shift them. Then go up to the
FIRST CLASS LOUNGE with your passport and disembarkation
card filled in. Don't delay or you will find a queue, hours long,
waiting to go through Immigration. You disembark from the FIRST
CLASS HALL; that is why you leave your bags there.

C) If there are not many passengers, nobody bothers about
class, so sit in the first or second class, as you please. There is
nowhere to read in third class. Do get a good book, the journey
is incredibly boring.

Will you really spend Monday night with me? No man should
be so lucky.

G.

On 8th November, he was by the pier, waiting for me. He
had found a place for us in Manchester. Nothing else in the
world mattered.

Thirty-three

*Gerry and Joan survey All Saints. No official welcome on our return
from the tours. An old house lent to us. The company move in, take
part-time jobs, salvage lighting equipment from a crashed plane. Our
life in the old house, now named the Schloss, rehearsing* As You Like
It *for schools. Corin (Peter Varley) walks out. Can Gerry replace him?
He is exhausted. We go away, return to buy a truck for fifteen pounds
and acquire rooms at 177A Oxford Road, Manchester. George Cooper
joins us. Five of us pick tomatoes and sell them. We have enough cash
to set us up. Jack Evans appears. To Scotland and the People's Festival,
Edinburgh. Manchester will not license All Saints as a theatre.*

We were standing gazing at the building which would solve
all our problems. All Saints, Manchester.

'Imagine it lit up at night like Blackpool Tower and every
kind of entertainment going on in and around it. You tried the
Trades Council?'

'And invited them to have a "welcome back" drink with us
at Tommie Duck's.'

'I didn't see them.'

'They weren't there.'

We'd been walking round all day looking for somewhere to
house the company.

'We haven't tried Cheetham Hill. We could have a word
with Dr Schloss.' Gerry had known the good doctor all his
life, a clever, eccentric man with a mathematical genius of a son.
It was no use looking for him at his surgery. He was never there;
he met his patients on the street and that's where he found us, on
the corner of Bury Old Road.

'The prodigal returns. What's wrong this time?'

'Nothing. We were just taking a stroll,' said Gerry.

'*La Recherche du Temps Perdu?*' I chimed in before he got going
on his favourite author. 'We're searching for a house.'

'You can take that house, the one with no railings, if you like.
I can't get rid of it.'

'We've no money.'

'Put it in order for me and you can have it rent free . . .
for six months.'

'You're on,' said Gerry, and hugged Dr Schloss.

The tocsin sounded: 'Company meeting Monday 9.30 a.m.
No prospects. Every man for himself. Joan and Gerry.'

The house was large, its many rooms empty and neglected.

'I think I'll stay with my parents,' said Howard. 'Our six
months'll be up before we get it clean, and all our gear arriving
from Sweden, where's that going?'

'There's plenty of room,' said Gerry.

Benny and Chick, Camel and Maggie arrived first, chose their
rooms and started scrubbing.

'What do we live on?'

'Work.'

'Part-time,' said Camel. 'We can play schools, afternoons.
There's a Forest of Arden waiting to be cut down in the back
garden.'

'School dinners!' said Benny, hungry already. 'J.L. will be
all right. She can feed in the BBC canteen, now she's back there.'

'Thanks,' I said. 'I'm having a great time in that can of worms.'
It was the same old game, my *Visits to* . . . the Longdendale Valley,
Ilkley Moor. . . . Well, at least Teesdale was new to me, disused
lead mines, all the farmhouses painted white, as decreed by some
forgotten seigneur. I amused myself collecting fragments of an old
song and got Jimmie a job completing it:

> *Fourpence a day, me lads*
> *And verra hard to wark*
> *With never a pleasant look*
> *From a scruffy-looking Turk*
> *His heart it may fail*
> *His conscience may give way*
> *And he'll raise us our wages*
> *To fivepence a day.*

Done! And Jimmie came back to the fold. He moved into the big room on the first floor, with Jean. The only snag, there was no bed. Every rostrum was needed for *As You Like It*.

Chick, who always looked kind-hearted, actually was. He gave up his feather-bed and rigged up a hammock. Jean at once started unstitching the bed-tick – strange, but she was a notoriously fussy housewife.

Making a roster to accommodate housework, wage-earning and *As You Like It* was no easy matter. Jacques (Benny) would be ready for bed after stacking newspapers all night just when Orlando (Denis), who'd decided to rejoin us, wanted to finish reacting to the seven ages of man and skip off to the washing-up at Lyons.

I was glad to escape to the wild moorland above the Long-dendale. One day, as I was walking at the top of Wild Boar Clough, I saw a mass of metal half-buried in the blaeberry and sphagnum moss. Then I came across the wreck of a giant spotlight. I walked about, found others, also some twisted iron spot stands. Then . . . part of an aeroplane, a broken wing, a pulverised cabin. Enough . . . but those lamps . . . they could be invaluable. It wasn't possible to carry one back with me – the descent was rocky, often precipitous. I'd have to alert the gang.

Of course Camel and Gerry didn't believe me. 'You're sure they're theatre lamps?'

'They're bashed and battered, but . . . Yes, I'm sure.'

'We'll take a look,' said Camel and I drew a map for them.

When they got back in the evening, 'It was an American plane,' said Gerry, 'carrying equipment from some army entertainment in Germany, by the looks of things.'

'Ran slap into that rocky headland. The mist on these moors plays tricks.'

'You'd think the locals would have heard the crash.'

'But decided there'd be nothing worth pinching.' We'd heard stories of crashed planes looted, fingers cut off for the rings on them.

'I hope there were no dead.'

'The Yankee airforce would have been up there like a shot.'

The following Sunday the whole company set out for Bleak

Low. We had to climb crouched in the shelter of the clough
for fear of the keepers. We were trespassing; that magnificent
moorland belonged to the Manchester Water Board.

T he descent was a feat, negotiating the rock falls in pairs,
the loot too heavy and awkward for one person to manage.

It was a relief when we boarded the tram for Piccadilly, M/C.
When we arrived there a policeman held up the traffic to let us
cross the road, a bedraggled crew.

'What are they at?' asked a middle-aged lady.

'They're going to reconstruct a train crash,' her husband told
her.

Camel closeted himself with those lamps at every opportunity and hammered them into shape. They were christened the
Big Yanks and served us well. They're probably still in use at
Stratford, E15. Tom Driberg called us ghouls. 'Now, I suppose,
you'll be waiting for some troop train to crash so that you can steal
the uniforms.'

W e weren't eating very well. Those school dinners would be
welcome. John Blanshard and Julia had rejoined us. Peter
Varley was back from Prague where he had found no work
at all.

It was time for the directors' meeting, long overdue, and the first
booking of *As You Like It* had been brought forward. The house was
bristling with activity, domestic and artistic. The meeting was to
be in Jimmie and Jean's room, so it was all hands on deck, scrubbing and polishing and arranging pads and pencils on seats. The only
thing was, Jimmie had taken to his bed. 'I'm afraid of pneumonia,'
said Jean. 'Can't miss the meeting,' said Jimmie. Jean was just going
to prepare a poultice when the doorbell rang. We heard Julia say,
'Welcome' and at that Bill Maclellan in his kilt, Chris Grieve, his
hair standing on end, and James Ford, smiling benevolently, came
marching up the stairs. Julia made a pot of tea and we settled to
the business in hand, the first being Gerry's report. He listed the
debts, tried to cast a rosy glow over the school bookings, and read

a letter from Wedgwood Benn to Tom Driberg:

Yes, Ewan MacColl is a poet and if the acting and production
are up to standard, the Arts Council should certainly give them
a grant, but I have contacted Llewellyn Rees and he tells me that
opinion about the Workshop is divided, that they have not given
a performance since their return to England, but when they do,
some of us will attend.

Then he handed out some of the notices from Sweden and
Czechoslovakia. 'They are all here,' he said. 'Not one is unfa-
vourable.'

Chris Grieve spoke bitterly about Arts Council's record. The
other two, Ford and Maclellan, were also critical. Freddie Piffard
had been unable to attend.

Gerry dealt with the lack of interest in All Saints. Each director
suggested names who might help and promised to do all in their
power to publicise the situation. Then came the crux. Gerry swallowed hard. 'For the sum of one hundred pounds a woman called
Nina is making us bankrupt. . . .'

Jimmie gave a yelp and rolled over.

'I'm sorry, Jimmie, but . . .'

There was a groan and a muttered curse.

'It was the mention of Nina,' said Jean.

'It's this bloody teapot in the bed,' said Jimmie. There was
a curious silence.

'Strange,' said Chris Grieve, 'but Ewan has no trace of a
Scottish accent.'

'Not surprising,' I said, 'since he was born and brought up
in Salford.' The air turned blue round Jimmie. Jean began to cry.

'I think it's time for the tea break,' said Camel, and they
all went down to the kitchen.

'Why did you tell them I was born in England?'

'Weren't you?'

'And what's this hideous object doing in my bed, Jean?'

'You said we had to sell anything to help pay the debts but

that was my grandmother's silver teapot. . . .'

Gerry and I tactfully withdrew. Peter Varley waylaid me on the stairs to resign. Pilgrim Players had offered him more money. That wouldn't be difficult: all we were doing was feeding him and trying to get him to take his share of the manual work.

'These hands were made to paint,' he told me, holding them out for inspection.

All very well, but Corin? I suddenly remembered. It was our first performance tomorrow. He'd have to stay for it. But, no, he just went. Who the hell could play it? Thank God, there was Gerry. I went to our room. The door was locked. I panicked. I shouted. The door opened, he stood there – not a hair on his head.

'What have you done?'

'Shaved my head. It was either that or cut my throat.'

'Why, love? Why?'

'The debts,' he said.

The irony of it was, Peter Varley had refused to play Corin without a bit of false hair made up to look like Gerry's. Gerry wore it under a knotted kerchief looking like a sailor in *Treasure Island* and played the part.

A part from Gerry in Varley's false bit, bankruptcy, Arts Council's latest snub and Sean O'Casey changing his mind and giving the rights of *Cock-a-doodle Dandy* to someone else, there was definitely something wrong with us. Gerry and Kerstin had achieved the impossible with the Czech and Swedish tours, but we were worse off than when we set out.

People's theatre? If they want it let them do it themselves. . . .

My thoughts were interrupted by Chick. 'Gerry is in hospital with pneumonia,' he said. 'They picked him up on the street, unconscious.'

'Enough is enough!' I said. 'He is killing himself.'

A s soon as Gerry was well enough we took a break. 'You once told me that we would make the best of life.'

'I have a hundred pounds and I owe a hundred and sixty-six,' he said.

'Forget it. Let's take the hundred and go.'

We went, heading for France, with a tent, two sleeping bags, a Primus, a change of clothes and a bar of soap. We hitchhiked. We breathed the fragrant air of the warm South and heard the evening din of the *cigale* for the first time. The roads were hot and dusty, the lorries left us behind. We regarded the folks who ate and drank in the cool cafés with envy, but we could camp on the high white rocks above Cassis and plunge into the clear water of the Mediterranean, sleep at night among the stars.

We made it to Florence, saw Masaccio's 'Expulsion from the Garden of Eden' and slept on bales of hay at a farmhouse outside Milan. The neighbours found us. Who were we? Were we for peace? How many children had we? Was Gerry hot stuff?

When communication gave out they sent a boy to the next village to bring someone who spoke English. And next morning, when we were given a lift to Milan we looked back to see '*Sta casa per Pace*' painted in giant letters along the farmyard wall: 'This house for Peace.'

Near Milan we were shown where Mussolini and Clara Petacci had been strung up by the heels. Near Viareggio we rode through avenues of bougainvillea on a farmcart, while the driver let the reins play and the old horse took his time. Gerry was cock of the walk everywhere.

'My friend from England,' said one truck driver, when we came on his colleagues in some lay-by in the middle of the night. And Gerry was given a swig of wine and introduced to '*Mille Fiore*'. The proceedings ended up with a mellifluous rendering of '*Avanti Populo*'.

We returned after our glorious hike, thinner but a lot happier, our only regret that bottle of Chianti, purchased with our last lire, crashing to smithereens as Gerry ran across the road to accept a lift at the northern frontier of Italy.

We crossed Switzerland in a car with no brakes and breakfasted near Vesoul, thanks to an old man who dropped little red apples into my lap as we sat by the roadside looking for a lift. We made it and caught the cross-channel ferry by the skin of our teeth, landing in Dover, ravenous.

'Two of BR's best sandwiches and two teas,' said Gerry, who had kept a couple of bob in reserve.

'Nothing like the old country, is there?' said the railway man.

By now we were expert hitchhikers and we made the Schloss in nine hours flat. The front door wouldn't open for the pile of bills awaiting us.

'Don't look.'

But Gerry skimmed through them to see if there was anything about All Saints. There wasn't.

There was a card from Scotland, where half the company were working on a farm, and another from Camel and Maggie, who'd hitched all the way to Timbuctoo. They should have been back by now. I found one with a Swedish stamp. Gerry tore it open. Kerstin was trying for another tour. He shook his head. 'Not yet, but she's optimistic. Refuse to give up, she says. "You have the whole Workshop behind you, you know what you're talking about. We'll win." '

Our lovely optimist! Meanwhile, home on the range . . .

'Not for long,' said Gerry. 'Our six months is almost up.'

'Let's get hold of a truck, live in it, drive to South Wales and get some bookings there. The Czech miners liked us, Nye Bevan recommended Ebbw Vale to us.'

'Where do we get the truck?'

'Look in that paper – what's it called?'

'*Exchange and Mart*.'

Camel and Maggie arrived, looking pretty scraggy and not at all sunburnt. Gerry rang the papers and they made a few quid with their story. Then someone told him that a lot of old GPO trucks were being auctioned. He took every penny in the kitty and went along.

Triumph. Used truck, in good condition, sold to Theatre Workshop for fifteen pounds.

We talked over a Welsh recce, studied the map and re-covered our unquenchable optimism. Camel was keen – he was half Welsh anyway. Gerry kept smiling to himself too. He'd had good news from somewhere, but he was such an oyster. It wasn't till we were scrubbing out the back of the truck that he came clean.

'I met a bloke at the auction, a second-hand car salesman – we can have the rooms over his shop at a very reasonable rent.'

'Where?'

'177A Oxford Road.'

On the sunny side! A home when we come back from Wales. I don't think Gerry had ever driven a truck before, but whether he had or not his style was definitely influenced by the driving he'd seen in Italy. No hands, seventy m.p.h. and a song to carry you along. I was navigator with a map spread over my knees, but at that pace, my eyes were glued to the road.

When it grew dark Gerry decided I should get in the back and sleep. 'You're tired.'

'So are you.'

'I'll pull in when we get to Abergavenny,' and he stopped while I climbed into the back. I must have dozed off at once, because the next thing I knew the Primus stove was rolling about, the truck was keeled half over and two puzzled faces were surveying me through a gap in the tarpaulin curtains. Cops!

'You hurt, missus?'

'No, just sleeping.'

They were so surprised to find me there that they helped right the truck, gave us a telling-off and let us go.

'Please let's take a rest at the first lay-by, Gerry.'

'Sure.'

Our prospecting went well. BBC contacts, random encounters at petrol pumps and union meetings. We were back in Manchester within a week with a tour pencilled in for later in the year.

Meanwhile, Camel had rustled up a team, including his sister Anne, and transferred our worldly goods to 177A Oxford Road, Manchester.

An envelope caught my eye, the address beautifully written. It was from George Alphonsus Cooper of Leeds – a request for work. Finding our address showed a certain initiative, but he couldn't have chosen a more inopportune time. I wrote at once, telling him there was positively nothing doing. And my reply? A roar of laughter in the street outside where Camel's sister was trying to repair the frame on our new old truck.

'Who have you got with you, Anne?' I stuck my head out of the window and there was a broad-faced, suntanned character wearing khaki shorts, army boots with khaki socks, still laughing.

'Indian Army,' he said, patting his bald pate and using a pukka British Raj accent.

'Come on up,' I said. There was no sign of any baggage but something told me we were receiving our first house-guest. Then Camel and Gerry appeared, dusted white like two millers.

'They've been trying to blow a hole through the cellar wall,' I explained politely.

'Convinced there's an empty space on the other side,' said Camel. 'Would do for storage space.'

'Not enough dynamite,' said Gerry. 'Want to have a look?'

George Alphonsus went with them and I put the kettle on and went to see how Anne was getting on.

'It's a bit shaky, still,' and she demonstrated.

'Never mind. Come and have a cup of tea.'

At that moment our guest stuck his head out of the window and asked Anne if she'd like to share a chicken farm with him.

'Are you staying?' she asked.

'Looks like it. I've been put in charge of the printing works.'

He meant our silk screen and the second-hand press Camel had bought for three pounds. Over a mug of tea, we learned that George had once worked in an architects' office; so Anne wanted to know if he could make a stable frame for a truck. He drew a truck with a handsome canopy on the table.

'Could you fix one like that?'

George grunted, but for the next few days we heard nothing but giggling as those two collaborated on the shaky frame problem.

'Fixed!' said George.

'Thank God,' said Maggie. 'I was beginning to think we were stuck here for life.'

'We can't move without capital,' said Gerry.

'I've been trying to get through to one of you for days,' said I.

'Not another one of your bright ideas?'

'Yes – a tomato syndicate.'

'What's that?'

'Well, tomatoes are fivepence a pound in Ardwick; out in the country they're giving them away. We harvest a truckload, sell them at threepence a pound and make enough to launch ourselves again.'

'What do we use for petrol?' asked Gerry.

'We each put in a pound,' said Maggie.

'Couldn't afford it,' said George.

'It's an investment,' said Maggie.

The pressure cooker was hissing. We adjourned for a hotpot and afterwards packed for a weekend's camping in the Vale of Evesham. We all forked out, except George.

'Where's your quid, George?' said Camel.

'I haven't got it.'

'Everybody's got one pound somewhere. What's that in your pocket?' Camel made a grab at George and George could hardly escape up the stairs for laughing. Maggie handed Camel a carpet-beater and the chase was on.

When Camel came down, 'Did you get it?'

'He gave up, just curled up on the printing press and giggled.'

'But did you get his money?'

Camel opened his grubby fist, and there it was – a clean pound note neatly folded.

George sat at the open end of the truck all the way to Evesham and glared at the shaky frame when Gerry took one of his Brands Hatch swerves. We arrived in one piece, harvested a truckload of tomatoes and turned towards home and fortune. Maggie was voted cashier. She hired a barrow and sent us forth to spiel and sell in the back streets of Ardwick. At the end of the day, she passed a critical eye over our poster. 'At threepence a pound people think there is something wrong with them.'

'Make it fourpence,' said Camel.

Next day we did better, made enough to finance a second trip to the Vale of Evesham. Only this time it rained so hard we had to take shelter under a tree. It was loaded with pears. 'It's a pity to let them go to waste,' we told the farmer.

'You can have 'em if you can pick 'em,' he said.

Sure enough, each pear was guarded by a whacking great wasp but we gathered enough for the whole company to make merry at

Christmas – with Camel's special vintage perry.

The Tomato Syndicate netted enough to finance the opening of the next Welsh tour. Kerstin arrived back from Sweden with the promise of a second visit to Scandinavia . . . and our friends in Scotland were demanding instant participation in their People's Festival which would put the old Edinburgh Festival in the shade.

'Epworth Hall already booked for you.'

Just before we left for Scotland, a fragile, saturnine being walked into our lives.

'Jimmie Miller around? Tell him it's Jack Evans from Moscow.'

'I used to write to you years ago,' I said. 'You advised me not to come there.'

'Because they only want people who're a bourgeois success: Bernard Shaw, André Gide, people like that.'

'What were you doing there?'

'I studied Shostakovich and Khachaturian, wrote music, then when war came I was a war correspondent for Reuter's.'

'Why ever did you leave?'

'I didn't leave. I was expelled. "Rather a million thrown out, than one spy left in." '

'And here?'

'Can't sell my music. I'm working as a labourer. Doesn't change very much, the old place, does it? After seventeen years you've the same old mob running things – left and right. I watched the Socialists waving their big red flag on May Day, only they'd got the day wrong. What's Jimmie doing? We all expected great things of him.'

We told him how Jimmie had not exactly become a bourgeois success, but his singing was much admired. He wanted to know what he sang and was shocked when he was told. 'I had enough of ethnic art in Russia. The only folk song I can appreciate is Gregorian chant.'

Jack was a tonic. We were invited to his home, a small house in Moss Side. The living-room was furnished Russian style and lined with books. There was a harmonium, on which he composed. We learnt that he had a Russian wife and child in Moscow. They were not allowed to leave with him. It wasn't long before he threw in his lot with us, wrote music for all our plays and when we could raise an orchestra, became our Musical Director. For which he fished out an old dress suit which looked as if it had spent the best days of its life in some Moscow pawn shop. Nevertheless, with his slim figure and slender hands, he looked elegant, if a little *déjà vu* – a dead ringer for the devil in *The Master and Margarita*. Often he was homesick for the old restaurants and drinking shops where he'd spent his time swapping yarns with kindred spirits. He enjoyed spy stories, like the one about the Japanese comrade lecturing on espionage at the Marx-Lenin Institute. In the middle of this he'd laugh so much as he switched from Japanese to Russian that we'd give up. 'What's funny, Jack?'

'That's what he did, the Japanese, he burst out laughing. "How do you know I'm not a spy, comrades?" he said and laughed some more. After that he was never seen again.'

But his *bête noir* was an English journalist, 'used to write for the *Manchester Guardian*. Now he writes for the KGB,' he said.

Jack came of a musical family, one brother played the cornet in the police band, while Jack himself was strictly classical and erudite. They grew up in a two up, two down near Salford docks and Jack had not lost his Salford sense of humour. 'Did I tell you about the day we went to Stalingrad? Well, what was left of Stalingrad. We were from all over the world – journalists. Our guide was a veteran of Smolensk. "Breakfast at four, gentlemen," he told us. "And the road's heavily mined." Poor chap, he trod on one himself, he was so excited. It was a special occasion, you see. We were lined up by this mound of rubble, blinking our eyelids to stop them freezing together, when this line of Germans straggled out of a bunker. Last of all a thin man in an overcoat – von Paulus. The bloke next to me straightened up to attention and lifted his cap. He caught pneumonia. He was from the *New York Herald Tribune*.'

We arrived at the Epworth to a right royal welcome – bagpipes playing, Hamish Henderson making a speech in Lallans and a reception at the Italian café next to the hall. Then to work – Jimmie's cage to be poised in space for *The Other Animals*.

It was beginning to look good when Benny tapped me on the shoulder. 'Have you forgotten who's opening this festival?'

'We are.'

'No! Agnes Walker, world-famous pianist, pupil of the great Lamond, wife of our director, Bill Maclellan. And where's she going to sit?'

'At her Bechstein, I suppose.'

'And where's that going?'

'You have a point. . . . In the cage, I suppose, if it'll go.'

It did.

And the next afternoon I would have to explain to the lady that we couldn't rig the set in time for the evening performance after her recital. I found her in a dressing-room, stuffing little mounds of cotton wool down the bosom of her very pretty dress. 'How do I look?'

'Ravishing.'

'It's terrible to be flat-chested.'

She was so preoccupied with her appearance that I didn't get a chance to explain the cage. The first she knew about it was when she stepped into it. In fact, she played beautifully and was delighted with the reception she was given. It wasn't till the evening papers came out with 'AGNES WALKER ENCAGED' that she flew into a rage. Luckily I was held up listening to Hamish Henderson performing an exegesis on an old Scots song and missed the fireworks.

'She doesn't realise it's another language, with different roots,' he told me, towering above a little lady from California, magnificent in his Highland regalia.

' "Johnnie gars my tail toddle" – that is to say, "causes my pudendum to rotate," ' and as he spoke he illustrated the point by gently undulating his backside, which made his sporran waggle a little.

The little lady looked quite pleased, which was reassuring. We were reviving *Perlimplín* and I had been wondering whether Edinburgh would prove as puritanical as Kendal.

'I have felt your warmth and your weight, delicious youth of my soul. . . .'

Kerstin, Howard and I were going through the lines in an

annexe to the Epworth. We came to Belisa's erotic aria, sung to
her lover. As Kerstin reached top C the Devil himself appeared –
small, dark, clothed in black, with pinstripes (and cloven hooves, I
decided after). 'Quiet, woman! You're destroying the peace of the
Sabbath!'

'So sorry, but I didn't know it was the Sabbath.'

'Are you a heathen?'

'An actress.'

'A service was being conducted on the other side of this door
till your obscene caterwauling disrupted it.'

'We'll go,' said Howard.

'Just as well, else I'd have you evicted.'

The next item on the agenda was a flyting or musical debate,
if you like, between Pipe Major Ross from the Castle and
Donald Bain, exponent of bagpipe blues.

Bain began with a short lecture and a divertimento on the
pipes. Cries of 'Bravo!' 'Jazz!' 'Down with militarism!' Pipe Major
Ross rose from his seat and began a classic rendering of 'The
Campbells are Coming'. The place was in an uproar – booing,
shouting, stamping. I hurried up on to the stage to hide any props
which could be seized and smashed in the threatened riot.

That confrontation, such as it was, divided Scotland. 'BAIN
CHALLENGES SCOTLAND'S ROYAL SCHOOL OF PIPING.' 'REVOLT AT THE
EPWORTH.'   'SCOTLAND'S   SACRED   HERITAGE   BESMIRCHED.'
And day after day the correspondence columns were full of
controversy. All we got was a bill:

    – for damage to three school benches
    – breakage of one Chinese vase plus yellow chrysan-
    themums
    – five window-panes smashed
    – one bust of Robert Burns (terracotta) hurled against
    a wall, destroyed

plus a letter stamped 'Arts Council'. More rebuffs? It wasn't.
It was from Ian Hunter, their Scottish Director, inviting our

participation, official participation, in the next Festival.

Last but not least, from C. Harrison, Regional Licensing Officer: 'I regret to inform you that a building licence for the construction of a new theatre at All Saints, Manchester, cannot be granted in view of other high-priority work which must be fitted into the building programme.'

Thirty-four

*To Wales on New Year's Eve 1950. The truck breaks down. We
spend the night in it. Hitchhike to Fleur, no lorry, too late to play
anyway. The Welsh tour with Uranium 235; hounded by the police.
Harry Greene joins us at Rhymney and comes with us on our second
Scandinavian tour. Oscar Tapper becomes our archivist. Tom Driberg
is engaged to be married. Gerry has a fling with an attractive girl.
Alan Lomax, the folk-song collector, invades us. I escape him. Gerry
attends Tom's wedding.*

We set out for our first Welsh tour on New Year's Eve. We
were to play mining villages with Jimmie's new play, *Landscape with Chimneys*, a story of squatters and their eviction.
We carried a well-packed load, the company and a new addition,
a shy young woman called Shirley.

We weren't far from Shrewsbury when it started snowing,
lightly, pleasantly at first, but it wasn't long before it began to settle
and the lorry came to a sludgy halt. Gerry tinkered with the engine,
we all got out and pushed. It was no use, she wouldn't budge. We
began stomping up and down to restore circulation. There was a
row of houses on the other side of the road but no one came out
to offer help. All the windows were dark. Were they all abed? Or
dead?

Howard decided to push on in the hope of finding a garage; one
or two joined him – anything to get away from frozen inaction. The
rest of us climbed back into the lorry and huddled together.

Some time later we thought we heard a distant church bell
chiming.

'Happy New Year, everybody!' It was the new girl, Shirley,
and what was she holding up?

'I thought we might need it,' she said.

Good rum; a little sleep, a fitful, uncomfortable night. When
dawn broke we were frozen.

'You'd better all push on,' said Gerry. 'Head for Wales, but first find a garage and send help. With any luck I'll pick you up on the way.'

It was an empty world that morning. Lifts were few and far between. It was broad day when we found a mechanic willing to go back and help Gerry. I was walking with Babs (Barbara Young), who'd not been with us long, and Benny, who was playing the lead in *Landscape*. It was evening before we straggled into Fleur, the mining village where we should have opened that night.

'We had a company stranded here for five weeks last year,' said our sponsor, chairman of the local Labour Party. 'By the time they left we knew their entire repertoire by heart.'

Howard's party was the next to arrive.

'We gave up when we couldn't find a garage open in Shrewsbury,' said Howard. 'Found lovely digs, though; two screws there, they'd come to top some poor bastard in Shrewsbury gaol.'

I think it was Babs who sighted the lorry as it came sliding along the icy road. We all rushed out to give Gerry a cheer.

Then to a good Welsh supper and a warm bed.

The show was lively next night and we swore we'd never forget the warm-hearted people of Fleur as we set off next morning for the frozen hills. Each night we played in a different village. I gave notes by torchlight in the back of the lorry as we rode back to base. The police took exception to our newly-painted lorry – green with red borders. George had done the lettering, 'The International Theatre Workshop', with a list of towns where we'd played abroad. The kids had improved on it with Cwm chalked in next to České Budějovice, Bargoed with Bratislava and so on, right down the list. Gerry was summoned:

- One Belisha beacon, bent, in Tonypandy
- A lamppost knocked down in Porth
- Two policemen spattered with mud in Pentre.

'That lorry's not fit for the road,' said the Superintendent as he walked into one of our warm-ups.

'What's all this?'

'Movement, isn't it?'

'Left Wing movement?'

So that was it. Ever since the Stockholm Appeal they'd been scared of peace breaking out.

'We're playing *Uranium 235* in a chapel on Thursday. Would you like two tickets?'

We were all lodged in miners' homes, feeding like fighting cocks. Our landlady was a widow. She looked rather strict, very proper, but I couldn't help noticing that two gentleman slept in her bedroom.

'It's my pension. . . .' she explained. I nodded wisely, though I couldn't for the life of me work it out.

At Rhymney we had a great night and many willing hands helped with the loading afterwards, but as we pulled away, 'Hey! Stop!'

'What's wrong?'

'I'm coming with you.' And he did. His name was Harry Greene, young and good-looking. We called him 'the poor man's Tyrone Power'. He was also very talented.

Ten days later I was leaning over the rail of the *Kung Gustavus V*. We were on our way to Bergen and our second Scandinavian tour and Harry Greene was with us.

'Don't do it,' said Howard.

' "Never go back," someone told me once.'

'Who?'

'George Bernard Shaw.'

'Well, they wanted us. "Bring us your atom bomb play," they said.'

'And with Niels Bohr in it, do you think we can play Copenhagen?'

'They'll lynch us. Still, it won't be our first failure. I still have nightmares about *Alice in Wonderland* at Barnsley and the miners throwing pennies at John Blanshard.'

'Or the orchestra that could only play "I'm Forever Blowing Bubbles" when Jack Evans tried to conduct his music.'

'We all remember our failures rather than our successes.'

As it turned out, *Uranium 235* was a rapturous success on that tour. The critics went over the top:

> The producer, Joan Littlewood, was seen only in small, but very important parts. What a woman this must be who handles all the different media of the stage with such a brilliant touch. She is a woman of real greatness, worthy of our admiration and reverence. A woman of whom the English theatre can be proud. As an artist she is worth the entire Old Vic. Her name should be written in letters of fire until the blinkers are burned off the eyes of the English theatre public.
>
> SVEN STAHL

> It is their dream of a people's theatre which Theatre Workshop realises in their hard struggle against commercial theatre which regards theatre simply as an industry. With an intimate dialogue between performers and audience, they engage their public and arouse their imagination, so that they become part of the play. This company is a unity, there are no stars. And so it should be when you not only work together but live in such a way that theatre becomes your life.
>
> ERWIN LEISER

There were many more and after a highly successful tour, back to Merrie England.

The plan of work went up on the noticeboard at 177A:

> – Jimmie's new play *The Travellers* is nearing completion.
> – Joan's adaptation of Gogol's *The Overcoat* is ready for analysis; Jack Evans has written the music.
> – *Landscape with Chimneys*, *Paradise Street* and *Uranium 235* must be kept up to scratch.
> – We leave for County Durham in a week's time.

I'd added the usual work roster, everybody taking their share of cooking, shopping, cleaning, tea-making, typing and work on the plays.

'I'm chuffed at being part of this company,' said Harry Greene.

'I'm glad to hear it,' said George C.

'Every moment is a new experience.'

'Try making this bloody printing press work if you want a new experience.'

Gerry wanted copies of the Scandinavian crits for the North-East and Howard was clamouring for a dozen to send to Arts Council.

'Don't forget the Co-op,' said Gerry.

'I've a friend who's brilliant with a printing press.'

'Where is he?'

'In Cardiff at the moment.'

'Well, bring him here.'

'Girry!' That was George (he never could say 'Gerry'). 'Some MP on the phone.'

'Switch it through. Could everybody make less noise?' The noise abated slightly.

'We've got to get hold of a copy of *The Times*. That was Tom Driberg.'

'Where? Nobody reads *The Times* round here.'

Doreen phoned David and he brought us Rosalie's father's copy. Nobody could see anything special in it.

In the evening Tom phoned again: 'Did you find it?'

'No.'

There was an explosion of wrath at the other end. 'Do look in the announcements!'

The pages were turned. Gerry roared with laughter.

'What's so funny?'

'Tom's getting married!'

Unbelievable, but Doreen was delighted. 'We'll all have to be bridesmaids. . . .'

David drowned her with a recording of Jack Evans's music for *The Overcoat* which we would be rehearsing on the road.

Next morning we all met in the top room for the first reading. Jack Evans arrived, carrying Russian books with illustrations of the

St Petersburg of Gogol's day. While the company was browsing I went to the window, and the view of Ardwick which hadn't changed since Mrs Gaskell's day.

Gerry was below, standing by the truck. A girl joined him. It's not . . . It was. What did he want with her? She should be up here. He was lifting her into the cabin. She was smiling. They were going to make love. I knew it.

Jack was giving a talk on Gogol, thank God. I couldn't have taken over, my mouth was dry as a bone. I took refuge in the kitchen and waited for the sound of the lorry returning. It was one o'clock. They weren't back. There was a burst of laughter upstairs. They were breaking for lunch.

Still no lorry when we reassembled. Another hour and a quarter before they walked in. She was still smiling. No apology. They sat down at a distance from each other but every so often their eyes met and he would glance towards the window.

The phone was ringing. Howard was shouting, 'Tea break!'

'It'll be for me,' said Harry G.

'What's her name, sweetheart?' asked David.

'She's a he, and it'll be Oscar.'

That crowned it. Everybody started ribbing Harry, so he went to the phone and closed the door.

'That you, Oscar?'

He told him how to find us, then, 'Watch it when you get here. These buggers think we're having it off. . . .' Camel and Gerry burst out laughing. They had only been listening on the extension.

Oscar proved to be a big portly chap with an infectious laugh.

'I've fixed you a bed in the storeroom,' said Harry over the Irish stew.

'Thanks. . . .'

'Oh, it's only a rostrum.'

That night I stole downstairs with a blanket and the *Fleurs de Carron* Gerry had given me for my birthday and slept in the lorry.

In the morning Camel asked Oscar if he'd slept.

'Fine,' he said. 'I can sleep anywhere, though I've never been wakened by the appearance of a rosy pink bottom before.'

'That'll have been Doreen. She's too shy to undress anywhere else.'

Gerry disappeared again, taking his girl with him. I found I was chain-smoking and not eating. I was being a fool. It was a relief to load the lorry, to be off.

Camel and Howard wanted to know what was wrong with me. What could I tell them? I couldn't say how much Gerry meant to me. Each night I slept in the lorry.

'I'm going to Newcastle with her tomorrow.' It was Gerry waiting for me outside the hall at Stockton. 'She has a rehearsal,' I said. Then I saw her, on the other side of the road. Her eyes were on me. She knew what I had said.

> *If I were a catfish, swimming in the deep blue sea*
> *If I were a catfish, swimming in the deep blue sea*
> *I'd stop those women crowing over me,*
> *Hey Hey Hey Hey – Hey.*

Next morning we were all assembled. Jack was playing us his music when she walked in. We'd just finished trying the first mime sequence.

'You missed an important rehearsal.'

'Did I?'

'If that's how it's to be, you'd better go.'

She walked out. A few seconds later, Gerry approached me.

'What has she done to you? Why be so inhuman?' He walked away.

We were supposed to be staying at Mr and Mrs A's that night. Camel took me aside. 'They're friends of my mother's,' he said. 'She would be most upset if she thought you and Gerry had parted.'

'Am I to accept a *ménage à trois* with anyone he takes a fancy to?'

'No, just to behave as if nothing was wrong tonight.'

I walked to the house with Gerry and went straight up to the room where we were to sleep, leaving him to cope with the family. There was a small dressing-room adjoining the bedroom warmed by a gas fire. I closed the door, which had no lock, and wedged a chair under the doorknob. Then I waited. Hours passed. I had to be sure that everyone was asleep.

At last. I put out the gas fire, waited, then turned the taps full on. I lay down, placed a coverlet over my head and breathed deeply.

Oblivion.

Something shook me. It was Gerry. He threw open the window. 'Go to bed,' he said, and lifted me up.

> *If I were a headlight on that Eastbound train*
> *Lord Lord*
> *If I were a headlight on that Eastbound train*
> *I'd spend my time in cool Colorado Springs*
> *Hey Hey Hey Hey – Hey.*

The last de-rig of the town was always a ball. Our new friends would bring refreshments and help with the work. There'd be jokes and thanks and a promise to return – but this time we seemed to be at sixes and sevens. Gerry's girl was packing costumes on her own, Maggie and I were folding the velvets. David suddenly sprang off the ladder and came towards me. I thought he was going to hit me.

'A woman your age,' he said. 'If I hadn't seen it myself I never would have believed it. She's no more than a girl. I always thought you and Gerry were an example to us. . . .'

I couldn't take any more. I ran out into the street. I hadn't learned that it's always the cuckold who carries the can.

Gerry found me. 'It's not worth it,' he said. 'It's finished.' Again the girl was there, in the shadows. He went and took her arm, guided her away.

In the morning I managed to ask him how things stood.

'I took her up to the hills and tried to explain. "I thought we might have had a little affair," she said.'

'That's all?'

'That's all.'

So we were speaking to each other, but no longer lovers.

An invitation to Tom's wedding was waiting for us at Durham. Unfortunately it clashed with our weekend school at the 'People's Theatre', Newcastle, but Gerry would be free. He was happy to escape.

While he was away an American folk-song collector came looking for Jimmie, who was lecturing at Berwick-on-Tweed. It was a Saturday night, so he watched the show instead.

'You're never careless,' he told me afterwards.

'Oh yes we are.'

'Careless, like Picasso,' he said and brought out a Spanish guitar to strike a few chords as he announced, 'The name's Lomax. Call me Alan.'

He was a big, slommocky man, dark-haired, with a small, straight nose. He sang us a song about molasses, then explained the background and thrummed into a ballad which sounded Scottish. 'It was carried to the Appalachians by early settlers,' he said. By now the whole company was sitting listening and Mr Lomax was wound up. Next came a hollering song, in the style of a black singer. 'I loved the red-light area where they lived, they're pretty wonderful people,' he said, dropping his voice. 'My father, John Lomax, discovered Leadbelly. Pa was one of the earliest folk collectors. He visited a chain-gang and there was this guy with a scar from ear to ear. He'd nearly had his head cut off, fighting in a swamp. The other feller was dead. "I've written a song for you," he told Pa. "It's called 'Goodnight Irene'," and he sang it then and there.

' "That song should free him," Pa told the governor.

' "Not a chance."

' "Even if I were to be responsible for him?"

' "And keep him under surveillance, night and day?"

' "I would be prepared to do that."

'Pa won, but at our home in New York Leadbelly proved to be a wild one and nobody could control him – but Big Black Minnie – when she was around he was as gentle as a lamb.'

Lomax was a hit with the ladies, there was no doubt about that. Was it that Southern drawl? No, even when he sang:

I can lie with another man's wife
And aye be welcome to my ain

they went into raptures. He had a nose for lonely wives, he'd
made a set at Jean as soon as he saw her. But Jean was wondering
what was going on in Berwick and soon went home. I was amazed
to find I was then the target, but he didn't seem quite so gallant
with me; he played the admiring swain with the great J.L., which
I found embarrassing. To head him off, I talked. I didn't find him
in the least attractive. I recited the 'Ballad of Bamborough Castle',
then launched into the history of the Romans in Britain.

'You talk well.'

'I was trying to entertain you.'

'Then take me to the Roman Wall – my sports car's outside.'

'I'm going home.'

'At least let me give you a lift.'

Why not? It seemed the easiest way to be rid of him. But
no sooner were we in he car than he raced off in the wrong
direction.

'This isn't the way.'

'Why don't we enjoy a night together?'

'Thank you.'

'Don't tell me you live as you do without . . .'

'As a matter of fact, we . . .' I stopped myself. Why not take
him on, have my revenge on Gerry? Who broke our bond? Not
me.

He was pulling up outside a bed-and-breakfast place. A sleepy
landlord unbolted the door. Lomax signed us in. The landlord gave
me a dirty look.

My escort had hardly locked the bedroom door, when he
dropped his pants and threw back the thin, flowered bed quilt.
So, I was to be the umpteenth scalp to hang at his belt. How
exciting! Was it that bed quilt which turned my stomach? It was
old and worn, a faded puce colour, stained. I fled. It was cold,
windy outside. I found it refreshing.

Gerry walked in, still smiling at the memory of Tom's nuptials. He'd driven our brightly emblazoned truck into the venerable forecourt where MPs park their cars, waved his invitation at the startled cops who were gazing, dumbfounded, at George's red entablature and sauntered off to find the reception. It was already in full swing on the terrace. A throng of cameramen and reporters were trying to get near the newly-weds.

'Tom was relieved to see me. He'd hired the right suit, and wore a white carnation – should have been green, of course. The lady looked rather nervous, so I gave her a hug.

' "Do you like me Schiaparelli," she whispered.

' "I wish you health to wear it," I replied.

' "*Shalom*, luv. He made me embrace the Church, you know, catechism, baptism, the lot. We're going to Brighton for the week-end. He's very fond of Brighton. Have you got a drink?"

'Tom was getting himself a whisky and chatting up the wine waiter. "WEDDING OF THE YEAR" was the *Express* headline next day. It'll be all right as long as she doesn't try to get into bed with him.'

Thirty-five

*Our summer school at Appleby. A talented young man among the
students – Frank Elliott. His impressions of 'The Workshop'. Ask
him to join us. He attends a rehearsal in Edinburgh – overwhelmed
when he is asked to participate that very night. Beatrice Tanaka
describes the show. Oscar marries Camel's sister, Anne. Tom comes
to Edinburgh with his new wife. Gerry is writing a mining play.
Back in Manchester, he takes us down the pit where he once worked.
A strange character invades us.*

August 1951.
Theatre Workshop is holding a summer school at Eden
Grove, near Appleby, Westmoreland. Young people from
all over the UK are coming to find out how we work.

The place itself was very pleasant, with immaculate lawns and
gardens. It was beautiful weather, so we worked in the open air.
Frank Elliott came, a young man from Horden in the North-East.

> It was the first time I'd met Joan and her company.
> I was sorry it only lasted a week, but in any case that
> was as much of an annual holiday as I could afford. I
> worked for the LNER for four pounds, six shillings
> and eightpence a week, but it was a pensionable job.
> I was safe for life. I'd done my military service, every-
> thing that was expected of me. The idea of a theatrical
> career never entered my head, though I'd made one or
> two stabs at acting in an amateur company, my main
> assets being useful muscle and the ability to learn
> lines. A five-ton Bedford truck stood in the station
> yard at Appleby, a big, burly fellow at the wheel. A
> good-looking young man jumped down.
>
> 'You Frank? I'm Harry. That's Gerry, our business
> manager.'

He may have been their business manager but he looked more like a truck-driver to me. Harry looked as if he were on holiday, green shorts and yellow sweater. I asked him what he did.

'Designer, odd job man, carpenter, actor.' You obviously didn't do just one job in this outfit.

The school was a pleasure. Joan gave us exercises to overcome our initial shyness. They were more like charades, but they broke the ice and we began to know each other. It wasn't long before we had the confidence to try everything demanded of us.

During the week Joan asked me if I would like to join the company. I'd only just met her. Who was this woman asking me to change my whole life? And for two pounds, ten a week. I thought of my future, my security, but after all this was Joan Littlewood and she was inviting me to join her and quietly, I was ever so glad about that.

Frank went home to give in his notice and joined us for the 1951 Edinburgh Festival. I'll let him tell his story:

As I approached the Oddfellows' Hall, insecurity overwhelmed me. I walked in and there was Joan coming to meet me and Harry winking at me and George, who'd been the hit of the school, still in his khaki shorts, still laughing. Then Gerry hove into view, descending by stepladder from a trap-door in the ceiling.

'We're going to run through a revised version of *Uranium 235*,' said Harry.

'You'd better watch,' Joan added.

When it was all over, I was in a state of shock. The magnificence of that performance was something I shall never forget. I've never seen anything to compare with it. The house lights came up, the actors – now themselves – moved slowly towards the edge of the stage. Somewhere behind me a match flared. It was Joan lighting a cigarette, adjusting her woolly cap and gathering her papers.

'Fine,' she said, as she moved towards her company and I waited for the superlatives to flow, 'let's go back to the dance entrance in Scene One.'

That was almost the beginning of the play. They went over it, polished it, then went on to analyse, argue and re-enact bits from every scene. Altogether it took longer than the performance.

'Frank will be playing Death tonight,' said Joan.

I prayed that there was another Frank somewhere about.

'This is Frank. . . .' Smiles, salutes.

'I'd get away while the going's good if I were you, Frank.' That was George.

'He's got the idea, now he'd better try the costume.'

I was handed a black battledress, a blackened steel helmet and a skull-like mask. At least nobody would know me under all that. A patient Howard walked me through all the scenes I was in. Camel showed me the lighting. That was it. Death, thank God, had no lines.

A student from Brazil, Beatrice Tanaka, wrote about us in her diary:

I found my way to an old-fashioned hall with a balcony. An usherette was running up and down, showing people to their seats. Without warning bells, or three bangs, the play began. I dropped on to the nearest bench. Then I had to concentrate, as a millennium rolled by, voiced in a multitude of accents, none of them the Oxford English to which my ear had grown accustomed.

Just when the argument became clear, someone near me started to protest, 'I've paid to be entertained, not lectured.'

The actor playing the scientist started to answer her.

'Theatre is not the place for politics,' she shouted.

'Oh yes it is!' I shouted back, and at that others began to join in.

'Perhaps you'd like to finish the argument in the interval,' said the scientist.

As the lights came up I recognised the heckler. It was the usherette. I was really mad at her and glad when she didn't come back for the second half. I loved the play – it was circus, ballet, gangster film pastiches – I can still see two Spanish Republicans crouched on the battle line, armed only with rifles, while bombers zoomed overhead and in the background a half-circle of people stood reading out sports news and trivial items from newspapers.

At the end Energy asked, 'Which way are you going?' There were protests, applause. He went off and brought a woman on stage.

Who is it? The director? No. It's the usherette. It's Joan.

When we met, I apologised for making a disturbance. 'That's just what I was trying to provoke,' she said. I thanked her for the lesson and Energy gave a laugh that shook the rafters. Energy was Gerry. We became great friends. My life was changed by that Edinburgh afternoon.

So was Oscar's – Harry's friend. He was Front of House manager in Edinburgh and met Camel's sister, Anne, who became his wife.

'Only because she is very tall, and I was taller,' he told me.

Even our old enemy *The Scotsman* changed its tune:

> This is no ordinary production. In comparison with this most acting is uninspired. This is the only striking event at the Festival.

And we packed them in.

The Festival is always fun, but more so when Tom Driberg was around, and he had already installed himself at the Caledonian with his new bride. Leaving her to her own devices, he tracked us down.

'Where does one lunch?'

'We've found the very best place,' said Gerry.

So Tom hailed a taxi. 'To the British Restaurant,' said Gerry. The menu was chalked up on a blackboard outside.

> TODAY'S SPECIAL
> Mince and hash
> Stewed prunes and custard
> One and six
> Cup of tea, twopence extra

Tom loved it – for all his snobbish act in posh places, he didn't mind where he ate, if he enjoyed the company.

When we got back to the hall there were two men lying under a tarpaulin on the pavement.

'Isn't that a public right of way?' Tom asked them.

'Yes, but we're trying out the fall,' said Harry Greene.

'Oh good. The first?'

'The one in Gerry's mining play.'

'Who is that?' said Tom. 'He's rather good-looking.'

'That's our Tyrone Power. Are you coming in to the rehearsal?'

'Of course.'

And he sat in all afternoon, writing notes on used envelopes. After the evening performance Gerry ordered spaghetti *al dente* at the Italian restaurant next door, and afterwards, as we drank our *capuccino*, the patron placed a glass cake-stand on the table, with the usual jam tarts and madeleines, but in the centre a chocolate cake crowned with a crystallised violet, oozing cream at the cracks.

Tom was delivering his criticisms, pointing out mistakes in grammar, incorrect ritual – but I was imagining the taste of fragile chocolate.

'Isn't anybody going to have a cake?'

'The chocolate one looks good,' said Gerry.

'Madly synthetic,' said Tom as he picked off the violet and ate it.

'Tom!'

'Charbonnel et Walker's is the only place for chocolate,' he said, turning the cake gingerly with his fork, but when you looked again – he'd eaten it.

Everybody was waiting to see Ena, but it wasn't till the last night of their stay that he produced her. We were all at the bar in the Festival Club when she breezed in, wearing a little cloche hat and a broad smile. The company crowded round, introducing themselves. 'Leeds,' said Tom. 'Rag trade. Should mean a few bespoke suits. The whole thing was John Freeman's idea, he said she'd straighten out my finances, make a going concern of Bradwell. But all she's done, to date, is dress for dinner and water the roses.'

I drifted across to Ena's corner and asked her how she was doing.

'Me, luv? Nothing upsets me. Mind you, he's very brilliant, but I'm always the same, always the same,' and she went drifting towards Gerry. They seemed to get on, right away.

'Luv?' said Tom. 'North country, I suppose.'

Gerry had completed the first draft of his mining play. It was set in the pit where he'd worked at Pendleton, Lancashire. I liked his simple, direct style; it was a change from the razzle-dazzle which had been our hallmark. Jimmie saw a script lying about one day and read it. 'Not for Scotland,' he said. 'Audiences here, for a variety of reasons, prefer pedantic plays. They like to feel they are in the mainstream of European culture.'

'Where's that? Personally I want to hear the miner's voice.'

'You'll abolish the rôle of the playwright altogether,' said Howard, who'd been listening.

'They've managed that for themselves,' I said. 'Where are our playwrights?'

I still cherished the romantic idea that they might develop among bright actors as they had in Elizabethan times.

Before working on Gerry's play I wanted the company to experience the magnetism of the pit, always there despite the underlying sense of danger. 'It is theatrical,' I said. 'That swift descent into the nether regions . . .'

'She's off,' said Harry Greene.

Oh, he works down below . . .

He was doing his pub tenor.

In the dark dreary pit
So that folks like us by the fireside can
cheerfully sit . . .

Oscar began harmonising with him:

Though he works down the mine far from Heaven's
glorious light!

'Crescendo! Now everybody. . . .'

And his face may be black, yet his big heart is . . .

Gerry and Frank Elliott gave them the bird.

Back in Manchester, Gerry arranged for us to visit Pendleton pit. They didn't want women, but I insisted on going. Nothing could have persuaded the miners to allow their womenfolk to visit the coal face. I don't think it was superstition, as people said, but because they didn't want wife or mother to see the conditions in which they worked.

Nobody spoke as the cage plummeted into the depths. Our guide, a deputy, was waiting for us. We followed him along the rails, till we had to bend to avoid banging our heads and walk lopsided not to trip over the cables. Even so, despite the protecting helmets, we gave ourselves some sharp knocks.

Occasionally a miner passed us. ' 'Ow do?' he'd say, or, ' 'Ow are ye makin' oot?' In my jeans and rambling boots they seemed to take me for a bloke.

As we approached the coal face the heat and noise increased. Camel was in the lead, his beard white with dust, his red singlet clinging to his sweaty torso. He came to a stone wall – there was a gap in it, he thrust his head into it.

The noise of the machinery died down. A miner's head appeared.

'Bloody 'ell, where is 'e?'

'Who?' It was a voice from the other side.

' 'Owd Nick. I've just seen 'im.'

We never ceased to check on details in our search for authenticity – our sound effects, courtesy of BBC sound archives, tools and helmets lent by the National Coal Board – but it was a mistake taking Gerry's play to the North-East: coals to Newcastle.

'We'd sooner see how the other half lives,' I was told. And, 'We who live to please, must please to live.'

Thirty-six

One morning, at 177A, I noticed a seedy-looking character hanging about in the street. He walked round the lorry, checked up on the building.

'Looking for someone?'

He wore an old camel-hair coat, his shoes were down-at-heel, but he looked better close to – clear grey eyes, a sharp, quizzical look.

'Can I help?'

A stream of words, from the corner of his mouth . . . funny accent. Was it Scouse?

'Did you say David Scase?'

'. . . terseemers Littlewood.'

'That's me. You said you were from a theatre?'

'Chorltenrep.'

Chorlton-cum-Hardy, an exclusive suburb of Manchester, was the last place where you'd expect to find a repertory theatre and this chap was the last person you'd expect to find in any theatre.

'Urry Corbit's the name. What would I be expected to do?'

It was very difficult to decode him.

'I'm afraid we can't take anyone on at the moment.'

The response to this was totally unintelligible and he turned on his heel and went.

I checked up on him with David, who'd produced at the Chorlton Theatre.

'Strange bloke, spends all his spare time at the flicks, that's where he learns his acting. Give him a part and he'll give you an impersonation of this week's film star.'

I liked the sound of Mr Corbett and wrote asking if he'd like to string along with us for a while. He appeared on our doorstep the next day.

'There are suttin difficulties . . .' A lot of gibberish, from which 'a load of Reds' emerged.

'You mean you're a Red?'

More gibberish. Then, 'Me brother's in the Labour Party.' I couldn't make out whether he wanted us to be Reds or not.

'And there's the question of wages.'

'Equal shares, but we guarantee you a roof over your head, plus grub.'

'Fags?'

'If you're lucky. Look, make up your mind; we're leaving Monday.'

'Would I act?'

'What else do you do?'

As it turned out he couldn't wait to get away. Avis Bunnage, his best girl, came to see him off. She didn't say much, just stood on the pavement, smiling, till we were out of sight.

'Bloody good artist,' said her young man. 'Better than me.'

Harry couldn't sit still on the journey. He was up and down like a jack-in-the-box, abusing the driver, Gerry, issuing naval commands, singing:

> *Eileen – Oh me heart is growing grey*
> *Ever since the day you wandered far away. . . .*

He kept us lively all the way to Eaglescliffe.

We had been offered hospitality in all the towns and villages of the North-East. Harry was delighted with his first hostess who called seedcake 'man's cake' and presents 'pressies'. He was a very good mimic, enjoyed meeting new faces and fell in love with someone or some place every day. After the show we'd given at a teachers' training college, we lost him altogether. Camel was fastening the tail-board of the lorry before we noticed.

'Search party,' said George and all the men jumped out and made for the woods.

'Damn it, now we'll never get home,' said Camel. At that moment, Harry came sauntering along the driveway on his own.

'They shouldn't keep women cooped up in these places,' he said. 'They get sex-starved.'

The North-East tour went well, but my dream of a Theatre Workshop was beginning to pall. Six long years and no sign of a place we could call our own. A letter came from Norman and Janey Buchan. They had booked St Andrew's Hall, Glasgow, for a fortnight of *Uranium 235* and 'the seats were going well'.

'I've had enough. How many times have I patched up that show? Let Jimmie cope with it.'

I wired him. He replied by letter:

You will accuse me of selfishness if I say I could no more produce *Uranium* than I could conduct a symphony and St Andrew's will present tremendous problems. I can drill crowd scenes, but when it comes to revealing the organic rhythms of the play, I'm lost. *Uranium* needs a producer of genius if it is to be anything more than a cabaret.

Get the show on, I will be your assistant. It will only take a couple of weeks, then you could go. Pity. Glasgow is our only chance of a permanent home. Pity to wind up the Workshop. I will finish *The Travellers* next Wednesday. I could join you then. Any chance of a sub? I am broke, as usual.

Why not go to East Berlin when you leave? My German royalties are at your service.

My love to you,

                                            Jimmie.

What could I do? I gave in, swearing that this would be my last stint.

We hired a basement in Lower Mosley Street, Manchester, and worked fast. At the end of the first week we were settling down before a run-through of the first half when Gerry walked in, followed by Harry Greene.

'I've told Sam Wanamaker he can sit in,' said Gerry.

I was about to protest, when Sam himself strolled in; with a smile and a wave he found himself a chair and sat down.

That first half went like wildfire, and at the end Sam walked up to me and kissed me.

'You did have a funny look on your face when he did that,' said young Babs.

'I was embarrassed.'

Sam was chatting to Gerry, asking if he could bring his leading man to see the second half. Gerry glanced at me. I shrugged. Might as well be hung for a sheep as a lamb.

Next day Sam turned up with, of all people, Michael Redgrave, the man who had reneged on us in 1940. He greeted me like an old friend. I was stunned. I left quickly at the end. Sam told Gerry that Redgrave was 'very impressed'.

Next morning we left for Glasgow. I was surprised when Harry Greene took the wheel.

'You're not driving, Gerry?'

'Don't worry. Harry knows what he's doing.'

'He has no licence.'

'He has now. I was showing him the ropes while you were rehearsing.'

Gerry stayed behind and Harry got us to Glasgow on time. Norman and Janey had performed miracles; tickets for the show had sold like hot cakes. The first-night audience was wildly enthusiastic. Someone handed me a telegram. Gerry was in hospital.

I took the first train south, leaving Jimmie and Howard in command. Gerry had been operated on for a torn bowel. How long had he been in pain, without saying a word to anyone? It was always, 'Gerry will fix it', 'Ask Gerry'. Even in Glasgow Harry Greene said to me, 'Sure, I made it, but I wished to God

Gerry had been with me. I missed his strength. He makes you feel secure.'

'He must have a long rest,' said the doctor. 'He's been overdoing it.'

Where could we go? We had no home. 'What about Cassis, Gerry? We were happy there.'

'It won't be warm now.'

Provence in April? As soon as he was out of hospital we would head for the south he loved.

Gerry was right about the weather. We walked out of the station at Marseille into a downpour. On the perilous bus ride along the clifftops to Cassis you couldn't even see the Med. Arrived there, we found the narrow main street flooded. Our former haunt, the bar of the 'Vingtième Siècle', was still there and crowded with workmen drinking and singing.

'They've been rained off,' said Madame Rosetta. 'And you know what builders are. You look as though you need this,' and she poured two glasses of rich red. 'From my father's own vineyard.' And what were we doing in such wicked weather? One of the workmen charged across the room and stuck a red oleander into her deep cleavage. 'No hotels,' she said. 'Too dear. Take a room and eat here.' At that, first one, then another recommended a good address. We thanked them all and, the rain having slackened, went out to look around. We settled for a third floor in a side street. From the window you could see the sea if you leant far enough out. Far below a woman was calling.

'Mel – an – ie, *viens, vite!*'

'It's stopped raining. Let's walk a little,' said Gerry.

Thus a quiet routine began. We would walk a little, sit by the sea and read, eat at Rosetta's and drink her good wine. After supper Gerry liked to walk around the harbour, inspecting all the boats. The days drifted by, only punctuated by Gerry's visits to the post office, just in case. . . .

One day we sat on a white rock watching the churning waters rise and fall in the hollows far below. The sand-red, giant Cap Canaille towered against the endless blue of sea and sky.

'Let's never go back, Gerry.'

One day, it was at the end of the first week, he came looking for me on the beach after he'd been to the post office. 'We have to go back,' he said, waving a telegram at me. 'Sam is putting on *Uranium* at the Embassy, Swiss Cottage, in two weeks' time. Howard has agreed it. We have to go back at once.'

'I've taken your best shirts to the laundry. They won't be ready till Monday.'

'Get them back and hurry. We have to catch the night train from Marseille.'

Goodbye Cassis. We're bound for . . . Paris . . . Gare de Lyon . . . Gare du Nord . . . Boulogne . . . Dover . . . London, Victoria.

The posters were already up.

EMBASSY THEATRE

Michael Redgrave
presents
the sensational success of the Edinburgh Festival

Theatre Workshop
in
Uranium 235
A morality play for the Atomic Age
by
Ewan MacColl
produced by
Joan Littlewood

'The most exciting theatre I have ever seen'
Sam Wanamaker

opening
Monday, May 12th at 7.45

They were all at the theatre, waiting for us. Gerry asked about the lorry first.

'I'm afraid the brakes gave out,' said Harry Greene. 'We went straight through a fence, keeled over and stuck on the top of a steep railway embankment.'

'Anybody hurt?'

Howard thought he had a broken finger. 'We only missed a couple of dates. Never mind, Gerry, with this first-class booking, we'll be able to buy a new lorry.'

The rest of the company didn't look particularly happy, but then they were all Northerners, not particularly impressed by Swiss Cottage. Sam was very pleased with the progress he had made, reeling off a list of stars who would be attending the première. Had we anybody in mind?

We could only think of *Theatre Newsletter*, and Sam had never heard of them.

Our show did not set London on fire but some rich friends of Sam's gave a first-night party for us. I'm afraid we were hopelessly *de trop*. We'd no best clothes, no small talk. We sounded more like North country comedians than smart actors. I was glad to run for the last bus to our digs in Kentish Town.

The critics didn't make much of us. Ken Tynan decided that our actors were 'in chains'.

The profession gave us the warm applause they reserve for their own when we put on a matinée specially for them. Afterwards Lewis Casson came up on stage to thank us, praise the production, especially the movement, dance and mime, but felt he couldn't be equally pleased with our vocal technique. I couldn't help thinking that he meant our accents. I'd never made any attempt to iron out local accents; if the vowels were distinctive, that was all right by me; class accents were adopted when the rôle called for them.

Taking it all in all, we were ill at ease in NW3. Sam was going off us too. He'd set great store by the critics' good opinion. I thought he'd underestimated reactionary England. He'd believed that we could capture a typical London audience. So had Gerry. Determined to conquer London, he'd sold us to the owner of the Comedy Theatre. We played a few weeks there – and flopped. The enthusiasm whipped up by Sam had melted away. The public who came couldn't make head or tail of us.

So – on the road again – back to Scotland. Were we destined to become the Scottish National Theatre? Gerry was beginning to think so. In Glasgow he found a fine house empty at 15 Belmont Street. The trouble was, nobody knew who owned it.

As usual, friends helped and the owner was located. His name was Bert Pickard, an eccentric millionaire who had stood as Independent candidate for Maryhill, refused to pay his taxes and, when he was summonsed, came to court wearing a policeman's helmet, fitted with traffic lights. Threatened with imprisonment he paid his income tax, in farthings.

Gerry ran him to earth and told him our story. The upshot was, we moved in, paid a peppercorn rent and settled. Each couple had a room with WELCOME or GO AWAY on the door. There was the usual hassle over furniture, but we were used to that.

Jimmie was away more and more, taking on singing dates, so Jean moved in with us, bringing their two-year-old son Hamish. Avis kept promising to come, but Harry Corbett was talking about marriage again and she didn't know what to do for the best.

We took it in turns to cook for a week. We arrived at the Labour Exchange together in a second-hand shooting brake which Gerry had borrowed. It was in better shape than the Bedford.

George and Harry G. (we'd adopted the G. to distinguish him from Harry Corbett) shared a room and liked to get up early and fry up all the leftovers for their breakfast. This attracted young Hamish who would appear every morning in the basement kitchen and join them.

'Why is the floor moving?' he asked Harry G.

'Cockroaches,' was the reply, which intrigued Mish and when he heard the neighbourhood ladies talking about their pets, 'We've got cockroaches,' he boasted.

Harry G. was our champion scrounger. He always came home with a bagful of fruit, jam, broken biscuits. 'Cooper's,' he'd say. 'The girls are crazy about us there. Mackenzie's is best for sausage and mincemeat and an occasional bone or pig's foot. But it's all fellers. We should send our girls along.'

George suffered a sea change when he was cook of the week. We all handed in a pound on Fridays, but with George all we got was potato soup, every day, potato soup. By Thursday, there was open revolt: 'Grub tomorrow, George, or there'll be an *auto-da-fé*!'

'Remember the Tomato Syndicate,' said Camel.

On Friday he served up fish and chips and on Saturday turkey with bread sauce . . . plum duff for afters.

We always had wine in the evenings, fourpence a glass. Gerry had come to an arrangement with an Italian restaurant down the road. Wine at cost price in return for publicity in our programmes. . . .

Jean worried – about the cuisine and the cockroaches, but most of all about the effect of our way of life on her young son. He had so many minders. She took her morning class in the kitchen (it was the largest room). If you took charge of Hamish you were let off the exercises.

'Did you have a nice time this morning, darling?'

'Yes, thank you, Mum. I killed a lion.'

'Who was your minder?'

'George.'

Jean tackled him straight away.

'Nothing to worry about, Jean. We were getting bored in the BBC waiting-room, so Mish played the Big Game Hunter and shot me dead.'

'What were you doing at the BBC?'

'Oh, they'd seen us and wanted me to act in something or other. I told them I couldn't do it, it would clash with our work.'

An hour with Karl and Hamish would come back with his mouth so full he could hardly speak. 'Want some bubble gum, Mum? Karl bought me a gobstopper so that he could read the papers in peace.'

And after Camel he'd have his pockets full of pebbles and seeds.

Our life found its own rhythm, as usual. The only snag was that Harry C. had never been able to take early morning calls.

'Come on, Corbett! Up!'

'What's going on? It's still dark.'

'You're holding us up, Harry.' Very reluctantly, he'd gird his loins and sally forth into the raw morning. . . .

'What's this place? It's padlocked anyway.'

'Jean's got the key.' (She'd had enough of the cockroach kitchen and had found a better place.)

'Why are we creeping into this kip?'

The beat of a drum answered him, and 'Ready? Leap and shake. This will warm you. Off with your trousers, Harry.'

'I've only just put 'em on.'

'Run. Leap. Arch your backs this time. And again. Higher. Arms and legs extended, Harry.'

Usually when Harry was going to bed, George Alphonsus would be getting up and we'd hear a bullying baritone in the bathroom.

'Gerrunder that shower!'

'It's c-c-c-cold!'

'Gerrunder!' More babyish squeals and protests which would suddenly break into 'Bzz Bzz Bzz Busyline'. Rose Murphy to the life.

One weekend, Harry Corbett went to Manchester to bring Avis back. This time he was determined to be married, and he fancied Chris Grieve for the job. Chris was a JP.

'We should tidy his room before they arrive,' said Jean. 'It's a tip. Let's give it a spring clean.'

We all went to work, scrubbing and polishing. George was against the scrubbing, said it ruined the wood.

'It looks very bare,' said Jean. 'Everybody will have to make a contribution.' Harry G. repaired a rocking-chair he'd found in the cellar and Maggie brought a china daisy in a hand-thrown pot and at the last moment Jean produced a crocheted white coverlet. 'Just for the first night.'

Jean would cling to her illusions. She set the seal of approval on the bridal chamber with a heart-shaped cushion and we all retired. It was late, they might arrive at any moment.

We were all up early; George, as always, the first. He found Jean listening by their door. 'Don't worry, luv,' he said. 'Your counterpane's OK. They're sticking out.'

'What's sticking out?'

'Harry's boots.'

'Where's Harry?'

'In 'em.'

'And Avis?'

'She didn't come.'

Harry assured us that Avis would be with us in time to play Toinette in *Le Malade Imaginaire*, which I'd asked Morris Blythman, a dominie friend, to translate for us. As yet I'd seen no sign of it. I'd have to prod him and while I was at it, Harry needed prodding too. Up till now he'd given us nothing but his Hollywood impersonations. *Twelfth Night* was the school play in Scotland, so that would be our bread and butter, but I'd get *Le Malade* on as soon as I could lay hands on it.

I prefer Ben Jonson's comedies to Shakespeare's, but Andrew Aguecheek might be just the part to jolt Harry out of the rut he was in. It was interesting checking up on the politics of the time, finding how the class structure worked. Aguecheek, a poor relation, accepting board from a rich relation, Lady Olivia. It may have been her duty to support him but she would never marry him. Sad, this lonely character who was 'adored once'. Could he just accept what life was bringing him?

'Play him seriously, Harry. Forget that he's played as a funny character.'

He tried. 'It's dull,' he said. 'I know where the laughs should come.'

'Keep going. You're still behaving like a comic. Don't worry about being boring, play his own idea of himself, a real suitor.'

At the first run-through, unforseen moments surfaced.

'Don't hang on to them. Never repeat. New things will happen.'

The first public performance was in a large hall packed with boisterous schoolboys. If ever an audience was ready for the kill, it was this one. I had a word with Harry just before curtain up, something I disapprove of, but the roars of those kids were quite savage. They wanted blood.

'Stand your ground, Harry.'

'What are you talking about?'

'Don't let them kill Sir Andrew.'

'What time is it?'

'You've another minute.'

'Beginners please.'

Was the curtain up? There was such a din out front I couldn't hear the dialogue. I went round to the circle to watch. Sir Andrew's entrance . . . catcalls, wolf-whistles. He just stood there, lost – roars of laughter. He didn't react, he held on to the character so painstakingly evolved and at each simple, true reaction the boys yelled with delight. Not once did he fall back on an easy laugh. He looked vulnerable and the sadder he looked the more those kids roared.

I was thrilled. This was the performer I'd been waiting for. Afterwards we met in the passage.

'Don't ever tell me what to do again. Come to that, don't speak to me again.'

'Harry. Listen. . . .'

'No! Never again.'

The kids were stamping and clapping. 'Can't you hear them? They're calling for Sir Andrew.'

We went back to Belmont Street in the Alvis and he never looked at me.

I waited anxiously for the next performance. Again, it was miraculous. Harry never went back. He couldn't. Once you have experienced the thrill of risk, the elation which often comes with fear, the beaten track is no longer inviting.

At last *The Imaginary Invalid*, beautifully packaged, arrived. A first reading is always an event so we foregathered in Jean's tidy room and took turns reading aloud. Good actors seldom read well, but this was chronic – was it those alexandrines, which the translation had tried to duplicate? Whatever it was, the play sounded turgid. There were too many inactive verbs and too many adjectives. We took a break.

After lunch I suggested having a crack at one or two scenes. 'Let's try to capture some of Molière's sparkle.' First, we mimed a scene to Couperin's music, then, when we'd caught the gist of the story, we threw in one or two phrases. It was working but the company had to leave to play a school in Rutherglen. I decided to stay and take that script apart by myself.

By supper-time I was prepared to abandon it. Our Scots poet was too pedantic, his version would never work. There was only one answer – rewrite. I began and worked far into the night.

In the morning we went on breaking up the scenes, using my night thoughts when they helped, or throwing them into the waste-paper basket. Either way, they helped.

'What's our dominie going to say to all this?' asked George.

I hadn't given the translator a thought, all that mattered was a good show.

'Mine's lighter and funnier, isn't it?'

George grunted, tied tassels at his knees and swished Angélique's feathered head-dress. He was playing Thomas Diafoirus, her papa's choice for a suitor. I burned the midnight oil each night, trying to whip up a soufflé which had fallen flat. Time was short.

The first night was upon us before we knew it. Gerry was away and God knows who'd found time to work on publicity. Curtain up. The auditorium was pitch black. The music played, the company did their best, but there wasn't a single laugh. What a dull lot. During the interval I looked through the peep-hole – there was nobody in the hall. Was it the wrong night? Had nobody tackled publicity? Oh Lord! Morris and his wife had just sat down and they didn't look very happy. Well, hardly a word we'd uttered had been his, and with no audience to show him where the laughs should be . . .

Well, I said to myself, at least they won't stay till the end.

But they did, and waylaid me. 'Aye,' said Morris. 'Better if you return to London, ye might be appreciated there.'

His Scottish accent was more pronounced than ever and his 'London' sounded like 'Sodom'. I might have told him we'd no wish to return to London. I might have said that our version of the play only needed a good audience, but I didn't. I felt sorry as he turned on his heel and left. His lady wife never even looked at me. Then I thought of Avis, as Toinette, George's Thomas, Harry C.'s Cléante, Howard's Purgon and started to laugh. It had all been worthwhile.

I never saw Morris again and he made no attempt to protest publicly during the run of the play. We played good houses. He must have read the crits.

LIVELY CLASSICS

At the moment they are playing a new translation of Molière's *Malade Imaginaire* with that fresh, unhackneyed acting and imaginative production, which give Theatre Workshop the 'cachet' of the better Continental studio theatres.

The Scotsman, 9th December 1952

THEATRE WORKSHOP *THE IMAGINARY INVALID*

This versatile and accomplished body presented Molière's *Le Malade Imaginaire* in a new translation last night. So distinguished was their performance that it is to be hoped that they will soon acquire fixed headquarters in which to give their enterprise a local habitation and a name.

The salient quality of the acting was teamwork. Even the most subsidiary character had something to contribute and was encouraged to do so. The leading parts were woven into the play's texture with easy authority without monopolising the limelight. The highly satisfactory result was the impression of a fellowship of players sharing an enjoyable experience with the audience.

If Joan Littlewood's production had a fault it lay in the stress on the farcical. A little restraint here and a dash of astringency there would have served Molière's ironical purpose better. Otherwise, Miss Littlewood deployed her forces with admirable economy and missed few cues for laughter. Her version incorporated pantomime, ballet and realism in brilliantly imaginative terms.

Thurso Berwick's French was less suspect than his name. The dialogue was faithful without being slavish and had the great merit of propelling the theme fluently, wittily and with dramatic bite. John Blanshard's Argan was effective, George Cooper made Thomas Diafoirus, his prospective son-in-law, a figure of irresistible fun. Harry Corbett endowed Cléante,

the lover, with a glissade of satirical sighs. But
notable as these players were, it fell to the ladies
to realise the full Gallic salt and pungency of the
comedy; item Barbara Young, luscious as Béline, Maggie Bury working wonders of vivacity as Angélique,
Avis Bunnage knitting a plot and sub-plot together so
resourcefully as Toinette.

Glasgow Herald

One day, Ewan MacColl, James H. Miller, Jimmie, call him
what you will, prime mover, inspiration, Daddy o't, walked out,
quit, buggered off – and, not to put too fine a point on it, resigned.
Theatre Workshop had been his life, his pride and joy, the vehicle
for all his plays. Whether improvised in the back of the lorry or
on some God-forsaken railway station, Jimmie's songs had always
lifted our spirits: 'I've a little baby, he's the apple of my eye' when
his son Hamish was born; 'I'm a rambler from Manchester way'
when we were all squatting on Edale Station waiting for the train
that never came. Or, in the early days:

> *To the old place down at Deansgate*
> *Where Theatre Workshop dwells*
> *With Les Preger, Patience Collier and the rest. . . .*

Where was he going?

To join the 'Hootenannys', one of the many groups of folk
artists who'd become fashionable. Folk-songs and singers were in
demand at this time and the Hootenannys offered real money. He'd
never earned money with his plays in England and all the hopes and
dreams of his youth had faded, but abandoning Theatre Workshop
to sing in London pubs – what a waste!

When he first took to folk-singing, Jimmie had abandoned his
own good baritone for the cracked voice of some old farm labourer
and in time evolved an authentic, original style, quite synthetic,
but much admired. He strongly influenced Jean Newlove, his wife,
among others. For a time she dropped Laban in favour of Irish and
Scottish folk dances.

His going saddened some of us, others were relieved, having recovered from the first flush of his influence. Gerry told him, 'You have been with dedicated people who will go on long after your Hootenannys are forgotten.'

It would soon be Christmas and there would be no school shows during the holidays.

'I could pick up a few bob playing Father Christmas in Leeds,' said George to Harry G.

'Speaking for myself personally, I'm hitching to Rhymney to enjoy a slice of real home cooking.'

Nostalgia for Ma's cooking caught on. One by one they drifted away, all except John B. He'd taken up with a local lass, Isabel, and was loath to go. As the house emptied, the cupboards filled. It was our friends bringing Christmas offerings for poor Theatre Workshop. John was embarrassed and very honest. He pointed at the forest of empty bottles in the cockroach-filled kitchen.

'And not a drop to drink,' said Hamish Henderson and went and brought us a bottle of Scotch. John B. gave up, cooked the turkey and invited Isabel to dine. After which we lived on turkey.

'Why don't you take the rest of the stuff and head for home?' said Gerry. 'It will only spoil by the time the gang returns.' So he did, and I think Isabel went along with him.

'Let's picnic on Christmas Day,' I said. The house felt so empty.

'Picnic? At Christmas?'

'Yes, by the sea. It'll be beautiful.'

He thought I was daft, but he fell in. We packed a good lunch, took the whisky and headed north.

'To Oban,' said I.

Gerry's thoughts were always with the warm South, the northern sea was steely grey, flecked with wild white horses, and it was freezing. We lunched in the old Alvis and while we sat there a seal bobbed up above the waves, not twenty yards from the shore. She crowned our strangely mixed-up year – success and disappointment, and at the end of it – no change.

Ah well, 'We're here because we're here, because we're here, because we're here.'

Part Three

1953 – 63

Thirty-seven

We move from Glasgow to London E15. The state of Theatre Royal.
The generosity of May and Bert Scagnelli. Gerry asks West Ham to
accept us as their Civic Theatre. They cannot. We live and produce
plays on the barest minimum. The Safety Curtain falls during a per-
formance of The Alchemist. *Harry Greene snatches George Cooper*
from danger. Harry Corbett and Avis Bunnage camping in France
with Gerry and me during an enforced break. Farming, rehearsing in
Tom Driberg's barn for The Travellers *in Edinburgh. Harry Greene*
and Karl Woods given four pounds to take them there and construct the
set in situ.

Eight of us managed to squeeze into the old Alvis when we set
out for Theatre Royal, Stratford-atte-Bowe, London, E15 – a
dump, as we already knew, but as you've gathered, we were
incurable optimists.

A Sunday in February 1953, the roads empty, the wind nipped
our ears as we hurtled along. As usual, Gerry was shouted at for
driving too fast. And we're hungry. . . . And is there any chance
of a bit of kip in a clean bed tonight?

'It's all been taken care of,' said Gerry.

'Put me down at the Sally Army,' said Karl. 'I'm sick of
the landscape. . . .'

'In England's green and pleasant land,' George Luscombe started
to sing but was howled down. George had just joined us and from
henceforth would be known as George L. to distinguish him from
Cooper, George C.

'It's not so much fighting for your ideals that's tough,' said
Karl. 'It's the company you have to keep.'

Gerry announced that we were in Shakespeare country.

'Any chance of a chip shop?' That was Harry Corbett.

Hours later, with cramped backsides and wet collars we tumbled
out of the old jalopy.

'Eight hours from Belmont Street. Not bad,' said Gerry.

There were no lighted windows to be seen, every door was shut. We were in suburban London on a wet Sunday night.

'A baked potato would do me,' said Babs as she wandered off.

'There's no point in trailing down the lane.'

'This is Angel Lane?'

We were at the side entrance to the Theatre, a sloping passageway with whorls of dirty paper swirling around in it. Along the lane, we could see the outline of small shops with uneven roofs. Somewhere people were singing, 'Shall we gather at the river, The beautiful, the beautiful – the river. . . .'

And here we were, at Theatre Royal, Palace of Varieties, twenty quid a week rent. Gerry pulled aside an iron grille and we walked up the murky tiled passage till we came to four narrow doors with stained-glass panels and heard George Cooper's laugh. He'd beaten us to it, hitchhiking. There he was, supping tea with Harry Greene behind an otherwise empty bar.

'Welcome to the Royal,' said Harry.

'Anything to eat?' we replied.

'There's a pot of tea, milk and sugar.' Funds didn't run to anything more.

'There'll be grub first thing in the morning,' said Gerry.

'Have an early night, make the best of it,' said Harry G.

'Where do we kip?'

Harry, who'd been there a few days, had made a sleeping plan.

Harry C., West Wing front, double. Is Avis coming?

'She'll arrive by bus tomorrow.'

West Wing, middle floor – the girls.

'What's all this wing business?' asked Harry C.

'Dressing-rooms, far side of the stage. Wing sounds better.'

'Come and take a look at the stage,' said Camel, clanging open a heavy, barred door. We went and found ourselves in enormous gloomy space. Gerry switched on the house lights – dress circle, stalls, four boxes, two on either side of the proscenium arch and a gallery, neglected, decaying, but graceful.

'Hullo!' somebody shouted. 'Hey there!'

Good for sound.

The place reeked of perfumed disinfectant and cat piss. The

curtains in the boxes were grey with age but the place merited something better than cheap variety.

'First call, eight in the morning . . . the Black Squad.' Gerry's organising voice.

We knew what that meant. We could smell the urinal under the stage and the auditorium was littered with orange peel and sticky papers, the stage floor greasy with dirt.

George C. was gazing up at the proscenium arch. 'We'll be lucky if we get our six weeks out of it,' he said. 'That lintel is holding the place up.'

John B. appeared from the West Wing, smiling. 'I've the bridal suite,' he said. 'Very cosy. Dressing-Room 2. No windows.'

'You have a bed?'

'No one has a bed.'

'You're not supposed to bed down in a theatre. It's illegal.'

'Have you all got a sleeping bag or a blanket? Anyone with spares share with a neighbour.'

'I swept the dressing-rooms,' said Harry G., 'but they need a thorough clean. And don't forget, if the Fire Officer should show in the morning, all signs of occupation must vanish. I'll warn you over the tannoy.'

'What's the code?'

'Walter Plinge,' said Harry C.

As a matter of fact, I'm quite sure that the Fire Officer knew perfectly well that we were all sleeping in that building, but he never let on. He actually became our best friend in Stratford.

'Is there a shower?'

'There's a pipe under the stage. It's a bit crude, but it'll have to do. . . . Well, what do you expect for twenty pounds a week?'

'What about cooking?' John B. asked.

'Gas ring in the main bar, another one in the gallery bar and a large one in the loading bay for heating glue.'

'Look at this! In the excitement I quite forgot.' John B. brought out a tin of biscuits. 'Home-made, my last effort in the cockroach kitchen. Any more tea in that pot, Harry?'

'Not really.'

'Fix us another brew, love.'

'The milk's run out.'

Harry C. wandered in. He'd been inspecting his quarters. 'Too far from my work.'

'You're only on the second floor, Harry.'

'Right folks, Black Squad eight. Lights and costumes eleven. Lunch one o'clock.'

'Where?'

'In the top bar.'

'What's the show?'

'*Twelfth Night*. And don't anybody go disturbing Wardrobe. All the costumes have to be made ready.'

'Where's Wardrobe, and who's running it?'

'A new girl, Josie Wilkinson, top floor. West Wing. And knock before you enter – it's also her bedroom. The washing machine will be working after the show, if anybody wants to use it.'

Nobody seemed in a hurry to retire. They all went nosing around. Karl discovered a cherub over the door to the dress circle. 'First time I've ever seen a working-class cherub,' he said.

George Luscombe was brooding in the gallery. 'We have a theatre, if only for six weeks. At least it'll mean less energy spent loading and unloading.'

Camel and Maggie were hoisting their rucksack up a ladder. 'Where are you going?'

'We're in the prop-room. It has air, there's a hatch that leads to the roof.'

Gerry and I had a small, low room at the top of the building and it had a window. It was to be our home for many years. So everyone had some place to call their own and we knew how to respect each others' privacy. The stage was for work and play and the roof, our garden. You could get to it by a hatch in the flies; you didn't have to go by Camel and Maggie's prop-room. There were fifty steps to climb up a wall ladder. It was worth it.

The Black Squad's worst job was the boiler. We utterly failed to get it to light. Luckily the weather wasn't too bad. If it worsened we'd have to ask our audience to wear their warmest clothes.

First thing Monday morning, Gerry bought a sack of potatoes and two pounds of mincemeat and John's Isabel arrived in time to make us a pie for lunch. Bless her, she sang like a lintie while she peeled the spuds.

On the second day Oscar Tapper appeared and disappeared into the cellar with Harry G. They were making a poster for the front of the theatre. Harry had conned lining paper and paint from the blokes in the do-it-yourself on the High Street. They had it posted by lunch-time.

Theatre Workshop
presents
A season of Great Plays
First production
Twelfth Night
by Will Shakespeare

Oscar also knew how to cut stencils in waxed paper and made smaller posters for the local shops.

Our first meal, served in the gallery bar, couldn't have been merrier if we'd been picnicking on a Derbyshire moor. We sat on the gallery seats, our plates on our laps, surveying the stage, clean now, all set for the afternoon's run-through. Avis had just walked in to play Maria. We couldn't go wrong.

Harry G. walked across the stage with an armful of toilet rolls and disinfectant bottles.

'Where did all that come from?'

'Our first patron. We need gallons of the stuff but there was no cash. I phoned the biggest firm in the book, Ibcol, and got the boss. You'll never believe this: he turned out to be one of Sam Wanamaker's friends, Harry Ibbotson. Remember, when we played at Swiss Cottage last year? He's given me two hundred and fifty quid into the bargain.'

No sooner were blessings called down on Harry Ibbotson than everybody started clamouring for a hand-out. Things were looking up, but unfortunately it rained during the run-through and the Oscar–Harry poster sagged. The paste, made with flour, had washed away. Harry G. seized one of the small posters and dashed off to rustle up an audience, but there were only two hours till curtain up.

Gerry came to me. 'Harry G.'s working against time on the publicity,' he said. 'You'll have to play his part.'

'Feste? I'm the wrong sex.'

'There's no one else.' When eight o'clock struck there was hardly anybody in the audience but we gave of our all and at the end our diminutive audience applauded to the echo.

'It will pick up,' we said.

The box office was silent, but there was friendship and goodwill on the street. George C. and Karl got paid work decorating local shop fronts. Harry G. became a signwriter. He'd whistle down the lane when cues were coming up. The owners of Café L'Ange, Bert and May Scagnelli, adopted us. After a week of shepherd's pie, May proposed a Café L'Ange lunch each day. We could pay, she said, on the Monday mornings when all the cash was in. We accepted thankfully.

Later, their cayf became the coffee-house for all the gossips and theatre lovers who'd managed to track us down, Bert's home-cured ham and good roast beef being not the least of the attractions.

Doreen, our blonde beauty, had left for Australia just before we moved to Stratford-atte-Bowe; the other girls were spoken for. At every company meeting, the cry from the men was: 'Not enough women.' Avis, Babs, Maggie and me – hardly a chorus line, but we were hot stuff. 'Tell your friends,' said Avis, every night at the curtain call. The only thing was they didn't seem to have any friends. Well, we were in the poorest borough in London, and though we didn't know it, nobody had ever made the old Royal pay.

'Charles Dillon has applied for a licence to build a permanent theatre in Angel Lane,' said the local vicar. That was in 1884 when West Ham was a fast-growing township. 'No doubt his only object is to gain an honest livelihood, but the very position of the proposed theatre will necessitate a low kind of drama; the place will become the resort of the worst characters of the neighbourhood.'

All the local clergy, schoolteachers, employers of labour and Catholic priests agreed with him and presented a petition to the Bench against the grant of a licence, but Dillon won and the theatre opened with Lord Lytton's *Richelieu* on Wednesday 17th December 1884.

The local critic was favourably impressed, but the gallery cracked nuts throughout the early scenes so that Dillon had to appear before the curtain and rebuke them: 'I will not have the beautiful lines of this play spoiled by your rude behaviour. Treat me fairly and I will treat you fairly.' He gave them *The Streets of London*, *The Colleen Bawn*, *Hamlet*, *East Lynne*, *Richard III*, *Don Caesar de Bazan*, *The Devil in Paris*, *The Shaughraun*, and *Belphagor*, paid his actors one and six per night and instructed them to dress well on and off stage.

We gave them *Twelfth Night*, *Colour Guard*, *Paradise Street*, *Hindle Wakes*, *Juno and the Paycock* and *The Imaginary Invalid*; for pay, a share of the takings, dressed them well on stage, though they looked like 'the worst characters of the neighbourhood' off.

Gerry wrote to the Town Clerk of West Ham on 14th April 1953:

THEATRE ROYAL

STRATFORD - LONDON, E.15

Licencee : J. ROWLAND SALES, F.V.A.   Manager : MARyland 3260
General Manager : GERALD C. RAFFLES   Box Office : MARyland 1075

THEATRE WORKSHOP

EUROPE'S OUTSTANDING GROUP THEATRE IS PRESENTING
BRITAIN'S MOST EXCITING REPERTORY OF PLAYS

THEATRE WORKSHOP LTD.

Directors: JAMES F. FORD
        WILLIAM MacLELLAN
        FREDERICK PIFFARD
        HUGH McDIARMID

General Manager :
        GERALD C. RAFFLES

Artistic Directors:
        JOAN LITTLEWOOD
        EWAN MacCOLL
Musical Director:
        JOHN EVANS
Stage and Lighting Director:
        JOHN BURY

Dear Sir,

A Civic Theatre for West Ham

We would like to suggest to the Borough Council that we be accepted by the borough as its Civic Theatre. In many years of playing throughout Great Britain, Europe and Scandinavia, Theatre Workshop has gained an international reputation. Here, at the Theatre Royal, we are doing our best to resurrect this beautiful and graceful building from being the sad and last resort of third-rate variety and striptease shows, into a theatre worthy of its place as the only theatre in the borough. The building should serve not only West Ham but also the million or so people for whom it is the nearest live entertainment.

We have been presenting, and intend to continue to present, a mixed programme of the great classics of the past, the classics of the last generation, and really new, modern plays with contemporary themes. We want to revive and preserve all that is best in the theatrical traditions of our country and of Europe.

The performances which we are presenting are of as high a standard as can be seen anywhere in this country with settings, costumes and music, designed and created specially for each production.

We can offer you – ready-made – a Civic Theatre which can even now be a source of great pride to the borough, and within a comparatively short time recognised as one of the most important theatres in the country.

If you will accept this idea in principle, in practical terms we need your aid in the way of publicity, and by making available to us one penny or two of the sixpenny rate which the borough is entitled to use for cultural purposes.

Would it be possible for me to appear before your committee to explain our ideas in more detail and to answer any questions you may have?

Thanking you in anticipation of the favour of an early reply,

Yours sincerely,

pp THEATRE WORKSHOP

Gerald C. Raffles
General Manager

The reply came by return:

Dear Sir,

Theatre Royal – Civic Theatre for West Ham
I have to inform you that your letter regarding the above-
mentioned matter, which I received on the 15th instant, was
submitted to and considered by this Council's Finance Committee
at their last meeting.

Whilst the Committee showed considerable sympathy with the
aims of the Theatre Workshop, and appreciated their endeavours to
secure for the benefit of the Borough a Civic Theatre which could
be the venue for the performance of cultural works, they regretted
that they were unable to recommend the Council to make any grant
for the purpose you have in mind.

As you will doubtless appreciate this Council are primarily
concerned that no additional burden which can be avoided shall
be placed upon the ratepayers of this Borough and for your
information I would mention that, bearing in mind the high
rate levy, the Council have not, up to the moment, exercised
their power under the Local Government Act, 1948, to provide,
or participate in, any entertainments which might have the effect
of expending even a fraction of the permitted amount to which you
refer.

The Committee indicated that they would be prepared to assist
you, where possible, in the matter of publicity, providing that this
could be done without cost to the Corporation.

Yours faithfully,

G.E. Smith
Town Clerk

Despite the rebuff, we decided to stay. After all, we'd nowhere
else to go.

The shopkeepers and stallholders in Angel Lane were friendly
enough. Bill Pohl, the butcher, told us stories of his barefoot
childhood; Dai, the fishmonger, swore that Gerry was a Taffy
too; Les Back at his vegetable stall, gave us the bird every time

we went by; and Mrs Egg advised us to find a proper job as she sold us four penn'orth of bacon.

Next door to us, on Salway Road, in a two up, two down, lived Mrs Ivory. She kept a fruit and veg stall on the forecourt of the Lion and you'd see her at first light stacking mounds of shining apples, hanging bunches of grapes, sorting the spuds and caulies bought at Stratford market. Mr Ivory walked very slowly and always wore carpet slippers. His lady wore her hair in coiled plaits which just showed under her sateen toque, her long blue apron over her black serge coat. She had fine gold earrings and one gold tooth which showed when she smiled . . . but she never smiled at us.

'Parking their old rubbish on the pavement outside our 'ouse,' she'd say. Harry G. and Camel often worked on the street when it was too dark inside, or if their noise was disturbing rehearsals.

And what rehearsals! I have never known anything like them, before or since. Our release from the slogging routine of one-night stands – load, unload, rig, warm up, perform, de-rig, unload – gave us more time and energy for our real work. We still shouldered the labour between us – repairing seats, curtains and carpets, cleaning out the boiler-room, cellars, urinal; hand-printing posters, distributing them, sticking them up in the tube station, when we could, and fly-posting all over Stratford. We made the sets, props, costumes and meals and still found time to read and train – and we were lucky if we received three pounds a week.

Yet there were moments I will never forget – Avis Bunnage as Louka in *Arms and the Man*, singing the song Jack Evans found for her:

> *I remember in my childhood*
> *We were sweethearts for a day*
> *But alas, now you've grown up dear*
> *All your love has flown away*

her voice as luscious as a ripe, dark plum. George Cooper as Sergius, carefully lifting the washing on the line and avoiding a chicken as he made his entrance through the back yard of the Petkoff house. Harry Corbett who, in *Red Roses for Me*, after shutting himself away for a fortnight with a concertina, produced an Ould Brennan whose feet barely touched the floor.

And the saga of Harry Greene's tree which lived and flourished on stage throughout the run of the Sean O'Casey. I said I needed a tree; Harry G. said he'd find one and disappeared with Karl. I didn't see them again till next day when they reappeared with Gerry and a tree twenty feet high.

'Where were you?'

'In the nick,' said Harry. 'I tried everyone we knew who had a garden, but none of them had the right tree or could even spare a tree, so we made for Epping Forest. There I saw a beautiful alder, just the right size, so I got out my saw and told Karl to dog out. Next thing I knew two forest wardens were standing looking up at me.'

'I was stretched out on the grass reading me book,' said Karl.

'You'd fallen asleep,' said Harry.

'What was the book?' I asked.

'Byron.'

'And I had to vouch for them,' said Gerry.

'Told the law he'd never seen us before in his life,' said Karl.

'I should have left you there. I gave the sergeant a couple of tickets for the show instead. Did you bring the tree?'

'It's on stage,' said Harry. 'Better send the Chief Warden of Epping Forest a ticket as well.'

In fact, the Chief Warden became one of our best friends. Best? Only friends – we hadn't many. All the neighbouring boroughs – Barking, Bethnal Green, East Ham, Ilford, Leyton, Poplar, Romford, Shoreditch, Stepney, Stoke Newington, Walthamstow, Wanstead and Woodford, all turned down Gerry's *cri de coeur*, all of them, and brusquely.

Despite the tiny audiences, who looked as poor as us, the work went merrily on. Good humour and daft jokes made up for what we lacked in caviare and champagne.

George Cooper and Harry Corbett became our chief sparring partners as one day Richard Harris and James (David) Booth would be.

For a long time after Sir Andrew Aguecheek, Harry C. was ill at ease with me. He'd never listen when I was giving notes. 'Take anything down that might interest me,' he'd say to Avis, and off he'd go. But most of the moments I'd questioned would have been re-worked at the next performance.

George C., on the other hand, wouldn't remember a thing from one rehearsal to the next. He'd just start again on a different tack.

'What happened to all those marvellous ideas we worked out yesterday?' asked Harry one day when they were working on Bluntschli and Sergius.

George didn't reply, he just sat there dreaming. I never saw George nettled or angry.

They were both clowns, George as agile as a monkey and light on his feet, Harry a master of swordplay, wrestling, any kind of fighting. When George knew he'd made a good invention he'd embellish it, play variations on it till he had his audience helpless with laughter. At a long-drawn-out lighting rehearsal he'd suddenly come to life. When he was playing Jove and Harry, Mercury in Giraudoux's *Amphitryon 38*, they were standing by the open trapdoor on stage. I wanted Camel to throw light up from the cellar so that they appeared to be gazing down at the world. Suddenly George stepped into the empty space – I shut my eyes, waiting for a sickening thud, a scream. Instead there was a roar of laughter. I looked; he was standing there posing on the other side of the trap. How did he do it? God knows. He was born a rubber ball.

In *The Alchemist* he narrowly escaped with his life. In Act II, Scene i, he was carried on as Sir Epicure Mammon in an open sedan chair accompanied by Surly (Harry G.):

> *This is the day, wherein, to all my friends,*
> *I will pronounce the happy word, be rich,*
> *This day you shall be . . .*

The iron safety curtain came crashing down and would have killed him had Harry G. not leapt forward, seized him and snatched him out of danger.

Everything in that old building had been neglected. Now, to

our horror, we found it was dangerous, but all the lessee was worried about was the advertisement curtain which was lifted seven minutes before the performance began. Too soon, he said and would we please make out our cheque for the rent, twenty pounds per week, to him personally, not to his company.

Ben Jonson's English was our riches. Howard as Subtle, Harry C. as Face and the incomparable Avis as Dol Common revelled in the play and at the end when the gang splits and Subtle kisses Dol with:

> *My fine flitter-mouse,*
> *My bird o' the night; we'll tickle it at the Pigeons*
> *When we have all, and may unlock the trunks,*
> *And say, this's mine, and thine, and thine, and mine . . .*

I wondered if he meant the same Pigeons as the old pub of the same name on the Broadway – for Stratford was always famous – as in the old ballad:

> *She came till she went to Stratford-atte-Bowe*
> *Then she knew not whither or which way to go*
> *So she kept on her journey until it was day*
> *And went into Rumford, along the highway.*

In *Richard II* George C. played Bolingbroke, Harry C., Richard. By this time Harry had developed such a command of inflection and rhythm that his rather light voice was no drawback, the meaning was as clear as a bell.

In the prison scene, Act V, Scene v, Harry C.'s Richard, dressed in sackcloth, tethered by his right ankle to a stake centre stage, could only circle slowly round as he spoke his thoughts:

> *I wasted time, and now doth time waste me;*
> *For now hath time made me his numbering clock;*
> *My thoughts are minutes, and with sighs they jar*
> *Their watches on unto mine eyes, the outward watch,*

> *Whereto my finger, like a dial's point,*
> *Is pointing still, in cleansing them from tears,*
> *Now sir, the sound that tells what hour it is*
> *Are clamorous groans, that strike upon my heart*
> *Which is the bell; so sighs and tears and groans*
> *Show minutes, times and hours; but my time*
> *Runs posting on in Bolingbroke's proud joy,*
> *While I stand fooling here, his Jack o' the clock*

The action gave a double poignancy to the words.

Howard Goorney worked with me each night, after supper, mastering the breath control needed for John of Gaunt's dying speech, that mounting list of virtues England had lost, so often rendered as a paean of praise:

> *This royal throne of kings, this sceptr'd isle,*
> *This earth of majesty, this seat of Mars,*
> *This other Eden, demi-paradise,*
> *This fortress built by Nature for herself*
> *Against infection and the hand of war,*
> *This happy breed of men, this little world,*
> *This precious stone set in the silver sea,*
> *Which serves it in the office of a wall,*
> *Or as a moat defensive to a house,*
> *Against the envy of less happier lands,*
> *This blessed plot, this earth, this realm, this England,*
> *This nurse, this teeming womb of royal kings,*
> *Fear'd by their breed and famous for their birth,*
> *Renowned for their deeds as far from home,*
> *For Christian service and true chivalry,*
> *As is the sepulchre in stubborn Jewry*
> *Of the world's ransom, blessed Mary's son:*
> *This land of such dear souls, this dear, dear land,*
> *Dear for her reputation through the world,*
> *Is now leas'd out, – I die pronouncing it, –*

With sustained delivery on these lines, the words 'leas'd out' gain a terrible strength and one feels that Gaunt has expended his last breath on his prophecy.

Our preparation for *Richard II* had a marked effect on George Luscombe, our gifted young Canadian – it cured him of a misplaced respect for the English Establishment. As Thomas Mowbray, Duke of Norfolk, he was tripping over his words in rehearsal. What was wrong? He had such a good ear. I had an idea.

'John Neville is playing *Richard II* at the Old Vic this afternoon,' I told him. 'I would like you to go and watch and bring me back a report. There's a seat fixed.'

He looked at me, puzzled, but off he went.

He came back cured. He couldn't stop impersonating the stylish English actors with their cut-glass accents.

Tom Driberg, as always a faithful follower, came on the Saturday night and sat in his usual seat, the nearest to the bar.

'I thought the lines you spoke rather appropriate,' he said afterwards. I was playing the Duchess of Gloucester.

'Which lines?'

'Weren't they about Theatre Royal? – Empty lodgings and unfurnished walls. . . .'

'Oh!

> *'Unpeopled offices, untrodden stones*
> *And what hear there for welcome, but my groans?* . . .

'Of course. Thank you, Tom.'

However, our fame reached three Russian writers who were visiting London. Here is a translation of the letter I received from Boris Polevoi:

Dear Miss Littlewood,

At the end of January, I and my friends, the Soviet writers Marshak and Klistratova had the pleasure of visiting your theatre. *Richard II* was playing. Its production struck us by its original treatment, its sharpness and artistic profundity. Samuil

Marshak, considered in our country one of the best translators
of Shakespeare, said to us then in a friendly discussion that that
was the way, probably, that plays had been put on in the past
at the Globe Theatre. I myself am not a Shakespearean scholar,
but I found great pleasure in this production for a quality it had
of freshness, honesty and impassioned craftsmanship, as well as
for the enthusiasm which fired the acting both in the leading and
minor roles.

We were particularly affected by your speech at the end
of the evening, in which you pointed out that the press was
ignoring the work of your theatre and in which you asked the
audience to tell their friends about your work. We three Soviet
writers have honestly carried out this request of yours and in our
lectures and talks on our visit to Great Britain, have spoken many
friendly words about your theatre, about the craftsmanship of your
actors, which is out of the ordinary; actors who have bravely come
out against academic theatrical routine. It gives me pleasure to
send you an article about your theatre, published in one of our
authoritative newspapers, *Sovietskaya Kultura*.

Please accept greetings from distant Moscow from a friend
of your small, great theatre.

Signed,

B. Polevoi

Greetings from John Moody, Drama Director of Arts Council.
He would have to be sure of our financial stability before any
assistance was forthcoming.

Heigh-ho. We're stable enough on our feet.

'The only company that trains,' said the convert, Harry C.
'They don't even limber up before the show in other theatres.'

I hoped he wasn't in danger of becoming a fanatic. There was
only one cure, send him on a Laban crash course. The opportunity arose when we played Charles Fenn's *Fire Eaters* and Harry
C. wasn't needed in it, neither was George C. I packed them both
off.

They came limping back a fortnight later.

'How did you get on?'

'Great,' said George C.

'Super,' said Harry C. 'Marvellous birds.'

'The only thing was,' said George, 'there was this old girl who could do everything better than me, turn cartwheels, stand on her head. She had a hold on you like a police dog.'

'Was she a student?' asked Jean Newlove.

'No, she was grey-haired.'

'You don't mean Lisa Ullmann, one of Laban's best teachers? She's by no means old.'

George kept up the exercises he'd learned. Harry C. buried himself in a book on crystallography, borrowed from Laban. Harry had picked up most of his education in Theatre Workshop. He'd only been to an army school in India, where his father was a sergeant; orphaned and sent back to England, a kindly old aunt in Wythenshawe adopted him. He kept out of trouble till he was called up, but, once in, there was no holding him.

'Our 'Arry's in the Marines,' his aunt told the neighbours. 'Spendin' his Christmas on a farm in Australia. 'E's the lucky boy.'

That farm was a detention camp. Our 'Arry had been on the trot. He was shacked up with an Aussie bint when they found him. Back in Manchester, after the War, he put his name down to take up medicine, but they wouldn't have him, not enough schooling, so he took up with a pretty nurse instead. From there it was a short jump to a dentist's daughter – Avis. And she was a part-time member of the local Chorlton Rep. He always stayed a little in love with his past conquests and was always perfectly frank. 'I won't be around for long,' he told Avis, at the outset.

George had started work in an architect's office, but was called up and posted to India. His troopship was only halfway there in 1945 when the amazing news broke:

'Labour's in!'

'What do we do, Cooper? Chuck the officers overboard?'

'Don't chuck the CO in. He's a socialist.'

George's CO was Ramulsen from Leeds. He and his men landed in some remote corner of Rajputana where there was nothing much to do. So he commandeered a Toc H hall and gave lectures on political economy.

'Why don't we 'ave a general election, sir?' asked one of the lads.
'Good idea.'

And they did, and hotly debated the burning issues of the day
. . . an England without unemployment, a home for every family.
Meanwhile more leave, more pay. Only a few scowed off now and
then to dance in the woods with the local hermaphrodites.

George ran into his CO after the War in Leeds.

'Is it true that you're boss of the local CP nowadays?' said
George.

'Right, lad,' said Ramulsen. 'Someone's got to put 'em on
the right track.'

We hardly seemed to be on the right track at Stratford-atte-
Bowe. Gerry appealed to all the neighbouring councils – Barking,
Beacontree, Chigwell, Chingford, Dagenham, Leyton, Romford,
Walthamstow and Woodford: do you need a theatre here in the
East End? And the answer came ringing back – No!

We had a pile of debts and an income which would hardly
sustain a flea circus. In June 1954, we split. Gerry couldn't feed
us through the summer months when theatres are always empty,
separately we might survive. We went camping in France and took
Harry and Avis with us. It never stopped raining and Harry got
more and more miserable. He'd taken his teapot with him but even
that didn't help. He longed to be in one of those warm restaurants
eating a posh French meal. He and Gerry tried to find work in Les
Halles and failed. So Avis went to the British Consul and borrowed
the fare home. If we didn't reassemble soon we'd be finished, for
ever.

'Come to Bradwell,' said Tom. 'Now that the weather's fine you
can camp out, rehearse and earn enough in your spare time, with
farmwork, to get yourselves to the Edinburgh Festival. If Jimmie's
play is finished . . .'

'*The Travellers*? Yes, it's finished, but we get no spare time
with J.L.'

'Nonsense. We'll have the life of Riley at Tom's with manual
work and creative work, like the monks of old.'

Bradwell-juxta-mare is a forgotten corner of Essex, unfashion-
able, serene, set in the flat, misty landscape which borders the

River Blackwater.

When Gerry drove the old Bedford into Tom's elegant drive the Chinese ducks on the pond by the gate rose up and took refuge among the trees. Tom and Ena hurried out of their Tudor setting to receive us and show us the vegetable garden.

'Help yourselves,' said Tom.

'And bring a few for us,' said Ena.

Then we were walked to the back of the house and, crossing a sloping lawn, came to a ditch.

'Ha-ha,' said Tom, 'not ditch. It prevents the cattle from straying.'

'But there are no cattle.'

'Quite.'

We looked back at the house, two floors, eight windows, alcoves with urns trailing blue lobelia, a belvedere – perfect eighteenth-century.

'Adam. The two parts, Tudor and Adam, were formerly separated by a carriageway, but that has been built on. I'm afraid I'm slipping into my lecture – I take parties of visitors round at the weekends. It helps pay for the dry rot.'

'Where do we rehearse?'

'In the barn.'

'Outdoors would do,' said George C.

'In inclement weather?' And Tom took the lead back to the potting sheds and up the rickety stairs to a loft smelling of apples.

Harry C. wanted to organise the farmwork and set off straight away to prospect. He returned in time for supper. 'All out for horse beans at the crack.'

'Till when?'

'Till we finish the field.'

'What about rehearsals?'

'We're being paid for the beans.'

Luckily that bean-field was near the sea, so, after a back-breaking morning under the hot sun, we'd fall into the water and swim – then to the barn and Jimmie's *Travellers*. It made exciting reading, but by the time we'd got to the end everybody was asleep.

'Early to bed tonight,' said Harry C. 'We're stooking tomorrow.'

But John B. lit a bonfire after supper in the field beyond the ditch where we pitched our tents and we sang till midnight. On the Saturday evening Tom invited us into the library and left us to browse among his books or listen to his collection of early jazz records.

We didn't see much of Ena; she had her own apartment somewhere in the house. Occasionally she'd come in when we were cleaning up in the wash-house.

'Sure you're all right?'

'Fine, fine.'

'I hear you laughing; you always seem to be laughing.'

She was quite transformed since Edinburgh. She would tremble every time Tom looked at her, usually as a prelude to some cool denunciation, then her stomach would heave and she'd go away.

The company worked on the play with complete concentration, lived mainly on vegetables and looked trim and fit, but the problem of the set had not been tackled. *The Travellers* takes place on a train speeding across Europe.

'We'd do better to film it,' said George C. 'How are you going to get first- and third-class compartments and a corridor on one stage?'

'Build your train on a central aisle, and seat the audience on raked seats on either side of it.'

'Like a cockpit?'

'Yes, one of the advantages of not playing on a formal stage.'

Harry G. made some sketches.

'It'll have to be built *in situ*,' he said.

'Could you build it?'

'How much money have we got?'

'Four pounds.'

'Four pounds? You'd be lucky to get that set for four hundred.'

'We may not have money, but we do have friends in Scotland. Would you tackle it, on your tod?'

'It'd be easier with Karl. He's a good worker.'

'Well, there isn't a part for him in the play and this morning he went out to shoot our supper and I found him crying over a dead rabbit. See what he says.'

Harry G. took the four pounds and Karl and set out for Edinburgh. It was more than a week before I heard from him:

Dear Joan,

We arrived here after two days' thumbing. I tried the first
name on your list and was given the phone numbers and addresses
of many friends.

Our luck was in. Barry, our next contact, said we could build
the set in his factory. Karl is already humping some iron there. We
found it on a dump. It will have to be cleaned and cut into lengths,
then we must find someone to weld it.

Norman and Janey Buchan have been great; they've not spared
themselves in their effort to help. They've found people to assist
with every aspect of the work. Will I ever get through telling people
about our cause? But we meet with such kindness from all sorts –
journalists, joiners, businessmen. It's unbelievable. Sometimes it's
hard to take – and I have to swallow hard.

We are sleeping comfortably and eating regularly, again thanks
to good friends. The work goes well. After a week in Barry's
factory the set is taking shape. We will have to upholster the seats
for the first-class compartment.

When it has all seemed hopeless someone has come along and
lifted the veil. Why should tough businessmen with factories to
run and profits to make take such care of us?

I only owe a few bob for nails.

Yours

Harry Greene

P.S. Great news – Barry will transport the whole set to the
Oddfellows Hall the day before you arrive.

P.P.S. Karl is talking politics with Janey. I wish I knew as much
as he does. But then his father named him after Karl Liebknecht,
that must have given him a good start.

Thirty-eight

The Travellers *in Edinburgh. Obraztsov plays E15:* An Enemy of the People. *George Cooper's* Schwejk *transfers to the Duke of York's, our* Arden of Faversham *and* Volpone *to the International Festival of Theatre, Paris. George's Volpone proclaimed the finest piece of acting since Orson Welles performed there. Nina makes us bankrupt for a hundred pounds. Arts Council withdraw an offer of a hundred pounds. George Cooper and Harry Corbett leave us.* Mother Courage *in Barnstaple, Devon. The* Italian Straw Hat *with the original music. The* Big Rock Candy Mountain *for Christmas. Third Scandinavian tour. Bankruptcy discharged.* Edward II *at E15. Visit from Jean Vilar.*

I t was a happy reunion in Edinburgh. Harry stood by his fantastic *Travellers* set, smiling, till Gerry clapped him on the back and nearly knocked him over. 'Good on you, Harry!' he cried. Karl ducked.

After we'd folded our tents at Bradwell, as we were crossing the ha-ha, we saw all the graceful windows of the house lit up, as for a ball. 'To show you where you belong,' said Tom.

Edinburgh was always the peak of the year for us and we were all excited by *The Travellers* and the superb set Harry Greene and Karl had made. Anne Bury and Oscar Tapper arrived with their first-born in time for the opening night. The audience acclaimed us and so, despite their political differences, did the press:

A TRAIN TWISTS ON A ONE-TRACK STAGE
The Travellers, Oddfellows Hall
The idea of this raw political melodrama is to shock.
The stage is set on a platform along the middle of the hall, laid out to represent a corridor train. The passengers come from all over Europe: a Scottish engineer, a Czech writer, an Italian worker and so on.

Where is the train going? Towards war. It is a
symbol for the modern crisis. Some passengers try
to stop it. Others, blindly or wickedly, want to go on.

The piece is powerfully acted, and has some good
scenes. Frank Elliott, a Durham miner's son of twenty-
two, is astonishingly good as an American soldier.

The author's obsession with warmongering America
and the worst outrages of the Nazis betrays a violence
of mind quite inconsistent with his pacific charter.

But that violence often rings the theatrical bell.

JOHN BARBER

After the first performance Howard took Anne and Oscar's baby
in his arms, made the sign of the Cross on her forehead, then the
Star of David, the Crescent and the Hammer and Sickle. 'Best to
be sure,' he said.

'But what's her name?' asked Avis.

'Caroline,' said Anne.

Back in Stratford we set to work at a hell of a pace. Not
content with a new play every fortnight we gave classes in a
local school for anyone interested, put on children's theatre on
Saturdays, organised jazz, calypso, skiffle, ballads and blues and
folk concerts on Sunday evenings.

The neighbours would sit by their doors listening to the music,
but only a thin trickle ever passed the box office and the seats were
at give-away prices – sixpence to two and six. The street kids made
money, blackmailing the owners of the posh cars which began to
park along Salway Road. 'Mind yer car for a couple of bob, guv?
It's liable to get scratched, down 'ere.'

'The only reason we haven't sold out,' said Harry C., as he went
looking for dimps in the stalls, 'is because nobody's asked us.'

We thought things were looking up when Sergei Obraztsov,
the Russian puppeteer, came to perform at E15 one evening. Word
got about and the place was packed. At the end, when he asked
for questions, he was answered with a roar, 'Yes. When are you

coming back?'

The gallery was full when we played *An Enemy of the People*. There was a local scandal over the state of the water at the time and we played the public meeting (Act IV) with Theatre Royal as setting and Dr Stockmann's family in a box. The audience joined in, many shouting support for Dr Stockmann. Even May and Bert from the Angel café came along to join us.

The locals often asked us to play *The Good Soldier Schwejk*. In George Cooper we now had the perfect Schwejk, and with the tunes we'd picked up in Czechoslovakia and Ern Brooks' cartoon settings, we were ready. It was a memorable first night. People crowded on to the stage to admire the drawings and talk to the actors after the show. Even Milton Shulman, the critic, was among them, his only criticism that my revolve was too small.

'It works,' I said. 'In any case, it's the only one we've got.'

A few critics were finding their way to E15 and as we couldn't afford newspaper advertising we were glad to see them, whatever they said. With *Schwejk* we were offered a fortnight at the Duke of York's.

I was summoned to the owner's office after our first night there. 'I wanted to meet the woman responsible for the horrendous piece of work which has disgraced my theatre.'

'Sorry you didn't enjoy it.'

'I was sitting next to John Gielgud and saw him hanging his head in shame.'

'Really? When was that?'

'When you had one of your soldiers micturating on stage.'

'He was only pretending. Anyway, it was a natural act among a group of soldiers waiting by a stranded railway truck, and he was way up against the painted wall with his back to the audience. From what I know of John Gielgud, I'm sure he would laugh at your reaction.'

The show transferred to the Embassy, Swiss Cottage, where we had the support of refugees from Nazi Germany who lived in the district. Meanwhile at Stratford I put on *The Chimes* with Barbara Brown and Israel Price, a recent recruit, to strengthen a company put together at random. In this case it included a rather gauche young man with a friendly face. 'Best thing you can do is fuck off to Hollywood and be a star,' I told him. 'You don't need to know anything about acting there.'

'Best advice anyone ever gave me,' he said, later, when he made it in a film called *Alfie*.

Gerry was given a subsidy of one hundred pounds by Arts Council in 1954 and West Ham promised us a hundred more if we could raise five hundred from the other councils. They were all socialists, but our survival was of no interest to them.

We were attracted to one of the finest plays in the English language, the neglected, anonymous *Arden of Faversham*, now possible because an actor who could play Arden had wandered into a rehearsal of *The Long Voyage Home* asking for a job. A wild scrum was taking place on stage as I asked the slender, handsome young man his name.

'Maxwell Shaw.'

'If you can get in among that lot, tell them your name and that you're joining the crew. The job's yours.'

After weighing them up for a few seconds he did just that.

'He knows how to time a line,' said Harry C., who was studying Mosbie, Alice Arden's lover. Alice was played by Barbara Brown. Arden, her husband, is pursued throughout the play by the blundering hired assassin, Shakebag (George Cooper). As for the poetry, Gerard Dynevor was convinced that Marlowe had a hand in the writing, it had the ring of the master. And then, there were the names.

Most of the scenes we set against three giant trees and the acting was superb. But the transport workers went on strike and the audience dwindled. Gerry disappeared with a portfolio of photos under his arm and set out as he had done so many years before, for Paris. This time to visit Claude Planson who was organising the International Festival of Theatre, held there annually. He came back, wildly excited. 'It's us,' he cried. 'We're representing England in Paris!'

'What with?'

'*Arden* and . . .'

'*Volpone*,' I said. 'The finest company in England plays the finest comedy.'

The excitement was at boiling point not only in the old Royal, but in the enemy camp also.

'Not those East End scruffs!'

'And they're a bunch of Reds!'

'They haven't enough money to transport the sets, let alone themselves.'

A kindly West End impresario offered to lend us the necessary, if we would put his name on the publicity – 'Presented by . . .' No fear! We'd sooner carry our traps on our backs. Which we did.

Gerry arrived at the French Customs looking like Samson, a *Volpone* pillar under each arm. The *douanier* smiled and held the crowd back for him.

Despite the fact that the English Ambassador was too occupied to attend our first night at the Théâtre Hébertot, we woke next day to find Paris at our feet, and, helped along by Claude Planson, our Ambassador appeared next night for *Arden of Faversham* and strolled on to the stage at the end with 'An eighteenth-century forgery!' pitched in his parliamentary voice. Then he invited us to cocktails at the Embassy, which Harry C. declined.

Next night, Ben Jonson, and 'Since Orson Welles, nothing has been seen to rival him but George Cooper's Volpone.' Gerry's dearest wish – success in Paris – had been granted him, but we hadn't the fare home. All the other companies playing at the Festival had been subsidised by their governments. Claude saw the plight we were in and found the francs we needed.

Back at E15, a surprise awaited us.

FROM MARTIN'S BANK LIMITED, MANCHESTER 4:

12th May 1955

A notice in the *Manchester Guardian* today shows that on 5th May a Petition for the winding-up of your Company was presented by Miss Nina **** and that the hearing of it is to take place on 23rd May next. Until the result of the hearing is known we must therefore stop the account of Theatre Workshop Limited and all cheques presented will, unfortunately, have to be returned unpaid.

Yours faithfully,

J.D. Townby
Manager

Arts Council withdrew their offer of a hundred pound guarantee against loss with our next play.

Theatre Workshop Ltd was wound up and somehow Gerry managed to prevent our precious property falling into the hands of the Official Receiver. Our situation was desperate, but we had to carry on. We had already made the costumes and sets for *The Legend of Pepito*, but now the props were beyond our means. It was set in Mexico. We needed beautiful rugs, hand-thrown pots. Well, wasn't the imagination the most powerful weapon in our armoury? We would imagine them, make a virtue of necessity. Yet there was a cloud hanging over the company. Was it a reaction after the triumphs of Paris?

Gerry phoned me at the lunch break. Could I come to his office? Harry C. was there, but he didn't look up.

'Harry's going,' said Gerry.

'To earn some money,' said Harry in his old between-the-teeth way.

'Will you be playing your Richard at the Devon Festival, as planned?'

'Yis,' he said, after a slight pause, got up abruptly and left.

'Tynan's got at him,' said Gerry. 'He brought Peter Brook to see *Richard II*. They gave Harry a Soho lunch and promised him a part in *Hamlet*.'

So that was why he'd been talking as if the Workshop was all washed up. It had been, 'Who'll buy the stuffed fish from the bar? How much will the switchboard fetch?' It would make it easier to go.

Harry had hardly left the room when George Cooper walked in.

'You off too, George?' I said.

'Lovely money,' he was using his squeaky, baby voice. 'Lovely grub!'

At that moment, I swear, I heard my heart crack. . . .

Gerry mentioned the Devon Festival. We had contracted to play *Richard II* and *Mother Courage* there. We needed the money. George agreed to stay that long.

Why had they chosen to go now? Now, just when we could break through? We'd stood together through thick and thin. In any case, what will happen to them, out there, in the jungle?

Well, that's their lookout.

There was still one more treat to come.

I had to play Mother Courage. When Brecht gave us permission to perform his work, it was on the understanding that I should play the heroine, but now, without our two stalwarts, I was faced with replanning the company's future programme. I gave Mother Courage to a good actress and got on with the job.

This came to Brecht's ears. Either I played the part or his permission would be withdrawn. I took over twenty-four hours before curtain up. I had no choice.

I might have got away with it but for that ****-*** hen. I had to pluck it in the first scene and it was stinking. The smell from its backside turned my stomach. Mother Courage had to stop herself vomiting for wellnigh half the play.

George and Harry went their way. Gerry changed our legal name to Pioneer Theatre Ltd and John Bury let us use his name for trading.

In 1955 we stood in the ruins of the castle which Gerry had kept standing against every storm till now. Our world looked empty. We gathered the old guard round us, the faithful who'd stayed on – and looked for new faces, among them Brian Murphy. It all seemed new and strange. Then on my birthday, one by one, they came to me and each one handed me a rose. Who thought of that? Who told them the day?

It was Max, tough, unsentimental Max.

We had to open a new season but I hadn't gathered enough strength to work on something new. We revived Lope de Vega's *Fuente Ovejuna*. And, for the next show, *The Italian Straw Hat*, Gerry traced the original music in France, rather than use Gilbert and Sullivan, as at the Old Vic.

Claude and Sue Marks designed and painted the sets. Avis as the Countess and Max as Ferdinand were brilliantly funny and my local students filled the many small parts faultlessly.

We were putting on *The Big Rock Candy Mountain*, by Alan Lomax, for Christmas and he came along to join in the fun, the nicest Alan this time, with a sackful of catchy tunes and 'Rambling Jack Elliott, the Singing Cowboy' in tow. Mind you, Rambling Jack had never seen a cow in his life, being born and bred in New York. All the same, his cowboy hat and boots caused a sensation in Angel Lane and brought the kids in. In fact, they followed him wherever he went.

Then, early in 1956, Kerstin Lind brought off another coup and we set sail for Bergen – with Gerard Dynevor replacing Harry C., Max instead of George as Shakebag – and the incomparable Barbara Brown still with us as Alice of Faversham.

When we returned the bankruptcy was discharged and Theatre Workshop could hold up its head again! We were ready for *Edward II*. I'd wanted to tackle it ever since *Richard II*. Now we had Max for Gaveston, Peter Smallwood came back to play the King before departing for the priesthood and Dudley Foster joined us.

We mounted the play on a sloping ramp which covered the whole stage, the outline of England painted on it and the northern coast of France. Gerry played Mortimer, he and his henchmen clothed in steel grey and black to contrast with the flamboyant colours of Edward and his retinue.

My *coup de théâtre* was Edward's murder – only his face was seen above a cloak held across his body and as the red-hot iron was supposed to enter his bowels the music gave a terrifying shriek.

Jean Vilar came to the show. His company was playing in town. Armand Gatti came with him. Afterwards Vilar wanted to know, Why is it always the women who resurrect the theatre in England?

Thirty-nine

Brendan Behan and The Quare Fellow. *His fare sent to Dublin twice; he drinks it. I shape the script without him. Richard Harris joins us. Paris wants* Schwejk; *this time Max Shaw plays it. The Quare Fellow transfers to the Comedy. Gerry and Joan visit Eduardo de Filippo's theatre in Naples and France Jamnik's theatre in Ljubljana. Gerry wasting away, we return with all speed to Manchester. He is taken to hospital – severe diabetes. Camel takes up the reins at E15, produces three plays financed by Dudley Foster's father. Another rebuff from Arts Council. An invitation to play the Moscow Art Theatre. Jimmie has an unfinished play. It cannot be finished in time. We mount* Macbeth *instead, with Glynn Edwards, and play Zürich en route for Moscow.*

While we were playing *Edward* a tattered bundle appeared on my desk. It was from Ireland and addressed to Ewan MacColl, who had forwarded it to me. The typing frequently went careering off the page, there were beer stains and repetitions, but you'd hardly read five pages before you recognised a great entertainer.

'Bring him over,' I said to Gerry.

There was no phone number on the script so Gerry wrote an invitation. After a few days the reply arrived: 'Drinking with some Toronto Irish. Send us an injection.'

'Who is this geezer?'

'We met his brother in Glasgow. Hamish Henderson knows them, a famous Republican family.'

Gerry sent the fare again but our new-found Rabelais guzzled that one too. The next letter carried a ticket in an AA map.

If the play was to go on, I couldn't wait for the author. It badly needed pruning: where one good story was sufficient, he'd added four or five. The title, *The Quare Fellow*, was the nickname given to the prisoner about to be topped for murder, and yet you never stopped laughing. Even the hangman told funny stories. I felt I was taking liberties with the man's work, but where was he?

He turned up on a Saturday afternoon, while *Edward* was still playing. I was told that he was in the bar, so I went to say hello. His friend, Jo McGill, was with him, but there was no mistaking our author, a good-looking Irishman, with a coxcomb of black wavy hair, a Roman nose, a few teeth missing and a pronounced stutter. He seemed incredibly shy – so did his friend Jo, for that matter, and Behan had brought him along because the thought of meeting a crowd of strange English on his own would be too much for him.

I didn't know it then, but it was the first time Brendan had visited England since his enforced stay in Borstal. Gerry had to apply to the Home Office for a dispensation which would allow him to stay for his play.

I handled the meeting as delicately as I knew how and invited them both to stay for the evening performance.

'How did you like that first speech of Gaveston's?' I asked B.B. at the interval.

'Like it? I translated it into Irish and claimed it as me own.'

Afterwards he declared that, after the Abbey, it was like watching a jet-propelled bomber.

Gerry found digs in a little house along by the railway siding, and B.B. moved in with his lovely wife Beatrice, who'd stayed with Kathleen McGill when he came to look us over. They found the simple lodging rather primitive. 'No electricity,' said Beatrice, 'in the great city of London.'

I ran the first half of *The Quare Fellow* for Brendan on the Monday morning. What would he make of it? There wasn't an Irishman in the cast. Brian Murphy was from Portsmouth, Max was a Polish Jew via Paris, Glynn Edwards a West Country man, Gerard Dynevor Welsh and the young prisoners Cypriots, but they were all wild about the play. Henry Livings, who was playing the Irish-speaking prisoner, had been studying the Irish language. There was a sense of occasion as the house lights dimmed. I sat in the front row of the gallery, listening for any sign of disapproval from the author, but all I heard were chuckles and occasional cries of, 'Me life on you.'

At the end, Duncan, a journalist, who'd come to interview Brendan, appeared at the dress-circle door, with his two pet poodles.

'I see you laugh at your own jokes, Brendan,' he said.

'Yes, but I don't fuck me own dogs,' B.B. replied.

After lunch, the company assembled in the bar and Brendan talked. He didn't mention the play but told us stories of quare fellers he'd known and Pierrepont who'd hanged them, of scows and villains and his own attempts at escape. He never once described the prison or its routine; it was as if he couldn't be bothered with the four walls, and the restrictions.

What's more, he approved of my cuts: 'Better without all that old rubbish,' he said. The 'old rubbish' was Catholic schmaltz, a throwback to boyhood.

The cast lived in that play. The only thing was, we'd nobody to play Mickser, in the prison-yard scene. It couldn't be just anybody, the way the play was shaping up. Time was getting short, I was rehearsing the scene, when a big lairy feller came striding across the stage, grinning. 'Mickser!' I cried.

'Sure,' he said. He stayed and the name stuck. His real name was Richard Harris, from Limerick.

In that theatre, on the first night, there were many Irishmen, among them three hundred years of prison sentences. Over in the pub, the Irish-speaking contingent spent the evening drinking. Brendan's Governor from Borstal was in the stalls with his wife.

'How did you like it?' B.B. asked the Irish-speakers afterwards.

'It was great, Brendan,' they told him. He was tickled pink. 'Seeing all the boys together again,' they added.

Ken Tynan captured him in the bar. 'Where were you, Brendan, when the quare feller was being topped?'

'Wanking over a copy of *Picturegoer*,' said B.B.

That party was still going strong at four in the morning, when Gerry and I left to go to bed.

Malcolm Muggeridge wanted an interview on TV the following day to include the scene in Act I where Dunlavin (Max) is having his legs massaged with meths by the screw Regan (Dudley Foster) and taking great swigs of the stuff when Regan isn't looking.

Neighbour (Gerard Dynevor) meanwhile grows furious as the supply of alcohol diminishes.

B.B. was in safe hands so I went on with rehearsals for *Schwejk* (without George). It had been requested for the year's Paris Festival. About four o'clock there was an urgent message: 'Come at once. Problems. BBC.'

Avis took over and I rushed to the TV centre. Everything seemed calm when I got there. Muggeridge looked relaxed, Brendan was half-asleep beside him.

'All went well at the rehearsal,' said Max, 'but some fools took him into the refreshment room. . .' The red light went on.

I glanced round at the other characters to be interviewed. They were waiting in open cubicles. Brendan snored. Muggeridge gave a Satanic smile. The red light came on. A flock of debs came twittering on to the central area, accompanied by their middle-aged chaperone. Brendan sat up with a start –

'I'd like to fuck you, the lot of you!' he shouted.

I hoped that with his broad accent, they wouldn't understand, but they did. They disappeared, all of them, in a flash. I'd never seen any group of people disappear so quickly.

'Did you see what I saw?' asked Muggeridge, but before I could reply two British generals in khaki, with medals, spit and polish, the lot – began talking about bomb disposal. This delighted Brendan.

'Disposed of 'em did you? I've planted more bombs than you've had hot dinners, you pox bottles.'

Muggeridge didn't seem in the least put out by these sallies, though next it was Brendan's turn to be interviewed.

'I'll kneel behind his chair, out of sight,' I whispered, 'in case he keels over.'

The meths-drinking came first and the scene went well, accompanied by cries of encouragement from the author, off screen. Then came his scene.

How wild it was, on camera, I've no idea. I was holding on to Brendan who was muttering whatever came into his head; while I prayed for it to end. End it did, with B.B. and me bundled out of the studio.

'Come on, we'll take a taxi,' I said, trying to steer him along.

'If we ever get out of this poxy place,' he replied. For we were lost in a labyrinth of passages, studios, red lights, lifts. At last we came up against a heavily barred door.

'This looks promising,' I said, but all I got back was a sleepy mutter.

'Hi Joan!'

It was the great lumbering old sergeant I used to know when I was in and out of the BBC all the time.

'Hi Sarge. Let us out, will you?'

'Sure thing. Saw you on the monitor just now Bean,' he said. 'Great stuff.'

Whether it was *The Quare Fellow* or the drink that put Brendan on the map I'll never know, but next day every bus or taxi that passed us slowed down to shout, 'Hi Brendan! You was properly pissed on TV last night. Good on yer!' And the play was safely launched, sold out, by the time we set out for Paris with *Schwejk*. This time the Workshop was at the Sarah Bernhardt, a most beautiful theatre. Avis had been given the divine Sarah's dressing-room and she was in her element. When I walked in on her she was still exploring. She'd just discovered a bath-tub, which looked like Napoleon's tomb. It was hidden behind japanned doors.

I spotted a panel which looked as if it moved. It slid back to reveal a secret stairway.

'For her lovers,' I said.

'Keep it open,' said Avis.

The dressing-room's *Côté Jardin* overlooked the Seine and the wide sky of Paris. Our new Schwejk, Max, was dressing there. He was in his element, talking elegant French, impressing the birds and conquering Paris. By now Paris was inclined to love us all.

Would London ever change its attitude to us?

The Quare Fellow transferred to the Comedy and then went on the road. It was 1956 and we'd had a crowded year.

'I need a break,' said Gerry.

'Sure, but who will keep the show up to scratch?'

'Avis has already offered.'

'I hope it won't take away from her acting.'

London was a-buzz with stories of our success:

'Have you heard about that East End lot in Paris?'

'She can have anything she wants, there.'

'Yes?'

'The place is at her feet.'

We left them to it, packed the old Alvis and headed south. 'Sunshine and swimming in a warm sea,' said Gerry, but the nights were chilly and the morning skies leaden. We were loath to leave our sleeping bags.

'Let's push on . . . Italy . . . Rome. Too many churches . . . Rain.'

It was a relief to pitch our tent on the warm grey ash of Pozzuoli.

'Naples tomorrow, and Eduardo de Filippo.' He'd invited us to his theatre when we met him at the Paris Festival. He survived like us, in the slums of a bent city. It was certainly bent – leave the motorway, walk underneath in the shadows and there you'll see the child whores, the pimps, pickpockets and hustlers, and, if you look hard, Eduardo's theatre. We only found it when we spotted a poster for *Bene Mio Core Mio*. It was all we had hoped for, as true, lively and witty as Eduardo himself.

After Naples, the ruins of Pompeii looked almost habitable. The survivors of the first earthquake had been rebuilding their homes when Vesuvius erupted again. It must have been so good living in this provincial city, soon after the death of Christ, that the inhabitants were loath to move away. Many artefacts which had been unearthed gave a clue to the life here – suits of gladiators' armour, graffiti on the stone walls: 'I fancy Uzbek, the Persian,' 'Julius is my delight.' The narrow paved streets still bore the deep ruts of chariot wheels and on either side you could see where busy shops once stood, several with the Star of David chiselled into the stone wall. In the marketplace stocks had been found. We visited the baths where delicately erotic wall paintings were still intact and we saw the calcified bodies of a young man and woman, covered in lava during the act of love.

'Poor things, clinging together for comfort.' That was Tom Driberg's mother, when she brought him here as a boy.

After Pompeii we turned north. It was time to make tracks for home. And late in the evening we were rigging the tent when an American yelled, 'Hey there! What do you think you're doing?'

'Putting up our tent.'

'I'm talking about Suez. You Brits in Suez.'

We'd no idea what he was talking about. We hadn't bought a newspaper since we left London.

'Who's in Suez?' We felt ashamed of our ignorance.

'France and Israel, they're sending troops in. They've been plotting with your Anthony Eden.'

'Well, for a start, he's not *our* Anthony Eden,' said Gerry.

'How are we going to get home? There'll be no oil.'

'Egypt was about to nationalise the Suez Canal when we left the UK.'

'That's the point, isn't it?'

It's hard to be blamed for the sins of one's government, but that's the way of it.

There was a September chill in the air as we decamped early next morning. In Florence Gerry stopped to drink at every fountain. In Venice there was such a downpour we had to skip from bar to bar. St Mark's looked like a blurred Impressionist painting. The Alvis was flooded, our sleeping bags soaked.

'We can't sleep out.'

'We should start the trek north.'

'We may never come this way again. Let's take a look at Yugoslavia.'

And in the late afternoon, we made for the frontier.

The first signpost I saw read, 'Trieste 40 kms.'

'We should stop off there, in honour of Richard Burton.'

'It'll be too late, it's already dark.'

All we could see on either side of the road were huge boulders.

'We seem to have missed the town.'

'Where next?'

'Ljubljana. It isn't a densely populated country.'

On . . . between banks of darkness which could have been hills or clouds. Once we saw glimmering lights far away. We weren't going to find a camping site, that was for sure. As soon as we came upon human habitation, Gerry pulled up and went looking for lodging. He found a room, clean and spacious. I hastily packed a night bag and followed him in. He was already stripped and under the shower.

'Gerry, what's happened to you? You've gone so thin.'

He turned to glance at himself in the mirror, but only laughed.

'Let's go home,' I said.

'After we've seen the town. It has a famous theatre.'

We went there next day. France Jamnik, the director, wanted to know all about our theatre. Were we free? During the war, each brigade of the Yugoslav Resistance had its own poet. Now they put poets in gaol.

'What happened?'

'When it was over, good people went home to take up their lives, and the running of the country fell into the hands of the second-rate.'

Gerry asked him if he'd like to work in England for a while.

Next morning we left early, taking the route by fairytale Bled, which France had mapped out for us. In the foothills of Austria we ran into a flurry of snow. Soon it began to form a carpet and the old Alvis coughed. I was afraid she was going to stall and she did, on a steep incline. We pushed and heaved and shovelled the snow from under the wheels but before long Gerry was exhausted. 'We must find help.'

We trudged on and up, where the snow lay in deep drifts, and at last we saw a log hut. There were people there, smoke was rising from the chimney. It was a mountain rest for woodmen and lumberjacks and we were given a seat by a blazing log fire and a mug of hot toddy. Four of the men collected a coil of rope and drove down the hill to rescue the Alvis. After a while they reappeared with our poor old jalopy in tow; what's more, they managed to start the engine, but by now darkness had fallen and they advised us to stay the night. 'Better to see where you're going up here.'

So we dined on strong sausage and boiled potatoes and slept under a warm coverlet. In the morning our hosts wouldn't look at our money. 'You're always welcome,' they said as we prepared to go.

Then it was up hill and down dale, but the hills were mountains and the valleys deep and I had only one thought: let the Alvis hold out till we get to England, then to Manchester to a doctor. There was one he trusted there – a schoolfriend.

We stopped in London to park the banger, buy tickets for

Manchester and phone Tom Driberg. His secretary was very cagey: 'He's abroad.' That's all she would say.

We guessed where he would be. After the dramatic reappearance of Guy Burgess and Donald Maclean at the National Hotel, Moscow, in February 1956 Tom had written care of the same hotel asking Guy for an interview. They had known each other when Tom was on *The Week in Westminster* and Guy was BBC representative at the House of Commons. Just before we left England Tom was surprised to receive a favourable reply. He was too good a journalist to miss the Burgess interview, so we were pretty sure that Moscow was where he would be.

As soon as we met Gerry's doctor he whipped him straight into hospital. Ralph, Gerry's elder brother, offered me hospitality and I waited three long days before I knew the truth.

'Diabetes,' said Gerry when they brought him home.

'It would take more than that to get a Raffles down,' said Ralph. 'It just means he can't make love so much. Don't let it worry you, J.L.'

When we were alone Gerry said they'd given him a taste of what would happen if his diet wasn't balanced with the insulin intake.

'You have to take insulin?'

'An injection every morning, after a urine test.'

'And the diet?'

'No wine, for a start. It's full of sugar.'

That would be hard, but a life without Gerry? Impossible. I held him in my arms. His flesh felt soft. It had never been like that before.

'How long will it take to cure him?'

'Perhaps two years,' said the doctor, but he was lying. Gerry was never cured.

I did not know then about the terrifying bouts of hypoglycaemia to come, but I knew we could not go back to the rough-and-ready life we'd lived for so long. We couldn't even leave his brother's home till the doctor was satisfied that Gerry's condition was stabilised.

John Bury took up the reins at E15 and met with an Arts Council attack straight away:

Where was the local support Gerry had predicted?

Where were the returns for last year?

Where was the budget for next year?

'You will have to wait for the Raffles' return,' John Bury told them.

Gerry's younger brother, Eric, invited us to his home for Christmas but we felt we would be *de trop*.

'Not at all,' said Gillian, his wife. 'I'm preparing a special diabetic Christmas for Gerald, to welcome him back to the fold.'

It sounded slightly menacing, but after all, we'd nowhere else to go. In fact the meal was excellent and Gillian's father proposed a toast: 'To the Queen, God bless her! You know she's giving her Christmas message in Yiddish today.'

It wasn't long before Gerry was fretting to get back to E15. 'I can't leave it to Camel.'

'We must find somewhere to live, first. Camel won't mind holding the fort a little longer.' In fact he had a faithful team with him – Dudley Foster and his wife Eileen Kennally, Glynn Edwards and Yootha Joyce, Brian and Carol Murphy, Avis, Josie Benson, Barry Clayton and Peter Smallwood.

Dudley's father had financed *Captain Brassbound's Conversion*, *The Playboy of the Western World* and *The Duchess of Malfi*, then he drew the line. It was January and the draughty old place still had no heating. Anybody and everybody tried their hand but that boiler would not stay alight. Camel appealed to Arts Council:

We have no boiler, half the seats in the auditorium are beyond repair. It is an imposition asking people to pay to come in. Your suggested grant of five hundred pounds a year is unrealistic.

A reply came by return:

I don't think there's the slightest chance of Arts Council voting you any money for redecoration and the Drama Panel does not consider our offer unrealistic.

'Better go foreign till the weather improves,' said Camel.

Letters went to every contact we had in Europe – Germany wanted Littlewood, Switzerland offered three days, Holland was thinking about us, Romania, Bulgaria and China told us to keep in touch. Then, a letter from Moscow – the Art Theatre during the World Youth Festival!

I asked Jimmie if his new play, *So Long at the Fair*, would be ready. 'Sure,' he said.

When we drove across Blackheath to discuss the production at his new home in Croydon, an old-fashioned fair was in full swing . . . tin trumpets blowing, side drums banging, galloping hobby horses and gilded dragons. A good omen?

Jimmie said his play would be ready in a week. On the way back we stopped on Blackheath. Gerry had noticed 'Flat to Let' on an old house there. The next day he investigated.

'How was it?'

'Perfect. Nobody will ever find us.'

'Did you take it?'

'Of course. The owner was weeding the garden when I got there, she showed me round, quoted the rent and I accepted.'

We moved in – ourselves, one bed, one bookcase with books and a desk. Gerry's mother helped us with bedding and Tom came in a taxi to give us good advice.

'You do know, I suppose, that rooms have to be cleaned every day?'

'Anyone would think we'd never lived in a house, Tom.' As a matter of fact, we hadn't.

'I would have preferred the Paragon, but this is quite roomy.' I knew he was considering moving in, his bachelor flat in Bloomsbury was being requisitioned.

'We'll be having a house-warming soon,' I said.

'A party?'

'No, a reading of Jimmie's new play.'

'But you've no chairs, where will they sit?'

'On their backsides.'

When the day came the play was by no means finished. Dudley Sutton and Richard Harris seemed familiar with the first scene. Obviously they had already heard it. Was Jimmie so pleased with his opening, or just stuck? It was extraordinarily vivid – a demobbed soldier's reaction to the adverts as he rides down the escalator to the tube train. It was fiery, vivid and Jimmie read it beautifully. Richard hugged himself with delight. It was a monologue any actor would glory in, but there was no dialogue, not till the second scene when the soldier joins his comrades and they wander round a fair. Here, there was a hint of several sub-plots. Was it to be another *Bartholomew Fair*? Difficult to analyse, impossible to stage in a Palladio-style theatre.

The company listened quietly. Several of them had known the seduction of *The Other Animals*. The reading petered out. Nobody actually said 'What's the plot?' and Jimmie said nothing. We dispersed with thanks and good wishes.

When they'd gone, I asked Jimmie how much time he needed. After all Webster took two years over a play.

'I can't write to a deadline,' he said.

'Well, we'd better say goodbye to Moscow.'

What could we play? I couldn't think. Next morning Dudley Foster approached me. 'Are we going to Moscow?'

'If only we had a play about the evil assumption of power.'

'You believe in evil?'

'Certainly I do.'

'So what the hell do we play?'

'*Macbeth*,' I said, without thinking.

'What will Jimmie say to that?'

'I don't know, but he'd make a marvellous *Macbeth*.'

Dudley looked non-committal. I invited Jimmie to Blackheath and put the idea to him. He flew into a rage. All his early dislike of the classics surfaced. He mounted his agitprop horse and called me a bourgeoise.

Someone was knocking at the door. 'When are you going to get some covering on your floor? We can hear every word downstairs.'

Jimmie washed his hands of us and I got on with producing *Macbeth*. I wondered if Joe Stalin had a Russian translation and who could play it? Richard Harris had fire in his belly, but his speech rhythms were pure Irish. I'd have to stay up all night showing him how to use the iambics. Glynn Edwards looked impressive but his gentle nature shone through, whatever he did.

For better or for worse I chose Glynn and set about stripping the play of the usual trimmings – no Highland mist, no bagpipes, no dry ice for the weird sisters, mine were three old biddies with a penchant for fortune-telling, such as you might meet at any time on a road to the isles.

Macbeth's return to the witches (Act IV, Scene i), a scene sometimes attributed to Middleton, we played as a nightmare, Macbeth tossing and turning on his bed, imagining the old women in the room with him and seeing the pageant of kings only in his mind's eye. This way it made sense; as usually played it is an illogical pantomime, whoever wrote it.

On the train to Zürich, our first date, I wrote the programme notes: 'Shakespeare's Macbeth bears no relation to the leader of that name who figures prominently in Scottish history; with Gruach, his wife, he led his people on a long march to avoid the English invader. . . .' Here the train pulled up with a jolt and I caught a glimpse of Brian Murphy and Richard Harris as they hurried along the platform. I picked up the thread. . . . 'Shakespeare was more concerned with the problem of usurpation than with a heroic figure unknown to him, and therefore of no interest. . . .' We were on the move again. 'The play has been obscured since Elizabethan times by the demands of popular actors such as Edmund Kean; and designers bent on pageantry.' There was a scuffling in the corridor. It was Lady Macbeth hanging on to Banquo's (her husband's) coat-tails.

'I warned them,' she said.

'Who?'

'Brian and Richard. I knew they'd be left behind.'

'So now can I have my coat back?' said Dudley, and disappeared.

'I'm trying to finish my notes!' I shouted. 'Nobody else leave the train, please.'

My notes and that train advanced by stops and starts, but by the time we heard, 'Next stop Zürich, five minutes' wait,' I'd finished.

'Where?' said Avis, waking from a long snooze.

'We've arrived! And there's a brass band to meet us.'

There was, and the flags of Great Britain and Switzerland

fluttered in the breeze as Gerry and Joan, Avis and Olive, Dudley and Eileen stepped down on to the platform.

'Where's the rest of us?'

Olive, our Lady Macbeth, smiled sweetly. 'Well, Glynn went to look for Richard,' she said, 'and Frances Cuka went to look for Glynn and Roger went to look for Frances . . . and . . .' Olive was quite new to the company, but didn't seem put out.

'Okay,' said Gerry. 'Just keep smiling. Somebody make a speech.' And he went off to try and locate our lost sheep. The Committee of Welcome were looking rather puzzled.

'Don't worry. We'll all be here tonight,' I told them. 'Meanwhile, I'm starving.'

It was the half-hour call when we heard a noisy crowd approaching the theatre. It was the rest of our gang, escorted by a gang of rowdy students, who turned out to be our audience! I was still staring at the vast, dim stage, draped in black velvet – it looked so funereal, needed another dozen lamps.

The show was funereal too. Glynn went slow. The students barracked. Nobody knew enough German to shout back. Nothing took fire, except my temper.

I bollocked everybody. It was lively enough on the next two nights.

Forty

To Moscow! To the great Moscow Art Theatre, the acme, Mecca, pinnacle of theatrical art. The gauge was changed at the frontier, then we steamed on into the new world. Every time the train stopped and that was often, there were speeches of welcome and large bunches of red flowers. At one station, among towering pine trees, a very tall man in a battered old hat stepped out from the shadows and began to sing. It was the voice of a Chaliapin, deep and thrilling, like the forest. It was all very moving, but we were getting hungry.

'Has anyone got any grub?'

No one had anything to eat. What a feckless lot we were! Even when we reached Moscow and the bus was waiting to take us to the theatre and, we hoped, refreshment, one of the girls wanted to speak to the engine-driver.

'My Dad's an engine driver' was all she wanted to say, but as he didn't understand a word of English a translator had to be found, while our bellies kept on rumbling. Even at the sight of that world-famous sign MXAT all we could think about was food. It was waiting for us, laid out on a long table, black bread, wurst, cheese, wallies, red caviare and Russian tea. We helped ourselves while the smiling *regisseur* waited to show us round.

Each dressing-room had a brass plaque on the door bearing the name of some famous Moscow Art performer.

'Which is your leading lady?' he asked.

'We don't have one – Lady Macbeth may be playing the skivvy tomorrow.'

'Who is Skivvy?'

'Maid of all work,' said Eileen Kennally and had her hand kissed and her name pinned up on to the most imposing door. There was a lot of hand-kissing and a lot of star treatment. Whenever we stepped out on to the street, a crowd would gather, ready to escort us anywhere. Gerry and I became separated from the rest and at once we were captured by Muscovites who marched us to the head of a bus queue and placed us there, as they recited a list of English football teams. All we could reply was 'Dynamos.'

Moscow was a city of contrasts – St Basil's in all the colours of boiled sweets opposite GUM, their big store which wouldn't have looked out of place in Stockport; Tolstoy's old house in soft green against high-rise blocks in china white.

'We're pulling them down next week.'

I hoped the drama of Moscow wouldn't weaken our performance.

It didn't. The famous stage inspired us and at the final curtain, among a hot-house of bouquets and nosegays, a host of young people surrounded us.

'Why the twentieth-century costumes?'

'Why no scenery?'

'Where is the English classical style?'

Every member of the company was being plied with questions.

'Speaking the verse with its inherent rhythm is classical.'

'The poetry sets the scene.'

'The modern costumes serve to underline the eternal problem of evil rule and usurpation.'

We were told to go and see Oklopkov's *Hamlet* and with fraternal greetings and the pledge of eternal friendship, we were escorted to supper.

For a long time I'd worshipped Oklopkov from afar. Any friend about to visit Moscow would be asked to bring back a complete account of his work. R.J. Finnemore saw *The Iron Flood* and found himself cutting bread for the play's guerrilla band and finishing up on stage with them. The next night he saw Pogodin's *Aristocrats* and tried to show us how a girl had descended a mountain slope on skis, bending this way and that, ski sticks in hand. 'Masked figures should be dancing by,' he said, 'brushing me with branches, scattering handfuls of paper snow.'

'Chinese theatre,' I said.

'Fascinating,' said Ronnie Finnemore.

I made for the Oklopkov Theatre at the earliest opportunity. I was surprised to be shown into a conventional Victorian auditorium, then the curtain rose, on time, to reveal night on the battlements, spotlight shafts suggesting moonlight as they slowly faded in and out. The ghost is always a challenge to the lighting man. Shakespeare made us use our imagination.

> *But, look, the morn in russet mantle clad,*
> *Walks o'er the dew of yon high eastern hill*

and that in the afternoon at the Globe. Next, the court, authentic period setting, and well-grouped courtiers. I know the play by heart, but I was having some difficulty in identifying the characters. Who is the fat man in the corner wearing black bloomers? Not . . . It is! Gertrude must favour 'He's fat and scant of breath' in the duel scene rather than 'faint'! Bit risky at this point so near to 'Oh that this too, too solid flesh would melt.'

I timed this speech. It took ten minutes! Why this slow delivery? Perhaps Ophelia will liven things up.

No! It's unbelievable. A middle-aged woman walks on, an underling brings her a harp and a stool. She sits and tries a glissando. This is Ophelia! Her ladies appear and dance around her to some Slavonic air. The scene hasn't begun yet. I can't take much more. Two-hour traffic? At this rate we wouldn't be home till midnight. Where's the Oklopkov of yesteryear? He had been made Minister of Culture.

Edging out of my seat, I escaped to the ice-cream parlour where a poorly dressed young man accosted me, thrusting a piece of paper into my hand, his name and address on it, in Cyrillic writing.

'My painting,' he said, 'you must see it.'

How long had he been waiting there?

'You paint here?'

'I change scenery here.'

'I will try to come.'

Next day we went to the National Hotel to leave a packet of curry powder for Guy Burgess. We had hoped to have good news for him, his dearest wish was to return to England. He couldn't come to terms with the Soviet Union. He hadn't been long in Moscow before he was writing to the head of the KGB, Beria, denouncing the secret police for their uncivilised behaviour. Luckily for him the letter was intercepted by a sympathetic official, otherwise we would have heard no more of Guy. Tom kept trying the Home Office, pointing out that Guy's mother was old and ailing. Guy would phone our home in Blackheath once or twice a week for news; we were still hoping for a change of heart when we left London. As it happens we did not believe that he was a traitor, but even if he were it would have been an act of mercy to let him pass the rest of his life in England instead of dying of boredom in the Soviet Union.

Moscow was basking in a summer heatwave, so we stopped at one of the many open-air cafés to enjoy an ice-cream and watch the world go by. 'Is today a holiday?' I asked the head waiter.

'Every day there are some on holiday,' he said. 'There is no official Sunday.'

We lunched in a station buffet, where roast sucking pig and Russian champagne were served at a marble-topped counter, yet through the open door we could see hundreds of peasants squatting on the platform, patiently waiting for their train. All the railway stations were christened 'Vauxhalls' by the Scottish architect who designed them.

We visited Moscow's Selfridges – GUM. It was very quiet apart from the cacophony in the music department, where young men in Red Army uniform walked up and down trying the accordions. The cashier totted up the price of our wooden pigeons on an abacus and we made for the exit. A Red Army officer, his wife and children with him, was rebuking some boys for making the revolving doors turn too fast and surprisingly, they were quietly listening.

Gerry was constantly at the Bulgarian Embassy checking on

the tour of their country due to take place after Moscow. I found time to visit the young man who'd waited for me at Oklopkov's theatre, our guide having translated his name and address. He lived in a high-rise block built for students. He smiled when he saw me and let me into a small room, made smaller by the stacks of boards leaning against the walls. He started turning them over, only pausing to move his bed-roll. Striking paintings were revealed – a ravaged Madonna, emaciated hands, pleading hands.

'I remember the siege of Leningrad,' he said. 'It was my home.'

The paintings stunned me, as if I were seeing Goya's 'Horrors of War' for the first time. I asked him to stop at one, stranger than the rest. A man stood in the foreground watching a funeral, an open coffin being carried through a barren landscape.

'It is his own funeral,' the artist explained. 'And there at the back is the man, as a boy.' That painting held me. It had a unique atmosphere, no influence of contemporary art had touched this young man. How could it? He'd had no contact with modern art.

'You like it? Take it! Take them all. It's my only chance.'

'Your only chance is a foreign dealer.'

'You could take them to him among your properties.'

'The Customs in England and Russia have a detailed list of everything we brought with us.'

'My only chance.'

'English critics think Russian art is Lenin addressing the people or that giant aluminium statue of a young man and woman which breaks down into cubes for transport.'

'I would cut my paintings into cubes if they could go to England.'

I thought of him when we landed at Dover and the Customs Officer turned over every page of my copy of *Macbeth*.

In London I tried to interest one or two dealers in the paintings I described, but nobody fancied a trek to that obscure Muscovite hostel.

Sergei Obraztsov, the pupper master who had played at E15, when he heard that we were in his home town, invited us all to tea.

His apartment was on the first floor of an old-fashioned house in nineteenth-century Moscow, where many of the original members of the Moscow Art company had lived. He showed us souvenirs from all over the world – a Mickey Mouse from Hollywood, a Chinese lantern from Peking, little sticks which opened to form a paper sun. . . .

'From a souk in Calcutta,' he said. 'And did you notice my mice?' He pointed to a wood carving of mice, holding a captured cat tied up with strings.

A buxom woman came in carrying a large cake which looked like a painting in a child's story book. 'My nanny,' he said, as she placed the cake in the middle of a round table set for afternoon tea. 'She baked it for you this morning.'

Nanny seemed to understand what he was saying and with a friendly gesture, invited us all to take our place at the table.

'Will you do the two billiard balls making love?' asked Lady Macduff (Olive Macfarland – too young to play the part, but so good it didn't matter).

'I'm afraid someone is using them for their proper purpose,' said Sergei, 'but I could do for you the operatic bass singing *Boris Godunov* when he was rather the worse for drink.' And he pulled out a glove puppet who looked like a sponge and sang.

Over tea he mentioned his many years as an actor.

'Why did you leave live theatre for puppets?' asked Dudley Sutton.

'My puppets are alive,' he said, and at that his table napkin began to dance. Afterwards he told me that he'd had to give up theatre because he disagreed with the party's cultural diktat. Then he changed the subject. He didn't want to spoil a merry tea party. We were very sorry to say goodbye. As we got up to go I repeated the question thrown at him by the audience at E15: 'When are you coming back?'

Outside, as we moved down the front steps into the street, flowers and petals floated down round us. We looked up – at every balcony friendly neighbours waved goodbye.

Adieu, dear hearts. . . .

On Gerry's first free evening (he was playing Malcolm in *Macbeth*) we decided to try for a typically Muscovite entertainment.

'*The Fountains of Bakhchisaray* by Zakharov,' said Gerry. 'Just the job.' Out of respect for his Russian grandfather we did the thing in

style – and took a taxi. The building was imposing, a wide flight
of steps led up to the façade which was suffused with pink light.
If only we'd brought that opera cloak from the wardrobe, the one
lined with white satin.

There was a palatial bar beside the foyer with a tessellated
floor and Corinthian columns.

'Champagne?' said Gerry.

'I don't mind if I do. Cheers.'

'Have another.'

By the time we'd finished the bottle we were floating. The
enormous orchestra tuned up as we found the way to our places
and the curtain rose to melodious tinkling music. Soon I had to
close my eyes as wild Bashkirs and ferocious Turks fought like
furies, their armour glittering, swords flashing, heads on lances
passing till, thank God, we moved to a peaceful garden where
the fountains of the title flowed with . . . I could have sworn –
real water.

More battles, more gardens, but all the time the fountains
played on. Gerry loved spectacle and transformation scenes but
by the end of the first act he was fast asleep.

'Gerry, wake up! There's a cast of thousands taking a curtain!'

'You said you were cutting the company down.'

'Do wake up, love, you were snoring very loudly.'

'Sorry. It's so relaxing here where the show has nothing to
do with us.'

'How are you, Joan?' It was definitely an English voice. I
turned, startled. A tall, rather heavily built man was looking at
me. With him, a group of smiling dignitaries; they looked rather
like the Bashkirs in the show. The intruder thrust a card into my
hand; it was in Russian. 'Do come by for a dish of tea one day. I'd
love to talk,' and he was gone.

'Let's go, Gerry.' I felt uneasy, trying to place the man. He
was from the remote past, Manchester perhaps. Who could it be?

We walked home and forgot the mysterious stranger.

Macbeth was attracting a young audience. It was only the
old-fashioned theatregoers who decided we weren't classical and
though they didn't talk about it the students seemed to grasp the
parallel with their own political leadership. Their English was

remarkably good. One of them asked me the difference between a tarn and a lake, then kept me up half the night checking through Samuil Marshak's translation of Robbie Burns.

Gerry and I spent pleasant hours wandering through sunny Moscow, or sitting in one of the quiet squares where people go to read. We visited Tolstoy's house, now a literary club; the librarian, once a famous author, had been demoted by the Stalinists. He was very proud of the books in his care and talked of the glories of Russian literature. We looked in at the National Library, the biggest in the world, they said, and took a boat trip along the Moscow River.

'Aren't you going to visit your mysterious stranger?'

'Should I?'

'If only to satisfy your curiosity.'

'Your curiosity, Gerry. I didn't think he looked all that interesting.'

Anyway, I went. It was quite a smart apartment. In Moscow modern flats tend to be rather skimpy. The gentleman opened the door to me himself.

'It's you. Good. Do come in.'

We entered a book-lined room, the walls and upholstery apple green. A Russian woman sat at a large table typing.

'My wife,' said my host.

'How do you do?' I said. He spoke to her in Russian and she gathered up some papers and left the room.

'She'll make tea for us.'

His attitude to me was cool but courteous. He sounded brusque with his wife.

'I'm afraid you have the better of me.'

'You mean you don't recognise me?'

'Well, if we ever met it must have been a long time ago.'

'Cast your mind back . . . to Manchester, or more recently to the Polevoi article.'

That voice. That rather literary manner. 'You're not . . . You used to write for the . . . ?'

'*Manchester Guardian*,' he said, and in my head Jack Evans's words came back to me, 'Now he writes for the KGB.'

'You always kept your cards close to your chest,' I said,

remembering how he'd been considered very right wing. 'You called us left-wing buttresses, remember? We were to be seen each lunch-hour propping up the pillars outside the Central Library.'

'What a good memory you have.'

'Yes – Rafe Parker.'

'I didn't forget *your* name. You seem to be doing rather well for yourself.'

'Not as well as you,' I said. Now that I knew who he was, I scrutinised him. 'That man is a spy,' Jack had said.

'They'll tell you I fill my petrol tank at the American Embassy,' said Parker. 'Wouldn't they, if they had the chance?'

The wife came in with tea and he gave his orders. I felt uncomfortable. He tried old-times chat, but I wanted to escape. Maybe Jack Evans had been wrong. Maybe not. In any case I didn't like what Rafe Parker had become. I'd never liked him much anyway. I wondered if *he* could get back to Britain to see his mother.

This wasn't the only strange encounter in Moscow. A few of us were attending a meeting in the House of Trades Unions when a working man, aged about fifty, approached Gerry and me.

'Wincott's the name,' he said. 'Len Wincott.'

'Not Able Seaman Wincott, Invergordon Mutiny?' I said it almost as a joke. It seemed unlikely.

'I took the rap,' he said.

'Weren't they scared you meant to join up with the unemployed and march on London?' Gerry asked.

'That was our intention.'

'So you claimed sanctuary with the Workers' Republic.'

'Workers Republic my ****. The swine, I'd no sooner landed here than they slung me in gaol.'

'In gaol. What . . .' but I checked myself in time.

'Bastards, I told them, wait till the English get here – they'll put you in your place.'

He spoke very bitterly, yet there was this twisted patriotism in him. Strange from this Red revolutionary.

On the day of our departure for Bulgaria Camel and Gerry went to the station early to be sure our truck had been shunted on to the right track. We'd labelled the crates in English, French and Cyrillic, too many companies had lost everything at railway junctions. Camel went down the line to check on the truck while Gerry filled in the necessary forms at the stationmaster's office. After a few minutes he came running out waving the papers.

'Camel,' he yelled. 'Get her back.'

Our truck was already clanking out of the station, on the line for Sofia.

'What's wrong?'

'They've cancelled the Anglo-Bulgarian Friendship week. They're having Soviet-Bulgarian Friendship instead.'

Forty-one

A script from Henry Chapman, You Won't Always Be On Top.
*Unproducible, no plot, shape, no sex-an'-violence, but some quaint
turns of phrase. The enjoyment of making possible the impossible. We
do it. The show goes on. Visits from plain-clothes cops. I'm invited to
East Berlin. Sir W.E. Williams of Arts Council friendlier than his
colleagues, but no money unless local boroughs cough up. Directing at
the Maxim Gorki Theatre. France Jamnik takes my place at E15. The
joy of working with the German company. I meet Ernst Hoffmann
again. He was my Friedrich Engels in a radio play I wrote in 1939.*

On the way back to London we took good care not to lose sight
of that truck, or the company. Olive was arrested at the DDR
frontier; she'd mislaid her visa. We left her there – it would
be easier to free her through diplomatic channels in London than
tangle with the German police.

Back at the theatre Gerry waded into the bills, Camel sifted
the requests for auditions, I picked out two plays from the stack
– a page or two would tell me if the author had an ear.

'There's some panicky weather comin' over from Beachy 'Ead.'

'Where's our sillyborn ganger got to?'

'Suppin' tea with the Pension Mush?'

'I can eat an apple wi' my false teeth.'

'I can eat an apple wi' me own teeth.'

'Give us a bunk up.'

'Don' be silly.'

'I don' weigh no more than a li'l ole blackberry . . .'

'We've four hundred quid to come,' said Gerry.

'When?'

'Next year. Barking, Leyton, Shoreditch and Walthamstow
offer us a hundred each.'

'Can they spare it?'

I escaped. I wanted to study that Beachy Head script, *You*

Won't Always Be On Top. There was no plot, no drama, just men going to work on a building site in the rain on a Monday morning, and the story of their day. We would have to cope with bricklaying, pipelaying, carpentry, scowing . . . the whole stage area from the back wall to the stalls, from side exit to loading bay, would have to be transformed.

It was a challenge, to express the inexpressible with a few well-worn sayings picked up from a previous generation – but feelings as profound and strange as yours and mine. The author, Henry Chapman, obviously knew the building job.

First, to take a look at the real thing. There were building sites all round us. A pint with a ganger over at the Lion and we were in. Of course the actors wanted to try their hand at everything.

'They're as comical as a pantomime,' said one of the carpenters.

'We do know what work means,' said Dudley Foster.

'Why did you give it up, tosh?'

'The pay's better,' said Dudley. He became our foreman Brickie, laying real bricks right up the back wall. Brian Murphy, head carpenter, measured up, sawed and did his joinery at floor level. Mickser ran a wheelbarrow across the site from time to time. The ganger was here, there and everywhere. We invented a few characters and situations when the play needed livening up – a cultured architect appeared under a large umbrella, a trades union representative came to address the men during the lunch-break and we had to do something about Henry's tea-boy. 'He's a Christlike figure,' he told Dudley Sutton who was playing the part and Dudley's face fell. He tried looking holy, the rest took the piss, so he floated in draped in a white sheet . . . and gave up.

'Henry,' I said, 'can't we just make him mad about Handel's *Messiah*, and forget the saintliness?'

He agreed. In fact he joined in the ad lib sessions, liked the way the show was developing and helped it along.

At one rehearsal Mickser paused with his wheelbarrow beside the big hole centre stage, the trap door, well masked, which we'd left open.

'Fill that in,' said the ganger.

'Sure,' said Mickser, but next day he took it into his head

to christen the hole with a watering can. 'I name this hole . . .' and he'd name some London landmark like Piccadilly Circus, or St Paul's cathedral, threatening collapse at the time. Every day in the lunch break Brian would read an item from the morning paper which struck him as amusing.

One day Mickser sang 'She walks through the Fair'.

'Let's keep it in,' I said. 'We'll find a place for it.'

A young man with his leg in plaster strayed in. 'I'm on the sick list,' he said, 'so I thought I'd see what you're up to,' and he promptly sat down and joined in a game of cards. . . .

'Cor, I've got a hand 'ere more like a foot.'

'You're on, if you can find yourself a job,' I said. He picked up a pipe and started tapping on it. It was 1957 and during the run, the Russians launched the first Sputnik. Stephen Lewis, the pipe tapper, put her to good use, hoisting his pipe like a telescope as the curtain fell. 'She's slowing down,' he said.

I didn't want a fixed show; leaving it open to fresh ideas seemed more important than polished repetition. On the other hand, extempore happenings were not allowed to spoil the rhythm of the mainstream. We would check up on the situation if this threatened and either cut the ad lib or develop it.

One night, two plain-clothes cops were sighted, taking notes. Ruth Parham, who ran the bar, spotted them as soon as they came in.

'As long as they paid for their seats,' said Gerry.

They turned up again two nights later. I knew that show inside out but I still would have been hard put to it to note everything that was being said and done.

The show proved very popular. It reminded the locals of *The Ragged Trousered Philanthropists*. Robert Noonan (Tressell was his pen-name) had influenced Henry, who had been involved in the reissue of Noonan's work in 1955. The earlier editions had been politely censored.

We ended the run in high spirits: as usual, a drink from the bar, a bit of horseplay then an all-night de-rig. There was always a moment of regret as we took apart the set we had lived in for two weeks, but in two days' time we'd be in another. On with the show.

And the Wind Blew, our next play, came from the north of

Brazil, where people were praying, night and day, for rain. Edgard da Rocha Miranda, the author, was very keen for his play to be seen in London, but none of the commercial managements was interested. I loved the play and the folk tunes his wife played for us, on the accordion. She also gave us beautiful fabrics from Brazil. Camel surpassed himself with the set and Mickser gave a remarkable performance as Monsignor Gusmao, who prayed with his people. Unfortunately, in the late fifties English people were unaware of the dramatic situation developing in so many South American countries. A few years later and *And the Wind Blew* would have been highly successful.

When the show was safely launched, I paid a visit to East Berlin, where I was shortly to produce *Unternehmen Ölzweig*, a German version of Jimmie's *Operation Olive Branch*. Maxim Vallentin, intendant of the Maxim Gorki theatre, met me at Schönfeld airport and drove me to the Hotel Adlon, a distinguished and impressive old place whose back windows looked out on West Berlin. I knew of Maxim's work with the 'Red Megaphones' and was delighted to meet him. France Jamnik from Ljubljana was to take my place at E15.

My two days in East Berlin, or rather in the Maxim Gorki theatre, were very satisfying. I looked forward to working there. Back home I found Gerry waving a cheque for three hundred pounds at me.

'Where did you get it?'

'It's a donation.'

Arts Council got the same reply when they asked him where it came from.

'A donation is a donation – period,' said Gerry and asked me what I thought of *Man, Beast and Virtue* with Mickser and Olive Macfarland. I loved Pirandello, gave them all my blessing and looked out my German grammar.

Gerry tried to call a meeting of local authorities before I left. Dagenham and Romford wrote that it 'was not worth their while to attend', West Ham agreed to come and to our amazement Sir W.E. Williams and Mr Jo Hodgkinson arrived from Arts Council. Williams addressed himself particularly to the representative from West Ham.

'We have a high regard for the adventurous and courageous policy of this company which, in our view, makes a unique and timely contribution to the drama of our time. I have just learned that the local authorities' contribution amounts to no more than five hundred pounds. This means a serious danger of Theatre Workshop going down. We are prepared to give one thousand pounds, if the local authorities, between them, will contribute as much.'

We were also given a cheque for a hundred pounds by Arts Council, with which they had guaranteed *And the Wind Blew* against loss. It was signed 'Anthony Field' – a friend at last. He had known our work in Manchester and liked it.

I was going away happy in the belief that our relationship with Arts Council would be easier in the future, but at the last moment I asked Gerry if he could spare Camel for a while? He had finished designing the Pirandello, spoke German and, what was more, understood my peculiar language. Like everyone else, I relied on Gerry to keep the Workshop afloat. Some seemed to believe that he had access to a goldmine, others that he could work miracles, which he did.

'At least you won't be able to rewrite the script in German,' he said, as he waved goodbye.

A small delegation from the Maxim Gorki met me at the airport. Camel was to follow later. We drove through quiet boulevards, made slightly sinister by parked railway trucks.

'What's in them?'

'Sets. The theatre stores are overflowing.'

We came to Maxim Gorki. *Das kleine Theater unter den Linden*. It was not pretty; it had been built during the War, but there was a warmth of welcome the moment you stepped inside. The rehearsal schedule was already posted. Digs? I liked the sound of Frau Schlissel's rooming house in a popular quarter, about a mile from the theatre. I was right. It was perfect – warm and friendly, the walk to work fascinating.

I was up early the following morning – East Berlin was a dawn city. I liked the look of the café on Friedrichstrasse Station. It was rowdy with local youth, the '*halb starkers*', laughing and shouting, some prancing about just to show off their red corduroy boots. I ordered a large black coffee and a slice of apple pie.

Outside, a giant news panel spanned the railway bridge bringing us the world's news. Sometimes a word would be so long that you couldn't wait to see the end of it.

At the theatre I was by no means the first to arrive. The company had been in tracksuits since 9.30, limbering up for the rehearsal. A lighted desk had been placed in the middle of the auditorium for me. I didn't go near it. The company was assembled on stage and I joined them there. I must say some of the older men looked a little apprehensive. Michael, a charming young man, introduced himself as my translator. He was a poet with an excellent command of English. Klaus, 'I am your dramaturg,' and Fritz, 'I, your assistant.'

I'd always wondered what a dramaturg did for a living and I soon found out. He undertakes the research which in the Workshop involves the whole company. The result is handed to the actors with a strong suggestion as to how the work should be interpreted. I didn't like the sound of it, but thought it better to wait and see how it worked out before voicing my opinion.

At 2.30 we broke for coffee, several actors taking a schnapps with it. I didn't. I don't drink during the day and I don't care for spirits anyway. At 3.00 we all moved to a neighbouring church hall and I was amazed to find our set, props, music and effects already there.

'Now we improvise,' I said and Michael duly translated.

'What does she mean?' the oldest actor asked his neighbour.

'Keep *schtumm* and look wise,' was the reply, for which I didn't need the translator.

'Let's play a scene from the late War,' I said. A simple queue in a canteen was chosen and I was amazed how well it went, particularly with the young actors. Certainly introducing improvisation was a lot easier than cutting the script. 'The text' was sacred and every word of Jimmie's draft had been conscientiously translated. What's more the slightest cut was resisted; you'd have thought I was taking their life's blood.

At 6.00 p.m. we broke to allow the company time to prepare for the evening performance.

Next day I found a canvas chair on stage.

'Could you please have that removed?' I asked the Stage Manager.

'It is for the director, you,' he said.

'But it's in the way.'

Jimmie had added a chorus of soldiers to the original. All the actors had lived through Hitler's War. I hoped to incorporate some of their experiences. Once the idea caught on, the improvisations became very lively, but those actors made the lines in Jimmie's text sound as fresh as improvisations. It was a joy to work with this company.

Michael conscientiously translated everything I said, but he'd had no experience of theatre and his instructions sounded too dictatorial. He told me that the actors had to have clear-cut, exact instruction. I could see danger ahead. I would have to try and communicate directly. I started using my few words of German and when I dried up, I clowned. If an intellectual problem arose Klaus was the one to translate. He hadn't missed a single rehearsal and knew exactly what I was getting at.

When Camel arrived, I told him what a smart assistant we'd found ourselves.

'I thought he had a Theatre Workshop look on his face,' said Camel.

On the third morning I found a sleeping bag on stage, the script on a cushion beside it. I burst out laughing. The Stage Manager, a wiry, dark chap, was another one who understood me.

'What were you,' he asked me, 'a dancer?'

He was a great Stage Manager. No matter what I asked for, it would be on stage in two minutes.

I'd started work with the soldiers to make my approach to the work clear, and because the men had so much to contribute to the scenes which parallel War-time Germany, but on the third day I ran into a new snag. Jimmie had introduced a deserter into a scene where Athenian soldiers were retreating, and the deserter spoke Lallans. Great care had been taken with the writing, but I could tell that the German actor was using some kind of mummerset. I stopped him and explained that it was better not to use debased German; the deserter should use a language with different roots. Would the Bavarian tongue be the answer? The actor didn't see the point, Klaus was unsure – in the end we used Swabian. At least it sounded better.

I added a scene where soldiers shuffled away from the Front, their feet swathed in sacking, as at Stalingrad, and those actors were magnificent. As it turned out they had all been anti-Hitler, some had been in camps, some had been through the hell of winter soldiering in Russia, but of course they hadn't expected to use their experience in a Greek comedy.

One day Camel sat in for one of the senators, while the actors watched the scene. Camel told me he was overwhelmed by the authenticity of the characters around him. If Manfred Borges, Albert Hetterle, Walter Jupe, Helmut Müller-Lankow, Willi Narloch, Heinz Scholz and Kurt Steingraf could play in English, they would conquer the world.

The actresses were not only talented but admirably equipped for this seductive play. They were slightly athletic, a little too competent at the outset, but when they softened down . . . perfect. The theatre of East Berlin was rather serious at that time and not very sexy. Brecht kept sex where it belonged – in the covered waggon. So Myrrhine giving her husband a sponge-down with cold water, when he desperately wanted to make love to her, brought the house down.

I had fun with Lampito, the girl from Sparta, too. First, I gave my impression of the tough CP rep, who attended my East-West press conference. It went down very well. All the actresses were dying to play the part.

'Mocking a Party member?' said Walter, who was Party representative in the company.

'Why not? Is the Party above satire?'

I hadn't much time for socialising, but I had to find Ernst Hoffmann, who'd played Friedrich Engels in a radio feature, 'The Classic Soil', which I'd put together way back in 1939. He came from the same town as Engels and was the only refugee in England elected to a trades council. I traced him to the Humboldt University, where he was professor of political science. I suggested meeting at the Actors' Club. I'd eaten there several times and it was quiet and comfortable.

Ernst looked exactly the same, slim, fair-haired, serious and

still young. I guess he always will be. We were at ease right away,
the years which had separated us ceased to exist. He was absorbed
in his work, enthusiastic about his students, the new generation. I
told him how Olive Shapley, who'd directed our programme, had
been victimised by the BBC. She had let me quote whole passages
from Engels' *Condition of the Working Class in 1844* and that wasn't
on, especially as I'd pointed out that things were hardly any better
a hundred years later. That I'd been banned throughout the War
years didn't surprise him.

'And now?'

'Our politicians are still of the shopkeeper class. If you ask
for an improvement in living conditions, you are an outsider, you
don't count.'

'I too was troubled,' he said, 'when the small shopkeepers
here accused the DDR of trying to destroy them. I'm afraid
it's a universal ill.'

The head waiter came to the table. I began asking for steak
cannibale but Ernst took over, ordering in German.

'I know what she likes,' said the waiter in English. He sounded
irritated and possessive. He obviously knew who Ernst was and
distrusted what he stood for. We regained our spirits over a
glass of good red wine and Ernst proposed a toast, 'To all our
hopes.' I wished that my hopes had been as simple as in 1939.

As we sat reminiscing and yarning, a group of theatricals
walked in.

'They're from the Berliner Ensemble,' said Ernst.

I'd no desire to meet them: for me Brecht's influence on
the German theatre was anything but life-giving. I crossed
that club off my list. The next time we met it was at Ernst's
home.

The music had been specially written for *Unternehmen Ölzweig*.
The composer was young but his music was old hat.

'Why all that pastiche Weill? Don't you want to write your
own music?'

'Well, I've spent three years at the Academy, trying to.'

'Why not try the streets, the fields or the factories, for a
change? Anywhere but the theatre or the concert hall.'

He disappeared. I didn't see him for days. I turned my attention to the sets and costumes. First, a costume parade. Enter the soldiers. Christ! Mini-tunics with frills, helmets with horses' tails, dyed red arty leggings. Willi Narloch started dancing, scattering imaginary petals. I seized a pair of shears, bent down and cut off Willi's frills. 'Excuse me,' said I.

'*Bitte*,' said Willi.

'Horse tails out,' I said. 'Batter your helmets and patch your leggings. Do it yourselves, as soldiers would.'

There was a suppressed squeak. The designer had just come in.

'You're in the wrong theatre,' I told him. 'You'd do better in London's West End or the Old Vic. They'll be much the same by now.' He pulled a face but I thought he rather liked the idea of going west.

The girls looked pretty but they lacked individuality. I told them to remedy that themselves. The senators and old men were okay. They were meant to look conventional anyway.

Next, the set. I'd only seen it on the drawing board. The stage carpenter took me to the workshop. He looked apprehensive, with reason. The design would have been perfect, for one of those wedding cakes, with columns and scrolls.

'Lop that off,' I said, 'and that, and that. Sorry, friend, I know you built the damn thing.'

'That's all right,' replied the carpenter. 'He who makes war pretty is not against war.'

Someone was following us around, picking up all the fallen pieces. It was the designer. 'Luckily I photographed it before the blitz,' he said.

It was time for dress rehearsals and there was still no music, but no one seemed to be panicking, there was no nervous tension. On the morning of the second run I found the young composer at the piano waiting for us. 'I'd like everybody to hear the new music,' he said.

We all sat down and listened. Yes, it was new. It was tuneful and it would be popular.

'Great,' I said, and cancelled the run so that we could use the new music. It gave the show a kick.

That evening I arrived back at Frau Schlissel's to find Camel's Maggie hanging paper chains. 'Where did you spring from?'

'I'm your Christmas present, with salami and potato salad, Limburger and a couple of Sylvaner thrown in.'

'It can't be Christmas. We open Christmas Day.'

'Well, tomorrow is Christmas Eve.'

'We must throw a party.'

'Not tomorrow,' said Maggie. 'Nothing stirs in Germany on Heilige Nacht.'

'But I must phone Gerry.'

'You'll have to wait till Christmas Day.' I did. Early in the morning I was waiting for the Post Office to open. When I heard his voice, I burst into tears.

'Merry Christmas, beloved one. How's the show?'

'It's going to be terrific.'

'Come home soon.'

'I will. Gerry!'

'Sweetheart?'

'Don't let the debts get you down. They can't hang us. If we lose the theatre, we'll still have each other.'

The Maxim Gorki threw a party on New Year's Eve and the Workshop threw a party to welcome me home.

In Berlin I staged my last protest. I refused to join in the festivities while my friends the stage-staff were segregated.

'The stage is for the artists.'

'Good; all the more reason to have the stage-staff there.'

I won. Soon we were all drinking and dancing together and to show there was no ill feeling they awarded me a medal: 'Best Director of the Year'.

In London Gerry invited the company to our new flat and they were impressed, especially by the red carpet he'd laid in the front room. I had a gift for each one, a portfolio of Chinese prints or an art book; for Hamish Miller MacColl a zither. Already at the age of seven, he was a promising musician. At the bottom of my case I had photos of the German version of *Olive Branch* with my beloved Gorki comedians.

'Joan and her Gorkis! You should have seen how France Jamnik worked with us, the performances he got out of Mickser and Olive.'

'Especially Ollie,' said Stephen Lewis. 'She turned in such

a performance that he still hasn't managed to tear himself away.'

'You mean he's still here?'

'That's right.'

'What are we doing next?' said Stephen.

'*The Celestina* by Fernando de Rojas. I've been working on it in Berlin, using Mabbe's translation.'

Actually, I wasn't sure that I'd made a job of it, the last days in Berlin had been distracting, people had begun to speak freely to me about the Soviet Union's treatment of German Communists who'd taken refuge there.

Forty-two

The Celestina. David (Jimmie) Booth found in our bar, plays Semaronio. Two detectives invade our rehearsal and hand me a summons for 'unlawfully presenting parts of a new stage play not allowed by the Lord Chamberlain', You Won't Always Be On Top. *Henry Chapman is to receive a summons, also Gerry, Camel and Richard Harris. We could be closed down. We need a lawyer. We circularise all our friends, receive donations, support – only Michael Redgrave is loath to associate himself with us, for fear we've been obscene. Wayland Young of the* Tribune *takes over the appeal, but is against contacting the* Daily Worker. *His QC is beyond our means. The notices may help – the only adverse one, 'the workmen, peculiarly uninteresting', Arts Council. Harold Lever, Chancellor of the Duchy of Lancaster, and Gerald Gardiner, Lord High Chancellor in Wilson's government, defend us, without fee. The result.*

For *The Celestina*, the young people were easy to cast and we picked up a new actor, David Booth. He'd arrived with a Christmas show, a twee story for babies written by two old lesbians. It only played matinées. He hated it. At all hours you'd find him propping up the bar, a cynical, witty, impossible character, lanky and agile, with his own peculiar way of tackling life, and acting. I gave him Semaronio, the artful go-between, and wondered what on earth I was going to do about the old procuress herself. I couldn't think of anyone who could tackle her.

One or two of the men who'd been so good in *You Won't Always Be On Top* were out of their depth with Fernando de Rojas or rather James Mabbe's translation of him, but I had lovely women – Ann Beach, Yootha Joyce, Olive Macfarland and glamorous Joanna Korwin. Finally I settled for Eileen Draycott as Celestina. She was the right age now. She'd been the star of Manchester Rep when I worked there.

One day in January when we were analysing Act One, two plain-clothes detectives stalked into the auditorium without so much as a by-your-leave.

'Yes, gentlemen?' said the ASM.

'Joan Littlewood?'

'At your service,' said I.

'Gerry Raffles, John Bury and Richard Harris? We're here to serve a summons on you all.'

'Whatever for?'

'That unlawfully, for hire, you did present parts of a new stage play entitled *You Won't Always Be On Top* before such parts had been allowed by the Lord Chamberlain, contrary to Section 15, Theatres Act, 1843.'

Old Eileen, standing on stage, went quite pale. I'd forgotten all about the building play myself.

'And the author?'

'A similar summons has been issued to Henry Chapman, aged forty-seven, builder's labourer, at Hastings. Now we should like to see the aforementioned.'

The ASM took them up to the green room. I looked at the piece of paper they'd handed me. The case was to be heard on 16th April at the West Ham Magistrates' Court. There was nothing to be done there and then, so we pushed on with the rehearsal; but every now and then the threat behind that summons kept recurring like the hiccups.

'Could they close us down?'

'If they fined us heavily, they could sink us.'

At the end of the rehearsal, we who'd been summonsed put our heads together. We needed a lawyer – and the money to pay him. Gerry phoned sympathetic journalists, we circularised friends till there was no money left for stamps. It felt like the last chapter, especially when the replies trickled in.

Joe Losey felt that as a foreigner and a refugee from the Un-American Activities Committee, he was not in a position to help. Sam Wanamaker, in Liverpool and in debt, would contact others. Michael Redgrave was loath to associate himself with us for fear we'd been obscene. His own improvisations had been 'arrived at with tact and in good taste'. He sent a small donation.

Sean O'Casey sent us two guineas; the Midland Fan Company ten pounds; Ted Willis five pounds; Unity Theatre five pounds; plus twenty-four pounds and fifteen shillings collected at the last two performances of *The Crucible*. Edward Percy and Henry Sherek sent us encouraging letters.

The Celestina was almost forgotten. Everybody was heart and soul in the campaign to save the theatre. I found time to go through the original Spanish with Robin Chapman and Jill Booty, his wife, who was a Spanish scholar. It was anti-clerical as only a Roman Catholic writer's work can be, priests running in and out of the brothel, constant mockery of the Church's hypocrisy. I intended to re-work the script but I couldn't find time. Would I ever get the chance again?

One morning a stranger presented himself at the box office. Wayland Young from the *Tribune*. 'Is the manager in?'

Gerry knew him at once, the drama critic most heavily involved in the fight against censorship. He asked if he might see the replies received so far and picked out a letter from Benn Levy, MP and playwright: 'Your case offers the worst possible opportunity for making a successful impression on the enemy.'

'Very sharp,' said Wayland Young. 'And what is your next move?'

'A public meeting.'

'Good. Meanwhile you'd better let me get on with the appeal. Have you any more circular letters ready to go out? May I have them?'

Gerry parted with them gladly and Wayland Young handed him the name of a QC who was just the man for us. Gerry managed to get him on the phone that afternoon but took care to ask his fee before going any further. 'Far beyond our means,' said Gerry.

Next morning a letter arrived by special messenger:

I have taken the liberty of extracting the envelope addressed to the *Daily Worker*. If our appeal appears there we shall forfeit all the sympathy we get from the substance of the case itself. I would also urge you, when you have your meeting next week with actors etc., to avoid contact with known Communists from Unity or elsewhere;

any contact like that would not only make it more likely you would
be convicted, but would make it quite impossible to keep a press
campaign going, after your case, in order to try and get the law
changed. We have forty pounds to date.

W.Y.

P.S. Newspaper criticisms of the building play would be useful.

We picked out the following:

> The extraordinary thing about this production is that
> it makes ordinariness fascinating. We are always hear-
> ing that the era of naturalism is over: Miss Littlewood
> proves that in this country it has never begun.
>
> Henry Chapman's play lacks every kind of form and
> shape except the form and shape of life. It happens on
> a building site and shows us the men who work there.
> They are neither sentimentalised nor shoe-horned into
> propaganda: they are simply *shown*, and that in itself is
> a revolution. Sometimes, individual voices are muffled
> in the mutually overlapping murmurs of a group of
> men working together, but the acting is so starkly
> authentic that words become secondary, as they do
> in life. We know, from their very tone and gait,
> what kinds of men are being presented . . . with
> performances as radically different from most West End
> acting as a documentary film is from a strip cartoon.
>
> The play is performed against and upon the most
> spectacular and elaborate setting I have ever seen in
> the legitimate British theatre. Using every horizontal
> square yard of the wings and every vertical square
> yard of the back wall, John Bury has reproduced a
> three-storey building in course of construction, com-
> plete with scaffolding, cement-mixer, workmen's hut
> and no-man's-land of plank-traversed mire. It is an
> astonishing achievement. Admirers of the films of
> Fellini or the latter-day Polish cinema will know the

kind of excitement to expect: the excitement of seeing
actors who look and behave like unobserved, uninhib-
ited human beings. On a lower level, there can be
few playgoers who have never succumbed to the
fascination of watching a hole being dug in the road.
They, too, are not forgotten.

KENNETH TYNAN
Observer, 13th August 1956

Mr Chapman, who is a building worker himself and
obviously knows what he is talking about, has not
attempted the probably impossible job of whipping
this astounding text into a well-made play. There is
no plot, no shape, and the script rambles towards its
destination almost as erratically as its characters.

But the language and the people are vividly alive,
often wonderfully funny, occasionally touching, and
Mr Chapman has replaced the grip of a story-line
with something just as effective: accurately drawn
and absorbingly interesting characters.

Liverpool Daily Post, 13th August 1956

Ordinarily there is no especial dramatic virtue in
authenticity – the theatre, after all, can never compete
with motion pictures in this regard – but it is, I think,
essential to the spirit and atmosphere of Mr Chapman's
work, which is so freely constructed that its present
curtain-line is a cheerful reference to the Red Moon
that could hardly have been part of the original text.
The shapelessness is deliberate and right. . . .

You Won't Always Be On Top penetrates with casual
understanding into the human heart – it perceives, too,
the hopes and frustrations that weigh upon his characters outside their work. Thus one is a parent, irritated
because his child has been unjustly treated at school;
another is a hopeful punter who interprets every stray
phrase of conversation as an inadvertent tip for a horse;

a third is a youth employed as a tea-boy who dreams of conducting a great orchestra.

KENNETH A. HURREN
What's On, 18th August 1956

The new Theatre Workshop play is that great rarity, a play about working men. . . . It's not a profound comment on our times, but who cares about that? The profound comment is that such a play – an entertaining chunk of life about the way nine tenths of the British people live – should be such an unusual event.

Joan Littlewood's production superbly catches the rhythm and feel of a day's manual work: the cold, the greyness, the long stretches when people are only half speaking their thoughts: my boots leak, women are beautiful, it's taken mankind thousands of generations to get here. And the sudden gusts of quarrelling and reconciliation, the warmth of shared experience, the tolerance of quirks. The accents are real ones, and properly differentiated. . . .

This play is absolutely true to life; we are made to love what we see and to laugh at it and ourselves. And if that isn't the prescription for a good play, I don't know what is.

WAYLAND YOUNG
Tribune

In London last week we came upon a new English dramatist and that is an event. . . .

On occasion I have great admiration for Miss Littlewood, her fierce sense of mission, her theatrical ingenuity, the work she has accomplished in making Theatre Workshop in Continental eyes, no less than England's premier company. . . .

HAROLD HOBSON
Sunday Times, 13th August 1956

Infinitely the best London play of the month is at the Theatre Royal, Stratford-atte-Bowe. Henry Chapman's play is kicking with humour, richly observant, Chekhovian in its cartography. . . .

PENELOPE GILLIATT
Vogue, December 1956

I am sorry but I am unable to make head or tail of this play. It seems to me to consist of a series of disjointed and more-or-less meaningless conversations between a set of peculiarly uninteresting workmen on a building site. It also has the disadvantage of being so abominably typed that it is almost unreadable.

A member of Arts Council's Drama panel, turning down Gerry's request for a guarantee against loss.

Harold Lever, Labour MP for Cheetham, Manchester, since 1945, later Paymaster General and Chancellor of the Duchy of Lancaster in Harold Wilson's government, barrister by profession and financial wizard by adoption, our Business Manager when we played *Fuente Ovejuna* in Manchester during the Spanish Civil War and a great help when Jimmie and I were in court in 1940 over censorship, phoned Gerry asking what we had been up to this time. He proposed to bring Gerald Gardiner along to talk things over. Gardiner was Lord High Chancellor in Wilson's government, a theatre lover and, as it turned out, a lover of our theatre in particular. The upshot of the meeting was that both men offered to defend us, without fees.

April 16th, 1957, dawned clear and bright and when we crossed the Broadway, making for the court-house, we noticed groups of brightly dressed young people heading in the same direction.

The bench looked formidable and the police prosecutor's hair looked like patent leather. But those young people we'd seen outside were all crowded into the public gallery, and they gave us a wink or a smile as we took our places.

Tall, grey-haired Gerald Gardiner looked very distinguished and Harold Lever was grinning from ear to ear. Henry arrived from Hastings just in time for the first item on the programme, our two coppers reading from their notes. It was good comedy stuff, a complete muddle. Brickies were given carpenters' lines, carpenters the brickies'; 'mouthy mucker' had never had an 'f', and 'mush', 'gooper', 'run and jump' and 'fart' sounded rather endearing. You could take 'I'm going for a Tom Tit' whichever way you pleased. Henry himself was a Puritan. It was alleged that Dudley Sutton had made the dreaded V-sign, and Mickser had peed into the open trapdoor while impersonating Winston Churchill.

Several times we had to stifle our giggles, but it was the police prosecutor reading one of the 'indecent passages' that broke the ice.

'I quote,' he began, and he had beautiful diction. ' "Missus 'ad to go out last night, so I was left to look after the little girl, got to put 'er on 'er potty at nine o'clock, I 'ad." '

'On her what?' asked the magistrate.

'Pot,' said the prosecutor, '*pot de nuit*. "So I puts 'er on an' she looks up at me, sort of sideways; but would she pee? Not 'er. So I goes an' fills the milk jug with water and finds a damn great pudden bowl an' I keeps pourin' one into t'other, one into t'other an' she keeps lookin' at me, sort of sidey-ways – but would she bloody well pee? Not 'er. Well, what with all that water an' me tellin' 'er to go pee-pee, I 'ad to run like 'ell. But 'er? Not 'er! Not till the missus got back." '

There was an outbreak of coughing and spluttering, and the magistrate blew his nose as the prosecutor folded away his piece of paper.

Gerald Gardiner had a private word with Gerry and me. 'They tell me the magistrate has been in the building trade all his life,' he said. 'We'll see.'

We did! We got off scot-free, cautioned not to commit the same offence again. I danced out of that court-house and all the way back to the theatre. The sun was shining, the birds were singing.

To the bar! Drinks all round. That evening our smiling faces were in all the papers, five in a row. Our victory was the first real blow at the ancient institution of censorship.

Forty-three

G.B.S., J.P. Sartre and Paul Green, American playwright, almost unknown, certainly undervalued; an inimitable performance by John Bay in Unto Such Glory, *one of our best productions.* La Putain Respectueuse, *with Yootha Joyce, incomparable. A quick trip to the DDR to receive my medal. Return to find another wild script awaiting me. It could be worked on. I am alone in thinking so. I go ahead with my reluctant team and kick the script into life – the lack of stagecraft covered by Johnnie Wallbank's jazz links. Despite rejection by Arts Council and flabbergasted reviews,* A Taste of Honey *brings 'em in.*

The night before the court case we'd presented a double bill, *Man of Destiny* by G.B.S. and the G.B.S./Ellen Terry correspondence. We'd acquired a clever actor in Robin Chapman, who played Napoleon. David Booth was the innkeeper. (David was later known as James, there being a David in the profession already.) Mickser's G.B.S. was as little wild, but good value, and Jill Booty was a charming Ellen Terry.

After G.B.S., Paul Green. His writing shows such insight into the lives of black Americans that I always thought he must be black himself. Not at all, he was just an unsung white who'd studied at North Carolina University, where his first plays were produced. He was thirty-two before *In Abraham's Bosom* was given a professional production and won the Pulitzer Prize. In 1936, ten years later, his most ordinary play, *Johnny Johnson*, was produced in New York by the Group Theatre. Why was he so neglected? Perhaps because his plays need actors with a knowledge of the Deep South.

I had chosen *Unto Such Glory* which deals with a community of Shakers and an itinerant preacher, Brother Simpkins, whose speciality is the seduction of the wives of poor farmers who'd given him hospitality.

The production would have been impossible without John

Bay, an American actor introduced to us by David Booth. John combined an ear for Southern American with a taste for Greek classics; crouching in a fox-hole in Korea, he had translated *Prometheus Bound*. He was our Brother Simpkins, the rest of us – the Shakers.

The play is set in an America which Alan Lomax knows well and I asked him along to help us. He showed us the curiously stiff dance, jumping backwards and forwards, performed by the Shakers as they sang:

> *You gotta cross that lonesome valley*
> *You gotta go there by yourself*
> *Ain't nobody else can go there for you*
> *You gotta cross that lonesome valley by yourself.*

So in battered straw hats and faded cotton frocks, we praised the Lord and enjoyed the novel experience.

With the Paul Green we played a Sartre play, *La Putain Respectueuse*, more honest than his other plays, I thought, for usually he shies away from the sexy woman, but he was certainly much happier with this whore than with many of his heroes. Yootha Joyce played the part, a stunning performance. I knew she had hidden depths, but that dead-pan face, gently sinuous movement and cynical delivery. . . . It was unforgettable.

On May Day 1958 I returned to East Berlin to receive my medal and see what had happened to the production during my absence. I knew it would have gone slow – all shows do if nobody keeps an eye on them, but it had also been toned down. Unconsciously? Lampito, who'd satirised the die-hard Party member when I left, was now more ordinary, and the fast and furious sex in the Myrrhine-Kinesios scene had grown soft and charming. Even so, it was great seeing the beloved company again. They were deep in rehearsals for the sad and serious *Lower Depths* of Maxim Gorki.

When I got back home, among the pile of letters on my desk was one hand-written. I'd overlooked it in the excitement of Sartre and Green:

Dear Miss Littlewood,

Along with this letter comes a play, the first I have written. I wondered if you would read it through and send it back to me because no matter what sort of theatrical atrocity it might be, it isn't valueless so far as I'm concerned.

A fortnight ago I didn't know the theatre existed, but a young man, anxious to improve my mind, took me to the Opera House in Manchester and I came away after the performance having suddenly realised that at last, after nineteen years of life, I had discovered something that meant more to me than myself. I sat down and thought. The following day I bought a packet of paper and borrowed an unbelievable typewriter which I still have great difficulty in using. I set to and produced this little epic – don't ask me why – I'm quite unqualified for anything like this. But at least I finished it and if, from among the markings and the typing errors and the spelling mistakes, you can gather a little sense from what I have written – or a little nonsense – I should be extremely grateful for your criticism – though I hate criticism of any kind.

I want to write for the theatre, but I know so very little about it. I know nothing, have nothing – except a willingness to learn – and intelligence.

Yours sincerely,

Shelagh Delaney

The play was in a packet postmarked 'Salford', where I'd lived with Jimmie Miller when I was nineteen, the same age as this girl. Everybody was poor there and everybody seemed to be Scottish, Welsh or Irish. Hadn't there been a Delaney family opposite the Richmonds in Hartington Street when Gerry lodged there?

I skimmed the pages. A section of a street, the main entrance to a house, a living-room with two doors and a window overlooking the river, a bedroom, a kitchen. It needed a film unit.

I started to read. One or two quirky phrases caught my eye:

JO (*to her mother's boyfriend*): Throw that cigar away. It looks bloody ridiculous, stuck in your mouth like a horizontal chimney.

There wasn't much of a plot. Helen, a woman of forty, goes off with her rather unbelievable boyfriend, leaving her daughter, Jo, to spend Christmas alone. Jo goes to bed with a young Nigerian sailor who soon disappears. Some months later, Geoff, an effeminate art student, moves in, sleeps on the couch and takes care of the girl, who is now pregnant.

That was about all there was to it.

All the characters spoke in pedantic Salford style:

> HELEN: I hope you exercised prudent control over his nautical ardour. . . . The only consolation I can find in your immediate presence is your ultimate absence.

Although she said she was Irish, the mother talked like all the rest. When Jo announced her intention of finding work in a bar, it was:

> HELEN: What sort of a bar?
> JO: The sort you're always propping up.
> HELEN: So you've been called to the bar, hey? That is gratifying; I'm glad to see a daughter of mine devoting her time and energies to such a very necessary social service.

> HELEN: Her father's dead.
> BOYFRIEND: Oh well, there's a first time for everything. How long has he been in this unfortunate condition?

Nobody was ever short and sharp. I couldn't help trimming the sentences as I read. Then again, some of the dialogue sounded more like music-hall:

> HELEN: Are you afraid of the dark?
> JO: You know I'm afraid of the dark.
> HELEN: You should try not to be afraid of the dark.
> JO: I do try not to be afraid of the dark.

HELEN: And yet you're still afraid of the dark?
JO: I'm still afraid of the dark.
HELEN: Then you must try harder.
JO: I'll do that.

At times the mother, alone on the stage, appeared to be talking to herself. Wouldn't it make more theatrical sense if she talked to the audience?

Were the characters believable? The young people, yes, they could be, with work. Geoff would be the most difficult. Miss Delaney didn't appear to understand him:

JO: I want to know what you do. I want to know why you do it.

And it wasn't surprising that a girl of nineteen couldn't make sense of a woman of forty. The mother's boyfriend, Peter, with his white house, park-sized garden, tennis court, swimming pool and bottomless wallet, didn't make much sense either. If the author had reread her script, she certainly hadn't pruned it. It remained as it had been when it emerged from that unbelievable typewriter. Most of the scenes didn't develop, largely because all the author's thoughts were written down higgledy-piggledy. Was it worth salvaging? It was far too long. One would have to take care not to lose its freshness; but the only two artists who could bring the mother and boyfriend to life were not impressed.

'Wait till she's learned how to write a play,' said Avis.

'Teenage sex, a black baby on the way and a queer boyfriend. She's not so dumb,' said John Bay. 'But why is the writing so childish?'

They wanted nothing to do with it. I had a job persuading them, but I managed. Avis, with her sharp Manchester wit, made short work of the long-winded speeches. John Bay had less to go on, so he underscored his part with snatches of popular song. On his first entrance, 'Getting to know you, getting to know all about you,' to Helen. And for Jo: 'Who's got a bun in the oven?' He created a droll, comic character, extremely funny and very welcome in the rather lachrymose story. As Jo, Frances Cuka gave us a spoilt, attractive brat. Murray Melvin, who had been given a Co-op grant to study with us, was always making tea, tidying the green room, taking care of us – Geoff to the life. He got the part.

The ending was downbeat. Jo was whisked off to hospital to have her baby and Geoff lay down on the couch with a life-sized baby doll to commit suicide. We tried several alternatives. Avis ad libbed the best closing line, 'Can you cut the bread on it yet?'

How did Shelagh take all this? She arrived from Salford and stayed at Blackheath. She was going to watch one of the runs.

'Well, we've a lot of disjointed scenes,' said Avis, 'and that's about it.'

'Jazz will solve it,' I said. 'Johnnie Wallbank has a group – trumpet, guitar, drums and sax. He can link the scenes and set the mood.'

Johnnie used 'Everybody Loves My Baby', 'Careless Love', 'Dippermouth Blues' and 'Baby Doll'. I put in a song for Jo:

> *Black boy, black boy, don't you lie to me*
> *Tell me, where did you stay last night?*
> *In the pines, in the pines, where the sun never shines*
> *I shivered the whole night through.*

Shelagh sat through the first run with music. She didn't utter a word.

'What do you make of it?' I asked her.

'I think it's going to be all right,' she said. I don't think she noticed the difference between her draft and the company's adaptation.

The press floundered about.

Alan Brien in the *Spectator*:

> It has been alleged against Shelagh Delaney that she wrote down the first thing that came into her head. But this is her great achievement. The best English playwrights serve up the second thing which comes into their heads – and this is always the cautious thing, the decent thing, the thing which is bigger than both of

them. They are disinfected with enthusiasm, so they put on their rubber gloves before they even touch the tongs which touch life. White-coated and gauze-masked, they deliver the three-colour, box-office child whose proportions are exactly calculated to fit the cover of *Illustrated*. Miss Delaney is her own midwife and makes an awful amateurish mess of her confinement on the stage.

A Taste of Honey is a boozed, exaggerated, late-night anecdote of a play which slithers unsteadily between truth and fantasy, between farce and tragedy, between aphrodisiac and emetic. It is written as if it were a film script, with an adolescent contempt for logic or form or practicability upon a stage. . . .

Twenty, ten or even five years ago, before a senile society began to fawn upon the youth which is about to devour it, such a play would have remained written in green longhand in a school exercise book on the top of the bedroom wardrobe. . . . This is not so much dramaturgy as anthropology, demonstrated by a genuine cannibal. As such it is a hair-raising evening.

The Times:

Miss Delaney sets her play in the outskirts of Manchester. The plot suggests a mood of interminable and squalid pathos. . . .

Nothing could be less sentimental than Miss Delaney's treatment of emotionally charged events. The first act consists largely of a ding-dong battle between a mother and daughter, from which the brassy and hardened elder woman emerges as the more likeable; whereas the daughter remains locked in private discontent, the mother is constantly stopping to pass an affable word with the audience, or to become suddenly absorbed in a completely unexpected topic ('I wonder if I could turn you into a mountain of voluptuous temptation'). The dialogue is not written

to evoke emotion, it remains tough, humorous and
close to the ground.

The play was a success, the audience arrived along with agents and
newshounds, anxious to get the low-down on this teenage wonder.
Louis MacNeice, the poet, came, slightly abashed to find himself
watching 'this adolescent effusion'.

Shelagh took it all in her stride, giving interviews, considering
offers, opening her first bank account. . . . She was seen in the
right pubs coping with the latest drinks and entertaining her hosts
with laconic comments in her broad Salford accent. 'Carefully
cultivated,' said a London admirer.

She left our home to share a flat with Una Collins, our latest
costume designer. So Brendan and Beatrice moved in.

Forty-four

Brendan in London for the launch of Borstal Boy. *The first
hostage of our time killed in Cyprus. There is a play in it. B.B. says
he will write it, in Ireland, and goes. The Royal Court try to take
over Shelagh. Gerry tries Arts Council for a bursary for her. She is
given a hundred pounds. Graham Greene praises us and gives Shelagh
a typewriter. Brendan returns from Ireland, drinking. Gerry chases
him across Blackheath. He also attempts to stop Shelagh spending all
her money, which she resents. We try everything to make Brendan
write. He begins phoning bits of songs and jokes to the theatre. We
patch two acts together. Three days before opening night there is no
third act. We ad lib it. Shelagh's second play not good. I tell her to
study well-constructed plays. She says other people will work on it.*

Brendan had come to London to launch *Borstal Boy*, the story
of his life in that institution, and gave out copies in the Fleet
Street pubs till the supply ran out. The rest got *The Quare
Fellow*.

'Not mine,' he told them. 'The lags wrote it.'

'His wife, he means,' said one of his countrymen. 'He's as
ignorant as a bush.'

We were awakened on his first morning at Blackheath by
platefuls of rashers and eggs placed on our chests. Over a mug
of tea, we took a look at the morning papers. The same story was
splashed across every front page: 'BRITISH SOLDIER FOUND DEAD IN
NICOSIA. . . . EIGHTEEN YEARS OLD. . . . A HOSTAGE.' It was
the first time we'd seen that word in a newspaper.

'It's like something from the past,' said Beatrice.

'There's a play in it.'

'I know nothing about Cyprus,' said Brendan, 'but I do know
about Ireland. I was put in charge of a hostage once meself. But I
felt sorry for the poor bastard, so I took him round all the Dublin
pubs. "Paddy," he said after, "that's the best night out I ever 'ad." I

drew a circle round him 'cos I'd had a few. "Step over that, *acushla*,"
I said, "and you're a dead man." '

'Write it,' I said.

'I'd need to go to Galway.'

Beatrice packed and they were up and away. It was 17th
June 1958 before we heard from him:

Gerry, *a chara*,

I am down here, in Carraros, working very hard, six hours a day,
and doing nothing for relaxation other than swimming, sunbathing
and telling obscene and funny stories in Irish to the neighbours. I
am working on *Hostages* and think you may be able to use it. In the
meantime, I am again very skint, though I have the rent paid here
till the 30th, and if you could send us an injection I should (like
the late Adolf) make no further demands on your consideration.
I have not tasted one drop of alcohol in any shape this ten days past.

In the meantime, *salud*.

Love to you and Joan and all the coy.

                                                    Brendan

Love to you both from Beatrice.

It was great news about the drink, and the play coming along.

Honey was doing so well that the vultures were appearing.
Gerry was warned that George Devine of the Royal Court had
advised Shelagh to drop Gerry and transfer *Honey* to his theatre.

'If the play is to transfer, I'd sooner it went to the West
End than the Royal Court,' Gerry told him.

Despite the fact that Arts Council had rejected *Honey*, he
was trying for a guarantee against loss and a bursary for Shelagh.
Peggy Ramsay, play agent, wrote to Gerry:

Arts Council's record is completely black. I have a young author,
Robert Bolt, at present enjoying a success at the Haymarket with
Flowering Cherry. Last year, when he desperately needed help, I

sent his first, and far superior, play to the Arts Council. They rejected it with scorn and contempt. . . . They were equally cold about Beckett's *Godot*. I received a very rude letter, which they withdrew the moment he became a success. . . .

With every good wish for your company's continued life. . . .

On 24th June 1958 Gerry thanked her and explained:

I put Shelagh Delaney under a comprehensive contract to protect her from the trouble that Brendan Behan got himself into by signing up with the first agent who came along. But I hope, when all the fuss has died down, some literary agent will be sufficiently interested in Shelagh to take her in hand and help her in many ways which I cannot. When that time comes I shall not stand in her way. She is a working-class girl and her talents and writing are of the ordinary people. It is because of this that we like her and can do more for her plays than another British theatre.

As for Arts Council, they have never believed that a theatre could be a success anywhere but in a respectable middle-class district, and our survival for ten years without their help and for the last three years with their tiny grant has been a source of amazement, if not irritation, to them. They gave us no help at all until the Parisian critics acclaimed us. If all we had to rely on was help from Arts Council, I would give up.

On 25th June 1958 he received two reports on *Honey* from Arts Council's Drama Panel (unsigned):

1) This is a good bad play. It seems to have been dashed off in pencil in a school exercise book by a youngster who knows practically nothing about the theatre and rather more about life than she can at present digest. There is no self-conscious defiance of established technique. . . . Miss Delaney writes with the confidence of sheer ignorance . . .

2) . . . not a play of quality but unnecessarily crude and coarse. If it was the author's intention to shock, she has succeeded. None of the characters ring true and quite often they are completely inconsistent.

1) . . . Arts Council should support the management's enterprise in encouraging so promising a writer by staging her 'prentice work.

2) . . . reluctantly recommended because it has a sort of strength in its crudity.

Arts Council said they would award *Honey* a limited guarantee of between a hundred and a hundred and fifty pounds.

On 26th June, a letter signed 'Graham Greene' appeared in *The Times*. He praised the play, the production and the architectural charm of our theatre and suggested that if ten people were to contribute a hundred pounds in the forthcoming year, they would be doing as much as Arts Council had done in the past.

On 28th June, Mr McRobert, Deputy Secretary of Arts Council, wrote to *The Times*:

Help from the Arts Council in the past amounted not to £1,000 but to £2,350. Miss Delany's play has received an additional subvention. Miss Delany herself has been awarded a small bursary . . . one hundred pounds. After five years' trial at Stratford . . . We urged a fresh start in the hope of success.

A secretary should find out how to spell a writer's name. The fresh start urged on us was a tour of mining villages or joining one of their protégés in Leicester; and they threatened to withdraw all support if we did not move from Stratford, E15. We had been playing one-night stands in villages, including mining villages, from 1945 to 1953 and in all that time we had received nothing but opposition from Arts Council, though we had been invited to Norway, Sweden, Germany, France and Czechoslovakia and played to packed houses in the biggest theatres in those countries.

'The finest company to come out of Great Britain,' they said. But not in the opinion of Arts Council. If we were to survive we would have to sell ourselves in a shoddy market – the West End.

I wrote to *The Times* summarising our history, and on 1st July 1958, the letter was published. The last paragraph read:

We have not made money at the Theatre Royal, Stratford, E15, but we have established the beginnings of a people's theatre. The idea of a popular theatre in England needs more support, not less.

> Joan Littlewood
> Theatre Workshop,
> Stratford E15

Shelagh now had a new typewriter – a gift from Graham Greene. She used it to type a letter to Gerry telling him that John Osborne (author of *Look Back in Anger*) and 'some American' wanted her to meet them in New York, all expenses paid, and she wanted to go. Gerry couldn't forbid her, though he felt that she was young in the ways of the world and advised her to be wary. We heard no more.

In any case, we'd have to leave her to her own devices for a while: Brendan had returned, red-faced, his coal-black hair standing up in a coxcomb. He was back on the booze. Did he have *The Hostage* with him? No answer. Leaving Beatrice to unpack, he hurried off across the Heath – to his favourite hostelry. In their room, the desk looked bare, the *Irish Times* lay spread across the bed. I placed a wad of writing paper on the table and left.

That night . . . no Brendan. Beatrice didn't seem put out. 'He'll turn up,' she said.

He did. Early next morning, I spotted a hummock of green tweed by the gate in the back garden.

Gerry was taking his shower. As I went to our room to collect his clean underpants a great hullabaloo broke out. I was just in time to see Brendan disappearing down the iron staircase which leads to the garden and Gerry, bollock naked, running after him.

'Irgun Zvei Leuni git!' Brendan shouted as he charged across the garden and out on to the heath.

'You dirty Irish spalpeen, I'll kill you when I get hold of you!' shouted Gerry as he plunged after him.

It was a rare sight, the two of them racing over Blackheath, Gerry naked as the day he was born.

'Come in and put your clothes on, Gerry.'

At that Brendan started to laugh and Gerry gave up. He ran back to the house with a prickle in his toe.

'What was all that about?' asked Beatrice, breaking an egg into the frying pan.

'I don't know,' I said, as I threw Gerry a bath towel.

'He was into that cupboard, where the whisky is, at this hour!' said Gerry.

'I'm exhausted,' said Brendan, as he lurched into the room.

'Not with writing plays,' said Gerry.

'Bejesus, don't be tormenting me. Where's me rashers and eggs, Beatrice?'

She called out to us as we were leaving, 'He'll get on with the play today.'

At the theatre, Shelagh was sitting in the vestibule waiting for Gerry. 'I'm going to buy that red sports car I've had my eye on,' she told him.

'Who's going to drive it?' said Gerry. 'In any case, your money is in the bank and will remain there till you're twenty-one.' She said nothing but wrote him a note:

I've never liked being told what to do and I've no intentions of starting to like it now. You have no right whatsoever to order me about like some Industrial Revolution employer. I'm not going to crawl round people's backsides like some suckholing spineless fly. I've been offered a lot of money for the film rights of my play and I want that car.

And that was that! As if we hadn't enough on our plate without trying to control Shelagh. All the same Gerry managed to persuade her not to buy the car.

Later, Brendan phoned the theatre to say he would shortly be reading his new play to us. Some hopes! He went on exactly as before, turning up when he was hungry, and before the dishes were cleared away, clearing off God knows where, banging the front door after him.

I began rereading old plays. *The Hostage* was obviously a write-off, but we needed a new play. Originality was our trademark. What about Tom? Could he write a play for us? There's plenty of material for satire in the Labour Party. 'It would be equal to how many columns?' he wanted to know.

Brendan hardly bothered with us. We decided that he was spending his time with his pub buddies in Fleet Street.

Wouldn't he like to see Shelagh's play?

Some schoolgirl bollocks about a mother and her daughter's black bastard? Not interested, and why does she want to spell her name that way? And he disappeared again. Next time we set eyes on him was when he was brought home in a police car.

'Where did you find him?'

'At the wheel of the Woolwich Ferry – the captain was out for the count, drunk as a lord. Your friend seemed to think he was crossing the wide Missouri.'

'Are you preferring charges?'

'No, no. He's a card. It would be a shame to put him under lock and key.'

'Me life on you,' said Brendan, merry as a cricket. 'Now I can pursue me play,' and he was upstairs, into his room and seated at his typewriter before you could say 'Jack Robinson'.

That night he came roaring into the living-room, a sheaf of papers in his hand.

'It's Monsewer,' he said. 'He's great in English.'

'Is he the hostage?'

'He's the brother of a bishop, an English bishop, and so he remains till he decides to become an Irishman.'

'How does one become an Irishman?' Beatrice was puzzled.

'Can I get on with me story? He takes a correspondence course in Irish, plays Gaelic football on Blackheath and goes over to live in Dublin.'

'A brave man,' said Beatrice.

'A great patriot,' said Brendan.

'But how does the hostage come into it?' asked Gerry.

'Am I not coming to that? I've got to get Monsewer into the IRA first.'

'Well, get on with it, for Chrissake.' Gerry was getting desperate. Tom had sent him a folder marked *Scarborough Follies*. It read beautifully as an essay, but theatrically it was a non-starter.

No sooner had we reached the theatre than Brendan was on the blower. 'I've a bit of a song for that play of ours. Do you want it?'

'Sure,' said Gerry, reaching for his notepad. 'Shoot!'

> *'Oh the south and the north poles are parted*
> *Perhaps it is all for the best*
> *Till the H bomb will bring them together*
> *And there we will let matters rest.*

'That's the end of Act One.'

'Any more?'

'I've another bit written down somewhere.'

'Tell him I've started my own play,' I said, but Brendan had found what he was looking for.

'It's about the Kerrymen, in 1925, when they occupied five thousand acres of Lord Tralee's land and the IRA told them to get off, the social question would be settled when they'd won back the six counties. "Never mind the six counties," said the Kerrymen, "the five thousand acres will do us for a start." '

More scraps of paper would surface daily, bits of jokes, nonsense songs – 'Never throw stones at your mother, throw bricks at your father instead.'

'I've a great song for Teresa.'

'Who's Teresa?'

'The country girl who works in Monsewer's boarding house. The hostage is very taken with her.'

'Fine. So we've got him in, have we?'

We called the company together and told them that Sean

Kenny, the young Irish architect, would be designing the set and Brendan's young sister-in-law Celia would be coming over to play Teresa.

'But where's the script?' said Howard.

'There's only one at the moment,' said I. Was there? I'd been listening for the sound of that old typewriter for days and there had been only silence.

Then, one morning, uproar again. The sound of a door being kicked open: 'O'Beacháin!' It was Gerry's voice. Beatrice and I rushed out into the passage. Gerry was at Brendan's doorway, a large pistol in his hand.

'See that? If you don't finish that ******* play, I'll kill you.'

Brendan turned as white as a sheet. 'Put down that skit, you gunman,' he said at last. 'He's a dangerous bugger, that man of yours.'

I couldn't speak. I left the house and went to the theatre on my own. At lunch-time Gerry phoned to say that B.B. was working and the waste-paper basket was full of crumpled papers. There was no time to be lost. We had a long story about Monsewer, several short scenes between the hostage and Teresa and no Act Three.

The hostage was a cockney boy and Brendan had relied on the memory of his pals in Borstal but over the years he'd lost the cockney, the boy's part would have to be rewritten.

Murray Melvin, young and chirpy, was just the one to bring the part to life. Celia had arrived to play Teresa and she was lovely with her ivory skin and her copper-coloured hair. At first she and Murray really couldn't understand each other and this became an important element in the story.

As the play was set in a Dublin lodging house, we could introduce any of Brendan's characters as and when we needed them. We spent a lot of time recollecting his stories of pimps and patriots, whores and social workers, IRA men and gardaí with which he had regaled us over the years.

The most difficult part was holding on to the theme and sustaining the tension behind the jokes and laughter as the threatened execution of the hostage drew near.

The Saturday before we were due to open, we still had no Act Three.

While we were trying to solve the problem, a package arrived from Shelagh Delaney. It was her second play, *The Lion in Love*. I read it with growing disappointment. It had more characters, less appeal and even less shape than *Honey*. She had learned nothing from the company's adaptation of her first work.

Read a good play, an Ibsen for example, then analyse it, note the construction. Play-writing is a craft, not just inspiration.

Her answer came back by return:

If you aren't interested enough in my play to sort out the good from the bad, and generally put me right where I've gone wrong, then I may as well be working on it with the people who think that there is enough stuff there to be doing something with. I know you were only considering my play because more important things, like Brendan's new play, weren't ready yet.

Well, she would have to cool her heels for a bit. Sean Kenny's set was up. We had two days in which to construct a third act. The stage was strewn with symbols of Brendan's past: pistols, tattered flags, a map – mementoes of the Civil War; while piles of old books, beautifully bound, testified to the scholar, the connoisseur in him.

On the back wall of the stage, a young Irish artist was putting the finishing touches to a huge fresco of Dublin.

It was Seán's first theatrical set and tremendously evocative – which only made us feel worse. We sat there, imagining that it was the dead of night, that we were waiting for news of the prisoner in Northern Ireland. If they hanged him, the young hostage sitting there with us would die.

One couldn't sustain such a mood for the whole act. Brendan's characters would burst into hilarity if they were on their way to the scaffold. That would work, but let the IRA guard be seen

and there would be half-spoken fears, fragments of prayers. . . .
Kate O'Connor at the piano started playing moody music in these
breaks. It helped.

But how to finish the story?

Inspiration – a police raid. It was the only way out. Ad lib at
first. Katie played wild music as for a silent film; we'd sort out
the details later. Let's get the main movement. So, turmoil – fear,
violence, attempts to escape. Somebody fired a shot. The hostage
fell. A hush. Was he dead? Celia knelt by Murray's prostrate body.
Brendan had written a few bitter lines for Teresa, but Celia was
just kneeling there silently, unable to speak.

Try, 'He died in a strange land and at home he had no
one,' I said quietly.

The line came from the moment. Everybody on stage was lost
in the play. Celia spoke simply. Then Brendan came and added a
thought. The dead hostage should rise and sing, he said. Murray
tried it:

> *The bells of Hell go ting-a-ling-a-ling*
> *For you, but not for me.*
> *Oh death, where is thy sting-a-ling-a-ling?*
> *Or grave thy victory?*
> *If you meet the undertaker,*
> *Or the young man from the Pru,*
> *Have a pint with what's left over,*
> *Now I'll say goodbye to you.*

Forty-five

*The Hostage notices. Brendan changes a line in one of his songs.
And what about the Lord Chamberlain? We try for a war of the
theatres with the Royal Court. They won't play.*

A *COMMEDIA DELL'ARTE* PRODUCTION

Ireland, seen through the bloodshot prism of Mr
Behan's talent. . . . He seems to believe that all the
gaiety departed from the cause of Irish liberty when
the IRA became temperate, dedicated and holy. . . .

There are, in this production, more than twenty
songs, many of them blasphemously or lecherously
gay, some of them sung by the hostage himself.
Authorship is shared by Mr Behan, his uncle, and
'Trad'. Nor can one be sure how much of the dialogue
is pure Behan and how much is gifted embroidery; for
the whole production sounds spontaneous, a communal achievement, based on Miss Littlewood's idea of
theatre as a place where people talk to people, not
actors to audiences. These actors step in and out of
character so readily that phrases like 'dramatic unity'
are ruled out of court: we are simply watching a group
of human beings who have come together to tell a lively story in speech and song.

Some of the speech is brilliant mock-heroic, some
of it is merely crude. Some of the songs are warmly
ironic (e.g. 'There's no place on earth like the world'),
others are more savagely funny. Some of the acting is
sheer vaudeville, some of it is tenderly realistic. The
work ends in a mixed happy jabber of styles, with a
piano playing silent-screen music while the cockney
soldier is rescued and accidentally shot by a lodger

who defiantly cries, 'I'm a secret policeman and I don't care who knows it.'

Inchoate and naive as it often is, this is a prophetic and joyously exciting evening. It seems to be Ireland's function, every twenty years or so, to provide a playwright who will kick English drama from the past into the present.

Perhaps, more important, Miss Littlewood's production is a boisterous premonition of something we all want – a biting popular drama that does not depend on hit songs, star names, spa sophistication, or the more melodramatic aspects of homosexuality. Sean Kenny's setting is, as often at this theatre, by far the best in London.

KENNETH TYNAN
Observer, 19th October 1958

TRIUMPH AT STRATFORD EAST

. . . Let us ask, not only for the time to be passed enjoyably, but for a deeply felt emotional experience. . . . Brendan Behan's *The Hostage*, as given by the inspired, chuckle-headed, aggravating, devoted and magnificently alive company of Theatre Workshop. I do not know whether *The Hostage* is a masterpiece or not. It made on *me* the impression of a masterpiece. . . .

Do we demand a splendid scorn of the rules that govern lesser plays? Well, *The Hostage* has that all right. It crowds in tragedy and comedy, bitterness and love, caricature and portrayal, ribaldry and eloquence, patriotism and cynicism, symbolism and music-hall songs, all on top of one another, apparently higgledy-piggledy, and yet wonderfully combining into a spiritual unity.

Do we ask that the author should show his own mind, his own personal view, and not a copy of the conventions, nor even of the anti-conventions? Again

The Hostage does that. . . . It has lines alleging the brutality of the British in Kenya, in India, in Cyprus, that
strike an Englishman across the face like a lash; and it
has lines also about the fatal habit that the Irish have
of blaming their incompetence on the English, which
will cause no joy in Eire. Mr Behan will anger the
short-sighted in both countries; but to the discerning
he gives a magnificent experience. . . .

His portrait of the young English soldier is magnanimous. . . . The play shouts, sings, thunders and
stamps with life. And when the life of the unself-
pitying English soldier is over, Mr Behan finds for him
an epitaph that is classically restrained and beautiful.
A girl drops on her knees beside the accidentally shot
body and stills the boisterous tumult of this joyously
rowdy play with words of staggering simplicity. 'He
died in a strange land, and at home he had no one.'
Nothing finer of this kind has been written for two
thousand years, nothing since '*Ante diem periit; sed
miles, sed pro patria.*' The Irish, the southern Irish, the
IRA Irish . . . should treasure Mr Behan and be proud
of him. . . . The play is pro-British and it is pro-Irish
too. It is on the side of everything that is noble and
compassionate and brave. It stands up for good men,
even though they may be bewildered and absurd. It
has no hatred. It is an honour to our theatre.

To the credit for this, Joan Littlewood can cry
halves. This is a tremendously vital production.

Avis Bunnage I never see except with pleasure;
her offhand, irritated deflating of pretentiousness is
admirable. Howard Goorney is sound and very funny
as the rebel of 1916 who thinks that revolutionaries
are not what they used to be. Glynn Edwards,
kilted, romantic, fantastic, is the Harrovian whose
Irish patriotism lives in a rarefied atmosphere that
would choke commoner men. Murray Melvin as the
careless lad from the streets caught up in a tragedy
that seems preposterous to his bright, matter-of-fact

nature is very moving; he makes it clear that this boy's resources are small, but, such as they are, they are of a quality that we all might envy. Celia Salkeld as the girl who befriends him, is simple and kindly, and does not fail her big moment.

HAROLD HOBSON
Sunday Times, 19th October 1958

TRAGI–COMEDY OF IRISH POLITICS

The Hostage is Brendan Behan's second play about people's reactions in the presence of the shadow of death. The 'House Full' boards were out and an audience not totally Irish found the proceedings made a wonderfully exciting occasion. . . .

Mr Behan can create almost as pungent an atmosphere, a wit, and a bitterness of political satire as did the author of *The Plough and the Stars*.

There the comparison ends; this is a melodrama on a plot which no dramatist today dare treat realistically. In the end the young English hostage is shot – only to come to life again to join a rousing chorus which disabuses us of any notion of taking the play's politics too seriously. . . .

The script bubbles with wittily offensive comments on sex, politics, corruption and – sex. It is the most pungent to be heard in any London theatre now and its up-to-dateness includes cracking jokes about the Wolfenden Report and the Lord Chamberlain himself.

A.V. COTON,
Daily Telegraph

THE MOST PREPOSTEROUS, COMIC AND UNNERVING EVENING IN LONDON

. . . *The Hostage*, set in a bomb-shattered bedroom of a bawding house. The kilted and cloaked owner speaks Gaelic with an Oxford accent and bagpipes round the corridors marshalling the whores and pimps and drunks and queers into an imaginary Republican Army. Then one day the IRA actually appear. They quarter on him a young cockney National Serviceman. Around this boy the whole household revolves in an eightsome reel of songs and dances, jokes, anecdotes and arguments. The whole thing has the air of having been written that afternoon . . . while the Lord Chamberlain was out of town. And every point is hurled straight at the audience . . . which is as much part of the performance as the audience in a game of charades. Pat . . . the caretaker, acts as a sort of master of ceremonies, deflating each pomposity with a crafty corner-of-the-mouth comment. When the mad laird says he would hang crucified in the town square for the Cause, Pat is politely concerned: 'Let's hope it keeps fine for you.'

Underneath the compulsive grin of the born farceur, Behan forces us to re-examine our prejudices and assumptions. . . .

In the specific context of *The Hostage*, he is arguing that both the oppressor and the oppressed are slaves to their own illusions and the illusions their ruling classes force upon them.

ALAN BRIEN,
Spectator

ROARING AFFAIR

Mr Behan is the Dublin Dionysus. His present play is a sprawling, roaring, farcically tragic affair without one statement that escapes instant contradiction or one moment of dignity that is not twisted into mocking caricature. Halfway through the play a call goes up for the author: 'Brendan, Brendan. Where is Brendan?' But he's not to be found and the search is carelessly abandoned. 'Divil he cares one way or the other.' [Sometimes he was to be found and would go up on

to the stage and ad lib with the actors – anti-English
one night, anti-Irish the other, as the mood took him.
J.L.]

    . . . His only consistent aim is to be entertaining
and, in this explosively vital production, his success
is undoubted. . . .

    Only Irishmen can afford to spend their words as
he does nowadays – and it is worth noticing that the
most carefully shaped part in the play is not Irish, but
is that of the cockney soldier.

Times Educational Supplement

Brendan enjoyed *The Hostage*. When he saw it put together for
the first time, 'I like the Littlewood bits, too,' he said. Then he
changed a line in the Leslie–Teresa duet.

LESLIE: I will give you a golden ball
            To hop with the children in the hall
TERESA: If you'll marry, marry, marry, marry
            If you'll marry me
LESLIE: I will give you a watch and chain
            To show to the kids down Angel Lane
TERESA: If you'll marry, marry, marry, marry
            If you'll marry me
LESLIE: But first I think that we should see
            If we fit each other. . . .
TERESA (*to audience*): Shall we?

Angel Lane was the lane beside the theatre. Brendan would trot
along there every day joking with the stallholders, shopkeepers and
flower sellers. Sometimes their cracks would turn up in the show,
or in his interruptions which became a feature of the performance.
If the show eventually transferred to the West End, the ad libs
would have to go or the Lord Chamberlain would be down on us
again. Arts Council had already refused us a guarantee against loss
because, said a Mr Linklater, 'The script must be submitted to us
two months before it is performed.' It was no use arguing or telling
them that *The Hostage* would never be finished.

One day I thought we should start a war of the theatres, so halfway through the play, when the social worker and her fancy man have irritated everybody beyond endurance, I told Howard Goorney (the caretaker) to have them stowed in two dustbins to be labelled 'Return to the Royal Court', where they were currently performing Sam Beckett's *Endgame*. The Royal Court didn't respond. They were too soft-centred – very middle-class and proper, like their leader, the anti-Semitic George Devine. As for their John Osborne, 'Angry?' said Brendan. 'He's about as angry as Mrs Dale.'

Brendan had found Beckett an amusing partner when they were young in Dublin, but that was in the long ago.

That first run of *The Hostage* in the old theatre was a very happy time, not least because Arts Council promised a grant of a thousand pounds for the following year, and Paris wanted *The Hostage* for the 1959 Festival.

At the end of the run, Brendan sent a telegram from Ireland to the Cast of *The Hostage*, Theatre Royal, Stratford:

Go raibh míle maith agaibh uilig Stop And my humble thanks to the greatest company of actors in the proud language of Shakespeare, Shaw, Sean O'Casey and Brendan Behan.

So he had given us a thousand thanks in his beloved native tongue.

Forty-six

*Another packet on my desk. David Booth opens it. It's the genuine
stuff. Frank Norman, Fings Ain't Wot They Used T'Be. Donald
Albery takes Honey to Wyndham's. Arts Council asks what we're
making out of it. Lionel Bart falls for Fings. The order of scenes
has to be changed, the dialogue expanded and Lionel's songs added.
It emerges a winner. Many offers from West End managers, an
invitation to the 1959 Paris Festival. Frank hopes for Fings. Paris
wants The Hostage. Frank, Brendan and Shelagh come with us
to Paris. Acclaim. Brendan finishes up in gaol. In London we have
three shows in the West End and nothing at E15. Success is
draining us.*

There was a big sagging packet in my room. Penelope Gilliatt,
the drama critic, had sent it to me. Another discovery? I kept
moving it around because I couldn't face another rewrite job,
so soon.

David Booth breezed in one afternoon wanting to know what
we were doing next.

'Some beautifully written classic,' I said.

'What's this, then?' He had spotted the sagging packet.

'It's from Frank Somebody-or-Other.'

'Frank Norman. He wrote *Bang to Rights*,' said David. 'Great
stuff.' He was tearing open the envelope.

I had to go down to the stage for the nightly warm-up.

'Can I borrow this?'

'Sure. Don't lose it – could be his only copy.'

Gerry was discussing a transfer with Donald Albery, the first
West End manager ever to approach us. Apparently I'd been one
of the snags – he'd heard that I was rough and rude. He told Gerry
that he was surprised when he met me. Anyway, *Honey* moved to
his theatre, Wyndham's, on 20th January 1959.

Mr Linklater of Arts Council Finance had his ear to the

ground. He phoned Gerry. 'I want to see all *Honey* contracts,' he said. 'And what's this about a Theatre Workshop percentage of the film rights?'

Gerry was still on the phone, assuring him that the Arts Council guarantee would be returned, when David walked in with Lionel Bart in tow . . . our beloved, impossible Lionel, who started life as a designer, a song writer for Unity Theatre and the life of The Two Eyes in Soho, meeting place for the young poets and composers of the time. Gerry had engaged him to write a song for each one of our productions – but, 'Li's fallen for this Frank Norman piece,' said David.

'First time I've heard cockney as she is spoke,' said Lionel.

'What are we talking about?'

'*Fings Ain't Wot They Used T'Be*,' said David.

'Is there enough to go on?'

'Only needs songs, instead of verbals,' said Li.

'Well, who's the songwriter around here, Baronet?'

'I'd have to have a think-out with Frankie first.'

'Can this cockney show be ready when *Honey* transfers?' asked Gerry. 'Bearing in mind that Joan will have to tune it up for Wyndham's and find replacements for *The Hostage*.'

I decided that Li and the company would have to start on the songs while I got on with the other jobs. Jean Newlove could sketch in the production. They would have a strong company: David Booth, Ted Caddick, Glynn Edwards, Howard Goorney, Mickser, Yootha Joyce, Brian Murphy, two young lovelies, Ann Beach and Carmel Cryan – and Eileen Kennally, to replace Avis, who was vital to the success of *Honey*. At the end of the first week, I couldn't wait to see how they were getting on. At ten o'clock on the Saturday I attended their first run-through.

They'd tackled a number of scenes. Many of the characters were beginning to live. David was playing Tosher, a ponce, filling out the part with ad libs when the script was too thin. Li had revived one of his best songs from Unity Theatre days, but there was something wrong.

On my way to the Angel caff for lunch, I knew what it was. The scenes were written the wrong way round: things would happen, then they'd be discussed. As a result – the climax would be lost. In fact, it was the same old story. The structure had not been planned. Still, putting sections in the right order would not be as difficult as a complete rewrite, and Frank's language gave the writing an individual flavour.

Shaping plays was becoming my speciality. I spent the weekend shuffling the script around and arrived early on the Monday morning with a bundle of pages. We rolled them off and laid out a set of new scripts along the front row of the gallery.

From then on, I was hooked on *Fings*. Frank and Lionel were at all the rehearsals, and when more dialogue was needed, they'd be up there ad libbing with the rest of us. Li would take a brass, Frank the plain-clothes copper on the Soho beat, then they'd swap.

Mickser was playing the copper, Tosher's deadly enemy. Frank had written Tosher as an old geezer; David was creating a new character, young and lively, but when it came to a confrontation, there was no script. We itemised two or three radically divergent opinions and they ad libbed the scene. It was electric. They were friendly enemies in real life.

The rewrites mounted up. Hard on the typist, but good for the show. The songs Lionel made up during rehearsals were the best. In the middle of a scene he'd shout, 'Hold on! I've got an idea.'

And the song would happen, then and there.

Before long, we were all talking *Fings*. 'Fink I'll shoot round the manor and see what's buzzin' ' meant, 'I'm taking a stroll down the lane.'

We had a ball – Li's tunes spilled out over Stratford. The number 'Fings Ain't Wot They Used T'Be' became our theme song. We sang it on our way to Bert and May's at lunch-time and the locals took it up and added their own words.

*H*oney was doing well at W1, and *Fings* opened with a roar at E15. Within a week, eight or nine West End managements were after it. Then we heard that Paris wanted *The Hostage* in April and Albery wanted it afterwards at Wyndhams. *Honey*, he said, could go into the Criterion.

How was I to cut Murray Melvin in half? He was playing the hostage in Brendan's play and Geoff in *Taste of Honey*. The only solution would be to play in repertoire; but our poor old West End had never heard of such a thing.

So it was replacements!

Claude Planson came from Paris to see *Fings*. After the show he was whistling the theme song all round the theatre.

'You liked my show?' said Frank.

'Ver' much, but it makes me ver' cross.'

'How's that?'

'When I was learning English at school we had to practise th, th, th, till we acquired a permanent lisp. Now, it seems real Londoners can't say th either. So it's F, F, F, Fings.'

Frank was sweating on *Fings* going to Paris, but Claude had set his heart on *The Hostage*. We'd already invited Frank to come with us, and Shelagh and Brendan. They were our hope for the future and I wanted Paris to meet them.

We were still playing *Fings* at Stratford when the time came to prepare for Paris. The *Hostage* set had been dismantled; part of it had been needed for *Fings*. We had not forseen the overlap. Now we'd neither the money nor the time to build a new *Hostage*. What was to be done?

'Take the *Fings* set,' said Camel. 'The acting areas are more or less the same.'

We hadn't much choice. So, the *Fings* set was sent to the Gare du Nord with the company, Lionel and our three young writers.

I'll never forget Frank's face when he walked into the Sarah Bernhardt and saw his set on the stage. How stupid of me, I'd underestimated the suppressed rivalry between Frank and Brendan. They'd both written prison books, but Brendan's had been published a week before Frank's. They'd joked about it at the time, but I'd forgotten how, when we were working on *Fings* in the front room at Blackheath and Brendan had walked in, offering to help, Frank had gone red with resentment.

In Paris, Brendan didn't even notice the set.

'Your turn will come,' I told Frank. 'You will have the biggest success in London, bigger than Shelagh's, bigger than Brendan's.' And so it was. *Fings* entered the language. The bright young things started talking like Frank.

At the Sarah Bernhardt the curtain fell at the end of *The*

Hostage to cries of, 'Bravo! Author!' And the author, dressed in his green tweeds and open-necked shirt, strolled on to the stage. I was in the prompt corner, signalling the curtains. He brought the company forward to take a bow and again . . . and again. . . . And so it went on . . . and on. They wouldn't let him go. He announced, in French, Irish and English, that he was about to dance 'The Blackbird' and would Kate O'Connor kindly oblige at the piano?

Chord! Then followed a long, repetitious Irish jig. At some stage in its bloodstained history, Ireland's Church had banned any bodily expression which might be interpreted as aggression. So Brendan held himself stiffly erect while his feet performed the intricate footwork. After a while the chic Parisian audience began to click their fingers in time to the music. . . . I sat down. I could just see a corner of the stalls and the smartly dressed audience there. Suddenly there was a communal gasp. I looked: Brendan had slipped out of his jacket, was shrugging off his braces. And Jesus! He was fumbling with his flies. He was going to drop his trousers.

'Curtain!' I shouted. '*Vite. Rideau!*'

But the SM was so taken with Brendan's performance that he didn't hear me, and the upper reaches of the theatre were yelling encouragement. I was sorry to disappoint them but I had to get that curtain down before Brendan's tweedy pants reached his knees.

Of course he accused me of ruining his curtain call and was still shouting abuse when we left the theatre. Two or three members of the public, who'd been hanging around the stage door, joined in. I let them have it, in a few well-chosen words. A restraining hand was laid on my arm. 'Leave it to Gerry and me.' It was Claude Planson.

I felt quite put out. I was enjoying the row. Still, we'd been invited to a very good restaurant . . . and I was hungry.

It proved to be very elegant as well, waiters in tails, snow-white napery, gleaming silver and a marble staircase down which you made your entrance. All eyes were on us as we slowly descended. By now Brendan was pretty dishevelled – I thought they'd show us the door. They didn't. We were received graciously, and as we moved to our table there was a burst of applause. Any restaurant of standing in London or New York would have thrown us out. I was still in working clothes myself with a clipboard under my arm.

We ate well that night and toasted the theatre in Fleurie, Gerry's favourite wine ever after.

In the wee small hours when our party broke up, Brendan wanted to finish up at an all-night cayf in Les Halles, but when he flung open the door and challenged anybody and everybody inside to a fight, he was out for the count, straight away and lay bleeding on the sawdust.

Could Brendan ever win a fight with those dainty hands and that fat belly? He was always the one who finished up with a black eye or a tooth missing. He used to show us his favourite tackle. Head down! Charge! Like a butting billy-goat.

Despite such small reverses, Brendan was reluctant to leave Paris. We left him there with ever-faithful Beatrice to get back to *Fings* at Stratford.

'Shelagh is going to make a guest appearance,' said David.

'What as?'

'A Mystery. It'll make a better intro to "The Student Ponce".'

Enter Shelagh with suitcase. Tosher sidles up to her. ' 'Ullo, darlin',' he says. 'Just come over?'

'I don't have to say anything, do I?' said Shelagh.

'You just say, "Yeah." And I say, "Lookin' for a job?" And you say, "Yeah," and I say, "*Honi soit qui mal y ponce*." '

And that was how Shelagh made her first and last appearance on the boards.

During the show a call came through from Paris. 'Brendan's in gaol.' It was Beatrice.

'What's he done?'

'Nothing. You know he only feels safe on Aer Lingus. Well, we took our life in our hands for once with Air France. "Air Chance!" Brendan shouted, making his way towards the pilot's cabin. "Resume your seat, please," said the air hostess, but of course he wouldn't. So before we knew where we were, we were landing back at Orly and he was arrested.'

'Where is he now?' She didn't know.

'Phone Claude. He'll find him,' said Gerry.

He did, in a suburban nick with a lot of Tunisians, shouting '*Vive* Bourguiba'. 'The Tunisians were okay,' said Brendan afterwards. 'It was the French police I objected to.'

With difficulty and some expense, Claude got him out.

The drinking bouts were becoming more frequent. Before the success of *The Quare Fellow* he hadn't had the money. He'd lugged a cello to a pawn shop halfway across Dublin once to raise the price of a round. Now he could afford to drink and he wasn't writing. He just talked and sang – in any bar room, at any dinner table, in the street, anywhere.

'I respect kindness in human beings, first of all. Then kindness to animals. I don't respect the law. I have a total irreverence for anything connected with society except that which makes the roads safer, the beer stronger, the food cheaper and old men and women warmer in winter and happier in summer.' He loved giving interviews.

Frank was different. He enjoyed writing and learning. 'I know considerably more about theatre now than I did when I wrote *Fings*,' he told me. 'Of course, I'd no idea it would be produced as a musical. I saw it as a straight play, but as such I don't suppose it would have seen the light of day. Mrs Gilliatt told me to send it to you, but I was amazed when I heard it was to be produced at your theatre.'

It was the Frank/Lionel/Workshop combo which made *Fings* so successful, but I didn't say so. I only prayed for it to last.

Frank had never seen a theatrical performance when he wrote *Fings*. Theatre Royal, E15, was his first experience of showbiz. Had it been some smart set-up, he would not have felt at home, but Stratford was packed, night after night, with cockney people who, like Frank, had never been in a theatre before.

The critics, who had at last found the way to Stratford-atte-Bowe, seemed to be as bored with drawing-room theatre as we were. They enjoyed identifying themselves with these ponces, lags and layabouts. Frank's language, learned on the streets, in the nick or in Soho spielers, was a change from the drama school cockney, suitable for faithful batmen and moronic maids.

Fings would transfer sooner or later. Meanwhile . . . from rumbustious cockney to the jewelled English of that Jacobean genius, John Marston. . . . But it was no use telling our audience that he was imprisoned for making fun of James I or that his satires were publicly burned. They still preferred:

> *There used to be schools, tharsands of parnds*
> *Passin' acrorss the baize*
> *Tools flashin' ararnd*
> *Oh for the bad old days,*
> *Remember?*
> *Once in golden days of yore*
> *Ponces killed a lazy whore*
> *Fings ain't wot they used to be*

to:

> *The Dark is my delight*
> *So 'tis the nightingale's*
> *My music's in the night*
> *So is the nightingale's*
> *My body is but little*
> *So is the nightingale's*
> *I love to sleep 'gainst prickle*
> *So doth the nightingale.*

Rachel Roberts played Marston's Dutch Courtesan, our first guest artist. Avis, who'd played it for us years ago, was still in *Honey* at the Criterion. Mickser and David Booth were still with us and the theatre looked smarter: the Long Bar, presided over by Ruth Parham, only sold the best liquor, and Ruth herself looked more and more like Renoir's barmaid. Brian Murphy's wife, cool Carol, ran the snack-bar; Gerry insisting that only best-quality, fresh ground coffee should be served.

Our programmes carried the legend, 'In accordance with modern theatre practice, National Anthems will only be played in the presence of Royalty or Heads of State.' To our surprise, some of these gentry started visiting our shows, incognito, and when they were identified we still couldn't find the required anthem. Luckily Kate O'Connor could always improvise.

Letters arrived from all over the world asking, 'What holds you together?' 'What philosophy do you recommend?' Droll really, for Theatre Workshop was now hopelessly partitioned. Two shows in the West End, another soon to follow. You cannot train an actor overnight, let alone a company.

I engaged a young actor to replace Murray in *The Hostage*. He was a cockney and intelligent, but he'd never been called upon to move except in his own individual way. His feet were stuck in a slough of naturalism; there was no time to free him.

Once the three shows were launched in the West End I had to spend my time running from one to the other reviving tired performances, playing all sorts of tricks to combat the artist's deadly enemy – slowness, milking the part. Mounting a show is easier than keeping it alive. Success was going to kill us.

Forty-seven

Two strangers at E15. A script from Wolf Mankowitz – a package production? Gerry needs one. Next day, conventional auditions for small parts. Victor Spinetti's name mentioned, he is working in a nightclub. I go to see him and am very impressed. Wolf won't have a word of his play changed. Shall I quit? There's Victor, Roy Kinnear, Sheila Hancock in the cast and two of my own. They make it worth staying. To my amazement, this show follows the others into the West End. Arts Council lay claim to ten per cent of our profits. In fifteen years, they've given us £4,150. Richard Findlater quotes the grants awarded to theatres in Europe. William Saroyan comes to E15, improvising a play, Sam, the Highest Jumper of Them All. *He likes it. The critics don't. He answers them. We prepare* Every Man in His Humour *for Paris.*

One morning two men were waiting for me at Theatre Royal. The house lights were on. Our cleaners, Bea and Meg, were still busy in the stalls. When he saw me, one of the men seated himself at the piano and fished some sheet music out of his music case. The other sang, 'Come and have a gander at the Portobello Road.'

'I'm Monty,' said the singer. 'He's David. We've brought you Wolf's new musical.'

'Wolf?'

'Mankowitz.'

'We've a Mankowitz in the market here, a nice old chap.'

'May be Wolf's old man.'

'Leave the script with me. I'll read it later.'

'Sure. We'll call back in a couple of days; bring Wolf.'

Wolf turned out to be a big, unhappy-looking chap. He did all the talking. 'We have the cast, designer, music, all we need is a producer. We'd be pleased, flattered, if you'd . . .'

I didn't like the sound of a show all parcelled up. They

could see I was hesitating. Should they speak to Gerry? I was glad to postpone the decision. I wasn't mad about the text. On the other hand, Gerry was relieved at the idea of a package. Stratford was drained dry.

The very next day I arrived to find a number of characters waiting in the foyer looking very mournful. Wolf and Monty were sitting in the darkened auditorium, David was strumming at the piano.

I walked on to the stage. 'I understood you had the cast.'

'Not the chorus.' It was Monty's voice. 'Name, please.' I looked round. A middle-aged chap gave a bright smile as he was ushered on to the stage.

'What are you going to sing for us?'

The bloke tried a few staves, with the piano.

'Thank you, we'll call you. We have your agent's number?'

There was no, 'Hello, Goodbye, How are you?' Just, 'Next, please,' and the voices in the dark talking among themselves.

'Is he coming?'

'He's working nights.'

'We know what he can do.'

'Joan might like to look him over.'

'She can see him any night.'

'Do they let women in that place?'

The auditions went on. I looked in from time to time, but the whole procedure appalled me. 'If you know so much about it, why don't *you* get up on that stage and show us?'

'Are you talking to me?'

'I am.'

It was Wolf who'd been hectoring a timid-looking little blonde.

When they finished I asked for the address of the club where women might not be allowed in and that evening took the tube to Leicester Square. I had a job finding the place but a line of middle-aged men shuffling along the pavement led me to it. There was no difficulty about getting in. They were glad of my ten-bob membership fee. A flight of stairs covered with coconut matting led down to the show.

Three old strippers were unveiling while a gramophone, offstage, played 'All of me'. The star, the middle one, wore a carroty fuzz of hair and smears of black make-up round her eyes. When she turned her back and started wriggling out of her tight panties, there was heavy breathing on the front benches, a pair of opera glasses were raised as the cheeks of her bum appeared. Too late. The curtain fell, but rose again at once – a little lopsided, and there was the resident comic, applauding. He welcomed us to 'the place where it's all at'. I burst out laughing, at which the entire front row turned to look at me. They were all Japanese.

How that comic in his sweatshirt and football shorts kept his end up in that hole God knows.

'How many shows a day?' I asked the box office.

'Five, dear,' she said.

Cripes! The Portobello Road epic would be a rest cure after this. I told the combo that I thought we'd got a star. Too late, said the Wolf. We had to have a name or we couldn't have raised the cash.

I felt like throwing my hand in – but somehow the combo had managed to hook Sheila Hancock and Roy Kinnear. With the comic from the club, Vic Spinetti, we'd have a pretty good nucleus. If I added Harry Greene and Marjie Lawrence from the Workshop stable, I'd be able to face that show.

Not long before we opened, Wally Patch, a cockney comedian of the Old Brigade, called me into his dressing-room.

'It's this line,' he said. 'I can't make sense of it.'

'Well, change it,' I said. We thought nothing of changing whole scripts at E15, let alone one line.

'Change what?' said a voice I knew too well.

'A line.'

'Mine?'

'Who knows?'

'Well, he's not changing it.'

To my surprise, *Make Me an Offer* followed the three Workshop successes already in the West End.

1960
They will soon be renaming the junction of Charing Cross Road and Coventry Street, 'Littlewood Corner'.

BERNARD LEVIN

Salute General Joan, the indomitable, iron-willed genius. . . . New companies have shown that experimental plays, dealing with themes of vital significance, can bring in the young people who would never bother with the commercial trivialities of Shaftesbury Avenue. A case in point is the outstandingly brilliant work done by Joan Littlewood at E15. But her recent successes follow years of difficulty and personal privation – patient effort to maintain the highest standards faced with half-empty houses, years during which a meagre grant from Arts Council and subsidies from sympathetic local authorities had to be supplemented by the proceeds of overseas tours. For, ironically, productions from which the British public stayed obstinately away were acclaimed in the main theatres of Stockholm, Paris and Prague.

From *Design for Living*
A Labour Party publication, October 1959

. . . In Western Germany, every theatre seat sold costs the public budget 7s.6d. Nearly one hundred towns share in the £8,500,000 which is devoted to theatre. Frankfurt-am-Main spends £400,000 a year on its theatres. This comes out of the rates. Two new theatres are being built which will cost approximately £1,300,000. In France, the government spends about £116,000 a year on five provincial drama centres (another £14,000 comes from the municipalities). It invests another £50,000 a year (approximately) on the Théâtre Nationale Populaire; and (in 1953) it spent over £1,340,000 on the four national theatres in Paris. In Denmark, the Royal Theatre in Copenhagen receives about £250,000 a year.

From *The Future of the Theatre*
by Richard Findlater

From August 1945 to March 1960, Theatre Workshop received a total of £4,150 from the Arts Council of Great Britain and a lot of criticism, but when we transferred a play to Wyndhams, Sir W.E. Williams, their Secretary General, laid claim to ten per cent of the profits. 'We want that *Taste of Honey* money,' wrote Jo Hodgkinson.

GERRY to ARTS COUNCIL FINANCE DEPARTMENT

30th May 1960

Dear Mr Lund,

By now you will have received a statement from our accountants, showing that profits from the exploitation of *A Taste of Honey* totalled £7,047.3.6. The percentage due to you is £704.14.4, and as we have already paid you £633.1.5, that would seem to leave the sum of £71.12.11 outstanding.

I would point out, however, that our current overdraft at the bank is today £4,922.10.8. Do you not think that it is a little hard to force us into paying out money which we could use to keep the company afloat? Our present position is not exactly the healthiest.

Yours sincerely,

Gerald C. Raffles

We were heartened at Stratford by the arrival of a master of improvisation, William Saroyan, who believed that we had broken the ice in London. We assembled a good team: Murray Melvin, *Honey* having finished its run; Griffith Davies, a treasured performer from Wales; Ori Levy, star of Israel; Claire Isbister; Robert Henderson, who with William Sherwood had been in *The Quare Fellow*; and Johnnie Wallbank, who had set *Honey* to music. Songs by Saroyan, dances by Jean Newlove. E15 was alive again. The work went well, Saroyan was happy. . . . Until he read the critics. When the critics panned our work we ignored them. Not so William Saroyan! He wrote a long letter and sent a copy to each one of them.

The Savoy Hotel
London

Dear Elizabeth Frank and Gentlemen,

I have read, with a great deal of interest, your reviews of *Sam, the Highest Jumper of Them All* or *The London Comedy*.

I hope you won't mind if I comment on one aspect of this work in a single letter rather than in fifteen separate ones.

At the same time, permit me to ask permission to reprint each review with the play when it is published, as I believe the reviews of a play are a part of it. The play failed to win any of you. I would rather it had bowled you over, but I am not displeased that it didn't, for I cherish failure and am wary of success, since failure makes a man interesting, while success only makes him courteous.

I have never had a play that has won all the drama critics of New York, but this is the first time that one of my plays has failed to win at least one or two of the critics. As there are fifteen of you, I am obliged to give this fact the importance it obviously demands.

Easiest of all would be for me to agree that the play is bad, or at any rate that it doesn't work, but that's a little too easy, and hardly honest or useful.

I consider this play necessary to the theatre which, to quote from the play itself, 'is the last arena in which everything is still possible'.

If this is not so, then the theatre, like the gun, 'is a toy for idiots'.

Because contemporary reality, unlike Shakespeare's, Molière's or even Shaw's, contains nuclear (or potentially unlimited) power, the theatre, in order to have any meaning or use at all, must at least try to work from this truth.

Fifteen years ago, the Hiroshima and Nagasaki bombs gave the dramatists of the world (and everybody else) clear instructions which, as far as I know, have not been heeded. As a dramatist, 'I have tried. . . . It isn't easy. . . .'

The grand tradition of raging against 'fate or something just as bad' or against too much ice-cream in one part of the world and too little bread in another, or against one's own limitations, failures, desires or delusions, or against anything, just won't do any more. You may reason, but you may not rage.

Now, if art is to have any relation to reality – and I know of no other excuse for it – it has got to make drama (form, meaning, beauty, truth) out of grace – that is to say, serenity of spirit – intelligence, humour, wit, humility and self-criticism. If there is an enemy, he must be identified as one's self. It is useless to call the other fellow the enemy, while you carry on precisely as he does. This is the fallacy of propaganda, without which war, or any other form of hysteria, is impossible.

Apparently for the first time, man is in the possession of potentially unlimited power: whether used destructively or constructively, this power is giving us a new identity. Some of us are aware of this, and some of us aren't. When the identity of the whole race changes, as it has several times in several centuries, everything which is man's also changes, especially reality and, more slowly, art.

The use of force, even as a threat, is out. If it isn't, we may have to believe that, deliberately or unconsciously, we rejoice in the possibility at last of total self-destruction.

All of this high-falutin' stuff is in the play in the form of kindergarten drama and fun, which I staged in a stylised manner in the interest of clarity. The staging is in a straight line. Convolutions are intentionally avoided. There is no razzle-dazzle, no tom-tom beat, no alcoholics, no running, ranting, raving, or other hamming up. If man is always potentially a fraud, this is quite clear and therefore no harm is done.

Plays are for people, however. Drama critics are also people, and so you have a perfect right to protest that first and foremost, as they say, a play has got to be something effective in acceptable terms on the boards of a theatre.

Since the play for you wasn't, you have me there.

It was, and is, however, for me. I also am people, so where do we go from here? I write plays and you write criticism. There are fifteen of you and one of me. I am seriously considering the materials and themes of my next play: fifteen priests who wear hearing aids with three gear-shifts for volume, and shout about God and man, and shift gears.

I say *Sam* is a good play. I am sorry you say it isn't. One of us is obviously mistaken. Knowing the paltry little I know, I almost believe it is me.

Yours truly,

William Saroyan

The critics did not respond. No doubt the play will be acclaimed some time, somewhere else, and Americans will get over their respect for English opinion.

We glanced at our unhappy world to find the horrors of Sharpeville blackening the newspapers. To the credit of the entertainment industry every artist in London wanted to participate in a giant concert we arranged for the benefit of the victims.

We promoted Clifton Jones' New Negro Theatre and they opened with Paul Green's *No 'Count Boy* and Saroyan's *Hello, out There*. Then Claude Planson phoned from Paris: 'Bring us a classic, there's no English company with anything new.'

'A classic?' said Camel. 'They all need the inn yard, and the upstairs, downstairs.'

'Too expensive,' said Gerry. 'I'll tell Claude.'

'Why not improvise here?' said Claude.

'Might as well be hanged for a sheep as a lamb. I've always wanted to do *Every Man in His Humour*. Brian would make a dashing Bobadill and Victor could delve into his darker side for Brainworm.'

I loved the play and Ben wanted it to be 'as other plays should be:

> Where neither chorus wafts you o'er the seas,
> Nor creaking throne comes down, the boys to please;
> Nor nimble squib is seen to make afeard
> The gentlewomen; nor roll'd bullet heard
> To say, it thunders; no tempestuous drum
> Rumbles, to tell you when the storm doth come;
> But deeds, and language, such as men do use,
> And persons, such as Comedy would choose,

When she would shew an image of the times,
And sport with human follies, not with crimes. . . .
By laughing at them, . . .
Which when you heartily do, there's hope left then,
You, that have so grac'd monsters, may like men.'

Enter BOBADILL, KNOWELL *and* MATTHEW, *the gull.*

CAPTAIN BOBADILL: Were I known to her Majesty and the lords,
observe me – I would undertake, upon this poor head and life, for
the public benefit of the state, not only to spare the entire lives of
her subjects, but to save the one half, nay, three parts of her yearly
charge in holding war. And how would I do it, think you?

EDWARD KNOWELL: Nay, I know not, nor can I conceive.

CAPTAIN BOBADILL: Why thus, sir. I would select nineteen more,
to myself, throughout the land; gentlemen they should be, of
good spirit, strong and able constitution; I would choose them
by instinct; and I would teach these nineteen the special rules,
as your punto, your reverso, your staccato, your imbroccato,
your montanto; till they could all play very near, or as well as
myself. This done, say the enemy were forty thousand strong,
we twenty would come into the field the tenth of March, or
thereabouts; and challenge twenty of the enemy; they could not
on their honour refuse us. Well, we would kill them, challenge
twenty more, kill them; twenty more, kill them; twenty more,
kill them too; and thus would we kill every man his twenty a
day, that's twenty score; that's two hundred; two hundred a day,
five days, a thousand; forty thousand, forty times five, five times
forty, two hundred days kills them all, by computation. And this
will I venture my poor gentlemanlike carcase to perform.

EDWARD KNOWELL: Why, are you so sure of your hand, Captain,
at all times?

CAPTAIN BOBADILL: Tut! Never miss thrust, upon my reputation
with you.

EDWARD KNOWELL: I would not stand in Downright's state then,
an' you meet him, for the wealth of any one street in London.

CAPTAIN BOBADILL: Why, sir, you mistake me: if he were here
now, I would not draw my weapon on him. . . . but I will bas-
tinado him, by the bright sun, wherever I meet him.

EDWARD KNOWELL: Od's, so, look, where he comes. Yonder!

CAPTAIN BOBADILL: It is not he, is it?

DOWNRIGHT (*as he crosses the stage*): What peevish luck have I, I
cannot meet with this bragging rascal.

DOWNRIGHT *goes.*

EDWARD KNOWELL: Yes, faith, it was.

MATTHEW: I'll be hang'd, if that were he.

EDWARD KNOWELL: Sir, keep your hanging for some greater matter, I assure you that were he.

CAPTAIN BOBADILL: Had I thought it had been he, he must not have gone so: but I can hardly be induced to believe it was he yet.

DOWNRIGHT *returns, disarms and beats* BOBADILL. MATTHEW *runs away*.

So, he brought the *commedia dell'arte* to the London stage: his Captain was a dead ringer for the swaggering braggart he had probably seen in one of their troupes, when he was soldiering in the Low Countries.

Ben Jonson enjoyed settling old scores with his contemporaries. Matthew, who 'utters nothing but stolen remnants', was a dig at John Marston.

Brian Murphy was surpassing himself as Bobadill, Roy Kinnear was Matthew and Victor Spinetti had Brainworm to a T. Bob Grant, who'd been knocking around for a while, rejoined us to play Kitely. He'd favoured a cocked hat and a monocle when he first came to us, seeing himself as a new Ralph Lynn, but when provoked he proved to be a very intelligent actor.

The more attention we paid to detail, the more interesting the play became. It was exhilarating to watch the actors responding to the challenge of the language.

Forty-eight

Vic's nightclub won't release him for Paris. We close ranks and get by.
Bob Grant wins an acting award. Wolf Mankowitz backs Shelagh's
second play. We produce Sparrers Can't Sing *by Steve Lewis. The*
play does well. Brendan is said to be writing Richard's Cork Leg.
I go and see. He isn't. He records a passage – a disaster. He tries to
buy champagne – violence in the grocer's – the police – a court case
threatens.

Three days before we were due to leave for Paris Victor
dropped a bombshell. 'I won't be able to come.'

'That's unthinkable.'

'I know. I've been trying to get round them all week.' Victor
was in the late show each night at Winston's Nightclub.

'You'd only be away two nights!'

'I've never been abroad either, but I couldn't walk out on them.'

I sympathised. Then I realised what a mess we were in: one
couldn't introduce a new player at this stage of the war, and for
two nights only. It would have to be the usual solution – shuffle
the parts around, rely on doubles. The company was disheartened,
but Paris would lift our spirits. It did, till we walked into the Sarah
Bernhardt and saw a mountain of packing cases on stage.

'Do what you like with them,' said Jean-Pierre, the Stage
Director, by now an old friend.

We juggled with those packing cases, draped them, lit them
– and they still looked terrible.

No Victor, no set! But when we heard, 'Beginners, please,' and
the three bangs, we came to life and our newfound comedian, Bob
Grant, won a medal for his performance as Kitely.

Back home, with Victor restored to us and a practical set, we
enjoyed rare Ben Jonson, but our audience was composed, almost
entirely, of foreigners.

Gerry had found a letter from his old pal, Jo, waiting for him:

What's this I read in the *Daily Express* about Shelagh Delaney's next play being presented by Wolf Mankowitz? Did Joan decide that she didn't want to do it?

Hodgkinson

So all the talk about Arts Council never reading anything more plebeian than the *Daily Telegraph* is untrue. To be honest with you, we cannot face the prospect of having to pay out all our former losses to Arts Council if we did another Delaney play.

Raffles

Had Mankowitz adapted the script? Had Shelagh made something of it? We soon heard. An ASM, formerly in our company, had been engaged as director with Howard Goorney in the leading rôle. The script had not been touched.

We had decided on a play by Stephen Lewis. He had been around for the build-up of *The Hostage* and *You Won't Always Be On Top*. His play, *Sparrers Can't Sing*, was gentle and nostalgic. Its characters? Amiable layabouts, bird fanciers, gamblers and their offspring, just the way our locals saw themselves.

Victor sent one of the girls from Winston's to see us when we were casting.

'I'm a dancer, I've never acted,' she told him.

'That's all right,' said Victor. 'You'll see.'

Gerry met her at the door. I was laying out some newly duplicated pages in the gallery. I heard a great guffaw from Gerry and looked down to see a dainty young blonde grumbling about being asked to sweep the stage. There were no flies on that one. Another guffaw from the stalls.

'Hey!' I shouted down. 'What's happening?'

'Who was that?' she said.

'Joan,' said Gerry.

'Oh, is she going to audition me now?'

'You've been auditioned,' said Gerry.

I asked her if she could stay.

'I could start tomorrow morning.'

'And Saturday?'

'Saturday's a bit difficult. I was going to have my hair done.'

'When you could be rehearsing the best part in the play?'

'I know, but I was going to get married.'

Winston's supplied us with a constant stream of young women after Barbara Ferris. They could all sing, dance, ad lib, change clothes in a matter of seconds and, despite the most uncomfortable conditions, light up the scene.

The newly-wed Barbara played in *Sparrers* and stayed with us. So did Jenny Logan, Clovissa Newcombe, Toni Palmer, Val Walsh and Barbara Windsor – all super performers. I would say actresses, but too many lost souls from universities, *haute societé* and theatrical families have debased the word, so I'll leave it out.

On the other hand, there was no one around who could play a working-class gran. Didn't they figure in pre-Workshop drama?

'Let Stephen play it, in drag,' said Bob Grant. 'He loves taking off his old mum.'

Millie, a little barrel of a woman, appeared one day. In the right clothes, she would pass – till she opened her mouth. Strewth. She sounded like a 1920 LCC schoolteacher. Stephen volunteered to teach her proper English, and on the strength of that we took her on and she took a crash course in cockney.

Murray Melvin, Griff Davies, Sean Lynch and Barbara Ferris were the young ones. Roy Kinnear and Stephen Lewis two old bums – the funniest thing since Laurel and Hardy. The set was the Ben Jonson with brickwork added. It was more solid than the theatre. It had to be: every night Bob Grant performed acrobatic miracles, manoeuvring an iron bed-frame through an upstairs window. Soon the 'House Full' notice was up every night. The locals relished the old-time chat and our 'working-class gran' fooled everybody, even Lionel Bart, who gave her a lead in his next West End production, *Blitz*.

Meanwhile, how was Brendan getting on with his promised 'next'? Gerry phoned him.

'Fine,' came the reply. 'Will I sing you me latest song?' And his full-throated tenor came crackling across the ether:

> *It's me ould Irish tomb*
> *I'll be in there soon*
> *But first I will fuck you*
> *Beneath the harvest moon.*
> *No matter where you come from*
> *No matter where you be*
> *Remember that ould Irish graveyard*
> *And Father and Mother Macree.*

'What's the play called? Is it still *Richard's Cork Leg*?'

'Why not? Would you not have me honour James Joyce? Didn't he say, when they asked him why his new play hadn't caught on, "I should have given Richard a cork leg"?'

'You'd better go over and see if he's got anything down on paper,' Gerry told me.

I went and when I got to the Behan home in Ballsbridge, everything was much as usual. Beatrice was grilling four large steaks, Brendan was sitting in the dining-room discussing the flight of the Earls with Flann O'Brien, whose real name was Brian O'Nolan, but whose weekly column in the *Irish Times* appeared under the name Myles Na Gopaleen. A bilingual discussion was going on, not to be interrupted till Brendan roared, 'When will dinner be ready?'

'It's on the table now,' Beatrice called back. We adjourned to eat and refresh ourselves with draughts of claret.

'Good stuff,' said O'Brien. 'What year is it?'

'I never heard a Frenchman ask that question,' said Brendan. 'He only wants to know what degree it is.'

' 'Twas Irish merchants who first imported the claret,' said Flann.

'*Vin clair*,' Brendan corrected him. 'Only the English couldn't pronounce it.' After the meal he fell asleep and his guest took his leave. It was the first chance I'd had to ask Beatrice how the play was progressing.

'Oh, indeed, he's started it,' she said. 'But with the prospect of New York for *The Hostage* he's laid it aside for a while.'

'He'll never write in New York.'

'You'll get him in harness again.'

But the moment our playwright woke up, he insisted on taking us on one of his guided tours, first to the local, of course, where he had a crack and a couple of jars with a bandy bloke in leggings.

'What does he do for a living?' I asked.

'He's paid two pounds a day by an Englishman to feed his dogs and walk them.'

'Can't the Englishman walk his own dogs?'

'He could if he were here, but he's in England.'

Then we took a cab to an ancient graveyard on the top of a high cliff. 'This is where my play is set,' said Brendan, and he climbed on to the stone table above an old grave.

> *It's me ould Irish tomb*
> *I'll be in there soon.*

And he lay there, eyes closed, arms crossed. I walked away. The grass was tall and spikey. The cemetery was railed in. I watched the waves tracing thin lines far below. He was reading the tombstones now, or pretending to: 'O'Hare . . . O'Toole . . . My beloved came . . . and went.'

'How's the drinking?' I asked Beatrice.

'Not desperate. He got himself arrested in Greystones a while back. He went there to write. They found him lying by the roadside, talking to himself. They took him to court and he defended himself in Irish.'

'They speak Irish in Greystones?'

'The magistrate does.'

Back at Anglesea Road, I raised the matter of the play with him. 'You know, we're leaving for America very soon. You've a date on Broadway.'

'To hell with America. I've no wish to go there. It was they who depopulated Ireland. And what happened when we got there?'

'Ellis Island.'

'Have you relatives in the United States? How much foreign currency? Address . . . ?' and he fell asleep on the old sofa muttering, 'To hell with you and your friends in America.'

'He'll work tomorrow,' Beatrice said. I doubted it; but to my surprise she was right. He was up before any of us. I found him upstairs in his den, fresh as a daisy. 'Today's the day,' he said, rolling a new page into his typewriter. I picked up three or four others which had blown round the room when I opened the door. I glanced at them.

Scene: Yesterday's churchyard. Two old bawds are discovered.

BAWD I: There's some beautiful tombstones. Here's one put by a
   widow:

> *We were but one night wed*
> *One night of blessed content,*
> *At dawn he died, in bed*
> *My darling came and went.*

BAWD II: Came and went, dear, dear.

BAWD I: Here's another, O'Hare and O'Toole – turn off that
   radio.

BAWD II: Me little Japanee transistor?

Later, BAWD I *announces trouble in Hungary.*

BAWD II: Those Hungry Aryans are cannibals. My husband was
   eaten by Hungry Aryans out in Africa.

BAWD I: There's no Aryans in Africa.

BAWD II: God's curse on the hungry bastards, wherever they are.
   There was nothing left of him but a button and a bone.

I supposed they would be acting as chorus to the main action, but as yet there was no sign of main action, let alone a plot.

Brendan was chuckling, ' "Tougher than a jockey's balls", I'll work that one in.'

'But you must have a plot, B.B. What happened to the story you told me of Crystal Clear, the young whore whose body was found up in the mountains? Suspicion fell on the police, you told me, but it was all hushed up, nobody dared open their mouths.'

'Sure, and I'll bring her into it. I'll have the old biddies tending her grave. I'll bring General O'Duffy in, too. The only man who came back from Spain with more men than he went with.'

'What was he doing there?'

'Fighting for Franco. Now will you let me get on with me story?'

'You do that. I'll make a list of the eight plots.'

I got out of his way, looked through some of his other writing, *The Big House*, *The Catacombs*. Nothing had inspired him so much as the hanging in Mountjoy Prison or the death of a young British hostage. *Borstal Boy* too had one deeply felt death in it, his friend, lost at sea.

He threw another couple of pages at me. One or two improbable characters had appeared – Cronin, who'd been in gaol for rape and was letting his young wife die of starvation after giving birth to four children. 'She can live for a couple of days on her milk,' he said. The other invention was 'The Hero Hogan', another improbable who had apparently been sitting around in the churchyard, an IRA man disguised in a black beard and black glasses. More jokes:

> BAWD I: Will you give me a long penance?
> CRONIN: What harm if it's short, if it's thick?

No sign of a story.

'If anyone saw us cooking up a play they'd never believe it,' said B.B.

'You've plenty of jokes. I think we should record them and weave them into a first draft. You'll say a tape recorder is an easy way out but it's worth a trial.'

'I've a couple of songs I'd like to record.'

He'd always taken his subjects from real life, but at the moment nothing seemed to inspire him; the success of the plays, all those interviews, had cluttered his mind. I went out to look for a tape deck.

It wasn't easy. Ballsbridge wasn't rich in gadget shops. After traipsing around I finally found one, in, of all places, the local hospital. It was a cumbersome job, a prototype. They said I could have it for a few days and didn't even ask for a deposit. I struggled back to Anglesea Road with the heavy gadget – and that was the easiest part. I couldn't get the damn thing going. Gerry would have solved it in a minute. Brendan found me switching and winding and unwinding.

'Are you going to spend the rest of the morning fucking about with that fucking Sonnabox? It's a great day. We should be up in the hills.'

'I've seen the hills.'

'Today you haven't.'

I was so fed up, I gave in. We went on a pub crawl, such a one as only Dublin can provide – a merry-go-round of fiddlers, tipsters, gas bags and loners, old ladies with well-darned mittens and gentle dockers. Beatrice joined us at a quiet boozer that looked like a grocery store and there we downed a creamy Guinness and made for the hills.

> *Down by the Salley gardens,*
> *my love and I did meet*
> *She bade me take love easy*
> *as the leaf grows on the tree*
> *But I, being young and foolish,*
> *with her did not agree.*

Someone was singing in the parlour of the pub under the hill. Another voice joined in and together they sang of the white, orange and green. 'We'll never get him out if he goes in there,' said Beatrice.

There was nothing Brendan liked better than an impromptu *ceilidh*, so in we went and he sang till the cows came home. It was hard to say goodbye.

Next morning the den was aired, the tape recorder switched on. The day promised well. Brendan seized the microphone and launched into a sparkling recitative. When he paused for breath, 'I want to hear that,' he said.

'Nothing easier, but why don't we push on a bit first?'

'After I've heard the "me" bit.'

Before I could say more, he bent over and pressed the nearest button. Nothing happened. He tried the one next to it; a little red light came on and there was a mad squeaking. I tried. The squeaking stopped, thank God.

'All's well.'

I pressed the first button. The tape went whirling round, shooting up into the air, in a hopeless tangle.

'Jesus!' cried Brendan. 'Stop the fucking thing.' He pressed every button he could find. The tangle was mounting at a terrifying rate. Suddenly he seized it, as one might grasp a dangerous snake, and began wrenching it from the machine, yard after yard. Finally it broke, and hurling it to the floor he stormed out of the room.

Oh dear. For a second or two I contemplated the chaos; then I, too, left the room. I found him on the phone which hung in a small cubbyhole under the stairs.

'Beatrice!' he shouted. She was in the kitchen and answered him quietly.

'They're proposing to cut some of the lines in my radio play.'

'Who's they?'

'Radio Eireann.' And he slammed the phone down and made for the front door.

'Go with him,' she said.

I caught up with him along the road. We didn't say a word. At the corner he hailed a taxi. 'Stephen's Green,' he said.

Nobody spoke. Unusual, because all the taxi drivers in Dublin knew him. Most of them, finding him footless, had driven him home, at one time or another.

When we pulled up, Brendan made for the pub.

'Are we going to drink?'

'If you want to eat?' I didn't, but grub might take his mind off the booze.

'Bailey's is the place,' he said.

It was. I was given a plate of roast beef and a glass of house wine. Bailey's was the meeting place for Dublin's writers and artists. The owner, John Ryan, liked good company and if you couldn't pay it would go on the slate.

While Brendan was at the bar, someone muttered in my ear, 'Your man stole Frank O'Connor's work for his *Hostage*. Did you know that?'

Brendan heard. 'That's a lie, you pox bottle,' he shouted. He was red with anger.

'We've a date, Brendan, remember?' I said, and picking up his overcoat made for the door.

'You've taken my coat,' someone shouted. So I had to go back. When I reached the street, Brendan was disappearing into a high-class grocer's. I ran to catch up with him.

'Bubbly,' he said. 'For Beatrice. It's my birthday.' And he made for the drinks shelves at the far end of the shop. A lordly assistant wanted to know what he could do for us. Brendan was scanning the wine shelves.

'We want a good champagne,' I said. A bottle was reached down.

'Supermarket stuff,' said Brendan. The salesman collected another from a lower shelf.

'That's no fucking good either,' said Brendan dismissing it with a gesture.

A second assistant flung himself between Brendan and the champagne. 'That's enough, guttersnipe.' He spat it out as a third assistant grabbed Brendan's right arm, twisted it and started kneeing him towards a door at the back of the shop.

'The street door's that way!' I shouted. 'Where are you taking him?'

'Isn't it terrible?' said an old lady who was looking at the tinned fruit.

'Call the *gardaí*,' shouted the lordly one. I followed the men into a small office. One of them, the third, I think, was punching Brendan in the face; the other two were holding him down.

'Stop that!' I shouted, punching the nearest man as hard as I could.

For a moment they stopped. Brendan reeled against the wall. Two policemen were entering the shop. The assistants were righting the desk which had been thrown over and picking up sheets of paper, a cigarette packet and an intercom telephone.

'Fine fucking birthday,' muttered Brendan, blood streaming from the corner of his mouth.

'Let me take him home,' I said. 'He's not well.'

The two policemen were upon us.

'He's a blackguard,' said the second assistant. The police seized

Brendan and frogmarched him to the front door. They obviously knew who he was.

'Where are you taking him?' They were bundling him into a police car.

'Harcourt Terrace.'

I found a cab across the road and gave that address, but when we arrived he wasn't there. 'He's at College Street,' I was told.

Brendan was in the hands of the police for eight hours, without the refreshment of a glass of water, without the blood being washed from his face. As he said himself, 'Fine fucking birthday.'

Still, they'd probably give him a state funeral, when the time came.

Anger passed over Brendan like the shadow of a cloud; passers-by could calm him, pacify him and set him on his way.

'They won't take him to court.'

'Oh they will,' said Beatrice.

'Then I'm his witness.'

Forty-nine

The Hostage is opening in New York. Gerry and I go ahead to contradict the bad press Brendan has been getting. A curious radio interview. The company and Brendan arrive, he is mobbed by press men. The backers worry about our accents. We play a joke on them. A brush with the Stage Manager. The first-night audience. Next day, Vic visits Lee Strasberg's studio. Dudley Sutton looks for Khrushchev's boat. Studs Terkel corners me. We meet Libby Holman. Tom Driberg to the Labour Party Conference, Scarborough – Gerry and I to London, Brendan and Beatrice remain in New York.

August 26th, 1961. Gerry and I on Pan Am, Economy, 13.00 Heathrow to Idlewild. We are travelling ahead of the company to try and counteract the bad publicity Brendan has been getting in New York. 'DRUNKEN PLAYWRIGHT IN WINE-SHOP BRAWL', 'IRISH PLAYWRIGHT BRINGING HIS *HOSTAGE* TO BROADWAY', 'WHEN IRISH EYES ARE BLOODSHOT' – columns of it.

We have been in the air two hours and no sign of food. Gerry must eat soon or he will be disorientated. It's a bumpy ride and the enormous plane is jam packed.

'We advise you to keep your seat-belts fastened.'

You can see nothing out of the windows; we must have flown over Ireland. I'd no idea flying would be so boring. I started thinking about Brendan. Why had they treated him so brutally?

'Just get me back over there!' It was the voice of the American lady two seats away. . . .

He had looked smart, that last day in court, clean white shirt, hair well-brushed, shoes polished. I got up to try and do something about Gerry's meal.

'Resume your seat, please.'

I sat down grumpily. Those shop assistants hinting at his reputation.

'We are encountering a certain amount of turbulence. Lunch
will be served as soon as possible.'

Saroyan was right. It was no use railing against injustice, but
yet . . . it was the fat policeman who'd saved the day: 'The last
time I arrested him, Your Honour, he gave me five pounds for the
police orphans.'

Lunch arrived at last and we attacked the plastic lids with
Gerry's penknife. It was a long, uneventful flight and when,
eventually, we bumped down to Idlewild airport, a party of
American ladies applauded. . . .

Outside? Steam heat. Steam rising from grids in the tarmac-
adam, yellow cabs tearing by or screeching to a halt and yelling
at each other in an unknown tongue. Bronze sky. Howling sirens,
grey boxes with slits on all the window-sills – buildings that
reached so high they converged.

'There are a lot of bird fanciers,' I said to the cabby.

'Yeah, two of 'em shot dead today.'

'Bird fanciers?'

'Blacks, stealing steaks. You from Australia?'

'No, but those!' And I waved at all the window-boxes.

'That's air-conditioning plant, ma'am.'

When we pulled up at the Bristol, West 48th Street, Gerry
coped with the strange money. . . . It was now past midnight but
looked like bright day.

'Thank God, there's an eatery,' said Gerry. 'Two hamburgers,
please.'

'Thousand Islands on the table. Coffee? Reg'lar?'

'Thanks.'

The place was all white tiles and wisecracks. I must have
fallen asleep there, for I've no recollection of getting to bed.

When I woke it was dark outside, but I stepped out of the
window on to a flat roof and could just discern the Empire State,
towering above us. This morning Gerry would be tackling the
newspapers, I would be giving radio interviews. A slip of paper
pushed under the door gave us our programme.

I washed and dressed hastily, wrote Gerry a note and left.
My first date was early and I was nervous. At the radio station I
was shown into a small basement studio. A pale, very tired man,

in his shirt-sleeves, was whispering hoarsely into a microphone –
ashtrays piled high with cigarette butts served as paperweights
and there were cartons rimmed with the stains of black coffee
everywhere. He turned a lack-lustre eye on me and nodded to
a chair on the other side of the table.

'A lot of people are kissing you this morning, Joan. . . .'

That threw me. Why should anybody be kissing me? Nobody
knew who I was or what I was doing here. . . .

'First time in New York?'

'Yes,' I said, 'and I've come to have a word about Brendan.'

'Enjoy your stay.'

'He's a remarkable man. Ireland should be proud of him.'

'I'm sure they are. It's a great shame that he wasn't here
for the St Patrick's Day parade.'

'His show is a parade. I only hope we shall see you at the
Cort theatre one night.'

'Sure – and you are very welcome to our city. Ever seen the
inside of a radio station? Have a look round the building. Mrs
Vanderpump will be pleased to conduct you.'

'Thank you, but I do have several interviews today.'

'Good girl. Mrs V.! Molly!' Nobody answered. 'By the way,
your calligraphy. It has a name, hasn't it?' He was holding the
note I'd just written with our address. 'Very unusual. You don't
type?'

'No.'

A sad man came in carrying a small fish tank. 'Butterfly fish,' he
said and smiled. Mrs V. appeared carrying the morning papers. 'A
lot of people will bless your name this morning, Vance,' our host
was saying to the fish man.

I beat a retreat. 'I don't think I made much of a mark on
your boss, Mrs V.'

'Too soon,' she said. 'You're not hot yet.'

We were hot by the time Brendan and the company arrived,
long overdue, but the crowd of reporters still growing. When the
plane, with the shamrock on its tail, touched down, Brendan was
the first to appear. Even before the landing steps were in place, he
was at the door smiling and waving. The rush was on. He was lost
in a forest of cameras and microphones. I caught a glimpse of him

trotting across the tarmac, an enormous green rosette in his button-hole. The company looked a bit shaky. They'd been fourteen hours in the air. Two nuns and a priest brought up the rear.

We moved to the Arrivals gate. And who was the first to appear? Patience Collier. She was playing the social worker, Miss Gilchrist, in New York, and gave us all a queenly smile.

'Oh those rude Customs officers,' she said when she saw me. 'Do you know what that awful man said to me?'

'I can't imagine.'

' "Open your bag." '

'And what did you say?'

'I said, "Say please," but he merely repeated himself. "Open your bag." ' 'Not till you say please.'

'And did he?'

'No.'

'So what did you do?'

'I simply stood there till there was quite a long queue.'

' "Ma'am! Please! You're holding up the line." '

' "Thank you," I said, and opened my bag.'

Brendan appeared next and I saw that he had 'Up Down' in the middle of his green rosette. Then came the reporters: 'Take it easy! Stand back there!' Gerry was trying to control the situation.

But Brendan was surrounded. What did he think about alcoholism, teetotalism and every other -ism? Was he an IRA man?

'Yes, but they sentenced me to death in me absence. "Right," I said, "You can shoot me in my absence." ' And he burst into song:

> Oh, had he died by Pearse's side
> Or in the GPO
> Killed by an English bullet
> From the rifle of the foe
> Or forcibly fed, where Ashe lay dead
> In the dungeons of Mountjoy
> I'd have cried with pride
> At the way you died
> My own dear laughing boy.

'Michael Collins,' he said. 'My song. It's in the show.'

How did he rate the latter-day Irish poets?

> *We that have done and thought,*
> *That have thought and done,*
> *Must ramble and thin out*
> *Like milk spilt on a stone.*

'William Butler Yeats, for all time,' he said.

Gerry insisted on the interviews continuing elsewhere and we moved to the VIP lounge.

'Are you queer, Brendan? We've thought so, since *Borstal Boy*. . . .'

'Well, if I had to choose between Michelangelo's David and Whistler's Mother . . .'

What was he going to do in New York?

'Visit the Empire State Building in honour of King Kong and swim at the Jewish boys' club.'

'Why there? You're not a Jew.'

'But I'll be the only one with a foreskin.'

The questioning went on for four hours. Every time Gerry moved in to put a stop to it the newshounds bayed for more, and by now B.B. wanted to give it to them. He ran his fingers through his tousled hair, in his element, entertaining that tough audience. We had to drag him away.

'In the name of Jesus and His blessed mother, am I not to have a look at the place before I go for a kip?' We took a taxi and toured New York.

'This is something like a city; but where are all the bars?'

We dropped in at Jimmy Gemmens, the place for serious stand-up drinking, and there it was we finished up in the after-glow of dawn – or dusk.

Our theatre was on 48th and Gerry and I went along next morning to look it over. The lights were rigged, the set was up. The company had a day off, a run-through being scheduled for the following morning. One of our backers turned up and after the usual greetings I asked if everything was going according to plan.

'Everything's going well – it's just the problem of the cockney boy and the Irish girl. We're afraid the audience won't understand them.'

'But they don't understand each other. Getting to do so is the story of the play.'

'I don't want to interfere, of course, but I have found a speech coach.'

'You mean you want them to speak perfect American?'

'Oh no. I don't want to lose the flavour of Brendan.'

'We all talked Brooklyn when we were kids – learnt it at the pictures. New York will enjoy a bit of real English.'

'Or ask for their money back.'

'I guarantee you they won't do that – Celia and Alfie are too good.'

'I shall be at tomorrow's run-through with my partner. We'll decide then.'

I wasn't worried about the accents, or the show. The run-through was simply to accustom the company to a different stage. But all artists are vulnerable and I didn't want the hostage, Alfie Lynch, and his girl, Celia Salkeld, upset.

When we arrived next morning our two backers were already there, seated in the stalls. We started on time and everything went smoothly. The hostage is seen for the first time at the end of Act One. He is shoved on to the stage. His army uniform was too small. No wonder – Victor Spinetti was in it. And who was that swamped in Victor's IRA mackintosh? Alfie Lynch! Teresa, the shy country girl, was not young Celia, slim and lovely, but sturdy, middle-aged Patience Collier. Celia appeared as seedy Miss Gilchrist. I'd swapped them all around.

Our backers didn't say a word. They just left. I never saw their speech coach.

After the run-through a burly man in a lumberjacket was waiting for me. 'I'm Stage Manager here. You can drop that goddam flag on the deck, if you like.' He pointed to the Union Jack. 'And that one! And that! Any of 'em. But not Old Glory!'

He was referring to a very important moment at the end of Act Two when the hostage is given a newspaper and all the other characters are shouting patriotic slogans and waving their national flags. As Alfie reads out loud the news that he is to be shot, the flags are lowered. They droop and fall to the floor.

'Is any flag worth the taking of one life?'

I didn't change it, it was too important to me, and I heard no more from that Stage Manager.

The first night? From the moment the curtain went up on a wild Irish jig, the audience was with us. They understood the symbolism of the flags, they understood us.

'Are you really having a ball up there?' someone shouted.

'Sure. Come and join us,' Victor replied.

We were used to interruptions; at Stratford we'd encouraged them, enjoyed them and hoped the same thing would happen in New York. It did, and to put the lid on it, who should come smiling through the pass door at the final curtain? Our beloved Tom Driberg. He had never missed one of our first nights and this was to be no exception. Theatre Workshop in New York! Triumph for Brendan, the company and each and every one of us.

We celebrated in style – Irish stew, drink, as much as you could take, and a *ceilidh* band. Every actor had a pretty girl on each arm; each actress an attentive lad, or one or two, or three or more – well! When those Broadway babies said good night it was tomorrow morning and the wage slaves were hurrying to work along the sweaty streets. Tom flagged a lift to his hotel on a milk float.

The neon lights went out, the tops of the tall buildings were appearing above the mist. The big ads were sombre grey now, their flashing bulbs switched off. I stopped to admire the Camel hoarding puffing real smoke. To bed, but not for long – today each to his own devices, until the hour call.

Dudley Sutton went down to the docks to see if the Soviet ship carrying Nikita Khrushchev had arrived. He was coming to address the UN. No, not yet. But the stevedores had prepared a welcome for him, 'Go Home, Red Rat,' in giant letters on the wall. Fidel Castro had already arrived. They put him in the Waldorf Astoria, but he'd moved out and gone to stay with some compatriots down in Spanish Harlem.

Brendan went for a swim, ate a steak and laid off the booze.

He was to give a lecture at the College for Catholic Girls – Victor had located the Actors' Studio and wanted to see Lee Strasberg in action.

Brendan was delighted with the Catholic girls. He'd found his Tir n'a n'Óg, he said. 'Spent the afternoon with Marilyn Monroe, myself,' said Victor.

'Bejaysus, where?'

'Studying the Method.'

'Which one's that?'

'Lee Strasberg's.'

'Used to wash for our family.'

Gerry and I had been in the theatre all day. While he was away making phone calls, a friendly, smiling character walked in. 'I'm Studs Terkel,' he said, 'and I know who you are. I'd like to know what you're after.' On the spur of the moment, I told him. I let rip, came out with all my thoughts and ambitions. 'The world is your oyster,' he said at the end.

'Were you taping that?'

'Yes, but I won't use it if you don't want me to.'

I didn't say no. I liked him. We became great friends.

Later that evening, we met up with Tom. 'Alan Lomax has invited us to a singalong, do you fancy it?' said Gerry. 'It's somewhere over on the East River.'

'I'd have to ask permission of the FBI, if we're leaving Manhattan.'

'Why?'

He sighed. 'You do know that I'm on the National Executive of the British Labour Party.'

'Yes.'

'And you have heard of MacCarthy and his Un-American Activities Committee?'

'You don't mean you're Un-American?'

'No. But the British Labour Party is.'

'And you think you'd have to "name" our host and Alan Lomax might finish up in a chain gang? Perhaps we should just take a stroll along the Great White Way.' Which we did, till we were halted by a crowd on the sidewalk, listening to a voice coming from the dark, 'Oh, the shark has pearly teeth, dear. . . .'

'It's Satchmo!' It was. We stayed listening till Gerry declared that he was hungry.

'We could try Libby,' said Tom.

'Who?'

'Camel cigarettes.'

'Did she think up that ad?'

'No, she married Mr Camel himself. Shortly after, they found him dead beside the icebox. She was the Number One suspect.'

When we located her maisonette, she was at the piano, murdering the 'St James Infirmary Blues'. 'So you took up singing,' said Tom, after she'd embraced him.

'One has to do something.' And she wiped away a tear. 'You know it came out that he was . . .' She waved a limp hand.

'Really?' said Tom. 'Have you eaten, dear?'

'I don't; only on alternate days. It's for my chords.' And she opened her mouth wide. Gerry's stomach gave a terrific gurgle.

'You may find something edible in the icebox.' Tom went and looked, but there was only an old sliced loaf in cellophane. 'That woman is worth millions,' said Tom as we sat in the local Kwikfood eating saveloys.

All too soon, Tom had to return to England for the Labour Party Conference at Scarborough. Nye Bevan and kindred spirits were opposed to Hugh Gaitskill and Tom supported them. We accompanied him to the airport.

At 3.15 in the morning, the phone in our room rang. It was Tom. 'Engine trouble halfway across the Atlantic. We had to turn back. Free drinks, of course, but tiresome having to locate the FBI at this hour.'

'Must you?'

'I must report my whereabouts. I'm in some Godforsaken hole a long way from Manhattan.'

A quarter of an hour later, the phone rang again. I let Gerry answer it. 'Did you get them, Tom?'

'Of course. I apologised for disturbing them at this ungodly hour, and explained that owing to an act of God I had landed here without their permission.'

'I'd have liked to see their faces,' said Gerry.

When Tom arrived at the conference, the vote had been

taken, Harold Wilson had thrown in his lot with the Bevanites and England was all set for another split.

So were we! The SM at the Cort theatre showed me a cutting announcing the Broadway production of *Taste of Honey* by Shelagh Delaney. No mention of Theatre Workshop, a conventional new cast and a director who'd let it be known that I'd ruined 'Shelagh's lovely, poetic play'. He can't have read it. I had the only original copy.

On top of that, Brendan was back on the booze and all the Irish pubs were beginning to bar him. Nevertheless, he and Beatrice came to Idlewild to see us off. Gerry and I had to return to England. The Maxim Gorki theatre in Berlin wanted us to stage our production of *Sparrers Can't Sing* there.

As our flight was called, Brendan gave each of us a hot, greasy hand and, half-drunk, sang his ominous song:

> . . . *me ould Irish tomb*
> *I'll be in there soon* . . .

The rest was drowned by the amplifiers. 'This is the final announcement.' I was so relieved to get away. As the plane reached the dark night, far below a million lightbulbs formed the shape of a Christmas tree.

Fifty

Study Danton's Death *by Büchner, which we cannot afford. We take* Sparrers Can't Sing *to East Berlin. Harry Corbett directs an Alun Owen play while we are away. John Junkin falls for* They Might be Giants *by Jim Goldman. Hal Prince finances it. The author attends rehearsals. To a man, the critics damn it. Disgusted, I quit theatre and Gerry. Sidney Bernstein arranges for Malcolm Muggeridge to interview me on TV. I go to Nigeria to work with Wole Soyinka, meet a young architect who sees me off. Goodbye, Europe.*

I was rereading Büchner's *Danton's Death*. Its scenes are vivid images in a dream which haunts me as the French Revolution haunted him. It occurred only forty-six years before he was born, when St Just was twenty-two. Danton and Robespierre were only thirty-five when they were guillotined. These characters, drawn with such sensitivity, would have to be played by young men – and the production? Invisible.

I longed for the time and money to work on it. Meanwhile the Maxim Gorki theatre was waiting to see our production of *Sparrers Can't Sing*. This simple story, set in London's East End, charmed the East Berliners with its truth and humour, perhaps as a change from their more serious dramaturgy.

Gerry had persuaded Harry Corbett to direct a play while we were away. I was delighted to see Harry back. He had chosen *Progress to the Park* by Alun Owen and collected a team of young artists, including Tom Bell and long-lost Billie Whitelaw. He made an excellent job of the play and, rather surprisingly, proved a very good educator.

John Junkin, son of a local policeman, had wandered into the theatre one day – a witty young man who was turning his hand to writing. He was intrigued by the unread scripts in Gerry's office and sat around reading them.

'Hey! Listen to this!' We were dispersing after Harry C.'s notes one lunch-time. Some had already left, the rest sat down, one after another.

'What's the name of it?'

'*They Might Be Giants*, by somebody Goldman.'

'The dialogue's very American.'

'There's a letter from Hal Prince with it, offering financial assistance.'

That clinched it. A meeting was called and we read the American saga right through. It's about a doctor who imagines he is Sherlock Holmes and a Doctor Watson, Mildred, who is inveigled into hunting Moriarty with him through wildest New York. It presented many problems set-wise, and the author was uncompromising: 'The action never stops, no pauses. The set changes are written into the play.'

Unfortunately, the company was already in love with the damn play! And there was that financial backing. I'd find a solution to all those set changes if it killed me.

I found a clue in an old Italian book of set designs. Try this one: 'Construct a number of small revolving circular rostra and connect them. Each one must support a prism of three screens. As they turn, a new vista is revealed, unseen hands change the screens upstage while the play is progressing.'

We made it work and Gerry clinched the deal. Harry C. and Avis played Sherlock and Watson; the company doubled and trebled the other parts between them. Then the author arrived, a lanky young man with glasses, from Chicago. He sat in the stalls at every rehearsal, just cracking his fingers, till Barbara Ferris came on stage in her nurse's uniform, then he'd sigh.

At the third rehearsal, we discovered the verse, carefully concealed under the smart dialogue. We became quite obsessed with this scatty play and its secret poet. It came as a shock when, to a man, the critics turned it down. Jim Goldman didn't fight back like Saroyan, but rewrote his play as a film with George C. Scott playing Holmes, and I'm sure he couldn't have been as good as Harry Corbett.

At first, I raged against the critics, then I gave them up. London was finished anyway. We could do better anywhere else. We couldn't do worse.

What was the straw that broke the camel's back? I'm not exactly sure. It could have been that night when I was sitting outside Olivelli's, in Gerry's car, and Tom Driberg joined us. A cynical remark was passed – about E15 – or the play. . . . All I remember is getting up and going, just going . . . wandering about . . . lost.

In the small hours, I found myself near the block of service flats where Jim Goldman had lodged. I asked if they had any accommodation. I was shown to the flat he had recently vacated. I fell on the divan and slept.

Tom found out where I was, don't ask me how. He was, after all, a newshound. He was also kind. It was fine summer weather. He took me to Bradwell, found me a garden chair, brought out his finest wines and played my favourite jazz records. I told him I wasn't going back to E15.

Next day he heard that Malcolm Muggeridge was cutting short his summer holiday to interview me on TV. Who fixed that? I'd never liked interviews. The truth was that Tom had told Sidney Bernstein my story and Bernstein had recalled Muggeridge. All right, I'd give them their interview and tell the truth, for once.

I did.

Muggeridge was charming. We fenced politely for a minute, then he tried to blame ungrateful actors for my departure. I laughed so much at the word 'ungrateful' that my woolly cap fell off and to retrieve it I knelt on my stool, turning my backside to the camera. The camera crew started to laugh.

'Let's turn the camera on them,' I told Muggeridge. 'Nobody ever sees the crew. Shall we change places with them, see if they do our job better than us?' I was on my favourite subject, wasted talent, lack of opportunity, old-hat education and the lack of joy in learning and living. I heard later that some of my swear words were cut before the interview went out, but I was away by then. I'd decided to go to Nigeria, find Wole Soyinka and film his most beautiful play *The Lion and the Jewel*. Sidney Bernstein paid me a hundred pounds for the interview, and gave me a first-class air ticket to Australia – one way. David Astor sent me a red leather suitcase and thanked me for the pleasure I'd given him over the years. *Reynolds News* paid me fifty pounds, I've forgotten what for.

The time had come to go to Blackheath and say goodbye to Gerry.

We sat in the car in the middle of Blackheath. 'You won't stay alone,' he said. 'You're too sexy. You'll find someone else.'

I hardly heard, I longed to be away. He dropped me at the bus-stop and he was near to tears. I took Wole's play to Harry Saltzman's office and he promised to read it that day. I said I'd return in the evening and whether he liked it or not I was going to Nigeria. I went to the tropical outfitter's in Charing Cross Road to look for boots. I was afraid of snakes.

'Are you an explorer, ma'am?' asked the gentlemanly assistant.

In the afternoon Tom had invited me to visit Lady Illingworth's house in Grosvenor Square with him. It was open to the public for one day, before coming under the auctioneer's hammer. Tom loved old houses and he was an amusing guide. I was a little early and waited in the foyer. It was quite bare apart from a tall, hooded sedan chair in the corner by the window. There was a young man in a grey suit sitting in it. One couldn't help noticing him, his hair was unusually long in that period of short back and sides and though I turned away I could sense that he was trying to draw attention to himself. He walked towards us, when Tom arrived. They knew each other, but without so much as a 'How d'you do' the three of us started exploring the house. I didn't find it very interesting, except for the Victorian kitchen, which reminded me of my grandmother.

'Dull English taste,' I said, 'whether in Grosvenor Square or SW9.'

The young man snorted.

'He's an architect,' said Tom. 'Shall we adjourn for a drink?'

At the Connaught he alighted on a celebrity right away. The architect knew it was Herbert Read. I didn't want to get involved. Harry Saltzman's office was within walking distance but I mustn't be late. Soon I bade everybody adieu, made a rendezvous with Tom for later and went. As I hurried along the street I heard footsteps. It was the architect running after me, holding up my Canadian purse.

'Thank you,' I said, and went my way.

My prospective producer was wild about the play, wild about Wole and Nigeria. It would be the first all-black film to be shot in Africa and when I told him I was on my way there he hit the roof and asked if I was going by Paris? Might he have my address there? I thought quickly and gave him the name of the small hotel on the Seine where Gerry and I had once stayed. I would really have to get cracking.

Tom was already at table when I arrived at his favourite restaurant, the architect and another young man with him. They were deep in mounds of pasta *al dente* and the architect was calling for snails.

'God, what a bore!' said Tom. 'Cambridge!'

I wanted to tell him how pleased I was about Saltzman and the play, but he was already paying the bill.

'If you really go,' he said, 'Senegal is a must. Drop in at the Bar de la Paix in Dakar, the head waiter is an old flame.' And he was gone.

What was I to do with the two young men? Bill and Cedric, they were called.

'I'm afraid I have to go,' I said, but to my dismay they both got up to accompany me. They didn't stop at the entrance to the flats either, but followed me and made themselves comfortable in my room. I went and took a bath. When I came back one had gone, but the architect was lying on my bed.

'I have a farewell present for you,' I said and gave him a large Danish silver brooch, Jim Goldman's farewell present to me, anything to get rid of this difficult young man. He pinned the brooch to his left lapel. 'I thought that fellow would never go,' he said. This was the crunch. Either he left, or I would. Neither of us left.

At first light he went. He was gone half an hour when the doorkeeper phoned to ask if he should be let in. I said yes. I should have said no.

'That brooch,' he said. 'I lost it in the taxi. Do you have your visa for Senegal?'

'No, and why have you come back?'

'I only went to change my collar.' He wore a very uncomfortable-looking stiff collar. 'I'll drop you at the Embassy. I have to call at Peter Jones. They have some new china which is supposed to be well designed.'

I was still waiting for my visa when he appeared yet again. 'After this I have to phone Paris,' I said, but when we left he was still with me.

'Why are we going towards Westminster Abbey?'

'Homage to rare Ben Jonson,' I said. He'd never seen the stone, so I took him to it. He wasn't interested.

I hailed a taxi. 'Goodbye,' I said. 'I must collect my things from the service flat.'

'What about the visa?'

'I'd forgotten. Yes, I'll have to wait till tomorrow.'

'Wait at my place. I'm never there. The key's under the milk bottle. There shouldn't be anyone in.' He gave me the address and I hurried away. As I paid off the taxi a smiling American got in. 'That interview! I've never seen anything like it. I could have . . .'

I escaped. That TV had made me very popular all of a sudden.

The flat was in a neighbourhood strange to me, quiet, leafy side streets, and a busy cosmopolitan thoroughfare where nobody was speaking English or even eating English. Why go all the way to Nigeria? Just move round the corner. Maybe this Cedric was right.

His home was two rooms on the top floor of a Victorian house which had been divided into many dwellings, all utterly silent. I located the key in a disused cupboard, effected an entry after a lot of fiddling and walked into a white room with a black divan. It was peaceful. I slept.

Cedric coming in woke me. As I got up he switched on his television and lay on the divan watching.

I made some slighting remark about the programme and was snapped at.

'You need some fresh air,' he said. We went out and took a walk through back streets. The evening sun shone brightly, the gardens were tangled with dying roses. We came to a country-style pub on a corner, sat outside, drank wine and he was gone. I was getting used to these sudden comings and goings and sat planning my own exit. If I didn't go soon I'd never go.

'I was phoning to say I wouldn't be coming. . . .'

'Don't let me interfere with anything.'

He didn't say so but obviously he'd been cancelling a date with his girl. Later over a pizza in a fast-food joint he declared his love for me, pulling such a silly face that I almost laughed – certainly I didn't believe him. I knew a repeat performance when I saw one.

Arrived in Paris, with visa, French money and new red leather case, I taxied to my Left Bank hotel through pouring rain. There was a message from Saltzman. Lunch next day? They showed me to my room. It wasn't overlooking the Seine where I'd been with Gerry, but a cupboard of a place with a dirty window overlooking a wall of peeling plaster. I'd change hotels as soon as my plans were made. Meanwhile I phoned all the contacts I'd written to about the film. Some of them had given me up. 'You didn't follow through.' 'Where have you been?' Had I been drifting since I left Gerry?

It was still raining next day when I went to meet Saltzman and his partner, Cubby Broccoli, *chez* Lipp. Harry did all the talking, Cubby said nothing. We got nowhere. The meal wasn't very good either.

Back in my miserable pad I got so depressed I couldn't even read. I would have given anything to talk to Gerry.

You've burned your boats. There's no one left.

In the middle of the night I thought of my new friend, the architect. 'A client is someone who comes to you in distress,' he had said. He didn't sleep at night. I could talk to him. I got up and dressed. The night porter was asleep but I found the key to the door of the hotel. I walked across Paris to the General Post Office. The streets were empty, the pavements still wet, but in the huge hall one counter was open. There you could put through a call, night and day.

I gave the number and waited. There were several ominous clicks, then silence. No, it was ringing. It rang and rang. No answer. Is he there?

'*Pas de réponse, madame.*'

'*Continuez, s'il vous plaît. L'appareil, c'est loin de lui.*'

And it rang on and on. He would be in some strange bed. Not there.

'*Merci.*' Phone down. Back through those damp streets to that cold, empty bed. The night prowl had disturbed me, and that strange young man, now lost for ever.

In the morning I sent a telegram. Why not come to Paris for the weekend? See me off? Then I looked for another hotel, found one and sat at a pavement café, taking a coffee. The sun came out. Whatever happened, I wouldn't spend another night in that human hutch. I went to pay my bill, collect my case and found a telegram waiting for me. He was coming. I couldn't believe it. The world changed. I might well have missed that telegram. But now, what could one do with him in a day, in Paris?

I was at the airport in good time, had a long wait before the London passengers came through, after Customs. I couldn't see him. The extraordinary thing was that I'd forgotten what he actually looked like. Was that him? I waved. Someone was beside me.

'I felt like an animal in a compound.' He was in a grotty mood. 'No mention of how little time we have,' he said.

I took him straight to l'Hotel des Étrangers on a corner of the Boul' Mich'. I'd already moved in, which was just as well. The manager looked amazed when he saw us together. Then I dropped the key of our room down the lift shaft and our door had to be opened with the master key. To crown it all, the bottle of champagne which I'd left cooling in a bucket was smashed. How on earth had that happened?

'I don't like champagne anyway,' said the architect. 'Let's go out.'

So we went, and took the bus to the suburban village of Maison Alfort, standing all the way on the open platform at the back. There, we took a walk round the old-fashioned place, already with high-risers among the trad. But if I dared voice a word of criticism, or even interest, in architecture, my head was bitten off.

He wouldn't ride back on the Métro. He wanted another bus ride. Then, back at the hotel, he fell asleep. I'd planned a fish supper in Les Halles but at midnight he was still asleep, fully clothed, lying across the bed. It wasn't till the small hours that he woke up.

'Too late,' I said.

'Just right,' said he, and out we went.

True enough, the place I'd chosen was still open, crowded with market porters and a sprinkling of American tourists determined to catch the night-life of Paris. We ate well.

Late next morning we took the Métro to Ménilmontant and my companion surveyed the plugs, fixtures, rails and dispensing machines as if he was thinking of buying up the Métro system. He knew where everything had been manufactured and whether it was good value. I could not match his know-how when it came to choosing a place to eat. Ménilmontant might hold its own in Parisian working-class history but on this Sunday afternoon it had nothing to offer.

'Better make for Montmartre,' said the architect in the tone of an expert. He was wrong. By the time we got there, mid-afternoon, hungry as hunters, we were glad to fall into the nearest ordinary, eat *boudin* with sauerkraut and drink plonk. Luckily there was a pin table which kept my companion happy.

I don't think he had a very happy weekend in Paree. Apparently he'd once had a French fiancée he'd never made love to, thoroughly disliked French architecture and couldn't speak one word of the language. Ah well, we'd be leaving early the next morning and I'd be glad to get away. In Rome I was to make the connecting flight to Lagos. Cedric was due back in London. 'My work!' I packed, paid the hotel, checked my money – and couldn't find my passport. I turned the room upside down, unpacked and packed again, but it had completely disappeared. So had my young man. Where could he be? I'd seen him casting a jealous eye on a bar with pin tables on the other side of the road. That's where he'd be, and my passport with him.

So he was, and smirking like a Cheshire cat as he handed me the precious document. I began slapping him with it. He pointed to the clock.

How he made his plane, I'll never know.

'No goodbyes,' he said, as his last call came through.

I had an interminable forty minutes to wait for my plane. Still, this was it. I was on my way at last. I wouldn't even look at Rome. I'd send a postcard to Gerry and reserve the best seat for my flight to Lagos, if possible stopping off at Dakar as Tom had advised. I might as well see all I could of the Dark Continent.

Goodbye, Europe, goodbye, my world.

Part Four

1963–74

Fifty-one

*Senegal. Exploring Dakar. The French colonials. The museum of
the slave trade. On to Lagos. No Wole. No public transport. A lift
through dangerous territory – a makeshift bed. The next day searching
Ibadan for Wole and better quarters – witch-doctors – ju-ju – dances –
a cultured concert – friendly people in a café. Mr and Mrs Hendrickse
say I can rent their house.*

The lights are dimmed. All I can see is the dull gleam of the
engines. We must be over Portugal. Soon the black void will
hide Africa.

The air from the ventilators feels warm. We are over the land
again. Africa – a vast, strange, sweating animal. We are coming
down. Already? My heart is in my mouth. Down through long,
low layers of cloud to Dakar.

We all stand and wait while a woman carrying a sickly baby in
a cot leaves the plane. Then we form a line and wait for our luggage. A barefoot *douanier* lounges by a shed and mosquitoes whine
around my head. It takes half an hour to get me and my suitcase
through the customs, a porter grabs both, thrusts us into a taxi and
jumps in himself. There is already an Arab-speaking gentleman
squashed into a corner. We deposit him, then we whisk about
till we come to a hotel with an elaborate frontage. There I have
to borrow from Reception to pay the porter and the taxi-driver. I
have only English money and a little French. 'And the price of the
rooms?'

'All rooms have all comfort – air-conditioning, running water,
baths, 4,000 francs.'

'A week?'

Reception did not deign to reply. 'Boy' was commanded to take
my luggage to the only room left and there the price was posted up
on the door. Also there was a putty-coloured insect on the lamp and
a black thing crawling out of the bathroom. The cold water tap ran

warm but there was no hot. What did it matter? All I wanted was sleep.

Someone was resting a heavy arm across my chest. It was my own arm. The boy had gone. There was a hammering in the passage and streaks of pink in the sky. It must be morning. I tried to take a bath, gave up, went and found some hot coffee, new bread and apricot jam instead.

First, to Air France. Change twenty pounds. Outside the sky is overcast. It's hot and clammy. Of course this is the rainy season. It will be like this till the end of September. My clothes are sticking to me. Why on earth did I put on stockings? There's a French pharmacy. What I need is some good soap and *eau de toilette*. You can bet your life there'll only be Lifebuoy and lavender water in Nigeria. The girl is really nice. She even gives me a little vial of Soir de Paris – a free sample. Well, I have spent – at 680 Dakar francs to the pound – nearly nine pounds with her. She gives me advice as well. 'You have only one day? But you must visit the island of Coree, where the French first landed. There are frequent trips.'

On the way to the docks I sent a telegram to Wole. It took a lot of time, spelling out the words, and cost me 2,993 francs, but I had to let him know when to meet me. Then I found myself in the middle of a market, with fruits and vegetables of every shape and colour – on a mound of pumpkins an enormous black woman was lying asleep. The red meat doesn't smell too fresh and there is a distinct smell of shit by the roadway. The women are beautiful, the colours they wear – turquoise, rose, silver, cerise – tinsel on tulle, stripes of gold on transparent veiling. Their skirts float, their waists are tight and their breasts are loose under the corsage. And those giant turbans! Like butterflies. Lord knows how they stay on. The older women wear tight plaits, not nearly so pretty. The young ones tinkle as they walk, bracelets, anklets, silver and gold and earrings that would do credit to Cartier's . . . but they're all false. An old woman holds out her hand. She is blind, her eyelids are sunken over the empty sockets. A huge pair of antlers bars my way. 'Fifteen dollar, madame.'

'Thank you.'

'Best Swiss watch, two 'underd franc.'

It's all so enchanting that I miss the boat. It's these lovely women. Did the French stop off here because of them? Or are they so beautiful because the French stopped off?

I book a passage for later – eighty francs, *aller et retour*. The locals, I notice, pay thirty. I'd passed a bistro with a beaded door near the docks. They might sell food. A Senegalese in white shirt and trousers was trailing a French broom across the pavement when I found it again.

'Bonjour, monsieur. *On peut manger ici?* Eat!' And I made eating gestures. I had to stop; he was looking at me as if I were demented. Then he dived through the beaded curtain. A moment later a weedy little Frenchman appeared.

'Can I 'elp you, madame?'

'Food,' was all I could say.

'At your service, madame. Please enter.'

The Senegalese was circling his broom round the bar-room floor creating little mounds of dust. 'Aly!' the proprietor barked at him in Arabic, obviously telling him to prepare a table, though it sounded more like a man bullying his dog.

'*Oui, Monsieur Pierre,*' Aly replied, almost saluting.

'An *apéritif*, madame?'

I took a pastis which they say is good in the heat. I didn't like the taste.

'What weather! Three wives I have lost through it.'

'I'm sorry.'

'White women, of course.'

'Poor things. What did they die of?'

'They didn't die, madame. They went back to France, couldn't stand the blacks either. They do smell, you know.'

Aly was spreading a paper tablecloth. I could see that his white pants were not pants at all but a white cloth knotted somehow under his crutch.

'Too many Mussulmen,' said M Pierre. 'You can't get a look in for Lebanese and Syrians. Another pastis?'

'No, thank you.'

'I give us another five years at the most.'

'Where would you go?'

'Brazil. That's the place.'

'But there are many blacks there.'

'Not on top.'

Aly brought a well-turned omelette and a dish of green salad.

'You are staying long, madame?' And he turned his fishy eyes on me. 'Stay 'ere and I will cook you anything you wish – eight 'undred a night.' His hand brushed my breast, accidentally, as it were, and he swallowed another pastis.

'I have a boat to catch.'

'A boat.'

'And tomorrow I am for Lagos.'

His watery eyes filled with tears. 'I have something for you,' he said as he went to the refrigerator and produced a solitary peach. 'From France,' he said, his voice deep with emotion.

I paid, gave Aly a tip and at the beaded door looked back to see M Pierre's face, streaming with tears.

I caught the ferry to Coree by the skin of my teeth. The old tub was already heavily loaded when I jumped aboard, and rocked violently as we left the harbour. An English tramp was coming in and a lonely fisherman in a pirogue was riding the wash. I was still sweating though there was a strong breeze across the water.

Looking back at Dakar – the squat oil refineries and anonymous blocks – we might be anywhere, with that lowering sky, at the mouth of the Thames even. I was standing near the prow among piled-up sacks and crates. A crew member asked me to go below as the sea was getting rough. I caught a glimpse of a black cliff lashed with breakers way ahead of us. As I help the ladies with their babies to the black den below decks, they give vent to little grunts and sighs, then as a particularly heavy breaker sends us flying one of them explodes with laughter and at once the rest join in. As we rocked across the breakers, I sat next to a beauty in eggshell blue holding her baby tightly and I saw that those Cartier earrings were quite cruel, the lobe and rim of the ear pierced seven or eight times and a gold circle inserted in each hole. One girl's left ear was quite badly lacerated, she had plugged it with cotton wool. Another had eight circles inserted in her baby's ears and the child was hardly eight months old. He also had a bracelet on each arm, one gold, one silver, and a gold chain round his neck. It was partly hidden by a little roll of fat. The mother wore four silver bracelets, one on each wrist, one on each ankle, and a little girl passed me with such heavy circlets in her ears that she had tied them up with black cotton to lessen the weight.

They all massage their gums continually and have gleaming white teeth, but it is those profiles which are so unusual, Florentine profiles on dusky heads and long necks.

At the landing stage, the beauties lean over the rail to hand their bundles to waiting children. I'm the last off, but several of the girls wait for me and we stroll along the stone pier together. Friends and relatives are waiting, as if their daughters and sisters had been away for a long time. They clasp hands when they meet and smile. The prettiest young woman clucks her tongue and smiles at everyone.

I am told that I must see the memorial to twenty French doctors who lost their lives fighting the plague of yellow fever.

'When was that?'

'Many moons ago.'

'Seventy-eight,' says one old fellow. 'Eighteen seventy-eight.'

'The Musée de Mer,' cries another. 'First the Musée de Mer. Once it was the Governor's residence, now it houses a dead octopus – a local octopus,' he added.

'I wish to visit the History Museum first,' I said. I'd heard about it from the girl in the pharmacy. Two small boys came up to me: guides, they said. The sky was a dome of blue and the grass almost smelt green. We passed a torn poster advertising films at the local cinema, one starred Jean Gabin, the other was in Arabic.

The History Museum had originally been a French colonial mansion. It was well kept, with a pleasantly proportioned front staircase, where two small boys sat playing draughts with beer-bottle tops. They darted forward to greet my guides with cries of delight. For me there was a polite '*Bonjour*'. I wondered how I would get into the museum with four youngsters at my heels, but they made no attempt to come with me, neither were any of them looking for tips.

Inside it was much as I'd expected – fragments of ground stones in showcases with frayed labels; potsherds identified in careful French calligraphy, the ink now brown; accounts of Portuguese expeditions questing for spices; pictures of shipwrecks, along the

Gold and Ivory coasts, some of them German – but at last that which I had really come to see – a diagram of a slave ship, showing the disposition of the captives. I began to make a sketch of it as the words of the old ballad 'Andrew Hollander' ran through my head:

> Scarce eighteen inches to a man
>   was all they had to go
> The plague and fever came on board,
>   swept half of them away
> We dragged their bodies up on deck
>   and hove them in the sea
> 'Twere better for the rest of them,
>   if they had died before
> Than to work under brutes of planters
>   in Cuba, for ever more.

A gallows ballad sold as a broadsheet, after a hanging. Nearby, in a showcase, the manacles of the captives were displayed, and a portrait of William Wilberforce, the English Tory MP who in 1792 introduced a bill to abolish the slave trade. No picture of Toussaint l'Ouverture who freed the black slaves of Haiti and finished his days in one of Napoleon's dungeons. Yet once there was a time when the black African was a romantic hero in the London theatre. I have an eighteenth-century play in which the hero, an African prince captured by slavers, is exposed for sale in a Cuban market only to see his paramour, a black princess, dragged to the stand to be auctioned. Their ensuing escape occupies four acts.

When I came out the two small boys were still playing draughts.

'You were in the Slave House,' said one.

'I know.'

'What language have you?'

'English.'

'And have you any property?'

'The contents of my pockets.'

I showed them what I had. The only thing that interested them was my box of Swan Vestas, so with suitable warnings I gave it to the eldest, who disappeared. The others said they would accompany me to the boat, and we began the descent, passing little houses with courtyards. We saw two small boys and their baby brother trying to bath an indignant goat, while chickens pecked corn under the family bed.

Above us, on a cliff-top, there was an ancient cannon hanging with rusty chains. Once it was the harbour's only protection against invasion. From where we stood, the harbour looked no more than an inlet surrounded by an embankment of black stones. I ran down the steep hill, afraid that the ferry-boat would leave without me. I was out of breath, but I made it and turned to see my guides waving goodbye as we headed for the open sea.

It was late when we tied up at Dakar. The place looked deserted, apart from a few vendors, hoping for a last minute sale. 'Ivory beads.' Gold-heeled slippers . . . and an old man paring the soles of his feet with a cutthroat razor. A wave of sky-blue silk billowed over his head, and a black beauty reached up to touch it, her squat little breasts with their tiny nipples tinged with mauve escaping from her bodice. She felt my eyes on her, turned and took my hand.

'You are lost. I will take you to the town.'

We crossed a railway line, a field of tall, prickly weeds, and at last I saw a faint light ahead.

'Is that a restaurant?'

'It is a lighted shop. Shall I take you to a restaurant?'

We went on, passed the lighted shop; a small boy was standing there, gazing at rows of fishing rods. In the dark, the town was unrecognisable. Without people, I couldn't tell where the busy market had been. We turned a corner.

'There! La Coupole! First class!'

A white candle and two shadowy figures sitting at a small table in an empty street.

'Thank you.'

From outside, the restaurant looked shut, deserted, but the door opened to a busy scene. Several smart Senegalese playing dice, two Chinese gentlemen sitting at a table sipping tea from tiny bowls, the bar was lined with happy drinkers and the barman looked at me askance. Suddenly, Madame, seated at a half-hidden table, summoned me to her with an imperious gesture. She was glittering with jet beads and looked like La Goulue.

'*Assis, Médard. Assis, mon chien!*' But Médard, a large Alsatian, was already sitting.

'You have to be careful.' She glanced at the Senegalese. 'All they think of is shafting white women.' Médard was growling in a rather menacing way. 'Quite right, *mon chien*,' she said. 'A woman alone.' She scratched his ear and drained a glass of cognac.

A man shuffled in selling safety pins. He was blind. She nodded to the barman. He seized the blind man's arm and guided him to the door, but I saw him slip the man a coin, muttering something in Arabic.

'So where have you been today?'

I told her.

'Where you have been nobody white goes.'

'Nobody noticed me, I'm quite sure.'

'Oh, yes they did. We all heard where you were.'

'Well, I'll be gone tomorrow.'

'Paris?'

'Lagos.'

'Lagos! Then you must have a good meal tonight. Boy!' (The waiter was at least fifty.) 'One *plat du jour* and a carafe of house wine.'

I asked her if she'd have a drink with me.

'I only drink cognac.'

I paid for her cognac and moved to a table. When the food arrived it was dressed up to look *très français*, but the meat was poor stuff and the wine watery.

Back at the hotel I found they'd closed the shutters in my room, but it was humming with mosquitoes. Dammit! One stung me just when I was about to swat it. There were more black things in the bathroom, and a thin gold creature was emerging from under the bed. I ripped off a sandal. This is going to be a massacre! I hate being stung. I laid about me, ruthlessly. I'd never killed anything before in my life.

Early next morning, the taxi-man came to my room for the baggage. It was still dark.

'Twelve hundred,' he said when we got to the airport.

'How much?'

'Twelve hundred.'

'But the taxi is paid for by the airline.'

'And what about the baggage?'

'In any case I have no money left.'

I had budgeted to the last penny, but now I was forced to change my precious pounds. Dakar cost me fifty-one pounds, ten shillings, and I had to carry a lot of useless Dakar francs around with me.

Lift-off. Next stop, Nigeria, the giant of Africa.

The land below – grey and scrubby. Here and there patches of red soil – village clearings, a few trees – the land where the zebra once roamed and I have toothache. Ah – a glimpse of the sea, between the cloud banks. We're still climbing. From now on it will be boring. When will they have jets on this route? I went through my Dakar receipts. Apart from the toiletries, six hundred for food, a hundred and eighty coffee and cognac, seventy wine, seventy-five a pack of Gitanes. How much since I left Gerry? I was horrified.

Abidjan. Two big-bellied US Army planes on the Tarmac. I fumble for the map. Accra, Cotonou, Jos, Kano. . . .

Two nuns who've travelled so far dressed in black, emerge from the toilet, all white.

'Are we nearly there, sister?'

'Twenty minutes Cotonou to Lagos,' says the younger nun.

Lagos. At last. My seat-belt is fastened long before the sign comes up. Everybody begins collecting their traps. The Nigerian lady in the seat ahead ties a flowered chamber-pot to her travelling bag.

At the airport a smiling crowd is waiting, all the women seem to be in indigo blue.

'Is somebody expected?' I ask a policeman.

'Move along, please.'

'They are seeing their relations off to UK,' says the lady with the chamber-pot.

Formalities. This way. . . . Health. Have you had your shots? Immigration. What do you intend doing here? Letters of introduction? I mention the film and get a permit for thirty days. Customs. Any cigars, cigarettes, perfumery? I produce three squashed packets of Gitanes and they wave me on. A boy in khaki with no shoes snatches up my case and throws it into a taxi.

'Hey, stop! I've no money. . . .'

A car labelled Ibadan University comes pushing through the crowd. This will be Wole. It is empty.

'To the money change,' I tell the taxi-driver.

'It's shut,' he says, revs up and drives off.

'Stop! Stop! My case.'

'Pay the porter,' he shouts.

'Who?'

'Me,' says the boy in khaki.

A smart policeman brings out his notebook.

'Can you tell me where I might find a message?'

'What does it say?'

'I don't know.'

'Why not?'

'Because I haven't received it yet. People do have messages delivered here?'

'Which people?'

'Oh, forget it. Just tell me the way to the nearest bank.'

He brightened up at that, and we set off, the boy in khaki shouting that he'd recovered my case. The bank was shut. I mentioned Wole's name to the policeman. He went straight to his box and put through a call to Ibadan University.

After three wrong numbers, 'He's in town,' he said.

'Which town?'

'I'll try again.'

There was a tea bar open. I'd been hanging around for two hours. I went in and ordered a large tea. It was served in a thick cup with a dark blue border.

'Sixpence.'

'Do you change English banknotes?'

'Certainly, miss.' And they gave me change for twenty pounds in Nigerian currency.

Outside, the policeman, the boy in khaki and the taxi were standing waiting.

'One pound,' said the taxi-man, 'two shilling for the porter and one shilling waiting time.'

I gave him five bob. 'That's your lot,' I said. 'Now I have to find a hotel.'

'Hotel, seven pound, fifteen shilling,' he replied.

'With a telephone.'

'Jump in.'

That was how it came about that I tasted my first Nigerian meal at the Railway Inn – fish and chips, pot of tea, bread and butter, two and sixpence.

Four young men in white received me, Joeferry, Boniface, Joseph and George (their names were stitched to their breast pockets). They carried my case to a bungalow which was making a terrible noise.

'Air-conditioning,' said the tallest, George, and disappeared. He returned holding a lavatory chain.

'I've changed my mind,' I said. 'I'd rather get to Ibadan.'

'We're not Yoruba,' said Joeferry, 'we're Ibo. The Ibo work harder.'

'Good. Do you have the times of the trains?'

'Joseph!' said George, but Joseph was disappearing. Is there any food? 'This way please,' said George and I was taken to a large room, crowded with empty tables. Joseph returned. 'Eight pound, ten shilling,' he said, 'Smart taxi.'

'Are there no trains?'

'Tell him six,' said a man who was frying fish. He turned out to be the Manager.

'Do you have the phone number of the railway station?' I asked him.

'Waste of time,' he said and turned back to his fish.

I decided to phone Ibadan University. It took an hour.

'Wole?'

It was a bright female voice at the other end. 'Oh yes, he's here.'

'Could you take a message for him?'

She began taking it down but was interrupted.

'Hello! Hello! Correction – Wole was here, three, no four days ago.' And she hung up.

Joseph was waving a piece of paper at me. 'The railway station number,' he said and, to my amazement, I got through at once.

'Two pound ten shilling, takes two hours, leaves six o'clock, evening.'

'But it's ten past five now.' There was a nasty echo on the line.

'Make it up to Agipi, you can catch 'im there. Go right away. No, hold on.' The station sounded quite empty.

Five minutes later. 'That's right. Go right away.'

'Joseph! Taxi, pronto.'

'That train takes five hours, if it runs at all,' said the Manager, placing a large plate of fish and chips in front of me. 'Take it easy and I will fix you a lift. You'd be lucky to get a seat on the train and if someone was going further than you, they'd get your seat.'

'Thank you, and could you possibly switch the fans on?'

'They're on.'

I ate my high tea.

'You sleeping here tonight, miss?' It was Boniface.

'No. I must get to Ibadan.' I lit a cigarette. Boniface held out his cupped hands for one. I offered the packet. He snatched it and made off.

Six thirty. Six forty-five. Seven o'clock. Seven fifteen. It was twenty to eight when a tall, bearded man walked in, made for the bar and helped himself to a beer. 'Coming?' he said, and in less time than it takes to tell I was climbing into the front seat of a roomy Humber; there was somebody else settled in at the back.

The road was bumpy and lonely till we came to an avenue of palm trees and passed an open truck. It had a crowd of smiling passengers aboard. They all waved at us.

'Mammy waggon,' said the back seat. We passed another one, parked by an open fire. It was plastered with Biblical texts.

'There's a smell of meat roasting,' I said.

'Venison,' said the driver, 'but we're not stopping.'

And we drove on into the darkness, with only the din of the crickets for company.

In each village there was a busy market, the stalls lit by wicks burning in earthenware bowls.

I asked if they knew Wole.

'Steve should,' said the back seat. 'He's assistant Director of TV in Ibadan.'

'You'll find him easily enough,' said the Assistant Director. 'Everybody knows Wole.'

We passed a badly wrecked car. 'Nasty accident,' I said.

'Very,' said the back seat. 'Highwaymen. The driver of that car saw a tree fallen across the road in front of him. When he looked back another tree fell. He was trapped, robbed and murdered.'

'Now you know why we don't stop,' said Steve. 'I don't know where we're going to park you tonight. Have you got a shakedown, Femi?'

'The wife's entire family have just moved in,' said the back seat. 'Sorry.'

At last, from the crest of a hill, we saw lights on TV towers. We were approaching Ibadan, the biggest town in West Africa. There were no neon signs, no necklaces of light indicating roadways, only streams of bicycles and soft-stepping women with large bundles on their heads.

We came to a busy depot where trucks and mammy waggons were assembled preparing for an all-night trek. Femi bade us good night.

'I have to call at the TV station,' said Steve. 'After that, to find a bed for you.'

The TV building was a model of Tropical Architecture, straight from the drawing boards of Bloomsbury. Steve wasn't gone long. 'Some idiotic all-woman Brains Trust going on,' he said. 'Why must they always take their cue from London?'

'And their architecture,' I added. 'What are all those artistic holes in the wall for?'

'The mosquitoes,' he said. 'And the roof leaks, and those window slats have been inserted the wrong way, sloping inwards instead of outwards – to let the rains in more easily, presumably. Why don't they come and stay in the place before they start designing, preferably during Hammert'ang?'

'What's that?'

'The wind from the Sahara. It gets in everywhere, leaves a

layer of sand when you take your bath. And as for you tonight, all I could find was the Lafia Rest House.'

Any place would be welcome, I was dropping on my feet, but when Steve unfastened the padlock and shoved open the door, such a musty smell overwhelmed me that I could hardly bring myself to enter. . . . No furniture, no bath, no WC, no plumbing at all, just a huge bed under a heavy mosquito net.

'Don't open the shutters,' said Steve.

As soon as he was gone, I dabbed my face with *eau de toilette* from Dakar and climbed up on to the fusty old bed.

I didn't get much sleep, I longed for daybreak, dreamed of flinging open the door to fresh air and sunlight; but when the dawn did come, the sky was bronze and the clouds were dark and lowering. I was out as soon as possible, walking in what I took to be the right direction. It was a long time before I saw a soul. Eventually, a law student picked me up and drove me to the University.

'When did you post your letter?'
'August 16th, in Paris.'

'No letters for Soyinka, are there, Aziz?' The Arab 'boy' shook his head.

'Which box number did you use?'

'I had no box number.'

'Then how could you expect the letter to be delivered to the addressee?'

'And the telegram from Dakar, did that require a box number?'

Aziz already had the door open for me.

'Hi, Banjo's the name.' I was in the corridor among a crowd of students. 'Saw all your shows at E15. For you, I would sweep the stage. Don't forget the festival tonight.' Before I could ask him if he knew of a room somewhere, he was gone. Better make for the old town; there would be nothing in the university area. It was a long walk, but entertaining, especially when you came to the shops. 'Morris of London, drapper. London diploms.' 'Hair stretching.' 'The Bible sold here. Moody books.' 'Do not be barren, have babies shortly

17a Henry Chapman's *You Won't Always be on Top* with (*left to right, on scaffolding*) Glynn Edwards and Brian Murphy; (*on ground*) Peter Doughty, Dudley Foster, Richard Harris and Henry Chapman. Setting John Bury.

17b *Unternehmen Ölzweig* at the Maxim Gorki Theater with (*left to right*) Gerd Ehlers, Alfred Müller, Walter Jupé and Heinz Scholz.

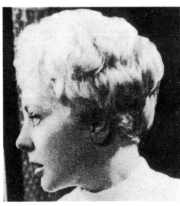

18a Valerie Walsh.   18b Carole A. Christensen.
18c Griffith Davies (among our glorious birds).
18d Jane McKerron.   18e Barbara Ferris.

19 Toni Palmer and Barbara Windsor.

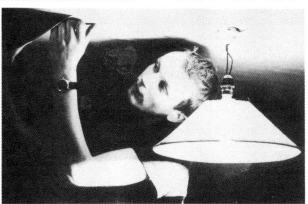

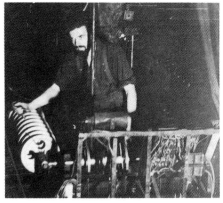

20a Ivor Dykes, slides, lights, sound – what you will.   20b Carol Murphy and Jo Benson.
20c Dick Bowdler, electronics and programming.
20d Chick Fowler, stage director.   20e John Bury at his switchboard.

21a *Oh What A Lovely War:*
'We don't want to lose you, but we think you ought to go.'

21b Avis Bunnage:
'I'll make a man of every one of you.'

21c Joan in action.

22a Brendan Behan on Sean Kenny's set of *The Hostage*.

22b *Oh What A Lovely War* in America with (*left to right*)
Frank Coda, Myvanwy Jenn, J.L., Fanny Carby and Linda Loftus.

23a Gerry, the rock on whom we rested.

23b Joan among the ruins of Salway Road E15.

24a Cedric Price, Architect.

24b We set about cleaning that abominable site.

after visit here.' 'Madam Adivendo. Wedding dresses. Wedding cake.'

Everyone who passed me said, 'Good morning, madam,' or 'akabo' which means 'welcome', and the children would touch my hand. 'Peeled skin,' they'd say.

In the cloth market two women were having a tug of war with a roll of calico. The younger one, she couldn't have been more than sixteen, was crying as she hung on to it. The other one was stronger and harangued the crowd as she held the roll under her arm. The crowd was delighted, nobody tried to intervene. Above us Frederick Lugard's statue surveyed the horizon.

'He was a strong man,' said the cloth vendor, 'governed us with an army. He should be here now.'

I wanted to sit somewhere; the day was hot and heavy and I was thirsty. I saw three men sitting drinking in a yard. They wore Nigerian costume but they looked like Jewish intellectuals.

'You want a beer? Three shilling.' A girl had appeared and was eyeing me suspiciously.

'Try a Pepsi,' said one of the drinkers. 'It's non-alcoholic and cheaper.' He wore a bright green shirt patterned with orange flowers, had tribal cuts across his cheeks and horn-rimmed spectacles. The girl brought the Pepsi, poured it and held out cupped hands. 'Sixpence,' she said. 'Are you a native of England? You are welcome nevertheless. My name is Juliana. What are you going to give me? If you don't give me anything I will go from here. Will you give me that wallet?' She pointed to my Canadian purse. 'No? Will you give me that, then?'

My soiled handkerchief! I offered her a sixpenny piece and she knelt on one knee to receive it. She told me how she rose at five each morning, performed her household duties, then came here to serve till eleven o'clock at night.

'My father is dead, my mother lives forty miles away.'

She brought me a cardboard disc to keep the flies out of my glass. 'Take your ease,' she said.

Two of the drinkers rose to go, pocketing what was left of their Pepsi-colas. Neither of them left a tip.

I asked Juliana how much she earned.

'Two pound, ten shilling a week. This is a good day for

me that I met you. Will you come back? I will have rice for you.'

I offered her the rest of my Pepsi. She took two sips. 'That's enough for me,' she said and moved away.

I was out on the street before she noticed I'd gone. She ran after me and took my hand. 'Will you come back tomorrow?'

'It depends on the gods.'

The gods can be useful sometimes. I hoped they would lead me to a furnished room. Nowadays half a million people live in this town but no one, anywhere, has a sign up saying 'Rooms to let'. I was hungry. I'd noticed the menu at the University. Meatballs in Turkish sauce, jam roly-poly – ten and six. Too heavy and in any case too far away. There was no sign of any sort of public transport apart from the mammy waggons.

I made do with some nuts, sat by the roadside and wrote to Gerry. As I finished I was aware of a young man standing looking at me. 'My name is Isaac,' he said.

'I'm pleased to meet you.'

'What are you doing here?'

'Looking for lodgings, when I've posted my letter.'

'I will accompany you.'

He found the Post Office without much difficulty but lodgings? He had no more idea than I had. He held my hand when we crossed a road and pointed to anything that might interest me.

'Look, miss.'

DO NOT ENCOURAGE CORRUPTION. FOR CARRYING 112 LBS YOU PAY THE PORTER 3D.

By the time we'd walked from one end of the town to the other, my left sandal was decomposing.

'I must go home, Isaac.'

'Are you trying to deceive me? Did you not tell me your home was on the black heath? How can you go there now? I have put myself to inconvenience to assist you. What will you do for me?'

'I will certainly show you my town as you have shown me yours.' He looked at me distrustfully. I held out a silver shilling. He snatched it and was gone.

There was nothing for it but to make my way back to the dreaded Lafia. I was too tired to walk any further. I think I'd got as far as the fuel market when a station waggon came hooting by with a white woman at the wheel.

'Hi! Can I give you a lift somewhere?' She stopped in the middle of the road.

'Saw you with Steve Rhodes at the TV station last night. I'm Lynn.' I got in first, then told her that I didn't know where I was going. 'You might as well come to the Festival of Arts, if you've nothing better to do.' Without waiting for a reply she drove on through the teeming streets.

'Come and have a drink.'

We'd stopped by a dull, very English civic building; chairs were being set out inside as we made for the bar. Over a Cinzano and for me, a ham sandwich, she asked what I was doing in Ibadan. I told her.

'Forget it,' she said. 'Even if you've a fortune at the back of you. There's too much corruption. Where are you staying?'

I told her.

'You'd better come and bed down at my place. You won't find anything better. There's a girl sleeps on the floor in my office, happy to have a roof over her head. Let's go and see how George is getting on.'

George, her boyfriend, was setting up a camera in the middle of the chairs. 'Turn that lamp down, you stupid bastard,' he shouted. 'Down! Not up!'

'How's it going, love?'

'It isn't.'

'Come and have a quick one.'

He gave her a dirty look and went on fiddling with his lenses. A line of boys danced on to the stage to drum-beats.

'They start dancing while they're still on their mother's backs,' said Lynn. 'See that boy with the beautiful belt? His parents won't let him go to school for fear it interferes with his dancing.'

'Stop that bloody drumming. I can't hear myself think.' George again. Lynn left him to it and we went back to the bar. Steve Rhodes was there with Orlando, a colleague.

'We've got news for you,' he said. 'Wole is in Venice with a Mr Driberg.'

'A Pan-African conference,' said Orlando.

Wole in Venice! What was I doing here?

'I thought at first that you'd come for my ballet with drums,' said Steve.

George blew in. 'Who's this?' He meant me, but didn't wait for an answer. Banjo's head appeared round the door.

'Mr George . . . Mr George! The audience is coming in.'

'Switch the lights on. I'll be there in a jiffy.'

A bell was ringing. Banjo left. Lifelong habit sent me hurrying back into the hall. The stage was in deep gloom, the auditorium packed. George followed after.

'The master switch, you bloody idiot, the master switch!'

Several heavy clankings backstage, then lights blazed on, the drums beat, the dancers leapt on to waves of applause. The MC couldn't make himself heard, not till the dance ended. And then all I got above the din was . . . 'Walter de la Mare, set to music by Armstrong Gibbs.' A pianist, in white dinner jacket, sat at the piano adjusting his stool. The audience listened politely, trying not to cough, but woke up again when the Benin dancers appeared, all pastel pink and coral.

When they were through I'd had enough. Steve and Orlando were still in the bar, tapping out complex rhythms together on the counter.

Steve had received his musical education in Frankfurt and loved to air his knowledge.

'The Minister's just got up to speak,' said George, as he came trailing in with Lynn. 'He's getting the bird already. Listen.'

'He was trying to tell them about their rich cultural heritage,' said Lynn. 'Millions for TV, nothing for schools and hospitals.'

Steve resented this and started to argue.

'Oh, can it. I'm for bed,' she said. 'Come on, I'll drop you off at the Lafia.'

'Forget yours truly, as usual,' said George.

On the way she told him why I was there.

'I'm your man,' said George. 'Just finished a ten-year stint in Ghana. Boy, that's the place.'

'Are you coming in for a drink?' I asked when we pulled up.

'I'll come for a piddle,' said George.

'Take everything he says with a pinch of salt,' said Lynn,

as he went round the back. 'They wouldn't allow his latest film to be shown in Ghana. Now he's here on sixteen a week, doing a schoolboy's job. Your shutters are open,' she sounded shocked and started to close them. 'Isn't there a night watchman?'

'I haven't seen one.'

'You can't stay here. It's not safe.' All the same she didn't renew her offer of a shakedown at her place. Just as well, I couldn't have put up with the boyfriend for long.

'You ready?' he shouted.

And they were gone.

Next morning I decided to try British Council. They might know of a room. Eventually I found them in a smart little building beside a grassy patch. An old woman was sound asleep there, her head resting on her bare arm. Nearby a Mussulman was kneeling in prayer.

'Nice quiet corner,' said the watchman. 'They like it here.'

'Yes. They look completely relaxed.'

'They're dead,' he said. 'They all come here to die.'

A bell was ringing somewhere, accompanied by a shrill cry. Some sort of Requiem? No, I traced the sound to its source. It was a Medicine Man. An assortment of unidentifiable objects was laid out on a square cloth on the bare ground in front of him. He was holding up a hank of black hair, part of the scalp still attached to it, and spieling in an unknown tongue. Shrill birdsong was heard. The Medicine Man leapt round, startled – exorcised a pot covered with cowrie shells. The whistling ceased.

An old man draped in brown sidled out of the crowd and whispered to the Medicine Man. He was given something which looked like snuff, after it had been carefully weighed on a minute balance scale and tipped into a twist of paper. Others came forward to buy. I wondered if he could cure my toothache. He produced a football rattle and I walked on till I came to a market, run by women. I'd seen some of them on the road earlier, walking swiftly, head held high, one managing a single iron bedframe on her head. All very well being a sightseer but I was here to work. Where? I'd nowhere to sleep, let alone write.

As if to cheer me up several drummers came dancing round me. As the drums beat faster, I clapped in time. Someone chuckled, that happy, infectious chuckle, so typically Yoruba. One of the dancers approached me and began a limbering, knee-shaking movement which I thought would topple him into a back somersault. 'You have to place a piece of silver on his forehead,' said an onlooker. I did, and with a long jump the dancer was gone.

I must find somewhere to make notes of everything I'd seen. It would all be useful in the film.

The gods must have heard my prayer. I came upon a café with chairs and tables. I sat down and brought out my notebook. 'You should try our kebabs, they are the best in town.' A Lebanese gentleman was smiling down at me.

'Oh I will, please bring me one. . . . and a brandy, if you sell liquor.'

The brandy appeared at once. 'I am not English myself, but English people come here and they will speak to you,' said my host.

Hungry bugs were already biting my bare legs, but I forgot them when a skewerful of succulent kebabs arrived. After I'd mopped my plate I began scribbling, hoping that I wouldn't be asked to leave. I wasn't. It was wonderful, a chair, a table and the occasional hum of conversation as people came and went.

It must have been some time later when I heard English voices, two men were making for the bar. The Lebanese gentleman was saying something about me, but I couldn't catch what he was saying. The younger of the two men approached me. 'Are you Joan Littlewood?' It came as a shock to hear my name. 'I'm Peter. That's Vivaldo, from Brazil. We're anthropologists. I saw *The Hostage* in London. What on earth are you doing here?'

I told him as Vivaldo came to meet me. 'You're not, by any chance, Vivaldo Costa Rica?'

'I must confess, I am.'

'My friend, Beatrice Tanaka from Brazil, mentioned you to me.'

We drank to this small world. Of course they knew Wole and began telling Wole stories. Vivaldo said he preferred *The Trials of Brother Jero* to *The Lion and the Jewel*.

'He's not only our finest poet, he's our sea-green incorruptible,' said Peter. 'You should start a Theatre Workshop here.' Without Gerry and my precious team? Impossible.

A young couple arrived. Peter knew them. 'Mr and Mrs Hendrickse.'

'Good,' said Vivaldo. 'Now we can go to the Independent. Are you coming, madam?'

As we threaded our way through the darkening streets a tree decked in coloured lights reminded me of a cockney pub at Christmas. 'That's a ju-ju tree,' said Vivaldo. 'Magic.'

'Magic?'

'Of course. Don't they believe in it in London? We even have a German convert here. He lives in a hut, no better than a hen-house, but he's surrounded himself with ju-ju trees. The locals won't go anywhere near the place. His wife went one better, she embraced the Shango cult, and went to live with a native chief aged ninety. Now she's a high priestess. The native chief went down with colic during the rainy season and the German worried. If the chief dies, the high priestess is supposed to die with him.'

'Did they recover?'

'She did.'

'Did she have colic?'

'She recovered from both – the colic and the old chief.'

We passed what remained of an elegant house, the façade crumbling, but the proportions graceful.

'Portuguese,' said Vivaldo.

Then we entered a courtyard where people sat around eating and drinking while dancers crowded the central area. You danced alone, or with a partner. If any one, or two, gave a particularly exciting display everybody else dropped back, watched and applauded. The drum rhythms were intricate.

'What sort of dancing is that?'

'Ju-ju,' said Vivaldo.

A girl in blue tulle came, took my hand and tried to get me to dance. I longed to join in, but I drew back. Peter, who'd been watching, tried to tempt me on to the floor, again I refused. But there was no refusing a fat black lady, draped in cloth of gold.

'Do what I do,' she commanded.

So I kicked off my sandals and danced, circling my shoulders and hips as she did, at the same time slowly bending my knees and winding my hands, first outwards, then inwards. Her movements were smooth as silk, but by God it was killing my thighs. Then when she unwrapped her cloth of gold and revealed her lithe black body, totally naked, I laughed so much that I had to sit down. Above us, the open sky. A balcony on three sides of the upper storey. It was the perfect Elizabethan inn yard.

Mr and Mrs Hendrickse were asking for news of Wole. I told them all I knew and they told me their story. They were refugees from the Cape, paediatricians unable to live in the political climate of South Africa. They were going away on the following Friday till 2nd October, would I like to rent their house during their absence?

I couldn't believe my ears. I felt like dancing all night, and I'd been so tired earlier.

'Let's take you home,' said Peter. 'Enough excitement for one day.'

'You've a day off tomorrow, Peter. You can show her around.'

'That is my intention,' said Peter, and with 'good night' and 'see you soon', we were gone.

Fifty-two

In the morning I decided to see the Hendrickses as soon as possible, and be sure they meant it about the house. I made myself as presentable as I could and set out.

'Going some place, miss?'

It was a cheeky-looking taxi-man in a broken down old banger. I told him the address.

'Seven and six.'

'Three and six.'

'For you, miss, five shilling.'

'Three and six.'

'Four.'

'Europeans five bob, locals sixpence. Don't come the old acid with me, brother.'

He laughed so much he nearly fell out of his cab. It had no doors anyway.

'What's so funny?'

'Jus' that you talk funny, miss.'

'So do you.'

He was still chuckling when he managed to get his vehicle to move.

'Get in, miss.'

We went bumping along the road, but at the first stretch of rising ground she stalled.

'Juice,' he said, and seizing a petrol can and funnel, made off. I'd half a mind to leave him to it, but I'd no idea where I was. Maps were almost unknown in Ibadan. Fifty minutes passed before I heard him coming back and then he spilt so much petrol telling me how he came by it that I was reconciled to losing the Hendrickse house, the film, everything – till I noticed that we were actually moving again.

'I will wait for you,' he said as we drew up.

'I wouldn't. I might be here till next Christmas,' and I handed him four bob. He inserted his starting handle, gave it a pull and tried to turn the engine over. Nothing happened.

Mrs Hendrickse came hurrying down the garden path to see what was wrong.

'Water!' he said. She found a watering can and led him to the garden tap.

'You'd better come back to town with me,' she said afterwards.

I accepted, gladly, and we discussed my tenancy *en route*. Happily Peter was waiting for me. He was used to flexible time-keeping and we set off on our expedition without further ado.

'I'd planned to take you to Benin,' he told me, 'but unfortunately all the bronzes are in Europe, touring Germany. . . .' I was disappointed, but said nothing. 'There is always plenty to see. In a moment or two we'll look down on Ibadan.'

I turned to see a mass of ramshackle roofs of corrugated iron and rusting zinc. 'In the days of tribal wars it was a walled town,' he said. 'Nobody ever got within twenty miles of it.'

Leaving the town, we passed a hospital built on a hillside; outside it a queue stretched right down to the front gate. 'I've known them wait there for four days.'

'There aren't enough doctors?'

'Too many young men prefer to study law or accountancy. Still, that hospital was started by two doctors, a Nigerian and an Irishman.'

The bush was flat, with hills like islands, unusually symmetrical, rising above the stony soil.

'Is the land fertile?'

'Spit on it and something will grow.'

'Why is there so much malnutrition?'

'Lack of education, shortage of fruit and beans, giving the children cassava, rather than rice. It's not necessarily poverty. A rich man's child was taken to hospital dying of squasia. He was told to give his wife more money. Two years later his second child died of malnutrition. It's hard to get people to change their ways, especially when it comes to food.'

We were at a village and stopped by a well guarded by carved gods.

'That's Ogun, the god of war.'

'And the one hung with garlands?'

'Peace.'

So here, in this remote village, the people feared war.

'Civil war.'

Some of the carvings were frankly erotic. Peter was talking to a woman standing at the door of her home. He returned with a carving about twenty centimetres high. 'The symbol of a sacrificed child,' he said, handing it to me. 'Formerly, when twins were born, one had to die. Sacrifice was not thought cruel. When a king died he received news of his kingdom from subjects despatched to the world of the dead on the point of a spear.'

A village elder approached us. He knew Peter. They greeted each other in Yoruba, then we were led to an open shed which sheltered an old motorbike. The elder bent down and lifted two floorboards. At once a gang of youngsters came scampering in and peered into the darkness beneath the floorboards. There was a crocodile there. 'His home is being repaired,' said the elder. 'That's why he's here.'

'Is he the village mascot?'

'He's the village pet,' said the old man.

'You're not frightened of him?'

'Oh yes, we are. But do we not often cherish the creature we fear and destroy that which we love?'

Back in the car Peter was silent for a while.

'This is a chaotic, muddled-up country,' he said, 'and democracy is as yet but a word, but there is such promise in these gifted people. I have been here twelve years and they still astonish me.'

A group of villagers came dancing along the narrow road. We'd no alternative but to leave the car and join them.

'We are making for the chief's house,' we were told. 'Our festival would not be complete without him. He is a popular chief.'

His house had a beaded doorway and we stood in a gathering quietly waiting for him. In so many places it's unpleasant to be in a crowd, but here the people were gentle and there was a scent of sandalwood and wild herbs in the air.

A voice spoke from behind the beaded curtain and the villagers listened reverently, as if to a god. It was the chief, and when he emerged he smiled at us, a benign smile, as if he blessed us. Then he led us to the village shrine and there was unspoken prayer under the trees. It reminded me of the god of peace we'd seen earlier.

Next day a neighbour came in a jeep to take me to my new home. On the way I made a list of jobs to be done: Number one, the synopsis of the film.

Life ran smoothly at the Hendrickses. I rose early, worked regularly, ate simply, got to know the strange insects and birds, but still feared snakes. I was afraid to walk in long grass at night, till one Sunday morning when my next-door neighbour came to tell me that the snake-charmer had arrived.

'It's now or never,' I told myself and went to the front gate to meet him. He had a long, grey specimen hanging round his neck; its fellow was in the basket, and I hoped he'd be content to stay there. The charmer transferred his boa constrictor from his own neck to my neighbour's. Her smile grew fixed. It must have been doped, poor thing, for it didn't stir, but hung there, lifeless. All the same I declined the pleasure of wearing a live boa.

'At least touch it,' said the charmer.

I felt a fool. I had to show willing. Gingerly I put out my hand and stroked the reptile! It wasn't cold, or smooth, more like touching an elephant's skin.

I paid my share of the fee, rushed back into the house and got on with that synopsis. I was having trouble with the language. Certainly the first version couldn't be in Yoruba – a phrase here and there perhaps, but we would have to use English or limit the film's appeal. I had been cutting some of Wole's words. He was in love with words, English as well as Yoruba, but film, after all, is mainly visual. I only hoped he would like what I'd been doing. There was also the different attitude to time in Nigeria – only yesterday a neighbour had sent me a present – a pineapple. I thanked the messenger who brought it to my door.

'No trouble,' he said. 'It gave me the chance to enjoy my cousin's party.'

'So early in the morning?'

It had started the previous morning. Nothing is urgent here, everything will come about in its own good time. These people will not change. We must.

That afternoon I was tidying the kitchen, barefoot, in my shorts, when I heard someone coming through the back garden. I knew who it was, at once.

'Yes, who is it?' I said.

'Me!'

And I looked up at that wicked, smiling face. 'Wole.'

'Himself.'

'Can you prove it?'

He was very surprised to find me there. He'd received none of my communications, had no idea I was in Nigeria.

'What was this conference?'

'Pan Africanism, silly business – a lot of sentimental people extolling the virtues of the African soul.'

Wole had no such illusions. Lucky for him that Tom Driberg had been there and introduced him to a few amusing people, including Lady Daisy, who had no buttocks.

'At least Cunégonde had one.'

'Daisy says she's better off with none. "They spoiled my line," she said. "I leave no impression on a cushion now when I sit." ' Wole was having fun imitating the lady's dewdrop accent. I was congratulated on managing to reach Ibadan and finding myself such smart quarters.

'Now, let's eat.'

His jeep was at the door and we sped along to the café where I'd eaten the kebabs. Wole knew it well. We ate our fill, cracked a bottle of Chianti he'd brought back with him and exchanged news and gossip. 'Tomorrow will you show me the village you had in mind when you wrote *The Jewel*?'

'I invented it.'

'And the people who live in it?'

'Well, I'm not God. In any case I think it was the Devil who invented Chief Beroke.'

'Beroke really exists?'

'He'll be celebrating his hundredth birthday any day. His people are giving him a hundred-gun salute. The government'll be sticking pins in his image. He's just ruined their scheme for a three-lane motorway. "Not through my land," he told them, got up in the middle of the night and threw down all their markers.'

'Did he really have so many wives?'

'More than Solomon. Quite a few of them are still around.'

'Perhaps he could play himself.'

'We'd never control him.'

'And the girl, Sidi?'

'Stars have been shining in the firmament for a million years without being discovered. Somewhere there is a Sidi waiting for us. Meanwhile, I would like to introduce you to my parents.'

Abeokuta, Wole's home town, had a wild reputation, like its most famous son. I looked forward to visiting the source and meeting his parents, who must be remarkable people. On our way there Wole started telling me stories about the history of his home town. 'In the wars with Dahomey we were on the frontier,' he told me. 'That great hill, covered with cactus, was our protection. When the enemy arrived on the scene the household troops would be ordered to storm the heights, while the king sat fanning himself with his fly swatter.

'It was the custom in those days for the first prisoner taken to be castrated. Our men were waiting with sharp knives at the summit of the hill.

'Exhausted but defiant, the heroic first warrior arrived, was taken and stripped, but the executioners blushed. He was a woman. The king of Dahomey had swapped his household troops for Amazons.'

He had another story about a ruthless female chief who had

sold the flower of Abeokuta's youth to the slavers and told their sorrowing parents that they'd gone to God.

'How did she get away with it?'

'She held up bloodstained garments belonging to the young men – bloodstained, but the blood was from betel nuts.'

A gentle man, with snow-white hair, walked towards us as Wole's jeep pulled up. It was Mr Soyinka, lithe and tall, like Wole. Mrs Soyinka stood in the doorway of their home, smiling, waiting to welcome us. Would I care to refresh myself after the journey?

I said yes, for the pleasure of her company – there was such a relaxed, friendly air about her.

The table was already spread outdoors, with so many delicacies that I felt she must have been up all night preparing for our visit. We sat to a long and pleasant meal, talking of the good things of life – friendship, man's handiwork and his expression in music, poetry and sculpture. I learned that Wole's father was a Christian, a vicar in fact. Surprising that this turbulent spirit should have been nurtured in a quiet Christian home. Were they not afraid for him? Sitting there in that calm, happy atmosphere I felt that they were just very proud, and of their other son, a doctor, and the daughter, who was studying to be an architect.

Wole wanted to discuss the increasing commercialisation of Yoruba art with his father. A young artist, son of a village craftsman, had recently gone to London to carve a figure for the outer wall of a newspaper office. 'Here he was essential to his village, like the blacksmith and the shoemaker, there . . .' Wole's gesture was frustrated and angry. As always he was prepared to make a lone stand against hypocrisy and graft.

On our way back I asked him if I could meet Chief Beroke.

'He wouldn't receive us,' said Wole. 'I will show you a chief's palace more interesting than his.'

And he did, though when we approached it I thought there was nothing there – but then leaves stirred, shadows moved and there it was. We walked into an area of slatted light. It was a controlled

arbour, which changed as Wole adjusted a woven screen with a
long pole.

'You can be open to the elements, or sheltered, as you wish,'
he said.

'Even the fierce Hammert'ang cannot disturb us,' said an old
man who was seated by a pillar playing chess. His opponent
greeted Wole and nodded to me.

'Would it interest you to see further?' said the old man.

'Indeed it would.'

We passed through roomy corridors which could serve as shelters or verandahs and I saw how the ventilation system worked. I
had seen it before, long ago, in the galleries of a coalmine. There
the air was kept circulating by the raising or lowering of curtains of
sacking. Here the curtains were of raffia, in both cases manipulated
by long canes. I found the furniture of strikingly good design. You
lounged or lay down on three adjustable
planes (see little drawing) your
head and legs both resting.

It had been a glorious day and as we said good night I gave
Wole my synopsis.

Next morning he came by early. He liked what I'd done.
'You've cut out a lot of unnecessary verbiage,' he said. I was
surprised, and very pleased.

'Let's make a list of advantages – and disadvantages,' he said.
'You'd better take a look at any local actors who might be used.
There are two girls who weren't bad in the University production.'

We tracked them down. They were lively and attractive, but as
soon as they heard the word 'film', they were transformed. Who
would design their costumes? How much would they be paid? And
their billing? Then we went to a bush village where a singer lived.

'Don't mention the film this time,' said Wole. So we took
a few snaps of palm trees and river banks and hung around.

'I'd like a picture of his house,' I said.

'Good day,' Wole cried to him.

'*Akabu.*'

'How is our friend, Nganwunze?'

'You come too late. He was a great singer, but he was murdered
by jealous friends.'

'Do you mind if we snap your house?'

'No, no. And you may have me in it.' He moved to the front of his homestead. 'For five hundred dollars.'

'Thank you.'

'Bushman,' said Wole. 'Better to find our cast in London.'

'I know the perfect Sidi, but she's from Haiti, only speaks French.'

He threw the script at me.

We visited Lagos to talk over our problems with a school-teacher there. Word got round that Wole was in town and the room was soon full of budding *cinéastes*, philosophers, gossips and their hangers-on.

Suddenly the door was flung open and an imposing-looking character walked in leaning on a tall stick. He had a commanding air, a bush hat and a moustache. 'About this Soyinka project,' he began. 'I'm inclined to see it this way' – and he broke into a very funny impersonation of Chief Beroke. It was Wole, of course.

'Settled!' I cried. 'It must be a one-man show with Wole playing all the parts.'

I wanted to visit the Lagos parliament before we left: the only democratic government in Africa, a leading Labour MP had told me in London. It looked like Westminster, but sounded like a black caricature of it. It was a farce, and graft ruled even more obviously than at home.

'There will be no support from this lot,' I said. 'Have you an agent, Wole?'

'No. Have you?'

'I had.'

'You mean Gerry. Well, if you don't want to finish up with Lynn's George on camera and a cast of bushmen, we'll have to find backers in the UK or USA. Beard Saltzman in his den.'

'Yes.'

'I've only used half this ticket. Can I exchange it for a flight to London?'

'No problem. Sorry to see you go, though.'

He handed me a ticket to London, economy class. Wole had

made his own arrangements. On the way back to Ibadan I was navigating and I missed a turn-off. 'Sorry.'

'You nearly landed us in witches' country. My girl's mother lives near here.'

'Is she a witch?'

'Yes.'

'Then you'll end up marrying the girl.'

As a matter of fact he did, and the night before I left I stayed with Laide. Wole had driven me to her rooms after I'd said goodbye to my friends in Ibadan.

'I'll be back in no time,' I told them.

Fifty-three

Icy London in the small hours — everyone away. The architect? He never sleeps — meet up in an all night café. Toothache treated. Saltzman visited. Terrible news of Gerry. To Salisbury hospital. He is on danger list and worrying about Brendan. To Dublin, to find he is now a complete alcoholic. Gerry determined to quit hospital. He must not. I see three Workshop actors, attend opening of the Establishment, a club in Greek Street. Gerry is driven to Blackheath. Two days later, he is in a local hospital. Brendan disowns me. Tynan wishes me to confront Franco Zeffirelli on TV.

London Air Terminal. Four a.m. The other passengers have all dispersed and I'm alone in a neon-lit hall, shivering in the unaccustomed cold. I daren't phone Blackheath. I've no money for a hotel. None of my friends know I'm coming back. In any case who would answer the phone at this hour? Cedric perhaps, he often works all night.

My footsteps echoed as I crossed the hall. Slowly I dialled the number. Let it ring. No answer. Sound asleep, or not there. I walked around. There wasn't a soul in sight, not a paper stand, a coffee machine, or even a seat.

Should I try again? Was there no one else? No one. I tried again, dialled very slowly. . . . Hold it. It's ringing. Hold on, it takes time to put on the light, cross the room, and . . . there's no one there. I'm sunk.

Round the icy hall we go – round and round. Dial again. Bang the machine to recover the pennies. I will go on ringing. I will ring till somebody answers. I phoned, at intervals, till morning.

'Hello!'

'It's me. I'm back and I'm very cold.'

'You must have been phoning for a long time.' (How did he know that?)

'Not really.' (Three hours. It was now nearly seven.)

'There's nowhere open at this time.'

'There's an all-night café in Fleet Street where the newspaper men go.'

'I'll meet you there in a quarter of an hour.'

'I've no money.'

'I'll be there.'

It was packed and steamy when we walked in, the same old cakes with coconut whiskers – the dark tea. I found two places at a table and began to fish in my shoulder bag for a small carved figure I'd brought back. As my friend brought the tea, I felt two bleary eyes fasten on to me. It was a bad actor from Dublin I'd used in the West End version of *The Quare Fellow*. To arrive back from Lagos and come face to face with him! Too much.

I started talking about the sacrifice of the twin child. My companion wasn't even pretending to listen. 'If only I'd had a night's rest,' was all he said.

I felt pretty desperate. 'If only I had somewhere to go,' I said.

'There's always the flat.'

I'd dragged it out of him. I knew that. Outside it was misty and very cold. He hailed several cabs before one stopped. As we rode through grey London I mentioned my need for an adventurous cameraman.

'We've been through that before,' he snapped.

In his bare flat he lit the gas fire and brought out a blanket. I went to the window and threw the precious little idol out into the night. I never saw it again. Then I lay down on the black divan.

'I mustn't sleep,' I said to myself. 'Just rest; you have to see Saltzman and before that . . . the dentist. . . .'

At nine o'clock I got up and made my phone calls. The flat seemed empty. Max, my dentist, said, 'Come at once.' Saltzman: 'Come later.' I borrowed ten shillings in silver which I found lying about in the kitchen, took the keys and left.

An abscess on my tooth was removed straight away; my mouth was still frozen when I arrived at Saltzman's and handed him the synopsis.

'Where's Wole?'

'In Paris. He'll be arriving tonight.'

'Then let's meet tomorrow, first thing.'

'I have to return to the dentist first thing.'

'Make it nine o'clock. You can put the dentist back.'

I was about to leave when: 'Sorry about Gerry.'

'What about Gerry?'

'The accident.'

'What accident?'

'Don't you know? On his boat, an explosion.'

'Where is he?'

'Salisbury.'

'I must go.'

'You can't. There's the film. Listen a minute, I'm getting you an office, the best team in the business. Are you serious about this film? Is Gerry to keep you away from me again?'

'I must see him before I do anything. I'll be back as soon as possible. . . .'

The hospital wouldn't let me speak to Gerry. I checked the times of the trains – phoned the dentist, but he would not let me go to Salisbury without further treatment. I left messages for Wole all over the place, went to the bank, returned to the flat and washed my clothes. Every time the phone rang, I rushed to answer it. So stupid – who could possibly be phoning me? Who would know where I was? The calls were mainly from young women trying to locate an elusive lover, but he didn't show up that day, nor that night. Next morning, just as I was leaving, he walked in, brewed himself a pot of coffee and wanted to know where I'd been. I told him where I was going and immediately he became charming, full of solicitude.

'I wish him well,' he said. 'I hope it's not too bad. Would you like me to see you to the station?'

'I have to go to the dentist first.'

In the end he came with me and saw me to the train.

Nothing prepared me for the sight of Gerry. Before being allowed into the ward at Odstock Hospital I had to wear a mask. He was lying under a cage with a sheet draped over it. He didn't say a word, just looked at me. He was terribly badly burned. The butane gas container he used on his boat had exploded, the flames filled the cabin. He had protected his face, his eyes, so his poor arms . . . and his legs. . . . His legs and feet were especially vulnerable because of the diabetes.

He looked at me and he was crying. I sat by him and told him all the interesting things I could think of about Nigeria. I don't know whether he heard me, whether he was even listening. He didn't speak till just before I was leaving. 'I didn't think you'd come back.'

The man in the next bed told me how very depressed Gerry had been. 'If ever he speaks, it's about you.' He spoke with quiet understanding, perhaps because he too had survived a frightful accident.

I prayed that Odstock knew all there was to know about the treatment of severe burns, for he certainly couldn't be moved.

I cannot forgive myself for what happened to Gerry, nor can others.

'You went away and look what happened,' his sister told me.

Yes, I went away, just when he'd completed the purchase of the old theatre which had cost him so much hard work and anguish. When I summoned up enough courage to visit the place the poster 'JOAN QUITS HER WORKSHOP' was still pinned to the wall in his office, and in his Accounts Book he'd drawn a red line on the day I left and torn out the rest of the book. Every titbit of gossip about the break-up had appeared in the popular press. Tom's nose for a story was sharper than his feeling for Gerry and me.

It wasn't sexual frustration which had driven me away. Gerry was the most satisfying lover you could imagine. It was because I could not face the prospect of passing the rest of my life in that crumbling old slum. Long ago I'd set my sights on a very different kind of place.

I returned to Odstock the following Friday. He was no better. 'He's pining to be out of here,' said his neighbour.

I knew it would be useless asking if he could come home, but I tried.

'As soon as it's possible,' said the doctor.

I told Gerry, and that Jane McKerron, his secretary, would be visiting him during the week. 'She's taking good care of E15,' I said. I didn't mention the film.

'He only wants to hear about you,' said the neighbour. I'd been trying to work in an office at the Film Technicians' Union, with phones and typewriters going, reporters who'd run me to earth bursting in. Gerry wouldn't want to hear all that. He had always protected me when I was working. I hadn't realised how successfully, till now. I couldn't sleep. I missed my home. In the evenings I moved from pub to club, talking, just talking. I didn't drink much. I never have. I was irritated with Saltzman. Wole didn't like the agent I'd found for him and Gerry was agitating to be let out of hospital.

'What would you do at home?'

'Read. Listen to music.'

'You're still on the danger list. Please be patient a little longer.'

He contrived to get a phone to his bedside, sent a case of wine to the harbour-master at Beaulieu who'd rescued him, and a bunch of roses to Jane McKerron.

He wanted to know what was happening to Brendan. I booked a return flight to Dublin. Cedric and a male lover tagged along at the last moment. Brendan was on the booze again and resorted to his usual entertainment – the pub crawl, with songs in the car.

'Unbelievable!' said Cedric.

'He's from a different world,' said the friend.

Neither Gerry, Nigeria nor Theatre Workshop interested B.B. He was now a complete alcoholic.

Back in London, word went round that I was out of work and offers were coming in from the most unlikely places. I wasn't interested, but when I heard that three of my favourite actors were appearing in Cambridge, I longed to see them again. I'd have to go. Surprisingly, Cedric offered me a lift and made a rendezvous at a rum place near St Anne's Mansions. It was some sort of Architectural Centre. The foyer was in silver. It looked like a *fin-de-siècle* gin palace; the next room was done up like a Tudor snug, the next had fruit machines. All the rooms were fitted out as pubs, the only thing was – there was no drink in them. I'm finally convinced that architects are all crackers. I told my friend when he turned up.

'Right! Let's go! The car's waiting.'

'Why are you going to Cambridge?'

'I often do. I was at college there.'

'So Tom said.'

'I lay on my bed most of the time, eating Edam cheese.'

In the car, he started to make fun of theatre, which provoked me into telling him about my idea of space where everybody might learn and play; where there could be every kind of entertainment, classical and ad lib, arty and scientific; where you could dabble in paint or clay; attend scientific lectures and demonstrations; argue; show off; or watch the world go by. It should be by a river. We need the ebb and flow of water to keep us in time. I went rambling on – talking of air balloons and cake walks, cake bakes and vegetable shows . . . but he wasn't listening. I was wasting my time with this weirdo who seemed to spend his leisure jumping from bed to bed like a Spring Heel Jack.

As we drove into Cambridge, I saw the names of my favourite actors on a theatre poster – James (David) Booth, Griffith Davies and Roy Kinnear.

'Stop here,' I told the driver.

'Thought you'd finished with all that.'

'I have. If you want to meet up with us later, try the curry place nearest the theatre.'

The show was more or less over. David was already in the bar. 'Thought you'd gone native.'

'Have you come back to make our lives a misery again?' said Griff, as he came rolling in. Roy was behind him smiling. We had a drink, then went and ate curry, drank brandy and turned our friends over. It was some time before I remembered Cedric and went to look for him. He was wandering along the street, half-seas-over. I pushed him along and into the restaurant. David handed him a glass of brandy and as soon as he'd knocked it back he started reviving his anti-theatre number. I introduced him.

'Where did you find him?' asked Griff.

'God knows,' I said.

'Ap Rhys, a Welshman!' cried Griff, 'A fellow countryman.'

'Where are you going?' said Roy.

'Back to the smoke, where else?'

'I'll take you,' said David. As we left, the Welsh contingent started harmonising together. Roy was fast asleep.

As we approached London and the prospect of another day

in that noisy office, I asked myself what I was doing. All I needed was an adaptable cameraman and with my far-famed gift for improvisation, a flexible work plan.

As if to remind me of my responsibilities, a letter arrived that day from Nigeria. I owed the Hendrickses fifteen pounds and what were they to do with the red leather case I had left with them, pending my return?

I could hardly go back at the moment. Gerry had decided to quit Odstock and Jane McKerron was already at Blackheath with Pat Patricks, our wardrobe mistress, preparing the place for him. My assistance would not be welcome there. Neither of them had approved of my escape to Africa.

Well, tomorrow Gerry would be home, I'd only one more evening to pass on my own. Tom phoned to tell me it was the opening of 'the Establishment', a new club in Greek Street and Sean Kenny had designed it.

It was all black and white: black walls, black furniture . . . so that when Wole arrived we mistook him for the invisible man.

Tom's moon face floated in the darkness.

'Very chic!' he said and disappeared altogether, as the old Duchess of Argyll fell over a chair trying to reach him.

Two smaller moons appeared. They turned out to be an overexposed bust. 'Have you seen my lover?' she was asking.

'I don't have a torch,' said Tom.

Sean appeared and was congratulated all round.

'Who is that with his nose in that young person's cleavage?' Tom wanted to know.

'It's my lover boy,' said the bust.

'The Architect!' said I.

'You pulled out all the stops,' he was saying to Sean. 'Here, these should prove useful,' and he handed me a pair of white gloves. 'Happy birthday.'

My heart sank. It was the first birthday I'd spent away from Gerry.

Wole was pouring us all duty-free cognac. 'Your health,'

he said to me. Tom was being introduced to Billie Whitelaw. 'Billy?' he said. 'How confusing.'

I went to Blackheath to meet Gerry. He was arriving at lunch time the next day. The flat looked remarkably spick and span.

The girls had been busy. As the car turned into the drive I caught a glimpse of him, heavily bandaged. His friend Ray, a boat builder from Hamble, was driving. He had to be carried upstairs and asked to be taken into the front room, his favourite room. I went and phoned the local doctor.

Ray went into the living-room to take a snack before leaving. 'The harbour-master says he's still drinking his health,' he said.

'His health, Ray? He's hardly fit to be out of hospital.' I was right, the doctor had him transferred to Lewisham Hospital on the Monday.

'I thought he was a goner,' he told me afterwards. 'It's a miracle he's alive.'

Lionel Bart came with me to see him and the family arrived from Manchester. They insisted on moving him to the London Clinic right away. That did it. The gutter press was on to us in a flash. 'MANAGER OF WORKERS' THEATRE IN SMART LONDON CLINIC' with overblown estimates of the cost of the place. No mention of the weeks he had lain at death's door in Salisbury or the faulty container which had caused the accident.

Out of the blue the architect phoned me. He was ill, he needed medicine, a hot-water bottle, hot drinks. All he had were fair-weather friends.

He wasn't alone in that – Brendan phoned the BBC to inform them that we were to receive nothing from their forthcoming production of *The Hostage* as the work was entirely his.

Good, that lets me out. From now on, he can write his own plays – so can Shelagh. He had once told her, 'We are both creatures of Joan's imagination.' Perhaps they were.

Jane handed me a pile of letters which had arrived during my absence, many from people wanting information for a thesis on theatre, one from a nun in the Mid-West, invitations to work in out-of-the-way places. Port au Prince sounded interesting. Saltzman didn't seem to be making much progress with *The Jewel* in Nigeria; perhaps we could shoot the film in Haiti. Creole would sound good and Mathilde de Beauvoir would be perfect as Sidi. More fun than *Henry IV, Part I* which Peter Hall was offering me. And had I seen John Gielgud as *Othello*? That was Ken Tynan.

'No, and I couldn't think of a more perfect piece of miscasting.'

'Would you be prepared to appear on telly and say so?'

'Of course.'

'With Franco Zeffirelli?'

'What's he got to do with it?'

'He directed it. Would you be prepared to go and see it?'

'I suppose it might be as well.'

'It's at the other Stratford.'

Fifty-four

With the CND, I attempt instant direction at the Albert Hall. An offer from Peter Hall. Contretemps. Zero Mostel – a Falstaff? And Un-American? On a delegation to Cuba but quit in Prague, after days of delay and no lights on the plane. Meet Maurice Goldsmith of Science Policy Foundation. Return to Blackheath. I'm with Gerry and my godchildren, Hamish and Kirsty MacColl, again. Resolve to master film-making with Sparrers Can't Sing. *Gerry kidnaps me. To Israel – Athens en route – Israel offers work.*

While considering Tynan's proposal, I became involved in a rather different production – with Canon Collins, who'd asked me to stage the rally he was organising at the Albert Hall in aid of Nuclear Disarmament. Remembering the sketches and songs which had worked so well in the huge meetings at the time of the Spanish Civil War, I was determined to make it a lively affair and made my dispositions.

On the great night, the vast building was packed to overflowing. I was installed in a box near the platform with a cue-board to hand, all wired up and ready.

To thunderous applause, Canon Collins and his fellow speakers filed in and sat down, looking solemn. The good Canon made the opening speech – earnest, sincere – and overlong. When the coughing and the shuffling became obvious – I pressed the cue button. . . .

With a warlike whoop, the four Alberts appeared, a comedy team who let loose their 'happenings' all over London, whether in parks, pubs, or even theatres. They leapt on to the platform, dressed in Boer War uniforms. They were pulling a small cannon. Drums rolled as a Union Jack popped out of it. Bruce Lacey yelled, 'Charge!' – a smoke bomb exploded and a fierce war dance commenced.

J. B. Priestley, who'd been sitting next to Canon Collins, got up and moved to the back of the platform. As if on cue a bugle sounded, the war dance ceased. 'Peace!' somebody shouted and the Alberts started to embrace each other, then everybody within reach.

Priestley came forward to speak, looking rather ill at ease, but after a shaky start got into his stride with good, blunt, Yorkshire plain-speaking. After a while, though, realising that he was becoming repetitive, he began looking at his notes. That was enough. A highly professional singing voice took over – 'As Long As He Needs Me', and Georgia Brown appeared to a wild gust of applause. She walked past J.B. smiling, finished her song and walked off.

I'd plenty more in store. I'd circularised all the London theatres, and put the word about. Everybody was keen to come along and liven up the meeting. A.J.P. Taylor got a march-past of Scottish pipers and the applause for Pete Seeger was accompanied by a paper snowstorm. There were poems and songs and when the theatres closed the back stairs were thronged with artists ready to do their bit.

I sent a note to Canon Collins: 'How long have we got the hall?' The reply came back at once: 'Bring things to a close.'

It was easy. The band played a bit of the dear old Beethoven's *Ninth*, there was an outbreak of fraternisation, everybody seemed to be hugging and embracing someone. I felt good, went backstage humming away to myself, but I came upon a wall of ice. Such looks! Such frozen silence! I had warned Canon Collins that there might be happenings.

Ah well, improvised direction was not the success I'd hoped for. I'd better take Gerry's advice and stick to normal theatre. So I went to Stratford-upon-Avon and argued with Zeffirelli on camera at eight in the morning. He called me a Puritan, but he was half-asleep, he'd been up so late. On the train back to London, I remembered Peter Hall offering me a production of *Henry IV, Part I*, and decided to take a look at his theatre, the Aldwych.

I tried the loading bay entrance, as it was wide open. Three or four cleaners were there, refilling their buckets, so I passed the time of day with them.

'Who are you?' It was a man's voice, sounded like a foreman. 'Come on. Out! What do you think you're doing 'ere?'

'Let go of me! Sex mechanic! I was thinking I might work here till I met you.'

One of the cleaners started giggling. I left.

Next day I had a meeting with Peter Hall about casting. 'Don't think I hit it off with your odd-job man,' I said. 'You might be seduced at Stratford East but no one would be rude to you.'

'I'll have a word with our man. He's usually very reliable.'

'In any case, I'm not so sure I could work here without a sprinkling of technicians and actors trained my way; though the biggest problem is Falstaff. You do know that Zero Mostel is arriving tomorrow?'

'Of course. Leslie, my wife, is in the same film. We're both very pleased that all that Un-American Activities business is over.'

'He'd be great in the part.'

'An American Jew playing Falstaff?'

'An actor playing Falstaff. I'll talk it over with him. I'm meeting his plane tomorrow.'

'You'll be seeing my actors on Monday.'

Zero liked the idea of playing Falstaff. 'The film will re-compense me,' he said. 'Peter Hall's company won't have any money.'

On the Monday, I arrived at the Aldwych early and told the Stage Doorkeeper to direct the actors and actresses to the market pub nearby when they arrived. I'd already arranged for snacks to be set out along the counter and told the publican to charge the drinks to the theatre. We'd always managed to provide drinks at E15 if the company was feeling low.

I stood by the bar for a quarter of an hour before anyone arrived. Then it was a pale young actor, who tried to order a coffee straight away. Another quarter of an hour and another timid-looking chap turned up. Had they expected to meet a Gorgon? It took a few drinks and some hairy old theatre yarns before the place took on the atmosphere of an actors' bar.

The first young man was in the middle of a very good imitation of Robert Speaight's Hamlet the night he forgot to fasten his flies and resisted everyone's attempt to make him decent. He'd got to Speaight saying, 'Such a sight as this becomes the field . . .' when Peter Hall walked in with Peter Brook behind him and, of all people, Zero.

'We've been sitting in the stalls since ten o'clock, waiting for your auditions,' said Hall.

'I don't hold formal auditions. I like to get to know people.'

'What are you doing here?' I asked Zero.

'He asked me to audition,' he replied quietly.

You could have knocked me down with a feather. Whatever administrative ability Peter Hall might possess he was, without doubt, one of the worst – no, give him his due, the very worst – director in the UK. Nevertheless he must have had ample opportunity to see Zero's work on stage or screen.

'Your little finger, please Zero,' I said and, raising it to my lips, blew. Zero grew and grew and as the company applauded we floated out into Tavistock Street and out of Peter Hall's life for ever.

Hollywood changed its mind about Zero. They wouldn't have him in the film after all. When I told Hall's wife, Leslie, she was indignant. 'We'll not take it lying down,' she said and asked Zero why he had been declared Un-American.

'For standing godfather to Paul Robeson's son,' he said.

Next day, she called me back. 'I've spoken to the producer,' she said. 'And the only trouble is – if we all come out in sympathy, there'll be no picture.'

There was no picture for Zero. He went back to New York and his wife and got on with his life – one of the happiest men I ever knew.

At Christmas-time, for the first time in years, our old theatre was closed. Gerry, not yet fully recovered, went to Manchester to stay quietly with his parents.

I was invited to join a delegation of lawyers, politicians and artists going to Cuba. I'd met two of the party: George Elvin, leader of the Film Technicians Union and D.N. Pritt, QC, the distinguished Socialist MP. Cheddi Jagan's wife and the rest were strangers to me, though I'd met Cheddi when he was premier of British Guiana. We all looked suitably solemn as we introduced ourselves on New Year's Eve at Heathrow.

Our plane was delayed. We were to travel to Prague first and from there take a Cuban plane to Havana. But the plane from Cuba had not arrived. We hung about, occasionally strolling over to the Arrivals/Departures panel, looking for a sign till even the most patient among us gave up. We dispersed, leaving a telephone number.

Where could I go? Tom was in Bradwell. I phoned Cedric. As usual, there was no reply. I took the bus to his digs. He was out in the road, having a snowball fight with a friend.

They didn't put off much time with me, they were going to a party, but they let me in and told me to make myself at home. I curled up on the black divan, slept fitfully, phoned Heathrow early. Castro had only three planes: he was making an official tour in one, the other two were grounded, owing to the weather, but I was asked to return to the airport.

Two more days dragged by while we waited for news. When take-off was finally announced, I was in some remote bar at the airport with Robert, another architect, who was trying to convince me that you could judge a building by its face.

We got some dirty looks when we found the others. They'd already boarded the plane for Prague.

That beautiful city looked sadder, more neglected than when we'd played there in 1947, but I heard singing coming from the bar at our hotel and joined a party of working men who were drinking there. Of course I started airing the few Czech words I remembered and was just giving my soulful rendering of 'Sadila' when someone called out: 'Discussing dialectical materialism?'

It was the sociologist from our party, a superior intellectual. I invited him to join us, but he wouldn't. There was another couple of days' waiting before the airport bus came for us. I was last across the Tarmac as usual. It had always been Gerry who went first and claimed a seat by the window for me.

Bags were being stowed and seat-belts fastened as I found a

seat, but the plane was in complete darkness. I pulled a book out of the side pocket of my Bergen pack and went to sit down. I pressed the overhead button – no light. I tried again – nothing. I called the steward.

'The electricity is cut,' he said.

'So I see. When is it coming on?'

He shrugged. I sat down, expecting lights at any moment. Instead it was: 'Fasten your seat-belts. No smoking till the plane is . . .' I'd had enough. I didn't even like that solemn delegation either.

'Just a minute,' I shouted. 'We've sixteen hours' flying time ahead of us. When are the lights coming on? I want to read.'

'The electricity is cut.'

'In that case, I'm getting off.'

'You can't. You've been through the formalities.'

'Nobody mentioned crossing the Atlantic in a black-out. Open this door, please.'

The plane was circling the airfield as I stood there. An argument broke out in rapid Spanish. It was the pilot talking to Control.

'I am not a prisoner. Open this door,' I shouted for all the world to hear.

The eyes of the entire delegation were on me. The plane drew to a halt.

'*Bon Voyage!*' I shouted as the door slid open. 'Bye bye,' and I descended to be greeted by a waiting policeman.

'You are under arrest.'

'*Čest práci.*'

I was interrogated till I fell asleep.

When I awoke, hours later, I was on a plane bound for London and a sunburned stranger smiled and began lecturing me about the lack of science training in schools. He had a very attractive wife.

'We've been on a Christmas ski-ing holiday in the High Tatra, she said. 'A perfect place.' By the end of the flight I had heard all about her husband's 'Science Policy Foundation'. His name was Maurice Goldsmith and through him I met Gordon Pask, the doyen of Romantic Cyberneticians.

Bump, bump. Heathrow. Okay. Taxi! Take me to Blackheath.

Gerry and Camel were sitting together in deep discussion when

I got there. They looked quite startled to see me. I left them to it and wandered from room to room, straightening a picture here and there, flicking the dust off books. I was looking through the discs when Gerry appeared in the doorway.

'Where the Hell have you been? And who's this cunt you've been sleeping with?'

I couldn't answer.

'I've come back to work. . . . Not at Stratford.'

'Please yourself. You always do. I'm taking flying lessons, anyway.'

I was shocked. He can't have told them about his . . .

'Hamish and Kirsty are coming to stay. They'll be here any minute.'

'I'll have to buy a new bed for Hamish.'

'That's up to you.'

'Do you want me to go?'

'This is your home. . . .'

The arrival of the kids put a stop to further fretfulness. Hamish wanted to be out in the snow right away. 'It'll be deep in the park,' he said.

Gerry went to look out the old toboggan.

'Not much daylight left,' said Camel.

'Don't let's waste time then,' said Mish, and he and Gerry went on ahead leaving Camel and me to trail along with Kirsty. When we arrived at the hilltop where Greenwich Observatory stands, we found Gerry and Hamish taking turns to toboggan down the steep slope which leads to the Queen's House. I don't know which of them was enjoying it most.

Camel asked Kirsty if she'd like to look in at the Banqueting Hall.

'Yes, it's too cold to be standing about.'

The long hall looked splendid, with lighted candles in branched candlesticks all along the tables.

'I used to eat here every day when I was in the Navy – a midshipman.'

'I can still smell the onion soup,' said Kirsty. She was gazing at the Baroque ceiling adorned with the virtues of James I.

'Rubens,' said Camel.

'And poor old Thorburn. His painting was paid for by the square yard,' I added.

Walking home quietly, across the snow-covered park, I felt at peace with the world and my future was very clear. The heavy stone laid on the theatre by the Puritans had still to be lifted. Could I restore a trampled plant and when it was strong enough, let it grow free?

'With all these activities you're proposing?'

'If film-making is as easy as all that, show us how. Splice a tape, film a night sky, a rose opening, a bird with its young. . . . You've talked enough about *The Lion and the Jewel*. Wouldn't it be better to try your hand with something simpler? *Sparrers*, for example. At least the setting would be familiar.'

I mentioned the idea of a *Sparrers* film to one or two people, phoned around to see if anything was stirring on the Nigerian front. All quiet! I sent the Hendrickses the money I owed them and gave myself a week's leave: William Empson, reading his poetry; P.M.S. Blackett lecturing on science in the Third World; my architect attacking prestige barriers at the ICA; Nureyev dancing at Covent Garden; lunch with Francis Bacon at The White Tower one day, supper with Orson Welles at The Pink Elephant, the next. To break the ice I told Orson how much I'd admired his *Macbeth* film.

'Speak again, bright angel,' he replied. 'I'm asked to leave dinner parties if it's even mentioned.'

'Deny thy father and refuse thy name!' I cried, in accents which might have graced the Old Vic and climbed on to a chair.

'Down from there!' yelled the Manager. 'And out! You're upsetting my clients.'

'Be but sworn my love,' said Orson, giving the angry man a bear hug, 'And I'll no longer be a Capulet.'

And we went. Francis and I had been shown the door yesterday and I didn't want it to become a habit. Already David Booth was going around telling everybody that I was taking a look at a couple of films, after which, nobody would be able to teach me anything about film-making. I'd be drummed out of Soho if that went on. I decided to look into the business.

Dugald Rankin, a friendly film producer, showed me a Nagra and Orson Welles told me about his new Moviola.

'I'd rather have the Nagra,' I told him.

It was the latest recording gadget, no bigger than a two-tiered chocolate box and simple to use.

'I've got you a producer,' said David Booth one day. 'A great admirer of yours.'

'Oh good.'

A soft-spoken bloke appeared and the air turned blue with new words – dub, post-synch, optical, magnetic – new to me. Then, *Night Mail*, Crown. . . .'

'Excuse me, wasn't that before the War?'

'Before the Flood,' said David, and produced a runner-up, Mac, his charming, successful, very slick agent. 'Much more with-it.'

'What's new?' asked Tom one day, descending from the clouds in his chariot of fire.

'Where have you been?'

'With Glenn, in the highest heaven of invention. What are you up to?

'Planning.'

'Work?'

'A project.'

'Well, whatever it is you've got into your head, Cedric Price has his entire office working on it.'

I was dumbfounded. I didn't know. I'd often raved about my Abbaye de Thélème. I'd never been more serious about anything. Since childhood, I'd been adding to the list of delights this century owed us, but I'd never found anyone to work with me on it. Now this young architect was actually trying to realise it. I began listing all the activities that would be possible in a palace of the future.

I was still thinking about it all when I found we were racing along the M5 in Gerry's car.

'Where are we going?'

'I think you've forgotten what life is for, getting up at dawn each morning to phone that cunt. You're with me, and that's all that matters.'

'Where are we going?' I asked the smiling steward as he handed me a glass of golden wine.

'Athens, ma'am.'

Gerry had laid on one of his specials. We slept that night in a mobile at the foot of a cliff. It opened with the heat and closed at night. Meals and drinks were brought to us across the rocks and rivulets of a sunny beach. We swam before breakfast and took our coffee under the trees. I made notes and wrote letters. Gerry just swam. For the first time, I saw how scarred and disfigured his legs were.

Even in that paradise, my dream would not leave me, whether speeding along the winding coast road, or watching the struggling fish newly caught in a rock pool – the image would not fade.

A brief stay by the shores of the Aegean and we flew to Tel Aviv. Gerry had arranged it all – a room in the Hotel at Herzliya, letters to our friends. There was a bouquet from Ori Levy in our room when we arrived and Ori, the superb actor who had worked with us for a season at E15, arrived himself next morning after breakfast. He gave us a list of places to be visited and invited us to a party at his apartment that night.

Gerry wanted to know where he might find the orange trees planted for his barmitzvah and Ori wanted to talk politics. Formerly he'd been a completely non-political creature. During the conversation he let slip the secret of our visit. He was hoping that I'd accept the offer of a theatre in Israel. He had to go to a rehearsal and we were left to our own devices. First, to get the feel of the place. There was no escaping politics. Eichmann was being tried in Tel Aviv and people talked of nothing but revenge. I have always admired the gifted Jewish people, but I found the Sabra (those born in Israel) aggressively nationalist, and the theatres, the Kameri and the Habima, very old hat. The only theatre worth a light was in Jaffa, in a hammam, where the story of the first Jewish settlers was told, with songs and sketches backed by old photographs projected on a screen. There were only four performers, two male, two female. We were so impressed that we went back next night to see their other piece, which dealt with the Palestinians in Israel. We were shocked to learn that they were living under curfew. We went to their villages to see for ourselves.

The Israelis joined the club. Eichmann was executed and the young performers we'd seen in Jaffa left the country, never to return.

Had Gerry thought to lure me back into the theatre in Israel? I told him it was not on.

'You seem to prefer the Muslim world. Let's visit Istanbul on our way back.'

'So long as they don't want me to direct plays there.'

'They want you everywhere.'

We celebrated Gerry's thirty-ninth birthday in a hotel in old Istanbul. Outside, the narrow streets were crowded with street vendors, bootblacks, mountebanks and beggars. You could scarcely move for them.

A pleasant voice, speaking English, accosted us. 'Can I be of some assistance?' And began berating the horde of beggars in rapid Turkish. The crowd dispersed, we invited the lady to take a coffee with us and saw, for the first time, a dainty child clinging to her skirts.

'My daughter, Funda,' she said. 'My name is Nesrin.'

We exchanged aery nothings and there was a little flirting as we ate Turkish delight and sipped Turkish coffee. Nesrin invited us to take a trip along the Bosphorus with her next day. 'I will come to the hotel for you.'

And so she did. We took a pleasure boat passing filigree buildings in the old town, glimpsing the angular concrete of the new Hilton on a high hill.

Lapping water. Sunlight. The great rusting hull of a Russian tanker, protruding from the Bosphorus. 'It's been there for years,' said Nesrin. The boat anchored by a well-kept garden bordering the water's edge. 'This is an eating place,' said the lady and she told Funda to show us the garden while she ordered.

It was my first experience of meze. I know of nothing like it: dainty tit-bits, savoury, tasty, sweet and sour, designed to arouse your appetite and satisfy it. To Gerry's delight there was wine too, in a swan-like jug embossed in silver. He looked so happy, as if he could stay here for ever but that evening back at the hotel he had news for me.

'Your film friends want you back in London!'

'My film friends?'

'That's right. You must know that a telegram came for me.' I didn't know.

'It seems everybody is mad for you to make a film.'

'Except you.'

'Right.'

'I have been hoping to talk to you about the one thing which really interests me.'

'And I've been hoping for you to come to your senses and do what only you can do. For God's sake stop wasting your time with half-baked charity, or sociology, or whatever they call it nowadays.'

'Nesrin offered us a stay at her summer home on the Golden Isle.'

'What about your friends in London.'

'I can't believe that crew has managed to set up a film, but if it's true, I'm committed.'

Fifty-five

Setting up the Sparrers *film. A base in Cable Street. Disagreement at outset – my chosen team edged out – the wrong cameraman – my Nagra sound recorder out. A party for the crew, actors and locals – the Krays turn up. Shooting goes badly – the cameraman slow. A top-level meeting holds up filming. I fly to New York with Shelagh Delaney for two days. On my return, 'Your film is overrunning, the cameraman has left, the producer has been sacked.' Good! 'Who's my new producer?' 'Andy Mitchell.' Very good. With the new cameraman, we shoot sixty per cent of the film in eight days – but I am not allowed any re-shooting. Give the story to the press. Lionel writes a song for Barbara Windsor. Gore Vidal and the fair Elaine.*

In less time than it takes to tell we were back in gloomy London and I was boozing at the Swiss pub with two young men whose work I greatly admired, Hugh Raggett and David Watkin of Transport Documentaries. Then I'd transfer to the Intrepid Fox to meet the soft-spoken producer and the smart agent; shoot in and out of the Film Finance Corporation and sign up with the ACTT, proposed and seconded by two technicians I'd never seen before and listening gravely to the Guarantee of Completion people without once letting on that I'd never taken so much as a snapshot in my whole life, neither had I strung two sentences together as yet, let alone a filmscript.

'That's okay. Steve Lewis is already tapping away like a woodpecker.'

'Where?'

'In a room at Father Grosser's Settlement in Cable Street.'

He was, on a small table in a neat little flat, all black and white.

'Where did all this come from?'

'Tom Driberg spoke for the flat and Una Collins and I fixed it up. I've been waiting for you to come back and work on the adaptation with me,' said Stephen. 'We should be able to improvise.'

On the mantelpiece there was a telegram: 'Welcome to filming – Dugald Rankin.'

I spent a sleepless night in that flat, watching the lights from passing lorries drift across the ceiling. By morning I'd decided to mingle a few locals with my Workshop gang – May from the Angel café; Rosie from Goide's bakery, the one who always sent you away with a pound of strudel when you'd only gone in for a slice; Queenie from the Iron Bridge who sang 'Can't Help Loving that Man o' Mine' while she drew your pint. Who could act such characters?

By lunch-time Steve and I had finished half a film treatment and were planning a coming-out party in the flat, with the crew, the actors and everybody we knew in the district. Our film was going to be a humdinger all the way.

I had several sites in mind and asked David Watkin to take a few shots of them. Soft-spoken Donald had eased himself into the producer's seat. He might need prodding but I didn't think there was harm in him. The script was finished; all we needed was a work-plan adjustable according to the weather: move to indoor locations when it rained, outside when it was fair. In fact a sunny summer was forecast.

'Let's get going.'

'We'd like to introduce you to the press, first,' said Donald.

'Don't bother. They all know me.'

'Next Tuesday. Soho Court.'

'Sorry. I won't be there. I don't like interviews.'

Tom published the story: 'Press party without guest of honour.' The ball was in their court.

'It seems that Greene is now free,' said my producer.

'Who's Greene?'

'A highly experienced lighting cameraman.'

'But we already have a cameraman,' said I, thinking of David Watkin.

'The general feeling is that a new man – an untried director —' Untried!

'This isn't some inexpensive East End theatre show. We have had to raise a great deal of money for this film.'

'I appreciate your kindness.'

We'd hardly parted when Watkin and Hugh Raggett approached me. Hugh had cut David's films and worked with John Schlesinger on *Terminus*.

'Is something wrong?'

'Yes. We feel ill at ease with your associates.'

'So do I, but surely we can work together.'

'It is being made impossible for us. Donald Taylor, instructed by you, booked David but sacked him after three weeks, a week before the main shooting begins.'

My heart sank.

'He made the excuse that David had provided no close-ups but in fact he had already booked Max Greene.'

'I'm afraid you've got a lot on your plate,' said David. 'We don't want to make things worse for you. We'll work together one day.'

I was frustrated and furious. Should I give up? I tried, but I was legally committed. Accept a *fait accompli*, or else . . .

'Mr Greene is highly regarded in the film world.'

I arranged a read-through, hired a room over the local pub. Una and I got there early, swept and dusted the place and arranged chairs and ashtrays. Una posted this notice: 'The artists will act the story of the film, so that you will have an idea of the style I have in mind and feel able to co-operate.'

The crew trailed in, looking completely lost. 'We don't need to know the story to make the props,' I heard one say. Mr Greene arrived last, found a secluded corner and settled down.

I gave three bangs for fun and the company rose to it. Barbara Windsor got laughs and wolf-whistles all the way through and Roy Kinnear had them in stitches. I glanced across at Mr Greene. He was buried in the *Sporting Life* and obviously had no intention of wasting his time watching a bunch of silly people. This highly experienced cameraman was hardly a man after my own heart, but I had to make a team out of this clanjamfrie or the film would be a disaster.

My launch party would break the ice. We made a huge bowl of punch and a cauldron of curry. When the front door was opened, the neighbourhood poured in: The Krays, looking sleek, Yootha looking glamorous, the Krays' minders and Yootha's admirers.

David Booth with Maurie, his six-foot-two baby-minder, laughing at his jokes; Wozzo and Bugsie, Marleena and Christabel. Barbara's Ronnie turned up with two or three yobbos, but vanished when he saw the Krays. Barbara came in later with the Misses Pelham, two very strait-laced sociable workers she'd picked up on the doorstep.

What a salad! Cops and robbers, do-gooders and cony-catchers, racists and humanists – anything could happen.

Limehouse Willy introduced himself: 'One of the Krays' minders,' he told me, then added under his breath, 'Very naughty boys.'

A bloke nobody knew never left the doorway, but stood there, watching everybody. He wore a soft black trilby, a black bow-tie and a black velvet jacket.

'Looks a bit dodgy,' said David. 'Do you want Maurie an' me to sweep up?'

'Don't worry,' I said. 'They're all going to be in the film. They're mad about show business.'

If you look carefully at the scene in Angel Lane, the one where David is careering along beside Barbara with their baby in the pram, you'll see quite a few of the boys. That's Limehouse Willy, polishing the antique tray.

The producer never noticed the unusual extras; they were paid off by the Extras Union who were too scared to ask questions.

'What happened to that bloke in the black velvet jacket?' I asked Limehouse Willy one day.

'Safe in the arms of Jesus,' he said.

Tom Driberg didn't turn up. He'd already been photographed with the Krays and didn't like it. I was relieved that Gerry had decided to stay away: he didn't approve of my mixing with such types. I was wrong. He came rolling in on his own and stood drinking brandy. Well, so long as Price didn't turn up. He'd been dubbed the arch-enemy, luring me away from theatre, and they were a pair who would be frightened of nobody, not even of each other.

The ranks were thinning. David had already disappeared with Yootha and Maurie was looking lost. I began collecting dirty glasses, stubbing out smouldering dimps and retrieving plates of half-eaten curry left in corners. One of Una's *Celestina* designs was hanging lopsided on the wall. I went to adjust it. Someone's hand forestalled me, sticking a drawing-pin into the cork panelling.

It was Cedric! Oh my God, where's Gerry? He's here some-where. My mouth is as dry as a bone. I'm going. I vamoosed, didn't stop till I was out in the cold air.

When I went back, hours later, the flat was utterly deserted, the windows were fleeing open, nothing was smashed. I felt desolate – lonely. Someone must have steered those two apart. I'd know all about it one day.

The filming started at long last. It went slowly, a few easy shots to begin with. I made a schedule to cover the whole film. It was flexible enough and my Nagra could record anywhere.

Why this large sound team, with van?

All this – 'Sorry, old man, let's try again. The mike was in shot.'

'Take Five.'

'Afraid we caught a bit of that plane going over.'

'Take Six. . . . How's that? Is it a wrap?'

'Why don't you use my Nagra?'

'Union rules.'

Dugald Rankin, my old friend who'd come along to have a look, took me aside. 'Don't you know why a Nagra is four-sided?'

'No.'

'So that four Union men can play cards on it.'

My Nagra was out.

So was my work plan.

'Not precise!' said the agent.

We sweated it out in Goide's bakery during a heat-wave and turned blue for three days on the Sewer Bank while Mr Greene waited for the sun. When the producer turned up with the editor to be, I let fly: 'Sir, for inflexible planning, discouraging initiative, dampening talent – in fact for crass incompetence, you take the cake.'

'I have a world-famous editor with me . . .,' he began but, seeing the world-famous editor looking rather shocked, 'She's always like that,' he said.

How the hell did he know? He'd hardly ever set eyes on me. As he moved away to blow his nose, 'Donald is famous for his charms,' said the editor.

'Oh is he? And anything else?'

The editor, like Mr Greene, was a mittel-European, that was the right accent to have in those days. Greene was in fact Mutzi Grünbaum and the editor, Oswald Hafenrichter.

'Remember that you are dealing with a first assistant, second and third assistant, camera, props, costumes, hairdressing – you can't just improvise,' he told me.

'Thank you, but I am used to dealing with several stage shows simultaneously,' I said.

'Birdsong. Take Five,' cried a burly young man and a mike, on a long pole, narrowly missed our noses.

'Take my name off the film,' cried a shrill voice. It was Polly, the hairdresser, Grünbaum's girlfriend.

'What now?'

'Miss Windsor's hair in yesterday's rushes.'

'That's the way I want it.'

I'd already had enough trouble with that shot. Barbara running the length of a side street, afraid the boozer would be shut before she got there. In the script it should have been shut; in reality – it wasn't. My first assistant, having forgotten his instructions, was still standing dreaming by the lamppost. Take One, so well rehearsed, was ruined. I'd already discovered that either you got what you wanted with the first take or it took five or six more and still lacked spontaneity. Oh, this cock-eyed film business! Cooked breakfasts as soon as we arrived on site, coffee break, lunch break, tea break, overtime. Wednesdays and Fridays work stopped at 5.50, Mondays, Tuesdays and Thursdays at 6.20. If at 5.50 you were in the middle of a shot, the first assistant would shout, 'Calling the quarter.' Which meant an extra half hour's pay for everybody. If you asked for the quarter at lunch-time, they got an hour's pay. When Mr Greene spent the whole afternoon trying out different gelatines on the windows of a pub location, I made a phone call.

'Sir! As the cameraman insists on turning every location into a studio and the first assistant you found me falls asleep in the fresh air, and it takes four days to produce a prop, you'd better move us into a place designed for this job, or *Sparrers* will cost you a million.'

Monday morning, 8.30 – Studio I Merton Park. Pub scene. Full cast, make-up, costumes.

Barbara was on set first, nattily dressed as always, but walking sideways?

'Are you all right? Turn round.'

The left side of her face was black and blue. She had a black eye and a swollen lip.

'We can't shoot on that. Get Make-up to have a go.'

'They already have.'

'How did it happen?'

'The pots fell on me.'

When the technicians turned up they were moody and irritable. Apparently they'd been enjoying the freedom of the outside.

I managed the master shot of the pub scene without closing in on Barbara and got Queenie Watts and her gang in the can, but there was an awful atmosphere on the set. I overheard Chuck Sewell talking about settling the score with Barbara's bloke, who was a slob if ever there was one, though she'd kill you if she heard you say so. . . .

Suddenly, in the middle of the scene, David hurled a glass at the family group standing by the bar.

'David! You can't do that.'

'Why not? It made them shut up.'

'It's not in character. Your character could get attention without that.'

He promptly walked off, threatening to turn in the part. It took another outburst and a lot of soothing syrup before he would consent even to try the take without the glass smashing, but when he did, it was good.

It was a Thursday, Barbara's bruises had scarcely faded when a notice went up: 'No Shooting Friday.'

There was a lot of whispering. All I heard, or rather overheard, was: 'Over the budget.' 'Mutzi gone?' 'They're replacing her.' 'A new producer?' 'The film won't get finished?'

I phoned Elstree's hatchet man, Andy. He watched the costs as if they were his life's savings. 'What's going on?'

'A very important meeting, top level; can't give you the strength at the moment.'

'That's okay. I'll take the weekend off. I could do with a break. See you Monday.'

I'd directed *Sparrers* at Stratford in a couple of weeks and rewritten it. After half a year on the film I'd bugger all to show for it.

I blew all my spare cash on a return ticket to New York. Shelagh Delaney decided to come with me.

The earth does look fair when you're high above it, as the cosmonaut said. The world was still marvellous outside that murky old studio . . . with the spacemen circling it, Professor Rotblat counselling us to preserve it, and Shelagh and Joan off to NY NY for two glorious days.

I had an idea that the Arc might be there with his plans, though I wasn't sure. And what if he were? I'd be like some old nightingale of Oscar Wilde's – singing, with my heart on a thorn.

Yes, he was staying with his friend, Jim.

Shelagh and I signed in at the Bristol and went to call on them. The apartment was stuffy, as if they'd had a twenty-four hour party and the guests had just fallen asleep. A girl called Barbie was dozing in an armchair.

'She appeared on the doorstep with a yellow chrysanthemum,' said Jim.

'I was a present,' she said, sleepily.

The Arc was making flagrant passes at Shelagh and she wasn't enjoying it.

'I'm tired,' she said.

'Go and lie down, then,' said Jim. She found a divan in the next room and stretched out on it. I went and put my arms round her and stayed there till she was asleep, then I tiptoed away.

I walked the streets, stood with a House Painters' picket for a while, made my way back to the Bristol to phone Zero and my friends Gerry Feil and Jim Goldman, then dialled the apartment and asked for Shelagh.

'Why not me?'

'I don't want you.'

'I flattered myself you came to New York to see me.'

'Then you were wrong.'

'Your coming was the nicest thing that's happened here. You keep me sane.'

His technique was good but I'd heard it all before. Jim's words came back to me. 'Can't you do anything with him? He's sexually disgusting.'

'I'm going to Coney Island on the subway. And I want Shelagh to come.'

'Can't I come?'

'I'll be with a crowd.'

'I'm coming anyway.'

And he did. I sat in a different carriage, rode the Ferris wheel with Gerry Feil and fell asleep on the way back. I must have been walking in my sleep because next thing I knew we were all in this all-night saloon somewhere on the East Side, and the drink was flowing.

'I'm selling up tomorrow. Drinks on the house.'

As it turned out, it wasn't his house, or his drinks.

'Jim never stopped talking about you and how kind you were to Shelagh.' It was Jim's friend and he was pouring brandies in my room at the Bristol. How any of them got there I don't know.

'I wasn't kind,' I said, 'and you'll all have to go. Everybody out. My friends are giving a party for me and I need some sleep.'

When I woke up, he was still there.

'What about Staten Island?'

'What about it?'

'We could take the ferry.'

'Zero and Kate are giving a farewell party for me. I don't want to miss it.'

'You can't go yet, you've only just arrived.'

'I know, but I have to be back at work.'

'Trouble is I'm so busy listening to myself that I seldom hear what other people are saying.'

'I have to buy some wurst and potato salad.'

'You can do that on Staten Island.'

We went, and it was great. The wind on the river and the talk about palaces on the waterside and gardens of light. . . . In the end I'd only time to pack, pay the hotel, look in at Zero's party, flag a lift to Idlewild and just make the plane for London.

Shelagh was there somewhere, waving goodbye, and I could smell something smouldering. It was a tip of lighted Gauloise, on my suede jacket. The hostess put it out as she fastened my seat belt.

O n the Monday I phoned Andy, first thing.
       'You know your film is over-running?'
    'I'm not surprised at the rate we've been going.'
'Not only that, the cameraman's gone, the producer had to be got rid of and the agent's broke.'
'It's been a balls-up from the outset. Who's my new camera-man?' I said.
There was a splutter from the end of the phone. 'There's been quite a lot of humming and ha-ing about completion.'
'With more than half still to be shot, he'll have to look lively, whoever he is.'
'Desmond Dickinson is free.'
'And the producer?'
'Me.'
If he expected me to be put out, he was wrong. Andy was brisk and efficient, what's more he came out with his criticisms. Till now the atmosphere on the film had been like the murky background of *Venice Preserv'd*.
I'd scarcely put the phone down when the agent called me. 'I think it would sound bad if word got about that Donald had been sacked, bad for the profession at a time like this. . . .'
'It's nothing to do with me. I have a film to finish.'
I took to the new cameraman; he worked fast. We sped around in his little Deux Chevaux, picking up bits that saved whole sequences, but when it came to re-cutting Reel Eight, Andy wouldn't budge.
'It would cost two thousand,' he said.
'But Desmond has shot sixty per cent of the film in eight days; that has saved you money.'
'Andy should have screen credit,' said Ossie.
'Not at Donald's expense,' said Andy.
'And Desmond can't hold a candle to Mutzi,' said the agent. I left them to fight it out and bought myself a cutting coat (a chef's jacket from Denny's) and hung it on the cutting-room door. I'd looked

forward to it, the winding, splicing and checking on the Moviola, saving dull footage with a neat cut, editing to music. . . . I placed Hector, my robot, on the work bench.

Alas, reality wasn't nearly so much fun. I'd sit for hours on the high stool beside the great editor, while he experimented with some intricate arrangement. Once, after sitting there a day and a night and into another day, I woke myself up falling to the floor.

Summer turned to autumn and we were still cutting. Every morning, including Sundays, I would leave Blackheath in time to catch the seven o'clock train from New Cross. Gerry would give me a lift: when I returned at eight or nine o'clock at night, he was usually at the theatre.

Reel Eight haunted me. If Andy didn't give in, there'd be trouble.

I asked Harold Lever to take a look at my contract. Tom told me to sell my story to the papers. 'The only way to get what you want is by publicity,' he said and phoned the *Daily Mail*. 'Six p.m. at the Café Royal – don't be late.' The journalist who turned up was knowledgeable about film.

'Fight for what you want. You would in the theatre. David Lean is still cutting when the first reel is on screen at the pre-mière.' A bit of film mythology, but it cheered me up. I dropped in on Tom to put him in the picture. He was dictating to one of his catamites, young and good-looking of course, but a bit spotty – 'Just acknowledge this one,' he was saying, 'It's from Gore. Tell him I'll reply when he recovers.'

'Is he ill?'

'He's in love.'

'It does happen.'

'With a woman! And he expects me to deliver his absurd letters to her, personally.'

'Why?'

'She's married to Ken Tynan.'

The thought of Ken and Gore fighting over the fair Elaine made me laugh.

'It really isn't funny,' said Tom. 'He was a dear friend.'

'He's not dead!'

'As good as. Anyway, Tim's famished. I'm taking him to

the Lebanese restaurant where the owner has the biggest cock in London.'

'Have you measured?' I fled before he could open a counter-attack.

Next morning the *Mail* ran a story about my adventures in Wonderland and the phone didn't stop ringing – friends, enemies, newspapers, magazines, Andy and Mac and Old Uncle Grade himself. . . .

'Tell Tom Driberg to stick to politics,' he shouted. 'I'll sue him.'

I kept my cool till he calmed down.

'Not blamin' you, darling,' he said. As far as I'm concerned, you've only got to name your film and the money's there.'

Andy was next. He exploded. 'That thing in the *Mail* . . .'

Lionel Bart was delighted. 'It's given me an idea,' he said. 'A song for Barbara, "Ain't It a Shame Sparrers' Can't Sing". You can have it for fifty quid.'

I asked Harold Lever to put it to Andy. He did. 'It's a bargain' said Andy. Two days later camera and sound were on location by half past eight in the morning and the sun was shining.

Some time later Barbara stepped out from the balcony window wearing only her Baby Doll nightie. She looked edible. She was miming the words, the song had been pre-recorded.

Take One. Action. Before the clapper board went in Andy yelled, 'Cut!'

'What's wrong?'

'The Censor will never allow it.'

'Allow what?'

'That nylon nightdress.'

'What's wrong with it?' asked Barbara.

'Nipples!' said Andy. The crew groaned.

'Come and look through the camera. See what I mean?'

'There was no trouble in the studio,' said Barbara.

'No, it's the sunlight,' I said.

'It's the wind bringing them up a bit,' she said. 'Can we get on?'

'How?' said Andy. 'Change the nightie and we spoil the continuity and we can't just shoot her from the neck up.'

Bernie from Make-up had an idea and disappeared, but returned shortly carrying a very long paintbrush and some white paste in a saucer.

'Lift your nightie, Babs.'

She giggled and lifted it. I can still see her standing there, holding her nightie aloft, gently pleasured while Bernie blotted out the little rosy buds with delicate strokes.

Fifty-six

Christmas in Casablanca. To Marrakech in an old, hired banger.
The Casbah and belly dancers with red noses. Beyond the walls, the
Berber entertainers. The remains of a harem. Among the sands, a
forgotten Jewish tribe. Our lives in danger – to the desert – across the
mountains, making for Agadir. Stopped by the floods – we must take
the long road back. Gerry exhausted.

Now the leaves were falling, soon snowflakes would be blotting
out Blackheath. 'And we haven't even taken time off to see
Guthrie's *Alchemist*.'

'Never mind that. What's more important, we haven't seen
the sun,' said Gerry. 'Pack your bikini.'

As we headed south it grew wintry. In Marseille it was snowing
for the first time in fifty years.

'Tunis or Casablanca?'

'Morocco's warmer.'

We were surveying posters blue and gold in the travel agent's.

So it was Moorish arches and feathery *fer forgé* ortolans, aromatic
bread, raisins with marzipan for Christmas dinner. Midday was
briefly hot, the nights were cold.

'Further south,' said Gerry and we headed for Marrakech
in an old banger. In each field by the grey-brown sea, there
was a small domed tower, marigolds and faintly mauve convol-
vulus bloomed by the roadside. We passed walled-in farmyards
and turreted houses, shepherds in earth-brown cloaks watching
over their sheep, young boys offering asparagus for sale. The
skyline was broken by the jagged silhouette of the Atlas Mountains.

We stopped for an Arab coffee, but we were served Nescaff.
Two dark-eyed girls looked at us and giggled, then sent the waiter
across with a note for Gerry. '*Meilleurs voeux,*' it read, 'Solange *et*

Marie.' He smiled that smile he kept for pretty girls and bought them a packet of chocolate biscuits.

We'd still a long way to go, though Gerry had driven as fast as the battered old car would carry us and when, at last, we reached Marrakech, it was very disappointing, dusty bougainvillea in the middle of a roundabout which led to French suburbia – red-brick villas with stucco additions.

'There must be another Marrakech,' I said.

There was, but first we had to find a room for the night. There wasn't much choice and after rejecting several airless lodging houses we drove through formal arrangements of trees and shrubs to an imposing hotel entrance. The hallway was empty but for a small French clerk in Reception. Reluctantly he thumbed his ledger and found us a room with a balcony. While we waited, a greasy smell was wafted to us from the nether regions with the sound of men playing a dice game.

From our room we could hear low chanting in the distance. The sky was now pale green and the trees in the garden looked dark, almost sinister.

'Let's take a look at the Casbah.'

We found our way to the old walled town, built in 1064. The women we passed were veiled, swathed in black. If you looked at them they dropped their eyes. There was no sign of an eating place in the narrow paved streets, now almost deserted. After wandering for some time we came upon an arched entry with a lamp above it. It led to a square room with mats, low cushions and coffee tables. It smelt of damp and was none too clean, but we sat down and waited. Finally, half-cold kebabs in pitta bread were placed before us and to the clash of cymbals seven middle-aged ladies arrived, flimsy drapes scarcely hiding their woolly jumpers (lime green, brown and puce). Their noses were red or graced with dewdrops. They were very gauche, not a patch on those mock Arab dancers that busk round Leicester Square.

We made tracks for our hotel, a bath and bed.

I was wakened before seven next morning by the astonishing colour of the sky – bright green, paling and turning to pink as I watched. From the balcony I could see a dignified old woman standing quite still in the garden; she wore a patterned scarf round her head. Lifting a blue enamel coffeepot, she drank wine-red liquid from the spout, and behind the neat box hedge an old gardener emerged from one of those small domed towers. I caught a glimpse of his bed of straw. Neither of them spoke.

What a divided town! In the souk we passed dark caves where silversmiths were fashioning jewellery and graceful vessels; further on the public way narrowed and small boys stood turning spools of thread this way and that, feeding it to men who worked in semi-darkness – the weavers.

A small boy approached us. What were we looking for? On the spur of the moment I said '*Touizats*' – the tiny cymbals belly-dancers wear on their fingers. Jean Newlove had asked us to look out for them. He took us on. I don't think he knew where to look. We came to the ironworkers' forge amidst smoke and grime. It was a mediaeval Hell. Mediaeval? Older than that. These people looked scarcely human. The boy was weary. The search was fruitless. He took his leave.

'How much do we owe you?'

'Give me what you think,' he said.

On the way back we stopped to admire the silverware displayed for tourists. To buy the kohl or the *touizats* prized by the natives you'd have to speak Arabic.

Outside the walls of Marrakech there was a different world. A letter-writer, seated on the ground, was tapping the keys of a prehistoric machine while his client gazed at the sky as he dictated a long letter in guttural Arabic. Nearby, a young man was having a tooth pulled, while a row of patients, waiting their turn, sat gossiping.

There was a hen's head lying in my path and Gerry narrowly avoided a mess of bloody guts and innards. We were near the butcher's. An old man's legs were stretched out stiffly in our way, their owner was having his head massaged by a dark-skinned man in a white turban.

A group of women passed us holding their veils between their teeth. Veils? Black tat. Do they think they look attractive, bundled up like that? Most of them wear plastic footwear, luminous pea-green under those rusty black shrouds.

We turned back. My God, that old man is being cupped and

bled by the man in the white turban. The wound looks horribly wide and red as the blood is sucked out. The patient catches my eye and gives me a look which says, 'Clear off.' How he must feel the need for privacy sitting there amidst swarming flies.

A man passes carrying goatskins, the goats' heads still attached. Not surprisingly, the young men wear perfume. They kiss each other when they meet and often walk together holding hands. A young man accosts us: 'Berber market?' Without waiting for a reply he leads us across the debris, past a circle of attentive listeners. . . . 'The storyteller,' he says, 'he relates tales from the Koran.' But we move on, drawn to a larger circle, where the crowd is three or four rows deep. There is a sudden roar of laughter. 'Berber people,' says our guide.

Wild drumming broke out and a group of entertainers started to dance. Their leader was a tall man with a serious face and gold teeth. He never stopped clowning.

'What is he holding?' A long hairy tail. He was holding it to his behind, wagging it wildly and chasing the women with it.

'They're not women,' explained our guide. 'They are men dressed as women.'

Gerry was pursuing a man in red who wore a wide hat trimmed with bobbles and bore a yoke which carried goatskins and bronze goblets.

'The water carrier,' said our guide, whose name was Ahmed.

The Berbers, marvellous clowns, have warmed up their audience, who now respond with whoops of delight. The leading man performs acrobatic feats and makes naughty suggestions to real ladies, but in such a droll way. This is my sort of theatre. Anything could be said or performed here by anybody. Ahmed beckoned me, but I could not move; I was reluctant to leave these incredible artists.

'They leave their sheep, their goats and their women and come down from the hills, travelling from village to village, singing and dancing to entertain us,' said Ahmed.

I went back to hear the storyteller. I didn't know his language, but I was held spellbound by his story of seven great feats of derring-do which had to be performed before his hero could attain the object of his desire. An old woman with leprous white lumps round her eyes was listening with rapt attention. Occasionally the listeners smiled, but they never laughed. A very old man, with corrupting flesh, had the cynical look of a French Academician.

The light was going, the dark mass of mountains looked like clouds on the distant horizon. As I passed the Berbers a boy from the audience produced a clout of grey cloth, twisted it into a penis shape and pretended to shove it up his own backside.

Next day Ahmed was waiting outside the hotel and insisted on taking us to a palace to see the King's 'reservoirs', the gaol where his prisoners were held (we saw their iron collars) and the tower, once his harem. It was high and forbidding with tiny windows surrounded by spikes.

'They never got out,' said Ahmed.

'Who?'

'The women. They weren't allowed.'

He seemed quite pleased about it and Gerry, intrigued, wanting to know more, asked him if he really wouldn't see his bride till he took her to bed, after the wedding. Ahmed grinned. He was twenty-five, but apparently quite content to leave the choice of a partner to his parents, confident that they would choose the best-looking, the richest and most useful partner for him.

'No wonder they're all queers,' I said.

Somewhere children were chanting the Koran. It sounded like the multiplication tables we used to sing at school – twice two are four, twice three are six – rather sad.

I wasn't sorry when we loaded the car next morning and took the long road south again.

The sides of the valley were formed of laminated, slate-coloured strata, the river bed was dry, this world was made of slag, shale and dark red cinder. Ten kilometres to Tazenakate.

Some of the rocks on the wayside looked as if they'd once been blackened by some volcanic eruption.

At a stony, remote crossroads we pick up a woman who looks like a gipsy. She carries a pot and a large bundle. As she gets in she blesses us to the seventh generation – at least that's what it sounds like – our knowledge of Arabic is, to say the least, limited and conversation soon peters out.

She tells us where to stop. Before she gets down she kisses Gerry's hand. The further from the town, the freer the women's manners. Here they go unveiled and only cover their face when a stranger appears.

On the verge of a rocky desert we draw up. Gerry pulls out a map, a boy appears as if from nowhere.

'Guide?' he asks. 'My name is Abdi. I am six. My father is dead, my mother is away from the house.'

'Quarzazate, Oraquar, Ajdz . . .' mutters Gerry. 'This language is as zazzy as the sunsets.'

'Is there anything of interest here?' I ask. The boy is cute.

'Tombs,' he replies, 'the old Jews . . .' and he ran to the edge of a slab of rock and pointed. I followed and found myself slithering down a steep bank of pebbles. Gerry came rushing after me making a small avalanche. We came to a halt by a ruined arch, half-buried in sand. Presently an old man peered out and beckoned us. Gerry stooped and passed under the arch. We found ourselves in a low tunnel smelling of dog piss and musty air. The old man lit the way with occasional matches till we came to a shaft of natural light and turned into a small courtyard, paved unevenly. An old woman stood there as if waiting for us; she was tiny and light but hump-backed and swathed in grey.

At the old man's command, in a language which was not Arabic, she opened a rotting door. Door? Four or five lengths of planking, nailed together. Behind it, a hole in the rock face hung with a scrap of mauve curtaining. The old man plunged his hand behind it and brought out – Talmudic scrolls.

'This is a synagogue?'

The old man seized a decayed book, adjusted the leaves, kissed it, and turned on the old crone angrily. Now I notice that, though she is dressed like a beggar, the few strands of hair I can see are hennaed and her eyes dark with kohl.

These two belonged to a tribe of bird-like people who have lived and worshipped here since before Christ.

Outside, Abdi was waiting for us. A crowd of older boys were jeering at him. They threw stones as he approached us.

He ran for it. 'He is not an official guide,' one of them told us.

'We don't need a guide for the desert,' Gerry said. The boy looked at us and smirked.

The mountains looked forbidding as we drove south. I felt they could move at any moment.

'Could they?'

'Well, Agadir is on the map,' said Gerry.

The villages were fortified, the valley had many conical hills, with paths spiralling round them. Children stood by the roadside holding out lumps of glistening spar. Miners were trudging home from work.

'We mustn't miss the sunset. There's a hill beyond this village, the view would be great up there.'

'Anything to please Joan.'

He left the valley for the winding road. At first we saw groups of villagers stepping across the scree. We were on one of the spiral roads we'd noticed further back. It was lonely. The road wasn't much more than a track. Suddenly, two comical-looking characters cropped up, one had a spanner in his hand as he waved us down. I supposed they'd had a breakdown. The other one, who had a wall eye, wanted to know if they could ride up the hill with us.

It was growing dark, the sun would be setting any minute. There must be a village at the top of the hill.

Gerry indicated the back seats and they started chatting away to each other in Arabic.

The road is very stony and steep and there isn't a hint of a village ahead. In fact it's so steep that I'm afraid if the car stops it will roll backwards. There are no lay-bys where we might safely park.

I turn to our passengers: 'We will be walking the rest of the way.'

The wall-eyed one says they will accompany us. The other one mutters something.

Suddenly Gerry shoves open the back door on their side. 'Out!' he shouts. 'Get out!' and leaves the car to confront them.

The wall-eyed one, out first, stumbles across the scree, then with a mixture of bravado and sheepishness, strides downward the way we had come, his companion following him. There was no suggestion of their moving upwards.

'What was wrong?'

'Did you see what he was hiding? A bloody great knife. I'd been keeping an eye on them through the mirror.'

Assassination on the bare mountain! And they'd spoiled our sunset.

After that we stuck to the river road. The rushing water was brown and in full spate. Gerry pulled in by a quarry and we watched what was left of the sunset, pale and yellow tonight.

The people we saw in that valley looked desperately poor. From time to time the road would disappear, swamped by puddles, deep and wide; dirty water splashed over the windscreen as we raced on. The trees looked purple and black, the river, silver. At last things improved slightly – the borders of the road were painted white. Was this a vestige of French colonialism?

'If you want to go any further, you'll have to hire a camel.' It was the proprietor of the rest house, the last outpost before the desert. There was no hotel. 'Even the royal family have to stay here, when they come this way,' he said.

'If they have to travel the road we came by, I guess that can't be often,' I said.

We were shown to a small room with thick walls. It was stuffy, over-furnished, and dense with tropical plants which caught your ankles and brushed your breast as you passed.

The bell rang for supper. We were served steak and tinned peas, swimming in slightly rancid butter. Afterwards there was nothing to do but go to bed. The yellowing newspapers in the rack were in Arabic and there was no radio, only the sound of the distant drumming which had been going on all evening.

'Shall we take a walk before turning in?'

Outside the drumming was louder. It was clearly coming from the desert side. We decided to leave the walled village and make for the source of the rhythmic beat, but we trod carefully – it was pitch dark.

No sign of any human activity. The world was sealed against the invader, night. That persistent drumming was all we had to guide us. Our feet slithered softly in the sand, occasionally striking a stone. Gerry thought he could make out the outlines of a village. We moved faster, a lantern swung across the darkness to reveal men, women and children seated round the drummer.

As we approached, all heads turned to watch us and an old man in a white turban brought two chairs and graciously indicated that we should be seated. Everyone else was sitting on a rug or carpet. We sat rather self-consciously. Other musicians and singers joined the drummers, and a boy brought two small glasses of mint tea on a silver salver. It tasted very sweet – for Gerry, strictly forbidden – but he sipped it, smiling as the concert continued.

The entertainers must be Berbers, they resembled the troupe at Marrakech. The elder who'd welcomed us carried a long wand and at the slightest hint of a misdemeanour among the boys sitting at the front of the gathering they'd get a whack on the head with it. He was a handsome old man, his brown cloak hung in rich folds. He obviously commanded respect among the villagers but there was no sign of anger or irritation against the children, just paternalism in action.

The night wore on and we were tired, but it would have been discourteous to leave before the show was over. We had arrived there, complete strangers, and been treated as honoured guests. When we finally rose to go, they bade us farewell with gentle courtesy, and gathering up their rugs and carpets made for their homes, taking the Berbers with them.

Making our way back in the darkness, we mistook some old ruined fort for the rest house – and when we finally located our night watchman, it was to find that the electricity had been cut and we were given candles to light us to bed.

Next morning Gerry announced that he was going to cross the mountains to Agadir. There was a perfect hotel there with gardens, good food and a swimming pool, and he'd checked the route with our host.

'Will we be able to swim in the ocean?'

'I should think so.'

Despite my misgivings – I didn't want him to drive so much – I had to fall in. If only he would take a holiday without a car, but the best I could do was insist on getting out to take a little exercise every hour or so – and he hated it. What could you do with him?

For a while the journey was uneventful – map-reading, looking for food, until, at a sharp bend in the road, we came upon a crowd standing by a flooding stream. They smiled at us and pointed to the notice, '*Oued en crue. Route barrée*'. And we saw the abandoned cars waiting by the roadside.

'There's no other route,' said one of them as we surveyed the ten feet of swirling water between us and our route onward.

'The only other way to Agadir is by the coast, and there's no telling that the road's open there. These floods are widespread.'

'Four and a half hours this way to Agadir. Lord knows how far, if we had to go back to the coast road.'

'It'll be barred that way too,' said the pessimist.

'We've no alternative but to go back,' said Gerry. 'And we're running out of petrol.'

'You can buy essence four kilometres along the high road.'

'We'd better get going,' I said.

No one likes to give up, go back on their tracks, but it was goodbye Agadir, a swim and a good meal. We were both so disappointed that we became desperately cheerful and by the time we reached Talamine and filled up with petrol we were quite light-headed.

Then, after searching enquiries, we found there was nothing for it but to go all the way back to Quarzazete and by mountain roads.

Those mountain roads, sometimes with a sheer drop on either side of us and hairpin bends, were frightening. And the sky looked evil. Even when the moon came out from behind the clouds it was only for an instant. We were descending barren hillside to a rock-strewn plain. One could not have imagined a more forbidding place – moon landscape – monotonous too – and dangerous. Gerry said nothing. I knew we'd a long way to go.

I tried 'I spy' to keep him awake, not that there was much to spy, and when it grew too dark even for that I tried telling stories. He still didn't speak. It's a terrible drive, he's just concentrating on keeping awake, as on we go . . . on and on. . . .

Even the memory of that drive puts me in a cold sweat. But everything comes to an end, and when we stumbled into some little hotel, starving and thirsty, we were far too tired to eat.

Gerry fell asleep on the table, spilling a coffee cup. I needed help to get him upstairs. Why do we get into such situations? Well, Gerry did check the route at Zagora, and with two planks we would have crossed that gushing stream. Would we?

'Forget it. Let's sleep.'

I woke in the night with a start, to escape from a nightmare – I was in London, trapped at the top of a high building which was on fire.

Gerry suggests we picnic today. He must be worried about money. He never worries till we're almost spent up. One day he'll say, 'Well that's it. We haven't two ha'pennies to rub together.'

And I'll say, 'We'll have to sing for our supper.'

And he'll say, 'I can always go back to navvying – less worry.'

We arrived at the airport and boarded Air Maroc's one Caravelle. It took us once round the airfield then it was, 'All off.'

Four white-coated mechanics drove up in a jeep. After an hour they left. One of them carried a small black box.

'*On y va?*' asked a tired Frenchman.

'*Tout de suite,*' said the boss of the mechanics. We waited another hour. The sky was grey when we left and the sea wild. There were French and English newspapers aboard, but nothing in them about the floods which had been devastating Morocco.

Fifty-seven

E15 needs a season of plays. Read a Vanbrugh and Genet, neither
suitable. Gerry plays me a tape, Songs of the First World War.
He wants them used in a play. Two writers have already tried and
failed, a third is working on it. Jacques Tati attends private showing
of Sparrers, offers me use of his studios at Charenton. A backer gives
me the go-ahead on needed pick-up shots. The third writer reads his
play to us. There are no songs in it. I could do better myself. Next
day, I dictate a first draft to Gerry. Say I can re-cut film and work
on the play at the same time.

'Fasten your seatbelts. In a few minutes . . .' And we descended through one, two, three layers of thick cloud.

Una and Pat Patricks had a meal ready at Blackheath,
but the heating was off and the house was icy. Outside, the
heath was covered in a thick coat of snow.

It was the first night of Robin Chapman's new play at Stratford,
but I had lost all interest in theatre. Gerry had hired a TV before
we went away. If bored, I could always see what use was being
made of the medium. On the other hand, there were plays to be
found for Gerry's season at E15. I picked up Cibber's version of
Journey to London, which Vanbrugh had left unfinished when he
died. I didn't think much of it. I'd just press the TV button and
see what was on. . . .

A shock. Harry C.'s face filled the screen. He was talking
in some stylised accent and there was a hideous old man with
him. . . . Harry, who had given us that incomparable Richard II,
and so many glorious moments of theatre; what had driven him to
this? I switched off and picked up Genet's plays . . . such style . . .
to enlarge our understanding of freaks who only merited a place in
Hirschfield's *Encyclopaedia of Sexual Perversions*.

The others came back shivering. 'The play was all right, but
the theatre? Brrr!'

Gerry wanted me to listen to some tapes. I put down *Le Balcon* and listened to Bud Flanagan introducing soldiers' songs from the First World War.

'I heard it while I was recovering from that accident.'

A male voice choir was milking the songs and the introductions were in schmaltzy cockney.

'He's so sentimental.'

'It's the songs that interest me.'

'Not me. In any case, you've already rejected one play using them, haven't you?'

'Gwyn Thomas is a good writer, but he was telling us things we already knew. There was a spate of anti-war books, plays and poems in every language after the First World War, but I don't believe any of them gave us the soldiers' point of view. I thought Charles Chilton might, since he collected the songs.'

'Any luck?'

'He took a fortnight's leave from the BBC, tried and gave up. His father died in that War, a young man of nineteen. Charles went to look for his father's grave – and came to the military cemeteries, mile after mile of white crosses. It had a lasting effect on him.'

'Perhaps he was too close to the subject to write about it.'

'Perhaps. I'm relying on my third choice now. He's already into the research, but he wants to clarify the theme with me.'

'You'd better be very clear about what you want.'

'I know that plays can't stop war – only the will of the people can do that.'

'Good luck anyway.'

Next day, Andy phoned to tell me there was to be a showing of *Sparrers* at the ABC cinema, Mile End Road, Monday morning.

'What is it in aid of?'

'The Censor is demanding cuts and you haven't seen the titles.'

Gerry gave me a lift and went on to the theatre.

A 1930s super-cinema at nine in the morning is not the most cheerful place in the world. I waited in the foyer beside an old generator, the air was heavy with the scent of lilac disinfectant and dust. Through the smeared window, I could just make out the entrance to the Krays' Kentucky Club on the other side of the road. The cleaners clattered in at about a quarter to ten, threw down their mops and buckets, and vanished. There must have been a hidden door in the wall. Off to make themselves a cuppa, no doubt. They'd scarcely gone when two house-painters arrived.

'Bangers, bubble an' bacon at the Essex Diner, eighteen pence,' said one.

'Cheers,' I said and went.

The Essex Diner does not merit description, but it took its time. The film had already started when I got back and I spotted Len, the dubbing editor, and went over to him straight away and asked if he could do anything about the sound. It was deafening. He said he'd try. Then someone jerked my woolly cap off my head. It was Ossie. The painters were sitting in the back row, smoking and making comments. Andy was with Ken Harper, a producer friend and a man I didn't know. Two big white chiefs from Elstree were puffing at their cigars. And was that Donald creeping in at the back? As the sound diminished, the chat took over.

'Shut up, all of you,' I shouted. 'Let's have a bit of quiet around here.'

Andy gave me a sharp look and he was pretty short with me afterwards. That *Daily Mail* piece was still rankling, I supposed, and Penelope Gilliatt had been quoting me on the British Film Industry while I'd been away.

'I simply couldn't understand all the fuss about Reel Eight,' said Andy. 'Could you, Ossie?'

'Not at all,' said Ossie dutifully.

'What are the cigar-smoking contingent doing here?'

'Elstree wanted to see what we'd got.'

'The Censor didn't like the film?'

'Oh yes, indeed. He passed Barbara's nipples, but he felt the word "perform" had a sexual overtone. It's your job to replace it – or Stephen's – where is he these days?'

'In a TV serial.'

Ken Harper was approaching with his companion. 'I like the way she mixes naturals with her actors,' I heard him say. 'My own technique exactly.'

It was Jacques Tati. He was very friendly and invited me to

use his studios at Charenton. I was delighted and went off to get myself a coffee.

I was at the dispenser in the lobby when a soft voice behind me murmured, 'It was Andy's fault that the film was so expensive.'

'Oh, bugger off,' I said and he melted away.

Later, over a plate of ham at the Café l'Ange, Gerry had to listen to my dramatised version of the scene at the showing.

'How's your war going?'

'An hour on Clausewitz and two hours of our third choice this morning.'

'Is he on to Clausewitz?'

'No, that was the MP, Ray Fletcher. He's an expert on the Kaiser's War, as he calls it. He's particularly strong on supply lines, railway computation; that War, he says, started by accident, but once started they couldn't stop it. He comes from a long line of German generals.'

'How did you find him under a name like Fletcher?'

'It was Tom. He has a nose for hidden anti-Nazis – and Nazis. Ray says Barbara Tuchman is best on the origins of the War and Liddell-Hart on strategy. Hart's first job was to notify next-of-kin when a soldier was shot for desertion.'

'How's your third choice faring?'

'Well, he's chuffed because Tynan likes his Zen Buddhist play, but he's still reading books about the 1914 War. He thought he might start it with a computer and finish with Papa Joffre and the whole Pentagon gang standing around listening for the computer's verdict. I think I managed to put him off that idea. On the other hand, he seems to be getting more and more obsessed with Haig.'

'That's not going to help him with the songs.'

That afternoon, one of the big shots from Elstree who'd been at the viewing, phoned me. 'I like your film,' he said. 'Go ahead with your eighth reel. Re-cut what you like, as far as I'm concerned.'

So I did. I moved into Soho right away, with a cutting-room, a studio for projection and Ossie, who nipped out straight away to see if the Colony Club was still going strong. He loved to hobnob with the cultured queers who drank there, all afternoon. Soho was much more entertaining than Bore'em Wood.

When we went to project Reel Eight, I took a look through

the glass porthole next door to see what was going on. 'Hey, Ossie! Come back here. Look! Bare bums!' They were too, one after another – fat ones, thin ones, wrinkled ones, hairy ones.

'It's Yoko Ono,' said Ossie. 'She thinks our bottoms are as interesting as our faces.'

'Who's Yoko Ono?'

'Nobody knows. She hangs out at the ICA, but what she does for a living is a mystery.'

I bought Barbara Tuchman's *1914* and started reading it on the train home. When I got there, Gerry looked crestfallen.

'What's up?'

'I've been hunting uniforms.'

'Uniforms, in a theatre! Not khaki, that cack colour!'

'How can you show war without it?'

'There must be a way.'

'The play's finished, by the way.'

'Already?'

'Yes, "Third Choice" leaves for the States next week and wants to read it to us before he goes. Would Saturday afternoon suit you?'

'I'll have to leave the reel.'

'Why do you go on fiddling with that film if you hate it as much as you say?'

'Because if there's the slightest chance of improving it I must go on. The public must have their money's worth.'

S aturday afternoon, cold outside, but the fire in the front room crackling and Charles Chilton and Gerry seated in comfortable armchairs. Charles had brought Mrs Chilton, the quiet, serious wife who had formerly been his secretary and still did a lot of his research. She'd found herself a seat, tucked away in a corner by the bookshelves. Charles was in a merry mood, talking about the old days at the Beeb, when he was producing the *Goon Show* and, as often happened, they had fallen out and would only communicate by passing notes to each other through him. . . .

Camel arrived and apologised for being late. When I dropped out of *Henry IV* Peter Hall grabbed him, but he would always answer a call from Gerry who liked to hear his opinions. If Gerry took to you, you could do no wrong; all the same, Camel was not at his best at readings. He would leave analysing to others, wait till we'd got an idea for the set then take it away and make it practical. Charles was still in full flight when Gerry's last hope appeared, bursting to read his play, impatient for Charles to finish, but Charles went on in his chirrupy cockney way.

Gerry made a formal opening, introducing the play. The author jumped out of his chair.

'I'm crazy about Gerry's idea for a War play,' he said. 'I've been to the Imperial War Museum, read thirty-two books.'

'The play,' said Gerry. 'Let's have it.' And the author looked so bright and enthusiastic that I think we all assumed that he'd done the trick. He strode up and down, playing all the parts, throwing in a commentary. He had an actor's vitality, if not his wit.

His play was clearly anti-War from the outset. It had a story, an unusual one – a young woman goes to the front dressed as a soldier. The War is already chaotic but Haig, in his château with the band playing on the lawn, is still making his infallible plans.

'If you're too anti-Haig, the audience will finish up on his side,' I muttered.

'Ssh!' said Gerry. 'This is a reading.'

The play also seemed to me anti-German. There was no mention of the fraternisation between English and German soldiers at Christmas 1914. The wild enthusiasm for the War was missing. At the beginning, there had been such patriotism, of course, the joy of escape from ordinary life, until the reality of the trenches struck home. It could have worked if there'd been a pro-army hero, like Schwejk, but the answer in this version was, 'Turn your guns on the warmongers,' and after all, that had been tried.

Everything went quiet, the reading was over.

'Where are the songs?' asked Charles.

I went to make coffee. I couldn't look at Gerry. When I came back, Charles had just finished speaking.

' . . . at least eight hundred.'

'Eight hundred what?' I asked.

'Songs,' he said.

There was a long silence.

'Is Joan going to produce it?' asked the author.

'There's nothing to produce yet,' said Camel, then excused himself, got up and went.

'We'll have to discuss it further,' said Gerry.

'Yes, but I'm for Hollywood on Tuesday. Still, I guess it can wait till I get back.'

Charles took his wife's arm. 'Can we give anyone a lift?'

'Thanks, but I'm not going your way,' said the author and he was gone. I don't think our reaction had pleased him.

Gerry and I sat silent for a long time. Occasionally he'd give a short, sharp stab at the fire.

'Why not let the songs tell the story?' I said at last. 'You could preface them with news clips to put them in context. We could add period dances or cartoon sketches here and there.' There was no response. 'There's no point wasting time and money on this last effort. I could do better myself.'

'Then do it.'

'All right. I will, but I want something to eat and drink first.'

We made a good meal and went to bed early and made love. Next morning, up with the lark, put the place in order, open the windows. Then Gerry sailed into the front room with a bottle of Alsace, *bien frais*, two Waterford glasses and a large writing pad.

I'd put the songs in order in my head and was confident that I had the whole thing under my belt. Gerry sat in an armchair. I stood by the mantelpiece.

'You do the writing, I'll do the talking.'

'As usual.'

'Here goes.'

Outside the sun was shining. It was a wonderful morning, good to be alive.

We worked without a break, sustained by occasional sips of the good white wine. There was no need to hold up for fine writing. All we needed was the songs in the right order, the facts and quotes.

Production ideas kept cropping up. It was three p.m., growing dark, when we stopped to eat.

'We've got the shape, but there's still a lot of research to be done.'

'I'm going down to the theatre to duplicate this.'

He was pleased with what we'd done. I could tell. So was I, but just as he was opening the front door I had a mad idea. 'Gerry! Stop! They must all be pierrots. The War is a pierrot show. It's the right period and, after all, war is only for clowns.'

He gave me a funny look and was gone. I wanted to develop the idea, argue it out with someone. I went to the phone and dialled a number without thinking . . . the wrong number. It was the Arc's voice which answered me.

'About time.'

'Oh, it's you.'

'Who else? I haven't seen you since New York. Where are you?'

'Didn't you get my card from Zagora?'

'No.'

'How are you?'

'Working, and I think I have the name for your mobile.'

'What is it?'

'The Fun Palace. It's so wrong, it's right.'

'I'll think about it, while you get on with it.'

I hung up. When Gerry came home I wanted so much to talk about the ideas behind the Fun Palace (I quite liked that name) but he was only interested in his War play.

'You'll have to produce it, Joan, there's no one else.'

'I can't divide myself in two. I must finish that reel.'

'Join us in the afternoons, we'll learn the songs in the mornings.'

'No, I must be there for the songs. Make it the other way round, theatre mornings, film afternoons.'

'I've got the beginnings of a super cast – Vic Spinetti, Griff Davies, Murray Melvin, Brian Murphy, Bob Stevenson for the choreography. . . .'

'They'll be marvellous pierrots. And the girls?'

'Ann Beach, Fanny Carby, Bettina Dickson, Vanne Jenn. . . . They can all sing.'

In fact, I couldn't wait to get them together, but I'd have to square Ossie. I stayed up till five in the morning making a detailed list of changes still to be made.

The critical first meeting for the War play took place in the Green Room at E15. Charles brought along the Musical Director and choir who'd performed the radio version and there was the nucleus of a company.

I read my notes and we played the tapes. Most of the characters listened politely but Victor and Griff kept groaning and taking the piss. When it came to 'Roses are shining in Picardy', the Musical Director's face crumpled into ecstasy. 'Lovely tune, that,' he said. Vic and Griff snorted in unison. After 'Pack up Your Troubles' it was, 'Lost your leg? Never mind, old son, keep smilin'.'

'Shut up, Victor.'

'Don't believe they sang that sloppy stuff,' said Griff. The BBC chaps looked uneasy.

Those songs took me back to childhood – red, white and blue bunting, photos of dead soldiers in silver frames, medals in a forgotten drawer, and that look as family and friends sang the songs of eventide – God, how I loathed those songs – but the pierrot show . . . dirty postcards and ice-cream cornets, sand in your plimsolls and paddling in your knickers. . . .

Fifty-eight

BBC Singers dislike changes. Technical requirements are many.
Mornings removing schmaltz from songs, afternoons cutting film.
BBC singers leave. John Gower (baritone), Colin Kemball (tenor)
stay. Gerry finds an army sergeant to drill actors. His language too
blue to be repeated. Ann Beach in tears over lack of script. With Camel
on design, Dick Bowdler on news panel, Ivor Dykes making slides and
Gerry collecting facts and figures, we shall have something.

'**O**kay. Everybody down on stage.' Might as well take the plunge.

'I don't want anything to do with it,' said Victor.

'Give us a chance. I disliked that singing just as much as you did,' I told him. Then I turned to the company. 'Imagine there's a trench running across the stage, you're in it, protected from the enemy by a wall of sandbags. A bombardment, which has been going on for two days, has just died down. Can you put yourself in that situation?' I turned to the brightest of the BBC bunch. 'Now try.'

'*There's a long, long trail a-winding into the land of my dreams,*' he started.

'It would be easier if you felt you were in that trench . . . but you're all wearing your best clothes. Come in outfits you can knock about in tomorrow.'

The girls did better, trying the old music-hall style, the men supplying the audience. Fanny, the *belle laide*, stole all hearts singing 'Itchy Koo'. She looked like the bow on a chocolate box.

On the tube to Soho, to the cutting-room, I made a list of requirements. Priority: a news panel, like the one that goes over the Friedrichstrasse in East Berlin. Gerry would find one, he could find anything, and he'd be the one to select the information which would move across it during the action. We'd need Dick

Bowdler, electronics engineer and musician, to maintain it in good order. We'd also need a screen and Ivor Dykes to make slides from old photos. As for the photos – everybody would have to collect them. The pierrot costumes must vary with each individual. Una could start working on a basic design, but she would have to watch the company at work to capture their individuality. David Scase was fully occupied at this time, running the Library Theatre, Manchester. Perhaps I could get that sound wizard at Elstree to tackle the effects.

When I got to the cutting-room, Ossie was very excited. 'The première's on the 26th,' he told me.

'Which 26th?'

'This month, February 1963!'

'Then we've no time for philandering. . . .'

'Except with me,' said Barbara, appearing at the door like the good fairy in the pantomime.

'Is that me in my nightie?' she wanted to know, squinting at a length of film hanging from the rack like a fly-paper.

Ossie found her takes and showed them to her on the Moviola.

'Corny, ain't I? Have you got that one of me close-up, the one Mutzi took three hours over?' Ossie located it. 'Can't see the highlights on me earrings, like you said.'

'Because you weren't wearing 'em. You forgot to put 'em on.'

'Oh yeah, that's right. Well, I mustn't hold up the good work. See you all at the première. Anybody giving a party after?' And she was gone.

Next morning, I had a go at those songs. I wanted to get rid of all that beautiful expression. 'Greasepaint', I called it. 'Sing it as if you were talking to someone.'

> *I don't want to be a soldier*
> *I don't want to go to war*
> *I'd rather stay at home*
> *Around the streets to roam*
> *And live on the earnings of a whore*
> *Don't want a bayonet in me belly*

Don't want me bollocks shot away
I'd rather stay in England
In merry, merry England
And fornicate me bleedin' life away.

'Notice the tune? Same as the song of the early days:'

On Saturdays I'm willing,
    if you'll only take the shilling
To make a man of any one of you.

Part of my trouble was the Musical Director. He loved milking those songs.

'Hey, Alfie! What sort of tempo is that? We're going to sleep here.' That was Brian Murphy.

Camel sidled up to me. 'The BBC singers are saying that they can't see anything wrong with the way they sang with Bud Flanagan. They're talking of pulling out.'

'Let them.'

'But what will you do without singers?'

'The actors can sing and any singers who stay will have to act.'

'We need good voices,' said Gerry.

At that moment Vic Spinetti was picking out 'Goodbye-ee, Don't cry-ee' at the piano. No one thought of Vic as a singer, but his quiet rendering of that song did the trick. A glorious tenor would have drowned it.

A spokesman for Charles Chilton's singers stopped me. 'The BBC is getting too demanding,' he said. 'I'm afraid we'll have to pull out.'

'What, all of you?'

'Most of us. I'm very sorry.'

Only one, the baritone who'd sung 'Long, Long Trail', wanted to stay. He was quite prepared to shed the schmaltz. So was Colin, the tenor who suddenly came over to our side. He had a lovely voice but waddled like a duck when he walked.

The girls were happy enough, flirting with the actors as they put over their sexy songs. Vanne Jenn, who was new to me, seemed less certain than the others.

'What kind of name is that?'

'I was one of the Jenn sisters.' I thought I detected a Welsh lilt in her voice.

'What is your real name?'

'Oh it's too Welshy.'

'But what is it?'

'Myvanwy Jenkinson.'

'But that's lovely. It's musical. Take it back and see how much lovelier your voice will be.' She didn't believe me. I gave her a copy of a letter from the Front, written by a young nurse. 'Read that to us and then sing, "Keep the Home Fires Burning" as if we were the women back home.' She did so and every night gave one of the most moving performances I have ever seen.

Despite horrified looks from Camel and Gerry, I tried some of our exercises. 'Start this morning blindfold,' I told them, producing scarves and handkerchiefs. 'Use your ears, your sense of smell – and touch. . . . Now, let's walk barefoot . . . as if on pebbles, on marble . . . on sand . . . mud. Good. Make the same efforts vocally. Don't worry about time, Gerry. You know there's no need to spend time directing formal moves when you have a trained company.'

The girls tightened their waists and picked up flouncy parasols, the men found walking canes and straw boaters. We moved in style to the music of 1914. We tried a promenade at the seaside. We heard the waves breaking, children laughing. . . .

I was working towards our opening scene: the hot summer, prelude to the Great War. Then I was stuck. I had to place the play in its political context. How? A lecture? No. Barbara Tuchman's book gave me an idea. A circus parade of all the national leaders, Victor as ringmaster, telling us their secret aims . . . and then . . . men marching to war.

'Don't think much of your soldiers,' said Gerry, standing beside me in the dress circle. 'They look like actors.' He was always very keen on authenticity.

That same day, a brisk little bloke in army uniform arrived. He was a drill sergeant Gerry had run to earth in the local barracks.

We were hardly ready for him, the canes and parasols from the promenade scene were still lying on the prop table.

'Not suitable for ladies,' he said, eyeing the girls. I led them away – with a wink. A minute later, we were creeping into the gallery and making ourselves scarce. We'd no intention of missing the fun.

'Men!' bawled the sergeant.

'Yes, Sarge,' said Big Baritone mincing towards him.

'Who's in charge 'ere? Hey, you!' He was pointing at Murray. 'Any rifles?'

'Afraid not, Sergeant. But we've been rehearsing a scene with sticks and sunshades. Would they do – as substitutes?'

'If you've nothing else,' said the drill sergeant. 'What's that thing on your 'ead?'

'A straw boater,' said Murray. 'A touch of period.'

'Never mind periods, get into line. Come on, you lot, look sharp. Attention! I said "Attention!" – slovenly lot of bastards, aren't you? Get into line there. Now then. By the right, dress. Cor, crikey, I didn't come down 'ere to muck about with a mob of fairies! And you there . . . get your 'air cut or I'll 'ave yer . . .'

No wonder he wanted the ladies out. The air was blue as he went on, bluer as he had the actors lunging and stabbing and twisting imaginary bayonets in the imagined enemy's guts. Compelling stuff, quite terrifying, as with blood-curdling cries the actors charged towards the audience.

Unfortunately, Murray was left behind. He stood still, clutching a parasol between his knees while he blew his nose.

This was too much for the instructor. 'What the ****ing hell d'you think you're doing? Get cracking, you 'orrible man.'

Murray leapt into the air with a shrill cry.

'That'll do! Get back! Come on, all of you. Back there. We're going to try that charge again. And this time I want to see you going for Jerry's man'ood.'

They tried, but the fiercer they looked the funnier it became. We had a job stifling our laughter.

Suddenly there was a terrible roar from below, followed by a flood of obscenities. Griff had broken loose, jumped down into the auditorium and was chasing Meg, our very attractive cleaner.

At that our long-suffering drill sergeant gave up, cast his eyes heavenwards, then went and treated himself to a pint in the bar.

'Well,' I said to the cast, 'the Old Contemptibles must have looked much like you, drilling with walking canes in the park. At the beginning the British Army had no more rifles than we have.'

'Could make a great scene,' said Vic.

'With all that foul language?'

'You couldn't understand a word our sergeant said when I was in the Welsh Fusiliers.'

'You mean you could play it in Welsh?'

'No. Gibberish.'

He did it and it sounded even worse than the real thing and much funnier. Of course, we kept Griff chasing a bird at the end, paid one of the programme girls a bit extra to be chased out of the theatre every night.

Colin had been waddling through the scene ruining the look of it altogether. I pulled him up: 'If I could co-ordinate you, it might have a remarkable effect on your voice too.'

'Nonsense, there's nothing wrong with my voice.'

'Want to bet? Do a jack-booted bully for me,' I said, and played some suitable music. It was funny, and it certainly wasn't a waddle. After a while, aided by blood-curdling commands from me, it became quite frightening.

'Try a sybarite, naked but swathed in silk.' I played 'Scheherazade'. A very voluptuous character emerged, smiling, unashamedly homosexual. Extraordinary, the cruel bully and the merry sodomite in the same man. 'Be yourself, be anything but a duck.' He was half angry, but at the same time delighted with himself.

Vic's walk was inhibited too. By now I'd worked with him for some time, but I'd never been able to get rid of those diffident feet.

'Return of the wounded,' I announced. 'Waterloo Station scene.'

'Can't see much point in it,' said Bob Stevenson.

'Coming after the drill scene? It's all a question of juxtaposition, Bob. Let's clown it first. Some custard-pie comedy music, please Kate.' Our brilliant, long-suffering pianist was present at all rehearsals. We couldn't work without music, or rather, Kate's music.

A minute later the scene looked like a First World War movie.

'Take it down now, try for truth.' It worked and for the first time I didn't recognise Colin: he walked slowly, feeling his way with his feet, a blinded soldier.

Annie Beach burst into tears. 'We're all lost,' she cried. 'We're getting nowhere. Can't we just do a straightforward play?' And she lifted a tear-stained face to me.

'If we don't get lost, we'll never find a new route,' I told her.

I hadn't converted them but we were making progress.

One morning as I walked in, even in the foyer I could hear a powerful Aussie voice preaching, 'Deerly beloverd brethrin, if yer don't modify yer voices, in the House of Gard, I'll 'ave you all on jankers.'

It was Bettina's impersonation of the Bishop of Sydney. There she was, standing on stage, legs akimbo, in black tights – and what legs! What a voice! And a face like a load of hay.

The company was egging her on. She gave me a right going over as I walked in. It was just the mood for the news I had. 'For this show we need the resources of a large newspaper and all we've got is us but . . . Gerry's found a news panel. It's coming today. If any of you want to see it working, we'll be trying it out after rehearsal, if Dick can get the hang of it.'

We gave Gerry a round of applause; Dick looked suitably confident and Ivor Dykes came up from the cellar to show us the slides he'd been working on. He was in that dark cellar night and day, shut up like a prisoner in an oubliette.

Gerry was assembling and collating the facts and figures which would flicker across the panel at a relentless speed while living, breathing men and women held the stage. The dead only appeared as numbers.

That evening and every evening from then on, Gerry, Camel, Ivor, Dick and I would edit the slides on a big screen, timing them with the songs and effects. Sometimes we'd work till daybreak. The balance between slides, news panel and performances was the key to the show. It was difficult to get it right, but when we did it doubled the effect made by the performers.

The girls were practising period movement with Bob Stevenson and Jean Newlove so I decided to have a crack at the fraternisation scene which would end Act One. It was all too easy to act, play results, as if we knew already what had happened, which, of course, we did.

I turned out the lights, told the men to move quietly. 'If you're seen or heard, you will be shot. Now, try to contact someone. You don't know them. In fact they are a hundred yards away. It's impossible.' There was a long silence. 'Careful,' someone had given a low whistle, 'a wrong move could mean death.'

'No past tense in the voice. You have no memory of such a situation. This is happening, a first time.'

It took a while. At last the enemy approached – afraid . . . treading a minefield of fear.

Colin's voice rang out, singing in German. 'Heilige Nacht', and as enemy met enemy and one of them held out his hand, Victor strolled downstage singing quietly:

> *Brother Bertie went away*
> *To do his bit the other day.*

We'd some sort of first half. I hoped the second half wouldn't be so difficult.

We'd been lost in the scene and hadn't noticed a stranger at the back of the stalls. It turned out to be Chuck Sewell. 'I'll be in this show for nothing,' he said. 'It's my great love, that period. I've a collection of helmets, medals, bayonets, shell cases . . . Didn't you know?'

I remembered my diktat: 'Don't let the actors fall in love with the play.' But Chuck was too good to miss. I found the solution, gave him Haig – he could hardly be in love with him.

Next day I asked Ossie if he'd fraternised with the Italian soldiers when he was in the Austrian Army.

'Sure. We exchanged lemons and melons, bread, too, sometimes.'

It was Saturday 16th February, my last day on the film. Ossie and I had worked all night to get Reel Eight in trim and we didn't wrap up till six in the evening.

At last! Now for full-time on the pierrot show. Then, come what may, the Fun Palace.

The second part would necessarily be gloomier, as the losses mounted on all sides. Frenchmen killed by arms manufactured in France and sold to Germany. Germans, by German guns. The facts had been published, but how many had read them? We must show the dealers in death at a top-level meeting. In Switzerland? The Mégève? On some grouse moor, maybe, annihilating droves of uneatable fowl while discussing profits. There was black comedy in this, if we could only hit it. One day we'd capture it, the next it would be as dry as dust. The actors were beginning to groan at the very mention of the scene.

'Never mind,' said Big Baritone. 'Every show has its grouse scene.'

Great Britain, France, Russia and Germany were sitting around the stage on shooting sticks, trying to make deadly statistics sound like merry quips, when Victor Spinetti wandered in. . . .

'Who's dead?' he wanted to know.

A row of funereal faces turned on him.

'Anything left for me?'

Brian (Great Britain) shook his head. 'You've been off two days.'

'If I'd stopped off a week, I'd've been out of the show altogether, I suppose. Okay, tomorrow I'll get a wheelchair and some dark glasses and give you an American armaments king that'll beat the lot of you.'

'Never! In any case, we're waltzing round a palm tree tomorrow,' said Griff, 'And the Stage Manager is the palm tree. It's in a pot on his head.'

'What's it supposed to be?'

'Buck House. We're all generals at this soirée in Buckingham Palace. Brian's Sir John French, with the Honourable Fanny Carby, Sir Henry Wilson's Big Baritone with Lady Ann Beach, Sir William Robertson —'

'That's me,' said Vic.

'You've got Baroness Jenkinson, and there's Chuck and Bettina as Sir Douglas and Lady Haig, but the servant problem is so severe in Theatre Workshop that the palm pot has to double as the butler.'

Fifty-nine

Sparrers film's East End première – I don't go – puzzling over presenting the Irish in the 1914–18 War. Company have mixed reaction to film. Good idea for church scene and title, Oh What a Lovely War! *Henri Barbusse book gives me an ending for it. First run, local people as audience. Souvenirs of that War presented to us. The show works. We are indebted to the unnamed soldiers who wrote the lyrics we sing.*

'Thank God we're getting off early tomorrow,' said Murray.

'What for?'

'It's the première.'

'Which première?'

'*Sparrers.*'

I phoned the Kentucky Club next morning and got Limehouse Willy. 'What's happening?'

'We're blowing up balloons.'

'And tonight?'

'The boys 'ave brought four 'undred an' fifty quids' worth of seats, an' we've got an extended licence . . . gala night.'

At lunch-time, I asked Gerry if he'd run me along the Mile End Road to see if the cinema had been smartened up a bit. I didn't mention the Krays or he wouldn't have taken me, but you could see a whacking great banner across the road a mile away: 'The Kentucky Club welcomes Princess Margaret to the East End.'

He did a U-turn and drove straight back to the theatre.

I was relieved. The second half was proving more difficult than I'd foreseen and there was still the crushing of the Peace Movement, Bertrand Russell and Mrs Pankhurst failing to convert the East End, the Irish problem, the munitions workers – there seemed no end to it. And I still had to get rid of the Musical Director's sentimental arrangements. Finding the way to sing those songs had been one of the major problems of the production. I wanted no decoration, no schmaltz, just the sincerity of the soldiers who wrote those words. The Musical Director was opposed to actors singing. I was opposed to beautiful renderings. My actors understood what that show was saying. I won. So did my actors.

I solved the Irish scene by turning it into a wild jig; danced by soldiers wearing khaki caps and the green kilts of the Munsters. Bob Stevenson, a superb dancer, led them, carrying a Union Jack. He was the last to be shot down. It was to be an attacking dance accompanied by the skirl of the Irish pipes and the sound of bullets whistling by.

Jean Newlove was something of an authority on Irish dancing. She told us that the jig had been a punitive dance until the Church intervened and took the aggression out of it. Bob and Jean working together seemed an ideal combination and it would leave me free to tackle the church scene which was to follow.

I didn't attend the film première but Andy rang me. 'Her Royal Highness didn't show up,' he said. 'Just as well – the Krays' mob were sitting all around the places reserved for the Royal party.'

'She missed her chance to meet the only Damon Runyon characters London can provide,' I told him.

Vic had enjoyed the film. 'Made me want to go and have a good fuck,' he said.

Fanny and Murray didn't agree. They'd walked in with that buttoned-up, 'let's spare her' look. They weren't going to let J.L. off lightly – not after all the things she'd said to them in the past.

I was working on the church scene in the green room, letting Jean and Bob have the stage. Big Baritone was at the piano trying the tune of 'I Wore A Tulip' with one finger:

> *I wore a tunic, a dirty khaki tunic,*
> *And you wore your civvy clothes*
> *We fought and bled at Loos, while you were on the*
>   *booze*
> *The booze that no one here knows*

You were out with the wenches, while we were in
    the trenches
Facing an angry foe
You were a-slacking, while we were attacking
The Germans on the Menin Road.

Haig, Myvanwy as the Nurse, Brian as Army Preacher, took their places. The soldiers entered to the tune of 'Onward Christian Soldiers', played on the harmonium, and sang:

Forward Joe Soap's Army, marching without fear
With our old commander safely in the rear
He boasts and skites from morn till night
And thinks he's very brave
But the men who really did the job
    are dead and in their grave.

The news panel would read:

BATTLE OF THE SOMME ENDS . . . TOTAL LOSS . . .
1,332,000 MEN . . . GAIN, NIL.

BRIAN (*as* THE PREACHER): Dearly beloved brethren. I bring
    glad tidings from the Home Front. The Archbishop of
    Canterbury has made it known that it is no sin to labour
    for victory on the Sabbath, and his Holiness the Pope rules
    that the eating of flesh on a Friday is no longer a venial sin.
    Likewise the Chief Rabbi absolves your Jewish brethren from
    abstaining from pork in the trenches.
       Tomorrow being Good Friday, we hope God will look kindly
    on our attack on Arras. We will now sing 'Waft, waft ye
    winds, waft, waft ye'. Hymns Ancient and Modern Number
    358.

Haig, the nurse and the chaplain sang the correct words, the soldiers their own version:

We are Fred Karno's army
The Ragtime Infantry
We cannot fight, we cannot shoot
What bleedin' use are we?
And when we get to Berlin
The Kaiser he will say,
Hoch, hoch mein Gott, *what a bloody fine lot*
Are the boys of the RFA.

PREACHER: Oh God, show thy face to us as thou didst with thy
angel at Mons. The choir will now sing 'What a Friend We
Have in Jesus' as we offer a silent prayer for Sir Douglas Haig
that he may be successful in tomorrow's onset.

And Colin sang:

When this lousy war is over
No more soldiering for me
When I get my civvy clothes on
Oh how happy I shall be!
No more church parades on Sundays
No more putting in for leave,
I shall kiss the Sergeant-Major
How I'll miss him, how he'll grieve.

HAIG: Well, God, the prospects for a successful attack are now
ideal. The people at home have given us the means to mass
every man, horse and gun on the Western Front. I am the
predestined instrument of providence for the achievement of
victory for the British Army. And I ask it, oh Lord, before
the Americans arrive. . . .

At this moment the holy atmosphere of our rehearsal was shattered by an outburst of angry voices. It was Jean and Bob, on
stage. I hurried down from the green room, followed by the men
in the church scene. Bob was stock still, white with rage. Jean was
lunging at him with a threatening fist.

'Jean! What are you doing?'

'If we're going to do it at all the jig should be authentic,' she
said.

'Nonsense,' said Bob, 'choreography is not documentary.'

'If you two can't collaborate, leave it,' I said. 'But you can hardly dance the standard-bearer yourself, Jean.'

'She thinks she can, ma'am,' said Bob. And that 'ma'am' was icy.

'I suggest we leave it for today. I've an idea for the cavalry charge and I want to try it.'

'Leave me out,' said Bob. 'I'll go over the steps for this on my own.'

Jean walked off.

'We need seven horses,' I said. 'Who can neigh and whinny?' Of course all the men started neighing, but it didn't sound bad. I'd found some small bells and jingling chains in the prop room and gave them out. Then the horses entered, rearing up on their hind legs and nearly throwing their riders. The cavalry governed their mounts with difficulty. What a charge! Surprising really, as the horses were only walking canes with bells.

Jean didn't turn up at the next Munster rehearsal. She'd gone off in a huff. Bob was there. He stayed. His dance, the whole scene, were both magnificent.

After a lot of argument, hard work and frustration, the second half was almost in the can. I had only to find the right finale.

Henri Barbusse gave it to me with his account of the French soldiers who mutinied because they thought it stupid to advance against certain death.

'You don't think, you obey,' said their officer. 'If you refuse, you will be shot.'

'Very well, Lieutenant, we follow you, like lambs to the slaughter.'

'*En avant!*'

They marched into No Man's Land baa-ing like sheep till they were all mowed down.

Later, when we played Paris, Claude Planson taught us a French soldiers' song which had been banned in the army. Our dead *poilus* come to life to sing for the first time in any theatre:

Adieu la vie
Adieu l'amour
Adieu à toutes les femmes
C'est bien fini
C'est pour toujours
De cette guerre infame
C'est à Craonne
Sur le plateau,
Qu'ils ont laissé leur peaux
Car ils sont tous condamnés
Ce sont les sacrifiés.

And the news panel flickered by with:

THE WAR TO END WARS . . . KILLED TEN MILLION . . . WOUNDED TWENTY-ONE MILLION . . . MISSING, SEVEN MILLION . . .

'No call tomorrow morning. First complete run-through two p.m., followed by notes. Seven p.m. – public dress rehearsal.

Everybody was in early next day. They found boxes specially constructed in the wings, one for each individual, so that all small changes could be carefully set – speed offstage was vital to the performances.

The run was efficient and flat. That was all right, the continuity made sense. For the evening run, we danced and sang to banish the demons and I took my usual place in the dress circle.

My heart sank. The evening was flat too.

Apart from playing several demanding rôles, Victor was functioning as a Master of Ceremonies. There were moments where he could have picked the show up. He didn't, he'd fallen back on his old self, diffident, sensitive but uncertain. Should I try giving it a kick at the interval? No. It was up to them tonight.

At the end I took it easy. 'Let's all go and have a drink,' I said. There was no need for a post-mortem – everybody knew it had been a dud.

'We'll have to run it again before tomorrow night's performance.'

'It's too late,' said Charles Chilton. 'It doesn't work, there isn't a single dead soldier in it. They're just playing for laughs and not getting them.'

'They will.'

Next day, I called Victor and Chuck Sewell aside. 'We're going through it again and I want you to sit this one out, Vic. Chuck will read in your part.' They both looked rather alarmed. 'Don't worry, it's only an experiment.' Vic sat beside me, watching a pretty disastrous run-through, flat with occasional bursts of frenetic energy.

'You see what it needs?' I asked him.

'I can see it all right.'

That evening, when local friends and neighbours were still coming in, I went round to Vic's dressing-room, something I never do.

'Go out there and just stand on that stage and talk to the people. No performance, no funny stuff. Ask them how they are, if you like, but do allow for a reply.'

That's what he did. And for the very first time, he was free, confident, easy, his feet had recovered at last. As a matter of fact, he's never looked back since.

I met Gerry on the stairs after. He was smiling broadly.

'It's rough,' I said, 'but it works.'

He gave me a hug.

'I don't suppose we could postpone the official opening?'

'Has there ever been a show you didn't want to postpone?' Next morning, I was giving notes when a local woman walked in. 'Saw your piece last night,' she said. 'Here, I've had this on the mantelpiece forty-five years. It was Dad's, for 'is Woodbines, he carried it with 'im wherever 'e went till 'e got killed.' She handed me a small tin box with 'Merry Christmas. Princess Mary' stamped on the lid. 'You can keep it,' she said.

Brian Murphy carried it in his pocket throughout the run of the play.

'Long walks an' short smokes,' said our boiler man. He'd been in that war too.

Oh What A Lovely War! awakened race memory in our audiences. At the end of each performance people would come on stage bringing memories and mementoes, even lines of dialogue which sometimes turned up in the show.

The ones who inspired and informed us were numberless but most of all we were indebted to the unnamed soldiers whose songs we sang.

We didn't postpone, but each day we dusted and polished that show. On the first Saturday after we opened I spent the morning tidying up at home. At lunch-time I heard Gerry coming along the passage. He had an armful of freesia, mimosa and daffodils for me and he smiled and kissed me. I put them all over the flat, the smell of the mimosa was everywhere. In the evening, after the show, we all went to Jimmie Ling's East West restaurant, down by the docks, to celebrate.

Jimmie had enjoyed the show, 'But why isn't your name on the programme?' he asked me.

'She's ashamed of us,' said Gerry.

Of myself more like it, running away for ever then turning up again like a bad penny.

'Put your name on the billing for Gerry's sake,' said Jimmie Ling and handed me a programme.

I wrote my name on it, then and there, and added, 'For Gerry Raffles, the only begetter of *Oh What A Lovely War!*'

Sixty

B esides presenting plays, whether during our eight-year stint on the road, or at Stratford-atte-Bowe, we were always ready to preach and play with any organisation that invited us. At one time a visit to a group of Nottinghamshire miners at their holiday camp was followed by a session with students at Malmö University. The camp was near Skegness and the miners had built it themselves – a roomy, wandering place, very pleasant. I arrived on the last Saturday of their holiday. There was a queue at 'Receptions', so I sat down and waited. There was a lot of coupon-tearing and rubber-stamping and a touch of chaos when a charabanc-load of families rolled in, merry after an outing.

My first session was on the following morning and I thought I'd better start making some sort of plan, but a rather harassed official located me, installed me in a chalet and took me along to high tea with the Committee. We had a good clash, as they say, and I felt quite at home.

Next morning I faced rows of smiling, expectant faces, and quite a few notebooks and pencils. . . . 'Before we begin, I was wondering what it was like here when you all arrived.'

A middle-aged chap cleared his throat and recited a list of collieries and the number of miners present from each one.

I congratulated him on his good memory. 'And can you remember who was in front of you in the queue at Receptions?'

'Oh yes, my brother.'

'And behind you?'

'Behind me?'

'Can anyone help him out?'

One or two tried, but others flatly contradicted them. As usual with this exercise, it took a long time to reconstitute the whole queue and even longer to give a true representation of the actual atmosphere.

'And what exactly were you queueing for?'

'Our cards.' 'The stamping.' 'Chalets.' 'You know, proper organisation.'

'We forgot the receptionist. That's a very important position.'

'There were two of them.' 'Don't bring them into it.' 'They did their best.'

'Anybody want to play a receptionist?'

It wasn't a coveted rôle. I appointed the two from the tail end of the queue. No sooner had they got the job than they started swinging their weight about.

'Less talking, there. We've a job on here. And [turning to me] we need a rubber stamp, meal tickets, a ledger, two chairs, a desk. . . .'

'Hold on,' I said. 'Improvise.'

It was amazing the number of ingenious stage managers who appeared – but they were stuck for the rubber stamp.

'Get a move on,' said Clerk Number One. 'We haven't got all day.'

One bloke found one in a desk, with a bell, the type that teachers use.

> FIRST CLERK: All right, let's be 'aving you. (*And she pinged on the bell.*) Name? Married or single? Colliery?
> SECOND CLERK: Chalet Number Six. (*And she pinged twice.*)
> FIRST CLERK (*ping*): Name? Married or single?

And so it went on. It was becoming boring, but suddenly a young feller came rushing in.

> YOUNG FELLER: Quick! Quick!
> FIRST CLERK: Get in line!
> YOUNG FELLER: There's a fucking chalet on fire!

Laughter, applause, some clucking from ladies present. I'm off,' said one. 'I came here for a lecture, not to play silly buggers.'

'I'll join you, love. My little girl'll be wanting to know where I am.'

'She's 'avin' the time of 'er life making sand pies on the beach,' said Bill, the one who'd brought the news about the chalet, but the good mum had already gone. One or two others were trying to remember funny incidents on that first day. There was the young couple who found themselves in the same chalet as a crotchety bachelor; the old feller who'd come to the wrong holiday camp. One fat, middle-aged bloke started making a political speech.

''E's being Ernie Bevin,' I was told. 'Ever seen a coalface, Ernie?' he shouted. 'They serve you tea an' buttered buns at ours.'

Then they all started heckling. It was obviously one of their party pieces.

'Let's try something we can all join in,' I said. 'What about the bus ride coming here?'

That worked. Everyone scrambled for their proper place on the bus (twenty-four chairs). Bill was the driver and shouted, ''Airpin bend, ahoy!' as he drove fast round unimaginable corners and the whole bus swayed with him. They whooped and sang and pointed out the landmarks. It was hilarious. Now they'd started, there was no stopping them. They played boring lectures and complaints about noise in the chalets after midnight; complaints about the grub – 'Cow 'eel agin?' Everything was re-enacted. Even I was amazed at the talent they displayed, and told them so.

'What do you want us to do, Joan? Go 'ome and paint like Picasso?'

'I'd sooner you painted like you.'

'Who's going to find the rent?'

'There may be other ways of making a living, apart from digging coal.'

'It's not so bad – the pit,' said Bill. 'I've seen worse.'

They postponed their departure on the Monday.

'We'd like a bit more *Candid Camera* to be going on with,' said Ernie Bevin.

'We've 'ad a right good time, lass,' said one of the ladies.

Next session? Malmö University in Sweden, a country where education is taken very seriously. You start school when you're seven and make your way, by disciplined stages, till you reach university or fall among ordinary mortals.

The invitation came as a result of the Workshop tours of the Scandinavian countries in '48, '51 and '56. In accepting, I'd said I would arrive early enough to inspect the hall and make a few arrangements. A formal delegation met me, looking slightly apprehensive. Had my forbidding reputation gone before me? Anyway, we proceeded smoothly to a large polished hall, where the resident Sparks was lurking. The delegation seemed reluctant to leave but I gave them a farewell smile and with one backward glance they were gone.

Rows of chairs had been set out. On each there was a piece of paper with a name and a coin on it – the students' way of making a reservation. I asked the Sparks for a lectern and we placed it down front. Then we slid the chairs away. They were linked together in rows. Next problem? The lighting. It was almost seven p.m. by the time I had everything the way I wanted it.

The doors opened on time, but the room was in complete darkness. The students groped their way to where the chairs had been, but there were no chairs. I tapped the lectern with a ruler and a bright spot shone on me. . . .

'Ever since man first descended from the trees,' I began, 'and penetrated the grasslands on his two hind legs, he has yearned for the unattainable, which we have named perfection. Could these two hands create – Could we have a little less noise please? – perfection? Is it not indescribable?'

There was a sudden crash and an abject apology, in Swedish.

'Thank you. I should think so. Never have I been subjected to such rudeness, inattention and incompetence in my entire career.'

The poor things were stunned into silence. I rapped on the lectern again and there was a burst of rock music from the back of the hall as a pool of rose-pink light appeared there. The music grew louder. I called for lights. My audience was revealed, standing around in forlorn clumps.

'Good evening,' I said and smiled. They responded all together, but quietly, as if dealing with a loony. I asked them if they'd like to avoid the evening as planned. There must be more rewarding things to do than sit listening to some foreign bird extrapolating on theatre. No one agreed. Nor did they disagree.

'While waiting for you to decide,' I went on, 'perhaps you would care to help me with a simple experiment. It only involves a change of identity. . . .' They looked doubtful, or worried.

'All you have to do is exchange some article of clothing, or an accessory, with the person nearest to you. Anything will do – not necessarily clothing, something which makes you feel distinctive – a watch, a ring, a piece of jewellery, shoes, spectacles.'

I started unpacking the chairs as the swapping began. I changed into a student's cap the Sparks had been wearing and gave him the English cap I always wore.

The students were making their exchanges very seriously. One bold young man was taking off his trousers and putting on his girlfriend's skirt. A cheeky blonde girl shook the brassière she'd just taken off and smiled. She wanted to give it to a healthy, sporty type, but he wasn't having any: he was after a T-shirt with 'Atlanta' on it. A very timid-looking brunette sat in a corner, held up her hand and pointed to the illuminated watch she'd acquired. A lovely Indian girl was trying to save her sari from a bookish chap in spectacles.

'Are we all set? Good. Music please. Have we a piano?'

'No, but I've a guitar in my locker.'

'Hans can play the mouth-organ.'

'Where's your trumpet, Sven?'

Several characters left to fetch their musical instruments. Sparks switched on some glamorous lighting.

'Let's change everything,' I said, ' – voice, accent, language – dance or relax, sing or spiel. Use the rock music till our home-made band assembles. . . .'

Two or three began dancing, the mood caught on – but suddenly a group formed in opposition.

'What about our lecture?' said their spokesman, a serious young man who'd been taking a lot of notes.

'Let's finish her experiment first.'

Sven was back. He blew a wild cadenza on his trumpet.

Guitar and mouth-organ joined him. Someone had found a drum.
Dancing took over. After a while the serious young man called a
halt. The room divided – the music won but this time with a
diminished majority. The serious young man approached me –
a one-man delegation.

'Leave it for the moment,' I said, 'and let's see what's
happening.'

We wandered round the hall together, weaving our way through
the small groups which were forming. One lot were condemning
the university authorities. Tonight was just bad organisation. What
they should be studying was the art of management. It could all be
traced back to the country's bad government.

The young man with the guitar started playing a political
song. His group split. Further on there was an aggressive peace
meeting. They should have had the hall tonight. The mouth-
organist started singing a satirical song about peacemakers. He
was making it up as he went along. An earnest young woman
broke away from the rest. She was in tears. Another girl put
her arm round her and led her into a corner. They began to
pray. Bit by bit others joined them; it became a regular prayer
meeting. Two young men stalked by, looking superior. They
installed themselves in a recess by the window. One of them, a
tall blond, started reciting. It sounded like an old Norse saga –
I thought I heard 'Skegge the Stately'. Anyway, whoever it was,
he sailed forth to conquer the sea, but by the sea was himself
conquered. Any one of these groups could have developed into
a significant force. Ideas were cropping up all over the place.
I was drawn to a very determined-looking crowd. They were
evolving a detailed plan of campaign for taking over the country's
educational system. A born leader was addressing them: 'We must
gather support by non-violent persuasion.' He was interrupted;
'Nonsense! The control system will use violent coercion, when
threatened. They'll have to . . .' The serious young man joined
them.

I left them to it – and sounded the tocsin. It took a long time
to gain silence. I thanked them for their co-operation and quoted
MacDiarmid:

All art risks being a destruction only
But while there is strength for creation
Destruction must be risked.

'Enjoy yourselves. Good night, and if tomorrow you remember anything that struck you as interesting during tonight's proceedings, please write it all down. I'll be most interested to read it.'

Next day, I heard that the fire brigade had arrived in the small hours, curious to know what was going on. The firemen were almost persuaded to join in. It was four o'clock in the morning when the hall was finally vacated.

I n 1961, in the East End of London, something had been stirring. Lou Sherman, Mayor of Hackney, invited the mayors of the neighbouring boroughs to join him on a boat trip along the River Lea. The Lea, before industrialisation, had always been a playground for London's East Enders and other pleasure-seekers. Pepys had taken his wife boating there. The mayors agreed that something must be done to restore the Lea Valley to its sylvan self, or part of its sylvan self – but it was to take a long time for Mayor Sherman to get any action on the scene.

1961 was the year I met Cedric Price, the young architect with the keen mind and an interest in accommodating change. When I'd blown off steam about the current vogue for quaint old theatres, he hadn't said much, but had gone away and designed the 'Fun Palace'. The first time I saw the plans was when I dropped in on him at his office, as if by chance, and asked how things were going. He became offhand, but nodded toward the drawing-board, before helping himself to a Cuban cigar.

The drawing was almost inexplicable. I could make out filigree towers, varied areas at different levels, there were galleries, gantries and escalators – it looked airborne.

'Can it be kept clean?'

'It's a self-washing giant.'

'And those things?'

'Moving walkways and catwalks. No, you're pointing at the radial escalators. They can be steered.'

'It's not easy to read.'

'It's a mobile, not a water-colour. And I am rather busy.'

'Good. I'll be off.'

I wanted to tell him I'd found the ideal site for the Palace, Glengall, on the Isle of Dogs. I'd seen it when I visited Dan Farson who lived nearby. . . .

'There's six acres of disused land on the riverside,' said Dan and took me to see it.

It was no use trying to tell the Arc. He was puffing at his cigar with his head down, but the more I thought about it . . . land, by a tidal river – and that river the Sweet Thames.

A few days later, he was there with me. 'I can see it,' I said, 'on festival nights – fireworks, water jousts, riverboats coming and going. . . .' But he was plodding over the rough land in his Wellington boots.

On 16th May 1963, he applied to the London County Council for use of the land. At the same time, Lou Sherman was asking the Civic Trust to prepare a feasibility study of the River Lea. His neighbouring mayors backed him up, without question.

W hen the news leaked out that Cedric Price was the architect of 'The Fun Palace', the design magazines of the world wanted photos of the plans. They all met with a refusal: 'It's a kit of parts, not a building,' he told them. 'I doubt whether it will ever look the same twice.'

That was true, but on fine mornings when I felt good, or at night by the river, I could visualise such a place, light, almost airborne, yet grounded in engineering skill, such as had never before been realised. I tried to explain the concept, I wrote and talked at universities and schools, to any assembly interested. I tried cyberneticians and politicians. I was glad when at last Cedric Price allowed his drawings to be reproduced.

'A new step in the world,' said Philip Johnson, the American architect.

'Better than I thought,' said Ian Mikardo, when I explained the idea behind the Palace. 'It's not just roundabouts and swings. it's the fun of learning.'

Price and I were summoned to a meeting of top-level London County Council officials and questioned closely as to the whys and wherefores as well as the architectural innovations. They were shown the plans.

'And how do you propose to finance it?'

'We hope to have government support. There is a sixpenny rate for cultural purposes. Also some private investor or syndicate will recognise the value of the experiment and support us. At the moment we are financing it ourselves.'

'There will have to be a great deal of discussion before you receive an answer to your request for use of the land at Glengall.'

It was 10th September when we received this reply:

> The chairmen of the committees concerned have considered the possibility of leasing the five and a half acres of land (including Glengall Wharf) in the Isle of Dogs for the Fun Palace project, but because of certain legal and planning difficulties, the Council is unable to make it available for this purpose. The chairmen were, however, impressed by the imaginativeness and potentialities of the project and the possibility of finding an alternative site is being explored. I should perhaps say that the possibility of finding riverside land of the area required, in that part of London, seems to be remote and the cost would be exorbitant.

So goodbye to the perfect site. We would never find such another. Could their decision be reversed? At least they were not unfriendly.

We were gaining support among the scientists: Professor Rotblat, who had helped us with *Uranium 235*, was for us; so was Lord Ritchie Calder. Dr Gordon Pask of Systems Research joined forces with us. He had known our work since the Liverpool days.

'Fun?' 'Seeking the unfamiliar, and ultimately transcending it.' The *New Scientist* published the following article in May 1964:

THE FUN PALACE by Joan Littlewood

Politicians and educators, talking about increased leisure, mostly assume that people are so numb, or servile, that the hours in which they earn money can be made little more than hygienically bearable, while a new awareness is cultivated during the hours of leisure. . . .

In London we are going to create a university of the streets – not a gracious park, but a foretaste of the pleasures of the future. The 'Fun Arcade' will be full of the games that psychologists and electronics engineers now devise for the service of industry, or war. Knowledge will be piped through jukeboxes. In the music area – by day, instruments available, free instruction, recordings for everyone, classical, folk, jazz, pop, disc libraries – by night jam sessions and festivals, poetry and dance.

In the science playground – lecture demonstrations, supported by teaching films, closed-circuit television and working models, at night an agora or Kaffeeklatsch where the Socrates, Abelards, Mermaid poets, the wandering scholars of the future – the mystics, sceptics and sophists – can dispute till dawn. An acting area will afford the therapy of theatre for everyone: men and women from factories, shops and offices, bored with their daily routine, will be able to re-enact incidents from their own experience, wake to a critical awareness of reality, act out their subconscious fears and taboos and perhaps find stimulus in social research.

A plastic area will be a place for dabbling in paint, clay, wood, metal, stone or textiles, for the rediscovery of the childhood experience of touching and handling, for constructing anything (useless or useful, to taste).

But the essence of the place will be informality – nothing obligatory – anything goes. There will be no permanent structures. Nothing is to last more than ten years, some things not even ten days: no concrete stadia, stained and cracking, no legacy of noble contemporary architecture, quickly dating.

With informality goes flexibility. The 'areas' that have been listed are not segregated enclosures. The whole plan is open, but on many levels. So the greatest pleasure of traditional parks is preserved – the pleasure of strolling casually, looking at one or other of these areas or (if this is preferred) settling down to several hours of work–play.

Besides the activities already briefly outlined, there will be plenty to engage imagination and enlarge experience. At various points, sheltered or open, there will be screens on which closed-circuit television will show, without editing or art, whatever is going on in and out of London, and in the complex itself: it will be possible to see coalminers, woodmen and dockers actually at work; Monkey Hill, the aquarium or the insect house at the Zoo, the comings and goings outside a local authority rest-centre, a Salvation Army hostel, the casualty ward of a hospital or a West End club; news panels will bring world and local news.

The curiosity that many people feel about their neighbours' lives can be satisfied instructively, and with greater immediacy than in any documentary film. . . . and an occasion of major popular interest – a Cup Final, happenings of international interest, or a royal funeral – would be presented on screens of maximum size. The visitor can enjoy a sense of identity with the world about him.

Many who start by wandering half attentively, or even sceptically, through the complex will be drawn into these and other elementary exercises in social observation. In what has been called the acting area, for instance, there will be no rigid division between performers and audience – a generalisation

of the technique used in Theatre Workshop for many
years.

As I have described it, it may seem very busy,
yet the general atmosphere will be one of relaxation
and, equally important and now technically possible,
there will be zones of quiet for those who don't feel
like listening to music or taking part actively in all
that is going on. Here they can watch, lounge about
and find enjoyment in wasting time.

The Fun Palace excited a good deal of interest in the scientific world and Gordon Pask decided to form a Cybernetics
Committee to act as a filter for ideas from other individuals
and groups and discuss the all-important problems of cost and
control. The following individuals agreed to serve on it and the
committee met regularly:

Roy Ascott, Ipswich School of Art
Chester Beatty, Research Institute
Stafford Beer, Sigma
Richard Bowdler, Fun Palace
Asa Briggs, Sussex University
R. Chesterman, Goldsmith's College
J. Clark, Bristol University
Tom Driberg MP
F. George, Bristol University
R. Goldacre
R. Goodman, Brighton College of Technology
Richard Gregory, Cambridge University
A. R. Jonckheere, University of London
Brian Lewis, Systems Research Ltd
J. Littlewood, Fun Palace
A. G. MacDonald, Scientific Advisers Branch, Home
Office
Mr and Mrs T. R. McKinnon Wood
Ian Mikardo, MP
R. Pinker, Goldsmith's College

Cedric Price, Architect
Gerry Raffles, Theatre Workshop
G. Slot
J. H. Westcott, Imperial College
M. Young, Institute of Community Studies

Chairman, Gordon Pask

Cedric Price submitted his plans to the Milan Triennale and published the following statement in the *New Scientist* alongside mine:

> This complex, which enables self-participatory educa-
> tion and entertainment, can only work – and then only
> for a finite time – if it is not only accessible to those
> living and working in the immediate neighbourhood
> but also, through its varied communication links, as
> a regional and national amenity.
>
> The siting exploits existing communication net-
> works and gives a clue to the potential enrichment of
> life through increasing mobility at present unrealised
> in large urban communities. The sense of confinement
> on the site is reduced by the deliberate extension of the
> visible limits.
>
> The activities designed for the site should be experi-
> mental, the place itself expendable and changeable.
> The organisation of space and the object occupying
> it should, on the one hand, challenge the participants'
> mental and physical dexterity and, on the other, allow
> for a flow of space and time, in which passive and
> active pleasure is provoked.
>
> The ephemeral nature of the architecture is a
> major element in the design, making possible the use
> of materials and techniques normally excluded from
> the building industry. Charged static-vapour zones,
> optical barriers, warm-air curtains and fog-dispersal
> plant are some of the methods employed, together
> with vertical and horizontal lightweight blinds.
>
> Within the complex, the public moves about, above

the largely unobstructed ground-level deck, on ramps, moving walkways, catwalks and radial escalators. All such equipment is capable of rearrangement – allowing multi-directional movement and random pedestrian grouping, yet capable of programming. The complex itself, having no doorways, enables one to choose one's own route and degree of involvement with the activities. Although the framework will remain a constant size, the total volume in use may vary, thus presenting a changing scene even to the frequent user. While individual enclosures such as theatre areas, workshops or restaurants have their own particular controlled environment, the total volume is capable of resisting or modifying adverse climatic conditions.

The nature of the enclosures and the degree of control required for these activities are so varied – including as they do large-volume activities such as rallies, concerts, conferences, theatre and screenings – that each is built up of separate units ('walls', 'floors', 'ceilings') as required. Inflatable enclosures are also used. The smaller enclosures are more likely to be self-contained: these are built-up standard-unit 'boxes' of reinforced plastic and aluminium, set on and serviced from open 'decks'. The construction and arrangement of such enclosures, together with the movement and positioning of fittings and equipment, are achieved by a permanent travelling gantry crane spanning the whole structure.

The movement of staff, piped services and escape routes are provided for within the open-frame, pro-tected-steel stanchions of the superstructure and cross-connected at service basement level, where service access and parking are located, together with the necessary plant.

The whole complex provides valuable site-testing conditions for a wide range of materials, equipment and constructional techniques.

Friends and supporters in NY NY wrote to me suggesting a likely venue there, but with the LCC on our side I felt we were bound to win in London. All we needed was publicity. I decided to make a film and, to raise the cash, wrote and directed half a dozen TV commercials. Then I approached the cameraman Walter Lassally. He said he'd be pleased to help.

Frank Norman had sent Gerry a new script, but I couldn't face the old Royal with my head full of the Fun Palace. I tried to persuade Donald Albery to let me convert his warehouse into a Clowns' Club as a temporary measure. It would give me free space and help Frank's play. Cedric Price made an original design for the conversion, but Albery found it too unconventional and rejected the whole project. I'd no alternative but to try and make the script stand up at E15. It didn't.

Frank liked the idea of the Fun Palace. He thought it'd stand more chance in America. 'They'd give you your head.'

'It's for my own country first,' I said.

Sixty-one

1964. Death of Brendan Behan. The LCC cannot accommodate the Fun Palace by the Thames, suggest Mill Meads at Stratford, E15. A plea for the F.P. filmed, a model made. Thomas North, Borough Architect of West Ham, against us. Jeremy Isaacs helps us. We are now a Trust, with Ritchie Calder, Buckminster Fuller, George Harewood, Yehudi Menuhin and myself, trustees. Try to interest Jennie Lee, Parliamentary Secretary to the Ministry of Public Building. Awaiting LCC decision on Mill Meads, plan a pilot scheme in Camden Town – it is turned down by local residents. March 1965 – still no decision from LCC.

On 4th March 1964 Shelagh Delaney gave birth to a daughter. A shy and very private person, she had been staying with us at our home in Blackheath.

'If it's a girl,' she'd said, 'I'll name her Charlotte.'

I wondered if she was thinking of the douce Brontë.

We'd hardly recovered from the new baby's appearance when news reached us of Brendan Behan's death, at the age of forty. Frank came with me to Dublin for the funeral. I was so angry with Brendan for dying that I felt like kicking that coffin. Someone, near to him, had smuggled a bottle of brandy into the clinic where he was supposed to be protected. It put paid to him. Death by drinking.

As we drove to Glasnevin through streets lined with Dublin's poor, an old man shouted, 'May he never get there!'

It's me auld Irish tomb
I'll be in there soon
*But first I will **** you*
Beneath the harvest moon.

B ack in London, Cedric Price had received a map of the Lea
Valley with a site at Mill Meads ringed in red. Would it be
suitable for the Fun Palace, Leslie Lane, Director of the Civic
Trust, was asking.

'It's an island on the Lea,' I said.

Charlie, the plumber at Theatre Royal, was delighted. 'Of
course you should be in Stratford. Three Mills? I grew up there,
caught tiddlers in the clear water under Pig's Hole and learned the
facts of life somewhere on that debris. Call it Mill Meads now, do
they? It's Three Mills.'

The Civic Trust informed Mr North of our acceptance. We
knew Thomas North of old – Architect and Planning Officer for
West Ham.

'All very well,' said Cedric Price, 'but Frank Newby wants to
know when he can start engaging staff.' Newby was the consultant
engineer. 'Where's the money?'

Enough loot to pay Frank's gang? From the film, maybe.
I shot round the East End with that first-rate cameraman,
Walter Lassally, and Kate, his right hand – picking up glimpses of
gambling clubs, poker games, pub striptease, picking the winner,
getting sozzled. It was pretty boring. I'd have to give the ending a
bit of zing.

'Pity we can't fake a shot of the F.P. on Firework Night.'

'We could if we had a model,' said Price.

'How much would it cost?'

'Nearly two thousand pounds, to do the job properly.'

I found it, but my purse was getting very light. Frank Newby,
Cedric Price and Steve Mullin constructed a delicate framework
with levels and bays and unfolding blinds. It looked superb.

'We need sparklers and some real clown faces at the back of it.'

I persuaded Barbara Windsor, Brian Murphy and Vic Spinetti
to come along in their pierrot outfits and clown some of the delights
of the palace. But where?

An angel appeared, in the person of Jeremy Isaacs, at that
time editor of *Panorama* at the BBC. He gave us the use of a
studio for a day, with camera crew, sets, accessories – everything
we needed. We finished with some super shots of those three love-
birds.

'Meanwhile,' said Dick, who always brought us down to earth, 'have we made formal application for Mill Meads?'

Who to? North or the Greater London Council, I wanted to know?

With the April 1964 changeover in London government the LCC became the GLC and passed the buck (Mill Meads, I mean) to West Ham, now named Newham, and its architect, Thomas North. 'He couldn't care less about us,' said Dick.

'That was in Theatre Royal days,' I said. 'This is different.'

We sent the application to the GLC and Newham. Sir William Fiske, the GLC's chairman, Sir William Hart, Clerk to the Council, and Sidney Melman, Chairman of Parks Committee, were a hundred per cent for us. Jennie Lee, Parliamentary Secretary to the Ministry of Public Building, was interested, but only just. Her husband, Nye Bevan, had been a friend, but he was long gone.

One day Dick turned up with the surprising news that the GLC still held Mill Meads, not Newham. Our spirits rose. 'Still, North hasn't actually opposed us,' I said.

But he had. On 9th October 1964 he'd written to Leslie Lane, Director of the Civic Trust, to tell him that a Teachers' Training College was claiming Mill Meads. On 18th October, Lane replied:

LEA VALLEY DEVELOPMENT
MILL MEADS

. . . The proposals by the Civic Trust were that this area should
be included in the overall scheme for recreational purposes. . . .
I think it would be a great pity if any of the land included
in the Civic Trust proposals were to be committed to other
uses.

Yours sincerely,

Leslie Lane
(Director)

The cat was among the pigeons. North and his teachers, harrying the GLC, would postpone their decision on us, if nothing worse.

I felt like following the example of the original Diggers and going
out with Newby to start claiming common land.

Price was more circumspect and prepared the following statement:

> The Fun Palace, originally planned for riverside
> London, has now been included in the Lea Valley
> Project, but the realisation of the scheme will take
> time. Meanwhile it is obvious that pilot schemes,
> parked temporarily on any available land, will be of
> great value as outlets for districts which lack modern
> entertainment and educational amenities. Pilots will
> also provide some specialised research for the main
> scheme.

It was published and I went out looking at docks, dumps and
disused allotments. I persuaded Commander Parmiter, Thames
Harbour-master, to take me on a trip up and down the river.

'Land?' said he. 'I dredge it.'

'Why can't the Government understand the crying need for
such schemes?' I asked him.

'Don't talk to me about politicians. They destroyed the British
Navy.'

I noticed some empty docks which looked promising and
earmarked a patch of land on the south side of Vauxhall Bridge.
I wrote the Port of London Authority. Nothing available. I tried
for Vauxhall. It was to be sold for a car park. L.G. Huddy, Town
Clerk of Hackney, expressed interest, so I went with Price to look
at the several small plots available in Hackney. We suggested different amenities on each one, but as it turned out he wanted one
central arts building.

I roamed far and wide, a land-hungry settler; tried Glasgow,
Edinburgh, Liverpool, while the designs went round the world.
I lectured in Helsinki, Aarhus, the universities of England and
Goldsmith's College, London. There and at the London School
of Economics we found our most helpful supporters.

'Time to form a trust,' said Harold Lever, barrister, old friend
and at that time Chancellor of the Duchy of Lancaster.

'You fix it for us, then,' I told him.

I had already asked Ritchie Calder if he would be one of our trustees when I was in Edinburgh and he'd agreed. I thought Yehudi Menuhin would accept, and he did. Buckminster Fuller was the father of mobile design, but he was away on one of his journeyings round the planet – so I wrote him hoping the letter would find him. And for the fourth?

'Try Harewood, for his great interest in music,' said Tom Driberg.

Enthusiastic letters began arriving from Liverpool, where we'd always had supporters, and David Scase was now running the Everyman Theatre. Eric Heffer, MP, was very keen, so was the City Architect and Planner, Walter Bor. Jennie Lee was coming to investigate the cultural amenities there and it was suggested that I should meet her. The general feeling was that we should not want for support in Liverpool.

Glasgow had been far more sympathetic than Edinburgh, but our good friends there were still living in the pioneering days of the Workshop. Even so, I was convinced that Glasgow would one day show them all. Frankly, Edinburgh was dead compared with Glasgow. Even the world-famous Festival didn't please the natives. It woke them up, but only to grumble. I found one enthusiastic supporter, Percy Johnson-Marshall, head of the local School of Architecture. We also shared an interest in the work of Patrick Geddes.

An all-out attack on likely sponsors was being plotted in London. By the time I got there, blow-ups of the design and world comments were being pinned up in an attractive studio. I was amazed at the number of countries welcoming the Fun Palace. The invitations were on silver cards, designed by Anna Lovell.

Dick, as usual, was critical. 'It's all art,' he said. 'We should be getting down to brass tacks. We haven't allowed enough time to prepare this meet, for one thing.'

All the same it turned out to be a brilliant occasion, distinguished visitors, good eats and drinks, well laid out, of course, and bright discourse from Price and myself. We were showered with congratulations and good wishes. A TV tycoon had worked out a rough costing for our communication networks. That was promising.

I had to return to Liverpool for the Jennie Lee meeting. The Adelphi Hotel, ten thirty a.m. I walked in on time, to find a crowd of journalists hanging about in the lobby. After a coffee and a couple of cigarettes I asked if something had gone wrong.

'No, no, she's in her room all right.'

'Why don't you go and tell her we're waiting, Joan?'

'Tell her we'll be drunk soon.'

I went. I'd always told my actors never to keep people waiting, if it could be avoided. I'd no idea that politicians could behave like film stars. The lady was in a white, flowery room seated at the dressing-table, making herself beautiful. She told me it was part of a journalist's job to wait.

Eventually we descended and I found I was part of a Grand Parade. I tried explaining the F.P. but the only thing she seemed to like about us was the word fun. She wanted everything to be 'gay and colourful' for the working people. I tried to explain that we'd chosen the word 'fun' almost as a provocation. I didn't stand a chance with my work–play symbiosis, she'd just turn on me a smiling face, prepared for the next happy encounter.

Cedric phoned to tell me that the Trust Deed was ready. The Charity Commissioners had accepted our four trustees. Sidney Melman, GLC Parks, had an alternative site for us and what was I doing idling my time away up north?

I made haste back and the first thing that met my eye was our new notepaper:

THE FUN PALACE

Architect Cedric Price
Chief Assistant Stephen Mullin
Quantity Surveyor Douglas Smith
Consulting Engineer Frank Newby
System Research Gordon Pask
Director Joan Littlewood
Administration Richard Bowdler
Trustees:

R. Buckminster Fuller

Lord Ritchie Calder
The Earl of Harewood
Joan Littlewood
Yehudi Menuhin

'We are now a certified Charitable Trust,' said Dick 'And where's this alternative site?'

'Hawley Road, Camden Town. Steve Mullin passes it every morning on his way to work,' said Cedric.

We went to have a look straight away. It was only a cock stride from the dreaded Round House, a huge mouldering building abandoned as a repair shop for railway engines and tried out as a theatre by Tony Richardson, Ken Tynan and other young hopefuls. You'd have to pull it down to get rid of the atmosphere of dirty engines that hung over it. Latterly it had become a resort for druggies and other unhappy citizens.

Melman's site was hardly inspiring – two patches of scruffy land, divided by a small road, with a railway bridge overhead.

'Awaiting development!' read Dick. 'Into what?'

Price wasn't nearly so pessimistic. 'How much land is there?'

'About two and a half acres,' said Dick. 'And there are problems.'

Our Arc seemed to enjoy problems. He applied for planning permission and set about solving them. First – the dividing road – a high-level bridge to unite the two plots, then an inflatable auditorium which could serve as a nursery school in the mornings, an old people's meeting place in the afternoons and in the evenings a theatre, cinema or concert and lecture hall. Acoustic baffles would control sound on the whole site. Equipment booths under a nylon canopy were for the use of primary and secondary schools during the day and at night an adult learning area with teaching machines. There was a children's play area – canopied – and an open-air classroom. The inflatable structures could be used by schools, technical colleges and institutes of further education to relieve the pressure on overcrowded classrooms and at weekends for entertainment. Mr Price was enjoying himself, adding overhead walkways, lavatories, a store for the inflatables, seats and electronic equipment.

A long, curved projection screen for cinema, multiple slide

shows and light projection would provide a changeable backdrop for dances and shows, movable cubes would offer privacy and serve as barriers.

I was still worried about noise. There were dwellings close by.

'Fifty per cent of the cost will go on acoustical control,' said Price.

Sidney Melman was very keen on our taking over, especially when he saw the designs. He even visited the local council. We gathered that he didn't get much change.

'You will win over the local citizens,' he told me.

So that was how I came to be taking the bus to Hawley Road on a wintry evening in 1965. I was heading for a meeting of the Hawley Road Tenants' Association. There wasn't a particularly friendly atmosphere in the small church hall. I'd brought some drawings and a plan, but nobody was very interested, they wanted to get on with the meeting. I explained the ideas behind the drawings, that the first consideration on this particular site was for the children – the very young, the schoolchildren and the teenagers. I said there was surely no need to harp on about the lack of facilities for training, for useful employment, the development of inherent talent. I did my best, confronted as I was by stony faces. Perhaps question and answer would work better, but instead of questioning me they just talked among themselves.

'A new attitude to time and space? What's she talking about?'

'I'll tell you what it's about, a lot of rowdies infesting the place day and night.'

'That's it. And they're supposed to be talking about a twenty-four-hour shift.'

'Thank Gawd I'm on nights.'

They'd heard some garbled version of the main project. I tried to explain the difference. I'd already told them that Hawley Road would be mainly a back-up for education. I explained the technique of noise control and how much the structures would enhance the appearance of the place. Everything was demountable and mobile, I told them, the whole site could be cleared in twelve hours, if necessary; except for the bridge, of course; that should remain, for safety's sake.

A philosopher on the front row interrupted me. 'If it's to be as pleasurable as you say, it's going to break the kiddies' hearts when you take it away.'

'Yes, if you're so clever,' it was the vicar's wife, 'why don't you come down here and give a hand with the youth clubs?'

'Because someone's making money out of this fun fair,' said the first speaker. 'That's the answer to that one.'

And so it went on, until the chairman decided to put the fate of Hawley Road to the vote. We were defeated, unanimously. No, there was one abstention.

'He was probably deaf,' said Dick Bowdler.

A report appeared in the *Hampstead and Highgate Express* on 12th February 1965. 'Parents, teachers and clergy in the parish of Holy Trinity, Chalk Farm, are alarmed,' it ran:

> 'Miss Littlewood's project would have the effect of destroying the existing church youth organisations, whose members would be weaned away and lost to church teaching,' said the vicar. 'I don't suppose the GLC will bother about that.'
>
> 'The building would attract the most undesirable type of rowdy and hooligan from other areas,' said an elderly resident.
>
> 'We have quite enough of our own to put up with,' his wife added.

A Mr Richard Perry of Nightingale Lane, SW12 wrote to the paper wishing me good luck and asking what the tenants of Hawley Road had, to be so precious about it.

Larry, the cartoonist, once drew me being burned at the stake by Newham Town Council. I took care to steer clear of the Hawley Road area after that meeting. We seemed to be up Shit Creek without a paddle. The only site the GLC had suggested was out. There was still no answer to our application for planning at Mill Meads. Nothing, not a sausage from the Silver Card Meet. Sidney Bernstein expressed great interest, but there wasn't a tinkle about investment.

A strong letter went to the GLC demanding an answer to our application for Mill Meads. In reply we were told we might expect a decision on 15th March 1965, but 15th March came and went, and there was no news. Sixteen days later we were informed that the decision had again been postponed. On 15th May Price gave notice of an appeal against the postponement, but I had already fled the country. On May Day I flew to Tunisia with Gerry. We had been invited to take part in an experiment at the Centre Culturel in Hammamet.

Sixty-two

To Hammamet, Tunisia, with Gerry, to teach as part of an International Summer School at Le Centre Culturel. We train Arabs and French students – a telegram from Dick Bowdler. Still no decision from County Hall – need cash. Interrupt work to return to London. Sign on for a commercial production. Cedric Price will appeal to the Minister regarding Mill Meads. Return to Hammamet. Twelve days later, the London County Council, now the Greater London Council, say Mill Meads needed for storm water tanks. That is not on, the land is scheduled Public Open Space. Our appeal will go ahead. Finish our training course at Hammamet.

We were met at the airport by Claude Planson and Beatrice Tanaka. It was Claude who had made us part of the annual Festival of Theatre in Paris. Beatrice had first seen us in 1953 on the Fringe of the Edinburgh Festival when she was a student. She was now a famous theatrical designer. As we rode, at breakneck speed, along the bumpy road to Hammamet, 'I shall run it as a cavalry commander,' said Claude.

'Which he was,' Beatrice added.

'What is it exactly?'

'A summer school,' said Beatrice.

'The first! The place has been kept alive by a Manchester man. Perhaps you know him, Gerry. Hourani, Cecil, very keen on music.'

'Didn't discover he was an Arab till he was twenty-eight,' said Beatrice.

'Lebanese,' added Claude. 'Supported Bourguiba at the end of the War, became his adviser.'

I was straining my eyes to see as much as possible of the strange countryside. Far to the right were the dark hills. Occasionally we passed a stall glowing with light, where pitchers and leather bottles were on display even at this late hour. Somewhere in that darkness there had once been sacrifices to Baal, the god of the Phoenicians – human sacrifice. By a stall brighter than the rest, we turned left towards the sea and drew up by an arch in a white wall. The door with its black studs swung open. We were in a lighted garden, fragrant with all the perfumes of Arabia.

'*Soyez les bienvenus,*' said a gentle voice.

'Monsieur Hedi,' said Claude introducing us. Then a tall, handsome man in Tunisian costume approached carrying a platter of couscous. Behind him, a young man in a white jacket with a dish of steaming vegetables and a third, black as the night, brought a basket of fruit.

'Grand Cheddli, Nouradinne and Aly Noir,' said Claude as they set our supper on a long table, gave a slight bow and vanished.

'Ah!' said Monsieur Hedi. 'Do you wish some wine?'

I looked round, but Gerry had disappeared. 'Yes, please,' I said tentatively, remembering at that moment that I was in the Prophet's world.

Gerry strolled back. 'Paradise,' he said, sniffing the air. 'I can smell orange blossom.'

We washed our hands quickly under the tap by the kitchen door and returned to find a bottle of red from Cap Bon and a small vase of eglantine by each place at the table. And Cheddli now had a flower behind his right ear.

Supper over, and time for bed, but Gerry couldn't wait to see the theatre. So Claude led us through a dark avenue where giant lilies shed a heady perfume and the sound of waves breaking on a calm shore grew nearer. We turned a corner and a concrete wall confronted us.

'Wait here,' said Claude.

A moment later, white light blazed across an amphitheatre. We moved into the arena, looking for the lions.

'We're by the sea, aren't we?'

'Ssh! So are the students' rooms.'

Gerry was examining the transformer switchboard. I discovered the projection box, built into the auditorium, and climbed to the topmost row of seats. In the moonlight I could see the dark towers of Hammamet.

'Where are the students from?' I asked as we walked back.

'Arab countries mainly, some from metropolitan France and her ex-colonies – a few odd ones.'

We slept in a white house by a white swimming pool, awoke with the dawn and the smell of woodsmoke. We grabbed two towels and ran straight down to the clear blue sea. The gardeners sitting round a small fire drinking tea looked rather startled.

Beatrice came to fetch us for breakfast. 'Georges Sebastien, a Romanian expatriate, designed everything here,' she said, 'except the theatre. That's René Allio's work.'

'The gardens are pure Arabian Nights,' said Gerry.

'Sebastien was more Arab than the Arabs and Hammamet the resort of world-famous sybarites. His lover died here and was buried somewhere in these grounds. Then he went away.'

'And now?'

'Lecturers from Russia, Poland, East and West Germany, Tunisia and one other from the UK – Peter Brook.'

Quite a cast, but my heart sank at the thought of all that verbiage. Thank God Gerry was taking the first session this morning. After breakfast I made off on my own, hardly noticing the tamarisk and oleander, the orange and lemon trees. I was contemplating escape when Gerry found me. I asked him how he'd got on.

'They wanted to know the whole history of Theatre Workshop. But you'd better get along; they're waiting for you.' They were sitting around in the sunny arena, notebooks at the ready.

'What do you think we should do first?' I asked, mainly to kill time.

'Say hullo,' said a thin, dark-haired boy.

'*Bonjour, madame,*' came the chorus.

'I think you should all introduce yourselves.'

'Well, I'm Raphael from Guatemala,' said the thin one. 'I'm Frederica from Poland.' 'Ollide from Marrakech, and that's my sister Léa.' They rattled off their names like schoolkids up for detention, except for one lone American who seemed to have finished up with us by accident. 'I'm Richard. I write music.'

'Wouldn't it be good to know more about each other? How

we came to be here? Where we come from? Perhaps where we're going?

'Well, I don't mind telling you that I'm going to be the best actress in Tunisia.'

'And in the past?'

'Don't let's talk about that.'

'Why not?'

'I want to forget it. School and parents. "Anissa! You're not concentrating! And Anissa! When are we going to find you a nice young man?"'

'And now?'

'Aly ben Ayed lets me work at the theatre and my parents don't approve at all.'

Zaaza butted in, a strong, broad-faced Tunisian, dying to talk about his happy boyhood among woods and streams and hidden wadis. He named every bud, every plant, every insect to be found there, and he knew how to trap a scorpion. About his future he wasn't too clear and he'd only come to Hammamet because two of his friends persuaded him.

I asked the rest what differences they'd noticed in the story-tellers' manner as the tenses changed. They hadn't noticed anything in particular.

'Watch carefully. Listen well.'

The stories went on, fascinating, some of them, but that was not the point.

'I know,' said Nidal from Lebanon. And she began to mime the difference, using a sort of Arabic gibberish. 'This is the past,' and she looked droopy and sighed, 'Here is the present,' and she was alert, as if about to dive, 'And here's the future.' Now she was the goddess carved on the ship's prow. Everybody clapped.

Richard looked lost. 'What am I doing here?' he said. 'I'm no actor. I was quite happy, lost at the airport, wondering where to go. I'd just seen my plane take off without me, when this forceful Frenchman kidnaps me and here I am. I know my past and future – music. Give me a piano and you'll never see me again.'

'But we want to,' said Frederica.

'Well said, Frederica.' This was Guy from Marseille. Without further introduction he began a long, rambling story, all on one note. Occasionally licking his lips and rolling his eyes, on and on he went. . . . I knew he was making it up as he went along; so, I think, did some of the others.

'We have to stop now, Guy. It's lunch-time.' There was a sigh of relief.

'Before we go,' I said, 'if you choose lies, you must be very clever. Everybody lies. Some of the most successful liars are con-men. Acting, too, is a special kind of lying and you'll have to study the minutiae of your rôle if you want to be convincing. Tomorrow I want you all to prepare a story. It's up to the rest to tell whether it's true or false.'

Lunch at the long table in the arbour with my new company was a babble of questions, jokes and wild suggestions. The afternoon was free for Gerry and me. A Russian lecturer had arrived and was giving a lecture on Stanislavsky. Gerry and I were being taken up into the hills by Cherif Khaznadar, a young Syrian director who knew where all the Roman sites in Tunisia were to be found and seldom returned from an expedition without a piece of turquoise Roman glass, a broken medallion or a fragment of pottery which would have been the envy of the British Museum.

The mornings began with exercises, first limbering up, then work on observation and memory.

'Make a wide circle. Throw this ball one to another. Now try the same scene – without the ball.'

They'd hardly got the hang of it before they started to play tricks and there were still details to be observed. . . . We'd try again the next day.

'Look at this tray.' And I'd whip off a cloth to reveal a collection of unusual objects. 'Note them quickly. You have only ten seconds.' Few remembered them all. 'We'll try that one each day.'

Blind Man's Buff? The blindfold one having to identify the people standing around him, with a light touch. Not on the face. 'Now move around everybody – quietly, don't speak.'

Soon they were up to their tricks again, the men faking breasts or baring their midriffs.

'All right. Now for space.' Each one found a doorway and stood there poised like the Vitruvius man. 'Lunge as far as you can reach, in every direction, try diagonals, high and low. Suggest a table plane surrounding you.' We touched every point of the compass we could reach without moving from the spot. I added music. Everyone invented a dance, some were comic, some silly, some graceful. They were all original.

'Have any of you brought musical instruments? This recorded stuff is not ideal.'

We leapt and twirled and almost flew about. We learned to identify the person walking behind us and named every sound we could hear.

Then to the imagination.

'Where shall we go today?'

'To the market,' said Karen, a Parisian girl.

'To the souk,' said Sarah, from Beirut.

'Yes, the souk!' the Arabs all agreed. We divided into two parties, shoppers and vendors, and tried it. The result was conventional and stagey. We definitely needed music. We tried with tambours and maracas. . . . It wasn't much better.

'Divide into three groups. Now, you people are the goods for sale. You must sing seductively to lure the shoppers. The vendors can sing a duo with you; you tell them what you are and what you're made of.'

This attempt was very funny until Mathilde, the black girl from Haiti, gave a shriek 'Aie! I'm frightened.'

'What's wrong?'

'I'm afraid she's going to eat me.'

'Why? What are you?'

'A salami sausage!'

I wanted to make use of the stories they had told on the first day. 'How would you like to dramatise your life stories?'

They looked lost.

'Improvise the dialogue, with partners of your choice. Then add songs, music, or poetry, if you're so inclined. Don't avoid critical friends, disagreement clarifies the argument. If you are sure you're right, stick to your guns, and let your critics play the opposition.'

They broke up into groups, but the arrangement didn't last long. Larger groups swallowed up smaller ones, who often wanted to be taken over. The French had the largest collection. Ollide and Léa, his sister, only wanted to work together. Richard was a loner. They all made off looking for a private place to work. Contact between groups was against the rules. I was allowed to visit, but not to comment. I had to cultivate a disinterested smile.

I crept up on the French first. They were arguing heatedly, throwing up bright ideas, then throwing them away without taking time to try them.

Zaaza was working in the woods with Mohsen and Mejhid, who came from a similar background. His story involved a lot of hiding and tree-climbing. They were in an enchanted wood where evil spirits lurked and they were young again.

It wasn't long, of course, before our golden rule was broken. I dropped in to see how the French were getting on: two were asleep, the rest were still arguing. As I was leaving, I only just managed to avoid someone crawling along behind the cactus hedge. I waited. The arguing ceased. The one who'd been approaching stealthily emerged.

'*Oui?*'

'*Formidables! Les Tunisiens sont formidables!*'

Spy business. And more came to light. Alain and Karen had chosen 'Chicago, Chicago, that wonderful town' as the theme song for their sketch. They'd heard Gerry sing it and approached him because they'd forgotten half the words. By the time this came to light he was producing their show, more or less.

A court of enquiry was set up. The French were let off, with a caution, and Karen pleaded so eloquently to retain Gerry that her wish was granted. This, I was sure, would cause no end of trouble. It did. From that time on any group needing special info could call on anyone they could get.

'We could do with a set of black tights,' said the French.

'Overruled.'

Life was fun, and often crazy. Jacques said he'd never laughed so much in his life. He was an orphan of the Blitz. As a child he'd been adopted by a French couple who found him wandering away from a burning ruin, too young to remember his name.

The morning session always finished in time for a swim before lunch. One day, as I plunged into the cool waves, Mill

Meads, our oasis in the desert of the East End, flashed before my
eyes. Planning permission? Our appeal against postponement? I'd
had no news and I'd long ago given up trying to get through to
London by phone. Talking drums would have been more reliable.
Cecil Hourani sent a cable from Tunis for me and received a reply
two days later. 'Decision on Mill Meads awaited. Meet pending.
Dick.'

I would have to be there and Gerry wanted to come with me.
He'd let the theatre to a new company; he had to check up on
them. Cecil and Claude were very understanding.

'You must come back,' said Claude as he handed us return
tickets.

Gerry was only too keen to come back. He'd fallen in love with
Tunisia and was considering the possibility of shooting Wole's *Lion
and the Jewel* there. I knew he wanted to steer me away from the Fun
Palace and a tempting offer which had been made to me before I
left. Tempting, not because I had the slightest desire to produce
conventional entertainment, but because the F.P. campaign needed
cash.

Peter Brook arrived just before we left for London and I warned
him against introducing any of his old-hat ideas while I was away.
In revenge, he swallowed a sheep's eye while we were at a Berber
wedding. I said it was only to put me down.

We arrived in London on 29th May. By 3rd June, Gerry was
back in Hammamet. He'd tuned up the admin at E15, given one
or two London wine importers a taste of Cap Bon (the French had
put an embargo on it since Tunisia became independent) and told
Tempting Offer that he wasn't offering me enough, and who was
writing the script?

I had found Dick in the doldrums. Mill Meads? We were
still waiting for a decision and we were losing a friend. Leslie
Lane was resigning as Director of the Civic Trust, 'The only
organisation concerned with the quality of life,' said Dick sadly.

'There'll be another good man in Leslie's place – and with
the four trustees we have now the GLC can't go on ignoring us.'

'We've no place for a Pilot.'

'I wouldn't say no to Hammamet,' and I told him about the
Centre. 'What's more, we're welcome there.'

'And Cedric's Palace? Sounds as if it wouldn't be needed in an Arab garden.'

'Perhaps you're right, but they've spoiled it with a crude amphitheatre. The Fun Palace is necessary anywhere.'

The Arc wasn't nearly so despondent. He just wondered how long it was all going to take.

'You're young,' I told him. 'And there's a cash injection coming. Only I must finish what I've begun in Tunisia.'

I phoned Tempting Offer and told him I accepted his proposition. He sounded happy enough, but was peeved when he heard that I had to return to Hammamet.

Zaaza was waiting for me at the airport, with Beatrice. It was good to see their smiling faces. Lectures were now in full swing.

'But I can't understand the ladies,' said Zaaza.

'They do have rather heavy accents,' said Beatrice. 'One's Czech, the other's Russian.'

'It's all about the great Moscow theatre. . . .'

'Peter Brook did at least try some improvisation and the German directors have arrived – one from the East, the other from the West, but they refuse to speak German, they will only talk to each other in French.'

Zaaza wanted to talk about his play and how it was developing. He'd persuaded Beatrice to help with the costumes. I made up my mind, then and there, to string all the students' contributions together and stage a grand finale to celebrate the first International Seminar at Hammamet.

At the Centre, Gerry was closeted with Cherif Khaznadar, the young Syrian, drinking *boukna* and arguing about lighting – and politics.

Next morning we swam early, as usual, but Mohsen was in the sea before us, washing his hair.

More lectures, so I escaped with Ollide and Léa. They wanted help with their story. We found a quiet spot by a marabout and they ran through a poetic duet, as delicate as they were, the fragile pair from Marrakech. By lunch-time I sensed a rift in the group. There was a changed atmosphere. 'I noticed an earring in your beard this morning. Whose was it?' 'Who was Marie France with last night?'

The two Lebanese girls, Sarah and Nidal, were sitting apart from the rest, chatting to each other in Arabic and laughing a lot. Nidal was such a beautiful girl, but she'd spent too much time in London, perfecting her English at RADA. There she had learned to sing 'There's a Hole in My Bucket, Dear Liza' and turn herself into a cross between a Bloomsbury peasant and a Chelsea Cleopatra.

'What's gone wrong?' I asked her.

'It's these poor Tunisians,' she said. 'The Lebanese are too affluent for them.'

'It's only jealousy,' said Sarah.

'Good. Then there's only one thing to do, make use of it. Play the invasion of Tunisia by the Phoenicians.'

Nidal laughed out loud. 'I'll be their leader.'

'We need a trireme,' said Sarah.

'We can make one. Beatrice will help us.'

Everyone helped and before long we had a walking boat, lifting over imaginary waves while the stout Tunisian defenders sang 'Tunisie Verte'. Richard, and Grand Cheddli on the drums, provided the battle music. All went well till Mounji, leader of the Tunisians, died a hero's death and Nidal, Queen of the Phoenicians, called for a truce. Reconciliation, hugging, embracing – a little too enthusiastic in some quarters – and a feast of Peace. Monsieur Hedi provided a *mechwe* and Mathilde tried to introduce a little voodoo into the proceedings and persuaded M Hedi to paint the goat she had provided, black. Revolt! Nobody was prepared to partake of a sacrificial goat!

Claude liked the idea of the finale, everybody was enthusiastic.

'Let's start with the café in Paris where we all met and decided to come here. *On y va?* I will write a song for the arrival in Tunisie,' said Frederica, '*Soyez les bienvenus parmi les chameaux.*'

'We've plenty to play,' said Nidal. 'It's a question of editing.'

'I want to play Malraux,' said Jacques, 'spreading culture.' Mohsen was giving a quite brilliant impersonation of Aly ben Ayed directing a play at the Tunisian State Theatre.

'I'll be a French lady doctor lecturing the Tunisians on birth control,' said Sarah.

'I'd like to finish my opera,' said Richard.

One unforgettable evening – it was the eve of the Prophet's birthday – we were working late in the arena; the afternoon had proved too hot. The Tunisians had been regaling me with stories of Aly ben Ayed's *Othello* and Maurice Béjart's ballet company.

'Don't you do anything that isn't of French or English origin? What was your grandfathers' entertainment?'

Jamil Joudi stepped lightly across the arena and looked up at the light tower where all the white moths of Tunisia were fluttering around.

'My grandparents,' he said quietly, 'they loved the Karragoz.'

There was an audible intake of breath. The Karragoz had been banned long since, but Joudi went on . . .

'Evenings in Ramadan . . . Shadow puppets, colours of wine and emeralds, golden oil, and hyacinth mauve. The finest leather stretched to transparency. The puppets dance, sing, speak, gesticulate, seen on a white sheet, stretched out like a cinema screen. There was this one family who had owned the puppets all their lives, and their fathers before them. They knew the old stories and dialogues and would relate them as they manipulated the puppets with long canes, but the best part was when, between times, they would improvise, mocking the rulers who oppressed the poor and the Jerbi who robbed them. The puppeteers themselves were poor. They were banned for their mockery.'

As Joudi spoke, some of the others gathered courage. One remembered half a phrase, another finished it, snatches of old songs came back to them. Mohsen remembered how even the wives and mothers were allowed to watch the puppets, 'after the evening meal of Ramadan,' Mounji added.

'Who were the Jerbi?' I asked.

'The grocers,' said Mounji.

Joudi remembered a satirical quip which once had all Tunisia laughing.

'Don't tell me about it, show it to me.'

'Joudi remembers it all,' said Zaaza.

'Give me a mat and a cushion,' said Joudi. 'Two cushions, I'm the Sumtsa. You are all coming to ask favours of me. You want something fixed? I'm your fixer.'

A ragged queue began to form. They pretended to be carrying gifts. A picture was emerging, a half-remembered scene was coming to life. They began laughing and prompting each other. I was watching buried treasure being unearthed. Joudi stretched out his hand . . . a Volpone.

Hardly a week passed before I was summoned to London again . . . crisis meet. A brusque interruption of my work at the Centre, but the F.P. was my breath of life. Nevertheless I would try linking all the scenes they'd worked on before I left. It would be a rough run-through, but we would learn a lot and they would know what to work on while I was away, and of course Gerry would be there. He was always a wise adviser. It was rough, but very exciting. If something went wrong, it became a joke.

We'd asked the villagers if they would like to attend – and quite a few turned up. At the end they clapped and shouted encouragement.

Each group of performers, intrigued by the accomplishment of the others, began congratulating and criticising, delighted and envious. That night a new element was born, competition.

It was on 13th June that I went back to London. The airport at Tunis was crowded with emigrants, waiting for the plane to Paris. Many of the women were carrying white bags, like pillowcases.

'What have you got in there?' asked Customs.

'Couscous,' was the invariable reply.

Dick was waiting for me at Heathrow. I thought it was lovely of him. Next day we faced up to the situation, with the Arc. Without a site no one would support us. We decided to take the problem to a higher authority. On 15th June a letter went to the Minister of Housing and Local Government from the Fun Palace Trust:

MILL MEADS, E15

As no decision has been received from Newham within the statutory period we are now appealing to the Minister.

Yours faithfully,

Cedric Price

A copy was sent to H.T. Woolcott, Associate Valuer at the GLC.

The first meeting of the trustees was to take place on 22nd June 1965. On the 21st I went with Cedric Price to see H.T. Woolcott at the County Hall. Afterwards Cedric wrote him a memo:

. . . I am concerned how little communication there has been between your department and those already in possession of information about the Fun Palace. Had we known that you were interested in detailed information on costing the Trust would have put your Department in direct contact with the Solicitor and Accountants for the Trust. . . . With reference to the Planning Appeal, I cannot recommend my clients to withdraw on the mere assurance that there will be negotiations with the GLC Engineers, since this is what I assumed, until very recently, had already been done.

There was no reply, so, twelve days later, Cedric Price phoned Woolcott to find out what was holding things up.

'Mill Meads is required for storm water tanks. There is no possibility of the tanks sharing the site with the Fun Palace.'

'Any use of the site by GLC Engineers will require the Minister's approval. Mill Meads is scheduled Public Space,' Price replied.

Woolcott suggested a meeting on site.

'The Trust has already expended several hundred pounds on engineers' and architects' feasibility studies. The appeal will go ahead.'

While at the County Hall we dropped in on our supporters, Sidney Melman, Peggy Jay and Sir William Fiske. Afterwards, we felt confident that the appeal would go in our favour. Dick wrote and told the trustees so. Next year Frank Newby would be digging the foundations.

Meanwhile, I couldn't stay. The young men and women in Hammamet were living for the evening of the finale. I took the next plane back.

During my absence Cherif Khaznadar had finished translating a

Babylonian text he'd brought with him from Syria. It was a poem with twelve couplets, each one dealing with a different phase of life, and presented as question and answer between servant and master. Everybody was talking about it.

'It has a beautiful rhythm, even in French,' said Nidal.

'We could stage it,' said Karen. 'Each couplet could be a scene.'

As we read the poem together I was reminded of *Don Juan* – Tirso de Molina's *Don Juan*. The Moors had been in Spain for seven hundred years – the Babylonian text might easily have been carried there and lived on.

The Centre was a hive of activity, exercises together, then each group to their hideaway to work? Play? They had become one. Mathilde, our belle from Haiti, was sitting on her own.

'What's wrong?'

'I don't want to be treated as a student.'

'But, daughter, we are students all our lives.'

She wasn't impressed. It takes a long time to overcome insecurity.

'You are a shaman,' said Claude. 'Even the intellectuals enjoy your games.' I thanked him. 'It makes a change,' I told him.

'These intellectuals! They're not used to enjoying themselves.' That last I said to myself.

I had to return to London for one more day. At last Dick had managed to assemble the other four trustees. We came together for the first time, friendly and optimistic. Dick handed fifty pounds to each of us, the sum demanded by law when a trustee enters upon his duties. We drank to the Fun Palace and surveyed our future hopefully.

I hadn't been afraid to leave my young team at Hammamet. They were confident now and could paddle along without Mother Duck. Soon we would have to leave them in any case. The blessed hours at Hammamet would be over.

Despite the excitement of preparing for our first and last night – the costume fittings, mostly improvised, music rehearsals, likewise, and the frantic search for props – we found time to go round the village and invite everybody to our *sambra*. It was the only word we'd found for songs and dances by moonlight, and when the great night came, postponed for twenty-four hours because the Minister who was coming from Tunis couldn't make it, excitement was bubbling over. The sight of the villagers entering the gardens with quiet dignity calmed us, the women swathed in white up to their noses, some wearing their luminous sandals in honour of the occasion. They were greeted by Hedi and his team, chose their seats and waited to see what Allah would send them.

Perhaps it was Anissa's story which really broke the ice. She herself had such warmth and joy in her that almost at once she had the audience laughing and giving her advice. At Zaaza's spooks some acted being frightened, others laughed and made ghostly noises. But the invasion of the Phoenicians had the young ones on their feet. Some joined in singing 'Tunisie Verte', others just shouted, 'Tunisia!' like fans at a football match. This was their world, their language, their place and I hoped it would always be so.

The French section gave us several sketches. One poked fun at the telephone system with Jacques Baillon as a happy Tunisian electrician, fixing the wires so that he could have a prolonged flirtation with his girlfriend while everyone else went mad, shouting their number. Very funny until Madame Hourani told me that the important politician who'd arrived was the Minister for Telecommunications.

Raphael, from Guatemala, drove the latest fast sports car (two plastic seats from broken chairs) across the Atlas mountains, with music and Regula, our Swiss Miss, by his side. They had an accident on the edge of the desert – 'Well, Joan wanted a happening.'

For her story, Sarah Salem chose the French song with 'Dominique-nique-nique' for chorus. Claude wanted to suppress it. He thought the word sounded like something rude in Arabic, but Sarah assured him he was wrong and won the day. Her story was quite charming.

Joudi's version of the Karragoz caused some raised eyebrows in the front row, but the audience loved it and hissed the wicked Sumtsa. Joudi was a marvellous actor and feared neither praise nor blame. I hope his courage and that superb performance helped to revive the shadows and their satirical comments. The old ban must have dated from darker days.

Our finale was unique: performers and audience alike were happy as children and when a love song in Arabic brought the *sambra* to a close, the audience called for music and everybody got up to dance, even the Minister.

The music died away and our guests departed. Gerry and I strolled back to the supper table where all our young stars were waiting for us. As we approached we were greeted with a round of applause. There had been so much pleasure, little pain, much joy but some sadness; only tonight was perfect. It would be hard returning to our problems in England.

Before leaving we gave a party for everybody including the team who had cared for us and spoiled us, Grand Cheddli, Jeune Cheddli, Nouradinne and Black Aly and of course Monsieur Hedi. I would have liked to kidnap them all and smuggle them back to England in my luggage, but I don't think they would have been happy there.

Sixty-three

Gerry visits Nigeria – proposes filming The Lion and the Jewel
*in Tunisia. My 'commercial' production, a non-existent script. The
composer's wild suggestions – a mixed cast – the choreographer and
George Cooper. I quit. My successor fares badly. Newham against
the Fun Palace. The Greater London Council for their storm tanks,
which were never built. We withdraw our appeal to the Minister for
fear of endangering the whole Lea Valley Bill, which is to go before
parliament. Deadlock. Gerry and Joan return to Tunisia, our only
Fun Palace, for the second year's programme.*

I n London I had to try and forget Hammamet. Gerry wanted to
live there, but first to visit Wole in Nigeria and suggest filming
his *Lion and the Jewel* in Tunisia. Wole was fussy about locations.
I had to face that Tempting Offer.

'You can't go back to theatre, Joan,' said a close friend.

I knew I couldn't, but I needed money desperately; the Fun
Palace couldn't be allowed to die for lack of a few quid. I signed
on and took an advance.

The very next morning I regretted it. I found I was under
contract to one or two good songs and no script, not even the
outline of one. Where was his secretary? The one who'd adapted
the book for his last 'sure-fire' success. He couldn't have found
backing with nothing. I knew I had a reputation for salvaging any
old thing, but I needed something to go on, if only an outline.
Worse still, our composer had undergone some sort of sea-change
since I'd worked with him. Success and other drugs had persuaded
him that he could do anything, including playing poker. A series of
all-night sessions set in – poker, not work.

'We're starting rehearsals next week. We need a script.'

'Okay. I'll play in the daytime and work all night.'

So I'd turn up with a pad and a stylo and find him at the
card table unable to tear himself away and losing, night after

night. There were three with him, dab hands at the game. One had been schooled in the Merchant Navy, another was a Tin Pan Alley sheikh who could play any game and the third, a con-man of course. Each morning one or other of them would send a note round, claiming what he was owed.

'How are you going to pay all that?' I asked one morning. 'With dolly mixtures?'

'I'll cut him in on the show. He's good at gags, used to write the best soap opera in the States.'

So this sharp poker player was introduced to the backers as part author. If they'd checked they would have found that he'd never written any soap opera and, as for his gags, the only one I ever heard went something like this: 'There's a man out there . . .' (declaimed with arm outstretched). The rest was lost. Somehow it got lost for ever.

First rehearsal. The usual smiles and kisses and high hopes all focussed on the genius, who lapped it up. He'd rowed in some of his favourite performers, so had I. They mixed like oil and water, but I hoped to overcome that as time rolled by. There wasn't much to read so the Musical Director played the songs to us. Next day and from then on we'd try to invent some fill-in between the numbers and the composer would arrive later and later. I felt like asking for my cards, but I'd taken their money and it was being spent. I'd have to earn it.

The second week – wild suggestions and dark glasses. 'Give him a fork-lift truck for his entrance.'

'You want to lose the mediaeval setting?'

Next day: 'I got an idea. Bring him in on a trapeze.'

'It'll take some time for the actor to master trapeze work.'

Idea abandoned, but a new tack. 'Those dolly birds [the chorus] should have everything they want.'

'Sure.'

Luckily he was due for a massage and didn't want to miss it, so we got on with the job, but he came back and changed everything. Time was getting short. It was an expensive show and the constant intervention was upsetting everybody. 'For God's sake, stay away,' I told him. 'Give us a chance to put something together.'

He went. We made some progress. At night I'd work at home,

noting the day's advance. It was anything but inspiring, half the cast were not used to inventing their lines.

One day I walked in to a dance rehearsal to see why the choreographer was taking up so much of our time and there was George A. Cooper, one of the artists I'd brought with me, a superb actor, lying on the floor, flat on his belly, while some chorus boy held him down with a foot on his neck.

'What the hell's going on?' No answer.

'George is playing a character respected by friend and foe alike. You are destroying George as well as the part he is playing. Cut it.' George got up and walked away.

Abraham Sofaer once asked his director, 'Am I playing the king in your production, dear boy?'

'But of course.'

'Then do you think you could stop these plebeians pushing and shoving me around?'

I had thought that with George and a few others we could get the better of this travesty of show business. We could not. At the end of the week, on the Saturday, I planned our first run-through. The composer got wind of it somehow and blew in to watch. To my amazement, it wasn't bad. It needed polishing and a few bright gags, but left alone we could have brought it off.

'About time I took over,' he said. Well, that was it! He wanted it to be his show entirely. . . .

'I'll be in Thursday.'

'It's all yours.'

That would crown it, I knew it, but it would be a relief to get away. George saw the show in, but left soon after me. My successor fared no better than me. When the composer had finally antagonised everybody, he was forbidden to attend rehearsals, but it was too late, the show was stillborn.

The only bright star in the set-up was Barbara Windsor, who gave a party for the cast to cheer them up.

When I returned, empty-handed, to my Fun Palace team, there were some long faces, but nothing to compare with the body-blow we received on 7th December 1965. A letter came from the GLC, well padded with verbiage. Newham (formerly West Ham) had, at last, come clean and voiced their doubts about *The Pilot Fun Palace project at Mill Meads*:

> It would attract large numbers of people from a wide area. The site was remote from public transport, access by public highway would be inadequate, improvement to the road pattern could have no priority. Remedial measures would be impractical and unjustified in view of *the temporary nature* of the project and the prior claims of other improvements.
>
> This site was procured nearly a hundred years ago by the Metropolitan Board of Works for main drainage purposes and was now urgently needed for storm sewage tanks and a pumping station. The new works must be constructed and in use by 1st April 1975. There is no other practicable alternative location, whereas the Fun Palace is not tied to the site or the locality.

The project was the Fun Palace at Mill Meads. It had never been referred to as a 'pilot'.

No reference is made to the mobile character of the Fun Palace. Was it not understood that the structure would be composed of prefabricated items requiring merely site assembly, which would take four to six weeks? Removal? Ten to fourteen days. The Fun Palace could be re-used elsewhere, thus long-term proposals for the site would not be jeopardised.

Theatre Royal, Stratford E15, is scarcely two miles from Mill Meads. The Fun Palace is a logical development of the work I had undertaken in the borough since 1953 and which, despite neglect and antagonism, had 'put Stratford E15 on the world map', according to their own brochure, published in 1992.

Today in 1993 there is no sign of storm sewage tanks, a pumping station or any other structure so urgently needed twenty-eight years ago. But then, Thomas North must have been a busy man. He hadn't even managed to find time to look at the plan of Ronan Point before it collapsed.

Newham also pointed out that 'however well the *building* was sound-proofed, the adjoining tenants would suffer some nuisance from the users and from the large car park that would be necessary'.

They might have taken into consideration the nuisance the Fun Palace might suffer from the adjoining tenants. When we moved into Theatre Royal, E15, we were pillaged and robbed, our wardrobe and stores broken into regularly, precious costumes and irreplaceable scripts destroyed. Any member of the audience parking a car in the vicinity of the theatre would be set upon by youthful blackmailers. Only constant vigilance saved us from being destroyed by fire as Hephzibah Menuhin's premises were at Bethnal Green. The local authorities had no solution. There was only one way. Educate the 'young savages' who, for the most part, could neither read nor write.

Carole Christensen, company secretary, evolved a system of teaching English with a typewriter and worked with local illiterates in her spare time. Harry Greene had always found out where the stolen goods were cached and invariably he recovered them.

The young savages were allowed into the theatre, if they behaved themselves. Saturday sessions were specially designed for them and took place behind locked doors. Incriminating truths often came out and I didn't want the children betrayed. Street kids are often called 'unsavoury elements' by the proper ones. Treated as such ourselves for so long, perhaps we understood them. Perhaps that was why we wanted to cater for them in the Fun Palace.

By 1975 our savages were designing and running their own festivals.

I n reply to the Price memo of 15th June 1965, the Ministry of Housing and Local Government proposed County Hall at ten thirty on 22nd March 1966 for the inquiry.

By 20th December 1965, no detailed designs for the storm water tanks at Mill Meads had been carried out. Nevertheless, when Mill Meads became the subject of an inquiry, the split between the GLC (Engineers) and the Lea Valley Development would be seized on by the press and bad publicity might endanger the passage of the Lea Valley Bill through Parliament. After a good deal of soul-searching we decided, in the public interest, to withdraw our appeal, and issued a press release to that effect.

Public-spirited? Or defeatist? Either way the Lea Valley Bill passed its first and second reading in the House without any mention of the Fun Palace.

'The only move you can make now is a petition to the Lords,' said Lou Sherman. 'You, Tom Driberg and Ian Mikardo should convene a gathering of councillors from Waltham Forest, Hackney and Haringey. You need back-up. It's no use bothering about Newham. You should never have settled there in the first place; half the councillors are members of the Transport and General Workers Union and the rest are Catholics. What can you expect?'

It struck me I'd have to stage a war of the councils as soon as the Fun Palace was functioning.

'So we've got to start all over again?'

'Yes.'

Robin Hope, our solicitor, agreed: 'Withdraw gracefully and find somewhere else.'

'Go through that charade again?' said Cedric Price. 'Four years of it. If someone came forward with the offer of a piece of land we might be interested, but they'd have to go down on their bended knees.'

So, all that was left of 'the world's step forward', 'the twentieth-century safety valve' was a model falling apart in Cedric's office and a collection of files already gathering dust. The pilot schemes too were falling apart. The design didn't fit the rule book. It wasn't a stadium. It wasn't a theatre, nor even a circus. A new attitude to free time? What's that?

The only place opening its arms to us was Tunisia. Hammamet wanted more; and after all it wasn't so far away. Dick Bowdler was willing to come and take a look. Even Camel was interested, and Gerry Feil, whom we'd met through Peter Brook.

There were lemons on the trees, narcissus and bougainvillea blooming everywhere when we came back to Hammamet.

Many of last year's students were returning, bringing friends and colleagues. Perhaps this year we could venture on a story which had never been told: 'The Adventures of Youssef, in the city where the streets are paved with gold.'

There was some magic in that place. Before we sat down to eat, someone started thrumming a guitar – and we were dancing.

Olé!

M Hedi hadn't finished welcoming us before he was dancing too. Cries of delight, such as you only hear in Arabia, greeted every newcomer. Cherif, bringing in his new young wife Françoise with their baby son; Latifa and Nadia stepping forward lightly with bowls of fresh, green salad and Grand Cheddli, grinning from ear to ear as he set down a giant fish, bedded in twigs of fennel and parsley. '*Le loup de la Mediterranée*,' he said.

Olé!

'My partner, Juan José,' said Raphael. 'He lives for his guitar.'

'What are we doing this year?' asked Nidal, who'd been the first to arrive.

'I thought of a quest,' I said, my mouth full of the delicious fish.

'To the end of the rainbow,' said Latifa, a new face.

'To happiness.' That was Anissa, looking prettier than ever. 'We know the whole world between us. . . .'

'Don't forget Spain,' added Raphael. 'We're going to the moon. We've our own system.' And he placed his fists one on top of the other, one *curé*, one general, one politician.

'Make it an Arab quest,' Zaaza spoke up quite firmly.

'That would mean he'd have to go to France,' Joudi reminded him.

'The *emigré* tourist!' That was Alain.

'There is the France of the *bidonvilles*,' said Cherif. But Nidal didn't know what a *bidonville* was.

'What it says, a *ville*, or rather a collection of shelters, improvised with *bidons*, that is large petrol cans, and necessarily *sans* sanitation.'

'Without water?' Sarah asked.

'The children queue with buckets, to draw water at the hydrants.' Cherif had obviously visited one of these places.

'What sort of people live there?'

'Poor Arabs, *immigrés*. They're not welcome in France. Every now and then the police bulldoze their shelters, flatten them into the ground. So they move on and make another *bidonville*.'

'Is that really true?'

'Next time you're in France, see for yourself,' said Cherif. 'They'll be difficult to find. Neighbours will deny their existence, though three and a half million Arabs live in them.'

'Don't let's make it sad,' said Anissa.

'Of course not, life's never altogether sad. Now I fancy a truck-driver's life. They seem to stay cheerful.' That was Alain, our roving Romeo from Picardy. 'Want to be my mate, Jean Daniel? Some travelling music, maestro, please.'

Juan José struck up a wild flamenco and, seizing a chair, Alain jumped into his dream lorry, shouting to Jean Daniel in Parisian slang never heard before on any stage, and driving bang into the table.

'Mind the cloth, Alain,' said Sarah.

'The snowy heights of the Pyrenees, you mean,' said Jean Daniel. 'We *are* in Spain, are we not? On our way. . . .'

'You seem ready to go, all of you.' Chorus of assent.

'But first we must tune up. It looks as if some of us have been letting ourselves go. Musical scales, movement scales. *On y va!*'

After lunch our hero was born and grew up fast. Those who'd been through it told us about *permis de séjour, permis de travail.*

'Permits to live,' said Juan José.

'Is our hero a Tunisian?' That was Mejhid.

'Why not a Spaniard, poor but honourable, like me?' said Raphael.

'An Algerian,' said Abdel Kader. 'We are the true heroes of the Arab world. We fought Imperial France and won. Fair play.'

'I would love to call him Pépé le Moko,' said Nadia. 'After my hero.'

'Make it Pepito and I'm yours, Nadia.'

'Well, for your cheek alone, you can have him, Raphael. So you'd better get busy and invent his village background.'

At that Juan José took over and we all did our best as Spanish peasants, much like any other peasants, I supposed. I made my mark by singing 'Fuente Ovejuna'.

When Juan José was satisfied, we all stood together to wave Pepito goodbye. God speed. Good luck.

Anissa was still worried about it being sad.

'Don't be so soft, Anissa,' said Alain. 'We're coming along in our truck in a minute, and we'll smuggle him over the border among our onions.'

So far so good. But next day everyone was clammering for a *bidonville*; so we had to find out more about them. We combed the village with some success. Nidal returned with a battered photograph of one and Joudi found out that Tunisian people settled with fellow townsfolk, so that even among the petrol cans there was a Sfax, a Nabeul, an Enfidaville, just as there is here at home. We piled up boxes and cans, anything we could find, and tried to imagine living in such a place.

'They barricade themselves in,' said Cherif. We needed sheets of corrugated iron and doors salvaged from demolished houses.

'Can't we have a *sambra*, like last year?' that was Anissa.

'We've got to get the background right first,' said Jacques Baillon, who was more serious than ever.

It took days to get the *bidonville* to ring true and when we were more or less satisfied, one of the characters, played by Zaaza, decided to invite three of his neighbours in to play cards, but his wife Latifa got very cross because they'd nothing to offer guests. She was so cross that Juan José came in with his guitar and played everyone into such good humour that suddenly we were tired of the *bidonville*. We were back in Tunisia, not sad any more, but singing. And so Anissa got her *sambra*.

Nidal stood up on her own and, in beautiful classic Arabic, began singing a story from the *Arabian Nights*. As the story unfolded, one by one we became part of it. She sang the naughty wife of a besotted husband. Every time he left the house a different lover would appear, and every time her husband returned she would quickly conceal the lover till she had quite a collection, each one in a different hideaway. Finally she was caught in the act and the lovers revealed themselves, formed a circle round the poor husband and sang an Arabic Ring o' Roses – or perhaps I should say, Ring of Jasmine.

'There's nothing funny about French bureaucracy,' said Jacques, as we moved on to the next scene. The *permis de séjour*.

'We can try.'

First, we went for the obvious and rubber-stamped everybody and everything but that didn't work. It just descended into horseplay.

Next, we filed everybody; but that was no good either. Jacques grew impatient and went berserk. He improvised a pair of pince-nez with twigs – mounted a rostrum and hurled abuse at everybody. He made us sit in rows, sharpen quill pens, dip them in ink, the right hand poised in the air until he gave the word. He was a monster of clerical exactitude, and drilled us into shape, a demon departmental boss in a Gogol nightmare. He hated everybody, not just Arabs and Jews, but Negroes, Indians, Chinese and Polynesians. He hated *all* outsiders and we had to enter their names and particulars in imaginary ledgers . . . fast!

Finally, to release us from his tyranny I called for music – luckily we had a piano now and the scene dissolved into Chopin – and a gently satirical dance of bureaucrats.

'Just when I was enjoying myself,' said Jacques. 'I never realised before that "players" meant just that – people playing.'

We'd jumped to the bureaucrat but we'd forgotten to get our hero to Paris. We had to go back. It was easy to make a boulevard or a Paris square. Motor horns would do. Just motor horns and infuriated drivers. '*Allez! Allez! Depêchez vous!*' cried Nadia. 'Beggars! Look at them! They just wander the streets like sheep. Sheep! Sheep!'

Poor Pepito, poor Juan José – they were only trying to cross the Place de la Concorde.

We had the empty arena of the theatre for décor and Jacques, now in thoroughly sadistic mood, invented a copper and accosted our two heroes, who'd managed to trap a pigeon and were hoping, at last, to eat.

'What have you got there?'

'An old roofer, officer.'

'And what are you doing with those twigs?'

'Making a fire.'

'What for?'

'To roast her.'

'Whom?'

'Jeanne d'Arc,' said Raphael, then, turning to the rest of us:

'We saw how to ride the Métro, without paying. You jump over the barrier, fast. José tried playing his guitar down there, but we were chased off. We rode the train to Billancourt. Up, up on your feet all of you.' Raphael chivvied us into a huddle. 'Let's show Nidal what it's like.' And he pushed everybody into a space no more than six feet by four feet. I could scarcely wriggle my way out.

'Here we go!' He mimed the doors closing and the rest swayed and lurched with him till they came to their imagined destination and there, they broke loose and belly-danced. Someone cried, 'There's the river,' and began to run. The rest pretended to bathe, to launder their clothes till Mohsen turned and cried, 'I'm for the real sea!' and made for the beach. Everybody followed and, keeping the character they'd invented, ran towards the cool waves.

Gerry wanted to speak Arabic this year. He'd taken a crash course in London and Sarah and Nidal heard him through his verbs each day. 'He's already better than the British Consul, who's been here since Independence,' said Nidal, but Gerry only wanted to talk to the locals in their own language. One day, soon after we first arrived, some poor people saw us passing and invited us into their home and up on to their roof, to watch the sun setting, and we hadn't enough Arabic to thank them properly.

'Once you leave the main road they don't understand a word of French,' he said. Now he could enjoy himself wandering round the village inviting everybody to join us at the Centre.

In ones and twos, they began to walk in, attracted by Juan José's music. They loved anything Spanish – the music, the dances – a race memory, perhaps, from the days when the Moors ruled Spain?

Soon the children appeared, shy at first, but intrigued. I was reminded of good times on the road, playing the villages in South Wales or Lancashire – with me minding the kids in the vestibule of the village hall – a procession coming to meet us in Bacup with fresh bread from the Co-op bakers, the old weaver pressing sixpence into my hand: 'For the theatre of the people.'

We hadn't sold out for money or glory, that wouldn't have been much fun. In Tunisia, I must admit, we ate regularly and well. So did our young colleagues, from poor homes, most of them, only two or three were comfortably off and they tended to throw away riches speaking English or French in preference to Arabic. Last year I'd told the two girls from Lebanon so. This year I was delighted to hear them speaking beautiful Arabic. They'd been delving into the history of their language.

As for our quest, after a good deal of trial and error we had a story. We called it *Who is Pepito?* It was a story without an end, except for the rejoicing at the end of each performance, when the stage would fill with men and women, questioning, or correcting, then dancing and singing with us.

Sixty-four

*Tunisia wants publicity for Le Centre. A well-known English
critic comes to see our work, says that England shouldn't let us
go. One more try in London. The Millwall Tenants' Association
give us their blessing, but we have nowhere to go. The* Evening
Standard *publishes the story. One bit of land is free, the debris
round the Theatre Royal, Stratford, left by the developers. We clear
it, Institute Learn-and-Play with local children and lost teenagers. We
have festivals, a zoo, a riding school, in defiance of Local Authority.
We call it 'Stratford Fair'.*

C ecil Hourani wanted the world to know about the Centre,
which had been his. The Tunisian newspapers had written
about Hammamet but when I heard that he'd sent to London
for a theatre critic, I shrank. 'Not here, too.'

The critic came. I disappeared. He was from one of the
Sunday papers. Soon everyone knew there was a stranger in the
house. I didn't want judgement on *Pepito*. I'd aimed to avoid 'What
did he think of us?' and the fizz of 'the first night', especially as the
show changed every night, sometimes radically. Too often I'd seen
spontaneity die, faced with destructive criticism.

'Could you draw or paint with a critical eye looking over
your shoulder? Or even a friendly eye?' I wasn't in the business
of setting up a smooth first night, invention frozen and canned
for export. Give me initiative and imagination, so powerful when
released, for evil or for good.

Our story often flowed over the physical limits of that amphitheatre, to the seashore, the dark woods or the gardens. You could
follow, if you felt inclined, or stay and guess what was happening
elsewhere. In any case the play would continue in several places
at once. The performers had been brought up on curtain theatre,
inherited from the nineteenth century. I was trying to recreate
some of the atmosphere of the mediaeval miracles and mysteries,

mobile, ubiquitous, knowing the onlookers would follow wherever they went.

Our public in Hammamet was greeted at the entrance by musicians; the Maison Blanche was open and lighted for those who preferred to listen to a lecture on classical music or just dispute; paintings by artists, Tunisian and French, were hung in the arbour. We hadn't yet managed closed-circuit television, mobile telephones, tomorrow's games, all that would come.

I knew that the visiting critic would be after a different story – the merits and demerits of the production by 'Littlewood in exile', especially after the clang with which the 'sure-fire success' had hit the deck. I wanted to protect my Arab fledglings from all that.

I'd tried in England – I hadn't succeeded but there came a time when word-of-mouth filled the house at Stratford E15, not the critics.

As sunset faded, our musicians struck up their *bienvenue*. That was it. Now I could do nothing to sustain the show. The performers were on their own. The journalist was already seated in the middle of the amphitheatre, on the third row, watching us disperse to our starting posts. The quest begins. The villagers scythe the corn – guitar music – Pepito passes, waving goodbye. I eyed the journalist now and then, surreptitiously. He looked quite kindly, but his eyes were fixed on where the curtain theatre would be, if we had a curtain. I hadn't buttonholed him to explain our approach; I'd left him to enjoy the delights of Hammamet, the sea, the sky, the good companionship. . . .

'Farewell, *Pepito*. Goodbye. God speed.'

Pepito ambled along. These youngsters had not succumbed to first-night fever. It was unbelievable. After a while I wandered off. I wanted to see how the gipsy encampment on the beach was faring. So relieved that our quest was happily launched that I sat down and gazed at a sky crowded with stars. The sea was wild, a few Berbers were cooking kebabs over a wood fire. It was Joudi and some of his gang: having finished their first *Pepito* contribution, they thought some of the audience might be hungry.

It wasn't till I heard the music for the finale that I returned to the arena. The critic had gone. Gerry, as if we were still at E15, had escorted him to the supper table. He'd probably be retired by now, writing his piece for London. But no, he was standing there, waiting for me.

'It was as perfect, of its kind, as anything you've done,' he said. I thanked him, but he went on praising me and said he was surprised by the audience reaction.

'I don't think that varies much with this type of entertainment, especially as they were hearing their own language tonight, not the classical Arabic usually used in Tunisian theatre.'

He said he was sorry about the Fun Palace.

'What about it?'

'The papers are saying that it's . . . well . . . finished.'

'It certainly isn't. Even tonight was part of it. They haven't understood what it's all about in England. Do they really prefer geranium beds and benches for the dogs to piss against? The Fun Palace is yet to come. If not in England, somewhere. It's a twentieth-century plaything: like a soap bubble, bright with colour, but not meant to last. Like us. Like our art.

'There is machinery which prevents the export of works by Rembrandt and Rubens. There should be some way of rescuing for Britain the art you have given, so superbly, to Hammamet.'

It was a gracious compliment. What a pity that, even tonight, he'd missed part of the fun, conditioned, like my young artists, to Palladio's theatre. Some of my Pied Pipers had gone into the woods, some to the Maison Blanche, some to the shores of the Mediterranean.

'You'd better draw your horns in,' said Gerry as we sat in the plane to London. 'You've spent all your money and most of mine. There's no more available. Settle down to what you know you can do. All this other is a dream.'

Okay. He was right. He'd won.

But when we got back home, there was a letter from the Millwall Tenants' Association for me. They wanted to see me. Millwall? The riverside . . . the Isle of Dogs. There were gardens there with the best view of Greenwich Palace to be had. Was the tide turning? At last.

I was received politely. The chairman led me to the dais. The small hall was quite crowded. These were people who, for many years, had been fighting the GLC for better housing and transport. Go easy now, Joan, I said to myself. They had heard about the Fun Palace . . . rumours, I supposed. There was quite a buzz when I was announced.

'Who called this meeting?' 'There's been a lot of talk.' 'What's all this about Glengall?' 'Glengall? We've been trying to have a park there for eight years.' 'That's right, there's nowhere for the kiddies to play.' 'Never mind a park; what about a few buses?'

I dived straight in, made no bones about my intentions and the urgent need for new solutions. A tough old docker heckled me: 'Sounds to me as if you're going to encourage a parcel of whores about the place.'

'They don't need the Fun Palace,' I told him.

'You seem to have plenty of money all of a sudden,' said a lady councillor. 'We've been allowing your theatre a hundred pounds a year for some time. Sounds to me as if you could give us some for a change.'

'There's government money for schemes such as this,' I told her. 'It has educational value. Of course it's your money; you've paid it over in taxes, but I can tell you that every country in Europe spends more on culture than we do.'

'I've nothing against culture,' said the tough oldie, 'so long as you don't touch our bowling green.'

I gave him my word and talked on, simply and directly, telling them about my fears for the next generation. 'Popular education is declining and so is government planning. We cannot afford to waste human talent. There is unexplored talent in each child. Let's get our priorities straight.' I appealed to them as citizens of a land where once untaught artisans had challenged the state and won, where once England had led the world in science and technology.

When I stopped the chairman looked straight at me. 'Well, Joan,' he said, 'I came here to tear you and this fun affair to pieces, but you've got something. Maybe your movement will bring us transport and better housing. I reckon we should back you up, fight for you like we've been fighting for that bridge down the road. Not that we can see much sign of it yet, though. Nevertheless, you yourself, personally, will always be welcome on this island. . . .' (He meant the Isle of Dogs, not Great Britain. I wasn't often made welcome there.)

Before declaring this meeting closed, he went on, 'I propose to present you with those sentiments in the form of a motion: "That we, the citizens of Millwall, members of the Tenants' Association, thank the speaker for coming here to address us and assure her of our support in her worthy mission." Those in favour? . . . Those against? . . . The ayes have it.'

I even got a few claps and my supporters were vociferous.

'You want to get 'old of the Bog,' said one, as I moved around saying good night.

'The Bog? You mean the mud chutes . . .?'

'The allotments by the mud chutes, he's trying to say.'

'If you think the PLA will let 'er get anywhere near those mud chutes, you're barmy,' said the first speaker.

'Did 'e say the PLA? I'll tell you what this 'ere Port o' London lot will give you. Bugger all. You go for Samuda Wharf, gel.'

'Samuda? Cutler, you mean.'

Well, I'd enough to go on. The very next morning I phoned the PLA, not for the first time. . . .

'Land? There's no land available. None at all.'

So that was that!

On 3rd March 1966, the *Evening Standard* published the following article by Judy Hillman:

> London's hopes for a Fun Palace have become exceed-ingly slim. Plans for this new type of mobile, tempo-rary centre have progressed well . . . but now Joan Littlewood's scheme has nowhere to go.
>
> A site was earmarked in the proposed Lea Valley regional park at Mill Meads, Stratford East. It is owned by the GLC, who were quite helpful. Now, however, its own engineers want part of it for future extensions to the Northern Outfall sewage works.
>
> There was to have been a public inquiry later this

month so that the Minister of Housing could decide on the strength of the two claims – public health v. public pleasure. The Fun Palace trustees have just withdrawn their appeal. 'It is felt that it would be unfortunate if the GLC were to appear at the public planning inquiry in opposition to even a part of the proposals for the Lea Valley regional development, since this might tend to encourage other objections and even prejudice the passage of the Bill,' the trustees comment. . . . They feel that the GLC is the only real hope of getting the whole Lea Valley project off the ground.

The Fun Palace has its supporters at the GLC, but if the GLC were to fight the Fun Palace at an inquiry, other people might gird themselves against other proposals for the river playground. And it might then end up drastically emasculated with a couple of paths for cyclists and the odd lick of paint on lock gates.

What exactly has gone wrong? Mr Cedric Price, the architect, first applied for planning permission to West Ham in the autumn of 1964. Nothing happened. With the changeover of Local Government last April it was passed to the GLC, who decided it was none of their business and it went back to the new borough of Newham.

They wanted to be sure that it really came within their aegis. And did it hold more than two and a half thousand people? Was it a sports stadium? The trouble was that the Fun Palace was new and it did not really fit the rule book.

In the end the project was passed back to the GLC who asked for an extension of time. However, just about then, the engineers did their calculations and realised they wanted about half the site for storm water tanks. Presumably, it would have been very expensive for them to look elsewhere. However, the Fun Palace could not be shrunk to fit the remaining land.

A public inquiry was fixed, but now the trustees have decided to give way.

The Camden Town pilot project, a very reduced version to go on two acres, has also been abandoned. The structures, including one that blew up with air like a giant tent, could have been removed in twelve hours.

However, local residents protested so noisily before anything happened that it seemed pointless to go ahead. It was, after all, meant to provide pleasure, not stir up rancour. . . .

And there was a photo of me, smiling, with the caption, 'Nowhere to go'.

Nowhere to go? I still had one place.

The houses and shops round Theatre Royal were being demolished. Angel Lane, with its poulterers, fishmongers, bacon shop, haberdashery and our beloved Café L'Ange, was under threat. This winding lane was used by Anglo-Saxon guerrillas to avoid the Roman highway. The old pub, the Lion, still stood, so did the empty school on Salway Road, but they wouldn't be there much longer. The corner beside the school, where once there had been houses, was now debris and Mrs Ivory's two up, two down beside the Theatre had already gone. You couldn't pass that corner without turning away from the broken mattresses, tin cans, wrecked prams, ruined refrigerators and unspeakable muck.

The state of the place and the children who played there were particularly distressing after Tunisia, where the government's first care was for the children and, faced with a shortage of teachers, the schools worked three shifts daily.

One Sunday morning I was out early and, equipped with stout gloves, a shovel and a wheelbarrow, set about clearing that abominable site. Before long a small boy joined me, then one of his friends, and soon after, a neighbour's child holding his little sister by the hand. The older boys and girls joined in later.

Someone told Gerry what was happening and he brought us brown paper bags, large and strong, and went to look for the local lorry driver. Three loads of rubbish were carted away that day, including the filthy mattresses, lifted with rakes and pitchforks.

There were council flats not far away. One or two inhabitants came out on to their balconies to see what was going on. No one came to help.

Working in all our spare minutes, helped at the weekends by student volunteers, it took three weeks to clean up that tip. Meanwhile Carole Christensen was collecting a team to repaint Angel Lane, hoping to save it from the bulldozers. She was an American girl and didn't know enough about our developers and corrupt councillors.

The neighbours, predictably, started complaining. 'That debris looked lovely before she came back – all that grass and rose-bay. . . . Now what's she doing?'

I was talking to some specialists from an asphalting firm which had generously agreed to provide flooring for us. 'Can we have those big coloured squares?' I asked. 'As in your brochure. This will be a first-class test-bed for your product.'

I got my squares. A giant chessboard appeared and Annabel Scase, David and Rosalie's daughter, painted the wall against the school white. Larry, our favourite cartoonist, came by one day and drew a schoolboy about to cane the headmaster, who was dressed in mortarboard and gown. Angel Lane was undergoing a spring clean at the hands of a squad of teenagers.

In case Newham decided to see us off, I took the precaution of filming that site as we found it. We worked and played there, drew and painted, until Michael Holt, a maths teacher from Goldsmith's College, came along. He had new ideas and set the children problems which they solved with coloured cubes, not too big to carry.

One day, worried by the prolonged silence outside, I went to investigate. The boys and girls were arranging their cubes in a strange pattern.

'Ask us another one, guv,' said Ray.

'Algebra!' said Michael, aside to me.

When the Whoopee Band was playing at the theatre (they earned their living in scientific labs, or as teachers – music was their spare-time occupation), Bif, the fiddler, would come out and join us. He taught the kids how to make maps by exploring Stratford. 'We're topologists now,' a boy called Dougie told me.

He had been one of the wildest in the gang. Geoff, aged nine, was proudly typing the next Sunday's programme. Carole had taught him to read and write with a typewriter. If his spelling resembled Frank Norman's, it was none the worse for that.

More houses came down. We took over a second site. It would be a long time before these patches of rubble were developed; meanwhile we would put them to good use.

Our old friends, the Newham engineers, uttered dire threats and closed the public lavatories on Sundays, so we opened the conveniences at Theatre Royal and Gaye Brown and Jenny King started campaigning for a Portakabin to afford shelter on the second site.

As time went by we took over three sites, the yard of the deserted school and, in winter, a boarded-up hall at 48 Martin Street. The older boys formed themselves into a club known as 'The Nutters' and were allowed complimentary seats for the plays, which they attended as critics. For despite our learn-as-you-will outside the shows went on within.

On Friday evenings the Nutters were invited to take over the stage at the theatre, from six o'clock till eight, for their 'posh night'. They were a scruffy lot and declared themselves proud to be so, but on Friday nights they'd be wearing lighting-up ties, polka-dot cravats, embroidered waistcoats and decorated dance shoes. You wouldn't have known them. Each Friday the Nutters would choose a different theme – and we would invent the appropriate décor with them. They also chose their own dance music and in time formed their own band. The girls held off till the last minute, attending to their own appearance and strolling in, heavily made up, often half crippled in their mothers' high-heeled shoes.

Our biggest advance was at the fall of Salway Road, when we took over two acres of debris. I gave my battalion two very large balls of string and told them to measure up the new territory and divide it into equal plots. They did so. We drew lots and everyone had a share. But equality did not last: within a week some commanded two or three plots while the former occupiers took to the gipsy life, having quickly consumed the supply of gob-stoppers or farting cushions for which they had bartered their estate.

Cleaning up and planning kept the site busy. There was no

time to worry about drop-outs and there was room for cricket and football as well as more esoteric pursuits. Lured by the games, Martin Langan, barman at the theatre, became a volleyball coach in the afternoons and Ken Hill, the playwright, stopped his word-spinning and strolled across the green . . . sorry, I mean the Salway plot, in his cricket togs. Beautiful Gaye Brown decided to defend the young ones and their dogs from passing meddlers such as the two thugs who called themselves security guards. They were employed by Taylor Woodrow to guard the building under construction which overshadowed the old theatre.

One day, working in my room, I heard their Alsatian barking; then a small dog yelping. I looked out of the window. A child was screaming; his dog was being attacked by the Alsatian. One of the guards began lashing at the big dog and tugging at its lead, which of course made matters worse. Then Gaye appeared and coolly thrust her fist into the Alsatian's jaw. The scared little dog was released and ran off with its master. Gaye came into my room, stood there – and then burst into tears. She was an actress and a singer . . . a brave country girl as well.

Lionel Bart turned up when we took over the playground of the deserted school and sat with a circle of budding song writers spinning lyrics. Mike MacCarthy appeared from nowhere and had the youngest citizens making up plays, and Jimmie Winston, who had a band called 'The Small Faces', involved himself in everything, a frontiersman in the bad lands.

On Sundays and during school holidays the team would picnic with the kids on our new-found territory.

'No need to throw good money away,' said one young angel-face. 'We can nick the stuff.'

'You can? How many of you know someone in the nick?' Every hand shot up.

'They've got spies, disguised as nuns, in that store,' I told them. 'You've got to be ultra smart to be a tea-leaf these days.'

Those kids knew the cops on the beat. They knew the bent ones and respected those who were straight, particularly 'Old Scottie', who was in fact very strict with them and knew how to keep them in order.

Before long we had to have our own police force, two were

elected each week. They only had to serve for a week, but even that was too long for Dougie.

'I'm sick an' tired of bein' law,' he told me. 'Can't I go back to villainy for the rest of the week?'

'Why?'

'Because it's more fun.'

'Punishment can be very severe, though, if you're caught and tried and found guilty.'

'Yeah, I know, but they're too slow to catch a cold.'

We already had our own court of law, and trial by jury. The worst punishment was banishment. Mind you, we'd no armed police or strong-arm defenders, but the court's decisions were respected. I saw a lad standing on the pavement outside the promised land, afraid to set foot on it. He'd been banished for three days for nicking an apple pie which some girl had baked for our Sunday picnic.

The friendly lorry driver who carted away our rubbish would often run us to Epping Forest on a Sunday morning, till one day he found his windscreen smashed, and strongly suspected one of our boys, a compulsive stone-thrower. A jury was summoned, our two policemen were sent to apprehend the suspect. The court assembled with due solemnity, but the prisoner was led in, looking quite unconcerned.

The accusation was read out by the Public Prosecutor, Dawn Day. 'Not guilty,' said Dean, the accused. The Defence rose to speak, but was thrown because he couldn't remember where he'd left his wig and Dawn was looking very smart in hers: she'd made it herself with horsehair and her sister's curlers.

'We don't seem to 'ave no witnesses,' was about all the Defence had to say.

The members of the jury were anxious to get away; they'd interrupted a game of rounders at the call of duty – so they retired at once, put their heads together and came back.

'Do you find the prisoner guilty or not guilty?' asked Ray, who was being very stern and solemn as the judge.

'Guilty!' said Nancy, leader of the jury. ''Ang 'im!'

The prisoner pulled a face at her. ''E's my bruvver,' she said.

'Where're we going to put the gallows?' asked the little boy with the dog.

'We're only pretending,' said Dean.

'Yeah, but we still gotta pay for that windscreen.'

'Why don't we do a pilgrimage?' said Dawn. 'We can put a rope round Dean's neck and collect for 'im on the way.'

'Where to?' asked Dean.

'St Paul's Cathedral,' I said, to bring the discussion to an end.

'A doddle,' Ray declared. 'St Paul's, 'ere we come.'

Doddle or not, it would take some organising. Luckily Christine, a harum-scarum motor cyclist, had not long since blown in and she fancied the job.

'Collecting boxes, banners, refreshments at two-mile halts. I'll need wheels. Departure Sunday next. Eleven ack emma. Friends and relations invited to give us a send-off.'

Thus it was that we assembled at eleven o'clock precisely, elder sisters in glad rags with us, bugle and side-drum accompanying us, and set off with banners waving along the Mile End Road. As we rounded the corner by Montague Burton's, the girls struck up with 'West Ham, we love you' (the football team, they meant, not the borough council). By the time we reached Aldgate East, and had two halts for pop, crisps and a singsong, we'd collected enough for two windscreens and the marching song had degenerated into 'Mademoiselle from Armentières' with unspeakable lyrics, derived no doubt from Lionel.

I broke away and took the tube to St Paul's. I'd already warned the Dean that an important pilgrimage would be arriving, but he was a bit of a VIP, and you know what they're like.

Just as I thought, he was nowhere to be seen. I took one look round, then decided to walk back and meet the marchers. They weren't far off, and definitely flagging. They'd walked nearly eight miles. But when we reached the steps of St Paul's the climax couldn't have been better. The faithful were just leaving after evensong. The doors were wide open and what with the lighted candles, the tall white lilies and the organ music – we were all ready to be born again. The kids stood there open-mouthed. I went in. If there was no Dean, someone had got to welcome them after that trek. I spotted this old geezer in a long black frock. He'll do. And I told him my sad story, cut it short though. 'Would he welcome them?'

'Of course, of course,' said he. 'I am a cockney myself. And this, you know, is the cockneys' cathedral.'

With that I ran to the door and hustled the pilgrims in. There was a formal welcome and then a guided tour. As we stopped by a glass case I heard Malcolm, ecstatic, 'Get them sparklers, I reckon they're real.' He was gazing at a jewelled monstrance, a chalice and a gold cross.

'Come, children,' said our guide. 'Now beneath this grill lies the vault where all that remains of Horatio Nelson lies buried.'

There were cries of protest. 'No, 'e don't!'

'Where is 'e, then?'

'Up a pillar in Trafalgar Square,' said Ray.

Christine was waiting outside in the car with all the banners and money boxes. We said goodbye to our new friend and as a reward for their long trek, the kids were given their fare home.

But the biggest event was yet to come – our Easter Fair. It wasn't the first, but it was special because this year the Nutters wanted to set it up themselves, and run it. Agreed by majority vote. At once the major site bristled with poles and flagstaffs, trestle tables, complete with vice, hammer and plane. Sawing and splicing, digging, planting and soldering went on from first light till the school bell rang, and resumed from the moment they were released till they were summoned home to bed.

Booths and tents sprang up, flagpoles, maypoles and coconut shies. The signwriter was kept busy: 'Test your Strength', 'Shoot the Jackpot', 'Catch a paper fish'. Would all these sideshows work? They did and I must say they looked highly original. Three school-teachers arrived on the great day, dressed as gipsies, and installed themselves in a wigwam which had once been a patchwork quilt. The tallest brandished a crystal ball. 'Come and have your fortune told,' she cried, in accents far from Romany – but she went down well with the juniors.

The theatre ran a talent-spotting competition all day and some of the mothers sold tea and rock buns on the second site. It was a great day, but some of the children were still not satisfied.

'That's our site,' one said. 'We don't want rock buns, we want a farm there.'

'A farm?'

'Well, animals,' said her friend.

'Where are we supposed to find them?'

'Everybody's got animals in Stratford. The council won't allow pigeons in our buildings, so we keep 'em in secret, on the roof. Everybody knows that.'

She was right. In the end we had pigeons, and chickens, two donkeys, three monkeys, a goat, a mynah bird and a tortoise; and Jimmie Winston brought a lion! One of the donkeys, Herbert, belonged to a lady bus conductor and he slept on the sofa in her front room (it was broken anyway). The other donkey belonged to Randy Ron who kept the do-it-yourself shop. Horace, the lion – he was only little – came from the pet shop owned by friends of Jimmie's. Gerry used to come out and smoke his pipe and talk to Horace every lunch-time, remembering, perhaps, the lion cub that nearly came to Ormesby Hall.

All the animals had good food and spacious shelters, airy and safe, built by the kids with the help of the theatre carpenter. Some went home at night. They all had good keepers. There was a queue for the job.

Animal Farm lasted through the holidays and the children from the school for the handicapped paid us a visit. Regent's Park was too far and too dear. Everybody was sorry when the time came to say goodbye.

Bertie Day, a ne'er-do-well like his father before him, was now a grown man, with a family of his own, but he came to me, almost in tears. 'Keep 'em 'ere,' he said. 'The kiddies are that pleased to 'ave 'em.'

'It's not possible, Bertie. The animals aren't ours.'

'Our kids ought to have horses to ride, while we're at it,' he went on.

All of Bertie's ideas were impossible. Still, it was worth a try, and sure enough, when the fair was over a string of horses appeared, led by a young woman in jodhpurs. She came every evening and taught the children to ride. I think it was Jimmie

Winston who was responsible. He had a way with the ladies.

We felt rich. When '48' was pulled down we acquired a large hut. 'The Who' came and played on the site and gave us a thousand pounds for 'The Invisible Fun Palace'.

On the last night of Animal Farm, Bertie Day surpassed himself. All the animals had gone, except Dobbin, the donkey belonging to Randy Ron, who was probably in the pub by the bridge. Bertie was going down there himself for a pint, so he decided to take Dobbin along with him. There was no Ron so he bought Dobbin a pint instead. As is the nature of things, a few rounds followed till Bertie decided he'd better take the donkey home, which meant the tube, because Randy lived with the aristocracy out Epping way.

No trouble at Stratford, you can walk straight onto the train, but at the other end a big black feller stood by the exit.

'You got a ticket for that there hanimal?'

'A donkey ticket? Yes!' But he hadn't.

''As 'e got a pedigree?' asked the Spade as Bertie searched his pockets.

'What? You should see it!'

The ticket collector got interested and Bertie filled him in.

Some time later Dobbin was leading him to a soignée little semi-detached where he stopped by the gate and brayed. Bertie rang the doorbell, not once, two or three times. He banged on the door.

'What the hell?' It was Randy Ron at the upstairs window.

'I've brought Dobbin home.'

'Well, take him back. I've just found my wife in bed with the lodger.'

'Tell 'er, Dobbin's got a bigger one than 'im!'

And that, as far as I'm concerned, is the end of the story.

P.S. Christmas 1974. Fine weather. Three of us invited the children to a picnic and presents if they'd nothing better to do. Gerry came. He sat outside the hut roasting chestnuts for us. It was his last Christmas.

Appendix One

Theatre Union Study Course, 1940. Each company member should prepare a paper or photomontage on their chosen subject.

FIRST SUBJECT:
HISTORY OF THE ANCIENT THEATRE: THE GREEKS

1. EXAMINE:

> The beginnings, the roots in primitive culture.
> Religious ritual.
> Secular mime and dance.
> The cult of Dionysus.

STUDY:

> The synthesis of historico-religious rites in the highly developed culture of progressive Greece.

TRACE:

> The development of acting as an art.
> The origin of the chorus.
> The origin of the protagonist.
> The development of play-writing as a literary form.
> The relation of Greek theatre to the people and to the State.

2. THE DRAMATURGY

Study the following works:

> Aeschylus: *Prometheus, The Suppliants, Seven Against Thebes.*
> Sophocles: *Oedipus Rex, Antigone, Ajax.*
> Euripides: *Trojan Women, Alcestis, Medea.*
> Aristophanes: *The Knights, Peace, The Birds.*

3. READING LIST

Les Matérialistes de l'Antiquité by Paul Nizan. Valuable for its understanding of the social implications of ancient materialism.

Aristophanes and the Practical Parties of Athens by M. Croiset. For useful data, conclusions drawn not important.

The Attic Theatre by Haigh. For technical background. General history.

The Greek Theatre and its Drama by Flickenger. Deals with technical problems from a theatrical p.o.v.

Greek Tragedy by Kitto. Makes connection between Theatre and Dramaturgy.

Aeschylus and Sophocles by J.T. Sheppard. Their influence on world theatre.

Aeschylus and Athens by Thompson.

Science and Politics in the Ancient World by Farringdon. Useful historical facts.

The Pelopponesian War by Thucydides.

Mediaeval, Renaissance, Spanish, Elizabethan or Jacobean drama could be taken as a subject, and comparable lists were posted. The few books available on the *commedia dell'arte* and the Chinese theatre were listed. It was considered mere philandering to read latter-day classics, let alone modern plays, unless you'd acquired a thorough grounding in the ancients. Restoration comedy was at the time considered chamber theatre and not to our liking.

Appendix Two

The Grosvenor Square Pesbyterian Church and School
at All Saints, Manchester.

This report is concerned with the conversion of the existing building into a theatre.

The church is an imposing structure, faced in stone, the architectural detail rich in character. It is situated within the central city area of Manchester, bounded by three of its busiest roads. There is hardly a section of the city or its suburbs which is not connected by bus service to points adjacent to the building.

The area is scheduled for development as the cultural and entertainment section of the city. The local authorities have intimated that they would be prepared to grant permanent life to the building, were it to be converted into a theatre.

No new construction is to be permitted in the area immediately surrounding the proposed theatre; grass walks and flower-beds are proposed instead. This would mean, as development proceeds, a pleasant aspect second to none.

The building can be divided into two main sections:
 a. The church itself
 b. The school rooms attached to it.
The church has a basement running under its entire length, which was used as an air-raid shelter during the War. The school is a one-storey building at the rear of the church, at present used by the Ministry of Food to store potato sacks.

Both buildings are solidly built and structurally sound though, due to neglect during the War years and also to Tortfeasors, some of the fittings are now dilapidated. Nevertheless, short of demolition, the structures will last indefinitely.

CONVERSION. The church is admirably suited to the requirements of a theatre: ample space for an auditorium which could seat between seven and eight hundred people, a large stage, a rehearsal room, adequate cloakrooms, and a bar and club room which later could be converted into a restaurant.

The school rooms would serve as offices, dressing-rooms, workrooms for set construction and wardrobe.

The following was added when Gerry secured drawings from Henry Elder MBE, ARIBA, AIAA, architect:

The estimated cost of conversion is based on the drawings attached. It should be understood that estimating without full details invites errors which although small in fact may, to a certain extent, be cumulative in character. It is suggested, therefore, that the figures given must be expected to vary to an extent of plus or minus ten per cent.

a.	putting the fabric in order		£1,400
	The Ministry of Works hold the building on a repairing lease and would presumably be responsible for a considerable proportion of this sum.		
b.	Constructural work below ground level		£2,500
c.	Constructural work above ground level		
	i.	An auditorium proper (with 850 seats)	£8,800
	ii.	Backstage	£700
d.	Other necessities:		
	i.	Heating	
	ii.	Lighting (stage and general)	
	iii.	Seating	
	iv.	Carpets	
	v.	Furnishings	
	vi.	Projection equipment etc., etc.	(?) £5,000

TOTAL COST OF CONVERSION	£18,400
(with 700 seats)	£16,175

Appendix Three

'Umeni Lidu – Art for the People' by Gerry Raffles,
General Manager of Theatre Workshop, who have just
completed a highly successful tour of Czechoslovakia.

Umeni Lidu – Art for the People – is the name of the cultural organisation of the Czechoslovak Co-operative and Trade Union movement. It sets out to develop a critical interest in art amongst the working class and tackles the problem on a very wide front. Its scope of activities includes both the active participation of workers in creative cultural activity on an amateur or part-time basis, and also the development of a critical appreciation of the work of professional artists.

This article is only concerned with the Theatre Section, but a similar drive is being made with painting, music and dancing.

The seats at most Czech Theatres cost from ten to fifty crowns – that is from one shilling to five shillings; this even applies to the theatres in the centre of Prague including the Opera. (At equivalent theatres in London, the average price is around nine shillings per seat and the top price can be anything from sixteen to thirty shillings.) Even so, approximately seventy per cent of the seats in the Prague Theatres are sold at less than the stated prices. Art for the People buys up sometimes whole performances, sometimes half or a percentage of the seats in the theatres, and sells them at a cheaper rate in factories and other places of work.

The loss incurred is made up partly by a discount given for the block purchase of the seats, partly by a subsidy given by the trade unions, the co-operatives and the Government. The seats are sold in the factories by the shop stewards, and voluntary Art for the People organisers. Special trains and buses bring workers from outlying districts to the theatres.

All nationalised industries in Czechoslovakia are taxed ten per cent of their profits and this money is used to buy seats at theatres and concerts, which are then given free to the workers in the industry. The money is also used to organise special theatre performances and exhibitions of art.

This year Art for the People has taken over six theatres in Prague, including an opera house. Here they will run festivals of all the leading provincial theatres, with as many as forty or fifty different theatre companies taking part. Here also, they will make a concentrated and special drive for the factory workers, to show them the theatre standards of the whole country and to stimulate criticism of the theatre amongst them.

The plays they sponsor range from conventional grand opera and Czech and foreign classics to new plays, some of them by the more politically conscious theatres.

Incidentally, a high percentage of plays performed are new. Every stimulus is given to writers, especially playwrights – every writer is guaranteed by law an extra room rent free at his flat or house in which he can write – and this is resulting in an ever-increasing supply of new plays of varying standards. Like all progressive organisations, Art for the People is very dissatisfied with the disparity between the standard of the work they produce and their aims, but they constantly try to reduce this difference by competition in festivals etc., bringing into comparison the work of different artists and thus stimulating criticism.

It is to this desire for a comparison of standards that we in Theatre Workshop owe the opportunity we had to tour Czechoslovakia. We played in sixteen towns, and everywhere were the centre of heated discussion in the press and with the local theatre artists about our methods and their own.

A few months before us, Louis Jouvet from Paris and a choir from Poland had toured the country, and this winter the Vachtangov Studio of the Moscow Art Theatre are to play in many of the towns we visited. All these tours were organised by Art for the People. This International exchange complements the national festivals which they hold and must result in a great broadening of the outlook of all the artists there.

Similarly with their dramaturgy: in Prague when we were there, four plays by Shakespeare and three modern American plays were being performed by Czech theatres, side by side with Polish, Russian, Swedish and both new and classical Czech plays.

Under conditions such as these a comparison of standards is really possible.

Art for the People intends to create theatre and art workshops all over the country – centres where artists can come to work out new ideas and forms, and where local amateurs can find expert help and advice. These will become the focal point of cultural activity in each area.

For amateur artists and actors, Art for the People finds suitable premises and facilities; helps financially with any necessary costs; provides professional helpers and advisers of the highest quality; organises visits to professional theatres; and stimulates a desire for ever higher standards.

In the words of Vaclav Kopecky, the Czech Minister of Information:

> All we do is directed by the desire to popularise culture, and to make it readily accessible to all classes, even to those who in the past have been intentionally and inhumanly excluded from cultural life. We wish to achieve a state of affairs in which the people will crave for a collection of poems, the sound of artistic music, the view of a beautiful picture, a visit to the theatre, all which, hitherto inaccessible, will become an absolute necessity. . . .

Art for the People is determined to succeed. Apart from their full-time organisers, they have large numbers of keen voluntary helpers who see to it that theatre seats are never left unsold through insufficient publicity.

In England, People's Entertainment Society, the cultural organisation of the co-operative movement, stands for exactly the same things as does Art for the People. If all co-operators were sufficiently aware of the potential importance of People's Entertainment Society, this could be as important to the British People as Umeni Lidu is to the Czechs.

This article was sent to Reynold News, *for the attention of the People's Entertainment Society. Neither body saw fit to reply.*

J.L.

Appendix Four

Rudolf Laban

I first heard of Laban when I was still a girl studying in London; intrigued and curious, I kept my eyes open for articles about, or photos of, his work. There was little to be found but gradually piece by piece I managed to construct some sort of Laban image for myself.

I gathered that he was, or had been: a Dadaist, a dancer, crystallographer, topologist, architect, composer, designer, choreographer – and had even earned his bread as a street cartoonist when he ran short of cash while studying at the École des Beaux Arts in Paris. He was born in Bratislava in 1879 when it was part of the Austro-Hungarian Empire. His father had been Feldmarschall Leutnant von Laban, military governor of Bosnia and Herzegovina. As a boy he had travelled from country to country with his father, watched the whip dance in Yugoslavia, seen whirling dervishes in Turkey, country Ländler on village greens and graceful waltzes and wild polkas in fashionable ballrooms; and he had heard the country cries and songs which inspired Bartók and Janáček. While still in his twenties he became the leading choreographer and dance master of the Weimar Republic with all the cultural richness of Serbia–Croatia–Turkey–Hungary–Austria – and Germany – at his disposal.

'So I tried to get the opera singers to move and the movers to sing, somehow,' he told me.

'Those big Brünnhildes, you got them to move?'

'A little. I remember after one particularly unsuccessful première, while the audience applauded wildly, I was crushed between zees two great sings.' And he did a very funny impersonation of a large lady enfolding him in her bosom.

While working on an idea for a dance theatre, he visited the classic theatres of Greece and Rome to measure the performance areas and test the sight lines. His design won the Gold Medal for Architecture in Moscow. Unfortunately the party line switched to Socialist Realism and his theatre was never built.

When the Nazis took over, Göring sacked him from his directorship of the Berlin State Opera and Goebbels denounced 'the erotic dances of the Jew Laban'.

'What else do you expect from these supermen in big boots? Dance is joy. So what? If they take the theatre from us, the town will be our theatre.'

In Vienna and in many other towns that is what he did. He set the whole town dancing, each profession or trade was given dance movements which symbolised their work. The smiths stepped out flourishing hammers, the shopgirls with streaming ribbons which flowed from arbours of flowers, the umbrella makers, young girls mostly, twirled coloured parasols in a dancing promenade. Concierges and athletes, milkmen, typists, butchers and bakers attended mass rehearsals. Volunteers decorated floats. And when the day came for Laban's 'Festzug', all Vienna celebrated.

In the eighteenth century Noverre, for his Ballet d'Action, had told his pupils to go to the fields and workshops for inspiration. Laban brought the people from the fields and workshops to the dance.

'Dancing will cure the warped psyche of our time,' he had said. And: 'Everywhere there is dancing. It is a universal language. We do not need translators.'

Then, like most artists, he contradicted himself by inventing a written language for dance.

'On the night tables of the ladies in eighteenth-century France,' he wrote, 'you would have found more choreographies than Bibles, which means that they could read the famous Beauchamps-Feuillet dance script.'

Laban's new script was so devised that, with it, you could script any series of movements, of work as well as dance.

Sound recording and the camera may have supplanted sheet music and descriptive writing, but Laban's dance notation is still a precise and accurate method of recording action.

For a long time there was no news of Laban, until one day we heard that he was working in France. I gave up hope of ever seeing him and consoled myself with the thought that at least our system of movement was derived from his, however patchily.

Laban's movement scales are very satisfying to perform. You touch each point in space which can be reached without elevation or propulsion. They are encapsulated in the icosahedron.

'What is that?'

'A twenty-sided shape. I knew it when I was a crystallographer – but it took me many years before I could get a dancer into one.'

We made models of his crystal, built one life-size and played around in it.

How difficult it is to translate movement into words, impossible I think. Can you express any element in terms of another?

Laban did not want his work intellectualised, yet he spent his life on system research. He started by dividing all human movement into eight fundamental efforts. Patrick Geddes in his time divided human activity into fundamental occupations, such as hunting, dam building, farming, mining, toolmaking, clothmaking, etc. How many have tried to analyse the few plots which are at the basis of all plays and stories? Eight, they say?

Inside Laban's crystal you can find the Vitruvius man, arms and legs akimbo, an encircling table plane defined by your arms outstretched – as you turn around there is the upward thrust of an arm preparing for a tennis service, and its opposite, the forward lunge of the discus thrower. High, low, narrow, wide. Direct, indirect, stab, point, smooth, press, flick, slash, wring, twirl. You see, I am trying to do the impossible, put Laban's 'efforts' into words.

We are working in an ephemeral medium where nothing lasts. Laban did not believe the camera could pin down his work. Neither do I. There is chemistry in the actual event which cannot be recaptured, and even if it is captured . . .

> *Yet should there hover in their restless heads*
> *One thought, one grace, one wonder at the least,*
> *Which into words no virtue can digest.*

After a session with Laban you began to look at the world with different eyes, as if it had changed its colours or its shapes, or you could see neutrons and protons instead of mass. You watched for the slightest gesture which would give away a secret. After a while, with some degree of accuracy, you could tell what people did for a living, or analyse their state of mind as they passed you on the street.

Whether in dance or any form of theatre, to create a character you must first divest yourself of your own characteristics, become a new being, live in a different time and place. With Laban it became possible. Is such art called for today, in the world of telly-typecasting where the dog or the spider is more entertaining than the clown?

To our great good fortune Laban remained in Manchester throughout the War and whenever possible we attended his studio.

One day he told us how, in 1913, he set out to create an International School of Living Art, and chose Switzerland as his milieu – there he would teach a form of dance that would 'involve the whole being, and give dance its rightful value as an art'.

'Within a year,' he said, 'the finest of my young dancers, French and German, were dead. They had lived and worked together, they died killing each other. I went berserk, waved the red flag, became a Bolshie.'

'What are you now?'

'A Platonist.'

'What was it that first attracted you to dancing?'

'I saw this man polishing the ballroom floor with a duster on each foot. That is the life for me, I said.'

When he came to Blackburn to see us, I was on tenterhooks all evening – his good opinion meant more to me than all the rave reviews in the world. If he decided we were just another bunch of mediocrities I would give up.

It wasn't a very exciting place and we weren't at our best, but he stayed. And he liked us. Mostly he was surprised at how much I knew without having trained with him.

I told him I'd always loved mime and dance, but disliked classical ballet intensely.

'Why?'

'I like action, ballet is all posing. I like men and women on the stage, ballet is sexless.'

He had seen the way I played with time and space, converting everyday actions.

'What about voice?' he asked me. 'Can my efforts theory be applied to the voice?'

'Yes, of course.'

He had discussed this problem with Kurt Jooss at Stuttgart and thought the dancers' range would be extended by the use of vocal efforts, though not in pure dance.

Jooss was of Laban's school and Laban's influence was strong on the bitterly brilliant *Green Table*, a work which, perhaps more than any other, was responsible for the switch from classical to modern dance. Modern dance, which had been derided by the classicists, now found its way on to the curriculum of even the most conservative school of dance, while in the American musical as well as in the work of Katherine Dunham, Michael Kidd and Martha Graham, Laban's influence has produced some of the most exciting dance this century has seen. He changed the course of history in the US, the Scandinavian countries, Holland, Switzerland, Germany, everywhere except London and Moscow where you can still see dying swans in tutus.

On his seventieth birthday we serenaded him with songs from Bratislava. He still walked with the jaunty air of a young Don Juan and had an eye for the pretty girls.

It was perhaps because we were taking too much of his time, or because we were involved politically, for whatever reason – to his companion and protector, Lisa Ullmann, we became a threat. It was not us, as individuals, rather it was the word: theatre.

She had seen what had become of the artists when Hitler took over in Germany and she lived in fear of repercussions here. Laban felt secure in England, she did not. She even felt that Nazi rule might come about here. All she wanted was peace and security for Laban, so gradually and carefully, she sidetracked him into education. 'Laban in the schools.' He was prepared to work anywhere. 'I've been teaching the loonies,' he said one day. And he had. He also went to work in the prisons.

Lisa wanted acceptance by the Education Authorities, a steady income, a regular life – and for him no temptations.

I thought it was a terrible waste. The theatre needed him but of course the theatre didn't know anything about him. In fact we were the only company in the country who regarded movement training as a necessary part of the preparation of a play.

I tried to find an architect with sufficient knowledge of German to go through Laban's notes and research, without success. Not long before he died, I asked how long it took to evolve his theory of efforts. 'It is only now beginning,' he told me.

Appendix Five

In the autumn of 1948, Theatre Workshop toured sixteen towns in Czechoslovakia, playing to packed houses in the largest theatres. They took with them plays by Molière, Chekhov and Lorca, and two new English plays by Ewan MacColl (Jimmie Miller). After Czechoslovakia came Sweden, and triumph at the Stockholm Opera House.

PRAGUE

Great success. Theatre Workshop . . . captured the enthusiasm of the audience by its simple beauty and richness of ideas. . . .

Lidovy Noviny

Thanks to Joan Littlewood's production, *The Flying Doctor* of Molière had a flavour of English humour in its riotously colourful scenes.

Lidova Demokracie

A happy evening with Theatre Workshop . . . . Glittering and elegant costumes, inventive choreography, and above all the movement of Joan Littlewood's production. Molière's wit sparkled among theatrical bubbles as Howard Goorney's Sganarelle leapt and turned with puppet-like agility. . . . The housekeeper was created with enormous richness. It seemed that the audience would never cease to bring the actors in front of the curtain after the performance.

Prace

Johnnie Noble: Effective and impressive. . . . Outspoken. Witty sound effects, excellent lighting. J.H. Miller's music is too good to be forgotten; it should be recorded.

Svobod Veslovo

With extreme skill and artistry the producer was able, with a few shining metal bars, to produce a décor of gaol. She uses light, movement and music to perfection.

Rude Pravo

The Flying Doctor as played by Theatre Workshop flew. It was a dancing, loving farce, produced and played with tremendous élan. The production was brilliant.

Mlada Fronta

OLOMOUC

These welcome British guests, real representatives and interpreters of the progressive thoughts of the British people, have a theatrical line so strong that it is almost the strongest artistic impression that we have ever known. In the charming comedy of Molière, shaped and played with a most subtle sense of theatrical detail, they were more perfect than anything we have ever seen – not merely as individuals, but as a whole. . . . They have it in their blood as well as their brains.

Johnnie Noble is a poem of the unnamed people on the north-east English coast. The poem grows on a black horizon and in the white light of the projectors or in the grim twilight, like one of those films which make us sometimes honour English production. It is so vivid, so real – we must learn from them.

Straz Lidu

STOCKHOLM

Theatre Workshop is almost perfect. In the crowded

theatre, the extremely conservative Opera House, the public applauded spontaneously.

Expressen

A packed and enthusiastic Opera House met Theatre Workshop in Stockholm. By this time, this ambitious young group has a great reputation in our country. The production is full of ideas.

Dagsposten

Some of the actors have great and important comic talents.

Dagens Nyheter

Theatre Workshop gave us a strong taste of English theatre, playing to a packed house. The production is worthy of great praise. It was an evening we will not easily forget.

Borås Tidning

Brilliant success in Gävle.

Svenska Dagblad

The foreign language has not stopped Theatre Workshop playing to packed houses, whereas most Swedish shows are usually partly empty.

Arbetaren

Theatre Workshop is a very interesting experience, contrasting strongly with the other English theatre, which is rather stiff and dull. It is a wonderful justification of group theatre.

Stockholms Tidningen

The audience was delighted.

Aftontidningen

Great success for British theatre pioneers. The whole production was brilliant. It was indeed a marvellous performance.

Valmlands Folkblad

Index